TRỊNH CÔNG SƠN &
BOB DYLAN

ESSAYS ON LOVE, WAR, SONGWRITING AND RELIGION

The Press at Cal Poly Humboldt

TRỊNH CÔNG SƠN & BOB DYLAN

ESSAYS ON LOVE, WAR, SONGWRITING AND RELIGION

JOHN C. SCHAFER

The Press at Cal Poly Humboldt showcases Cal Poly Humboldt research and scholarship with a broad scope of print and electronic publications including books, journals, conference proceedings, data sets, open textbooks, and more. The open-access works connect Cal Poly Humboldt with a worldwide community of researchers and scholars.

The photo of Bob Dylan on the front cover is by Rowland Scherman and appears courtesy of the National Archives. The photo of Trịnh Công Sơn appears by permission of the author.

The photo of the church used for the back cover is File #225979976 and was licensed from Adobe. The photo of Thien Mu pagoda is File #195723015.

Cover design by Colwyn Delany
Editing, typesetting, and layout by Colwyn Delany

The Press at Cal Poly Humboldt
California State Polytechnic University, Humboldt
University Library
1 Harpst Street
Arcata, California 95521-8299
press@humboldt.edu
press.humboldt.edu

Đợi chờ yêu thương trên cây thánh giá
Đợi xóa sân si dưới bóng bồ đề

Waiting for love upon the cross
Waiting to wipe out anger in the shade of the bodhi tree

Trịnh Công Sơn's "Waiting for the Day" [Đợi có một ngày]

CONTENTS

ILLUSTRATIONS

PREFACE

Most of my footnotes are bibliographical notes that indicate only the source of a quotation or of an idea or opinion. Some explanatory notes, however, add information about a person, song, issue, or event that I am discussing.

Unless another translator is indicated, all the lines and stanzas of Vietnamese songs and poems that appear in the folllowing chapters have been translated by my wife, Cao Thị Như Quỳnh, and myself. Our translations of twenty-three complete songs are indicated by an asterisk following their Vietnamese title, and can be found in Appendix D.

Translations of some poems by the New Poets, who are described in chapters 16 & 17, can be found in Appendix G. Translated poems have an asterisk after their titles.

In our translations of Trịnh Công Sơn's songs we have attempted to capture their meaning—not an easy task for reasons explained in chapter 19 ("Understanding Trịnh Công Sơn's Obscurity"). We have not attempted to write lyrics that could be sung.

Đặng Hoàng Lan has published the most complete collection of English translations of Trịnh Công Sơn's songs. See Đặng Hoàng Lan, Tôi ơi đừng tuyệt vọng [Don't Despair], (HCMC: Hội Nhà Văn, 2020).

For other English translations of Trịnh Công Sơn's songs see the following website, maintained by the Friends of Trịnh Công Sơn, where you can find translations of over seventy songs: www.tcs-home.org/english.

For good translations of fourteen of Trịnh Công Sơn's best known songs about war and peace, see *Love Songs of a Madman: Poems of Peace & War by Trịnh Công Sơn*, translated by Joseph Do Vinh Tai & Eric Scigliano, in *Việt Nam Forum* vol. 16 Not a War: American Vietnamese Fiction, Poetry and Essays, edited by Dan Duffy (New Haven, CT: Yale University Council on Southeast Asia Studies, 1997), 225-61.

ACKNOWLEDGEMENTS

My wife, Cao Thị Như Quỳnh, helped me in ways too numerous to list in full. She grew up in Trịnh Công Sơn's hometown of Huế where she attended Quốc Học Huế [National High School] and later taught English at the University of Huế. She helped me understand the impact Trịnh Công Sơn's songs had on young people in Huế. She also translated 23 of his songs (See Appendix D).

She also helped me in more mundane ways. For example, she helped me translate correctly some Vietnamese words and phrases used by Vietnamese scholars. She also checked first drafts of chapters to make sure I had added the correct diacritical marks to Vietnamese words.

My brother-in-laws, Cao Huy Thuần and Cao Huy Hóa, both devout Buddhists, helped me understand Buddhist concepts and the history of Buddhism in Huế.

Trịnh Công Sơn's sister, Trịnh Vĩnh Trinh, and her husband, Nguyễn Trung Trực, have gracefully granted us permission to quote lyrics from Trịnh Công Sơn's songs and include some illustrations from Trịnh Công Sơn's song books.

Barry Hillenbrand, a close friend since our time in the Peace Corps in Ethiopia in 1963-1964, and a correspondent for Time magazine in Vietnam in 1972-74, provided valuable advice and encouragement.

Dave Van de Mark, a friend and computer expert, was always ready to come at a moment's notice to help me solve computer problems.

Finally, I want to thank The Press at Cal Poly Humboldt. Kyle Morgan, Scholarly Communications and Digital Scholarship Librarian, was a pleasure to work with. Colwyn Delany, production assistant, was an excellent proofreader.

INTRODUCTION

When I was in college in the 1960s Bob Dylan and Joan Baez were at the top of my list of favorite singers. When I joined the Peace Corps in 1963 I took some of their LPs with me and listened to them in Debre Markos, Ethiopia where I taught English. When I returned to the US in 1965 and enrolled in the Harvard Graduate School of Education, everyone was listening to the Beatles. I did too but I didn't stop listening to Baez and Dylan. Then in 1968 I joined International Voluntary Services (IVS), a precursor of the Peace Corps that was established in 1953 by internationalists and religious leaders. Although it did not proselytize, Thierry J. Sagnier, author of a history of IVS explains, its roots were "firmly planted in the Christian pacifism of Mennonites, Quakers, and Brethren organizations."[1] When President Kennedy created the Peace Corps in 1961, he and Sargent Shriver, the first Director of the Peace Corps, studied the IVS model. I taught English in Vietnam for two years, one year at Phan Chu Trinh Secondary School in Đà Nẵng and one year at the University of Huế. Then I came home and worked in IVS's office in Washington D.C. for a year before returning to Vietnam where I taught two more years at the University of Huế under the Fulbright program. In Vietnam in the late 1960s and early 1970s, I listened to songs composed by Trịnh Công Sơn that he and a talented singer named Khánh Ly sang. Their songs and the songs of Joan Baez and Bob Dylan are woven deeply into my memory. When I think of this period, I remember one of their songs; when I hear one of their songs, I remember this period, a tumultuous one for Vietnam and the US.

The impetus for this book came later, in 2011, when I learned that on April 10, 2011, Bob Dylan was going to give a concert in Hồ Chí Minh

---

1. Thierry J. Sagnier, *The Fortunate Few: IVS Volunteers From Asia to the Andes* (Portland, OR: NCNM Press, 2015), xvii.

1

City and it would include songs by Trịnh Công Sơn, who passed away in 2001. The songs, I learned, would be sung by Vietnam's best singers. Joan Baez was not coming, nor was Khánh Ly, but the event still had, at least at first glance, a pleasing symmetry: Trịnh Công Sơn, often called "the Bob Dylan of Vietnam," and Bob Dylan himself coming together—if not in the flesh, then at least in spirit.

But then I read more reports and learned that the singing of Trịnh Công Sơn's songs was just a warm-up act for Bob Dylan. How could that be? One of Vietnam's greatest song composers reduced to a warm-up act? Worries I had about the concert were confirmed by reviews I read later. More than half—some reports said seventy percent—of the audience consisted of foreign visitors, expatriates or tourists, some of whom, bored by the Vietnamese portion, began yelling "We want Bob" in the middle of it.[2] Pre-concert publicity suggested that Bob Dylan was coming to Vietnam to remember and honor Trịnh Công Sơn, which made sense because many events were planned in early April to honor the tenth anniversary of Trịnh Công Sơn's death. Bob Dylan, however, gave no indication he had even heard of Trịnh Công Sơn. "The advance billing 'Bob Dylan's coming to Vietnam to show his appreciation for Trịnh Công Sơn' became more tactless," Duy Lân writes, "when throughout the program Bob never said a word about Trịnh Công Sơn."[3] The many Vietnamese journalists who called Trịnh Công Sơn and Bob Dylan "two harmonious souls" [*hai tâm hồn đồng điệu*] were quoting Rod Quinton, the Australian who produced and promoted the show. Though the show was promoted as "a chance for two harmonious souls to meet" they never met. Between the two parts of the show, Duy Lân says, "there were no common elements, no common language, no harmony, and most important no official recognition of Trịnh Công Sơn by the main actor, the mythical Bob Dylan."[4]

2. Duy Lân, "Bob Dylan ở Việt Nam: Thương nhau như thế quá mười ghét nhau" [Loving Each Other Like That Is Like Hating Each Other Ten Times Over], http://vn.news.yahoo.com/bob-dylan-%E1%BB%9F-vi%E1BB%87t-nam--th%C6%BO (accessed Apr. 14, 2011). Other Vietnamese who were present at the concert agree with Duy Lân. See Nguyên Thuận, "Trịnh Công Sơn và Bob Dylan: Tri ân hay hát lót?" [Trịnh Công Sơn and Bob Dylan: A Sign of Gratitude or Singing to Fill In?], http://www.vietnam-plus.vn/Home/Trinh-Cong-Son-va-Bob-Dylan-Tri-an-hay-hat-lot/20114/84995.vnplus (accessed July 5, 2012); and Linh Phạm, "Nhạc Trịnh 'lạc' trong buổi diễn Bob Dylan" [Trịnh Music Was "Lost" in the Bob Dylan Concert], https://web.archive.org/web/20110417073031/http://www.baomoi.com/Nhac-Trinh-lac-trong-buoi-dien-Bob-Dylan/71/6044594.epi (accessed July 1, 2012).
3. Duy Lân, "Bob Dylan ở Việt Nam."
4. Ibid.

2

A poster advertising Bob Dylan's April 10, 2011 appearance in Ho Chi Minh City.

Why did this happen? If Trịnh Công Sơn is the Bob Dylan of Vietnam, as many people have declared, then clearly the two singer-composers share some quality that the organizers could have focused on to harmonize the two parts of their concert. One obvious possibility would be the fact that both Trịnh Công Sơn and Bob Dylan wrote and sang songs opposing war. Concert organizers could not, however—for several reasons—unify their concert by highlighting this similarity. They no doubt expected an audience composed mostly of people born long after the war had ended. They wanted to create a festive atmosphere, something like the mood that prevails at outdoor rock concerts in the West where young people frolic together, drink beer, and dance to the music. Two of the corporate sponsors for the show were Jim Beam, the whiskey company, and San Miguel, a leading beer manufacturer. The concert was held on the football field of the Royal Melbourne Institute of Technology which is on the outskirts of Hồ Chí Minh City. The legendary Australian promoter Michael "Chuggie" Chugg asked Rod Quinton if he wanted to produce a Dylan show in Vietnam and Quinton obtained permission from the Vietnamese Ministry of Culture.[5] Organizers of the event understandably did not want to bring up the sad history of the war. Imagine the effect if one of the Vietnamese singers had sung Trịnh Công Sơn's "A Winter's Fable" [Ngụ ngôn của mùa đông], which contains verses like the following:

> One winter's day
> On a well-worn road
> A tank travels along
> A mine explodes slow
> People die twice
> Flesh and skin torn to pieces[6]

Imagine the effect of this verse from "A Song for the Corpses" [Bài ca dành cho những xác người], Trịnh Công Sơn's sad reaction to the deaths and destruction that occurred in his beloved home city of Huế during the 1968 Tết Offensive:

> Corpses lying all around in the cold and rain
> Corpses of the old and weak near those of the young and innocent
> Which corpse is my love lying in that trench
> In the burning fields, among those potato vines

Four of the songs in the Vietnamese set contain lines that mention the war but they contain no gruesome images.[7] If they are anti-war they are only gently so. For example, "Please Sun Sleep Peacefully" [Xin mặt trời ngủ yên], the first song of the set, contains the line "War has taken

---

5. Rob Schwartz, "Bob Dylan's First Vietnam Show From Stage Front," https://www.billboard.com/music/music-news/bob-dylans-first-vietnam-show-from-stage-front-1178398/ (accessed Jan. 8, 2012).
6. All translations unless otherwise indicated are by Cao Thị Như-Quỳnh and John C. Schafer.
7. See Appendix A for a list of songs by the two composers that were performed at the concert.

my friends." A stanza in the fourth song, "Sleep, My Love" [Em hãy ngủ đi] describes burning and withered forests, an image that listeners would understand as a reference to the use by US forces of Agent Orange and incendiary bombs to defoliate the countryside. Among the things Trịnh Công Sơn asks for in "Please Give Me" [Xin cho tôi], the twelfth song, are the ability to forget a new grave, a night without flying bullets, and a chance to build peace. In "Love Each Other" [Hãy yêu nhau đi], the closing song, Trịnh Công Sơn urges people to love each other "Though the night brings bullets / Though the morning brings bombs." Probably the organizers included these four songs because they were all written during the war but contain no images that would dampen the festive atmosphere. By including them the organizers hint at the most important similarity between Trịnh Công Sơn and Dylan—their reputation as anti-war sing-er-composers—before quickly moving on to the lullabies and love songs featured in the rest of the Vietnamese set.

Another factor, however—besides fears of dampening the festive mood—surely influenced the decision of the organizers to include only these quite mild anti-war songs. Culture managers in Vietnam object to Trịnh Công Sơn's anti-war songs because, in their view, he "opposes war too generally" [phản chiến một cách chung chung].[8] When asked in 2003 why so many of Trịnh Công Sơn' pre-1975 songs couldn't be performed, Lê Nam, head of the Office of Performing Arts of the Ministry of Culture and Information, explained that it was because in many of Trịnh Công Sơn's songs "the anti-war content is raised in a very general way, with no distinction made between a non-righteous [phi nghĩa] and righteous [chính nghĩa] war."[9] In other words, officials don't like Trịnh Công Sơn's anti-war songs because in them he does not embrace their war for national liberation.

But how about Dylan? Why didn't he sing one of his anti-war songs? Probably because these songs would not have been approved by the Vietnamese Ministry of Culture which routinely screens programs for public events. Dylan was criticized in the Western press for not singing his songs of protest and struggle at his shows in China and Vietnam. After his China concert Maureen Dowd, a columnist for the *New York Times*,

---

8. Nguyễn Đắc Xuân, *Trịnh Công Sơn: Có một thời như thế* [Trịnh Công Sơn: There Was Such a Time] (HCMC: Văn Học, 2003), 99.
9. Thu Hà, "Cái gì đã thuộc về nguyên tắc thì không có ngoại lệ" [There Are No Exceptions to Matters of Principle], *Tuổi trẻ* [Youth], Apr. 18, 2003.

wrote that "the idea that the raspy troubadour of '60s freedom anthems would go to a dictatorship and not sing those anthems is a whole new kind of sellout."[10] Dylan's anti-war songs aren't about Vietnam but some of them, when performed in Hồ Chí Minh City, could make the current leaders uneasy. Consider Dylan's song "Masters of War," for example, which includes these lines:

> *You [masters of war] that never done nothin'*
> *But build to destroy*
> *You play with my world*
> *Like it's your little toy*
> *You put a gun in my hand*
> *And you hide from my eyes*
> *And you turn and run farther*
> *When the fast bullets fly*

Hearing "Masters of War" some people might ask, "Who are those masters of war?" And if, in the midst of an Arab Spring, with insurgencies and civil uprisings occurring in the Middle East, he sang one of his most famous songs, "The Times They Are A-Changin'," people might ask whose walls he was referring to in these lines:

> *The battle outside ragin'*
> *Will soon shake your windows*
> *And rattle your walls*
> *For the times they are a-changin'*

Or what order he had in mind in these lines:

> *The order is rapidly fadin'*
> *And the first one now*
> *Will later be last*
> *For the times they are a-changin'*

Perhaps the fact that both singers sang anti-war songs couldn't be used to unify this concert, but that doesn't mean the two men don't resemble each other. Rod Quinton, the Australian producer of the show, referred to Trịnh Công Sơn and Bob Dylan as "harmonious souls." Just how harmonious are these two souls? Was Trịnh Công Sơn really the Bob Dylan of Vietnam? These are interesting questions. Trịnh Công Sơn is one of the most famous composers in Vietnam. Only two other composers

---

10. Maureen Dowd, "Blowin' in the Idiot Wind," *New York Times*, Apr. 9, 2011.

(Văn Cao and Phạm Duy) rival him in fame. His songs urging peace moved millions of Vietnamese during the second Indochina War. In the West Bob Dylan is a cultural icon whose name and songs are invariably mentioned whenever the protest movements of the 1960s are discussed. If Trịnh Công Sơn and Bob Dylan are two harmonious souls, then that would be something to learn from and celebrate. If they are not so similar, exploring how they differ may lead to illuminating insights regarding cultural differences.

Before considering whether Trịnh Công Sơn was the Bob Dylan of Vietnam I must discuss who first made this bold claim. One must understand, of course, that journalists and bloggers find Bob Dylans everywhere. One (unidentified) blogger lists singers around the world who have been tagged the Bob Dylan of their respective countries. The blogger includes this warning:

> Careful, folk/rock singer/songwriters of the world: There is a specter haunting you. If you're eminent back home, or just the first big rock guy in your language, vaguely political, or lyrically pretentious, or mischievous, possessed of bad voice, or accused of capturing a moment in your people's cultural history, then look out, my foreign friend for you are sooner or later gonna catch a comparison to Dylan. In recent times the simile has become so wild and virulent that non-musicians must be careful also.[11]

This website identifies singers around the globe who have had this tag applied to them—Vusi Mahlasela (South Africa), Cui Jian (China), Mohsen Namjoo (Iran), etc.[12]

And it was applied to Trịnh Công Sơn, but when and by whom is a mystery. In pre-concert interviews Rod Quinton, the producer of "Bob Dylan—Live in Vietnam," said that it was Joan Baez who dubbed Trịnh Công Sơn the "Bob Dylan of Vietnam." She did so, he said, "forty years ago" when she returned from a trip to Vietnam and was interviewed by an NBC-TV reporter. The interviewer, Rod Quinton said, asked her whether she had met anyone interesting on her trip, and she mentioned Trịnh Công Sơn, adding that he was the Bob Dylan of Vietnam. Quinton's story about

---

11. To back up his assertion that non-singers should be worried, this blogger quotes Bono's description of Steve Jobs: "He's the Bob Dylan of machines, he's the Elvis of the kind of hardware-software dialectic." See "Like a Ruritanian Bob Dylan," http://afteral-litcouldbeworse.blogspot.com/2012/01/like-ruritanian-bob-dylan.html (accessed Apr. 17, 2013).
12. Ibid.

Baez appears in other accounts.[13] I have not been able to find the NBC interview. Joan Baez made only one trip to Vietnam during the war and it was to Hanoi, not to South Vietnam where Trịnh Công Sơn lived. Nancy Lutzow, Joan Baez's personal secretary, confirmed this in an email.[14] Baez, who fervently opposed the war, went to Hanoi in December, 1972, as part of a delegation organized by The Liaison Committee. The announced purpose of the visit was to distribute mail and Christmas presents to American prisoners of war but clearly another goal was to promote the anti-war views of the organizers. After they arrived in Hanoi, President Nixon's Christmas bombing began and Baez and other members of her group sought shelter several times in bomb shelters.[15]

When I lived in South Vietnam in the late 1960s and early 1970s, members of non-government organizations and foreign reporters who had been in Vietnam long enough to know about Trịnh Công Sơn would say "He's the Bob Dylan of Vietnam" to explain his importance to newcomers. After Trịnh Công Sơn died on April 1, 2001, writers of obituaries in the West called Trịnh Công Sơn the "Bob Dylan of Vietnam," usually mentioning that that was what Baez called him.[16] The first person to compare Trịnh Công Sơn to Dylan—in print, at least—may have been a Vietnamese named Trần Văn Dĩnh (1923-2011). In an article about Trịnh Công Sơn that appeared in 1971, Tạ Tỵ cites an article by Trần Văn Dĩnh about Trịnh Công Sơn that had the title "The Bob Dylan of Vietnam." According to Tạ Tỵ, Trần Văn Dĩnh's article appeared in *Peace News* on November 8, 1968.[17] Trần Văn Dĩnh was from Huế, Trịnh Công Sơn's hometown. He served as Chargé d'Affaires in the Vietnamese Embassy in Washington from 1961 to 1963. When his diplomatic career ended he

---

13. See, for example, "Trải chiếu nghe Bob Dylan" [Spread Out a Mat and Listen to Bob Dylan], https://tuoitre.vn/trai-chieu-nghe-bob-dylan-431894.htm (accessed Apr. 9, 2011). See also this article written shortly after Trịnh Công Sơn's death: Bùi Bảo Trúc, "Về Trịnh Công" [About Trịnh Công Sơn], *Văn* [Literature] 53 & 54 (May and June, 2001), 59.
14. Nancy Lutzow, email to the author, Apr. 4, 2012.
15. Joan Baez describes her visit in *And a Voice to Sing With: A Memoir* (New York: Summit Books, 1987), 193-225. See also Jean Thoraval, "B-52's Pound Hanoi Area 9 Miles from City Center," *New York Times*, Dec. 19 1972; and Deirdre Carmody, "4 Who Visited Hanoi Tell of Destruction," *New York Times*, Jan. 2 1973.
16. For example, see "Vietnam Mourns Its 'Dylan,'" *BBC News*, Apr. 4, 2001, http://news.bbc.co.uk/2/hi/entertainment/1260527.stm (accessed Jan. 17, 2012); Shanda Deziel, "Passages," *Maclean's* (Apr. 16, 2001), 16; and Kathleen Adams et al., "Milestones," *Time* (Apr. 16 2001).
17. See Tạ Tỵ, "Trịnh Công Sơn và tiếng ru máu lệ" [Trịnh Công Sơn and Lullabies of Blood and Tears], in *Mười khuôn mặt văn nghệ hôm nay* [Ten Faces of Art Today] (Saigon: Lá Bối, 1971), 23-64.

remained in Washington and became a writer and teacher. During the Vietnam War, American journalists, politicians, and anti-war activists would all seek him out to learn more about the history and culture of Vietnam.

But it's not so important who first made the claim. The important question is whether it is true. Is Trịnh Công Sơn the Bob Dylan of Vietnam? "No, of course he isn't," is the short answer. The two men grew up in different cultures so of course they are different, as Trần Văn Dĩnh, or whoever it was who first said Trịnh Công Sơn was the Bob Dylan of Vietnam, surely was aware. Those who make this claim probably mean only to suggest certain similarities, particularly the fact that both men wrote and sang anti-war songs. So the real question becomes: Yes, both composers wrote anti-war songs, but are there other similarities? In fact, there are. Here's a list:

1. Both composers have been called poets, not simply songwriters.

2. Both have written song lyrics that listeners appreciate and accept as conveying important truths, but which they find very difficult to interpret. What Kurt Gegenhuber, a blogger and Dylanologist, says about Dylan's "poetic strategies" could also be said about Trịnh Công Sơn's: They "revolve around undecided meaning, meaning as an unfinished art for the listener to complete, meaning not as autocratic rule but as democratic process."[18]

3. Both have written moving love songs.

4. Both have been linked romantically to female singers who helped them become famous.

5. Both have articulated the hopes and fears of a young generation of admirers who praise them for saying what they themselves could not express.

6. Trịnh Công Sơn had, and Dylan is still enjoying, a long career as a successful singer-composer. In other words, both men have remained famous in their respective countries despite momentous political and cultural changes.

7. Both have been interested in and inspired by their respective

---

18. Kurt Gegenhuber, "The Celestial Monochord: Hollis Brown's South Dakota," https://www.celestialmonochord.org/hollis_browns_s/ (accessed Apr. 14, 2013).

religious traditions, primarily Buddhist in Trịnh Công Sơn's case, Judeo-Christian in Dylan's.

This lengthy list suggests the two men have much in common but some of these similarities are obvious and superficial and others, when examined more carefully, can be seen as obscuring some very important differences. In contrasting Trịnh Công Sơn and Dylan I shall discuss differences in personality and literary and musical traditions as well as religion. I conclude, however, that the primary reason why Trịnh Công Sơn should not be called the Bob Dylan of Vietnam is because he was a Buddhist and Bob Dylan is best described as a Judeo-Christian, a term I will discuss in coming chapters. They were both spiritual seekers, as similarity number seven above suggests, but the religious traditions that they interiorized are radically different and this difference has produced two composers who see themselves and the world differently.

Long before the Trịnh Công Sơn-Bob Dylan concert in Hồ Chí Minh City, I had grown tired of people saying Trịnh Công Sơn was the Bob Dylan of Vietnam. It has always struck me as a grossly insufficient explanation of who he was. In South Vietnam in the 1960s and early 1970s he was probably more popular than any political or military figure. He deserved, I've always thought, a better introduction than a one-line comparison to an American singer. Hearing this comparison repeated again and again in pre-concert publicity forced me to think more carefully about what bothered me about this identifying tag that Westerners have bestowed on Trịnh Công Sơn. The pages that follow contain the results of my reflection.

Edward Said describes Orientalism as a way of dealing with the Orient "by making statements about it, authorizing views of it, describing it, by teaching it, settling it, ruling over it: in short, Orientalism as a Western style for dominating, restructuring, and having authority over the Orient."[19] Orientalism is not a "'Western' imperialist plot to hold down the 'Oriental' world," Said says. "It *is*, rather than expresses, a certain *will* or *intention* to understand, in some cases to control, manipulate, even to incorporate, what is a manifestly different (or alternative and novel) world."[20] It may be overstepping to label "Orientalist" well-intentioned attempts to explain Trịnh Công Sơn by comparing him to Bob Dylan, but Said helps us understand that as we attempt to know the "other," we

---

19. Edward W. Said, *Orientalism* (New York: Vintage Books, 1978), 3.
20. Ibid., 12.

construct the "other." Naming and fixing someone in discourse, even in tags like "Trịnh Công Sơn is the Bob Dylan of Vietnam," is an exercise of power. But how will I, a Westerner, avoid naming and fixing Trịnh Công Sơn in my own discourse? Australian concert producers promote Trịnh Công Sơn as the Bob Dylan of Vietnam in their discourse and I, an American, promote him as something else in mine. How will my portrait of Trịnh Công Sơn be any less Orientalist than theirs? Perhaps it won't. My intention, however, is to understand, not to control or manipulate, and I will draw heavily on Vietnamese sources. These sources will enable me to convey how Vietnamese themselves view Trịnh Công Sơn.

Most Vietnamese, I should point out, are thrilled, not offended, when someone says "Trịnh Công Sơn is the Bob Dylan of Vietnam." They are proud when their own Trịnh Công Sơn is mentioned in the same breath as Bob Dylan, whom they know to be an internationally acclaimed composer and singer. Vietnamese reveal a touching—but in my view excessive—modesty when they compare Trịnh Công Sơn to Bob Dylan. Upon hearing that I was working on a book about Trịnh Công Sơn that compared him to Bob Dylan, a Vietnamese publishing company expressed interest in publishing it. They wanted it to appear in April of 2012, to coincide with another memorial concert to honor the singer. (Such concerts have become an annual event since Trịnh Công Sơn died.) I rushed to complete a short book, a much-abbreviated version of this one, and my wife translated it into Vietnamese. It was titled *Trịnh Công Sơn-Bob Dylan: Như trăng và nguyệt?* [Trịnh Công Sơn-Bob Dylan: Like a *Trăng* and a *Nguyệt*?].[21] I was pleased that my short book convinced at least some Vietnamese reviewers and readers that comparing the two singers was justified and interesting.

The original impetus for both the shorter book in Vietnamese and this longer book in English was that disappointing concert in Hồ Chí Minh City in 2011. I wanted to reach those expatriates who, during the Trịnh Công Sơn segment of the concert, yelled "We want Bob": I wanted them to know what they, and others who know nothing about Trịnh Công Sơn, were missing. Reading reviews of the concert, I thought of the famous line from the movie *Cool Hand Luke*: "What we have here is a failure to

---

21. John C. Schafer, *Trịnh Công Sơn-Bob Dylan: Như trăng và nguyệt?* [Trịnh Công Sơn-Bob Dylan: Like *Trăng* and *Nguyệt*?], trans. Cao Thị Như-Quỳnh (HCMC: Trẻ, 2012). ("*Trăng*" is a common way to refer to the moon in Vietnamese, and "*Nguyệt*" is a more literary word for moon. These words appear in Trịnh Công Sơn's "Nguyệt ca" [Moon Song].)

communicate." This failure to communicate moved me to write this book. The concert's promoters could have done more. Some acknowledgement of Trịnh Công Sơn's accomplishments from the Dylan camp would have been nice. But an outdoor music concert really is not the proper setting for a serious exchange about culture. To understand the cultural divide one has to talk about many things, but foremost among them, I believe, is religion. The first song that Dylan sang at that concert in Hồ Chí Minh City was "Gonna Change My Way of Thinking." Here is the seventh stanza:

> *Jesus said, "Be ready,*
> *For you know not the hour in which I come."*
> *Jesus said, "Be ready,*
> *For you know not the hour in which I come."*
> *He said, "He who is not for Me is against Me,"*
> *Just so you know where He's coming from*

Probably very few of the expatriates in the crowd spoke Vietnamese and so few understood Trịnh Công Sơn's songs. Most Vietnamese, even if they knew English, must have found Dylan's "Gonna Change My Way of Thinking" equally incomprehensible, or at least very puzzling. I quickly realized that to understand where Trịnh Công Sơn and Bob Dylan were "coming from" one had to talk about religious differences. In 1980 when Dylan was in Hartford, Connecticut, on his Gospel Tour singing his evangelistic Christian songs and trying to bring people in the crowd to Jesus, he said: "We're not gonna be talkin' about no mysticism, no meditation, none of them Eastern religions. We're just gonna be talking about Jesus."[22] In this book we will be talking about Jesus and Christianity, and also about the Buddha and Buddhism.

MY APPROACH

Songs are designed to be heard, not read; they are intended for oral performance. I will sometimes discuss a song's musical features—whether the tempo is quick or slow, for example—but I focus primarily on the printed lyrics, not on the music. I realize this is a limitation, particularly regarding Trịnh Công Sơn's songs, because although most English language readers of this book will have heard many of Dylan's songs, few will have ever heard a Trịnh Công Sơn song. My focus on words, not music, is not, however, in my view, a crippling limitation. Accessibility is not an

---

22. See Clinton Heylin, ed., *Saved! The Gospel Speeches of Bob Dylan* (Madras and New York: Hanuman Books, 1990), 100.

issue; one can easily listen to Trịnh Công Sơn's songs online. Vietnamese is written in a Roman script so one can simply type the Vietnamese title (with or without diacritical marks) in a browser. Recordings of Trịnh Công Sơn himself singing his songs are hard to come by, but mp3 recordings of Sơn and Khánh Ly singing at the Literature Café (Quán Văn) in Saigon in 1966 and 1967 are available on the Internet. These recordings were done with primitive equipment and the sound quality is not up to today's standards, but they are interesting because they reveal how Trịnh Công Sơn and Khánh Ly sang and interacted with their audience when they were on the threshold of fame.[23] Nowadays singers sing Trịnh Công Sơn songs accompanied by a large orchestra, but at the Literature Café there was just Trịnh Công Sơn strumming his guitar.[24]

If words and music are both available, why do I choose to focus on the words? Partly it is because I am a retired English teacher and feel more confident discussing a song's lyrics than its musical qualities. But I focus on lyrics primarily because I am interested in what Trịnh Công Sơn and Dylan are saying in their songs, and I believe the lyrics are the best place to look for clues. Both Trịnh Công Sơn and Bob Dylan have written songs that are difficult to interpret. Their malleability, their openness to different meanings, is one reason for their popularity and durability. Songs with clear and easy meanings appeal to only a limited number of people; songs that allow different interpretations enable more people to relate the song to their own lives. Songs with a catchy tune but simple and uninspiring lyrics may be briefly popular but not durable; they will fail the test of time. Both Trịnh Công Sơn and Bob Dylan have passed this test, and both have been called poets because their lyrics, like good poetry, both challenge and please their fans.

Let me explain my approach by contrasting it with Betsy Bowden's in *Performed Literature: Words and Music by Bob Dylan*.[25] In Bowden's approach the printed lyrics are only a rough guide to meaning which is determined, in each performance, by the voice of the singer and the accompanying instrumentation. Bowden argues that the ambiguity of Dylan's lyrics, the fact that they contain "unresolved oppositions,"

---

23. These videos are available at the website TCS-Forum. http://www.tcs-home.org/songs/mp3/quan-van (accessed Apr. 22, 2010).

24. See Appendix I for links to videos of famous singers performing Trịnh Công Sơn's songs.

25. Betsy Bowden, *Performed Literature: Words and Music by Bob Dylan* (Bloomington, IN: Indiana University Press, 1982).

allows performers to tilt a song toward a particular meaning—to resolve oppositions found in the printed lyrics.[26] Bowden analyses six different performances of one of Dylan's most famous songs, "It Ain't Me Babe." "In words on paper," she says, "the male narrator of 'It Ain't Me Babe' thoroughly rejects the romantic expectations of a woman who stands, at night, outside his bedroom window."[27] In other words, "on paper" the song is one of Bob Dylan's "non-love songs,"[28] songs for which "there is almost no precedent" because they "reject women because they are accepting of sex-role stereotypes."[29] Although Bowden acknowledges that the words on the page say that the narrator of the song "It Ain't Me Babe" rejects the woman, she argues that "some phrases in it suggest the narrator may reject Babe for her own good"; and she also finds "hints about the potential strength of Babe."[30] These hints of a kinder, gentler narrator and a stronger Babe are, however, only developed in one of the six performances of this song that Bowden analyzes—the studio performance for Dylan's 1964 album *Another Side of Bob Dylan.*

One way Dylan suggests a kinder narrator in this performance, Bowden says, is by playing his harmonica at a high pitch at the close of the song. The harmonica at the end, she says, leaves "the listener at a high pitch of anticipation, not finality. The song need not be over; each listener can resolve in her own way the ominous sentiments expressed by the minor chords of Babe's romantic expectations." The second way that Dylan, in his studio performance, makes the song kinder, according to Bowden, is by beginning sung lines "off the beats"—not where the music (Dylan's guitar) would lead the listener to expect. This technique puts the words in focus, forcing the listener to pay attention to Dylan's soothing words about Babe's ability, if she chooses, to make it on her own, to oppose "culturally accepted roles." According to Bowden, Dylan's offbeat guitar tells Babe: "Be a little offbeat—I'll show you how."[31]

---

26. Ibid., 2, 23, and passim.
27. Ibid., 107. See also 2.
28. I will have more to say about Dylan's non-love or anti-love songs in Chapter Six. Bowden says she found the term "non-love song" in an article by Ellen Willis that first appeared in *Commentary* 44 (Nov., 1967), 71-78, as "The Sound of Bob Dylan." Willis' article, with a different title, "Dylan," can also be found in *Bob Dylan: A Retrospective,* ed. Craig McGregor (New York: William Morrow and Company, Inc., 1972), 218-239.
29. Betsy Bowden, *Performed Literature,* 55.
30. Ibid., 114.
31. Ibid., 115.

Let me give one more example of Bowden's approach, her analysis of two different performances by Dylan of another well-known non-love song, "Just Like a Woman." Here's the first stanza of the song:

> *Nobody feels any pain*
> *Tonight as I stand inside the rain*
> *Ev'rybody knows*
> *That Baby's got new clothes*
> *But lately I see her ribbons and her bows*
> *Have fallen from her curls*
> *She takes just like a woman, yes, she does*
> *She makes love just like a woman, yes, she does*
> *And she aches just like a woman*
> *But she breaks just like a little girl*

Bowden analyzes a 1966 studio performance with a backup band for the album *Blonde on Blonde* and a 1974 solo performance with acoustic guitar for a concert in Los Angeles that appeared on the album *Before the Flood*. In both performances the narrator rejects the woman, Bowden says, but in the first he rejects her gently and regretfully; in the second he rejects her "venomously, maliciously, gleefully."[32] According to Bowden, Dylan changes the song from gentle to venomous primarily by altering the way he sings the word "girl." In 1966 he sings "girl" quickly, then gives way to a gentle guitar arpeggio. In 1974, in contrast, he drags the word out. In Bowden's graphic description he "makes a four- and then a three-syllable descent on 'girl.'"[33] In the last refrain he plays with the word even longer, "like a cat with a mouse," Bowden says. Instead of giving way to the guitar, as he did in 1964, in this later performance he "gives over none of his control to the harshly strummed guitar: he manipulates the word 'girl' and with it the narrative situation."[34] "Each 1974 'girl,'" Bowden says, "twists like a knife into the listener's gut, giving the lie to the song's opening line, 'Nobody feels any pain.'"[35]

I admire Bowden's close analysis of song performances and agree that vocal inflections and instrumentation can point the listener toward one of several possible interpretations, but Bowden suggests they can deny or negate what the words say, and that I find hard to accept. What I believe Bowden reveals in her analyses, and what I no doubt shall reveal in mine,

---

32. Ibid., 57.
33. Ibid.
34. Ibid.
35. Ibid., 58.

is that our background and beliefs influence our interpretations. Bowden describes herself as an independent woman who did not like being referred to as a "chick" when she protested the Vietnam War in Madison, Wisconsin in 1966. When she listened to Dylan's "Just Like a Woman," she says that it never occurred to her to identify or even sympathize with the "beribboned and curly-headed Baby being rejected by such a song's narrator." Instead, she identified with the male narrator. "Pronouns can remain neutral in performance, as they seldom can on paper," she explains.[36] Bowden says that before she saw the printed lyrics to "It Ain't Me Babe," she "had never thought of a male narrator and a female Babe."[37]

Bowden says that "in spite of vicious attitudes toward women in the printed lyrics of Dylan's non-love songs, those songs were helping me subconsciously articulate what kind of woman I did not want to be."[38] I accept Bowden's accounts of her own experiences, which certainly demonstrate that, as another Dylan scholar observes, "the meaning so many of us find in his [Dylan's] work is largely of our own making."[39]

One way my approach differs from Bowden's is that I do only a few close analyses of individual songs whereas her book is a collection of long, very detailed (and very thoughtful and intriguing) analyses of performances of Dylan's songs. My focus is much broader than Bowden's. She adopts what she herself describes as a New Critical approach—focusing narrowly on words and music and how they interact while saying little about Dylan's life or the cultural context in which the songs were produced.[40] In the 1950s the New Critics, scholars like Cleanth Brooks and William K. Wimsatt, argued against going outside the text to consider things like biographical information about the author or cultural context. The idea, Brooks says in his preface to *The Well Wrought Urn*, was to see "what residuum, if any, is left after we have referred the poem to its cultural matrix."[41] This is Bowden's approach in her early chapters. In later chapters, particularly in her discussion of performances of "Like a Rolling Stone," Bowden widens

---

36. Ibid., 56.
37. Ibid., 111.
38. Ibid., 56.
39. Michael J. Gilmour, *Tangled Up in the Bible: Bob Dylan and Scripture* (New York: Continuum, 2004), 103.
40. Betsy Bowden, *Performed Literature*, 73. Bowden differs from the New Critics, however, in admitting that she is reporting on how the songs affect her. "I have analyzed," she says, "what occurs in between a revolving black plastic disk and the eardrum-connected cells of my own brain." In this sense her approach resembles a literary critical approach called reader-response criticism.
41. Cleanth Brooks, *The Well Wrought Urn* (New York: Harcourt, Brace and World, 1947), x.

her focus somewhat by discussing how different audiences and historical contexts influenced each performance. In general, however, she focuses, as did the old New Critics, on the text alone—on the sound and words of a work, not the wider cultural context. In *Dylan's Visions of Sin*, the respected literary critic Christopher Ricks applies a similar approach.[42]

In this post-modern age, however, the pendulum has swung in the other direction. Critics now want to talk only about cultural context. According to the New Critics, to search for authorial intention by looking at evidence outside the text itself—in the "cultural matrix"—was to commit the "Intentional Fallacy."[43] Today, however, postmodern critics are so fascinated with this cultural matrix that they come close to suggesting that it, not an individual writer, produces a literary "text." "The text," Roland Barthes writes in "The Death of the Author," "is a tissue of quotations drawn from the innumerable centers of culture," and an author's "only power is to mix writings, to counter the ones with the others, in such a way as never to rest on any one of them. Did he wish to *express himself*, he ought at least to know that the inner 'thing' he thinks to 'translate' is itself only a ready-formed dictionary, its words only explainable through other words, and so on indefinitely."[44]

In the passage I have just quoted Barthes is talking about a "text," not a "work." Except when referring to Barthes' ideas, I won't distinguish these terms, but let me explain how Barthes uses them. In his system, a "work" is a piece of writing that has a clear author and a stable, relatively unambiguous meaning. A work is "readerly"; we consume it quickly and somewhat idly and passively. It does not take us long to process its meaning. "Text," on the other hand, refers to a piece of writing so full of "quotations" that it seems incorrect to ascribe it to a single author. Its meaning, generated by interaction among these different "quotations," is unstable. A "text" is "writerly"; we become actively involved in deciphering its unstable meaning. Writerly texts blur the distinction between writer and reader, not "by intensifying the projection of the reader into the work but by joining them [reading and writing] in a single signifying practice."[45] In other words, writer and reader work together to create the meaning

---

42. Christopher Ricks, *Dylan's Visions of Sin* (New York: Harper Collins, 2003).

43. William K. Wimsatt and Monroe C. Beardsley, "The Intentional Fallacy," in *The Verbal Icon*, ed. William K. Wimsatt (Lexington, KY: Farrar, Straus, and Cudahy, 1954), 3-18.

44. Roland Barthes, "The Death of the Author," in *Image – Music – Text*, trans. Stephen Heath (New York: Hill and Wang, 1977), 146.

45. Roland Barthes, "From Work to Text," in *Image – Music – Text*, 162.

of a text. Barthes distinguishes work from text but in *S/Z*, his analysis of Balzac's "Sarrasine," he demonstrates that even what appears to be a very "readerly" work is actually very "writerly"—composed of hundreds of references to prior texts.[46]

Though I am interested in what might be called "intention relations"—a song's relation to the intent of the composer—I also believe that we understand a song better when we are aware of how it relates to prior texts. All texts echo prior texts; all are composed, as Barthes says, out of a "tissue of quotations."[47] By "quotations" Barthes means references not only to known printed texts but also to various "cultural codes"—to proverbs, for example, or to common understandings and beliefs about the world. I will pay special attention to religious texts because I believe exploring them will enhance our understanding of songs by Trịnh Công Sơn and Bob Dylan. Religious texts—not just printed books but also morals and beliefs sanctioned by a particular faith—profoundly influence people raised in that faith, even those who are not especially devout. Dylan only rarely uses quotation marks when he quotes the Bible in his songs and Trịnh Công Sơn does not use them when he refers to Buddhist concepts. Dylan songs, not simply his explicitly Christian songs, are, however, full of traceable biblical allusions. Buddhism does not have a single "founding book" as does Christianity. There are hundreds of Buddhist texts, most written originally in Pali or Sanskrit, and most Vietnamese know them from translations from the Chinese. Vietnamese, however, have their own terms and expressions for Buddhist concepts and I—relying heavily on Vietnamese scholars and friends—shall try to explain how Trịnh Công Sơn uses them in his songs.

I am discussing songs, a special kind of text. Sometimes a song is one big and obvious "quotation," as when Dylan "covers" Blind Lemon Jefferson's song "See That My Grave Is Kept Clean" or Frank Hutchison's "Stackalee."[48] All songs include, however, smaller and less obvious quotations, those that Barthes says are "anonymous" and "untraceable" and so appear "without inverted commas"—with no acknowledgment

---

46. Roland Barthes, *S/Z*, trans. Richard Miller (New York: Hill and Wang, 1974).
47. Roland Barthes, "The Death of the Author," in *Image – Music – Text*, 146.
48. Dylan's version of "See That My Grave Is Kept Clean," a traditional spiritual, appears on *Bob Dylan* (1962), his very first album. There were no original songs on this album, only covers of traditional songs. "Stack a Lee" (Dylan changes the spelling) appears on *World Gone Wrong* (1993), another album of covers.

of their source.[49] In "Just Like a Woman" Dylan is clearly playing with the expression "just like a woman"; in "It's All Good" he toys with the expression in the title, one that had become common when this song was released in 2009; and in "Gonna Change My Way of Thinking" he gives the common expression "where one's coming from" an interesting double meaning. Note, also, the other quotation, this one *with* "inverted commas," of Matthew 24:42:[50]

> *Jesus said, "Be ready*
> *For you know not the hour in which I come"*
> *He said, "He who is not for Me is against Me"*
> *Just so you know where He's coming from*

Then there are quotations like Dylan's use of the structure and melody of the Child ballad "Lord Randall" for his "A Hard Rain's A-Gonna Fall."[51] This quotation is not exactly unknown or untraceable. Those who know this old Anglo-Scottish murder ballad will be aware of it, but no one knows who wrote the ballad. In any utterance, Barthes says, we hear "off-stage voices" whose origins are lost in the mist of time.[52] "O where ha' you been, Lord Randall, my son? / And where ha' you been, my handsome young man?" Certainly these lines were running through Dylan's mind when he wrote "Oh, where have you been, my blue-eyed son? / Oh, where have you been, my darling young one?"

Anyone who tries to understand a song composed in a language which he or she does not speak natively is aware of the importance of prior texts. That is, of course, my situation when faced with a song by Trịnh Công Sơn. Connotation enables a single word to evoke prior texts. Connotation, Barthes says, makes possible "a (limited) dissemination of meanings, spread like gold dust on the apparent surface of the text (meaning is golden)."[53] Limited, maybe, but important. In Trịnh Công Sơn's song "Moon Song" [Nguyệt ca] the speaker uses two words for "moon"—*trăng* and *nguyệt*—to refer to a woman that he has known. Early in the relationship, the narrator says, *trăng* was *nguyệt* and he was "like a happy kite," "like a flower that's just opened." Later, however, *trăng* stops

---

49. Roland Barthes, "From Work to Text," 160.
50. "Watch therefore: for ye know not what hour your Lord doth come."
51. A "Child ballad" is a ballad included in Francis James Child's *The English and Scottish Popular Ballads*, 5 vols. (Boston, MA: Houghton-Mifflin, 1982-98).
52. Roland Barthes, *S/Z*, 21.
53. Ibid., 8-9.

being *nguyệt* and we get a series of sad images—of rocks too tired to roll, of a tree bereft of branches. The song ends with these lines: "From the time you stopped being *nguyệt* / I stand alone."

Vietnamese whom I've talked to find "Moon Song," like most Trịnh Công Sơn songs, easy to appreciate but difficult to interpret. They know, however, things that a non-native speaker has to learn. They know that *trăng* is a Vietnamese word whereas *nguyệt* is a Sino-Vietnamese word, a Chinese loanword that has been given a Vietnamese pronunciation and incorporated into the Vietnamese language; and they know that *trăng* is not used as a girl's name whereas *nguyệt* is; and they know also that in general Sino-Vietnamese words like *nguyệt* connote learnedness—that using them makes one's discourse sound more literary and scholarly; and they know that *nguyệt* is used in compound words like *nguyệt lão* and *nguyệt hoa*, words that have romantic connotations. *Nguyệt lão* is the old man of the moon, who, according to a popular belief, sits in heaven and arranges marriages; *nguyệt hoa* literally means moon and flowers but connotes a frivolous or promiscuous love affair. Vietnamese also know many sad songs of failed love relationships that preceded this one. The so-called pre-war songs, *nhạc tiền chiến*, popular when Trịnh Công Sơn was becoming famous, are almost all about impossible, unrequited love (See Chapter Eighteen). Possibly Trịnh Công Sơn decided that by playing cleverly with the words *trăng* and *nguyệt* he could make his song about a failed love relationship a little fresher and more intriguing than older songs that tell a similar sad story.

The claim that I have been making is that the meaning of a song is intertextual. "To say a text's meaning is intertextual," Simon Malpas and Paul Wake explain, "is to claim that it derives its meanings from its relationships with other texts, for example through overt and covert allusions and references. Meaning is not, therefore, something which inheres in that text and only that text; it is relational. Similarly, no text is seen as autonomous; instead, every text is made up of many other texts."[54] This definition suggests that there is both a macro and micro aspect to intertextuality: a text *as a whole* relates to prior texts and at the same time is made up of allusions and references to other texts. The relation of Dylan's "Love Henry" (1993) to Dick Justice's "Henry Lee" (1932), and the relation of both songs to the Child ballad "Lady Isabel and the Elf Knight," represents

---

54. Simon Malpas and Paul Wake, *The Routledge Companion to Critical Theory* (London: Routledge, 2006), 208.

intertextuality at the macro level. Dylan's use of the expression "where he's coming from" in "Gonna Change My Way of Thinking" and Trịnh Công Sơn's taking advantage of the connotations of the words *trăng* and *nguyệt* in "Nguyệt Ca" represents intertextuality at the micro level.

Intertextuality at the macro level also includes the relationship of an artist's body of work to works created by his or her predecessors. Many of Bob Dylan's early songs caught people's attention because they were different from rock 'n' roll songs of the 1950s, songs that by the 1960s Americans had grown tired of. Trịnh Công Sơn's early love songs appealed to young Vietnamese in the South because they sounded newer and fresher than the pre-war songs of the 1940s and early 1950s. According to some critics, the ability to "defamiliarize"—to get us to see familiar things in new ways—is an essential skill for artists.[55] Both Dylan and Trịnh Công Sơn demonstrate this skill

One way both Dylan and Trịnh Công Sơn defamiliarize is by slowing comprehension, preventing listeners from processing the meaning of their songs too quickly and automatically—by making their songs "writerly" not "readerly," to use Roland Barthes' terms. Many of Trịnh Công Sơn's and Bob Dylan's greatest songs are writerly texts, not readerly works, and so knowing their intertextual relations helps us understand and appreciate them. I can't agree with Barthes, however, when he says that an author's (or composer's) only power is to arrange prior texts. (I suspect he exaggerates to get our attention.) Both New Critics and postmodernist critics, many of them inspired by literary theorists like Barthes, seem too eager to kill off the author, to divorce a text from its creator. Neither are interested in authorial intention. I believe, however, that although one can never be certain of the answer, one should still try to answer the question, "What is the author trying to say in this work?" It is too important and interesting a question to ignore. E. D. Hirsch, a rare defender of authorial intention, pointed out several decades ago that when the meaner is excluded from the meaning, "when we fail to conjoin a man's [sic] intentions to his words, we lose the soul of speech, which is to convey meaning and to understand

---

55. The concept of "defamiliarization" is associated with the work of the Russian Formalists, particularly Victor Shklovsky, who argued that writers make their works literary—that is, different from ordinary communication—by making them strange or unfamiliar. In Chapter Nineteen I argue that Trịnh Công Sơn used various devices to defamiliarize his songs—to make them different from pre-war songs. For more on this concept and the Russian Formalists, see *Formalist Criticism: Four Essays*, trans. and ed. Lee T. Lemon and Marion J. Reis (Lincoln, NE: University of Nebraska Press, 1965).

what is intended to be conveyed."[56] Hirsch points out that critics who dismiss authorial intention, including Roland Barthes, adopt a double standard, one for the authors whose works they criticize and another for their own writing. When analyzing a literary work, they disregard authorial intention, but after reading a negative review of something they have written, they respond, "That's not what I meant at all."[57]

Roland Barthes, however, insists that we give the authors and their intentions too much respect. Literary scholars and copyright lawyers have insisted, he says, that "the author is the reputed father and the owner of his work." They have insisted that we have "respect for the manuscript and the author's declared intentions." Less respect—but still too much, Barthes suggests—is shown the authors of "texts."[58] As I discuss the songs of Trịnh Công Sơn and Bob Dylan, however, I will be guided by the assumption that we don't give composers too much respect—only the respect they deserve—when we try to figure out what they are saying in their songs.

One final aspect of my approach has to do with context—two different contexts, actually: the historical and political contexts in which Trịnh Công Sơn and Dylan composed their songs, and the contexts of performance—the atmosphere that has prevailed in the various venues where their songs have been sung, and the relationship between singer and audience and between singer and other performers, for example. Both these contexts influence how a song is received. Information on the first context—the historical and political situation—is fairly easy to find; information on the context of a particular performance, unless one was in the audience, is, however, very difficult to obtain. One senses that Betsy Bowden is interested in both these contexts, but she has little to say about them. She does, however, have lots to say about vocal inflections and instrumentation—things that one can analyze by listening to sound recordings of performances. Although the information is hard to obtain, I will, when it seems important and when information is available, report on both the historical/political context and the context of performance.

Let me give two examples to illustrate how historical/political context and performance venue can influence how a song is received. When in 1975 Trịnh Công Sơn sang "Join Hands in a Great Circle" on a Saigon radio

---

56. E. D. Hirsch, *The Aims of Interpretation* (Chicago, IL: University of Chicago Press, 1976), 90.
57. Ibid., 91.
58. Roland Barthes, "From Work to Text," 160.

station soon after the city, and all of Vietnam, came under communist control, it was received differently than it was when he first sang it in 1968. On July 6 1963 at the invitation of the Student Nonviolent Coordinating Committee (SNCC), Dylan visited Greenwood, Mississippi and sang "Only a Pawn in Their Game," a song about the murder of Medgar Evers, head of the National Association for the Advancement of Colored People (NAACP) in Mississippi. On June 12, less than a month before Dylan went to Greenwood, Evers had been shot by a member of the White Citizens' Council in Jackson, Mississippi. Dylan sang at a voter registration rally on Silas Magee's farm for an audience of roughly 300 people—mostly local African Americans.[59] Surely this audience received this song differently than did the larger and predominately white audiences who heard it later in the North.

I have said that these different contexts can influence how a song is "received." But do these contexts change the meaning of a song? Betsy Bowden thinks they do. "It Ain't Me Babe" performed by Dylan in studio in 1964 is, she says, about a man rejecting a woman; performed as a duet by Dylan and Joan Baez at Philharmonic Hall during the same year it becomes, in her view, "a playful and teasing love song."[60] Dylan and Baez *were* romantically involved in 1964—"Now, me and Joan had this *thing*," Dylan told David Hajdu[61]—and chuckles and giggles can be heard on the recording; Baez does sing softly, letting Dylan lead her, as Bowden points out.[62] Clearly there is something different about these two 1964 performances, but is it a meaning difference?

In *Tangled Up in Blue*, Michael J. Gilmour says, "Something new is created every time a Dylan CD is played, and every time he walks out on stage."[63] But what exactly is that "something"? We have all had the experience of listening to an old song—often the same recording, the same performance that we loved long ago—and realizing that the song, as we say, "means something different" to us now. This book is in part a report of what the songs of Bob Dylan and Trịnh Công Sơn, songs so important to me when I was young, "mean" to me—and to Americans and Vietnamese—now. But it is also an attempt to place the songs in a

---

59. Robert Shelton, *No Direction Home: The Life and Music of Bob Dylan* (Milwaukee, WI: Backbeat Books, 2011), 130.
60. Betsy Bowden, *Performed Literature*, 15-116.
61. David Hajdu, *Positively 4th Street* (New York: Farrar, Straus and Giroux, 2001), 171.
62. Betsy Bowden, *Performed Literature*, 115.
63. Michel J. Gilmour, *Tangled Up in the Bible*, 104.

historical context and suggest—even if it's only an educated guess—what Dylan and Trịnh Công Sơn wanted to communicate when they first wrote their songs. I do not presuppose that they wanted to communicate a single idea, but I do assume they wanted to communicate something. I think it is important to see more than a little hyperbole in claims that a completely new meaning emerges at each performance and every time one listens to a song.

There are different ways to get at the issue raised by Dylan and Baez's light-hearted, meaning-changing (in Bowden's view) performance of "It Ain't Me Babe" and by the common experience of having the same song affect us differently in different times. One can see the Dylan-Baez duet as Barthes might see it, as an "intertext," closely linked to Dylan's original studio performance of the same song, a comment on it, almost a parody of it, a "text" that will be followed by other performances. Or one can use the distinction that E. D. Hirsch makes between "verbal meaning" and "significance," reserving the former term for the creator's original intended meaning and the latter term for what makes the text come alive for different listeners in different times.[64] Observing this distinction, when an old song—or even a not-so-old song—affects us differently when we listen to it again, we would say that its significance for us has changed, but not its meaning.

I think it is useful to lay out one's assumptions and mention the scholars whose approaches have shaped one's own, and that is what I have tried to do here. During my academic career I have been exposed to various ways of analyzing oral and written texts. I've studied approaches proposed by rhetoricians, linguists, and literary critics and theorists. It has been my impression that each approach has something to offer and so I have hammered together an approach that draws—I hope—on the best of all of them. I have not felt obligated to follow any single approach in a rigorous way. My goal instead has been to find interesting things to say about the lives and songs of Trịnh Công Sơn and Bob Dylan. My approach is a simple one: I study the songs of two songwriters—one Vietnamese, one American—to learn more about their respective cultures, and I study their respective cultures—paying particular attention to religious differences—to better understand their songs.

---

64. Robert Shelton, *No Direction Home: The Life and Music of Bob Dylan.*

I

WAR & LOVE

1

ANTI-WAR IN DIFFERENT WAYS

Although it is true that both Trịnh Công Sơn and Bob Dylan wrote anti-war songs, this is a good example of a similarity that hides some important differences. The war that Trịnh Công Sơn objected to in his anti-war songs was the war taking place in his country. He wrote his anti-war songs during the Second Indochina War which began in the early 1960s and ended with the fall of the American-backed Saigon regime in 1975. Americans call this the "Vietnam War." In Vietnam today it is referred to as the American War or the war to oppose the Americans (*chiến tranh chống Mỹ*). Anti-communist Vietnamese who fled to other countries when communist troops captured Saigon call it the war to oppose communism (*chiến tranh chống cộng*). The Second Indochina war was preceded by the First Indochina War between the French and their Vietnamese supporters and revolutionary troops inspired by Hồ Chí Minh. This war began in 1946 and ended in 1954 when French forces were defeated at the Battle of Điện Biên Phủ and the Geneva Accords divided the country at the 17ᵗʰ parallel.

Sơn wrote his anti-war songs during the Second Indochina War and in several songs he refers to specific battles and events that occurred during the war. In one famous song, "A Mother's Legacy" [Gia tài của mẹ],* written in 1965, he talks about twenty years of civil war but also about other wars that preceded it:

> *A thousand years slaves of the Chinese*
> *A hundred years slaves of the French*
> *Twenty years of civil war*

A mother's legacy to leave for her children
A mother's legacy, the sad country of Vietnam

It is this twenty year long civil war that disturbs him the most. He refers to it again in a song composed in 1967 called "A Long Day in the Native Land" [Ngày dài trên quê hương]:

An old person in the park
A crazy person in the city
A person lies without breathing
A person sits for twenty years
Watching flares turn the night bright
Young children have grown used to bombs
Vietnamese lie with their wounds

His reference to a civil war in "A Mother's Legacy," which ignores the involvement of Chinese advisors in the North and American soldiers in the South, is noteworthy. He mentions the internecine nature of the war again in the first stanza of another song, "Who Is Still Vietnamese" [Những ai còn là Việt Nam], written in 1969:

Open your eyes and look around
Who is still Vietnamese
A million people have died
Open your eyes and turn over the corpse of an enemy soldier
On it you'll see a Vietnamese face

If you turned over corpses on Vietnamese battlefields, however, you could see a white or black face. People of other races were killing Vietnamese, and some of these people were dying in the process. In referring to the Indochina Wars as twenty years of "civil war" Trịnh Công Sơn ignores the ideological and international dimensions of the conflict, including the fact that it was a part of the Cold War, a battle between communist nations and America and its allies. Trịnh Công Sơn's refusal to portray the war as a war of aggression by foreigners ensured that he would have trouble with the new socialist regime, which he did. In the view of the literary critic Đặng Tiến, however, arguing that the war was not originally a civil war is the business of politicians, not artists. The term "civil war," he says, had an "emotional basis":

The two words "civil war" [*nội chiến*] [in the song "A Mother's Legacy"] may not have made [rational] sense, but they had an emotional basis to them. They satisfied a psychological need of the general population that had not been politicized and had not received a political education—a population that was just sick at heart about people of the same race killing each other and so didn't search after the complicated origins of the problem.[1]

Trịnh Công Sơn was not engaging in a political discussion, he was writing songs, and he knew that focusing on the civil war aspect of the conflict, the fact that people of the same race were killing each other, was the most effective way to oppose the war. Trịnh Công Sơn also knew that although he had his protectors in the Saigon regime, if he became too provocative—if he attacked Americans in his songs, for example—then his protectors could not prevent him from being drafted or imprisoned. So he talked about a civil war.

Interestingly, however, even in "A Mother's Legacy," the song in which he refers explicitly to the war as a civil war, he seems—in the last two lines of the song—to hint at the international dimensions of the conflict. The concluding lines are: "A mother's legacy, a mixed-blood gang / A mother's legacy, an unfaithful horde." What gang and what horde is Trịnh Công Sơn referring to in these lines? Is it to people who are literally of mixed blood or to Vietnamese who have no foreign blood but have allied themselves with non-Vietnamese—to people who have not been true, who have, as the last line of the song suggests, been "unfaithful [*bội tình*] to their race, the golden-skinned race"? Perhaps Sơn is referring to Vietnamese who became allies of the Americans, or to Vietnamese who became allies of the Soviet Union and the People's Republic of China. Or to both. As I will explain in Chapter Nineteen, Trịnh Công Sơn is famous for writing obscure lyrics. Obscurity is for him primarily an artistic device, but in his anti-war songs it could also be a survival mechanism, a way to avoid being muzzled completely by the political regime in Saigon.

Support for the idea that by "mixed-blood gang" and "unfaithful horde" in "A Mother's Legacy" Trịnh Công Sơn means Vietnamese who cooperate with foreign powers can be found in another song, "Let the Native Land Smile" [Cho quê hương mỉm cười]. Trịnh Công Sơn never officially released this song though it is available in collections of his songs.[2] Here is the last stanza:

---

1. Đặng Tiến, "Trịnh Công Sơn: Tiếng hát hòa bình" [Trịnh Công Sơn: Voice of Peace], *Văn Học* [Literary Studies] Special Edition on Trịnh Công Sơn (Oct. and Nov. 2010), 192.
2. It is included, for example, in Ban Mai, *Trịnh Công Sơn: Vết chân dã tràng* [Trịnh Công Sơn: Footprint of a Sand Crab] (Hanoi: Lao Động, 2008), 225-226.

Our hands a million strong shatter servitude
Within our hearts trust is a weapon
We stand proud next to the animals with human faces
A pack of animals, lackeys for foreigners
Our feet a million strong walk on this land
Within our hearts is a new field of rice
We heat up our will as hot as the sun
Breaking the chains to let the native land smile

Note that in this song we find not vague references to a "mixed-blood gang" or an "unfaithful horde" but rather a specific condemnation of Vietnamese who have become lackeys of foreigners. In "Let the Native Land Smile" Trịnh Công Sơn would seem to be saying that Vietnamese should not serve foreign powers but it is not clear what foreigners he has in mind. Americans were the most conspicuous foreigners in South Vietnam, but he could be referring to Chinese or Russians, allies of the Democratic Republic of Vietnam. This song resembles Trịnh Công Sơn's movement songs like "We Must See the Sun" [Ta phải thấy mặt trời] and "Huế Sài Gòn Hà Nội" that I will discuss in Chapter Three, but these later songs, composed in 1968 and 1969, contain no references to foreign lackeys. In this and other anti-war songs Trịnh Công Sơn emphasizes the internecine nature of the war—that it involved people of golden skin killing other people of golden skin. His famous collection of anti-war songs, *Songs of Golden Skin* [Ca khúc da vàng], is therefore aptly titled.[3] In a song in that collection, "Night Now, Night Tomorrow" [Đêm bây giờ đêm mai], Trịnh Công Sơn sings: "Oh Vietnamese golden skin broken and crushed / That flesh and bone that is so sacred." In this sense Trịnh Công Sơn *did* oppose the war "generally" [*chung chung*], as officials in the current socialist government maintained. He didn't blame one side or the other. He simply mourned the fact that people of the same race were killing each other.

How general was Trịnh Công Sơn's objection to war? Did he oppose all wars? Vietnamese emphasize that all Trịnh Công Sơn's songs, even his anti-war songs, were love songs in the sense that they all are imbued with a deep humanistic spirit. This humanism, no doubt reinforced by his

---

3. At least two different song books titled *Songs of Golden Skin* [Ca khúc da vàng] were published. Early editions had twelve songs; later editions had fourteen songs. I have copies of both editions that I bought when I was in Vietnam in the late 1960s and early 1970s. Neither edition has a date of publication. The Trịnh Công Sơn-Forum website does not list the first publication; it indicates that the second edition was published in 1967.

Buddhist upbringing, would have—it seems to me—made it difficult for him to approve of any war. He focused on the war in his country because the situation was urgent: the war was tearing his country apart. Trịnh Công Sơn made it clear that he opposed all wars in an interview with a reporter from the *New York Times* in February of 1969. On February 8, 1969, the government of Nguyễn Văn Thiệu had issued a decree banning the playing of his songs and the distribution of tape recordings and sheet music. When the *Times* asked about the ban, Trịnh Công Sơn told the reporter: "Well, frankly speaking, I am against the war in general," he said. "I don't want to do what some people did: to draw a clear difference between just and unjust wars. Wars, any wars, bring about death and destruction and I am against war generally."[4]

If pressed for more evidence that he opposed war "generally," I would offer his "A Morning in Spring" [Một buổi sáng mùa xuân],* a song about a young child killed after he or she stepped on a mine. It seems motivated by a sympathy for others and an anti-war spirit that transcends national or racial boundaries.

Dylan wrote his anti-war songs from a different temporal and spatial perspective. He wrote only a few songs that are explicitly anti-war and no song, to my knowledge, that addresses the war in Vietnam specifically. Songs commonly identified as Dylan's anti-war songs—"Blowin' in the Wind" (1962), "With God on Our Side," (1963), "The Times They Are A-Changin'" (1963), and "Masters of War" (1963)—were all released before the Vietnam War became front page news in the US. Fearing a nuclear war, after Stalin's death in 1953 Khrushchev proclaimed a policy of "peaceful co-existence" with the US. In 1961, however, he pledged support for "wars of national liberation," seeing these wars as a way to advance Soviet policy objectives without risking military confrontation. Dylan wrote his anti-war songs before one of these wars, the Vietnam war, heated up and so his anti-war songs express a global cold war, not a country-specific hot war, perspective. He feared modern warfare would destroy the whole world, not just a single country. He looked at war from the perspective of someone who lived in a country with atomic weapons that, if used, could result in a nuclear holocaust.

---

4. Joseph B. Treaster, "Saigon Bans the Anti-war Songs of Vietnamese Singer-Composer," *New York Times*, Feb. 12 1969. See also Nguyễn Đắc Xuân, *Trịnh Công Sơn: Có một thời như thế* [There Was Such a Time], 100.

In his autobiography Dylan talks about being trained in grade school to take cover under a desk when the air-raid sirens blew. In the 1950s, underground fallout shelters were being built in the larger towns. "The threat of annihilation was a scary thing," Dylan says in his autobiography.[5] Confrontations with the Soviet Union—the Berlin Wall crisis in 1961 and the Cuban missile crisis in 1962, for example—heightened fears of a nuclear conflagration. Dylan addressed these fears most explicitly in "Let Me Die in My Footsteps" and in "With God on Our Side," both written in the early 1960s. The latter song has these lines:

> But now we got weapons
> Of the chemical dust
> If fire them we're forced to
> Then fire them we must
> One push of the button
> And a shot the world wide
> And you never ask questions
> When God's on your side

In the early 1960s Dylan was known as a writer of "protest songs," not "anti-war songs," because in his songs he protested a variety of political and social problems, not simply war. "Only a Pawn in Their Game" is about the killing of Medgar Evers, an organizer for the National Association for the Advancement of Colored People. In "North Country Blues," the speaker, whose father and husband worked in the iron ore fields in Dylan's native Minnesota, describes the suffering that follows when the mines close down. "Maggie's Farm" is about a laborer exploited by cruel employers. Although in "Blowin' in the Wind," a song sung by anti-war protestors, Dylan does ask "how many times must the cannonballs fly before they're forever banned," this song, as David Hajdu says, is "an all-purpose protest anthem" and could be—and has been—sung to protest many misfortunes and injustices.[6]

It is also important to point out that Dylan's period of political engagement was very short, only about two years —1962-63. When his album *Another Side of Bob Dylan* was released in 1964, he had already moved away from political songs to more personal material. In an interview with Nat Hentoff when he was recording this album Dylan

---

5. Bob Dylan, *Chronicles: Volume One* (New York: Simon and Schuster, 2004), 29-30.
6. David Hajdu, *Positively 4th Street* (New York: Farrar, Straus and Giroux, 2001), 117.

explained that there wouldn't be any "finger-pointing" songs in it. When Hentoff asked him what he meant, he said, "I looked around and saw all these people pointing fingers at the bomb. But the bomb was boring because what's wrong goes much deeper than the bomb. What's wrong is how few people are free. Most people walking around are tied down to something that doesn't let them really speak, so they just add their confusion to the mess."[7] "My Back Pages," one of the songs on *Another Side of Bob Dylan*, is generally interpreted as Dylan's good-bye to protesting and the writing of protest songs. Every stanza ends with the same refrain, "Ah, but I was so much older then / I'm younger than that now." In this song Dylan attacks his prior "protest" self for being too old—by which he means too consumed by self-righteous indignation, too serious, too quick to oversimplify complex issues. Other folk singers like Pete Seeger were very earnest and sometimes sanctimonious. Dylan may be suggesting a similarity between his earlier "protest" self and folk singers who preceded him. Here is the second stanza of "My Back Pages":

> *Half-wracked prejudice leaped forth*
> *"Rip down all hate," I screamed*
> *Lies that life is black and white*
> *Spoke from my skull. I dreamed*
> *Romantic facts of musketeers*
> *Foundationed deep, somehow*
> *Ah, but I was so much older then*
> *I'm younger than that now*

At the close of an interview that appeared in *Playboy* in 1966, Nat Hentoff asked Dylan this final question: "Now that you've more or less retired from political and social protest, can you conceive of any circumstance that might persuade you to reinvolve yourself?" "No," Dylan replied, "not unless all the people in the world disappeared."[8]

When Trịnh Công Sơn was writing his most famous anti-war songs in 1965, Dylan had already moved on to songs that were more personal than political. Dylan could stop pointing fingers at the bomb because bombs were not falling on his country, but Trịnh Công Sơn did not have that luxury. He continued to write anti-war songs, producing, by one

---

7. Nat Hentoff, "The Crackin', Shakin', Breakin' Sounds," in *Bob Dylan: The Essential Interviews*, ed. Jonathan Cott (New York: Wenner Books, 2006), 23.
8. "Interview with Nat Hentoff, *Playboy*," in *Bob Dylan: The Essential Interviews*, ed. Jonathan Cott (New York: Wenner Books, 2006), 111.

researcher's count, sixty-nine in all.[9] As for Dylan, he wrote many songs protesting flaws in people and in the society in which he lived but only half a dozen or so anti-war songs. This difference in quantity is important but so is a difference in tone and message. In his anti-war songs Trịnh Công Sơn continually counsels against hatred and resentment whereas Dylan, when he is protesting war or some other social evil, seems consumed by these emotions. Take, for example, what is probably Dylan's most famous anti-war song, "Masters of War." Dylan himself insists that it is not an anti-war song and in an interview in 2001 he seems irritated that people have given it that label. "Every time I sing it, someone writes that it's an anti-war song," he told Robert Hilburn. "But there's no anti-war sentiment in that song. I'm not a pacifist. I don't think I've ever been one. If you look closely at the song, it's about what Eisenhower was saying about the dangers of the military-industrial complex in this country. I believe strongly in everyone's right to defend themselves by every means necessary."[10]

President Eisenhower used the phrase "military-industrial complex" in a farewell address to the American people in 1961. He urged citizens to be vigilant and not let armaments manufacturers obtain too much power and influence. Many Americans accepted his advice as useful and timely. Many people also believe that arms merchants are engaged in a gruesome business. The desire for revenge shown by the speaker in this song, however, particularly in the last stanza, has upset some. This stanza disturbed Joan Baez and Judy Collins so much they refused to sing it when they performed this song.[11] Here's how "Masters of War" ends:

> And I hope that you die
> And your death'll come soon
> I will follow your casket
> In the pale afternoon
> And I'll watch while you're lowered
> Down to your deathbed

9. According to Michiko Yoshi, who wrote a thesis on Trịnh Công Sơn at the University of Paris, of the 136 songs that Trịnh Công Sơn wrote between 1959 and 1972, sixty-nine were anti-war songs. Đặng Tiến cites her study in "Trịnh Công Sơn: Tiếng hát hòa bình," 180.
10. Interview by Robert Hilburn, "How Does It Feel?: Don't Ask," *Los Angeles Times*, Sept. 16, 2001.
11. See Mike Marqusee, *Chimes of Freedom* (New York: The New Press, 2003), 70; and Robert Shelton, who reports that Judy Collins "refused to sing the final vengeful lines." According to Shelton, "Bob said her version blunted his intent." See Robert Shelton, *No Direction Home: The Life and Music of Bob Dylan* (Milwaukee, WI: Backbeat Books, 2011), 116.

And I'll stand o'er your grave
'Til I'm sure that you're dead

In his anti-war songs, however, Trịnh Công Sơn continually advocates forgiveness and an end to hatred. In "A Mother's Legacy" [Gia tài của mẹ]* (1965) Trịnh Công Sơn lists the calamities that have afflicted his country but urges the children of Vietnam to avoid a resentful, vengeful attitude. "Oh, children of the same father," he sings, "forget anger and resentment."

In "Rebuild People, Rebuild Homes" [Dựng lại người dựng lại nhà], a song written in 1968, the most violent year of the war, he describes how Vietnamese will rebuild their country when peace comes. He suggests that they must first rebuild themselves, a process that involves covering hatred with compassion:

We take to the road together
To rebuild love
Our mother's heart in olden times was as immense as the Pacific
Children are the rivers
Who today celebrate the removal of hatred
Who bring silt to cover the devastation,
And compassion [lòng nhân ái] *for the rose*

And in "Hue, Saigon, Hanoi," written in 1969, he sings,

For twenty years crying in misery
Hue, Saigon, Hanoi
Our Vietnamese hearts are sick
Hue, Saigon, Hanoi
Oh you, bombs and bullets
And you, greed, no weapons can destroy our people
Oh Vietnam
Wake up and let your eyes sweep away hatred

Neither Bob Dylan nor Trịnh Công Sơn wanted to be seen as speaking for any particular political faction. As his friend Allen Ginsberg put it, "Dylan didn't want to be anyone's trained seal." Trịnh Công Sơn's friend, the painter Bửu Chỉ, says that Trịnh Công Sơn didn't take sides, meaning he didn't support the National Liberation Front or the Saigon regime and their American backers.[12] It was, of course, easier for Dylan than it was for Trịnh Công Sơn to avoid being identified with a political faction. In the

---

12. Bửu Chỉ, "Nhạc phản chiến Trịnh Công Sơn" [Trịnh Công Sơn's Anti-war Music], *Diễn đàn* [Forum] 110 (2001), 30.

heated political environment of South Vietnam, it was not easy to stand on the sidelines. If Dylan expressed his worries about "the bomb" in his songs he wouldn't be imprisoned and his songs wouldn't be banned. If he forgot about the bomb and wrote personal songs, Joan Baez and other activists would be disappointed but he risked no serious repercussions.

It was more difficult for Trịnh Công Sơn to avoid becoming identified with one side or the other. Vietnam during the war was a highly charged political environment. "If today we look back at that time," says his friend Bửu Chỉ, "it is clear that he (Trịnh Công Sơn) walked between two sides, and at any time a bullet from one side or the other could end his life."[13] Bửu Chỉ does not exaggerate. While Trịnh Công Sơn and Khánh Ly were performing at the Faculty of Letters of the University of Saigon on December 20, 1967, several young men and a woman grabbed the microphone and began making a pro-National Liberation Front speech. The date is significant. The intruders wished to commemorate the founding of the National Liberation Front which occurred on December 20, 1960. People in the audience climbed on the stage and began pushing the intruders. A fight broke out and, according to Đặng Tiến, someone on the concert staff was shot. Then the NLF demonstrators vanished on motorcycles.[14]

Sơn's friend Bửu Chỉ and the writer Đặng Tiến argue that Trịnh Công Sơn succeeded in remaining neutral. Bửu Chỉ says that the only "-ism" Trịnh Công Sơn supported was humanism. "In his anti-war music, he had no political intention at all. Everything was done on orders from his heart."[15] Some people question whether Trịnh Công Sơn remained neutral into the late 1960s and I will consider their views in the next chapter, but one thing seems clear: throughout the 1960s both Trịnh Công Sơn and Bob Dylan were able to capture the mood of people in their respective countries, particularly the mood of young people. Their success in convincing the young that they spoke for them is one clear similarity between the two composers. Dave Van Ronk, a musician who was a friend of Dylan's, says that "if there is an American collective unconscious, Bobby had somehow tapped into it."[16] Another friend, Liam Clancy, a member of Irish singing group the Clancy Brothers, says Dylan was like the "shape changers" in

---

13. Ibid., 32.
14. See Bernard Weinraub, "A Vietnamese Guitarist Sings of Sadness of War," *New York Times*, Jan. 1, 1968; and Đặng Tiến, "Trịnh Công Sơn: Tiếng hát hòa bình," 190.
15. Bửu Chỉ, "Nhạc phản chiến Trịnh Công Sơn" [Trịnh Công Sơn's Anti-war Music], 30.
16. Dave Van Ronk in Martin Scorcese's film *No Direction Home* (2005).

Irish myths. "He changed voices. He changed images. It wasn't necessary for him to be a definite person. He was a receiver. He was possessed. He articulated what the rest of us wanted to say but couldn't say."[17]

Trịnh Công Sơn had a similar ability. When I arrived to teach English at Phan Chu Trinh High School in Đà Nẵng in 1968, my students insisted on my listening to Trịnh Công Sơn's songs in his collection *Songs of Golden Skin* [Ca khúc da vàng]. It was their way of explaining to me how they felt about the war. "His voice," Bửu Chi says, "was like an invisible thread that quickly unified the private moods and destinies of individuals living in Southern cities."[18]

---

17. Liam Clancy in Martin Scorcese's film *No Direction Home* (2005).
18. Bửu Chỉ, "Nhạc phản chiến," 30.

2

WAS TRỊNH CÔNG SƠN
A NEUTRALIST?

Both the government of the Republic of Vietnam and the current socialist regime have banned Trịnh Công Sơn's anti-war songs. When Trịnh Công Sơn first began composing, his songs were distributed on dittoed song sheets that Sơn and the singer Khánh Ly passed out at concerts. Other students would copy them into their student notebooks. Later, more professionally printed collections appeared, each one containing the words and music to around a dozen songs. When the war escalated in 1964-65, American troops poured in and with them came consumer goods, part of the US plan to boost South Vietnam's economy. Japanese Honda motorcycles and Akai and Sony tape recorders soon became readily available. The first tape recorders used in Vietnam were the large reel-to-reel variety which the Vietnamese called *Akai* after the brand name. They were cumbersome and expensive but were soon replaced by much more convenient and considerably cheaper cassette tape recorders. These developments led to a paradoxical situation: The same American escalation of the war that had provoked Trịnh Công Sơn to write antiwar songs also provided him with the means for their distribution and thereby helped make him a "popular" singer, in the American sense of this term. The government decree in 1969 that forbade circulation of Trịnh Công Sơn's songs—both tapes and sheet music—was easily subverted. Cassette tapes could be copied so fans could borrow a friend's cassette and make a copy. To circulate his printed song collections he used four different printing houses so if the police raided one, he could still get them printed.[1]

---

1. Trịnh Công Sơn, "Trời kỳ trốn lính" [My Draft Dodging Days], a 1987 essay reprinted in Nguyễn Đắc Xuân, *Trịnh Công Sơn: Có một thời như thế* [There Was Such a Time] (HCMC: Văn Học, 2003), 181.

Young people Sơn's age had to worry about being drafted. Sơn avoided the draft and managed to lead a fairly normal life by fasting and by taking Diamox before required physical exams. Diamox, a brand name for acetazolamide, removes fluid from the body and is used to treat congestive heart failure, seizures, and glaucoma. Apparently it reduced Sơn's weight, or maybe just his overall health, enough to enable him to flunk the physical exam. After three years, however, his health deteriorated and he adopted other draft dodging strategies. For a while he lived like a homeless person with other draft dodgers in prefabricated houses on the grounds of the Faculty of Letters of Saigon University.[2] It seems, however, that the police could have arrested Trịnh Công Sơn if they wished to. Đặng Tiến points out that the homeless area where Sơn was staying was near the Independence Palace, the seat of the Nguyễn Văn Thiệu government. Why the police did not arrest him remains a mystery. One theory is that he was protected by high-ranking members of the Thiệu government. Đặng Tiến says that Vice President Nguyễn Cao Kỳ was one of his protectors. He protected the singer, Đặng Tiến says, because he wanted to mend fences with those in the Struggle Movement in Huế, including Buddhist leaders—monks like Thích Trí Quang. The Thiệu-Kỳ regime had crushed this Struggle Movement in 1966. Đặng Tiến says that Nguyễn Cao Kỳ and Trịnh Công Sơn also were friends. He gave Sơn bottles of whisky, he says, and even let him fly to Huế on air force planes.[3]

In his songs Trịnh Công Sơn pleads for an end to anger and hatred. These facts would suggest that Trịnh Công Sơn supported neither side in the war—that he was a neutralist interested in peace. Not everyone, however, arrives at that conclusion. Communist party member and Huế historian, Nguyễn Đắc Xuân, who joined the National Liberation Front before the Tết Offensive of 1968 and still lives in Huế, has argued that after 1968 Trịnh Công Sơn "stood completely on the side of the Revolution."[4] Some Vietnamese in the diaspora who left Vietnam after 1975 argue that Trịnh Công Sơn did not remain neutral during the war and that he was, in fact, a communist sympathizer. Liên Thành, a former chief of police in Huế, goes further, arguing that the singer was an underground agent for the National Liberation Front. Though I believe the evidence suggests

---

2. Ibid., 180.
3. Đặng Tiến, "Trịnh Công Sơn: Tiếng hát hòa bình" [Trịnh Công Sơn: Voice of Peace], *Văn Học* [Literary Studies] 186 & 187 (Oct.-Nov., 2001), 187.
4. Nguyễn Đắc Xuân, *Trịnh Công Sơn: Có một thời như thế* [Trịnh Công Sơn: There Was Such a Time] (HCMC: Văn Học, 2003), 101.

that during the war Trịnh Công Sơn remained unaligned with either side, I consider other views in this and the next two chapters because one hears them often, especially in the overseas Vietnamese community. Two song collections, *Prayer for Vietnam* and *We Must See the Sun* figure prominently in discussions of whether Trịnh Công Sơn took sides in the war. Songs in these two collections, like those in *Songs of Golden Skin*, are anti-war, but they are anti-war in a different way. I will discuss them in the next chapter. I discuss the accusations of Liên Thành, the Huế police chief, in Chapter Four.

Five of Sơn's good friends were left-leaning, somewhat bohemian, activist intellectuals. These friends included Nguyễn Đắc Xuân (1937-), Hoàng Phủ Ngọc Tường (1937-), Đinh Cường (1939-2016), Bửu Chỉ (1948-2002), and Ngô Kha (1935-1973). Sơn spent a lot of time with these friends in the late 1950s and 1960s and remained close to them all his life. Some people argue that these friends pushed Sơn away from a neutralist stance and caused him to adopt positions close to those of the National Liberation Front (NLF). I will introduce these friends briefly and then consider arguments that have been advanced regarding their influence on Trịnh Công Sơn.

Nguyễn Đắc Xuân studied at the University of Huế and was active in the Struggle Movement in Huế in 1963 and 1966. He joined the National Liberation Front in July of 1966. Hoàng Phủ Ngọc Tường, also active in the Struggle Movement, earned a degree in philosophy from the University of Saigon in 1964 and then taught at the Đồng Khánh Secondary School, a prestigious girls school in Huế. He joined the NLF in 1966, one month before Nguyễn Đắc Xuân. Đinh Cường studied art at the School of Art in Huế and at the National School of Art in Saigon. He painted abstract paintings, several of which appear on the covers of Trịnh Công Sơn's song collections. He taught art at Đồng Khánh Secondary School and at the Huế Institute of Fine Arts. According to Nguyễn Đắc Xuân, Hoàng Phủ Ngọc Tường invited Đinh Cường to "participate in the Revolution" in 1966 but he declined because he was married and had children.[5] Đinh Cường left Vietnam in 1989 and lived in Virginia until his death in 2016.

Bửu Chỉ obtained a law degree from the University of Huế and then

---

5. Nguyễn Đắc Xuân, interview by Dương Minh Long, "Nhà Văn Nguyễn Đắc Xuân một chứng nhân của những năm sáu mươi ở Huế" [The Writer Nguyễn Đắc Xuân, A Witness of the 1960s in Huế], http://dongduongthoibao.net/view.php?storyid=561 (accessed Sept. 12, 2012).

became a self-taught artist. Active in the Struggle Movement in Huế in the 1960s, he was imprisoned by the Saigon regime in 1971. His early paintings, which are included in several collections of Trịnh Công Sơn's songs, are black ink drawings that depict the horrors of war. He died in Vietnam in 2002.

Ngô Kha studied Vietnamese literature and culture at the Faculty of Pedagogy at the University of Hue, where he also earned a law degree. He was a leading poet and activist who taught Vietnamese literature at the National Academy (Trường Quốc Học) and other secondary schools in Huế. An important leader of anti-government organizations, he was drafted into the Army of the Republic of Vietnam but continued to protest the war. He was imprisoned several times by the South Vietnamese police. After he was arrested in 1973, he never returned, and most people in Huế did not know what had happened to him. I will have more to say about Ngô Kha, including how he is believed to have met his death, in Chapter Four.

These friends were all left-leaning, but Trịnh Công Sơn was a very social person and had friends of different political persuasions. One friend, a man named Lưu Kim Cương, was a colonel in the Air Force of the Republic of Vietnam. He was killed in 1968 by a B-40 rocket fired by National Liberation soldiers while he was patrolling the outskirts of Tân Sơn Nhất Airport during the Tết Offensive. Trịnh Công Sơn mourns his death in a song called "For Someone Who Has Fallen" [Cho một người nằm xuống]. Another close friend was the artist Trịnh Cung, who now lives in the US. He was in the Army of the Republic of Vietnam and spent three years in a reeducation camp after the war ended. In 1959 Trịnh Công Sơn wrote a song, "Cuối cùng cho một tình yêu" [The End of a Love], that was based on a poem that Trịnh Cung had written.[6] His friendship with Sơn did not prevent Trịnh Cung from later criticizing his friend for his leftist views and his failure to support the Republic of Vietnam.[7]

People in the overseas Vietnamese community who argue that Trịnh Công Sơn supported the NLF provide very little scholarly support for this view. What one finds instead are accusations like those found in Nguyễn Thanh Ty's book, *On a Period of Trịnh Công Sơn's Life* [Về một quãng đời

---

6. Trịnh Cung, "Bi kịch Trịnh Công Sơn" [The Tragedy of Trịnh Công Sơn], *Văn* [Litera-ture] 53 & 54 (2001), 77.
7. Trịnh Cung, "Trịnh Công Sơn không quan tâm đến chính trị?" [Trịnh Công Sơn Doesn't Pay Attention to Politics?], Tạp Chí Da Mau, http://damau.org/archives/5055 (accessed Nov. 3, 2016).

Trịnh Công Sơn].[8] Nguyễn Thanh Ty was a classmate of Trịnh Công Sơn's at the Quy Nhơn School of Education from 1962-64, and later taught elementary school with him in Bảo Lộc in the Central Highlands where they boarded, along with some other teachers, in the same house. Both Nguyễn Thanh Ty and Trịnh Công Sơn received draft notices in 1967. Nguyễn Thanh Ty reported for duty but Trịnh Công Sơn did not, electing instead to become a draft dodger in Saigon. Nguyễn Thanh Ty suggests in his book that in the mid-1960s, when he and Sơn were both in Bảo Lộc, Sơn's leftist friends, especially Hoàng Phủ Ngọc Tường and Đinh Cường, took control of his mind and convinced him to write the anti-war songs that were later included in the collection called *Songs of Golden Skin*.

A few days before leaving Huế to join the NLF, Hoàng Phủ Ngọc Tường visited Trịnh Công Sơn in Bảo Lộc. Hoàng Phủ Ngọc Tường joined the NLF in June of 1966 so this visit must have occurred in late May or June. He not only visited Sơn, he also tried hard to change Sơn's view of the war. He describes his visit and attempt to get Sơn to take sides, to abandon his neutral position, in an essay written in 1971 that is included in his book *Trịnh Công Sơn and the Lyre of the Little Prince*.[9] He tried, he explains, to get Sơn to see the war not as one big, absurd, inhumane "mass" but instead to recognize that two different wars were going on—"a war of invasion of the Americans and a war to protect the nation waged by the Vietnamese. . . . On one side are enemy invaders, on the other our ancestors, our own flesh and blood. One war we must stamp out, the other war we are duty bound to wage till the end." For too long, Hoàng Phủ Ngọc Tường says he told Sơn, we [peace loving Vietnamese] have opposed the war by "grabbing all the chopsticks in one hand" [*vơ đũa cả nắm*], an expression used to criticize people who do not make careful distinctions. He compared the NLF forces and the Army of the forces of the Republic of Vietnam to a pair of shoes. You don't, he told Sơn, throw away both shoes when only one of the pair is dirty and hurts one's foot. "Think again," Hoàng Phủ Ngọc Tường says he told Sơn, "and consider what position you are choosing in your anti-war songs."[10]

"You want me to choose?" Sơn says, and then he tells his friend

8.　Nguyễn Thanh Ty, *Về một quãng đời Trịnh Công Sơn* [On a Period of Trịnh Công Sơn's Life], (Place of publication and publisher not listed: 2001).

9.　Hoàng Phủ Ngọc Tường, "Như con sông từ nguồn ra biển" [Like a River From the Source to the Sea], in Hoàng Phủ Ngọc Tường, *Trịnh Công Sơn và cây đàn lya của hoàng tử bé* [Trịnh Công Sơn and the Lyre of the Little Prince], (HCMC: Trẻ, 2004), 26-52.

10.　Ibid., 32.

about two people killed recently in the Bảo Lộc area. One was a young man named Hoan, perhaps an Army of the Republic of Vietnam soldier, perhaps just an innocent civilian. Sơn doesn't identify him clearly. He and Sơn were both students at Quy Nhơn Teachers' College. Sơn says that last week he sang a requiem for him at a church. Sơn had heard a poem Hoan had written about growing up in the war, "never knowing the face of love," and then two days later he died, presumably from some war-related incident. The other recent death was of a female guerilla soldier. On a recent trip to Saigon, Sơn tells Hoàng Phủ Ngọc Tường, he had seen her corpse on a rock above the road with her arms hanging down. She had been left there by ARVN soldiers. "It was horrible," Sơn says. "I could see her very white arms clearly, and I thought of that girl's hand that Hoan never in his life had a chance to hold." "Death overflows everything," Sơn tells his friend. "Choose what? I really don't know."[11] Hoàng Phủ Ngọc Tường wanted Sơn to support the NLF, though he does not explain what exactly he wanted him to do. Perhaps he wanted him to leave the area controlled by the Saigon regime and join him in the mountains, which was what he himself was about to do; or perhaps he only wanted him to stop writing sad songs that opposed war in general, songs that did not take sides—neutralist anti-war songs—and begin writing songs that supported the NLF.

Trịnh Công Sơn, in letters written to a young woman named Dao Ánh when he was in Bảo Lộc, emphasizes how sad and lonely he felt when he was there. I will have more to say about Dao Ánh and the letters Sơn wrote to her, which have been published, in Chapter Five.[12] She was the love of Sơn's life and clearly inspired many of his songs. Being separated from Dao Ánh was one reason Sơn was sad in Bảo Lộc, but Hoàng Phủ Ngọc Tường's description of Bảo Lộc and the school in which Sơn taught suggests other causes of his sadness. Bảo Lộc, a town well-known for the tea grown there, is in the central highlands of Lâm đồng Province. Sơn taught in an elementary school in B'Lao, a hamlet about a thir-ty-minute walk from the town. This hamlet, Hoàng Phủ Ngọc Tường says, was a "strategic hamlet" [ấp chiến lược].[13] Strategic hamlets were established during the Ngô Đình Diệm government as a way to pacify the

---

11. Ibid., 33.
12. See *Trịnh Công Sơn: Thư tình gửi một người* [Trịnh Công Sơn: Love Letters for Some-one], (HCMC: Trẻ, 2011), 229.
13. Hoàng Phủ Ngọc Tường, *Trịnh Công Sơn và cây đàn lya của hoàng tử bé* [Trịnh Công Sơn and the Lyre of the Little Prince], 27.

countryside. People living in these hamlets were to receive government funds for clinics and schools. People resented being forced to live in these hamlets. The fact that officials administering them were often corrupt was an added problem.[14] There were only three classrooms in Sơn's school. Some of the students were ethnic Vietnamese, the children of Army of the Republic of Vietnam (ARVN) soldiers stationed in the area, and some were children from ethnic minority families who had been gathered there, presumably because fighting was occurring in their home villages. Most of the students had no raincoats and steam would spiral up from their wet clothes giving the room a bad smell. Soldiers, who would enter the classrooms on Sunday nights to play cards, sometimes defecated on the furniture.[15] The school was near a church, Hoàng Phủ Ngọc Tường says, and Sơn could hear the church bell ringing for soldiers who had died on the battlefield. On his way to teach, Sơn would pass by a cemetery where crows were feeding on corpses.[16]

When Sơn was in Bảo Lộc, one of his roommates, a twenty-four-year-old man named Nguyễn Văn Ba, was killed when, on a trip to Saigon, he got out of the bus and volunteered to defuse a homemade mine in the middle of the road. The bomb exploded and a piece of shrapnel pierced his heart. Both Hoàng Phủ Ngọc Tường and Nguyễn Thanh Ty argue that Nguyễn Văn Ba's death, and the fact that if the road was now being mined he would not be able to go to Saigon on weekends to sing and see his friends, intensified Sơn's sadness.[17] His dismal time in Bảo Lộc, Hoàng Phủ Ngọc Tường says, "awakened in Sơn's soul the anti-war feeling that one finds in the songs he wrote at this time."[18] These songs were his "Songs of Golden Skin," the songs that made him famous.

After Sơn left Bảo Lộc and was living in the dilapidated temporary housing on the grounds of the Faculty of Letters of the University of Saigon, he began performing with Khánh Ly at a grass-roofed café on the school grounds which was called the Literature Café (Quán Văn). Hoàng Xuân Sơn, one of several young people who established the Literature Café, was a friend of Sơn's. In an interview, Bùi Văn Phú asked Hoàng Xuân Sơn whether Trịnh Công Sơn "supported or was on the side of the

14. See Stanley Karnow, *Vietnam: A History* (New York: Viking Press, 1983), 255-56.
15. Hoàng Phủ Ngọc Tường, *Trịnh Công Sơn và cây đàn lya của hoàng tử bé*, 27.
16. Ibid., 74-75.
17. Nguyễn Thanh Ty, *Về một quãng đời Trịnh Công Sơn*, 47-48, 126. See also Hoàng Phủ Ngọc Tường, *Trịnh Công Sơn và cây đàn lya của hoàng tử bé*, 75.
18. Hoàng Phủ Ngọc Tường, *Trịnh Công Sơn và cây đàn lya của hoàng tử bé*, 75.

communists." Before 1975, Hoàng Xuân Sơn replied, "Trịnh Công Sơn was not a communist. His songs, specifically his *Songs of Golden Skin*, had only an anti-war character to them. Although people said they aided the enemy, one couldn't deny their humanistic quality, the fact that they opposed an inhuman war of mutual destruction."[19] Hoàng Xuân Sơn left Vietnam and immigrated to Canada in 1981. He met Trịnh Công Sơn again when the singer came to Montreal in 1992 to visit relatives. At this meeting he sensed a change in his friend, but he is not very specific about exactly what this change was, mentioning only that he had a different way of "thinking, expressing himself, and reacting." He suggests this change was a result of his being "showered with favors" by the socialist regime. "From this time [presumably 1991]," Hoàng Xuân Sơn concludes, "it would not be an exaggeration to say that Trịnh Công Sơn belonged to the communists."[20]

In assessing the views of people like Nguyễn Thanh Ty and Hoàng Xuân Sơn one must understand that they suffered greatly from the takeover of their land by the communists. Trịnh Công Sơn dodged the draft but Nguyễn Thanh Ty did not, and when the Saigon regime collapsed and the communists took over, he was sent to a reeducation camp, along with other former officers in the Army of the Republic of Vietnam. Both Nguyễn Thanh Ty and Hoàng Xuân Sơn found it necessary to leave their homeland. Trịnh Công Sơn's songs no doubt did, as Hoàng Xuân Sơn suggests, turn many people against the war, and this pleased some people and angered others. His anti-war songs, Bửu Chỉ says, "got not a few young people to look at the inhumanity and cruelty of the war and encouraged them to hide from the draft or desert. In the eyes of those who held power in the old regime, Sơn was someone who destroyed the will to fight of the troops."[21] Many of those people whom Bửu Chỉ refers to now live in Canada, or Australia, or the US and they, and their families—even to this day—bear ill feelings toward Trịnh Công Sơn. They particularly resent the fact that when communist troops took over Saigon in 1975, Trịnh Công Sơn agreed to sing "Join Hands in a Great Circle" [Nối vòng tay lớn], a song he wrote in 1968, on a Saigon radio station. It ends with these lines:

---

19. Hoàng Xuân Sơn, interview by Bùi Văn Phú, "Hoàng Xuân Sơn: nơi tôi sinh sống thì hát nhạc Trịnh cũng nên dè dặt" [Hoàng Xuân Sơn: Where I Live You Should Be Careful about Singing Trịnh Music], http://damau.org/archives/19866 (accessed Jan. 15, 2012).
20. Ibid.
21. Bửu Chỉ, "Về những ca khúc phản chiến của Trịnh Công Sơn" [On Trịnh Công Sơn's Anti-war Songs], *Diễn đàn* [Forum] 110 (Sept. 2001), 31.

From the North to the South we all join hands
We go from deserted fields, cross mountains and hills
Pass by waterfalls high above
Hand in hand we cross mountain passes
From the poor countryside to large cities
Holding hands from blue sea to shining rivers
Joining hands in a circle of life and death.[22]

These lyrics may not sound provocative, but they are in the Vietnamese diaspora. To avoid unpleasantness, overseas fans of Trịnh Công Sơn do not talk about him with strangers or sing his songs in public. "Where I live [Montreal, Canada]," Hoàng Xuân Sơn says, "you should be careful about singing Trịnh music." By general agreement, Hoàng Xuân Sơn says, Trịnh Công Sơn songs are not sung at public events, for fear of provoking conservative members of the Vietnamese community.[23]

Unlike artists attached to combat units of the North Vietnamese Army and the People's Liberation Armed Forces, Trịnh Công Sơn did not experience battles firsthand. He was a civilian and lived in cities and towns controlled by the Republic of Vietnam. The dominant perspective of his early anti-war songs, his *Songs of Golden Skin*, is that of an empathetic city dweller—someone who does not live in the midst of the fighting but knows how it is affecting his people wherever they live, in the countryside or the towns. Both this perspective and his empathy are evident in "Lullaby of Cannons for the Night"*:

Every night cannons resound in the town
A street cleaner stops sweeping and listens
The cannons wake up a mother
The cannons disturb a young child
At midnight a flare shines in the mountains

His perspective was altered during the Tết Offensive of 1968 when communist forces entered the city of Huế and remained for twenty-five

---

22. The VietinBank, one of the four largest state-owned companies in Vietnam, adopted an English version of this song, with somewhat different lyrics, as their theme song. Here is the chorus:
We'll lead the way, finance Vietnam,
From north to the south, across this great land.
Our customers respond with glee,
The nation will prosper and so will we.
Forward, together, VietinBank-IFC!
See https://kzbin.info/www/vietinbank-ifc-song/q2qYZpVsiNF9i9U (accessed May 2, 2022).
23. Hoàng Xuân Sơn, interview by Bùi Văn Phú.

47

days. They were finally driven out by US Marines and troops of the Army of the Republic of Vietnam, aided by heavy American bombing. At the time it occurred, the battle for Huế was the longest battle since the Second Indochina War began and there were heavy casualties on both sides. Many of those casualties were civilians. After the battle, roughly 2,800 bodies, many of them civilians, were found in mass graves, leading President Nixon to call the communist's brief occupation of the city a "reign of terror."[24] Others suggested that many in those mass graves had been killed by American bombs. After the battle, bodies were found in a patch of land lying between the Perfume River and a part of Huế called Gia Hội. People in Huế call this area "Bãi Dâu," or "Berry Patch,"[25] and Trịnh Công Sơn, who was in Huế during and after the battle, mentions it in his song "Singing Above the Corpses" [Hát trên những xác người] which he included in later editions of his already famous *Songs of Golden Skin*. The song includes these lines:

> *This afternoon I went by the Dâu Patch and sang above the corpses*
> *I saw, I saw*
> *On the road an old father clutching the cold dead body of his child*
> *This afternoon I went by the Dâu Patch and sang above the corpses*
> *I saw, I saw*
> *Ditches where corpses of brothers and sisters were buried*

Trịnh Công Sơn's friends Hoàng Phủ Ngọc Tường and Nguyễn Đắc Xuân would later be accused of presiding over people's courts in Gia hội during the Tết Offensive and sentencing people to death. If these charges are true, they would be responsible for the corpses about which Trịnh Công Sơn sings in his song. Both men deny these charges. I will describe these accusations against Sơn's friends and their reactions to them in the next chapter.

---

24. President Nixon made this remark in a televised address to the nation on November 3, 1969. See Don Oberdorfer, *Tet!* (Garden City, NY: Doubleday, 1971), 232-233. For a complete text of President Nixon's remarks, see "Address to Nation on US Policy in the War in Vietnam," *New York Times*, Nov. 4, 1969.
25. For some reason Western writers and reporters have referred to this area as the "Strawberry Patch," but *dâu* (*Baccaurea sapida*) is not a strawberry and resembles a nut more than a berry. For example, Dan Oberdorfer refers to this burial site as the Strawberry Patch in his book about the Tết Offensive. See *Tet!*, 235.

3

PRAYER FOR VIETNAM &
WE MUST SEE THE SUN

*H*oàng Phủ Ngọc Tường's *Trịnh Công Sơn and the Lyre of the Little Prince* was published in 2004, but the fourth chapter, in which he describes his visit with Sơn in Bảo Lộc in 1966, is dated to August of 1971, when Hoàng Phủ Ngọc Tường was with the National Liberation Front (NLF) in the Trường Sơn Mountains west of Huế. In this chapter he suggests that he failed to move Sơn away from his neutral position during his visit with him in 1966. He argues, however, that Sơn eventually did take sides, or at least became more radicalized. When Phương, an undercover NLF operative in Huế and a friend of Hoàng Phủ Ngọc Tường's,[1] came to the mountains to attend a meeting in the NLF-controlled area where Hoàng Phủ Ngọc Tường was stationed, he sang for his friend some of Sơn's recent songs. Hoàng Phủ Ngọc Tường observes that in them Sơn's "familiar sad, blues-like melodies had been replaced by marching rhythms." In these songs, he says, "are images of people stepping away from weakness to enter a city in the midst of an uprising."[2] He is clearly referring to songs from two collections—*Prayer for Vietnam* [Kinh Việt Nam] and *We Must See the Sun* [Ta phải thấy mặt trời]—that Sơn wrote after the 1968 Tết Offensive. *Prayer for Vietnam* was released in 1968; *We Must See the Sun* was—it says on the second page—"finished at the end of October, 1969" and, presumably, released that same year.[3]

---

1. Both Hoàng Phủ Ngọc Tường and his friend have the same given name. Hoàng Phủ Ngọc Tường does not include this friend's family name.
2. Hoàng Phủ Ngọc Tường, "Như con sông từ nguồn ra biển" [Like a River from the Source to the Sea], in Hoàng Phủ Ngọc Tường, *Trịnh Công Sơn và cây đàn lya của hoàng tử bé* [Trịnh Công Sơn and the Lyre of the Little Prince] (Ho Chi Minh City: Trẻ, 2004), 44.
3. I say "presumably" because my copy of *We Must See the Sun* does not include the date of publication. Both of these song books were published by Nhân Bản (*Humanism*). The

Songs in these two collections are anti-war but differ from his *Songs of Golden Skin*. Most of the *Songs of Golden Skin* were mournful laments about suffering caused by the war. Songs in these later two collections may begin with images of terrible suffering, but then they move on to describe a vision of a happy, peaceful Vietnam. This vision is presented in a few songs in the *Songs of Golden Skin* collection, in "I Shall Go Visiting" [Tôi sẽ đi thăm] and "Night Now, Night Tomorrow" [Đêm bây giờ đêm mai], for example, but in these later collections it appears in almost every song. A typical example of this new kind of anti-war song is "Waiting for a Bright Native Land" [Chờ nhìn quê hương sáng chói], the second song in *Prayer for Vietnam*. Here is how it begins:

> *In this place I wait*
> *In that place you wait*
> *In a small house*
> *A mother also waits*
> *A soldier sits and waits*
> *On top of a deserted hill*
> *A prisoner sits and waits*
> *In the pitch black darkness*
> *Waiting for how many years*
> *Waiting for tomorrow when we'll wake among shouts of joy*
> *Waiting for hearts of hatred to disappear*
> *Waiting for peace to come*
> *Waiting for the bombs to be quieted*
> *Waiting to walk on roads without mines*
> *Waiting for roads that connect the three regions*[4]

The first nine lines above, which typically are sung very slowly and mournfully, remind one of songs from *Songs of Golden Skin*, but then in the tenth line the tempo picks up and the mood becomes joyful as a vision of a happy, peaceful future unfolds. Almost all the songs in *Prayer for Vietnam* and *We Must See the Sun* anticipate the joys that peace will bring.

The sun becomes an important symbol in these songs. Paintings by Trịnh Công Sơn's friend Đinh Cường of a reddish sun are featured on the

---

Trịnh Công Sơn Forum lists these same dates for these two albums. See https://www.tcs-home.org/songs/albums (accessed June 3, 2021).

4. The regions referred to are the South, the Central, and the North. The 17th parallel, which, during the Second Indochina War separated the Democratic Republic of Vietnam from the Republic of Vietnam, passed through the central region. In this line Trịnh Công Sơn looks forward with joy to a time when Vietnam will be reunified.

cover of both *Prayer for Vietnam* and *We Must See the Sun,* and the songs in these collections present a vision of a glorious future when the darkness of war is replaced by the brightness of peace. Black and white drawings by Trịnh Công Sơn's friend Bửu Chỉ, which are included between the songs, are of people marching under—or looking hopefully up at—a bright sun above them. The first song in the collection *We Must See the Sun,* which has the same title as the title of the collection, clearly identifies a bright shining sun with a bright peaceful future. "We must see the sun shining on this native land," the song begins. It concludes with these lines: "We must see, we must see / A bright shining peace around here."

Besides their sunny optimism, another striking feature of these songs is their activist message. Trịnh Công Sơn's *Songs of Golden Skin* were passive complaints, but these later songs appear to be "movement" [*nhạc phong trào*] songs—songs written to get demonstrators to take to the streets [*lên đường*] to demand a redress of grievances. "We take to the streets together / To rebuild freedom," he sings in "Rebuild People, Rebuild Homes" [Dựng lại người dựng lại nhà].

Đinh Cường's cover for Trịnh Công Sơn's song collection Ta phải thấy mặt trời [We Must See the Sun].

51

Bửu Chỉ's illustration in Ta phải thấy mặt trời.

In four songs Trịnh Công Sơn talks of "revolution" [*cách mạng*], a term that most Vietnamese would associate with Hanoi and the National Liberation Front.[5] In "Don't Wait for Anyone, Don't Have Doubts" [Đừng mong ai, đừng nghi ngại] he sings:

> *Please rise up brothers and sisters*
> *This life is full of darkness*
> *A million brothers and sisters sharing dangers and difficulties*
> *Building a revolution, building a new person*

In "Huế, Saigon, Hanoi"* he sings:

> *Oh, Vietnam*
> *How long before people remember to love each other*
> *A million feet of the young*
> *A million feet of their older brothers*
> *All three regions rise up for the revolution*

Many of these "movement" songs have a quick tempo and were designed to be sung forcefully. The following instructions appear on the

---

5. The songs in which Trịnh Công Sơn uses the word "*cách mạng*" [revolution] are: "Don't Wait for Anyone, Don't Have Doubts" [Đừng mong ai đừng nghi ngại], "Rise up, Viet-nam" [Việt Nam hãy vùng lên], "We Are Determined that We Must Live" [Ta quyết phải sống], and "Huế Saigon Hanoi" [Huế Sài gòn Hà nội]*. All four songs are from the collection *We Must See the Sun*.

title page of *Prayer for Vietnam*: "Songs in this collection with 2/4 time [six of the twelve songs] can be sung forcefully and quickly." On the second page of *We Must See the Sun* there are these instructions: "Perform forcefully according to the emotion of the words." Trần Hữu Thục, a journalist and literary critic from Huế who now lives in Worcester, Massachusetts, detects in some of these songs the influence of martial music (*nhạc chiến đấu*) of the North. Some songs, he says, are even "more forceful" [*mạnh hơn*] than the songs that communists who infiltrated the student anti-war movement in the South encouraged demonstrators to sing.[6] The black and white drawings by Bửu Chỉ, like the one included above, reinforce the "movement" and "revolutionary" theme of these songs. The shirtless men in this drawing, broken chains dangling from their wrists, are presumably prisoners who have just regained their freedom.[7]

Are these neutralist anti-war songs or songs designed to get young people to join the revolution spearheaded by the National Liberation Front? What is behind Trịnh Công Sơn's shift from gloom and pessimism to joy and optimism? How should we interpret this talk about "revolution"? Different observers provide different answers to these questions. We can look first at the views of Nguyễn Đắc Xuân, one of Trịnh Công Sơn's five left-leaning friends that I introduced in the previous chapter. Nguyễn Đắc Xuân began studies at the University of Huế in 1961 but, he explains in an interview with Dương Minh Long, most of his teachers were priests or lay Christians and he was a Buddhist so he "couldn't join in with University life in Huế at that time."[8] He was active in the Struggle Movement in Huế against President Ngô Đình Diệm in 1963 and against Prime Minister Nguyễn Cao Kỳ in 1966. Though not, apparently, a very close friend of Trịnh Công Sơn, he and Sơn knew each other and they had many mutual friends. When the 1966 Struggle Movement in Central Vietnam was crushed by the Thiệu-Kỳ regime, Nguyễn Đắc Xuân decided "there was no other way but the way of the Liberation Front."[9] In early July, 1966, he

---

6. Trần Hữu Thục has in mind songs like "Rise Up and Go" [Dậy mà đi], a musical version of a poem by Tố Hữu, a revolutionary poet who served in a variety of posts in the Democratic Republic of Vietnam. Tố Hữu worked tirelessly to ensure that art served politics. See Trần Hữu Thục, "Một cái nhìn về ca từ Trịnh Công Sơn" [One View of Trịnh Công Sơn's Lyrics], *Văn học* [Literary Studies] 186 & 187 (Oct.-Nov., 2001), 65.
7. Bửu Chỉ himself was imprisoned by the Republic of Vietnam from 1972 to 1975 for his anti-war activities.
8. Nguyễn Đắc Xuân, interview with Dương Minh Long. See *Đông Dương Thời Báo* [Indochina Magazine], http://dongduongthoibao.net/view.php?storyid=561 (accessed Sept. 12, 2012).
9. Ibid.

received a letter from his friend Hoàng Phủ Ngọc Tường, who had joined the Front a month before, inviting him to join him in the "liberated area." "I left immediately," Nguyễn Đắc Xuân told Dương Minh Long, "and easily became a part of the resistance."[10] Both Nguyễn Đắc Xuân and Hoàng Phủ Ngọc Tường returned to Huế in 1975 and both have written books about Trịnh Công Sơn.[11] Both are members of the Communist Party.

Some contemporaries of Nguyễn Đắc Xuân and Hoàng Phủ Ngọc Tường who live in Huế, and many more who live in the diaspora, do not like or trust these two writers. Both men have been accused of identifying people for execution when they returned to Huế with NLF troops during the 1968 Tết Offensive. Nguyễn Đắc Xuân admits he was in the city during the battle for Huế, but says that at that time he had been with the NLF for only a year and a half and had no authority to make decisions about who should be killed.[12] Hoàng Phủ Ngọc Tường says he was not in Huế during the Tết Offensive, explaining that he left Huế to join the NLF in the summer of 1966 and did not return to Huế until 1975.[13]

Hoàng Phủ Ngọc Tường has also been accused of forcing Trịnh Công Sơn to write a self-confession after the communist victory in 1975, and of sending him on work details to grow vegetables. Regarding the charge that he forced Trịnh Công Sơn to write a confession, Hoàng Phủ Ngọc Tường told Giao Vy in 2002 that in 1975 he was not a party member and did not have the authority to make anyone write a self-confession.[14] Nguyễn Đắc Xuân defends Hoàng Phủ Ngọc Tường. He explains that writing self-confessions [bản kiểm điểm] was a common practice within the NLF and that both he and Hoàng Phủ Ngọc Tường had written many themselves. Hoàng Phủ Ngọc Tường, he says, simply advised Trịnh Công Sơn on ways to write his self-confession so he could pass through the process quickly.[15]

---

10. Ibid.
11. Nguyễn Đắc Xuân, *Trịnh Công Sơn: Có một thời như thế* [Trịnh Công Sơn: There Was Such a Time] (HCMC: Văn Học, 2003); Hoàng Phủ Ngọc Tường, *Trịnh Công Sơn và cây đàn lya của hoàng tử bé* [Trịnh Công Sơn and the Lyre of the Little Prince] (HCMC: Trẻ, 2004).
12. Nguyễn Đắc Xuân, interview by Dương Minh Long.
13. Hoàng Phủ Ngọc Tường, interview by Thụy Khuê on July 12, 1997, "Nói chuyện với Hoàng Phủ Ngọc Tường về biến cố Mậu Thân ơ Huế" [Talking to Hoàng Phủ Ngọc Tường about the Events in Huế], Radio France Internationale, http://thuykhue.free.fr/tk97/nchpngoctuong.html (accessed Oct. 21, 2016).
14. See Giao Vy, "Huế lang thang trong tháng tư" [Wandering in Huế in April], *Diễn đàn* [Forum] 118 (2002), 32.
15. Nguyễn Đắc Xuân, *Trịnh Công Sơn: Có một thời như thế*, 101.

Nguyễn Đắc Xuân blames the writer Nhã Ca and her semi-fictional account of the Tết Offensive in Huế for spreading false rumors about him.[16] In Nhã Ca's *Mourning Headband for Huế* [Giải khăn sô cho Huế], there is a character named Đắc who, like Nguyễn Đắc Xuân, was a student who was active in the Struggle Movement and then joined the NLF. In Nhã Ca's book, however, the character Đắc is an evil character who commits acts of violence against former acquaintances during the battle for Huế in 1968. Nguyễn Đắc Xuân says that he met Nhã Ca in Hồ Chí Minh City after the war ended, and she admitted to him that she thought he had been killed in the battle and so felt she could fabricate and embellish his character to make her book more appealing. According to Nguyễn Đắc Xuân, the effect was devastating. Friends in Vietnam and abroad accused him and even his own wife suspected him![17]

In his book, *Trịnh Công Sơn: There Was Such a Time*, Nguyễn Đắc Xuân describes how in 1975 he and Hoàng Phủ Ngọc Tường came to the defense of their friend Trịnh Công Sơn in a crucial meeting with important NLF officials in Huế. Trịnh Công Sơn needed to be defended because, in the eyes of the new cultural managers in Huế, Trịnh Công Sơn had some black marks on his record. Those in the revolutionary movement viewed both Indochina Wars as one long resistance to foreign invaders, but, as mentioned previously, Trịnh Công Sơn describes the war that broke out in the 1960s as a civil war; and he had also written a song that memorialized an officer in the air force of the Saigon regime.[18] Trịnh Công Sơn was also a problem for authorities in the new government for other, more general reasons. After their victory in 1975, communist leaders of the Democratic Republic of Vietnam were intent on wiping out all vestiges of the "neo-colonialist" culture that had developed in the South. One object of their ire was what they called "yellow music" [nhạc vàng] by which they meant sentimental songs that "lead people into a state of suffering over love, the opposite of the ideal happiness that people expect to find in it."[19] Soon

---

16. Nhã Ca, *Giải khăn sô cho Huế* [Mourning Headband for Huế] (Saigon: Đất Lành, 1971). For an English translation, see Nhã Ca, *Mourning Headband for Huế*, trans. Olga Dror (Bloomington, IN: Indiana University Press, 2014).

17. Nguyễn Đắc Xuân, "Hậu quả của 'Cái Chết' của tôi" [The Consequences of my "Death"], http://sachhiem.net/NDX/NDX020.php (accessed Sept. 30, 2012); Nguyễn Đắc Xuân, interview by Dương Minh Long.

18. As explained in Chapter Two, the officer was Lưu Kim Cương and the song was "For Someone Who Has Fallen" [Cho một người nằm xuống].

19. Tô Vũ, "Nhạc vàng là gì?" [What Is Yellow Music?], *Văn hóa nghệ thuật* [Culture and Art] 5 (1976), 45.

after Huế was liberated, a banner appeared on a Huế University building that called for the overthrow of yellow music [đã đảo nhạc vàng]. Trịnh Công Sơn's friend Hoàng Phủ Ngọc Tường considered this banner to be an attack on his friend, the best known and most popular singer in Huế, and saw to it that it was taken down.[20]

Both Hoàng Phủ Ngọc Tường and Nguyễn Đắc Xuân were present at a meeting at the Association for Literature and Art of Thừa Thiên and Huế that was convened in Huế soon after the communist victory in 1975. The purpose of the meeting was to consider this question: Do Trịnh Công Sơn's contributions outweigh his offenses? Those attending were local writers, politicians, and education officials who had the power to set Party policy regarding the composer. Nguyễn Đắc Xuân describes the meeting in some detail in *There Was Such a Time*. Some participants brought up Trịnh Công Sơn's "offenses"—the ones mentioned in the previous paragraph—and then Trịnh Công Sơn's supporters spoke up. One "contribution" of Trịnh Công Sơn that they emphasized was the effect of Trịnh Công Sơn's anti-war songs on soldiers of the Army of the Republic of Vietnam (ARVN). Here is how Nguyễn Đắc Xuân summarizes the argument they made to support this point:

> It is true that Trịnh Công Sơn wrote many anti-war songs. He was called the number one anti-war musician at that time—just like Bob Dylan and Joan Baez in America. Trịnh Công Sơn was a musician of freedom: Unlike us he followed a general humanistic ideology. But he wrote songs in the occupied areas [i.e., South Vietnam] and those listening to those songs were Republican soldiers. A great many of President Nguyễn Văn Thiệu's soldiers deserted because they heard his song "Vietnamese Girl" [Người con gái Việt Nam]*.[21] But no revolutionary soldier deserted because he listened to Trịnh Công Sơn's songs. . . It was not for no reason that Thiệu gave the order to confiscate Sơn's songs.[22]

According to Nguyễn Đắc Xuân, another crucial element in their defense of their friend was Trịnh Công Sơn's songs in *Prayer for Vietnam* and *We Must See the Sun* and his close relationship to a fiery and fearless poet and anti-war activist named Ngô Kha, one of Trịnh Công Sơn's five friends mentioned previously. The songs and this poet are related, in

---

20. Giao Vy, "Huế lang thang trong tháng tư," 32.
21. I do not know why Nguyễn Đắc Xuân argues that it was this particular song that caused ARVN soldiers to desert. It is about a girl who loves her native land and dreams of peace. One day while walking to her village she is hit by a bullet and killed.
22. Nguyễn Đắc Xuân, *Trịnh Công Sơn: Có một thời như thế*, 99.

Nguyễn Đắc Xuân's view, because he believes Trịnh Công Sơn's songs in these two collections were heavily influenced by Ngô Kha's views and poems. It is Ngô Kha's influence, Nguyễn Đắc Xuân says, that explains why these later songs have a revolutionary tone and mood that is not present in his *Songs of Golden Skin*. Ngô Kha's influence, according to Nguyễn Đắc Xuân, caused Trịnh Công Sơn to move from a general, more neutral anti-war position to positions more in line with those of the National Liberation Front. Ngô Kha was a very close friend of Trịnh Công Sơn's. I will tell the story of his life and tragic death and consider how he may have influenced Sơn in the next chapter.

4

NGÔ KHA &
TRỊNH CÔNG SƠN

In 2009 Liên Thành, a policeman in Huế who had Trịnh Công Sơn's friend Ngô Kha killed, posted an article on the web titled "Trịnh Công Sơn and Underground Activities" [Trịnh Công Sơn và những hoạt động nằm vùng].[1] Liên Thành says he was moved to write this article after reading two articles that appeared on the web in 2009, both by friends of Trịnh Công Sơn, both formerly soldiers in the ARVN.[2] One article was by Sơn's friend, the painter Trịnh Cung, and the other by a man named Bằng Phong Đặng Văn Âu. Both writers suggest that Trịnh Công Sơn was not a neutralist but supported, or at least was sympathetic to, the goals of the National Liberation Front. Liên Thành goes further and suggests that Trịnh Công Sơn was an underground agent of the NLF. He supplies no concrete evidence. His approach is guilt by association. He mentions only one specific crime committed by Trịnh Công Sơn: helping his friends Hoàng Phủ Ngọc Tường, Hoàng Phủ Ngọc Phan (Tường's brother) and Nguyễn Đắc Xuân leave Huế in 1966 and join the NLF, a departure which was, Liên Thành says, "directly arranged by the Huế City (Communist)

1. Liên Thành, "Trịnh Công Sơn và những hoạt động nằm vùng" [Trịnh Công Sơn and Underground Activities], Khai phóng [Emancipation], May 28, 2009, http://khaiphong.org/showthread.php?1929-Tr%26%237883%3Bnh-C%F4ng-S%26%23417%3Bn-v%E0-nh%26%237919%3Bng-ho%26%237841%3Bt-%26%23273%3B%26%237897%3Bng-n%26%237857%3Bm-v%F9ng (accessed Nov. 1, 2016). See also Liên Thành, "Liên Thành trả lại một số thắc mắc trong bài về Trịnh Công Sơn" [Liên Thành Answers Some Questions Regarding His Article about Trịnh Công Sơn], June 30, 2009, http://biendongmientrung-lienthanh.blogspot.com/2009/06/lien-thanh-viet-bai-2-ve-trinh-cong-son.html (accessed Jan. 9, 2017).
2. Trịnh Cung, "Trịnh Công Sơn không quan tâm đến chính trị?" [Did Trịnh Công Sơn Not Pay Attention to Politics?], Tạp Chí Da Màu, http://damau.org/archives/5055 (accessed Nov. 3, 2016); and Bằng Phong Đặng Văn Âu, "Nhạc sĩ Trịnh Công Sơn—một thiên tài đồng lõa với tội ác" [Trịnh Công Sơn—A Genius Who Allied Himself With Cruelty], Tiền Vệ, https://www.tienve.org/home/activities/viewThaoLuan.do?action=viewArtwork&artworkId=8532 (accessed Nov. 3, 2016).

59

Committee [*thành ủy* Huế]."[3] These three friends of Trịnh Công Sơn left Huế because they knew they faced imprisonment or perhaps death if they remained in Huế. In June of 1966, the military and police forces of Prime Minister Nguyễn Cao Kỳ had put down the rebellion in Đà nẵng and Huế, and Liên Thành's boss, a ruthless police officer named Nguyễn Ngọc Loan, was jailing student protestors and others who opposed the Thiệu-Kỳ regime. Colonel Loan arrested Thích Trí Quang, who was taken to Saigon and imprisoned.[4] Apparently Colonel Loan ordered Liên Thành to arrest Trịnh Công Sơn's three friends and he failed, a mistake that still haunts him. "Letting these three men escape was," Liên Thành says in his book *Disorder in the Central Region*, "a very big mistake, one that I have regretted all my life."[5] It is possible Ngô Kha received no mercy from Liên Thành because he was a close friend of the three men that he let get away. Certainly in his books Liên Thành makes no attempt to hide his desire for revenge against anyone connected, no matter how tenuously, to the communist underground.

Liên Thành says he failed to arrest Sơn's friends because in 1966 he had not yet developed the "coldness" [*lạnh lùng*] that an intelligence officer needs to do his job.[6] Hoàng Phủ Ngọc Tường had been his teacher and, Liên Thành says, he had learned from his father and from Vietnamese culture generally that one must respect one's teachers. Not wanting to arrest his former teacher himself, he assigned the task of arresting Hoàng Phủ Ngọc Tường and his friends to an assistant. We know from his treatment of Ngô Kha, who was also a teacher of Liên Thành, that the police chief later developed sufficient coldness to be ruthless even to a former teacher.[7]

---

3. Liên Thành, "Trịnh Công Sơn và những hoạt động nằm vùng."
4. Stanley Karnow, *Vietnam: A History* (New York: Viking Press, 1983), 447-450.
5. Liên Thành, *Biến Động Miền Trung: Những bí mật lịch sử trong các giai đoạn 1966-1968-1972* [Disorder in the Central Region: Historical Secrets from the Periods 1966-1968-1972], 11th Edition (California: Ủy Ban Truy Tố Tội Ác Đảng Cộng Sản Việt Nam [Committee to Prosecute Crimes of the Vietnamese Communist Party], 2014), 145. (This book was first published in 2008.) See also Liên Thành, *Huế thảm sát mậu thân* [Huế—The Massacre of Tết Mậu Thân] (California: self-published, 2011), 211-213.
6. Liên Thành, *Biến Động Miền Trung*, 145-146.
7. Nguyễn Đắc Xuân states that Liên Thành was a student of Ngô Kha but he does not indicate when or in what school. See Nguyễn Đắc Xuân, "Vài điều về Liên Thành, Tác giả 'Biến động, Miền Trung'" [A Few Things about Liên Thành, the Author of *Disorder in the Central Region*], https://sachhiem.net/NDX/NDX017.php (accessed Oct. 30, 2016). A shortened version of this article, titled "Cái chết của Ngô Kha như tôi đã biết" [What I Know about Ngô Kha's Death], appears in Bửu Nam and Phạm Thị Anh Nga, eds., *Ngô Kha hành trình, thơ hành trình dẫn thân & ngôi nhà vĩnh cửu* [Poetic Journey, Engaged Journey, Eternal Home], 220-222.

Many of Sơn's friends were intellectuals—writers, artists, and teachers—and Sơn spent time with them at their homes and at cafés in Huế. It is no doubt true that most of these intellectuals were opposed to the war and we now know that some of them—Nguyễn Đắc Xuân, Hoàng Phủ Ngọc Tường, and Lê Văn Hảo, for example—later left Huế to join the NLF.[8] Liên Thành appears to assume that everyone who visited certain homes or frequented certain cafés were part of a vast web of communist agents who had, as he puts it, "sold themselves to the devil."[9] Clearly, however, communist agents were operating in Huế. One friend of Sơn's, a man named Lê Khắc Cẩm, who liked to read and translate English and French literary works, was working for the NLF. Liên Thành says that Lê Khắc Cẩm was "the cadre that directly controlled and guided" Trịnh Công Sơn.[10]

Lê Khắc Cẩm and Trịnh Công Sơn were obviously friends and they both worked together on a Christmas 1974 issue of *Đứng Dậy* [Stand Up] containing articles by friends and former students demanding that the government explain what happened to Ngô Kha.[11] Trịnh Công Sơn wrote the rough draft of a "Declaration" [Tuyên cáo] eventually signed by forty-six teachers, writers and artists, that appears at the beginning of the issue, as well as a letter addressed to Ngô Kha titled "A Letter for a Person Who is Now In Prison or Has Been Exterminated" [Lá thư gửi cho người đang ở trong tù hay đã bị thủ tiêu].[12] This letter created a stir

---

8. Lê Văn Hảo (1936-2015), a Huế University professor of Anthropology and Vietnamese culture and civilization, left Huế shortly before the Tết Offensive in Huế began. He was chair of a group called the Front Alliance of the People's Democratic and Peaceful Forces of Huế [Mặt trận Liên Minh các Lực Lương Dân tộc Dan chủ va Hoa bình Thành phó Huế]. Hoàng Phủ Ngọc Tường was the general secretary for this group and Nguyễn Đắc Xuân was given responsibilities for organizing young people. According to Liên Thành both Nguyễn Đắc Xuân and Hoàng Phủ Ngọc Tường were members of the Security Force to Protect City Districts [Lực lượng An ninh Bảo vệ Khu phố], a force which, he says, "brought death and suffering to the people of Huế for 22 days" during the Tết Offensive. See Nguyễn Đắc Xuân, interview with Dương Minh Long, "Nhà Văn Nguyễn Đắc Xuân một chứng nhân của những năm sáu mươi ở Huế" [The Writer Nguyễn Đắc Xuân, a Witness of the 1960s in Huế], http://dongduongthoibao.net/view.php?storyid=561 (accessed Sept. 12, 2012). See also Liên Thành, *Huế thảm sát*, 172-173, 688-689.
9. Liên Thành, "Trịnh Công Sơn và những hoạt động nằm vùng."
10. Ibid.
11. The entire issue of this journal is reprinted in Bửu Nam and Phạm Thị Anh Nga, eds., *Ngô Kha hành trình*, 159-214.
12. This "Declaration" and Trịnh Công Sơn's letter originally appeared in *Đứng Dậy* [Stand Up] 65 & 66 (Dec., 1974). Page numbers in ensuing notes, however, will refer to the Declaration and the letter as reprinted in Bửi Nam and Nguyễn Thị Anh Nga, eds., *Ngô Kha hành trình thơ hành trinh dấn thân & ngôi nhà vĩnh cửu* [Ngô Kha: His Poetic Journey, His Engagement, and His Eternal Home]. The Declaration appears on pages 166-167; Trịnh Công Sơn's letter appears on pages 187-194.

when it was republished in books and journals in 2003 and 2004 because it suggested that Trịnh Công Sơn was more fully engaged in the political struggle than was commonly known.[13] At first some readers, including Nguyễn Đắc Xuân, did not believe Trịnh Công Sơn wrote it because it contained communist jargon—phrases like "people's collective" [*tập thể nhân dân*] and "the problem of structural organization" [*vấn đề tổ chức cơ cấu*]. But it is clearly authentic. Nguyễn Đắc Xuân did some investigating and found out that Bửu Ý has Trịnh Công Sơn's handwritten drafts of both the "Declaration" and his letter to Ngô Kha.[14]

In the letter, Trịnh Công Sơn has harsh words for the *công an mật vụ trí thức*, the secret police targeting intellectuals. "Kha," he asks, "do you remember that once before we were the victims of an informer in this group?"[15] He describes the present situation as being terrible but suggests this is a good thing because people will see they have nothing more to lose. "When people realize," he says, "that they don't have anything left to be seized, that they can't be exploited anymore, then they rise up and take to the streets."[16] Trịnh Công Sơn uses the image of ripe fruit to suggest that the end of the current regime is near:

> Kha, probably you remember that we used to tell each other that we must wait for the day when the facts of the situation are like ripe fruit. Could it be that today that fruit we waited for is ripe? The fruit of poverty, hunger, death, unemployment, ruined fields and gardens, etc. which are all mutually affected by a society torn to pieces, by factionalism, by corruption, division, imprisonment, torture…. So, Kha, has not the time come for a new opportunity to appear?[17]

Trịnh Công Sơn wants to give Ngô Kha hope, but not provoke him to do anything rash. His warnings suggest that he is well aware of his friend's fiery personality. "We know you are eager like an uncontrollable horse," he tells his friend, "but try to be calm and cool, don't be over-hasty [*nôn*

---

13. It was republished in Nguyễn Đắc Xuân, *Trịnh Công Sơn: Có một thời như thế* [Trịnh Công Sơn: There Was Such a Time] (HCMC: Văn Học, 2003), 153-162; and in Lê Minh Quốc, ed., *Trịnh Công Sơn: Rơi lệ ru người* [Trịnh Công Sơn: Shedding Tears, Singing Lullabies] (Hanoi: Phụ Nữ, 2004), 26-35; in *Thơ* [Poetry], a supplement to *Báo Văn Nghệ* [Journal of Literature and Art], June 6, 2004; and in *Thanh Niên* [Youth], June 26, 2004, 178.
14. Nguyễn Đắc Xuân, "Sự thực 'Thư gửi Ngô Kha của Trịnh Công Sơn'" [The Truth about Trịnh Công Sơn's "Letter to Ngô Kha"], in Bửu Nam and Phạm Thị Anh Nha, eds., *Ngô Kha hành trình*, 217.
15. Trịnh Công Sơn, "Lá thư gửi cho người đang ở trong tù hay đã bị thủ tiêu" [A Letter for a Person Who is Now In Prison or Has Been Exterminated], in Bửi Nam and Nguyễn Thị Anh Nga, eds., *Ngô Kha hành trình*, 189.
16. Ibid., 190.
17. Ibid., 191-192.

nóng] like in the old days."[18] He repeats this warning not to be over-hasty two pages later.

Trịnh Công Sơn is clearly the author of this letter, but does this mean he was a member of the communist underground and that Lê Khắc Cẩm was his handler? Nguyễn Đắc Xuân, in his article about Trịnh Công Sơn's letter, says that he asked Lê Khắc Cẩm: "Was Trịnh Công Sơn a revolutionary agent [*cơ sở cách mạng*]?" "That's hard to say," Lê Khắc Cẩm replied. "But Sơn knew that I was an agent of the City Party Committee. To work with me means that he was working for the Revolution."[19] When asked about the revolutionary language in Trịnh Công Sơn's letter, Lê Khắc Cẩm says it could reflect the fact that "at that time we, including Trịnh Công Sơn, read a lot of books and newspapers sent from the war zone and also every night listened with admiration to the Hanoi radio station. There's nothing surprising about someone being influenced by revolutionary language."[20]

Clearly Trịnh Công Sơn and Lê Khắc Cẩm were friends and clearly they associated with each other, but it is interesting that Lê Khắc Cẩm, whom Liên Thành claims was Trịnh Công Sơn's handler, tells Nguyễn Đắc Xuân that he does not know whether Trịnh Công Sơn was a revolutionary agent [*cơ sở cách mạng*]. If he knew he was an agent, it would seem that in 2011, when Nguyễn Đắc Xuân interviewed him, he would have no reason to withhold this information.

Liên Thành's most stunning and perhaps most damaging accusation is not that Trịnh Công Sơn was a communist underground agent but that he, in return for favored treatment, agreed to supply Liên Thành with information about other agents, some of whom were Sơn's good friends. Liên Thành says that he gathered evidence that Trịnh Công Sơn was associating with known communist agents and when he confronted the singer-composer with this evidence, he agreed to supply him with information about communist underground agents [*Việt Cộng nằm vùng*] in Huế. In return, Liên Thành says, he gave Trịnh Công Sơn a paper, called an "Order for Special Assignment" [*sự vụ lệnh công tác đặc biệt*] that enabled him to avoid the draft and kept him from being arrested at anti-war demonstrations and music concerts. This paper was the carrot, Liên Thành says. The stick was imprisonment for two years on the island

---

18. Ibid., 190.
19. Nguyễn Đắc Xuân, "Sự thực 'Thư gửi Ngô Kha,'" 218.
20. Nguyễn Đặc Xuân quotes Lê Khắc Cẩm in "Sự thực 'Thư gửi Ngô Kha,'" 218.

of Phú Quốc and when these two years were up, Liên Thành says he told Sơn, he had the power to keep sentencing him for two-year terms if he judged the security situation required. He told Sơn that he had the power to renew his sentence again and again because of his high rank in the security forces—Chief Commander of the National Police, General Secretary for Administration of the Provincial Phoenix Program, and General Secretary of the Provincial Security Council.[21]

The crimes Liên Thành accuses Trịnh Công Sơn of committing would not seem to be crimes that would get one imprisoned indefinitely on Phú Quốc Island, but no doubt Trịnh Công Sơn knew Liên Thành had the power to do what he wished; that, as he told Trịnh Công Sơn, there would be no trial. He could simply imprison him, saying the "security situation" justified it. If Liên Thành's story is true, if Trịnh Công Sơn did agree to be some kind of double-agent, it could have been because he sensed he had no choice, that if he wanted to continue to write and sing songs opposing the war he had to make some deal with Liên Thành. It is significant that Liên Thành says that although Trịnh Công Sơn gave him names of some Việt Cộng agents, he revealed "only one-tenth of what he knew." "There were very important matters," Liên Thành says, "that Trịnh Công Sơn participated in and knew clearly and thoroughly, but kept quiet about, never told us." (Liên Thành says he learned about these matters from other sources.)[22]

I do not know what to make of Liên Thành's account. It was generally assumed, as I explained in Chapter Two, that Trịnh Công Sơn had protectors associated with the Saigon regime at various stages of his career. Đặng Tiến has raised the question of how a musician without proper military service papers could "rudely sing anti-war songs like 'Gia tài của mẹ' [A Mother's Legacy] at the Faculty of Letters right in front of majestic Independence Palace, songs with lines like 'A mother's legacy, a mixed-blood gang / A mother's legacy, an unfaithful horde.'"[23] These lines could refer not to people who are literally of mixed blood but to Vietnamese who have allied themselves with non-Vietnamese, to people who have not been faithful to their race—to people like those occupying Independence Palace!

---

21. Liên Thành, "Trịnh Công Sơn và những hoạt động nằm vùng."
22. Ibid.
23. Đặng Tiến, "Trịnh Công Sơn: Tiếng hát hòa bình" [Trịnh Công Sơn: Voice of Peace], *Văn Học* [Literary Studies] Special Edition on Trịnh Công Sơn (Oct. and Nov. 2010), 188.

So why wasn't Trịnh Công Sơn arrested? Some people think his friend Lưu Kim Cương, a colonel in the Air Force of the Republic of Vietnam, protected him early in his singing career. Nguyễn Thanh Ty, one of Sơn's roommates when he taught in Bảo Lộc, includes a dialogue in his book in which he and some of his friends talk about who Trịnh Công Sơn's protector might be. One friend says it was Lưu Kim Cương, who, he claims, gave Trịnh Công Sơn a "Certificate of Military Service" [Chứng Chỉ Tại Ngũ].[24] As explained in the previous chapter Lưu Kim Cương, an officer in the air force and a friend of the singer, was killed in 1968 and Sơn wrote a song, "For Someone Who Has Fallen" [Cho một người nằm xuống] to mourn his passing. The literary critic Đặng Tiến, however, believes that Nguyễn Cao Kỳ became Sơn's protector, partly because he wanted to curry favor with Buddhist elements in Huế.[25] But perhaps Trịnh Công Sơn's real protector was Liên Thành. Perhaps it was that "Order for Special Assignment," that Liên Thành says he gave Trịnh Công Sơn that kept him out of the army and out of jail. It's possible that the "Certificate of Military Service" that Nguyễn Thanh Ty's friend says Lưu Kim Cương gave Sơn was actually the "Order for Special Assignment" given him by Liên Thành. In a follow-up article to "Trịnh Công Sơn and Underground Activities," Liên Thành explains that this order worked all over the Republic of Vietnam. If Trịnh Công Sơn were stopped by a policeman anywhere in South Vietnam, all he had to do was call the police station in Huế and he would be released immediately.[26]

I am not qualified to assess the veracity of Liên Thành's account, but I will mention some aspects of his personality that are revealed clearly in his writing. I call attention to these aspects not to reject Liên Thành's story about Trịnh Công Sơn but to give readers information to help them arrive at their own conclusions. One thing that emerges clearly from Liên Thành's books and articles is his undisguised hatred for anyone associated with the National Liberation Front. Certainly some intellectuals were underground agents for the NLF, and certainly terrible acts were committed by people on both sides of the conflict, but because his works are so biased they read like propaganda tracts, not objective historical accounts. His book *Biến Động Miền Trung* [Disorder in the Central Region] is published

---

24. Nguyễn Thanh Ty, *Về một quãng đời Trịnh Công Sơn* [On a Period of Trịnh Công Sơn's Life] (Place of publication and publisher not stated: 2001), 115.
25. Đặng Tiến, "Trịnh Công Sơn: Tiếng hát hòa bình," 187.
26. Liên Thành, "Liên Thành trả lại một số thắc mắc trong bài về Trịnh Công Sơn."

by the Committee to Prosecute Crimes of the Vietnamese Communist Party. Liên Thành is chairman of this committee, which he established in January of 2010. His other book, *Huế—Thảm Sát Mậu Thân: Tội Ác Đảng Cộng Sản Việt Nam* [Huế—The Massacre of Tết Mậu Thân: Crimes of the Vietnamese Communist Party] is self-published.

Another personality trait revealed in Liên Thành's writing is a tendency to boast. A large part of *Biến Động Miền Trung* is devoted to the operation he led that succeeded in capturing a communist underground agent named Hoàng Kim Loan, a man whom Liên Thành describes as an exceptionally skillful spy and the "chief architect" of a network of underground agents in Huế and Thừa Thiên Province that, he says, numbered in the thousands. These agents were everywhere, he says: in every civilian, military, security, and police organization, in student organizations, in political parties, and in Buddhist pagodas."[27] According to Liên Thành, Lê Khắc Cẩm, the agent who he says became Trịnh Công Sơn's handler, was part of this network established by Hoàng Kim Loan. Capturing Hoàng Kim Loan was Liên Thành's crowning achievement. The capture took place as part of an operation called The Dawn Campaign [*Chiến dịch Bình Minh*]. The operation began on May 6, 1972, five days after North Vietnamese troops had taken the provincial capital of Quảng Trị, only 40 miles north of Huế. Those troops were now advancing on Huế. The road was filled with refugees who were also heading south. People in the city feared a repeat of the 1968 Tết Offensive and by May 6 many Huế residents had already fled south to Đà Nẵng, including a family with seven children in whose home I had rented a room while teaching at the University of Huế. I left Huế on May 2 and my future wife and her family left around the same time.

Vietnamese in Huế refer to this period as "The Fiery Red Summer" [*Mùa hè đỏ lửa*]. The battles in Quảng Trị and Thừa Thiên were one part of an offensive communist leaders called the Nguyễn Huệ Campaign [*Chiến dịch Nguyễn Huệ*] after a national hero who, in the spring of 1789, surprised Chinese troops outside of Hanoi and defeated them. Americans refer to this offensive as the Easter Offensive. During this offensive, communist troops attacked in three places: across the Demilitarized Zone in Quảng Trị Province, in Kontum in the central highlands, and along

---

27. Liên Thành, *Biến Động Miền Trung*, 254; "Liên Thành trả lại một số thắc mắc trong bài về Trịnh Công Sơn."

the Cambodian border in Bình Long Province. With the help of bombing by US forces, ARVN troops were eventually able to repel the attacks in all three regions. It was a prideful time for both military and civilian officials of the Republic of Vietnam, and no one was more prideful than Liên Thành. This pride is evident in a passage in *Disorder in the Central Region* in which he describes his capture of Hoàng Kim Loan, the master communist spy. Liên Thành refers to himself in the third person. Hoàng Kim Loan was preparing to perform again the tragedy of Tết 1968, a general offensive, another bloodbath, but, he says,

> Hoàng Kim Loan did not suspect that this time he would meet an opponent who had just turned 30, who was half his age, who had entered the profession [undercover work, spying] 18 years after him, but had the full ability, the full bravery, the iron will of a military officer in the Army of the Republic of Vietnam and was also a member of the National Police. This young officer broke up the plan of Hanoi and Hoàng Kim Loan.[28]

Then he says: "Basically I am humble but I must boldly speak the truth: That officer was I."[29]

Liên Thành had other reasons to be proud. He is the grandson of Prince Cường Để (1882-1951) whose personal name was Nguyễn Phúc Hồng Dân.[30] Prince Cường Để was a direct descendent of Nguyễn Thế Tổ, known as Gia Long, the first king of the Nguyễn dynasty. The Prince's father, Nguyễn Phúc Cảnh, was Gia Long's eldest son. In the early decades of the twentieth century Cường Để was involved in anti-colonial activities, cooperating with Phan Bội Châu, a prominent leader of the anti-colonial struggle. Liên Thành also had relatives who became monks who held high positions within the Buddhist hierarchy. The brother of Liên Thành's maternal grandmother, and his own brother, Liên Phú, were respected monks who held leadership positions within the Buddhist hierarchy. The older monk, Liên Thành's grand-uncle, was Thích Tịnh Khiết (1890-1973); the younger monk, Liên Thành's brother, was Thích Chơn Kim (1929-2017). Both monks were associated with Tường Vân Pagoda in Huế.[31]

Liên Thành was raised a Buddhist. His mother was, he explains, a very devout disciple of a monk named Thích Thiện Lạc, known locally as

---

28. Liên Thành, *Biến Động Miền Trung*, 254.
29. Ibid.
30. Ibid., 337, 475.
31. Ibid., 475.

Thầy Ngoạn, and she arranged for him to perform a *quy y* ceremony for Liên Thành and his siblings.[32] Liên Thành's relationship to Thầy Ngoạn became an issue in December of 1970, when he interrogated a recently captured high-level communist operative and learned that Thầy Ngoạn was working for the National Liberation Front and that his pagoda, An Lăng, located just over a mile southwest of Huế, was a refuge and meeting place for a communist cadre. Aided by two platoons of heavily armed police [*Cảnh Sát Dã Chiến*] in commando cars, Liên Thành raided An Lăng Pagoda, killed three NLF soldiers, and arrested Thầy Ngoạn. When Liên Thành's mother learned that her son had arrested Thầy Ngoạn, she had another son relay this message to him: "Release Thầy [Ngoạn]. Since when does someone go and capture the monk that conducted his *quy y* ceremony and gave him a Buddhist name? Only a child who has no filial piety [*con bất hiếu*]!"[33] But her plea fell on deaf ears. At a meeting of the Provincial Security Council [*Hội Đồng An Ninh Tỉnh*] to decide Thầy Ngoạn's punishment, one member proposed six months in prison, another one year, but Liên Thành says he convinced them to imprison him for two years on Côn Sơn Island.[34]

What turned this Buddhist into a ruthless police officer who ordered his former teacher to be killed and who, if Nguyễn Đắc Xuân and his sources are correct, five years earlier had also brutally murdered a childhood friend named Hồ Đăng Lương after he learned he had assisted the Việt Cộng?[35] One can only speculate, but it seems possible that Liên Thành was influenced by his father, a member of the intensely anti-communist Đại Việt Party [Greater Vietnam Party]. Additionally, he may be influenced by Nguyễn Ngọc Loan, a notoriously cruel GVN police chief whom Prime Minister Nguyễn Cao Kỳ sent to central Vietnam in June of 1966 to restore order after ARVN commanders sympathetic to the Buddhist Struggle Movement refused to use harsh means to squash it. Liên Thành, who was then an Assistant Chief of the Special Police in Huế, worked under Nguyễn Ngọc Loan.[36] (The "special" indicated it was it was a secret

---

32. Ibid., 363. This ceremony involves pledging to accept the Three Jewels [*Tam Bảo*] of Buddhism: Buddha, Dharma, and Sangha [*Phật, Pháp, Tăng già*]; and also to obey the Five Precepts [Skt. *pancasila*]: to refrain from killing, stealing, sexual misconduct, lying, and taking intoxicants. After making this pledge, the monk gives the person a Buddhist name [*Pháp danh*].
33. Ibid.
34. Ibid., 364-365.
35. Nguyễn Đắc Xuân, "Vài điều về Liên Thành."
36. Liên Thành, *Biến Động Miền Trung*, 476-477.

police [*mật vụ*] or intelligence [*tình báo*] unit.) A third influence on Liên Thành was probably the Phoenix program, the American program to root out Vietcong infrastructure which the American advisors pressured the Republic of Vietnam to adopt. Let me talk about these possible influences on Liên Thành in more detail. Liên Thành's accusations could damage Trịnh Công Sơn's reputation and so it is important to learn all we can about his accuser.

The Vietnamese Đại Việt Party, which was formed during World War II, began as a rival to the Viet Minh Front, an organization created by the Indochinese Communist Party. At first it sought help from the Japanese, who occupied Vietnam in 1945, but eventually it recruited anti-communist nationalists to resist the French colonial regime. After the division of the country in 1954 it was active in the Republic of Vietnam. In January of 1964, a young officer named Nguyễn Khánh and other young officers, called Young Turks by the Americans, staged a bloodless coup against then-head of state General Dương Văn Minh, one of the leaders in a group of generals who had overthrown Ngô Đình Diệm in 1963. General Minh, whom the Americans called "Big Minh" because he was six feet tall, was a southerner and a Buddhist. George Kahin explains that Nguyễn Khánh's group of Young Turks contained "ex-Can Lao Dai Viet Catholic officers."[37] "Can Lao" refers to a secret political organization that Ngô Đình Diệm and his brother Ngô Đình Nhu created in 1955 to control policy and protect their interests.[38] One of the Catholic Young Turks was Nguyễn Văn Thiệu. The coup in February 1965 that ousted Nguyễn Khánh from power was, George Kahin says, "led by Catholic officers, mostly with Dai Viet connections."[39] Kahin quotes from a C.I.A. report that describes these officers as "die-hard neo-Diemists and Catholic military militants disturbed at the rise of Buddhist influence, opposed to Gen. Khanh and—in a vague, ill-thought-out way—desirous of turning back the clock and undoing some of the results of the November 1963 ouster of Diem."[40]

It seems that Liên Thành got the job of Assistant Chief of the Special Police in Huế because he was recommended by his father and other Đại Việt Party members. Trần Việt says that after the fall of Ngô Đình Diệm

---

37. George McT. Kahin, *Intervention: How America Became Involved in Vietnam* (New York: Alfred A. Knopf, 1986), 230.
38. The full name of this organization was the Revolutionary Personalist Labor Party [*Cần Lao Nhân Vị Cách Mạng Đảng*].
39. George McT. Kahin, *Intervention*, 299.
40. Ibid.

the provinces of Quảng Trị and Thừa Thiên were "Đại Việt territory" [lãnh thổ Đại Việt] and so it was easy for the party to get one of their own appointed assistant head of the secret police.[41] Prior to taking this position, Liên Thành was head of a company of Regional Forces [Nghĩa Quân] in Nam Hòa, a district on the outskirts of Huế.[42] Three different sources say that Liên Thành ended up in the Regional Forces rather than becoming an officer in the regular army because he failed his first baccalaureate exam [thi tú tài một], an exam that one had to pass to enter the last year of secondary school.[43] Liên Thành, however, says that after Ngô Đình Diệm was overthrown, many in his class at the Thủ Đức army training center were transferred [biệt phái] to the Regional Forces.[44]

In June 1966, the most powerful person in Huế was Liên Thành's superior, General Nguyễn Ngọc Loan, the northern-born Catholic whom Nguyễn Cao Kỳ appointed to put down the rebellion in Đà Nẵng and Huế led by dissident ARVN officers who joined forces with those in the Buddhist Struggle Movement. Nguyễn Ngọc Loan achieved worldwide notoriety two years later when he shot a Viet Cong prisoner in the head on a street in Saigon, an event captured in a photo taken by Eddie Adams, a photographer working for the Associated Press. This photo has become an iconic image. It is one of the most famous photos of the war in Vietnam. Two years earlier in Đà Nẵng and Huế, Nguyễn Ngọc Loan had been just as ruthless. "Deploying tanks and armored cars," Stanley Karnow reports, "he systematically combed Danang street by street, slaying hundreds of rebel troops and more than a hundred civilians, most of whom had taken refuge in Buddhist temples."[45] Then he moved on to Huế where, Karnow says, "he jailed hundreds of students and other rebels, many of whom were to languish in prison for years without trial."[46] He also arrested Thích

---

41. Trần Việt, "Nguyễn Phúc Liên Thành, Chống Tôi Lên Tiếng" [We Raise Our Voices], Apr. 2, 2012, http://chungtoilentieng.blogspot.com/2012/04/phan-vii-nguyen-phuc-lien-thanh-theo.html (accessed Feb. 28, 2017).
42. Liên Thành, Biến Động Miền Trung, 474-475.
43. Nguyễn Đắc Xuân, "Vài điều về Liên Thành"; Phan Bùi Bảo Thy, "Liên Thành, kẻ sát nhân trong những ngày miền Trung biến động" [Liên Thành, The Assassin During the Days of Disorder in the Central Region], An Ninh Thế Giới Online, May 27, 2012, http://antg.cand.com.vn/Tu-lieu-antg/Lien-Thanh-ke-sat-nhan-trong-nhung-ngay-mien-Trung-bien-dong-303297/ (accessed May 4, 2017); and Trần Việt, "Nguyễn Phúc Liên Thành."
44. Liên Thành, Biến Động Miền Trung, 475.
45. Stanley Karnow, Vietnam: A History, 447.
46. Ibid., 450.

Trí Quang who went on a hunger strike and was later taken to Saigon.[47] Observing his boss's ruthless methods in Huế no doubt reinforced Liên Thành's own ruthlessness.

It seems likely also that the Phoenix Program was an important influence on Liên Thành. In *Disorder in the Central Region*, he includes a photo of himself standing in front of an advisor from the Phoenix Program named Louis Spalla while they were on an operation in Hương Thủy District outside of Huế in 1970.[48] Stafford T. Thomas, in his *Dictionary of the Vietnam War*, explains that the Phoenix Program was a GVN program but was established by the C.I.A., who provided the advisors. Simply put, the aim of the Phoenix Program, Thomas says, was to "neutralize" members of the Viet Cong infrastructure through "arrest, conversion, or death."[49] Frances FitzGerald, in *Fire in the Lake*, highlights an effect of this program that could have made someone like Liên Thành feel he had free rein to arrest and kill civilians like Trịnh Công Sơn's friend Ngô Kha. This program, she writes, "in effect eliminated the cumbersome category of 'civilian'; it gave the GVN, and initially the American troops as well, license and justification for the arrest, torture, or killing of anyone in the country, whether or not the person was carrying a gun."[50]

Despite Liên Thành's accusations, I do not believe that Trịnh Công Sơn was an underground agent for the NLF. It is clear that many of his friends sympathized with the NLF and that other friends, like Lê Khắc Cầm, could be considered communist agents. If Liên Thành's account is true, if Trịnh Công Sơn did make some kind of deal with this ruthless police officer, it does not mean that Trịnh Công Sơn was not a neutralist. It only proves how very difficult it was, especially for draft-aged young men, to remain neutral when just talking about neutralism and a desire for a peaceful solution to the war could get you labeled pro-communist and put in jail. Ultimately I believe to find out where Trịnh Công Sơn stood we should listen not to Communist Party member Nguyễn Đắc Xuân or to a power-crazed GVN police chief in Huế but to Trịnh Công Sơn's songs—songs like "Love Song of a Mad Person"* in which he expresses

47. Neil Sheehan, "Troops Move Tri Quang From Hospital in Hue," *New York Times*, June 26, 1966.
48. Liên Thành, *Biến Động Miền Trung*, 338.
49. Stafford T. Thomas, "Phoenix Program," in *Dictionary of the Vietnam War*, ed. James S. Olson (Westport, CT: Greenwood Press, 1988), 369.
50. Frances FitzGerald, *Fire in the Lake: The Vietnamese and the Americans in Vietnam* (Boston: Little, Brown and Company, 1972), 412-413.

love for soldiers killed in all three regions, and whispers their name and the name Vietnam, and insists that all Vietnamese are bound together by their "golden skin voice." And to his song "Singing Above the Corpses" [Hát trên những xác người] which he wrote after the Tết Offensive. In this song the speaker goes to the Berry Patch [*Bãi Dâu*], a place in an area of Huế that Vietnamese call Gia Hội. After the Tết Offensive, over 200 bodies were found there. Liên Thành accuses Trịnh Công Sơn's friend Hoàng Phủ Ngọc Tường of presiding over a People's Court in Gia Hội and sentencing 204 people to death. Trịnh Công Sơn, however, sees the pain of families who lost loved ones. He sees first a mother and then a father hugging the dead body of a child. And he sees also the divisions and the hatred that lead to the madness of war:

> *A mother claps her hands and cheers for war*
> *A sister claps her hands and cheers for peace*
> *People clap their hands to increase the hate*
> *People clap their hands to avoid repenting*

Mysteries remain regarding both Ngô Kha and Trịnh Công Sơn, but what seems undeniable is that Ngô Kha and Trịnh Công Sơn inspired and influenced each other. Many passages in Ngô Kha's "Long Poem for Peace" resemble passages from Trịnh Công Sơn's songs in the collections *Prayer for Vietnam* [Kinh Việt Nam] and *We Must See the Sun* [Ta phải thấy mặt trời] that I discussed in the previous chapter—songs like "We Are Determined That We Must Live" [Ta quyết phải sống], "Huế, Sài gòn, Hà nội" and "Vietnam Rise Up" [Việt nam ơi hãy vùng lên]. Here are the opening lines of Ngô Kha's "Long Poem for Peace":

> *Brothers and sisters meet happily as if just beginning life*
> *On this day when Vietnam gives birth to a new language*
> *Thirty million fellow citizens rise up*
> *Waiting like the great* trường sơn *mountains*[51]
> *For peace to return in people's hearts*

Here are lines 50-57:

> *We advance together*
> *Singing the song of a Reunified Vietnam*
> *In the midst of historic change*

---

51. The Annamese Cordillera, a mountain range that extends parallel to the coast from the northwest to southeast, forms the boundary between Laos and Vietnam.

72

We go from Nam Quan to Cà Mau[52]
From the Mekong, the Perfume River, the Red River
Phú Quốc, Côn Lôn, Ba Vì, Tam Đảo[53]
 From Huế, Sài Gòn to Thái Bình, Hà Nội
Our voices echo beneath the sky

Note the similarities between the above lines and these lines from Trịnh Công Sơn's song "Huế, Saigon, Hanoi":

From the Center, the South, and the North
People wait to light
Torches hailing freedom
Now the road leads to prisons
Where tomorrow we'll build schools and markets
Our people will till the fields and will be well clothed and fed
As hands help the country
As hands rebuild
The old hatred fades

And these lines from Trịnh Công Sơn's song "What do we see tonight?" [Ta thấy gì đêm nay]:

What do we see tonight?
Hundreds of flags flying
The forests and mountains spread the news to every region
The wind of peace blows in a thousand directions

Both Ngô Kha in his long poem and Trịnh Công Sơn in his songs talk about the wonderful things that will happen when peace comes: The bombing will end, hate will turn into love, and eventually the country—all three regions—will be unified. The Paris Peace Talks opened in May 1968. These talks dragged on for five years—the final agreement was not signed until January 27, 1973—but their beginning was cause for great optimism in both Vietnam and the US.[54] Trịnh Công Sơn's language sometimes sounds militaristic. His songs in *Prayer for Vietnam* and *We Must See the*

---

52. "Nam Quan" is a pass on the Vietnam-China border. "Cà Mau" is the name of a city and province on the southernmost tip of Vietnam.
53. Phú Quốc and Côn Lôn (also known as Côn Sơn) are islands in the South China Sea. (Ngô Kha was imprisoned on the island of Phú Quốc in 1966.) "Ba Vì" is a mountain range in the north. "Tam đảo" is the name of another mountain range in North Vietnam, a range with three high peaks.
54. Đặng Tiến argues that the opening of these talks helps explain the glorious visions of a peaceful Vietnam found in Trịnh Công Sơn's later songs. See Đặng Tiến, "Trịnh Công Sơn: Tiếng hát hòa bình," 190-191.

Sun are movement songs [*nhạc phong trào*]—songs to mobilize people. His intent in these songs, however, it seems to me, is to appropriate the energy inherent in militaristic language and channel it into peaceful projects. Like Martin Luther King, Jr. in his famous drum major speech, Trịnh Công Sơn wanted to be a drum major but a drum major for love, a drum major for peace and reconstruction, not war.[55] "We become part of a proud revolution [*cách mạng*]," Trịnh Công Sơn sings in "Vietnam Rise Up." But then come these lines: "We will seize a hundred building sites / We will build a thousand peaceful streets."

But how do Ngô Kha and Trịnh Công Sơn differ? The Struggle Movement in Huế was not completely, but in large part, a Buddhist movement. Ngô Kha, was, it seems, a Buddhist, and Trịnh Công Sơn has described the important role Buddhism played in his life in several articles and interviews which I will discuss in later chapters. Ngô Kha, however, was different. He encouraged students to burn American vehicles and filled his pockets with stones to throw at policemen.[56] Trịnh Công Sơn adopted a gentler approach. In songs like "Singing Above the Corpses," Sơn seems to be suggesting the need for what the Vietnamese refugee writer Viet Thanh Nguyen calls "pure forgiveness," the forgiving of the unforgiveable, the forgiving even of events like those that occurred at the Berry Patch during the Tết Offensive and the brutal murder of Ngô Kha in 1973. Pure forgiveness may sound unreasonable and unrealistic—mad even—but isn't it, Viet Thanh Nguyen asks, more sensible and realistic than perpetual war?[57] In "Love Song of a Mad Person"* and "Singing Above the Corpses" Trịnh Công Sơn suggests that it is perpetual war that is madness. He wants Vietnamese, as he sings in "Huế, Saigon, Hanoi,"* to "Step away for once from extermination / Build one common house for all."

---

55. Martin Luther King, Jr. delivered his sermon, titled "The Drum Major Instinct," at the Ebenezer Baptist Church in Atlanta, Georgia, on Feb. 4, 1968, two months before he was assassinated. In this sermon he told the congregation what he wanted people to say about him at his funeral: "I'd like for somebody to say that day that Martin Luther King, Jr., tried to love somebody. I want you to say that day that I tried to be right on the war question."

56. Hoàng Phủ Ngọc Tường, *Trịnh Công Sơn và cây đàn lya của hoàng tử bé* [Trịnh Công Sơn and the Lyre of the Little Prince] (HCMC: Trẻ, 2004), 41.

57. Viet Thanh Nguyen, *Nothing Ever Dies: Vietnam and the Memory of War* (Cambridge, MA: Harvard University Press, 2016), 290-291.

5

LOVE STORIES

Like Trịnh Công Sơn and Khánh Ly, Bob Dylan and Joan Baez became a famous couple. Both singer-composers benefitted from having such beautiful and talented singers popularize their songs. The image both couples projected, and the intrigue and curiosity generated by their relationship, helped promote the songs they were singing and the causes their songs were about. "Every crusade needs a great romance," the singer and activist Harry Belafonte said, referring to Dylan and Baez's contributions to the civil rights struggle.[1]

Descriptions by Vietnamese of the Trịnh Công Sơn-Khánh Ly relationship suggest that it resembled the Dylan-Baez relationship in some ways. "They traveled together," Đặng Tiến says of Trịnh Công Sơn and Khánh Ly, "and created the image of 'a couple,' a boy and a girl with a natural and guiltless friendship. . . . They had their native land, love, fate, duty to the country, and all the while 'Autumn passes, winter's far away, summer brings clouds, and love's a flying bird against the sky.'"[2] Trịnh Công Sơn and Khánh Ly sang to young audiences in university auditoriums and churches and did not charge for their performances. They created an "idealistic image [*hình ảnh lý tưởng*] for art," Đặng Tiến says, "especially for the art of singing, and this image encouraged an idealistic approach to humanity, love, and politics."[3]

---

1. David Hajdu quotes Belafonte in *Positively 4th Street* (New York: Farrar, Straus and Giroux, 2001), 183.
2. Đặng Tiến, "Trịnh Công Sơn: Tiếng Hát hòa bình" [Trịnh Công Sơn: Voice of Peace] *Văn Học* [Literary Studies] 186 & 187 (Oct.-Nov., 2001), 185. Đặng Tiến quotes lines from Trịnh Công Sơn's song "Calling the Four Seasons" [Gọi tên bốn mùa].
3. Ibid., 186.

Bob Dylan and Joan Baez performing at the 1963 March on Washington.
Photo by Rowland Scherman, courtesy of the National Archives

Khánh Ly and Trịnh Công Sơn performing in 1967.
Photo courtesy of Tommy Trương Collection

I never saw Trịnh Công Sơn and Khánh Ly perform together. Performance styles and dating and courtship customs differ greatly across cultures, making comparisons difficult, but comments like Đặng Tiến's ("a guiltless friendship") and things I've learned from Vietnamese friends lead me to conclude that Trịnh Công Sơn and Khánh Ly, like Dylan and Baez, projected an image of youth, love, and social commitment. In reality there were differences. Dylan and Baez were lovers but only for a short time, and Trịnh Công Sơn and Khánh Ly were never lovers. In an interview, Hoàng Xuân Sơn, who knew both Trịnh Công Sơn and Khánh Ly well when they were singing together, states clearly that Khánh Ly and Trịnh Công Sơn were not lovers. "Trịnh Công Sơn regarded Khánh Ly as a friend," he told Bùi Văn Phú, the interviewer. "He loved her the way one loves a younger sister in one's family."[4] Trịnh Công Sơn himself has said that he and Khánh Ly were just friends. Letters that he wrote to Ngô Vũ Dao Ánh, which she saved and which were published in 2011, make it clear that she, not Khánh Ly, was the woman he loved when he and Khánh Ly were performing together.[5] But nevertheless it also seems true that when both couples performed, romance—real or imagined—was in the air, and so was idealism, a sense that their singing was not just to entertain but also to make the world better.

In the late 1950s in Huế, Sơn fell in love with Phương Thảo, the sister of two brothers that he played music with, but she married a dean at the University of Huế. In an article published in 1969 Trịnh Công Sơn refers to this failed relationship as "an unfathomable disappointment," but he doesn't blame Phương Thảo. Such disappointments were common, Trịnh Công Sơn suggests, in Huế at that time.[6] Trịnh Công Sơn's close friend Đinh Cường, who discusses the end of this relationship in an article that appeared in 2001, explains that families in Huế "usually pay attention to social position and to [educational] degrees when they marry their children."[7] Singers were not high on the social scale and parents, who had

---

4. Hoàng Xuân Sơn, interview with Bùi Văn Phú, "Nơi tôi sinh sống thì hát nhạc Trịnh cũng nên dè dặt" [Hoàng Xuân Sơn: Where I Live You Should Be Careful about Singing Trịnh Music], http://damau.org/archives/19866 (accessed Jan. 15, 2012).
5. The letters appear in *Trịnh Công Sơn: Thư tình gửi một người* [Trịnh Công Sơn: Love Letters for Someone] (HCMC: Trẻ, 2011).
6. Trịnh Công Sơn, "Nhật ký ở tuổi 30" [Diary Written at 30], in *Trịnh Công Sơn: Một người thơ ca một cõi đi về* [Trịnh Công Sơn: A Singer-poet, a Place for Leaving and Returning], eds. Nguyễn Trọng Tạo, Nguyễn Thụy Kha, and Đoàn Tử Huyến (Hanoi: Âm Nhạc, 2001), 164-165.
7. Đinh Cường, "Gửi Sơn, Những đoàn ghi rời của người bạn ở xa" [For Sơn, Scattered Notes from a Friend Far Away], in *Trịnh Công Sơn: Cuộc đời, âm nhạc, thơ, hội họa, suy*

great power over whom their children married, wanted their daughters to marry men headed toward more prestigious careers. It was not easy for young women to resist parental pressure.

BÍCH DIỄM AND DAO ÁNH

In the early 1960s Trịnh Công Sơn fell in love with a young woman named Ngô Vũ Dao Ánh who lived near him in Huế. Before 1975 not many people knew about this relationship and only Trịnh Công Sơn's close friends understood how deeply he was affected by it. In 1960 Sơn wrote a song, "Diễm of the Past" [Diễm xưa],* a song that was inspired by Dao Ánh's older sister, Bích Diễm, and so many people thought that she, not her younger sister, Dao Ánh, was the woman that he was in love with in the early 1960s. It is no surprise that his fans were confused. "Diễm of the Past" was very popular and it helped Sơn become famous after it appeared in 1960. The song had her name in the title, so many people, at least Huế residents, assumed Sơn was in love with Bích Diễm. And, it seems, Sơn *was* attracted to her. She lived near him, just a short walk across the Phú Cam bridge spanning the An Cựu River.[8] Sơn's friend Đinh Cường lived near her family, and from his place he and Sơn could see the house where Bích Diễm lived. They would wait for her father to leave to teach and then visit her.[9] Her father, a northerner, who taught French at Đông Khánh, the girls' secondary school in Huế, and also at the Faculty of Pedagogy of Huế University, was very strict regarding his daughters. "He would look at us," Đinh Cường says, "very suspiciously, especially Sơn who had long hair and a wispy beard on his chin."[10] He clearly did not want a young man with no university degree to associate with his noble daughters.

In 1997 Sơn wrote a very touching and beautiful essay in which he explains how he was inspired to write "Diễm of the Past" (See Appendix E for a translation).[11] From the balcony of his family's apartment on Nguyễn Trường Tộ Street, he says, he would watch Bích Diễm walk to classes at the University of Huế. He makes clear that she was the inspiration for

---

tưởng [Trịnh Công Sơn: Life, Music, Poetry, Painting, Reflections], eds. Trịnh Cung and Nguyễn Quốc Thái (HCMC: Văn Nghệ, 2001), 54.

8. This bridge is also called the Bến Ngự Bridge.

9. Nguyễn Đắc Xuân, *Trịnh Công Sơn: Có một thời như thế* [Trịnh Công Sơn: There Was Such a Time] (HCMC: Văn Học, 2003), 68-70.

10. Đinh Cường, "Gửi Sơn, Những đoàn ghi rời của người bạn ở xa," 60.

11. This essay by Trịnh Công Sơn, titled "Hồi Ức" [A Recollection], first appeared in *Âm Nhạc* [Music] in 1997. It is included in Nguyễn Trọng Tạo et al., ed., *Trịnh Công Sơn:Một người thơ ca một cõi đi về* [Trịnh Công Sơn: A Singer-Poet, a Place for Leaving and Returning] (Hanoi: Trung Tâm Văn Hóa Ngôn Ngữ Đông Tây), 201-202.

"Diễm of the Past" but does not suggest he was in love with her. Sơn's sister, Trịnh Vĩnh Trinh, however, says that Sơn was interested in Bích Diễm before falling deeply in love with her younger sister, Dao Ánh.[12] She remembers, too, how this relationship—perhaps too strong a word—with Bích Diễm ended. It was in 1963, she explains, and Sơn was sick and lying in his room. Suddenly the house was filled with the smell of hyacinths (*dạ lan*). Bích Diễm, who was fifteen years old at the time, had brought the flowers and included with them a note to say goodbye and end their "relationship." After Bích Diễm sent this letter, her younger sister, Dao Ánh, wrote a letter to Sơn and had Ngân, a sister of Sơn's and a classmate of Dao Ánh's at Đồng Khánh Secondary School, deliver it to Sơn. In her letter she expressed her affection for Sơn and sympathy for the problems he was facing. Sơn replied and thus began a relationship that lasted Sơn's entire life.[13]

Trịnh Công Sơn wrote his essay about Bích Diễm almost forty years after he wrote his song "Diễm of the Past." In the minds of his fans Diễm had long ago assumed a mythic status. In his essay, Sơn himself suggests there was something unreal about her from the beginning. In his essay he describes a quiet and dreamy time that is vague and surreal [*liêu trai*].[14] "But," he asks, what are reality and dreams? "Truthfully," he continues, "when all is said and done, the former is an illusion of the latter. And after having those illusions for a rather long time, people who grow up in that small city [Huế] weave and embroider their own dreams."[15]

Bích Diễm was, of course, very real. She left Huế in 1963 to study in Saigon and later went to the US to continue her studies, where she married, had a family, and worked in a hospital in Los Angeles. In March of 2010, she returned to Huế where she spoke, very modestly and circumspectly, about Trịnh Công Sơn. "I never have dared," she told a reporter,

---

12. Giao Hương and Dạ Ly, "Công bố hàng trăm bức thư tình của nhạc sĩ Trịnh Công Sơn: Trịnh Công Sơn-Dao Ánh qua hồi ức của Trịnh Vĩnh Trinh" [Making Public Hundreds of Trịnh Công Sơn's Love Letters (Part 7): Trịnh Công Sơn—Dao Ánh as Remembered by Trịnh Vĩnh Trinh], Thanh Niên [Youth Online] https://thanhnien.vn/cong-bo-hang-tram-buc-thu-tinh-cua-nhac-si-trinh-cong-son-ky-7-trinh-cong-son-dao-anh-qua-hoi-uc-cua-trinh-vinh-trinh-post297058.html (accessed Apr. 12, 2011).
13. Ibid.
14. "*Liêu trai*," translated here as "surreal," does not refer to the twentieth century avant-garde movement in painting and literature. (Vietnamese use the compound word "*siêu thực*" to refer to this movement.) "*Liêu trai*" means "strange," "marvelous" or "other-worldly." The term comes from the title of a Chinese collection of strange tales, *Liêu trai chí dị* [Strange Tales Recorded in Liêu Trai], compiled by Bồ Tùng Linh at the end of the seventeenth century.
15. Trịnh Công Sơn, "Hồi Ức," 179.

79

"to accept that I am Diễm of the Past. I consider that to be too large—large beyond my ability to imagine. I don't know if it's true or false. But anyway, I think, as many people do, that it is a very beautiful love."[16]

We now know quite a bit about Sơn's relationship to Bích Diễm's younger sister, Dao Ánh, because in 2011 *Trịnh Công Sơn: Love Letters for Someone* [Trịnh Công Sơn: Thư tình gửi một người] appeared in bookstores in Hồ Chí Minh City, its release timed to correspond with the tenth anniversary of Trịnh Công Sơn's death.[17] It contains hundreds of love letters that Trịnh Công Sơn wrote to Dao Ánh, letters that Dao Ánh, who came to the US after the fall of the Saigon regime, had kept for decades. Most of the letters were written in 1964 and 1965 when Trịnh Công Sơn was teaching in Blao (Bảo lộc),[18] a small town in the central highlands, and Dao Ánh was in Saigon. Trịnh Công Sơn was lonely in Blao. Missing his girlfriend and saddened by the rapidly escalating war, he poured out his feelings in his letters to Dao Ánh as well as in songs. Some of his most famous songs were written in 1964-65, including his *Songs of Golden Skin*, the anti-war songs that were censored by both Republican and Socialist regimes. Trịnh Công Sơn clearly loved Dao Ánh and she apparently loved him. It is not completely clear why they went their separate ways but it appears that it was again a case of parents having other plans for their daughter. A letter Trịnh Công Sơn wrote to Dao Ánh in 1969 mentions a visit that Dao Ánh's mother made to Trịnh Công Sơn's house in Huế on April 2, 1969. Apparently she conveyed to Trịnh Công Sơn that Dao Ánh was marrying someone else. Writing Dao Ánh the day after the visit, Trịnh Công Sơn says:

> I won't write at length here about the thoughts that ran through my head all last night. I just want to tell you for the last time something I've held secret within me for a long time. That is my dream that I could have you next to me so we could go through a long life together. Now all that is not possible. The dream only exists within me, like a lamp that cannot be lit.[19]

---

16. Ngọc Văn, "Diễm của ngày xưa" [Diễm of Bygone Days], *Tiên Phong* [Vanguard], Mar. 14, 2010, http://www.tienphong.vn/Tianyon/Index.aspx?ArticleID=188748&Channe-lID=7 (accessed Mar. 20, 2010).

17. *Trịnh Công Sơn: Thư tình gửi một người.*

18. Blao is a ward of the city of Bảo Lộc, a town southwest of Đà Lạt.

19. *Thư tình gửi một người*, 309.

He doesn't fault Dao Ánh, perhaps because he realizes the decision was not hers alone to make. "I just feel sad," he says, "that we didn't have the power to make suggestions regarding this important matter."[20]

Trịnh Công Sơn's youngest sister, Trịnh Vĩnh Trinh, however, says that her brother told her many times that he was partially responsible for his breakup with Dao Ánh. "He said," Trịnh Vĩnh Trinh reports, "that at that time he couldn't provide a complete married life for someone he loved, so he didn't think about establishing a family. As for Dao Ánh, she couldn't wait a long time." Sơn's sister is a little surprised by the gentleness of her brother's reaction to the end of his relationship with Dao Ánh. "Everyone is sad," she says, "when the person one loves marries someone else, but his sadness was unusual and very kind-hearted [*nhân từ*]."[21]

Bob Dylan grew up in the United States, where parents had much less control over whom their daughters could associate with and whom they could marry. When he became a star, his problem was not finding women to love but keeping women away, preventing them from infringing on his privacy. In the next chapter on the personalities of the two singer-composers, I will mention some of the relationships that Dylan had with women when he was older. Here I will comment on his relationships with three women whom he loved and who loved him, and who inspired some of his most famous songs: Echo Helstrom, Suze Rotolo, and Joan Baez.

ECHO HELSTROM

Dylan's girlfriend in high school was named Echo Star Helstrom. Her parents named her Echo because she was born exactly fourteen years after her brother was born. Both Robert Shelton and Anthony Scaduto have interviewed her. In their accounts Echo comes across as a very likeable young woman. Dylan's parents, however, did not approve of her because—Bob's brother, David, told Shelton—"She was not Jewish and she wasn't from the right side of the tracks."[22] The Helstrom's house was a tar-paper shack on Highway 73, three miles outside of town. Echo hung out with a crowd some people called "greasers," kids who liked motorcycles and wore black leather jackets. A high school classmate of Dylan's told Anthony Scaduto that Dylan was part of the greaser crowd but Echo told Scaduto

---

20. Ibid.
21. Trịnh Vĩnh Trinh, in Giao Hương and Dạ Ly, "Công bố hàng trăm bức thư tình của nhạc sĩ Trịnh Công Sơn."
22. Robert Shelton, *No Direction Home: The Life and Times of Bob Dylan* (Milwaukee, WI: Backbeat Books, 2011), 43.

that wasn't true. "He didn't fit in with the bums," Echo said. "I knew the real bums. All my friends were the wrong-side-of the-tracks people, the dropouts, and Bob didn't fit in with them. He didn't fit in with anyone in town really."[23]

Though from different backgrounds, Echo and Bob shared an interest in rhythm and blues music. Echo stayed up until four in the morning listening to Gatemouth Page, Howlin' Wolf, Jimmy Reed and B.B. King. You couldn't hear these singers on stations in the Hibbing area, she told Anthony Scaduto. You had to stay up late at night and tune in to Black stations in Little Rock or Chicago. Dylan listened to these same singers and was delighted to learn Echo loved them too.[24] Echo's mother, Martha Helstrom, told Robert Shelton that Dylan had a small Ford and he and Echo used to drive to the top of Maple Hill where one got a good view of the Iron Range.[25] "They had their dreams to get married and live on Maple Hill," she said. "We were really in love," Echo told Scaduto. "Everybody laughs at kids when they fall in love, saying how they don't know what it all means or anything, but that's not true. Kids know."[26] Echo and Bob broke up in 1958 just as they were starting their senior year of high school. In 1969 they met again when Bob returned to Hibbing with his wife Sara Lowndes and attended Hibbing High School's reunion for the class of 1960.

It is generally assumed that Dylan's song "Girl from the North Country," is about Echo, probably because Hibbing, Minnesota, is a cold place where "the snowflakes storm" and "the rivers freeze" and a girl needs a warm coat "to keep her from the howlin' winds." It is included on his second album, *The Freewheelin' Bob Dylan*, released in 1963. Paul Simon and Art Garfunkel released a similar song, "Scarborough Fair," in 1965. Note the similarities in their opening stanzas. Here's how Dylan's song begins:

> *Well, if you're travelin' to the north country fair*
> *Where the winds hit heavy on the border line*
> *Remember me to one who lives there*
> *She once was a true love of mine*

And here's the first stanza of Simon and Garfunkel's "Scarborough Fair":

---

23. Anthony Scaduto, *Bob Dylan* (London: Helter Skelter Publishing, 1996), 20.
24. Ibid., 14.
25. Robert Shelton, *No Direction Home*, 44.
26. Anthony Scaduto, *Bob Dylan*, 19.

Are you going to Scarborough Fair
Parsley, sage, rosemary and thyme
Remember me to one who lives there
She once was a true love of mine

Robert Shelton says that both Dylan and Simon and Garfunkel were probably influenced by a version of an old English ballad sung by Martin Carthy, an English folksinger. Paul Simon and Art Garfunkel's "Scarborough Fair" was a bigger hit, but Dylan's "Girl from the North Country" is a beautiful song. Robert Shelton calls it "a tender love song of yearning nostalgia."[27] Dylan and Johnny Cash sing it beautifully as a duet on Dylan's album *Nashville Skyline* (1969).

Whether Echo Helstrom inspired "Girl from the North Country" is an open question. Robert Shelton says "there is great reason to believe it was inspired by Bonnie Beecher," a young woman and aspiring actress Dylan knew in 1960 in Dinkytown, a hip area of Minneapolis near the University of Minnesota.[28] Anthony Scaduto calls this song "Echo's song" but he also says Dylan's friends told him that Dylan had been carrying the song around in his head for a long time but didn't write it until Suze Rotolo, his girlfriend in Greenwich Village, went on a long trip to Europe. "This song," Scaduto concludes, "is about an earlier romance [with Echo] motivated by the loss of his present woman."[29]

SUZE ROTOLO

That "present woman" Anthony Scaduto refers to was Suze Rotolo. Her name at birth was Susan and her friends often called her "sooze." In the early 1960s she changed the spelling to "Suze" after seeing a reproduction of Picasso's collage *Glass and Bottle of Suze*. (Suze is the name of a liqueur.)[30] She saw Dylan perform at Gerde's Folk City in Greenwich Village and later they met at a folk concert at the Riverside Church in upper Manhattan at the end of July, 1961.[31] Suze was 17 years old. "I felt a strong attraction to this character," she writes in her autobiography. "It was as if we knew each other already; we just needed time to get better acquainted. And so we did

---

27. Robert Shelton, *No Direction Home*, 116.
28. Ibid.
29. Anthony Scaduto, *Bob Dylan*, 258, 129.
30. Suze Rotolo, *A Freewheelin' Time: A Memoir of Greenwich Village in the Sixties* (New York: Broadway Books, 2008), 105.
31. Ibid., 90.

over the next four years."[32] Dylan had his own apartment and Suze moved in with him after her eighteenth birthday in November, 1961.

Suze Rotolo, everyone seems to agree, was a beautiful, intelligent, talented, and socially conscious young woman. She is the girl on Dylan's arm in the cover photo of his album *The Freewheelin Bob Dylan*, released in 1963. "Suze," Anthony Scaduto says, "was fair with long-flowing hair the color of wheat." She was described, he says, as "kind of like a Botticelli woman by one who knew her at that time."[33] In *Chronicles* Dylan says that "she had a smile that could light up a street full of people and was extremely lively, had a particular type of voluptuousness—a Rodin sculpture come to life. She reminded me of a libertine heroine. She was just my type."[34] She was beautiful and she was smart. According to Scaduto, she "struck almost everyone she met as a highly intelligent woman, one of the brightest young women in the Village folk crowd."[35]

Suze no doubt got her social consciousness from her parents, who were both members of the American Communist Party. Her mother was an editor and columnist for *L'Unità*, a communist paper. Her father aspired to be a painter but couldn't support his family on an artist's salary, so he worked in factories and became a union organizer. They lived in Queens. Suze's father died when she was fourteen.[36] Suze met Dylan in the summer of 1961, when civil rights activists from the North headed south on buses on "Freedom Rides" to end segregation in Southern states. Suze was working that summer in the New York City office of the Congress of Racial Equality (CORE), which was organizing Freedom Rides. Fieldworkers in the South would send reports of sit-ins and beatings to the CORE office, which passed on the information to news outlets in New York.[37] In the early 1960s, Dylan wrote three songs that describe the murder of an African American by whites in the South: "Only a Pawn Their Game," "The Lonesome Death of Hattie Carroll," and "The Death of Emmett Till." Dylan's famous "Blowin' in the Wind," a more general protest song which urges people to notice and do something about suffering in the world, was released in 1962. Dylan also went to Greenwood, Mississippi in July,

---

32. Ibid., 92.
33. Anthony Scaduto, *Bob Dylan*, 90.
34. Bob Dylan, *Chronicles: Volume One* (New York: Simon and Schuster, 2004), 265.
35. Anthony Scaduto, *Bob Dylan*, 90.
36. Suze Rotolo talks about her family background in "Queens," the third chapter of *A Freewheelin' Time: A Memoir of Greenwich Village in the Sixties*. See especially pages 26, 29-31, 33.
37. Ibid., 87-90.

1963, to participate in a voter registration rally organized by the Student Non-Violent Coordinating Committee. He sang "Only a Pawn in the Game," his song about the death of Medgar Evers, a civil rights activist who had been killed by a member of the Ku Klux Klan a few weeks before the rally.[38] In her autobiography, Suze praises Dylan's civil rights songs, saying they were "not just newspaper stories rewritten in rhyme"; they were timeless songs about the human condition.[39] It seems clear that Suze was attracted to Dylan in part because she felt he shared her passion for social justice.

She was also passionate about art—literature, theater, and painting. In *Chronicles* Dylan said Suze was the one who got him interested in the poems of the French Symbolist Arthur Rimbaud.[40] Suze worked behind the scenes on a musical production of songs by Bertolt Brecht and Kurt Weill. Dylan saw the production and found it fascinating. He was, he said, "totally influenced" by the song "Pirate Jenny" which is about a maid whose town is taken over by men who arrive on a black freighter. When they ask her whether to kill some townspeople now or later she shouts "Right now!" In *Chronicles* Dylan says that if he had not heard "Pirate Jenny" it "might not have dawned on me" to write songs like "It's Al-right Ma (I'm Only Bleeding)," "Mr. Tambourine Man," "Lonesome Death of Hattie Carroll," "Who Killed Davey Moore," "Only a Pawn in Their Game" and "A Hard Rain's A-Gonna Fall."[41] This comment reveals Suze's influence—how she expanded Dylan's horizons; it also suggests how mysterious the creative process is.

Like her father, Suze liked to draw and Dylan said he picked up the drawing habit from her.[42] Before he became famous, some of Dylan's songs appeared in a magazine called *Broadside*. To accompany Dylan's "Masters of War," which appeared in *Broadside* #20, Suze drew a man carving up the earth while a family looks on. She also included a baby carriage on tank tracks with a rifle on the side.

Suze and Dylan went to art museums where, Dylan says, he admired works by famous artists—Velazques, Goya, Delacroix, Picasso, Braque and others. Suze's favorite artist was Red Grooms, an American artist best known for his pop-art paintings of modern urban life. He became Dylan's

---

38. See Robert Shelton, *No Direction Home*, 129, 130.
39. Suze Rotolo, *A Freewheelin' Time*, 90.
40. Bob Dylan, *Chronicles*, 288.
41. Ibid., 287.
42. Ibid., 270.

favorite too. "There was a connection in Red's work to a lot of the folk songs I sang," Dylan says. "What the folk songs were lyrically, Red's songs were visually."[43]

Suze Rotolo's cover for the February 1963 issue of Broadside.

Suze and Dylan broke up for a variety of reasons. In June of 1962, Suze's mother invited Suze to join her and her husband on a trip to Europe. Suze suspected her invitation was a scheme to get her away from Dylan, whom, Suze says, her mother did not approve of. He paid her no homage, Suze says, and she paid him none.[44] Dylan went to the dock to see her off. "When the ship was ready to sail and it was time for visitors to disembark," Suze writes, "we were still joking as we said good-bye. But

43. Ibid., 269.
44. Suze Rotolo, *A Freewheelin' Time*, 169; See also 176.

wisps of sadness and foreboding enveloped me as I watched him walk to the stairs, then turn and smile and wave."[45] Suze spent eight months in Europe, traveling and studying Italian in Perugia. When she returned to New York in mid-January 1963, Dylan was rapidly becoming famous and everyone was begging for his attention. Suze says that Dylan was becoming paranoid, and that she adopted his paranoia as people would befriend her to try to get to Dylan. "People crowded around," she writes, "wanting to be my new best friend or claiming to be my oldest best friend, and couldn't we all go hang out with Dylan?"[46]

Another factor in the breakup was Dylan's affair with Joan Baez, which I discuss in my next section. Rotolo heard about the affair from friends. "At first it was just gossip—then, of course, it wasn't," she explains.[47] Dylan apparently fully expected to keep both affairs going at the same time, confirming Howard Sounes' judgment that Dylan "became an inveterate womanizer in young adulthood and would remain so throughout most of his life."[48] Suze, who loved him, calls him "a lying shit of a guy with women, an adept juggler really."[49] By late 1963 Suze says she and Dylan "had ostensibly broken up" and they were no longer living together, but still saw each other when Dylan was in New York.[50] "Breaking up takes time," she explains.[51] In March, 1964, she became pregnant and she and Dylan had to make a difficult decision. They decided on an abortion, which, in the 1960s, was illegal. Finding a trustworthy doctor willing to perform a secret abortion, Suze says, was difficult but they found one.[52]

Another event in March of 1964 that strained Suze's relationship with Dylan was a bitter argument between Dylan and Suze's sister, Carla. Suze was no longer living in Dylan's apartment and had moved in with her sister, who was living in a cramped flat on Avenue B in the Lower East Side. In Howard Sounes' account, Carla came home from work and found Suze and Bob arguing, and then she and Bob got into a terrible shouting match. Carla told Dylan to leave, he refused, there was some pushing and shoving, and finally, Sounes says, "friends were called and finally Bob was

45. Ibid., 170.
46. Ibid., 275-276.
47. Ibid., 232.
48. Howard Sounes, *Down the Highway: The Life of Bob Dylan* (New York: Grove Press, 2001), 128.
49. Suze Rotolo, *A Freewheelin' Time*, 286.
50. Ibid., 288.
51. Ibid., 282.
52. Ibid., 280-281.

forcibly removed."[53] According to Scaduto, this event marked the end of Bob and Suze's relationship. After a couple of months she would see him and his friends when he came to New York, but she refused to go back to him.[54]

Suze places some blame on her sister. "The way I saw it," she says, "Bobby and Carla had some kind of rivalry for controlling interest in me." She knew, she says, that her sister "needed to be in charge—be the authority." But she also did not like the way Dylan treated her. "Bob wanted me to stay where I was," she says, "to be there when he got back from wherever he went without me, and to be with whomever he pleased while he was there. He'd plead with me to marry him, which made no sense to me the way things were; nor did I believe he was sincere."[55]

Bob describes the argument with Carla in "Ballad in Plain D," a song that Dylan has said he regrets recording.[56] In this song he says that he loved the younger of the two sisters, "the creative one," but "For her sister, I had no respect / Bound by her boredom, her pride to protect." In another stanza Dylan describes a shouting match between him and Carla: "Beneath a bare lightbulb the plaster did pound / Her sister and I in a screaming battleground." "That song just went too far," Suze Rotolo told the journalist Robert Shelton in 1968. "There's some things you just can't do no matter how much power you have."[57]

"Ballad in Plain B" reveals a great deal about Dylan's character—his inability to control his anger, his tendency to say cruel things and hurt people close to him. But in this song he reveals some remorse for his actions (though, he says, he's not yet ready to say he's sorry); and he makes it clear that he loved Suze. If he lied to her, he says, it was so he wouldn't lose "the could-be dream-lover of my lifetime."

Suze makes it clear that another reason her relationship with Dylan did not work was her determination not to be just a "musician's chick," a "string on his guitar."[58] The word "chick," she says, made her feel that she wasn't a whole person, that she was just one of Bob's possessions. This was, she explains, before the feminist movement began, before women had a

---

53. Howard Sounes, *Down the Highway*, 153.
54. Anthony Scaduto, *Bob Dylan*, 279, 174-175.
55. Suze Rotolo, *A Freewheelin' Time*, 278-279.
56. Howard Sounes, *Down the Highway*, 154; Liner notes for Dylan's compilation album *Biograph* (1985).
57. Robert Shelton, *No Direction Home*, 159.
58. Suze Rotolo, *A Freewheelin' Time*, 183.

"feminist vocabulary" to help them understand the predicament they were in. At that time a musician's girlfriend was a chick and if they married she became his "old lady." "I was very young, I was still forming myself," she says, "but I did know I wasn't a musician, nor was I a musician's 'chick.' And you could bet the neck of a Gibson I had no desire to graduate to 'old lady.'"[59]

Dylan's final word on what he refers to as his "alliance" with Suze is rather cold. He accepts no blame for their breakup. This alliance, he says, "didn't turn out exactly to be a holiday in the woods. Eventually fate flagged it down and it came to a full stop. It had to end. She took one turn in the road and I took another. We just passed out of each others' lives."[60]

JOAN BAEZ

Dylan and Baez first met in Greenwich Village in April 1961 at a folk music establishment called Gerde's Folk City where Dylan was performing.[61] She later told Anthony Scaduto, "He knocked me out completely. He seemed tiny, just tiny, with that goofy little hat on. And he was just astounding."[62] Apparently their love affair began in mid-May of 1963 when Baez and Dylan appeared together at the Monterey Folk Festival. Baez was at the height of her fame at the time and was the headliner, but Dylan was on the verge of stardom. His second album, *The Freewheelin' Bob Dylan*, was to be released on May 27. On it were what are now some of Dylan's best-known songs—works like "Blowin' in the Wind," "A Hard Rain's A-Gonna Fall," and "Don't Think Twice, It's All Right." After the concert they drove together down the coast to Baez's home in Carmel, and Bob stayed there with her for several weeks. Then he returned to Suze Rotolo in New York.[63] He also stayed with Baez in Carmel in the fall of 1963.[64]

In July, 1963, Dylan and Baez appeared together at the Newport Folk Festival. This festival, at which older singers like Pete Seeger performed with younger singers like Baez and Dylan, is now considered the highpoint of the folk music revival. Baez was eager to promote Dylan at this event. They appeared together at the opening and sang Dylan's "With God on Our Side" to close it. At this festival, reporters concluded, "Baez,

---

59. Ibid., 254-255; See also page 287.
60. Bob Dylan, *Chronicles*, 276-277.
61. Joan Baez, *And a Voice to Sing With: A Memoir* (New York: Summit Books, 1987), 83.
62. Anthony Scaduto, *Bob Dylan*, 76.
63. Ibid., 145-146.
64. Robert Shelton, *No Direction Home*, 134.

the reigning queen of folk music, had named Dylan the crown prince."[65] Professionally, Dylan benefitted more than Baez from their relationship, because he was still a relative unknown whereas Baez was already a star. Baez, who recognized his talent, helped people appreciate his genius. Dylan has acknowledged his debt to her, though somewhat grudgingly. "She [Baez] brought me up . . . I rode on [depended on] her, but I don't owe her anything," he told Robert Shelton in a March 1966 interview.[66]

Dylan and Baez sang "We Shall Overcome" together at the March on Washington on August 28, 1963, the event at which Martin Luther King, Jr. gave his famous "I Have a Dream" speech. An estimated crowd of 250,000 people were listening. Dylan and Baez were popular individually and were even more pleasing when they performed together. Many fans were inspired by their combination of talent, romance and social commitment.

David Hajdu says that the on-stage chemistry between Dylan and Baez was "unconventional," somewhat lacking in "sexual magnetism," and suggests that this was because as individual performers each of them projected an image that was "de-sexualized and androgynous." Dylan's public image was of a "boy poet," not of a virile male like, say, Elvis Presley.[67] Baez herself and other women have commented that they felt the urge to "mother" Dylan, perhaps because he was short and had a boyish mop of curly hair. Joan Baez told an interviewer that Dylan brought out the "mother instinct" in women.[68] Suze Rotolo mentions Dylan's "impish charm that older women found endearing."[69] Baez was the same age as Dylan but she couldn't resist the urge to mother him. "It was a funny thing," she told Anthony Scaduto. "I wanted to take care of him and have him sing . . . I mean, brush his hair and brush his teeth and get him on stage . . . I wanted to have as many people hear him as possible."[70] Robert Shelton suggests that Baez's mothering of Dylan was probably a "major mistake," but one can understand why Baez acted in a motherly way toward Dylan. She was already famous. She had a three-year head start on Dylan. In the beginning, Shelton says, Dylan "seemed to

65. Robert Shelton, *No Direction Home*, 132.
66. Bob Dylan, "Interview with Robert Shelton, from *No Direction Home*: March 1966," in *Bob Dylan: The Essential Interviews*, ed. Jonathan Cott (New York: Wenner Books, 2006), 88.
67. David Hajdu, *Positively 4th Street*, 171-172.
68. Joan Baez, interview for *No Direction Home*, a documentary film about Dylan directed by Martin Scorsese that first aired on PBS in 2005.
69. Suze Rotolo, *A Freewheelin' Time*, 10.
70. Anthony Scaduto, *Bob Dylan*, 146. See also, 210.

encourage her looking after him," but "eventually resented it." Dylan, he says, "didn't want to be treated like a kid anymore."[71]

Reporters called Baez the "queen," not the princess, of folk music and Dylan was the "prince," not the king. Expected gender roles were reversed when Baez took Dylan under her wing and introduced him to her fans at concerts. Baez was beautiful but also virgin-like—David Hajdu refers to her as a "virgin enchantress"[72]—and most of the songs she sang were deadly serious. Dylan himself says Baez "looked like a religious icon, like somebody you'd sacrifice yourself for and she sang in a voice straight to God."[73] Trịnh Công Sơn was also impressed by Baez—by "the sad sound of her voice and guitar playing." In a letter to Ngô Vũ Dao Ánh written in 1965 he mentions listening with his friends to recordings of her singing some songs, including Dylan's "With God on Our Side." Her singing voice, he wrote, "was like quiet weeping that called out to you."[74] I heard her sing in 1961or 1962 when she and Pete Seeger gave a joint concert in Woolsey Hall at Yale University. She came on stage, walking barefoot and carrying a guitar that seemed almost as big as she was. She was dressed in a simple white dress, no makeup, no jewelry, long black hair hanging down her shoulders. When she began to sing, her beautifully pure, crystal-clear voice filled the auditorium.

Joan Baez was no virgin when she met Dylan, and she and Dylan were lovers and lived together in California in 1963. All this is made clear in her autobiography. Most of their fans didn't know and didn't care exactly what their relationship was, though many were curious about it, just as Vietnamese fans were curious about the Trịnh Công Sơn-Khánh Ly relationship.

Dylan and Baez's romance didn't last in part, it seems, because Dylan lost interest in trying to make the world better; or perhaps because he thought one made it better through art, not political action. Or perhaps the relationship didn't last because Dylan was still in love with his girlfriend Suze Rotolo, and regarded his relationship with Baez as just a temporary fling.

Dylan wouldn't let Baez lead him into politics, not primarily because he felt his manhood threatened—though that might have had something

---

71. Robert Shelton, *No Direction Home*, 133-134.
72. David Hajdu, *Positively 4*th *Street*, 172.
73. Bob Dylan, *Chronicles*, 255.
74. Trịnh Công Sơn, *Trịnh Công Sơn: Thư tình gửi một người*, 229.

to do with it—but because, as he explains over and over again in his autobiography, he did not want to be a spokesman for any cause. The press,
he writes, "kept promoting me as the mouthpiece, spokesman, or even
conscience of a generation. That was funny. All I'd ever done was sing
songs that were dead straight and expressed powerful new realities."[75] Baez
had to persuade Dylan to appear with her at the March on Washington in
1963.[76] He never joined Baez at anti-Vietnam War protests though she
often begged him to do so. In 1972 she wrote "To Bobby," a song urging
him to join her and others in the anti-war struggle. "Like these flowers
at your door and scribbled notes about the war," she sings in "To Bobby,"
"We're only saying the time is short and there is work to do."

Baez clearly had political, as well as artistic, motives. She fiercely
opposed the war in Vietnam and throughout her life has supported a host
of other causes and organizations working to end war and promote social
justice. In the 1960s she founded the Institute for the Study of Nonviolence
in Carmel and resisted the war by refusing to pay a percentage of her
income taxes and by demonstrating at an induction center in Oakland to
support draftees who refused to be inducted. Given her enthusiasm for
social action and Dylan's reluctance to be a spokesperson for causes, it was
probably inevitable that she and Dylan would go their separate ways. In
early 1965, Dylan and Baez gave a series of concerts at universities in the
eastern US. A member of the tour told Anthony Scaduto that the tour didn't
go well, that there was "serious conflict" and "real blowups and everybody
was walking gingerly."[77] Dylan was growing tired of the folk scene and
was making a transition from folk songs to songs some people called
folk rock and others rock 'n' roll. Instead of playing an acoustic guitar,
which was favored by folk singers, he started using an electric guitar and
hired a band to back him. Baez wasn't enthusiastic about this new musical
direction he was heading in. She was also frustrated by Dylan's refusal to
join her in opposing the war. She was afraid, as she puts it in her autobiography, that he was going to be the "Rock and Roll King," leaving her to be
the "Peace Queen."[78] In 1965, very deep differences between them were
coming to the surface. Dylan, in answer to a question by Baez, mentions
the biggest one: "I asked him," Baez writes, "what made us different, and

---

75. Bob Dylan, *Chronicles*, 115.
76. Baez talks about her failure to get Dylan to join her at anti-war events in the documen-
    tary film *No Direction Home*. See also David Hajdu, *Positively 4th Street*, 182.
77. Anthony Scaduto, *Bob Dylan*, 189.
78. Joan Baez, *And a Voice to Sing With*, 95.

he said it was simple, that I thought I could change things, and he knew that no one could."[79]

One must also remember, however, that when Dylan was touring with Baez and staying with her in Carmel he was also still involved with Suze Rotolo. In 1964 Dylan was also seeing Sara Lownds, a fashion model who also worked at the Playboy Club in New York City. Lownds was a friend of the wife of Albert Grossman, Dylan's manager. Her father was a Jewish immigrant from Belarus. Her maiden name was Shirley Marlin Noznisky. She changed her first name to Sara after marrying a photographer named Hans Lownds who was twenty-five years her senior. Sara and Hans had a daughter, Maria, whom Bob and Sara raised after Hans, who did not want Maria to be raised by Dylan, abandoned his plan to achieve sole custody.[80]

"There is some question among those who were close to Bob and Joan," Anthony Scaduto says, "as to which came first, Bob's break with Joan or his meeting Sara Lownds."[81] Baez did not become aware of Dylan's relationship with Lownds until she accompanied him on a concert tour in England in May of 1965. Baez hoped that Dylan would invite her to perform with him in England, where he had many fans. She had invited him to perform with her in America where she was more popular and she thought he would return the favor. Dylan, however, ignored her.[82] Toward the end of the tour, Lownds flew to London to be with Dylan. Not aware of her arrival, Baez came to his hotel room in London to give him a gift, a blue Viyella shirt. When she knocked, it was Lownds who opened the door.[83]

It is possible that Dylan never loved Baez and that his relationship with her was motivated by financial gain. Her inviting him to sing with her early in his career certainly helped propel him into stardom. The queen of folk music performing with the new crown prince was an act fans could not resist. In 1964 and 1965, however, he did not seem to be as emotionally involved with her as he was with Suze Rotolo. He did not seem to mind being away from her for long periods of time. As we will see in Chapter Six both women are thought to have inspired Dylan to write non-love or anti-love songs but, critics suggest, Suze inspired true love

---

79. Ibid.
80. Howard Sounes, *Down the Highway*, 162-165.
81. Anthony Scaduto, *Bob Dylan*, 190.
82. Joan Baez, *And a Voice to Sing With*, 96; Howard Sounes, *Down the Highway*, 170-171.
83. Joan Baez, *And a Voice to Sing With*, 98.

songs as well. No one suggests, however, that the songs Baez is supposed to have inspired fit into this category.

Dylan is "terribly bright," Baez told Robert Shelton, "with a funny magnet inside him that makes you drawn to him. I mean I love Bobby, and I would do anything for him, ever. Whatever went wrong between us, I really don't know."[84] "I still wonder what Bobby thinks about me," she told Anthony Scaduto in 1996. "You're bound to do that with somebody you loved once and who, it seems, turned on you."[85] In 1974 Baez wrote "Diamonds and Rust," a song clearly about Dylan whom she addresses directly in the second person. In her song she calls Dylan the "unwashed phenomenon, the original vagabond" who "strayed into my arms." She mentions that Dylan was "good with words and at keeping things vague" and says she needs "some of that vagueness now" because

> *It all comes back too clearly*
> *Yes I loved you dearly*
> *And if you're offering me diamonds and rust*
> *I've already paid*

Forty-one years later, in a speech Dylan gave when he accepted an award from MusiCares, a charity associated with the Grammys, Dylan offered Baez something more: gratitude and love for her help early in his career. "She took a liking to my songs," Dylan told the audience at the Los Angeles Convention Center, "and brought me with her to play concerts where she had crowds of thousands of people enthralled with her beauty and voice. People would say, 'What are you doing with that ragtag scrubby little waif?' And she'd tell everybody in no uncertain terms, 'Now you better be quiet and listen to the songs.' And for her kind of love and devotion, I could never pay that back."[86]

---

84. Robert Shelton, *No Direction Home*, 134.
85. Anthony Scaduto, *Bob Dylan*, 203.
86. I quote from a transcript of the event prepared by Randall L. Roberts. "Grammys 2015: Transcript of Bob Dylan's MusiCares Person of Year Speech," Pop & Hiss, Feb. 7, 2015, http://www.latimes.com/entertainment/music/posts/la-et-ms-grammys-2015-transcript-of-bob-dylans-musicares-person-of-year-speech-20150207-story.html (accessed Sept. 9, 2018). See also Ben Sisario, "At Grammys Event, Bob Dylan Speech Steals the Show," *New York Times*, Feb. 7, 2015.

6

LOVE SONGS &
ANTI-LOVE SONGS

Both Trịnh Công Sơn and Bob Dylan have written love songs, but some of Dylan's most famous songs are what music critics and biographers call "non-love songs" or "anti-love songs" or "insult songs."[1] Robert Shelton says that Dylan may have invented the "anti-love song"— an unsentimental song in which male narrators "hit back at women who hurt, disappointed, or confused" them.[2] In these songs Dylan complains about annoying and possessive lovers—lovers that he seems more than willing to abandon. The terms "love song" and "anti-love song" are, I realize, problematic because love has many moods; a song in which the speaker is angry at and critical of a lover can still be considered a love song. Dylan's biographers and musicologists, however, use these terms, and they have their uses: They are one way of classifying Dylan's songs addressing women. At the end of this chapter I will describe another way, one suggested by Kevin Krein and Abigail Levin.[3]

---

1. Betsy Bowden calls them "non-love songs." See *Performed Literature: Words and Music by Bob Dylan* (Bloomington, IN: Indiana University Press, 1982). Michael J. Gilmour calls them "anti-love songs." See *Tangled Up in the Bible* (New York: Continuum, 2004), 29. Alan Jacobs calls them "insult songs." See Alan Jacobs, "It Ain't Me Babe," in *A Visit to Vanity Fair: Moral Essays on the Present Age* (Grand Rapids, MI: Brazos Press, 2001), 103.
2. Robert Shelton, *No Direction Home: The Life and Music of Bob Dylan* (Milwaukee, WI: Backbeat Books, 2011), 192.
3. Kevin Krein and Abigail Levin, "Dylan, Authenticity, and the Second Sex," in *Bob Dylan and Philosophy*, eds. Peter Vernezze and Carl J. Porter (Chicago, IL: Open Court, 2006), 53-65.

TRỊNH CÔNG SƠN'S LOVE SONGS

Trịnh Công Sơn lived in Huế, a very traditional town in many ways, where parents protected their daughters and had a great deal to say about whom they married. As a result men and women often could not marry the person they wanted to marry and so many people experienced what Vietnamese call *"tình yêu dang dở"*—unfinished or unfulfilled love, love that was not sexually consummated and did not lead to marriage. There are many sad songs of unfulfilled love in the history of Vietnamese songwriting but Trịnh Công Sơn's love songs are, in some people's judgment at least, sadder than the love songs popular when he began composing. These so-called "pre-war songs" [*tình khúc tiền chiến*], which I will discuss in Chapter Eighteen, are definitely sad songs but, as Khánh Ly, the singer who became famous singing Trịnh Công Sơn's songs, points out, "They didn't have a shadow of despair, they didn't have a pain that pushed one toward death. Pre-war songs were sweet and soothing. There were goodbyes but they were soft goodbyes."[4] Pre-war songs are sentimental. They are sad but their "soft goodbyes" remind listeners how sweet it is to feel so sad. Trịnh Công Sơn's love songs are full of goodbyes and some of them are soft, but many are hard. The tone is typically forgiving but very sad. That "shadow of despair," that Khánh Ly says was absent from pre-war songs hovers over many of Trịnh Công Sơn's love songs. Typically one hears whisperings of mortality, of life's impermanence, as we do in "How Many More Days" [Còn có bao ngày]:

> At night I lie and darkness looms
> At night I lie and hear life passing
> Whispering, whispering
>
> People who love each other
> Have lost each other in life
> One dark day
> Closes a thousand mornings.

Some of Trịnh Công Sơn's love songs have cheerful elements—a sprightly tune, for example, or some lines expressing the singer's enthusiasm for some attribute of his beloved. But even in these songs sadness enters before the song concludes. A beautiful and very popular love song called "Like a Flying Heron" [Như cánh vạc bay]* begins:

---

4.   Khánh Ly, *Đằng Sau Những Nụ Cười* [Behind the Smiles] (HCMC: Văn Học, 2015), 17.

Is sunshine as rosy as your lips?
Is rain as sad as your eyes?
Each small strand of your hair
Falls on life and makes a drifting wave
The wind's happy because your hair flies
The cloud sulks and sleeps on your shoulder
A shoulder slender and small
Like a heron returning to a place far away

Later in the song, however, it becomes clear that the two lovers are far apart and the song ends with the sound of a "thousand tears":

Is it happy where you are?
Is the sky blue where you are?
I hear a thousand tears
Falling to make a shining lake

Another song, "The Fragrance of the Quỳnh Flower" [Quỳnh hương] has a quick and cheerful tune and the lyrics at the start are upbeat.

I bring for you a Quỳnh flower
Is it the Quynh flower that's fragrant or your lips?

By the second stanza, however, the mood has already changed:

Tonight, this night
There's sadness with the kisses
In the moon garden
The fragile flowers close

Vietnamese listeners are not surprised by this change in mood. The Quỳnh flower, or night-blooming cereus, is a delicate flower with very smooth, silk-like petals. It blooms only once around midnight and then the flower withers quickly. For Vietnamese it suggests beauty but also impermanence. In this song the lips that kiss are associated with the petals of the night-blooming cereus: both close quickly, both are fleeting events.

In his love songs Trịnh Công Sơn typically mourns the end of love relationships, but accepts the fact that love, like life itself, does not last forever. The speaker in his love songs is typically sad and regretful but not angry or accusatory. There are exceptions. "A Lullaby for You" [Ru em]*, a song understood to be about Ngô Vũ Dao Ánh, contains the lines "A lullaby for you for nights in the past / A lullaby for you for betraying me"; and "Do You Remember Now?" [Này em có nhớ] begins with these lines:

> *Christ has abandoned humankind*
> *The Buddha has abandoned humankind*
> *So go ahead and betray others*
> *And go ahead and betray me*

This song, gloomy from start to finish, is atypical. Trịnh Công Sơn rarely speaks harshly of lovers in his love songs. In "A Lullaby for You" [Ru em],* after accusing his lover of betrayal, Sơn seems to regret his harshness. In the next stanza come these lines:

> *A lullaby for you for sweetness in the past*
> *A lullaby for you for unfortunate lives*
> *Loving you I love betrayal more*
> *Loving you suddenly loving-kindness and compassion fill my heart*

Typically in a Trịnh Công Sơn love song the speaker and the woman he loves are no longer together. Instead they are separated in one or more of the following ways: by time (the love occurred in the past), by space (the lover is now far away), or by emotion (a former lover no longer loves him). We see these separations in the songs just discussed. In "How Many More Days" the lovers have "lost each other in life"; in "Like a Flying Heron" the speaker asks if his love is happy where she is; in "Lullaby for You" he gifts his lover a lullaby though they "are far apart." Sometimes all three separations—time, space, and emotion—are mentioned in a song. Frequently, however, these time and space separations are suddenly collapsed as the speaker remembers a lover. This collapsing occurs in "Remembered Love" [Tình Nhớ]:

> *A love I thought I'd forgotten*
> *That my cold heart tried to ignore*
> *A person I thought faraway*
> *Suddenly has returned*

And in "Like Words of Goodbye" [Như một lời chia tay]*:

> *A rose from the past remains*
> *Next to my life here*
> *A little love passes like a hurried breeze*
> *I suddenly recognize myself*

I believe that Trịnh Công Sơn's love songs reveal a tug-of-war that was going on in his heart and mind. He resented lovers like those that he sings about in "Distant Love" [Tình xa], lovers that "have abandoned him like little rivers," but being a Buddhist he knew that resentment was to be avoided and loving-kindness and compassion were the virtues to cultivate. And he knew life had other joys, lesser joys than romantic love, perhaps, but still joyful: good friends and warm whiskey, pleasures that he mentions in several songs that I will discuss in the next chapter. It would be a mistake to paint Trịnh Công Sơn as someone constantly overcome by sorrow. He was, however, unfortunate in love, and for most of his adult life his country was at war and his people of golden skin were killing each other with help from foreign powers. In some songs it is difficult to separate romantic love from the singer's love of friends and his country. One can't be sure whether the speaker is suffering from unrequited love or missing people who have died, or moved away, or were killed in the war. Consider, for example "Let the Wind Blow It Away" [Để gió cuốn đi]*, a song written in 1971. The song begins:

> *To live in this life*
> *One needs a good heart*
> *To do what with do you* [em] *know*
> *To let the wind blow it away*
> *To let the wind blow it away*

Who is he referring to in the third line? The Vietnamese pronoun that Trịnh Công Sơn uses is "*em*." I have translated it as "you," but the pronoun "*em*" in Vietnamese can refer to a lover or wife, or to a younger sibling of either sex, or to oneself when talking to someone older. In the next-to-last line of the last stanza Sơn uses a different pronoun, "*ta*":

> *Love the day that's coming*
> *Though tired of life*
> *As long as there's life* [ta] *be happy*
> *Though someone is gone*
> *Though someone is gone*

"*Ta*" can be used to refer to oneself when one is talking to oneself, but it also can be used as an inclusive pronoun to refer to both speaker and audience. In this translation it is not clear whether he is talking only to himself or to himself and someone else, so I have not attempted to translate "*ta*." Vietnamese I have talked to about this song understand Sơn to be talking both to himself and to his audience, to his fellow Vietnamese.

Another song, "Each Day I Choose a Little Happiness" [Mỗi ngày tôi chọn một niềm vui]*, is similar to "Let the Wind Blow It Away" in some respects: Both songs are about how to be happy. In "Let the Wind Blow It Away," however, Sơn tells others what to do to be happy whereas in "Each Day" he explains what he himself does to be happy. Sơn wrote "Each Day" in 1977, a time when he was still adjusting to the new communist regime and had to work especially hard to be happy. It was the first song that the communist regime allowed Sơn to sing on television after it reclaimed Saigon and renamed it Hồ Chí Minh City.

Here is the first stanza:

> *Each day I* [tôi] *choose happiness*
> *Choose flowers and smiles*
> *I* [tôi] *pick wind from sky and invite you to take it*
> *So your eyes will smile like flying leaves*

The first-person pronoun Sơn uses is "*tôi*," a pronoun that refers to the speaker. It is the first-person pronoun that one uses to refer to oneself when addressing non-relatives. Thích Nhất Hạnh suggests that in this song Sơn is revealing the influence of his Buddhist faith, so I will return to it in Chapter Twenty-Five.

In some love songs Trịnh Công Sơn expresses appreciation for women he has loved even though they abandoned him. In "Thanks" [Tạ ơn] he mentions a lover leaving like "a wisp of gentle wind" but his song is a tribute to all the people who have enriched his life. Here are the final lines:

> *Though you came, then left, I still thank people*
> *Thank life, thank whoever gave me*
> *Love bright like a star that's fallen from the sky*

The singer is also full of thanks in "Thank Life a Little" [Cho Đời chút ơn]. In this song he mentions seeing a girl walking home and describes the happiness this sight brings him. Here is the last stanza:

> *Keep walking so the dawn will come quickly*
> *Thank life a little for the flap of that dress*
> *You are the perfume that makes the forest fragrant*
> *The song words for the world*
> *Down in the town a person thinks of you*
> *Dreaming the whole night in paradise*

Ban Mai, in her collection of songs by Trịnh Công Sơn, includes a footnote for "Thank Life a Little" in which she paraphrases comments that Sơn made about this song in an interview that she found on the web.[5] In

---

5. I have not been able to find this interview online.

this interview, she says, Sơn said that in this song "he was expressing his gratitude for all the young women who had enriched his life. In the line 'Thank life a little for the flap of that dress' he was praising love. Sadness is inevitably a part of love because a day will come when we will lose everything, so as long as we exist we have love and praise love."[6]

Trịnh Công Sơn, however, was not always forgiving when women he loved abandoned him, at least not right away. In "A Lullaby for You," he first accuses a lover, presumed to be Ngô Vũ Dao Ánh, of betrayal before "loving-kindness and compassion" fill his heart. Clearly it was hard for him to forgive Dao Ánh. In 1993, the same year he wrote "Thank Life a Little," he wrote "Repaying a Debt" [Xin trả nợ người] in which finally, twenty years after she "left and forgot" him, he forgives her. I discuss this song and events that inspired it in Chapter Seven.

DYLAN'S LOVE SONGS AND ANTI-LOVE SONGS

Dylan, unlike Trịnh Công Sơn, does speak harshly about lovers. Frequently the speaker in his anti-love songs is angry, mean-spirited, and defiant. In some anti-love songs the speaker criticizes character flaws in the woman he addresses. This anger and criticism are surprising because the more one learns about how Dylan treated women the more one thinks it is women, not Dylan, who should be angry and critical. People like Suze Rotolo who knew that Dylan could be "a lying shit of a guy with women, an adept juggler," probably were not as surprised by the meanness of Dylan's anti-love songs as others who did not know him personally.[7] Another surprising thing about Dylan's anti-love songs, however, is that they are more famous than his true love songs. Anti-love songs "Don't Think Twice, It's All Right," "It Ain't Me Babe," and "Like a Rolling Stone" are extremely well-known but kinder love songs like "Tomorrow Is a Long Time," "Tonight I'll Be Staying Here With You," "Baby, I'm in the Mood for You," and "I Threw It All Away" are not nearly as famous. It could be that Dylan's anti-love songs are better known because they are technically superior—more pleasing musically—than his kinder love songs, but I think their appeal also has a lot to do with the fact that in predominantly Judeo-Christian countries, self-righteous anger, particularly when it is exhibited by men, is a tolerated—even a respected—virtue. In Buddhist

---

6. Ban Mai, *Trịnh Công Sơn: Vết chân dã tràng* [Trịnh Công Sơn: The Footprint of the Sand Crab] (Hanoi: Lao Động, 2008), 222.
7. Suze Rotolo, *A Freewheelin' Time: A Memoir of Greenwich Village in the Sixties* (New York: Broadway Books, 2008), 286.

countries where anger is a "poison"[8] and compassion and loving-kindness are the supreme virtues, getting angry, particularly men getting angry at women, is not considered admirable behavior. I develop this point further in later chapters.

Before looking at Dylan's anti-love songs let us look more closely at some of his true love songs. "Tomorrow Is a Long Time," is what I would call a true love song. Howard Sounes says that it and "Don't Think Twice, It's All Right," which is clearly an anti-love song, were composed "in the wake of Suze's departure for Europe"[9] so it seems that the same circumstance (lover leaving for a long trip) can inspire two very different songs. "Tomorrow Is a Long Time" is a beautiful song with lines like these:

> *There's beauty in the silver, singin' river*
> *There's beauty in the sunrise in the sky*
> *But none of these and nothing else can touch the beauty*
> *That I remember in my true love's eyes*

Each of the three stanzas end with the lines "Only if she was lyin' by me / Then I'd lie in my bed once again." In discussing Dylan's familiarity with major English poets, Michael Gray mentions this song and suggests before Dylan wrote it he "seems to have come across" the following—often anthologized—fifteenth century four-line anonymous poem that has been given the title "Western Wind":[10]

> *Western wind, when wilt thou blow*
> *The small rain down can rain?*
> *Christ, if my love were in my arms*
> *And I in my bed again.*

Christopher Ricks agrees. This song, he says, "is a tribute to a loved one and to 'O Western Wind.'"[11]

Bob Dylan grew up in the United States, where in the 1960s young women were less protected by their parents and more promiscuous than women in Vietnam; and in the 1960s, Greenwich Village, where Dylan met Suze Rotolo, was perhaps the most freewheelin' community in the

---

8. In Buddhism Anger [Vn. *sân*; Skt. *dvesa*] is one of the Three Poisons [Vn. *Tam Độc*; Skt. *trivisa*]. The other two poisons are Greed [*tham*] and Delusion [*si*].
9. Howard Sounes, *Down the Highway: The Life of Bob Dylan* (New York: Grove Press, 2001), 120.
10. Michael Gray, *Song and Dance Man III: The Art of Bob Dylan* (London: Continuum, 2000), 54, note 17.
11. Christopher Ricks, *Dylan's Visions of Sin* (New York: Harper Collins, 2003), 413.

US. In "the Village" Dylan met young women whose parents had little control over them, women like Suze Rotolo, who, despite objections from her mother and sister, moved in with Dylan when she was 17 and later became pregnant with his child. Perhaps because he grew up in a time and place with sexual mores very different from those that prevailed in Vietnam, what I call Dylan's true or kinder love songs are not, like Trịnh Công Sơn's love songs, about unrequited or unfulfilled love (*tình yêu dang dở*) but rather about a yearning for an intimacy enjoyed in the past, a desire to be in bed with, or at least alone with, his love again. This desire is expressed in the song just discussed, "Tomorrow Is a Long Time," and also in "To Be Alone with You," "Tonight I'll Be Staying Here with You," and "I'll Be Your Baby Tonight." Here is the first stanza of "To Be Alone with You":

> *To be alone with you*
> *Just you and me*
> *Now won't you tell me true*
> *Ain't that the way it oughta be?*
> *To hold each other tight*
> *The whole night through*
> *Ev'rything is always right*
> *When I'm alone with you*

And here are the first and last stanzas from "I'll Be Your Baby Tonight":

> *Close your eyes, close the door*
> *You don't have to worry anymore*
> *I'll be your baby tonight*
>
> *Kick your shoes off, do not fear*
> *Bring that bottle over here*
> *I'll be your baby tonight*

Michael Gray calls our attention to a "moving-on theme" that is found in many songs in Dylan's early albums.[12] This theme, Gray suggests, can be traced to stories and songs about the lonesome cowboy that go back to the nineteenth century. This theme then was passed on to the twentieth-century hobo, which Dylan claimed to be at the beginning of his career. This impulse to keep travelin' on is strong in Dylan's early albums, Gray argues, where it co-existed with "the opposite impulse, the desire to stay and be

---

12. Michael Gray, *Song and Dance Man III*, 30.

entangled."[13] In early albums, however, this desire to stay did not "win," Gray says; in Nashville Skyline, however, it does. Most of the songs on this album, which was released in 1969, are about the desire to stay put with a lover—songs like "Tonight I'll Be Staying Here with You," which Gray says is "a deliberate announcement of the fall from restlessness."[14] The railroad in the fourth stanza, Gray says, symbolizes the always-moving-on lifestyle which, in this song, the speaker rejects:[15]

> *I can hear that whistle blowin'*
> *I see that stationmaster, too*
> *If there's a poor boy on the street*
> *Then let him have my seat*
> *'Cause tonight I'll be staying here with you*

I bring up Michael Gray's discussion of these two conflicting yearnings in Dylan's songs on his early albums—to leave for the open road, to be back in a lover's arms—because it reveals something about Dylan's love songs, namely, that in his anti-love songs the first yearning predominates and in his true love songs the second yearning reigns supreme.

Two highly praised true love songs, "Boots of Spanish Leather" and "You're Gonna Make Me Lonesome When You Go," are interesting variations on the pattern just described. In both these songs it is the woman, not the man, who is travelin' on. These are true love songs, however, not insult songs. They resemble Trịnh Công Sơn's love songs because in them the speaker has to come to grips with the fact that the woman he loves is moving on. In "Boots of Spanish Leather" there are two speakers, a woman and a man. Both speak sweetly and kindly to each other. This song is probably a reaction to Suze's long stay in Italy—from June, 1962, to January, 1963.[16] While they were separated Dylan and Suze exchanged letters. In her autobiography Suze says that Dylan's letters were "written by a young writer on the rise who is in love." They were, she adds, "very personal, full of pain, humor and storytelling."[17] The woman in the song, who is about to sail away (for Spain, not Italy), asks if there is anything she can send him "from the place that I'll be landing." The man says he doesn't want anything; he just wants her to return. When

---

13. Ibid.
14. Ibid., 31.
15. Ibid., 43.
16. John Shelton, *No Direction Home*, 153.
17. Suze Rotolo, *A Freewheelin' Time*, 178.

the woman persists, asking him if he doesn't want something fine from Madrid or Barcelona, he finally says she can bring him "Spanish boots of Spanish leather." Christopher Ricks, in an impressive ten-page-long analysis of this song, calls it "an indestructible song about the destruction of love." In it, he adds, "artistic self-discipline is inseparable from the self-control of the one who comes to learn what it is to be let down." There is bitterness in this song, Ricks adds, a "bitterness which will not let up," but it is "tinglingly contained."[18] Containing bitterness after a doomed love affair was difficult for both Trịnh Công Sơn and Bob Dylan. Trịnh Công Sơn was clearly better at it than Dylan, a composer well-known for his bitter anti-love songs, but in "Boots of Spanish Leather" he summons up enough self-control to keep his bitterness in check.

"You're Going to Make Me Lonesome When You Go" was apparently inspired by Dylan's relationship with a woman named Ellen Bernstein, an A&R (Artists and Repertoire) executive for Columbia Records. In "You're Gonna Make Me Lonesome" Dylan sings "I'll look for you in old Honolulu / San Francisco, Ashtabula." Ashtabula, Ohio, was Ellen Bernstein's hometown. Dylan spent most of the summer of 1974 away from his wife on a ranch that he had recently bought in Minnesota. Ellen Bernstein visited Dylan at this ranch that summer.[19]

"You're Going to Make Me Lonesome When You Go" is on Dylan's album *Blood on the Tracks* which was released in 1975. Clinton Heylin and other biographers argue that Dylan's troubled marriage was the underlying theme of the songs on this album.[20] The songs on it were composed in 1974, when Dylan's marriage to Sara was falling apart. The music critic Chris Willman refers to it as Dylan's "personal breakup album."[21] Although this album did include a song apparently inspired by Ellen Bernstein as well as "Simple Twist of Fate," a song about Suze Rotolo (a subtitle, "Fourth Street Affair," was later dropped) these two songs were distractions. "Dylan's marriage was in trouble," Heylin says, "and it is this which remains the underlying concern of *Blood on the Tracks*."[22]

18. Christopher Ricks, *Dylan's Visions of Sin*, 404.
19. Howard Sounes, *Down the Highway*, 282.
20. Clinton Heylin, *Bob Dylan: Behind the Shades* (New York: Summit Books, 1991), 240-241.
21. Chris Willman, "Dylan's Bloody-Best Album: 40 Facts About the 40-Year-Old *Blood on the Tracks*," *Rolling Stone* (Jan. 21, 2015). https://www.rollingstone.com/music/music-news/dylans-bloody-best-album-40-facts-about-the-40-year-old-blood-on-the-tracks-159901/ (accessed Apr. 13, 2018).
22. Clinton Heylin, *Bob Dylan: Behind the Shades*, 240.

An interesting feature of Dylan's true love songs is that many have a pastoral quality. They feature country scenes and landscapes far from the madding crowd, scenes like this one from "You're Gonna Make Me Lonesome When You Go":

Flowers on the hillside, bloomin' crazy
Crickets talkin' back and forth in rhyme
Blue river runnin' slow and lazy
I could stay with you forever and never realize the time

In "New Morning" the speaker arises with his lover in the country and asks her if she can "hear that rooster crowin'," see that "rabbit runnin' across the road," "feel that sun a-shinin'," see a "groundhog runnin' by the country stream"; and in "To Ramona" the speaker says he still wishes to kiss his lover's "cracked country lips." I will explore Dylan's praise of pastoral women further at the end of this chapter when I discuss Kevin Krein and Abigail Levin's view that in many of his love songs—both what I have called true love songs like "You're Gonna Make Me Lonesome When You Go" and anti-love songs like "Like a Rolling Stone"—Dylan is critiquing "urban materialism," "contemporary vanity," and "the false promise of consumerism as happiness."[23]

Dylan, Suze Rotolo, and Joan Baez were at the Newport Folk Festival in July, 1963. Suze had returned from her eight-month stay in Europe in mid-January. While she was gone Dylan had been seeing Joan Baez and had spent time with her in Carmel, California. Suze was becoming aware that the rumors of Dylan's affair with her were true. She also knew that in August Joan and Bob would be touring together. Knowing these things, however, surely did not prepare her for what happened at Newport when Baez came on stage and sang "Don't Think Twice, It's All Right," which she introduced in this way: "Here's another Bobby song. This is a song about a love affair that has lasted too long." Robert Shelton reports that when Rotolo, who was in the audience, heard this introduction, she "turned pale and got up to walk out. Ric Von Schmidt, a blues guitar player and folk singer who was a friend of Dylan's, went with her, trying to comfort her after this public gibe."[24] "Don't Think Twice, It's All Right" is one of Dylan's best-known works. It was the song that played in the White House in 2012 when President Obama presented Dylan with a Presidential Medal

---

23. Kevin Krein and Abigail Levin, "Dylan, Authenticity, and the Second Sex," 54, 64.
24. Robert Shelton, *No Direction Home*, 132.

of Freedom. The final lines seem designed to inflict maximum pain on the lover girl the speaker is discarding:

> *I ain't sayin' you treated me unkind*
> *You could have done better but I don't mind*
> *You just kinda wasted my precious time*
> *But don't think twice, it's all right*

Robert Shelton says that "Don't Think Twice" was "clearly about Suze."[25] Clinton Heylin says the song was "probably a direct response to the phone call from Suze, who was traveling in Europe, informing him that she would not be coming back around Labor Day as originally planned."[26] The song, Heylin says, "does a deliberately lousy job of disguising the very real hurt underlying those verbal put-downs, a Dylan trademark since his student days."[27] In explaining this trademark both Heylin and Anthony Scaduto mention Dylan's response to a girl named Gretel Hoffman, whom Dylan knew when he was a student at the University of Minnesota and hanging out in Dinkytown. Apparently Dylan and others, but not Gretel, thought she was his girlfriend. She began dating David Whitaker, a good friend of Dylan's. When they met after not having seen each other for a while she told Dylan she was marrying David. He stalked past her, then turned and said "Let me know when you get divorced."[28] In liner notes for his album *Freewheelin'* Dylan says that "Don't Think Twice" "is not a love song. It's a statement that maybe you can say to make yourself feel better. It's as if you were talking to yourself."[29] Getting mad, not sad, seems to be Dylan's way of avoiding pain.

Dylan's "Don't Think Twice" hurt not only his girlfriend Suze; it also irritated some of Dylan's friends who felt he should have given Paul Clayton more credit. Dylan took a couple of lines and his melody for "Don't Think Twice" from a song by Clayton called "Who's Gonna Buy You Ribbons When I'm Gone."[30] Clayton's song was an adaptation of a traditional ballad called "Who'll Buy Your Chickens When I'm Gone," which Clayton had unearthed while researching folklore in Appalachia. Robert Shelton describes Paul Clayton, one of Dylan's friends in Greenwich Village, as "a

25. Ibid., 117.
26. Clinton Heylin, *Revolution in the Air* (Chicago, IL: Chicago Review Press, 2009), 103.
27. Ibid.
28. Clinton Heylin, *Revolution in the Air*, 103; Anthony Scaduto, *Bob Dylan* (London: Helter Skelter Publishing, 1996), 36.
29. Quoted by Nat Hentoff in his liner notes for the album *The Freewheelin' Bob Dylan*.
30. Anthony Scaduto, *Bob Dylan*, 142; Clinton Heylin, *Revolution in the Air*, 102.

gentle, lost, earnest folk singer, whose knowledge of balladry was wide."[31]
The similarity between "Who's Gonna Buy You Ribbons" and "Don't
Think Twice" is obvious. Here's how Clayton's song begins:

> *It ain't no use to sit and sigh now, darlin*
> *And it ain't no use to sit and cry now*
> *Tain't no use to sit and wonder why, darling*
> *Just wonder who's gonna buy you ribbons when I'm gone*

As we will see in Chapter Eight, Dylan's biographers and his friends
describe him as a taker, not a giver. He was, Clinton Heylin says, "the
most casual of credit-givers."[32] Anthony Scaduto says that although
legally Dylan did not have to give Clayton credit—because the tune came
from a folk song in the public domain—Dylan's friends, whom Scaduto
interviewed, believed that morally Dylan should have made Clayton
co-author and given him half of his royalties.[33] Twenty-two years after
"Don't Think Twice" was released, Dylan, on the liner notes for his box
set *Biograph* (1985), acknowledged his debt to Clayton. It was too late to
help this troubled young man who greatly admired Dylan; he committed
suicide in 1967.

LIKE A ROLLING STONE

"Don't Think Twice, It's All Right" is well known, but another anti-love
song, "Like a Rolling Stone," is even more famous and has garnered
extravagant praise from Dylan's fans and biographers. It is, Robert Shelton
says, "often regarded as the greatest rock single of all time."[34] In 2015
Henrik Franzon, a Swedish statistician, analyzed published lists that rank
songs and determined that "Like a Rolling Stone" was the most highly
rated song of all time.[35] Dylan himself recognized its importance soon
after he wrote it. "If you're talking about what breakthrough is for me,"
Dylan said in a 1966 interview, "I would have to say, speaking totally, 'Like
a Rolling Stone.'"[36] Why did Dylan and why do his biographers consider
this song a breakthrough? In tone and theme it seems to resemble other

---

31. Robert Shelton, No *Direction Home*, 112.
32. Clinton Heylin, *Revolution in the Air*, 102.
33. Anthony Scaduto, *Bob Dylan*, 142.
34. Robert Shelton, *No Direction Home*, 196.
35. "Acclaimed Music—Top 6000 Songs of All Time," http://www.acclaimedmusic.net/
    year/alltime_songs.htm (accessed Mar. 1, 2018).
36. Bob Dylan, interview by Marvin Bronstein, Montreal, February 1966. Greil Marcus
    includes this interview in *Like a Rolling Stone: Bob Dylan at the Crossroads* (New York:
    PublicAffairs, 2005), 69-70.

anti-love songs written earlier—"Don't Think Twice, It's All Right," for example, and "It Ain't Me Babe." As in these earlier songs, the speaker is angry and criticizes a woman for various character flaws. Referring to an early draft of "Like a Rolling Stone," Dylan told Jules Siegel, a writer for the *Saturday Evening Post*, that "it was just a rhythm thing on paper all about my steady hatred directed at some point that was honest. In the end it wasn't hatred, it was telling someone something they didn't know, telling them they were lucky. Revenge, that's a better word."[37] What Dylan was angry about, what made him vengeful, is not clear. Anthony Scaduto says "Like a Rolling Stone" might have been written for Joan Baez or for his friend Bob Neuwirth but "more likely it was written for everyone Dylan believed had been trapped by the poison, including himself."[38] Mike Marqusee says the song's "high school rage seethes into a broader critique of all aristocracies—the rich, the famous, the hip, 'the princess on the steeple and all the pretty people'—and a warning to all those who forget that high status is transient."[39] Robert Shelton suggests he is attacking "anyone afraid to step out of his or her cocoon and into life's mainstream without guidance, parents, or structure or crutches."[40]

These comments by Dylan himself and by music critics suggest that "Like a Rolling Stone" is another angry anti-love song, which raises this question: What was new about "Like a Rolling Stone" and why did it become so popular? Music critics and historians offer one answer to both questions: Because it was a rock 'n' roll song, not a folk song, or at least a folk-rock song and not a pure folk song, and so fans, who were growing weary of earnest songs about social injustice backed by acoustic, not-electrified, guitars, welcomed the new sound and the new message. Dylan wrote "Like a Rolling Stone" in early May, 1966, when he and popular music were at a crossroads.[41] He wrote the first draft on his plane trip home from his English tour. The song emerged, he told Robert Shelton, from a six-page draft that was "very vomitific in structure," by which he apparently meant not carefully thought out but rather composed in a "stream of consciousness" manner.[42]

---

37. Jules Siegel, "Well, What Have We Here?" *Saturday Evening Post* (July 30, 1966), 39.
38. Anthony Scaduto, *Bob Dylan*, 212.
39. Mike Marqusee, "The Song that Got Away," *Guardian*, May 27, 2005.
40. Robert Shelton, *No Direction Home*, 196.
41. The subtitle of Greil Marcus' book about "Like a Rolling Stone" is "Bob Dylan at the Crossroads." See Greil Marcus, *Like a Rolling Stone: Bob Dylan at the Crossroads* (New York: PublicAffairs, 2005).
42. Robert Shelton, *No Direction Home*, 196.

Dylan was not in a happy frame of mind when he returned from England in May, 1966, after a world tour.[43] "After I finished my English tour," he told Jules Siegel, "I quit because it was too easy. There was nothing happening to me. Every concert was the same. . . . I'd get standing ovations but it didn't mean anything to me."[44] "I was playing a lot of songs I didn't want to play," he told Nat Hentoff in 1966. "I was singing words I didn't really want to sing."[45] He was determined to strike out in new directions.

The "British invasion" in 1964 by the Beatles and the Rolling Stones intensified an interest in rock 'n' roll in America. Regarding the Beatles, Greil Marcus quotes Dylan as saying, soon after their arrival in the US in 1964, that he "knew they were pointing the direction where music had to go." "That was the moment," Marcus says, "that took Bob Dylan out of his folk singer's clothes."[46] In naming his song "Like a Rolling Stone," Dylan appears to also acknowledge the influence of the Rolling Stones. Mick Jagger, Keith Richards, and Brian Jones, however, took their name from a Muddy Waters song "Rollin' Stone," first released in 1950, which contains lines like the following:

> *Well, my mother told my father*
> *Just before I was born*
> *"I got a boy child's comin'*
> *Gonna be, he gonna be a rollin' stone"*

When he wrote "Like a Rolling Stone," Dylan may have been thinking of this old rhythm and blues song or the British rock group's song, or both. Mike Marqusee points out that Dylan gives the rolling stone metaphor a different meaning. For the British group, Marqusee says, it "was a declaration of personal independence—a macho disavowal of responsibility or permanence of affection." In Dylan's song, however, the "rolling stone" becomes "a punishment and a prison, but also a common fate, an underlying reality."[47]

Dylan was also impressed by another British group, The Animals, who in 1964 released a folk-rock version of "The House of the Rising

---

43. This was not the trip immortalized in D. A. Pennebaker's documentary *Don't Look Back*. That earlier trip occurred in May, 1965.
44. Jules Siegel, "Well, What Have We Here?," 39.
45. Bob Dylan, "Interview with Nat Hentoff, *Playboy*," in *Bob Dylan: The Essential Interviews*, ed. Jonathan Cott (New York: Wenner Books, 2006), 97. This is a reprint of an interview that first appeared in *Playboy*, March 1966.
46. Greil Marcus, *Like a Rolling Stone*, 6.
47. Mike Marqusee, *Chimes of Freedom: The Politics of Bob Dylan's Art* (New York: The New Press, 2003), 154.

Sun." Dylan had released a more traditional folk version of this song in 1962, based on Dave Van Ronk's arrangement. According to Anthony Scaduto, The Animals' folk-rock version greatly impressed Dylan.[48] Some music critics refer to it as the first folk-rock song, but others say that distinction should be given to The Byrds' rock version of Dylan's song "Mr. Tambourine Man," which they released in 1965.[49] The Byrds sent Dylan an advance copy of their cover of "Mr. Tambourine Man." A "member of Dylan's set" told Anthony Scaduto that "for Bob it was like The Animals rocking 'House of the Rising Sun' all over again. Rock worked."[50] And it worked with songs that Dylan had previously recorded ("House of the Rising Sun") or both written and recorded ("Mr. Tambourine Man"). One can understand why Dylan, after seeing what these other groups had accomplished, was eager to move to folk-rock.

I should explain, however, that Dylan did not like the term "folk-rock," which was coined by *Billboard* to describe songs that The Animals, The Byrds, and Dylan were releasing in the mid-sixties. The term is "nose-thumbing," Dylan told Scaduto. "[It] sounds like you're looking down on what is fantastic, great music."[51] For Dylan, folk-rock was a good thing, a positive and exciting development. Why not use an electric guitar, he thought, if it produces a wonderful sound? Many people involved in the folk revival in the 1960s, however, were purists and wanted folk songs to be performed with traditional instruments. Many also held leftist political views. For the singer Pete Seeger, for example, and Irwin Silber, the editor of *Sing Out!*, folk songs performed with traditional instruments were protest songs, weapons in the class struggle and a way to oppose the commercialization of art. For some people involved in the folk revival, the electric guitar represented capitalism. In November, 1964, Silber wrote "An Open Letter to Bob Dylan" which appeared in *Sing Out!*. In it he attacks Dylan for abandoning protest songs. "You said you weren't a writer of 'protest' songs—or any other category, for that matter—but you just wrote songs. . . . But any songwriter who tries to deal honestly with reality in this world is bound to write 'protest' songs. How can he [sic] help himself?"[52]

---

48. Anthony Scaduto, *Bob Dylan*, 176.
49. Clinton Heylin, *Bob Dylan: Behind the Shades*, 133.
50. Anthony Scaduto, *Bob Dylan*, 188.
51. Ibid., 222.
52. Irwin Silber, "An Open Letter to Bob Dylan." The entire letter can be found at http://www.edlis.org/twice/threads/open_letter_to_bob_dylan.html (accessed Apr. 19, 2018).

In the 1960s during the folk revival, which I will describe more fully in Chapter Twenty One, songs called "folk songs" were what could be called "covers" of either old English and Scottish ballads, or of American blues, gospel, and country songs that were sung in the 1920s and 1930s and preserved in Harry Smith's *Anthology of American Folk Music*, a collection of six long-playing records (LPs) on which are found 84 American folk, blues, gospel, and country songs that were originally recorded from 1927 to 1932. The song "Mary Hamilton," for example, which Joan Baez sings on her first album, is a sixteenth-century ballad from Scotland. The song "See That My Grave Is Kept Clean," which Dylan sings on his first album, is a traditional spiritual that Blind Lemon Jefferson (1893-1929) composed and sang in the 1920s.

Another kind of song popular during the folk revival was the topical song. Paul Williams provides a concise definition. Topical songs, he says, are "retellings of real events, usually tragedies, usually with a moral attached or implicit."[53] Topical songs by a friend of Dylan's, a singer-composer named Phil Ochs, became fairly well-known in the mid-1960s. Ochs, who called himself a "singing journalist," was considered a master of the genre. He wrote "Talking Birmingham Jam" about the bombing of a Birmingham, Alabama church that killed four African American girls and the "The Ballad of Medgar Evers," about the civil rights activist who battled segregation at the University of Mississippi and was killed by a white supremacist. Dylan wrote topical songs also: "Only a Pawn in Their Game" about the murder of Medgar Evers; "The Lonesome Death of Hattie Carroll" about the 1963 Baltimore killing of 51-year-old African-American barmaid, Hattie Carroll, by a rich tobacco farmer; and "The Death of Emmett Till" about a fourteen-year-old boy from Mississippi who was killed by two white men reportedly because he was flirting with a white cashier.

In an attempt to account for the vindictiveness expressed in "Like a Rolling Stone" and two other songs also released in late 1965—"Positively 4th Street" and "Can You Please Crawl Out Your Window"—Mike Marqusee makes some interesting observations. He points out that this vindictiveness was already present in songs written during Dylan's protest phase—in songs like "When the Ship Comes In," "Masters of War," and "The Lonesome Death of Hattie Carroll." In "Masters of War," for

---

53. Paul Williams, *Bob Dylan, Performing Artist: The Early Years, 1960-1973* (London: Omnibus Press, 2004), 93.

example, the speaker hopes that the masters die soon and looks forward to standing over their grave. What has changed in these songs released in 1965, Marqusee says, is that in them vindictiveness has been abstracted from a political context and become "strictly person to person."[54] "Like a Rolling Stone," he says, is a "sustained six-minute epic of vituperation" which is "permeated by a kind of ecstasy of *schadenfreude*," a feeling of joy derived from seeing other people suffer.[55] In both "Like a Rolling Stone" and "Positively 4th Street," he adds, Dylan marries "vindictive glee to the adrenaline kick of rock 'n' roll."[56]

The crossroads that Dylan was at when he wrote "Like a Rolling Stone" was not just a question of whether to stick with acoustic guitars or sing backed by a band with electric guitars. Dylan, in his interviews with Nat Hentoff and Jules Siegel, made it clear that he was tired of singing the same old songs. In one interview with Hentoff he indicates that the songs he was tired of were protest songs, which he calls "message songs." Everyone knows, Dylan told Hentoff, that message songs are "a drag." "It's only college newspaper editors and single girls under 14 who could possibly have time for them."[57]

Dylan had already begun to tire of protest songs before this 1965 interview. Nat Hentoff had interviewed Dylan in October, 1964, when he was recording songs for his album *Another Side of Bob Dylan*. Before the recording session began Dylan told Hentoff that there were not going to be any "finger-pointing" songs on this album. "You know—pointing to all the things that are wrong. Me, I don't want to write *for* people anymore. You know—be a spokesman. . . . . From now on I want to write from inside me, and to do that I'm going to have get back to writing like I used to when I was ten—having everything come out naturally."[58] As an example of the kind of song he did not want to sing anymore Dylan mentions his topical song "The Death of Emmett Till." The journalist Anthony Scaduto praises Dylan for his "topical protest" songs that he wrote in the early 1960s. They "reached beyond political sloganeering," he says, and "many of them were touched with poetry."[59] Joan Baez also has praised Dylan's protest songs,

---

54. Mike Marqusee, *Chimes of Freedom*, 152.
55. Ibid., 154.
56. Ibid., 156.
57. Bob Dylan, "Interview with Nat Hentoff, *Playboy*," 100.
58. Bob Dylan, interview by Nat Hentoff titled "The Crackin', Shakin', Breakin', Sounds," in *Bob Dylan: The Essential Interviews*, ed. Jonathan Cott (New York: Wenner Books, 2006), 16. This interview first appeared in the *New Yorker*, Oct. 24, 1964.
59. Anthony Scaduto, *Bob Dylan*, 11. See also, 136.

saying that they are powerful as poetry . . . and as music."[60] Dylan himself, however, realized the limitations of topical protest songs. He realized that it was very difficult to make them poetic, and Dylan wanted to be a poet like Rimbaud. He had literary pretensions.

Before he went to England in April of 1965, Dylan had been working on *Tarantula*, a collection of prose and prose poems. Dylan planned to publish it with Macmillan, but set aside the project when he had a motorcycle accident in July, 1966. Bootleg editions were available earlier, but it was not officially published until 1971. *Tarantula* is an obscure book, many parts of which most people have found to be unreadable. Robert Shelton calls it "an enigma wrapped in a question mark."[61] Clinton Heylin says that "perhaps only *Finnegans Wake*" among works of modern literature "is as sustainedly unreadable as the prose sections of *Tarantula*."[62] *Finnegans Wake*, however, is considered high art, whereas *Tarantula* has garnered precious little praise.[63] I mention *Tarantula* because it reveals that prior to composing "Like a Rolling Stone," Dylan was determined to produce literary works. It seems likely that his lack of success with his novel made him more eager to write and sing songs that were poetic, more literary. He told Nat Hentoff that in the spring of 1965 he was so tired of singing his old songs that he contemplated quitting singing altogether. "But," Dylan says, "'Like a Rolling Stone' changed it all; I didn't care anymore after that about writing books or poems or whatever. I mean it ["Like a Rolling Stone"] was something that I myself could dig."[64] Dylan makes it clear that he did not see his decision to "go electric," to sing with a band that included an electric guitar, as selling out to the "Establishment." "Contrary to what some scary people think," Dylan says, "I don't play with a band now for any kind of propaganda-type or commercial-type reasons. It's just that my songs are pictures and the band makes the sound of the pictures."[65] With "Like a Rolling Stone" and other songs that followed, Dylan was, Mike Marqusee says, "proving he could reach a mass audience without compromising his vision." Then Marqusee quotes Dylan's friend Allen

---

60. Robert Shelton quotes comments Baez made in an interview with Nat Hentoff that appeared in *HiFi/Stereo*. See *No Direction Home*, 131.
61. Robert Shelton, *No Direction Home*, 166.
62. Clinton Heylin, *Bob Dylan: Behind the Shades*, 129.
63. Robert Shelton asked Gabrielle Goodchild, a literature scholar, to analyze *Tarantula*. She discusses its themes and writers whose influence she detects in it. Both Shelton and Goodchild urge readers to give it a try. See Robert Shelton, *No Direction Home*, 166-167.
64. "Interview with Nat Hentoff, *Playboy*," 97.
65. Ibid.

Ginsberg who comments that for Dylan, "it was an artistic challenge to see if great art can be done on a jukebox, and he proved it can."[66]

Another anti-love song, "Positively 4th Street," is also a song of hatred and revenge, a song that Clinton Heylin finds more mean-spirited than "Like a Rolling Stone"—so mean-spirited, he says, that it makes "Like a Rolling Stone" sound like the Beatles's sweet song "I Want to Hold Your Hand."[67] Christopher Ricks calls it "a masterpiece of regulated hatred" but appears to suggest in his fourteen-page analysis of this song that the speaker's anger is justified, because the friend or friends Dylan addresses in the song had no faith in him. "What matters, " Ricks says, "is that a friend has let you down."[68] Anthony Scaduto says "there is no line in all pop music filled with more hate than the last line of the song which sums it [the song] up: "If you could stand in my shoes you'd see what a drag it is to be you."[69] It is not clear whom Dylan is attacking in this song. Some people think it is Joan Baez, but most people believe it is the entire Greenwich Village folk scene. It has been seen, Mike Marqusee says, as "Dylan's fuck-you to the folk set."[70] 4th Street is a street in Greenwich Village that in the early 1960s was the center of the folk scene. Dylan himself lived on West 4th Street with Suze Rotolo and it is where the Gaslight, an important venue for folk music, was located and where Dylan sang when he first arrived in New York. "Positively 4th Street" was recorded shortly after the 1965 Newport Folk Festival, at which many admirers of folk music were upset when he performed with a band using electric instruments. Some people see his song as a reaction to the way he was treated in Newport. "Positively 4th Street," Clinton Heylin says, "sure sounds like the product of a post-Newport Dylan mighty pissed off for the second year running by those shouting, 'Which side are you on?'"[71] The sides he refers to are those who favored pure folk, protest songs, and acoustic instruments and others who were ready to rock and roll.

What actually happened at the 1965 Newport Jazz Festival when Dylan and his band took the stage is not clear. They had practiced secretly and had not told anyone about their plan, so the audience was shocked when they launched what Robert Shelton calls "a rocking electric version of 'Maggie's Farm.'" When Dylan began singing "Like a Rolling Stone," Shelton says,

---

66. Mike Marqusee, *Chimes of Freedom*, 144.
67. Clinton Heylin, *Bob Dylan: Behind the Shades*, 145.
68. Christopher Ricks, *Dylan's Visions of Sin*, 56, 65.
69. Anthony Scaduto, *Bob Dylan*, 230.
70. Mike Marqusee, *Chimes of Freedom*, 155.
71. Clinton Heylin, *Revolution in the Air*, 255.

people got angrier, some yelling: "Play folk music!" "Sell out!" "This is a folk festival!"[72] The heckling increased as Dylan sang a third song, "It Takes a Train to Cry." People who were there offer different opinions about what the audience was upset about. Clinton Heylin provides a balanced account drawing on interviews given by key participants, including Al Kooper, a member of Dylan's band; Joe Boyd, who was a sound technician; and Pete Seeger. Some people apparently were upset, as Robert Shelton suggests, because Dylan was not singing "folk" songs but others, including Pete Seeger and Alan Lomax, a folklorist and collector of folk songs, were upset because the sound was too loud and distorted. In other words, the quality of the sound was the issue, not the fact that Dylan was singing backed by a band using electric instruments. And according to Al Kooper, others were angry because Dylan sang only three songs.[73]

"Like a Rolling Stone" was a hit probably because it was released when both Dylan and his fans were growing tired of protest songs, but also because of what Mike Marqusee calls the song's "spirit of unmistakable freshness and energy" and its "diabolic exuberance."[74] It is a song of "hatred, bitterness, and revenge," Paul Williams says. "But it is so real, so deeply felt, that in a sense it conjures up that whole passionate state of being in which one lives this hard and cares this deeply."[75] The musical qualities of the song help to create this passionate state. Anthony Scaduto says that "when you heard 'Like a Rolling Stone' back then it was like a cataclysm, like being taken to the edge of the abyss, drawn to some guillotine of experience." Scaduto credits the "rock band" for creating tension: "It opened with a quick drum beat, and then organ and piano and guitar rolling over the listener, setting up an overwhelming sense of immediacy, drawing the nerves taut."[76] The inclusion of an organ riff that Al Kooper, usually a guitarist, had come up with was a last minute decision, one made pretty much by Kooper himself who moved to the organ when Tom Wilson, the producer, was on the phone.[77] Many music critics praise Kooper's contribution to the song.

Before leaving "Like a Rolling Stone," a few comments about Dylan's anti-love songs and catharsis—the idea that by expressing anger and

---

72. Robert Shelton, *No Direction Home*, 210.
73. Clinton Heylin, *Bob Dylan: Behind the Shades*, 140-146.
74. Mike Marqusee, *Chimes of Freedom*, 154.
75. Paul Williams, *Dylan—What Happened?* which is co-published by "and books" (South Bend, IN: 1979, 1980) and Entwistle Books (Glen Ellen, CA: 1979, 1980), 39.
76. Anthony Scaduto, *Bob Dylan*, 212.
77. Greil Marcus, *Like a Rolling Stone*, 110-111.

hatred one gains some control over these emotions. "Catharsis" comes from a Greek word meaning "purification" or "cleansing." In his *Poetics* Aristotle argued that tragedies bring about a catharsis of pity and fear by first arousing these emotions and then curing us of them. Aristotle saw catharsis working, the literary scholar J. Hills Miller says, "as a kind of homeopathic medicine: tragedy cures the disease by administering a controlled dose of it and then clearing it away."[78] The "catharsis theory," the idea that expressing anger or aggressive feelings is an effective way to reduce anger and aggression, has been debated by psychologists for decades. Freud's ideas about catharsis led to what is known as the hydraulic model of anger, the idea that anger builds up like hydraulic pressure until it is somehow released. Brad J. Bushman et al. report that the "scientific community has largely disconfirmed and abandoned the catharsis theory." These researchers blame "the popular mass media" for keeping this thoroughly debunked theory alive.[79]

In discussing "Don't Think Twice, It's All Right" I mentioned Dylan's comment that this song was something you could say to make yourself feel better. Getting mad, not sad, I suggested, was perhaps Dylan's way of avoiding pain. Music critics acknowledge that Dylan's famous anti-love songs are full of hatred and revenge, but they greatly admire the depth of passion revealed in them; and they suggest that expressing this hatred and revenge is cathartic. Paul Williams says "Don't Think Twice" is about "the transmuting of pain into something not only bearable but actually attractive;"[80] and he says "Like a Rolling Stone" is about a man repossessing his "selfness" and becoming whole again, reaching the point where he can say "I don't care, I am me again now, I AM." After this "translation" of "Like a Rolling Stone," Williams places the word "catharsis" implying that this word sums up the meaning of the song.[81] Robert Shelton says that "Idiot Wind," a song "generally acknowledged" to be the "big song" on the album *Blood on the Tracks*, is "a catharsis, a venting of personal anguish as well as a portrayal of a milieu where gossiping and backstabbing have replaced caring and believing."[82]

---

78. J. Hillis Miller, "Narrative," in *Critical Terms for Literary Study*, ed. Frank Lentricchia and Thomas McLaughlin (Chicago, IL: University of Chicago Press, 1990), 67.
79. Brad J. Bushman, Roy F. Baumeister, and Angela D. Stack, "Catharsis, Aggression, and Persuasive Influence: Self-Fulfilling or Self-Defeating Prophecies?" *Journal of Personality and Social Psychology* 76, no. 3 (1999), 368.
80. Paul Williams, *Bob Dylan, Performing Artist: The Early Years, 1960-1973*, 57.
81. Paul Williams, *Dylan—What Happened?*, 39.
82. Robert Shelton, *No Direction Home*, 301.

Some of the songs on *Blood on the Tracks* are believed to be about Dylan's marriage with Sara that was falling apart in the mid-1970s. Paul Williams acknowledges that "Idiot Wind" is, like "Like a Rolling Stone," "awfully negative" but calls it "one of the greatest essays on marriage ever written."[83] Robert Shelton compares it to Edward Albee's *Who's Afraid of Virginia Woolf?*[84] One can understand why. The speaker in "Idiot Wind" sounds like the character George in Albee's play. An idiot wind, the speaker says, "is flowing through the flowers on your tomb" and this same idiot wind "blows every time you move your teeth." The lines "You're an idiot, babe / It's a wonder that you still know how to breathe" are repeated three times. In the final two lines of the song, however, Dylan changes "You're" and "you" to "We're" and "we": "We're idiots, babe," the speaker says in these final lines, "It's a wonder we can feed ourselves." There are different versions of "Idiot Wind." Howard Sounes says that Dylan revised it to make it less autobiographical and mentions that Dylan has denied that the album *Blood on the Tracks*, the album on which it appeared, was autobiographical. Sounes reports, however, that Dylan's son Jakob has said that the songs on this album are "my parents talking."[85]

Though the catharsis theory seems to have been rejected by researchers, it could be true. "Idiot Wind" and other anti-love songs may be cathartic. They may purge Dylan, and in some vicarious way his fans, of hatred and anger, and perhaps that helps explain their extraordinary popularity. No doubt, too, Dylan's distinctive voice and the way he performs his anti-love songs, contributes to their success—the way, for example, in "Idiot Wind" he draws out syllables in words at the end of lines and gives the word "wind" a nasal twang. Perhaps also the extreme meanness Dylan displays in songs like "Idiot Wind"—the brazen way he attacks women—captures listeners by surprise and intrigues them. One wonders if songs attacking women as viciously as Dylan does in his anti-love songs would be as popular today. These songs were released in the 1960s and early 1970s, when the second wave of the feminist movement was gaining strength, but the battle against sexism was only beginning. Even now, decades later, very few music critics and Dylan biographers—almost all men—have asked the question I shall take up in my next chapter: Are Dylan's anti-love songs sexist?

---

83. Paul Williams, *Dylan—What Happened?*, 39.
84. Robert Shelton, *No Direction Home*, 301.
85. Howard Sounes, *Down the Highway*, 283-284.

7

BOB DYLAN & SEXISM

No one doubts the success of "Like a Rolling Stone"—the most highly rated song of all time.[1] What interests me is the fact that its vindictiveness did not bother anyone in the 1960s and it is still difficult to find any biographer or music critic who is bothered by it today. No one seems to ask why the most highly rated popular song ever is a vengeful and hate-filled attack on a woman. One wonders if these biographers and critics have not asked this question because almost all of them are men. Mike Marqusee does discuss the song's "vindictiveness" and "spitefulness." He suggests that this vindictiveness was already evident in songs Dylan wrote during his protest phase—in, for example, "When the Ship Comes In," "Masters of War," and "The Lonesome Death of Hattie Carroll." But in songs written later like "Positively 4th Street" and "Like a Rolling Stone," Marqusee says, "the spleen is strictly person to person."[2] He argues that in "Like a Rolling Stone" a "sense of millennial confrontation that riddled Dylan's protest phase here takes on a life of its own, abstracted from any but the most personal context."[3] For Marqusee the "unremitting spitefulness" of "Like a Rolling Stone" is only one of its "remarkable features," but he does notice a connection between the song's success and the spitefulness and vindictiveness it expresses.[4] His suggestion, however, that in "Like a Rolling Stone" and other anti-love songs vindictiveness has become "strictly person to person" is imprecise. It would be more accurate

---

1. "Acclaimed Music—Top 6000 Songs of All Time," http://www.acclaimedmusic.net/year/alltime_songs.htm (accessed Mar. 1, 2018).
2. Mike Marqusee, *Chimes of Freedom: The Politics of Bob Dylan's Art* (New York: The New Press, 2003), 153.
3. Ibid., 154.
4. Ibid., 153.

to say it has become "man to woman." In "Like a Rolling Stone" and other anti-love songs, Dylan is angry not at all humankind but at women. A straight man writing love songs is certainly going to talk about women, but why are so many of Dylan's "love songs" actually anti-love songs filled with hate and criticism of women for various character flaws?

Most scholars and teachers today are alert to sexism and so when I searched scholarly databases I expected to find a host of articles discussing Dylan's sexism and misogyny. I found very few. Some journalists and musicologists, however, do accuse Dylan of sexism and when they do they invariably discuss Dylan's song "Just Like a Woman," a popular Dylan anti-love song that many other singers, male and female, have covered including Joe Cocker, Rick Nelson, Roberta Flack, and Judy Collins. It is also controversial. In an article that appeared in the New York *Times* on March 14, 1971, titled "Does Rock Degrade Women?," Marion Meade, referring to "Just Like a Woman," says that "there's no more complete catalogue of sexist slurs than this song in which Dylan defines women's natural traits as greed, hypocrisy, whining and hysteria."[5] In a response to Meade's article, Robert Shelton admits that the title is a "male platitude that justifiably angers women," but he suggests that Dylan may be "ironically toying with" this platitude.[6]

Personally, I don't sense the irony. The speaker in this song talks about a "Baby" who is like "all the rest" (presumably all other women) in being foggy and taking amphetamines. She "takes," "makes love," and "aches" just like a woman but she "breaks just like a little girl." Alan Rinzler in *Bob Dylan, The Illustrated Record*, describes "Just Like a Woman" as a "devastating character assassination"—perhaps "the most sardonic, nastiest of all Dylan's putdowns of former lovers."[7]

Paul Williams, however, who focuses on the way Dylan performs the song on his *Blonde on Blonde* album, comes to a different conclusion. The performance of the song, Williams says, is "affectionate in tone from beginning to end; there's never a moment in the song, despite the little digs and the confessions of pain, when you can't hear the love in his voice." If you can't hear this tone, he says, "then there's nothing more to be said."[8]

5. Marion Meade, "Does Rock Degrade Women?" *New York Times*, Mar. 14, 1971.
6. Robert Shelton, *No Direction Home: The Life and Times of Bob Dylan* (Milwaukee, WI: Backbeat Books, 2011), 226.
7. Alan Rinzler, quoted by Paul Williams in *Bob Dylan, Performing Artist: The Early Years, 1960-1973* (London: Omnibus Press, 2004), 190.
8. Paul Williams, *Bob Dylan, Performing Artist: The Early Years, 1960-1973*, 191.

Oliver Trager points out that in the third stanza the speaker gives what is "at least a vague accounting of his actions and sensitivities" when he tells the woman that "Your long-time curse hurts/ But what is worse/ Is the pain in here." Dylan succeeds, Trager says, "in portraying a defensive but maturing guy genuinely sorry, but not solely guilty, for the way things have turned out."[9]

Oliver Trager says that "Just Like a Woman" was "purportedly inspired by socialite/artiste Edie Sedgwick" but could also be about Joan Baez or "any one of a number of femme fatales spinning in his orbit."[10] According to Trager, the reference in the lyrics to "her fog, her amphetamine and her pearls" suggests Sedgwick.[11] She was a part of Andy Warhol's group and had gained some fame by appearing in some of Warhol's films. Dylan, according to some accounts, had an intimate affair with Sedgwick around the time he was marrying Sara Lownds.[12] Later she entered into an affair with Dylan's close friend Bob Neuwirth.[13]

Richard Goldstein, who writes about pop culture, politics, and sexuality for *The Nation*, discusses Dylan's sexism in an article titled "Bob Dylan and the Nostalgia of Patriarchy."[14] "Hostility to women is a recurring theme in Dylan's songs," Goldstein writes, "from 'Like a Rolling Stone' to 'Idiot Wind.'" His love songs, he says, "bask in feminine submission," offering as an example "Sweetheart Like You," a song on Dylan's album *Infidels* released in 1983.[15] In this song the speaker asks "What's a sweetheart like you doing in a dump like this?" and answers:

> *You know, a woman like you should be at home*
> *That's where you belong*
> *Watching out for someone who loves you true*
> *Who would never do you wrong*

Dylan, Goldstein argues, is "not determined by machismo" but he appeals to men's "nostalgia for patriarchy," to their "ambivalent embrace of sexual

---

9. Oliver Trager, *Keys to the Rain: The Definitive Bob Dylan Encyclopedia* (New York: Billboard Books, 2004), 347.
10. Ibid.
11. Ibid., 348.
12. Ibid.; Clinton Heylin, *Bob Dylan: Behind the Shades* (New York: Summit Books, 1991), 153-154.
13. Oliver Trager, *Keys to the Rain*, 348.
14. Richard Goldstein, "Bob Dylan and the Nostalgia of Patriarchy," *The Nation* (Apr. 27, 2006). I read it online at *The Nation* https://www.thenation.com/article/archive/satellite-dylan/ (accessed July 15, 2021).
15. Ibid.

equality." He has escaped criticism for his "sexual politics," Goldstein believes, because "he is as critical of injustice as he is of liberation."[16]

Machismo attitudes were expressed by blues singers in the 1920s and 1930s, singers that Dylan loved and listened to for hours when he was a young man in Hibbing, which raises the question as to whether Dylan in his anti-love songs was expressing his own attitude toward women or simply participating along with many other singers and songwriters in the folk revival of the 1960s—or doing both at the same time. The speakers in many of the songs on Harry Smith's *Anthology of American Folk Music*, reveal a "machismo" attitude, a refusal to be tied down by possessive lovers. "Cause I was born in the country, she thinks I'm easy to rule / She try to hitch me to a wagon, she wanna drive me like a mule," sings Richard Rabbit Brown in "James Alley Blues." "Don't you never let one woman rule your mind / Said she keep you worried, troubled all the time," sing the Cannon's Jug Stompers in "Minglewood Blues." "Then, when you've been good, now / Can't do no more / Just tell her kindly / There is the front door," sing the Mississippi Sheiks in "The World Is Going Wrong," a song Dylan covers on his album *World Gone Wrong*. Dylan in "Don't Think Twice, It's All Right" and "It Ain't Me, Babe" expresses a similar refusal to be tied down and ruled by a woman.

As I will discuss in Chapter Twenty-One, Dylan loved these old folk songs. "Except for Roy Orbison," Dylan writes in *Chronicles*, the "playlist" when he began composing songs was "strictly dullsville . . . gutless and flabby. It all came to you like you didn't have a brain."[17] People were tired of Elvis Presley, Dylan says. Songs on the radio reflected, "nothing but the milk and sugar and not the real Jekyll and Hyde themes of the times" and so the old folk songs became, he says, "my preceptor and guide" into a different world, into what Greil Marcus calls "an invisible republic."[18] More on this republic later. I mention it here because I think Dylan in songs like "Like a Rolling Stone," "Don't Think Twice, It's all Right," and "It Ain't Me Babe" was to some degree channeling the sexism of the old blues singers. Many other popular singers and songwriters in the 1950s and early 1960s were as well. I believe, however, that there is a nastiness in these songs that is pure Dylan and clearly sexist. As Suze Rotolo says, Dylan could be "a

---

16. Ibid.
17. Bob Dylan, *Chronicles: Volume One* (New York: Simon & Schuster Paperbacks, 2004), 33.
18. Ibid., 34.

lying shit of a guy with women."[19] We should not be surprised to find that he treats them badly in his songs as well. Charles Shaar Murray, in a book about Jimi Hendrix, argues that for white performers in the early sixties like Dylan and the Rolling Stones, "the knowing sexuality of the blues" was "the perfect antidote to the sugar-coated romantic stereotypes of conventional pop" but, Murray adds, in songs like the Stones's "Play with Fire" and Dylan's "Like a Rolling Stone" the "reactionary stagnation of the social order was personified as female." Both these songs, Murray points out, "are sneeringly and contemptuously sung to a spoiled rich girl whose ways are acutely offensive to Jagger's and Dylan's (fictitious) proletarian integrity."[20]

Kevin Krein and Abigail Levin also argue that Dylan personifies social problems as female. They place the songs he wrote in the 1960s into three categories: protest songs like "Blowin' in the Wind" and "The Lonesome Death of Hattie Carroll"; "personal songs of love and loss" like "You're Gonna Make Me Lonesome When You Go" and "Don't Think Twice, It's All Right"; and songs in which "the political and the personal intersect" like "Just Like a Woman" and "Like a Rolling Stone."[21] It is this last category that interests Krein and Levin the most. Note that it includes both love songs and anti-love songs. Many songs in Krein and Levin's third category are full of pastoral imagery, which I have already identified as a common feature of Dylan's sweeter love songs. "You're Gonna Make Me Lonesome When You Go," the song Krein and Levin offer as an example of a category three song, has pastoral imagery—references to flowers on a hillside, crickets singing, etc. Krein and Levin argue that Dylan uses pastoral imagery to mount a critique of "urban materialism" and the "the false promise of consumerism as happiness."[22] The women Dylan praises and feels content with are women who live in the country and are not

---

19. Suze Rotolo, *A Freewheelin' Time: A Memoir of Greenwich Village in the Sixties* (New York: Broadway Books, 2008), 286.
20. Charles Shaar Murray, *Crosstown Traffic: Jimi Hendrix and the Post-War Rock 'n' Roll Revolution* (New York: St. Martin's Press, 1989), 63.
21. Kevin Krein and Abigail Levin, "Dylan, Authenticity, and the Second Sex," in *Bob Dylan and Philosophy*, eds. Peter Vernezze and Carl J. Porter (Chicago, IL: Open Court, 2006), 53-54.
22. This third category resembles Betsy Bowden's definition of what she refers to as "non-love" songs, which I discussed in Chapter Six. "There is almost no precedent" for these songs, Betsy Bowden says, because they "reject women *because* they are accepting of sex-role stereotypes." This only happens in certain performances, however. She says, for example, that this kinder, well-meaning rejection is evident in only one of six oral performances of "It Ain't Me, Babe." See Betsy Bowden, *Performed Literature: Words and Music by Bob Dylan* (Bloomington, IN: Indiana University Press, 1982), 55, 114.

caught up in the consumer culture. They are also "pastorally passive."[23] "The way Dylan describes them," Krein and Levin say, "the most active thing they do is grow their hair."[24] "Dylan feels safe and relaxed in the company of women," they say, "who do little else but lay across his big brass bed."[25]

The women Dylan criticizes are caught up in consumer culture. The woman in "Just Like a Woman" has her "amphetamine and pearls" but they don't give her strength, don't prevent her from breaking "like a little girl." The woman in "Like a Rolling Stone" has a diamond ring and she and her friends exchange "all kinds of precious gifts and things" but these consumer goods don't prevent her from being all alone "with no direction home." One can understand Dylan's anger at consumerism but why does he blame women for it? Krein and Levin suggest that Dylan "conflates" the evils of consumerism with women because it saddens him to see women, who, until recently, were not corrupted by the public sphere (because they were denied access to it), suddenly become corrupted. They argue that Dylan and other male members of the counterculture who were upset by consumerism and the troubles of the 1960s and 1970s—the Vietnam War, Watergate, the assassination of Martin Luther King, Jr.—tried to "fantasize a way out" by envisioning a pastoral world where they could fall in love with women who were uncorrupted by politics and consumerism. The penetration of these evils into that "protected private sphere" (women's lives), Krein and Levin argue, angered Dylan and motivated him to write songs like "Just Like a Woman" and "Like a Rolling Stone" in which he attacks women for succumbing to these evils, and also songs like "You're Gonna Make Me Lonesome When You Go," which praise women for being "pastorally passive."[26]

In the 1960s Dylan may have been concerned about the ill effects of consumerism on women, but it has not proven to be a lasting concern. As Krein and Levin themselves point out, in 2004 Dylan appeared in a television commercial for Victoria's Secret.[27] While Dylan sings "Love Sick" scantily clad women parade around him. (An article in Slate about

---

23. Kevin Krein and Abigail Levin, "Dylan, Authenticity, and the Second Sex," 61.
24. Ibid.
25. Ibid. The line "lay across my big brass bed" is found in Dylan's song "Lay, Lady, Lay."
26. Ibid., 62.
27. Ibid., 64-65.

this commercial is titled "Tangled Up in Boobs.")[28] He has appeared in other commercials as well, including one for General Motors in which he drives an Escalade. In 2014 during the Super Bowl, he appeared in a longer-than-usual commercial for Fiat Chrysler Automobiles. In an article in *Variety* about this Super Bowl ad, Brian Steinberg says that Dylan "has moved from 'Positively 4th Street' to absolutely Madison Avenue." "Somewhere," he says, "Woody Guthrie, Dylan's inspiration and muse, is shedding bitter tears."[29]

When I listened to Dylan's songs in the early and mid-60s I loved many of his anti-love songs, especially "It Ain't Me, Babe" and "Like a Rolling Stone." I never questioned the way the speakers in these songs talk to women. This was the period of second wave feminism, roughly 1960s-1980s. In the first wave the focus was on legal inequalities, including women's suffrage. In the second wave the focus was on cultural inequality and the role of women in society, but even during this second wave male musicians still, as Suze Rotolo observed, called their girlfriends "my chick" and their wives "my old lady."[30]

The feminist movement has increased our awareness of the need for gender equality. I do not believe, however, that attitudes toward anger have changed. At least, displaying it in speech and song is still more accepted in America than it is in Vietnam. Vietnam is a predominantly Buddhist country, and Buddhists do not consider anger to be cathartic; they see it as one of the three poisons, as something that will not only not heal you but will make you sicker, spiritually. In both his anti-war songs and his love songs, Trịnh Công Sơn urges his listeners and himself to avoid this poison.

Acceptance of anger and the belief that it is cathartic may explain why Dylan's anti-love songs are more famous than songs like "One Too Many Mornings" and "I Threw It All Away." Music critics and biographers praise these songs, but they are not as famous as "Like a Rolling Stone," "Don't Think Twice, It's all Right," and "It Ain't Me Babe." "One Too Many Mornings" and another true love song, "Boots of Spanish Leather," which

---

28. Seth Stevenson, "Tangled Up in Boobs: What's Bob Dylan Doing in a Victoria's Secret Ad?" *Slate* (April, 2004). *Slate* is an online magazine. See https://slate.com/business/2004/04/bob-dylan-shills-for-victoria-s-secret.html (accessed June 6, 2018).
29. Brian Steinberg, "Super Bowl: How Bob Dylan Jumped from Counterculture Icon to Car Salesman," *Variety* (Feb. 2, 2014). See https://variety.com/2014/tv/news/super-bowl-how-bob-dylan-jumped-from-counterculture-icon-to-car-salesman-1201083508/ (accessed Feb. 27, 2014).
30. Suze Rotolo, *A Freewheelin' Time*, 183, 254-255.

I've already discussed, both appear on *The Times They Are a-Changin'* (1964), Dylan's third studio album. They are the only love songs on the album, which contains mostly protest and topical songs, including the well-known "The Times They Are a-Changin'" and "With God on Our Side." Robert Shelton says both "One Too Many Mornings" and "Boots of Spanish Leather" are "linked to the loss of Suze."[31] Paul Williams claims that "One Too Many Mornings" is "a spontaneous reaction to what was happening in his relationship with Suze."[32] By including these two love songs on an album of protest songs, Dylan signaled to his liberal and radical followers that he was going to write and sing other songs, not just protest songs.

"I Threw It All Away" was included on *Nashville Skyline*, an album released in 1969 that is packed with love songs, all of them true love songs. It includes "Girl from the North Country," which Dylan and Johnny Cash sing beautifully together, and also "Lay, Lady, Lay," which became a hit single. The album sold well, primarily, Clinton Heylin says, because interest in it was generated after three songs from it were released as singles: "Lay, Lady, Lay," which was a top ten single, and "Tonight I'll be Staying Here with You" and "I Threw It All Away," which both reached the top one hundred.[33] *Nashville Skyline* began a trend that Robert Shelton calls "a retreat from significance, except the significance of an old truism: 'Love is all there is / It makes the world go 'round.'"[34] This truism is the first line of the third verse of "I Threw It All Away." Clinton Heylin says "I Threw It All Away" was "originally inspired" by Sara Lownds, Dylan's wife, but Dylan was still with Sara when *Nashville Skyline* was released in 1969.[35] He broke up with Suze, whom he refers to in "Ballad in Plain D" as the "could-be dream-lover of my lifetime," in 1964. Though Dylan blames Suze's sister and mother for the break-up, he was seeing Joan Baez at the time so it makes sense to think that Suze was the lover he talks about having thrown away.

If I had to choose one word to say why I like "One Too Many Mornings" and "I Threw It All Away," it would be "kind." Both of these songs are kind. There's no anger or hatred, just regret for lost opportunities. The speaker in "One Too Many Mornings" accepts some blame for the

---

31. Robert Shelton, *No Direction Home*, 153.
32. Paul Williams, *Bob Dylan, Performing Artist: The Early Years, 1960-1973*, 86.
33. Clinton Heylin, *Bob Dylan: Behind the Shades*, 196.
34. Robert Shelton, *No Direction Home*, 275-276.
35. Clinton Heylin, *Revolution in the Air* (Chicago, IL: Chicago Review Press, 2009), 389.

breakup: "You're right from your side / I'm right from mine," he says. The real problem is that time slips away, things happen, and soon two former lovers are both a thousand miles behind. I agree with Paul Williams that the harmonica solos between the verses in "One Too Many Mornings" are wonderful.[36] I also like the refrain that ends each verse: "One too many mornings and a thousand miles behind." Christopher Ricks calls it "one of those mysterious triumphs of phrasing that exquisitely elude paraphrase."[37] The speaker in "I Threw It All Away" also blames himself for the breakup:

> *I once held her in my arms*
> *She said she would always stay*
> *But I was cruel*
> *I treated her like a fool*
> *I threw it all away*

In discussing anti-love songs like "Don't Think Twice, It's All Right" and "It Ain't Me, Babe" I mentioned Michael Gray's point that these songs, written in the early 1960s, express an impulse to keep travelin' on, an impulse which he traces to songs and stories about the lonesome cowboy. But by *Nashville Skyline*, Gray argues, the opposite impulse, the impulse to stay, began to predominate. In "I Threw It All Away" the speaker regrets that he gave in to the impulse to travel on and—by describing beautifully what he has lost—makes a good case for staying:

> *Once I had mountains in the palm of my hand*
> *And rivers that ran through every day*
> *I must have been mad, I never knew what I had*
> *Until I threw it all away*

Michael Gray says this second verse "echoes the cowboy ethos succinctly by using, as his image for the discarded love's value, the scenery the lonesome traveler has around him, though it acts also as sexual imagery."[38] (Gray is probably referring to those mountains the speaker had in the palm of his hand.) The emphasis, Gray adds, is on "the problem of choice" and "the choice propounded is between loving and moving on."[39] The speaker in "One Too Many Mornings" faces this same choice. He too is at

---

36. Paul Williams, *Bob Dylan, Performing Artist: The Early Years, 1960-1973*, 90.
37. Christopher Ricks, *Dylan's Visions of Sin* (New York: Harper Collins, 2003), 60.
38. Michael Gray, *Song and Dance Man III: The Art of Bob Dylan* (London: Continuum, 2000), 32.
39. Ibid.

a crossroads: He looks back to the room where he and his lover have laid, then gazes at the street.[40]

As a kid growing up, I rode horses, went to western movies, and enthusiastically accepted the "cowboy ethos" and experienced the "gotta travel on" impulse. I grew up in the east but used a Western, rather than English, saddle. This same impulse led me to work summers at a ranch camp in Arizona when I was in college, to become a Peace Corps volunteer in Ethiopia after I graduated, and to go to Vietnam with International Voluntary Services in 1968. I don't regret those choices—they kept me from being drafted and exposed me to two fascinating cultures very different from my own—but I appreciate "One Too Many Mornings" and "I Threw It All Away" because these songs remind us of the value of staying home, especially if you have been lucky, like the speaker in "I Threw It All Away," to find someone who "gives you all of her love."

Both these songs are about losing intimacy that the speaker once enjoyed. In "One Too Many Mornings" the speaker is about to move away from the room where he and his love have laid. In "I Threw It All Away" the speaker once had those mountains "in the palm of [his] hand" and those rivers that "ran through ev'ry day." These are sad love songs but sad in a different way from Trịnh Công Sơn's sad love songs, most of which, as we have seen, are about love which is unrequited or unfulfilled [*tình yêu dang dở*]. Who can say which is more painful: never realized intimacy or lost intimacy? "One Too Many Mornings" and "I Threw It All Away" make a good case for the latter. As the speaker in "I Threw It All Away" says, "You will surely be a-hurtin'" if you lose someone who has given you "all of her love."

POSTSCRIPT

On May 23, 1976, Dylan performed at Colorado State University in Fort Collins. His performance was filmed by NBC for a TV special, *Hard Rain*, that aired, to mixed reviews, six months later, on September 14. The name of the TV show suggests Dylan's well-known song "A Hard Rain's A-gonna Fall" and it is also the name of a live show album of the concert that was released in mid-September 1976.[41] The album *Hard Rain* (1976) contains nine "remastered" songs that Dylan performed in spring of 1976, on the

---

40. For a very detailed (18 pages long!) analysis of "One Too Many Mornings" see Christopher Ricks, *Dylan's Visions of Sin*, 421-439.
41. See William McKeen, *Bob Dylan: A Bio-Bibliography* (Westport, CT: Greenwood Press, 1993), 274. See also Robert Shelton, *No Direction Home*, 320.

second segment of his Rolling Thunder Revue tour. Five of the songs on this album, including "Idiot Wind" and "One Too Many Mornings," appear as sung at his concert at Fort Collins on May 23, 1976; four of the songs appear as sung at an earlier concert in Fort Worth on May 16.

The title for this album, *Hard Rain*, is appropriate for another reason: It rained hard in Fort Collins during the night of the concert, which was held outdoors. The protective canopy over the singers and the band leaked. According to Rob Stoner, one of the musicians, the water caused shocks and the humidity sent their instruments out of tune. Dylan was in a bad mood, Stoner says, because although they had four days off before the concert it rained every day and so there was nothing to do except drink.[42] Then Dylan's wife Sara arrived unannounced with their children, perhaps to celebrate his thirty-fifth birthday, perhaps to confront him about his adulterous affairs. Their marriage was disintegrating and they would be divorced a year later. Joan Baez, who was performing with Dylan on this part of his tour, says that when Sara arrived she looked like "a mad woman, carrying baskets of wrinkled clothes, her hair wild and dark rings around her eyes."[43] According to Baez, Sara had a right to confront Dylan who, she says, "had picked up a local curly-headed Mopsy who perched on the piano during his rehearsals."[44]

Among the songs Dylan sang at this concert were "Idiot Wind" and "One Too Many Mornings." "Idiot Wind" had already appeared on Dylan's album *Blood on the Tracks,* but a writer for the British music magazine *Uncut* says that in terms of "paint-blistering bile," this earlier version is no match for the version Dylan sang at Fort Collins.[45] Dylan made this anti-love song even more hateful than it already was by changing "Visions of your chestnut mare" to "Visions of your smoking tongue," and by shaking his head from side to side when he sang the word "sorry" in these lines: "And I'll never know the same about you, your holiness or your kind of love / And it makes me feel so sorry."[46] He also made his love song "One Too Many Mornings" less loving by adding these four lines at the

42. Clinton Heylin quotes Rob Stoner in *Behind the Shades*, 283.
43. Joan Baez, *And a Voice to Sing With: A Memoir* (New York: Summit Books, 1987), 243.
44. Ibid.
45. Chris Willman quotes this article from *Uncut* but does not provide bibliographic information. See Chris Willman, "Dylan's Bloody-Best Album: 40 Facts About the 40-Year-Old *Blood on the Tracks*," *Rolling Stone* (Jan. 21, 2015). Rolling Stone website, https://www.rollingstone.com/music/music-news/dylans-bloody-best-album-40-facts-about-the-40-year-old-blood-on-the-tracks-159901/ (accessed Apr. 13, 2018).
46. Clinton Heylin, *Bob Dylan: Behind the Shades*, 284.

end: "I've no right to be here / And you've no right to stay / Until we're both one too many mornings / And a thousand miles away." These changes in wording can be clearly heard on Dylan's album *Hard Rain* (1976), a remastering of songs that Dylan performed on the second segment of his Rolling Thunder Revue tour.

Did Dylan make these changes to "Idiot Wind" and "One Too Many Mornings" because Sara was there to watch him? Is Sara, whose arrival surprised Dylan, the one who has "no right to stay"? No one can say for sure. Robert Shelton says that reinterpreting old songs was a "compelling interest" of Dylan's at this time so perhaps he had these changes in mind before Sara arrived.[47] Now, however, whenever I listen to "One Too Many Mornings" I can't help seeing Sara standing in the hard rain at Fort Collins.

---

47. Robert Shelton, *No Direction Home*, 298.

8

PERSONAS & PERSONALITIES: TRỊNH CÔNG SƠN

In later chapters I will discuss the very different literary, musical, and religious traditions that influenced Trịnh Công Sơn and Bob Dylan. In the next two chapters, however, I consider how the personalities of these two artists may have influenced their art. In this chapter I concentrate on Trịnh Công Sơn; in the next on Bob Dylan. Trịnh Công Sơn was in some ways a typical Vietnamese and Bob Dylan is in some ways a typical American, but both songwriters exhibit qualities that distinguish them from their contemporaries. Drawing on books and articles, I will attempt to determine the kind of person Trịnh Công Sơn was and the kind of person Bob Dylan has been and still is. Some critics and scholars object to the use of biographical information to understand literature and songs. Christopher Ricks, for example, the author of *Dylan's Visions of Sin*, advises others who have written or will write about Dylan in this way: "Don't track or trace him [Dylan]. Don't seek to interpret the life of his songs by resurrecting loathed people or loved people from his personal life."[1] Ricks prefers "close reading," the "back to the text" approach of the New Critics that I discussed in my introduction. In this approach one ignores cultural context and biographical information on the composer, focusing instead only on the song itself. "Don't break works of art back down into the biographical contingencies that contributed to bringing them into being but that are not their being," Ricks says.[2]

---

1. Christopher Ricks, *Dylan's Visions of Sin* (New York: Harper Collins), 192.
2. Ibid.

Unlike Ricks, I believe "biographical contingencies" are important and that we should listen to what those who "loathed" and those who "loved" Dylan and Trịnh Công Sơn (as well as more neutral observers) have to say about them. I believe that personality matters. It certainly matters if one is interested not only in the music but also the character of the two singers. It is necessary to answer the question: Was Trịnh Công Sơn the Bob Dylan of Vietnam? One important reason Trịnh Công Sơn was not the Bob Dylan of Vietnam is because, based on all the evidence I have been able to obtain, Trịnh Công Sơn treated people better than Bob Dylan has. For me that is an important difference between the two composers. But personality also matters if we are interested in learning what Bob Dylan's and Trịnh Công Sơn's songs mean.[3] I see no reason to rule biographical information out of court in interpreting works of art.

In discussing the personality of a composer (or poet or novelist) one must be careful to distinguish it from persona, the narrator or speaker who speaks in the song (or poem or novel). One shouldn't assume a one-to-one correspondence between the two. Literature teachers frequently warn their students that they should not assume that the person referred to in the first person is identical to the writer. In referring to the person who speaks in a literary work, one is supposed to use terms like "speaker," "narrator," or "persona." Persona is a Latin word meaning "mask." Writers and composers do, of course, assume various identities or masks in different works to achieve certain artistic effects. The man named Gulliver in Jonathan Swift's *Gulliver's Travels*, for example, is clearly not Swift. The "I" in the poem "Song of a Soldier's Wife" [Chinh phụ ngâm][4] clearly does not refer to the Vietnamese author (Đặng Trần Côn) who wrote it in Chinese or to the translator who translated it into Vietnamese (Phan Huy Ích): Both author and translator are men.

In lyrical poems and songs, however, things are not so clear cut. We generally assume, for example, that the "I" in William Wordsworth's poem about a visit to Tintern Abbey with his sister refers to the poet himself.[5]

---

3. In my introduction I have laid out my views regarding interpretation, including the importance of trying to determine the author or songwriter's intended meaning.
4. Written in the first half of the eighteenth century, "Song of a Soldier's Wife" is a famous poem known to all educated Vietnamese. The author assumes the voice of a wife who misses her husband, who is fighting on some distant battlefield. Huỳnh Sanh Thông has translated it into English. See *An Anthology of Vietnamese Poems* (New Haven: Yale University Press, 1996), 401–418.
5. Known as "Tintern Abbey," the full title of this poem is "Lines Composed a Few Miles above Tintern Abbey, on Revisiting the Banks of the Wye during a Tour, July 13, 1798."

When we hear a line like "I give her my heart but she wanted my soul" from Dylan's song "Don't Think Twice, It's All Right," we assume that the "I" refers to Dylan. And when Vietnamese hear Trịnh Công Sơn's song "Each day I Choose a Little Happiness" [Mỗi ngày tôi chọn một niềm vui]* they assume that the composer was referring to himself when he wrote it. We may be too quick to make these assumptions, but I believe most of us make them, and I don't think we are completely wrong to do so.

In discussing personae in literature, M. H. Abrams reminds us, however, that even when it seems clear that a speaker in a poem is the author we must realize that these "lyric speakers exist at some remove from the men [sic] who wrote the poems, and were devised to play a role in a particular situation and to help achieve a particular effect."[6] We should heed Abrams' advice and be aware that speakers in poems (and, I would argue, songs) "exist in some remove" from their creators. I feel, however, that some Dylan experts exaggerate the distance of that "remove." Mike Marqusee suggests that the "posture of rude resentment" that Dylan adopts in songs like "Positively 4th Street" and "Like a Rolling Stone" is a "mask," just as was the "Woody Guthrie accent" he employed for his "self-abne-gating songs of social protest." Both masks, he says, are the "authentic" Dylan.[7] I see his point but I would argue that Dylan's persona of rude resentment is much closer to the authentic Dylan than is his persona of self-abnegation. Clinton Heylin says for him each Dylan song is "a play, a script, and he'll be that guy from the song for the moment but [then] he'll switch back to Bob." Dylan's "greatest masterpiece," he argues, is his ability to get people to believe that he is 'involved' in the writing—that he cares for more than a moment about the causes and issues he sings about. We shouldn't assume, he says, that the "righteous thought" contained in "The Times They Are A-Changin'" existed for more than a moment.[8] Dylan's greatest artistic achievement may indeed be his ability to trick us into believing he cares about the issues he sings about, but my intent is to look not only at the mask but also the person behind the mask.

Betsy Bowden in her book on Bob Dylan argues for a sharp distinction between author and speaker, and she insists that we should not look at songs for biographical information:

---

6. M. H. Abrams, *A Glossary of Literary Terms* (Fort Worth, TX: Harcourt Brace Jova-novich, 1985), 136.
7. Mike Marqusee, *Chimes of Freedom* (New York: The New Press, 2003), 157.
8. Clinton Heylin, "A Preface in the Present Tense," in *Bob Dylan: Behind the Shades Revis-ited* (New York: Harper Entertainment, 1991, 2001), xv.

> The narrator in the lyrics of a Dylan song may show some attitude toward women, toward war, toward authorities, toward whatever. But the "I" in a song *is not* Bob Dylan. Like poems, songs can sometimes rework into artistic patterns the songwriter's own experiences. But a song is absolutely not biographical evidence.[9]

Bowden objects to mining songs for biographical information, but I am interested in moving in the other direction—in learning something about the lives of these two composers to better understand their songs. The "I" in a single song may not be Bob Dylan, but if one looks at a sizable number of works by a composer and finds a similar persona appearing in most of them, one can assume a relationship between that composite persona and the personality of its creator. Artists create art to express their feelings, attitudes, and ideas. Their "real" lives and their artistic lives are connected. As Professor Bowen says, composers "rework" their own experiences into "artistic patterns." One should not generalize from only one or two works, but if one looks at a body of work by a composer, patterns will emerge. Clearly the persona in a typical Trịnh Công Sơn song is gentler, less angry, and more forgiving than the persona in a typical Bob Dylan song.

TRỊNH CÔNG SƠN'S STAGE PERSONA

For public performers like Trịnh Công Sơn and Bob Dylan one can also consider their stage persona: the kind of person they project on stage, their manner of interacting with live audiences at concerts. One should not assume that singers are completely themselves when they interact with the audience during a performance. Live singing concerts are "acts." The word persona comes from the Latin word for the mask that actors used in classical plays. Some singers may mask their true personality during a public performance. As with personae in literature and song, however, I feel that a singer's stage persona offers clues as to the kind of person the singer is.

Trịnh Công Sơn did not perform publicly as much as Bob Dylan, who has been on a never-ending tour his entire adult life. In the mid to late 1960s Sơn was dodging the draft, sleeping in different places to avoid the police, and although it seems that people in high places were protecting him, even with protectors he must have worried about performing publicly. As mentioned in Chapter One, in 1967 a fight, provoked apparently by dem-

---

9. Betsy Bowden, *Performed Literature: Words and Music by Bob Dylan* (Bloomington, IN: Indiana University Press, 1982), 27.

onstrators belonging to the National Liberation Front, broke out while he was performing at a concert at the Faculty of Letters on Cường Để Street in Saigon in 1967. That ended Trịnh Công Sơn's concerts at public venues. The Thiệu government banned circulation of his songs in 1969 though cassette tapes were readily available.

After the war ended in 1975, the new communist leaders allowed only a small selection of his songs to be performed. Some officials accused him of opposing war too generally, of being a neutralist; others called his songs "yellow music" [*nhạc vàng*], their term for weepy, soft and sentimental songs. Gradually the Office of Performing Arts of the Ministry of Culture and Information has approved more and more songs, but many songs still are not allowed to be publicly performed.

I never saw Trịnh Công Sơn perform publicly, but Đặng Tiến says that when he appeared on stage, he "inspired love, not fear." He spoke in a voice that was "friendly, creating the illusion in many people that they were close to him, maybe not real close, but certainly not distant."[10] On the Trịnh Công Sơn website there is a recording of Trịnh Công Sơn and Khánh Ly singing at the Literature Café in 1966. The sound quality is not very good, but it is, as far as I know, the only recording of Trịnh Công Sơn and Khánh Ly singing anti-war songs at a live performance in the mid-1960s.[11] Here is how he introduces the song "An Old Man and a Child" [Người già em bé], a song, composed in 1965, about an old man sitting on a park bench with a small child as bombs fall on the town:

> We are very moved that you all have come here to hear us sing and we will try as hard as we can to satisfy you. Can you people sitting far away hear us clearly? [shouts of "Yes"] The first song I will sing is one I wrote in June of last year. I'm sure most of you here have heard it. It's "An Old Man and a Child."

Bernard Weinraub, a reporter for *The New York Times* in 1968 and 1969, apparently attended some of Trịnh Công Sơn's concerts. In an article titled "A Vietnamese Guitarist Sings of Sadness of War," he describes Sơn's manner on stage:

> At his concerts Trịnh Công Sơn steps on stage in a wave of applause. Timid, almost frightened, his voice is clear and gentle. He wears a white shirt open at the neck, tight pants and pointed black shoes.

---

10. Đặng Tiến, "Trịnh Công Sơn: Tiếng hát hòa bình" [Trịnh Công Sơn: Voice of Peace] *Văn Học* [Literary Studies] 186 & 187 (Oct.–Nov., 2001), 184.
11. Những bài hát tại Quán Văn 1966-1967 [Songs at the Literature Café], TCS-Home, https://www.tcs-home.org/songs/mp3/quan-van (accessed Nov. 16, 2021).

> As soon as he starts strumming his guitar and singing, the audience bursts into song with him. At most of his concerts young women in the audience weep during several of his songs.[12]

Bob Dylan's stage persona is very different. As we will discuss in the next chapter, Dylan typically does not interact with the audience at all, though he was talkative on his Alimony tour in 1978 and on his Gospel tour in 1979-1980.

TRỊNH CÔNG SƠN'S PERSONALITY

I've talked to many people in Huế who knew Trịnh Công Sơn and I've read scores of articles and many books about him. Some criticize his fondness for alcohol. Very anti-communist Vietnamese now living abroad do not like his anti-war songs, which, they believe, weakened the will of southerners to resist communist forces; and they feel that when the war ended he cooperated too quickly and too willingly with the new communist regime. But everyone seems to agree that he was a kind person, a man who loved and respected his mother, who honored the memory of his father (who died when he was 16), and who was a good older brother to his six siblings. Here is how his youngest sibling, the singer Trịnh Vĩnh Trinh, describes her oldest brother:

> We [Trịnh Vĩnh Trinh and her siblings] often say to each other that we don't praise him just because he's our brother. Clearly he was a special person. We keep asking ourselves how there could be a person so kind-hearted. He was soft and gentle about everything, even his way of teaching his younger siblings at home. When one of us did something wrong he would reprimand us by leaving a note on our pillow. Every time we saw a note on our pillow we were afraid. His way of expressing his anger was very different from other people, always soft and gentle.[13]

Sơn's friends agree that he was gentle and tolerant. "A gentle generosity and boundless tolerance," Sơn's friend Hoàng Phủ Ngọc Tường says, "formed the ever present core of Trịnh Công Sơn's artistic personality: They were his plan for salvation, his solution to the problems of war and hatred, his

---

12. Bernard Weinraub, "A Vietnamese Guitarist Sings of Sadness of War," *New York Times*, December 31, 1967.
13. Trịnh Vĩnh Trinh, interview with Giao Hương and Dạ Ly, "Công bố hàng trăm bức thư tình của nhạc sĩ Trịnh Công Sơn (Kỳ 7): Trịnh Công Sơn—Dao Ánh qua hồi ức của Trịnh Vĩnh Trinh" [Making Public Hundreds of Trịnh Công Sơn's Love Letters (Part 7): Trịnh Công Sơn—Dao Ánh as Remembered by Trịnh Vĩnh Trinh], https://thanhnien.vn/cong-bo-hang-tram-buc-thu-tinh-cua-nhac-si-trinh-cong-son-ky-7-trinh-cong-son-dao-anh-qua-hoi-uc-cua-trinh-vinh-trinh-post297058.html (accessed Apr. 12, 2011).

way of easing the anxieties associated with the human condition."[14] Other friends, both men and women, emphasize his kindness and gentleness.

In "Like Words of Goodbye" [Như một lời chia tay]* Trịnh Công Sơn sings "How can you know each private life / To love more and with more passion." To convey something about the kind of person Trịnh Công Sơn was, I discuss three topics: friendship and drinking, unfulfilled love, and his relationships with two talented singers, Khánh Ly and Hồng Nhung, who helped make him famous and were close friends of his. I see these topics as windows into Trịnh Công Sơn's "private life," but, as he suggests in his song, no one can know a private life completely. I believe, however, that my windows will provide glimpses into his life and help us understand him better.

FRIENDS AND WHISKEY

"Glasses of whiskey / I've drunk them always in my life" Trịnh Công Sơn sings in "Fading" [Phôi pha].[15] Trịnh Công Sơn definitely drank a lot. In his many love letters to Dao Ánh he often mentions drinking with his friends. He talks about his drinking so much that in one letter, probably in response to a letter from her expressing concern, he tells her "Don't be sad because I drink too much."[16] In another letter, written when Dao Ánh was in Huế and he was still teaching in Bảo Lộc but was in Saigon visiting friends, he talks about whiskey and emptiness:

> I don't yet have enough courage to return to Blao [Bảo Lộc]. It is still stormy. I just came back from Tự Do [Freedom Street in downtown Saigon] with [Đinh] Cường and Bửu Ý. Anh Cung [Trịnh Cung] has shaved and cut his hair and is going to Thủ Đức this morning. . . . We drank whiskey from the afternoon till now. Nothing helps me find emptiness [hư vô] better. *On trouver le vide dans le whisky* [One finds emptiness in whiskey].[17]

The word Sơn uses for emptiness, *hư vô*, can refer to the Buddhist concept of emptiness [Skt. *akasa*] but here he probably means simply a

---

14. Hoàng Phủ Ngọc Tường, "Hành tinh yêu thương của Hoàng tử Bé" [The Little Prince's Planet of Love], in *Trịnh Công Sơn: Một người thơ ca một cõi đi về* [Trịnh Công Sơn: A Singer-poet, a Place for Leaving and Returning], eds. Nguyễn Trọng Tạo, Nguyễn Thụy Kha, and Đoàn Tử Huyến (Hanoi: Âm Nhạc, 2001), 26.
15. The Vietnamese word for alcoholic drinks is "*rượu*," which includes home-brewed Vietnamese rice wine [rượu đế] and European wines, cognac, scotch, and bourbon. Trịnh Công Sơn's friends report that Sơn favored scotch and cognac. I will translate "*rượu*" as "whiskey."
16. See the letter dated Jan. 1, 1965 in *Trịnh Công Sơn: Thư tình gửi một người* [Trịnh Công Sơn: Love Letters for Someone] (HCMC: Trẻ, 2011), 125.
17. Ibid., 83, letter dated November 16, 1964.

deep sadness. One reason he is sad when he writes this letter is that his friend, the painter Trịnh Cung, has been drafted and is going to officer training school in Thủ Đức on the outskirts of Saigon. A little more than two weeks later, he visits his brother Hà who has also been drafted and is at the same training school. After returning to Bảo Lộc after this visit he writes another letter to Dao Ánh and tells her that he was again depressed and again saw life turning into emptiness, and again got drunk to forget it all. "Forgetting," he tells Dao Ánh, "is necessary at this time."[18] Sơn is depressed because he worries about his friend, but also because he fears he himself will soon be drafted, a concern he expresses to Dao Ánh in several letters.[19]

Whiskey certainly was a very important part of his life, a fact he makes clear in "Playing Games" [*Trò chơi*],* an essay Sơn wrote in the late 1990s when he had stopped drinking for health reasons. "There are a thousand and one games," Sơn says in this essay, "but for me the dearest and most splendid games are love, life, and whiskey." These three games, he says,

> . . . have chosen me and I have accepted them like the first and last choice of a fate that is neither colorful nor gloomy. . . .These games sometimes liberate me, help me rise up from dark and hellish holes of decline; and sometimes they press me deeply into suffering."[20]

In this essay Sơn bids good-bye to whiskey and in doing so makes clear how important it was to him and how difficult it will be for him to live without it. "Good-bye," he says, "to those glasses of warm whiskey in the morning, noontime, afternoon and night. My life is now free of games. A white colorless life. Playing the game of life without color forces me to find myself, to search for a face that does not look like the one in the past."[21]

Sơn's relationship to whiskey was complicated. Clearly for Sơn drinking and friendship were closely intertwined. When he was a young man in Huế, most of his close friends—Hoàng Phủ Ngọc Tường, Bửu Ý, Ngô Kha, and Đinh Cường—were drinkers. After 1975 he befriended and drank with artists who had supported the revolution. Two famous

---

18. Ibid., 95. Date of letter: December 3, 1964.
19. See, for example, the letters dated Mar. 21, 1965 (p. 179); Mar. 28, 1965 (p. 181); and Apr. 13, 1965 (p. 186).
20. Trịnh Công Sơn, "Trò Chơi" [Playing Games]. I do not know where this article first appeared. To my knowledge it has not been reprinted in any journal or book. It was written sometime in the late 1990s when Sơn's health was declining. Certainly it was written after 1995 when he visited a Martell cognac distillery in France, a trip Sơn mentions in "Playing Games." See Appendix F for a translation.
21. Ibid.

northerners, the composer Văn Cao and the writer Nguyễn Tuân, would stop by Sơn's house to visit and drink when they traveled to Hồ Chí Minh City. The poet Nguyễn Duy from Thanh Hóa, a former soldier in the North Vietnamese Army, and the soldier and writer Nguyễn Quang Sáng, a southerner from An Giang Province in the South, were also drinking buddies of Sơn's.[22] Typically in photos of these meetings Sơn and his friends have glasses in their hands and bottles of whiskey lie open on a nearby table. Sam Thuong reports that Sơn liked scotch—Cutty Sark, Chivas Regal, and Johnny Walker.[23] He also liked cognac.

Appreciating fine wine or other alcoholic drink has a long history in China and Vietnam. A short chapter in Hoàng Phủ Ngọc Tường's book about Trịnh Công Sơn is titled "A Whiskey Drinker" [Người uống rượu]. In it he quotes these lines from a poem by the Tang poet Li Bai "Sober men of olden days and sages are forgotten / And only the great drinkers [ẩm gia] are famous for all time." Trịnh Công Sơn, Hoàng Phủ Ngọc Tường says, was an "authentic drinker," an "ẩm gia đích thực."[24] Hoàng Phủ Ngọc Tường's comment links Sơn to ancient Chinese and Vietnamese scholars, officials, and poets who were connoisseurs of fine wine and whiskey. Sơn's friend, the northern writer Nguyễn Tuân, was an heir to this tradition. He wrote a very well-known book, *Echoes of a Former Time* [Vang Bóng Một thời], in which he describes members of the Vietnamese leisure class in the late nineteenth and early twentieth century. He talks about their passion for Chinese tea, fine wine, poetry, and raising orchids. *Echoes of a Former Time* evokes nostalgia for the good things in life and for traditional virtues—courtesy, modesty, a broad-minded attitude toward life. Probably Sơn saw himself as continuing in this tradition of connoisseurship. Sơn's friends knew he was a connoisseur of fine alcohol and after 1975, friends from overseas who came home to visit would often bring a bottle of fine cognac for him.

---

22. Nguyễn Quang Sáng also supported the communist revolution, first as a soldier in the 1940s and later as a writer and editor and a member of the Writer's Association [Hội Nhà Văn] in Hanoi and later in Hồ Chí Minh City.

23. Sâm Thương, "Những ngày cuối của Sơn ở cõi tạm" [Sơn's Last Days in this Temporary Abode], Trịnh Công Sơn Forum, www.tcs-home.org/ban-be/vinh-biet-anh-son/SamThuong (accessed Feb. 28, 2005). This article can also be found in *Trịnh Công Sơn: Ánh nến và bạn bè* [Trịnh Công Sơn: The Light of a Candle and Friends], ed. Tạ Duy Anh, et al. (Hanoi: Hội Nhà Văn), 117-131.

24. Hoàng Phủ Ngọc Tường, "Người uống rượu" [A Whiskey Drinker], in Hoàng Phủ Ngọc Tường, *Trịnh Công Sơn và cây đàn lya của hoàng tử bé* [Trịnh Công Sơn and the Lyre of the Little Prince] (HCMC: Trẻ, 2004), 115.

The French are connoisseurs of fine wines and cognac and Sơn, a graduate of French schools, was certainly exposed to French attitudes regarding drinking. In 1995 he visited the Martell distillery in France. Martell makes fine cognac and company executives probably invited Sơn because they had heard that Sơn appreciated their cognac. Other well-known people from other countries were invited including, Hoàng Phủ Ngọc Tường says, some princes. Sơn showed Hoàng Phủ Ngọc Tường a souvenir plaque that the Martell Company gave him. It was, Hoàng Phủ Ngọc Tường says, one of his treasured possessions.[25] In "Playing Games" Sơn talks in reverent tones about how cognac is made. He describes "the high oak barrels filled with an amber liquid" and how "in each of those fragrant drops a silent and mysterious life is developing each day, even each minute, continuing in the silent darkness a process that has been going on for hundreds of years."[26]

In "A Whiskey Drinker" Hoàng Phủ Ngọc Tường says that once when the subject of "new music" [Nhạc mới] came up, he told Sơn that there was no reason for Sơn to change. "You have a world [with your songs]. If you change you won't be Trịnh Công Sơn and that world won't survive." Sơn laughed and then quoted the line from Li Bai's poem that Hoàng Phủ Ngọc Tường cites in his article: "Only the great drinkers [ẩm gia] are famous for all time." Then he added: "I suspect that all I'll leave behind is one word: 'drunk.'"[27] Trịnh Công Sơn was joking, of course. But his joke makes one wonder whether Trịnh Công Sơn was a "problem drinker," or an alcoholic. This is difficult to determine. Hoàng Phủ Ngọc Tường mentions that Sơn would keep a bottle under the table and sip from it occasionally.[28] In his article "In the Middle of Saigon—Drinking Whiskey and Remembering Nguyễn Tuân and Văn Cao," first published in 1999, Sơn says that he had a private room that he used to drink alcohol, write music, and paint, a comment that suggests drinking was one of his three favorite pastimes.[29] Friends and admirers of the singer-composer mention his drinking. In his dharma talks about Trịnh Công Sơn, which I discuss in ChapterTwenty-Four, Thích Nhất Hạnh says that one day after Sơn drank three bottles

25. Hoàng Phủ Ngọc Tường, "Người uống rượu," 119.
26. Trịnh Công Sơn, "Trò Chơi".
27. Hoàng Phủ Ngọc Tường, "Người uống rượu," 119.
28. Ibid., 116.
29. Trịnh Công Sơn, "Giữa Sài gòn uống rượu—nhớ Nguyễn Tuân và Văn Cao" [In the Middle of Saigon Drinking Whiskey—Remembering Nguyễn Tuân và Văn Cao] in Trịnh Công Sơn: Tôi là ai, là ai . . . [TCS: Who Am I, Am I . . .], eds. Nguyễn Minh Nhựt et al. (HCMC: Trẻ, 2011), 171.

of some unspecified alcohol, his sister Trịnh Vĩnh Trinh asked one of Sơn's friends to help her get him to drink less. But he couldn't help her, Thích Nhất Hạnh says, because the friend was also a drinker.[30]

No doubt some of his friends and certainly his family worried about his drinking, but accepted it, in part, no doubt, because they realized that drinking had become an important part of his social and artistic life. Sơn, in his article about remembering Nguyễn Tuân and Văn Cao, says this about drinking: "Every day in one's life, when you've lifted up a glass of whisky, you have to drink it. Maybe you drink it because the whisky tastes good, or because the glass is beautiful, but first of all you drink it because of whom you are drinking with. But, in a deeper sense, you drink it to share with yourself the sweetness and bitterness of life [*ngọt bùi đắng cay*]."[31] Trịnh Công Sơn, of course, did not share that sweetness and bitterness of life only with himself; through his songs he shared these aspects of life with countless others. It seems that drinking was, for Sơn, in some ways a metaphor for life. In it, as in life, there was sweetness—the companionship of friends, for example—but in it too was sadness. "All of Sơn's songs are sad," Hoàng Phủ Ngọc Tường (somewhat cryptically) says, "and what carries this sadness is a glass of whiskey."[32]

Sơn mentions drinking in some of his songs, and when he does he associates it with the sweetness or the bitterness of life, or some combination of the two. In "Please Give Me" [Xin cho tôi], written in 1965, Sơn asks for the bad things related to war to end: mounds of fresh graves, nights when bullets fly, etc.; and the good things of peace to return: happy mornings, the sound of bustling children, and a little pungent alcohol [*thoáng rượu cay*]. In "A Children's Folksong of Peace" [Đồng dao hòa bình], a song written in 1968 after the Paris Peace Talks had begun and peace seemed obtainable, he calls for a joyful toast to celebrate the end of hatred and war: "Today let's drink a toast with warm whiskey," he sings, "To the happiness of mothers and fathers / To the happiness of children and wives and

---

30. See Thích Nhất Hạnh, "Thông điệp thương yêu của Trịnh Công Sơn" [Trịnh Công Sơn's Message of Love], Làng Mai [Plum Village], https://langmai.org/thien-duong/nghe-phap-thoai/pt-phien-ta/pt-su-ong-lm/binh-tho-nhac/noi-vong-tay-lon-trinh-cong-son/ (accessed Sept. 3, 2015). According to this transcript, Thích Nhất Hạnh gave these talks in 2004. I base my translations of Thích Nhất Hạnh's remarks on this transcript because it appears to be a carefully considered and edited version of his talks. All the talks are available on YouTube, https://www.youtube.com/watch?v=wZp6511RJIg (accessed Apr. 7, 2016).
31. Trịnh Công Sơn, "Giữa Sài gòn uống rượu—nhớ Nguyễn Tuân và Văn Cao," 173.
32. Hoàng Phủ Ngọc Tường, "Người uống rượu," 115.

husbands." In "The Garden of the Past" [Vườn xưa] written in 1993, the speaker seems to be drinking in that "deeper sense" that Sơn talks about—drinking to share with yourself the sweetness and bitterness of life. This song is a good example of Sơn's obscurity (See Chapter Nineteen) and is difficult to translate. It is about a man who has returned to the garden of a home where a woman he loved once lived. She has married someone else and is no longer there. In earlier times, when a woman married a man from another village she often went to her husband's village by boat. The second stanza would seem to evoke that idea:

> Do not let a heart that's faithful fade
> What boat carries away a beautiful woman
> With the boats headed out on the river
> Let's give a toast with a cup of warm alcohol [rượu nồng]

The next stanza begins: "For love relationships stormy and drifting / Let's one time drink a cup of sorrow." In an article about the women featured in Trịnh Công Sơn's songs, Khuất Đẩu cites these lines to make the point that in his songs Sơn expressed "a kind and compassionate" [từ bi]" and "tolerant" [độ lượng] attitude even to women who have abandoned and perhaps betrayed men who loved them.[33]

Sơn's romanticized view of drinking probably prevented him from realizing the dangers drinking posed to his health. According to Sơn's close friend Sâm Thương, who was with Sơn in his final days, cirrhosis of the liver was one of the diseases—along with diabetes, kidney failure, pneumonia, and problems with the digestive tract—that led to his death.[34] After 1975, Cutty Sark scotch and Martell cognac were hard to find. Food was rationed and rice was scarce. When out of rice, families had to eat a cereal grain called *bo bo* provided by socialist countries, which was hard to digest.[35] Unable to get good whiskey, Sơn and his friends sometimes drank *rượu đế*, home-brewed rice wine, and this could have contributed to his health problems. When glutinous rice was scarce, Đinh Cường says, sellers added an insecticide to kill the bacteria that made it cloudy.[36] Immediately after the fall of the Saigon regime, Sơn's family

---

33. Khuất Đẩu, "Người nữ trong nhạc Trịnh Công Sơn" [Women in the Music of Trịnh Công Sơn], in *Trịnh Công Sơn: Ánh nến và bạn bè* [Trịnh Công Sơn: The Light of a Candle and Friends], ed. Tạ Duy Anh, et al. (Hanoi: Hội Nhà Văn), 63-64.
34. Sâm Thương, "Những ngày cuối của Sơn ở cõi tạm."
35. John C. Schafer, Interview with Lê Thị Phương Dung, 2007, Huế.
36. Đinh Cường, "Gửi Sơn, Những đoàn ghi rời của người bạn ở xa" [For Sơn, Scattered Notes from a Friend Far Away], in *Trịnh Công Sơn: Cuộc đời, âm nhạc, thơ, hội họa, suy*

stayed in Saigon but Sơn returned to live in Huế in the family apartment on Nguyễn Trường Tộ Street. This was where Sơn drank the rice wine, along with other writers and artists—the painters Đinh Cường and Bửu Chỉ, the poet Lữ Quỳnh, and an art critic named Thái Bá Vân. "Oh, those times of drinking this poisonous, harmful rice wine," Đinh Cường says, "clustered together, talking and laughing, drawing portraits of friends and putting them all over the wall."[37]

After 1975, the new government attempted to use mass mobilization and collective effort, approaches which had helped them win the war, to increase agricultural production and avoid food shortages. Party members and government officials were expected to participate in "productive labor for self-sufficiency" [lao động sản xuất tự túc]. After the Association for Literature and Art [Hội Văn Nghệ] in Huế decided Trịnh Công Sơn's contributions outweighed his offenses, he became a member of the Association and so was required to participate in work projects. Some Vietnamese in the overseas Vietnamese communities claimed that Sơn had to go to a reeducation camp, some said he had been sent to a New Economic Zone, but both Đinh Cường and Nguyễn Đắc Xuân say that was not the case.[38] He was required only to participate in "productive labor" projects organized by the officials of the newly formed province of Bình Trị Thiên—a consolidation of the old provinces Quảng Bình, Quảng Trị, and Thừa Thiên. If participating in these work projects was reeducation, Nguyễn Đắc Xuân says, then the entire Party Committee and all government officials in Thừa Thiên Province and the city of Huế could be said to have had to go to a reeducation camp.[39]

The poet Vĩnh Nguyên describes doing productive labor and drinking rice wine with Trịnh Công Sơn after 1975. They worked in various locations in Quảng Bình, Quảng Trị, and Thừa Thiên.[40] For one project, he says, they traveled to a work site near Đồng Hới in Quảng Bình on bicycles, a distance of 105 miles. When they arrived at Đồng Hới Trịnh Công Sơn was tired and despondent. "How great it would be," he told Vĩnh Nguyên,

tưởng [Trịnh Công Sơn: Life, Music, Poetry, Painting, Reflections], eds. Trịnh Cung and Nguyễn Quốc Thái (HCMC: Văn Nghệ, 2001), 60.

37. Ibid.
38. Ibid., 59; Nguyễn Đắc Xuân, Trịnh Công Sơn: Có một thời như thế [Trịnh Công Sơn: There Was Such a Time] (HCMC: Văn Học, 2003), 107-108.
39. Nguyễn Đắc Xuân, Trịnh Công Sơn: Có một thời như thế, 106-108.
40. Vĩnh Nguyên, "Hồi ức về Trịnh Công Sơn" [A Recollection of Trịnh Công Sơn], in Trịnh Công Sơn Cát Bụi Lộng Lẫy [Trịnh Công Sơn: Resplendent Sand and Dust], eds. Trần Thùy Mai et al. (Huế: Thuận Hóa, 2001), 29-38.

"to have some rice wine." Stores were closed but Vĩnh Nguyên found some rice wine somewhere. When he saw the rice wine, he says, "Sơn was as happy as if he had met a girlfriend! His eyes sparkled strangely. That night Sơn grasped his guitar and told stories and sang a lot of songs."[41]

Sơn was also a heavy smoker. As I mentioned in my introduction, both my wife and I were in Hanoi when Sơn died on April 1st, 2001 in the Chợ Rẫy Hospital in Hồ Chí Minh City. (I was teaching English at the Vietnam National University.) A few days later, my wife and I attended an "Evening of Music to Remember Trịnh Công Sơn" at the old French opera house, now called the "Nhà hát lớn" (Great Singing House). Before the singing began, photos of Sơn appeared on a large screen and in almost every photo Sơn was smoking or holding a cigarette.[42] In short, Sơn, like many singers and performers around the world, did not have a healthy lifestyle. He died at the relatively young age of 62. Before Sơn's health began to decline, he would meet with Sâm Thương and other friends, often at the Givral Café on Tự Do Street in Hồ Chí Minh City. At these gatherings, Sâm Thương says, Sơn used to drink Cutty Sark, Chivas Regal, or Johnny Walker Black label, but in the late 1990s he drank only tea and so his friends switched to tea also.[43] In a song composed in 1966 called "Distant Love" [Tình xa], Sơn sings "Each lover abandons me / Like small rivers" but, he says, at least I still have friends and whiskey:

> *What's there to see this morning*
> *Never mind I still have friends*
> *A drop of whiskey will always be bitter and warm* [chua cay]

Note that Trịnh Công Sơn sees whiskey as bitter [*chua*] and warm [*cay*]. In this sense it is like life, a mixture of sadness and happiness. In his essay "Playing Games"* he develops this point further:

> Almost everyone has heard of the *tao* of tea. It is one of the high-class leisure games of old sages. The game of drinking alcohol is closer to real life. It is a friend, a lover. It is happiness and also sadness. It is words of comfort. It is a source of inspiration. It is sharing and returning a favor. To sum up, for people who know how to drink whiskey as an elegant game it is everything. Drink alcohol to love

---

41. Ibid., 31.
42. Đinh Cường visited Sơn in August, 2000, and says that at that time Sơn had given up smoking, but still drank a little whiskey. See Đinh Cường, "Gửi Sơn, Những đoàn ghi rời của người bạn ở xa," 68.
43. Sâm Thương, "Những ngày cuối của Sơn ở cõi tạm."

life and people more and to love even the ghost-like, firefly-like flickering of betrayal in love.[44]

Toward the end of his life Sơn had to reduce his drinking, but his friends were still there. In "Playing Games" Sơn says of all the games in life that one can play, the game of friendship causes the least grief. "It can be either a lot of fun or only a little fun," he says, "but it doesn't cause heartrending pain."[45]

UNFINISHED LOVE

When I lived in Vietnam, male friends would recite a short poem by Trần Tế Xương (1870-1907). Everyone seemed to know it. Here's an English translation:

> Tea, whiskey, and women
> These three idle past0imes are always troubling me
> Should I give up this one or that one
> I could maybe give up whiskey along with tea[46]

Toward the end of his life Trịnh Công Sơn gave up whiskey, or at least drank much less, and drank tea. In the previous chapter we saw that Sơn did not give up women; they rather gave up on him, in some cases, it seems, because their parents wanted their daughters to marry someone with a university degree and better career prospects than a man like Sơn, a long-haired musician who was hiding out, trying to avoid being drafted into the army. According to his friends, that is why his relationships with Phương Thảo and Dao Ánh never led to marriage.

These break-ups, however, occurred when Sơn was a young man. People wonder why, as he sings in "Distant Love" [Tình xa], each lover abandoned him "like small rivers." Though rarely expressed clearly—at least in print—they wonder if perhaps he was gay or impotent. In an interview, Bùi Văn Phú asked Hoàng Xuân Sơn, a friend who knew Sơn when he sang with Khánh Ly at the Literature Café in Saigon in the early 1960s, about these rumors. "You are a friend of the musician," Bùi Văn Phú said. "What do you think about his emotions and his psychological

---

44. Trịnh Công Sơn, "Trò Chơi."
45. Ibid.
46. Here is the Vietnamese: *Một trà, một rượu, một đàn bà / Ba thứ lăng nhăng nó quấy ta / Chừa được thứ nào hay thứ ấy / Có chăng chừa rượu với chừa trà*

and physical condition?" "I think they were normal," Hoàng Xuân Sơn answered.[47]

Bửu Ý was a very close friend of Sơn's. He told Phan Quỳnh Anh in an interview that he and Sơn would ride together in one rickshaw, sleep in the same bed, and talk all day about literature, music and painting. "Rumors spread that they were gay," Bửi Ý said.[48] In Vietnam, however, it is not uncommon to see two men holding hands as they walk along the street, or for two male friends to sleep together in the same bed. According to Bửu Ý, shyness may have hindered Sơn's relationships with women. He says that Sơn was shy and nervous in the presence of beautiful women: "When Trịnh Công Sơn was in a forest of flowers [beautiful women]," Bửu Ý says, "people would start to think it would be 'like a wolf among sheep,' but it wasn't like that. He was always gentle and well-mannered, but also uncomfortable, and even would stammer and stutter."[49] Sơn clearly felt more comfortable in the presence of his friends. "Fortunately in life there is romantic love [tình yêu] and also the love of friends," he once said. "Love of friends usually has a truer face than romantic love. There is also ungratefulness in the love of friends but not a lot. I feel that the love of friends is more valuable than romantic love because it can revive you from an unconscious state and revive a life one thought could not be recreated."[50]

It is important to remember, too, that prior to 1975 Trịnh Công Sơn was worried about being drafted. Bửu Ý was in the same situation. Bửu Ý eventually did get married, but not until he was almost fifty. "Both of us," he said in his interview with Phan Quỳnh Anh, "had people we loved. But we were both hiding out to avoid being drafted and so marriage was

---

47. Hoàng Xuân Sơn, interview by Bùi Văn Phú, "Hoàng Xuân Sơn: nơi tôi sinh sống thì hát nhạc Trịnh cũng nên dè dặt" [Hoàng Xuân Sơn: Where I Live [Montreal, Canada] You Should Be Careful about Singing Trịnh Music], http://damau.org/archives/19866 (accessed Jan. 15, 2012).
48. Bửu Ý, interview by Phan Quỳnh Anh, "Bửu Ý: Trầm ngâm ngồi nhớ bạn hiền, vợ yêu" [Thoughtfully Sitting and Remembering a Kind Friend, a Beloved Wife], https://cand. com.vn/Nhan-vat/Buu-Y-Tram-ngam-ngoi-nho-ban-hien-vo-yeu-i314686/ (accessed Jan. 9, 2014). The interview took place in 2011.
49. Bửu Ý, Trịnh Công Sơn: Một nhạc sĩ thiên tài [Trịnh Công Sơn: A Genius of a Musician] (HCMC: Trẻ, 2003), 65.
50. Different writers quote this comment without indicating its original source. For example, Đinh Cường quotes it in "Tình Bạn, Hồi Sinh Cơn Hồn Mê" [Love of Friends, Restoring Consciousness], Trịnh Công Sơn, https://web.archive.org/web/20150429054848/ http://www.trinh-cong-son.com/dcuong.html (accessed Mar. 26, 2015). Đinh Cường wrote this article on April 16, 2001, fifteen days after Trịnh Công Sơn died.

not appropriate for us." He adds, too, that "we thought living together was interesting, beautiful."[51]

Trịnh Công Sơn may have preferred the love of friends, but beautiful women were a part of his life and his songs. His friend Trịnh Cung says that all the women that Sơn truly loved were beautiful and all of them inspired him to write songs about them.[52] I have already discussed his early loves—Phương Thảo, Ngô Thị Bích Diễm, and Diễm's sister Ngô Vũ Dáo—but Sơn continued to fall for beautiful women later in his life. Bửu Ý says that in 1983 Sơn, who was living in Hồ Chí Minh City, wrote him a letter inviting him to come to his wedding to C. N. N.—Bửu Ý provides only the initials of her name—but, for some reason Bửu Ý doesn't explain, this wedding never took place.[53] Both Bửu Ý and Trịnh Cung also mention that in 1990-1991 Sơn fell for V.A., a beauty queen.[54] (Bửu Ý provides only these initials; Trịnh Cung provides no name or initials, referring to her as "a girl who was once a Vietnamese beauty queen.") This relationship ended around the time his mother died. This was, Trịnh Cung says, a very sad time for Trịnh Công Sơn. He suggests that in his song "Don't Despair, I Tell Myself [Tôi ơi đừng tuyệt vọng],* written in 1992, Sơn is expressing the deep sadness he felt at this time.[55] Don't despair, Sơn sings in this song. Accept the fact that "Autumn leaves fall in the midst of winter" and "golden sunlight fades like a private life."

Before *Trịnh Công Sơn: Love Letters for Someone* was published in 2011, the general public was not aware of his love for Dao Ánh, and the exact nature of his relationships to the female singers who sang his songs remains a mystery to most people. Regarding Dao Ánh, his sister Trịnh Vĩnh Trinh says her brother took some of the blame for his break-up with her. Her brother knew, she says, he could not provide anyone with "a complete married life."[56] Whoever is to blame, it clearly was a momentous event in his life. It seems possible that he never married because Dao Ánh was the love of his life, a love he deemed to be irreplaceable. One cannot

---

51. Bửu Ý, interview by Phan Quỳnh Anh, "Bửu Ý Trầm ngâm ngồi nhớ bạn hiền, vợ yêu."
52. Trịnh Cung, "Sơn Trong Trí Nhớ Nhỏ Nhoi Của Tôi" [Sơn in My Limited Memory], in *Trịnh Công Sơn: Cuộc đời, âm nhạc, thơ, hội họa, suy tưởng* [Trịnh Công Sơn: Life, Music, Poetry, Painting, Reflections], eds. Trịnh Cung and Nguyễn Quốc Thái (HCMC: Văn Nghệ, 2001), 42.
53. Bửu Ý, *Trịnh Công Sơn: Một nhạc sĩ thiên tài*, 32-33.
54. Bửu Ý, *Trịnh Công Sơn: Một nhạc sĩ thiên tài*, 34; and Trịnh Cung, "Sơn Trong Trí Nhớ Nhỏ Nhoi Của Tôi," 42-43.
55. Ibid.
56. Trịnh Vĩnh Trinh, Interview with Giao Hương and Dạ Ly.

read his letters to her, in which he pours out his heart for her, and not be impressed with the depth of his love. She clearly inspired many of his sad love songs. "A pretty girl named D. A. [Dao Ánh]," Trịnh Cung says, "was the longest lasting inspiration among the number of people that passed through Sơn's life."[57] Dao Ánh has lived most of her adult life in the United States. She married and had two children and is separated from her husband. She returned to Vietnam for a visit in 1993 and met Sơn. After this meeting Sơn wrote "Repaying a Debt" [Xin trả nợ người], a song which has the preface "Written for the Sunflower," Sơn's nickname for Dao Ánh. In this song Sơn faults Dao Ánh for betraying him, which suggests that twenty years later some pain remains. But he also suggests that all is forgiven. Here are the closing lines:

> *You betrayed me when you were young and naïve*
> *Young and naïve you left and forgot me*
> *Young and naïve you completely forgot my love*
> *After so many years suddenly this miracle*
> *The debt is paid, painful love is forgotten*
> *Twenty years have passed but it's still like before*
> *The debt this time we share in our lives*

In 2001, when it was clear to everyone that Sơn was dying, Dao Ánh returned to Vietnam and spent his last month with him. "Every morning each week," Đinh Cường says, "she would sit next to his wheelchair looking at Sơn until it grew dark and she returned home."[58]

Being unlucky in love was, in one way, a good thing: It inspired Trịnh Công Sơn to write some sad and beautiful songs about unfulfilled love. At that time, Nguyễn Đắc Xuân says, "It was really rare to see a young vagabond, his studies uncompleted, who had a lover from a well-to-do family. However, in my generation, it was precisely that separation which produced many silent, one-way loves and when they occurred in the lives of outstanding musicians like Trịnh Công Sơn these loves became immortal."[59] Trịnh Cung says that perhaps we should thank the women who spurned Sơn because they "created unending inspiration that enabled Trịnh Công Sơn to contribute some immortal love songs."[60] Sad songs of unfulfilled love exist in all cultures. It seems, however, that

---

57. Trịnh Cung, "Sơn Trong Trí Nhớ Nhỏ Nhoi Của Tôi," 42.
58. Đinh Cường, "Gửi Sơn, Những đoàn ghi rời của người bạn ở xa," 59.
59. Nguyễn Đắc Xuân, *Trịnh Công Sơn: Có một thời như thế*, 65-66.
60. Trịnh Cung, "Sơn Trong Trí Nhớ Nhỏ Nhoi Của Tôi," 42.

most of Vietnam's "immortal" love songs are sad songs of unfulfilled love. The so-called "pre-war" songs that were popular when Sơn first began composing were mostly about unfulfilled love (See Chapter Eighteen and Appendix G). Vietnamese audiences appear to have a built-in expectation that a love song will be sad, perhaps in part because the most famous poem in the Vietnamese language, *The Tale of Kieu*, is a story of unfulfilled love (See Chapter Fifteen). In the so-called New Poetry of the 1930s and early 1940s, which I discuss in Chapters Sixteen and Seventeen, there are many poems about the pain of unfulfilled love. "To love is to die a little in the heart," Xuân Diệu says in "Love" [Yêu].[61] Another contributor to this movement, Hồ Dzếnh, pushes this idea of unfulfilled love to an extreme. In a poem called "Hesitation" [Ngập Ngừng] he argues that unfulfilled love is superior to fulfilled love because "love loses its flavor once fulfilled." A pre-war song called "Love is Only Beautiful" [Tình Chỉ Đẹp], which may have been inspired by Hồ Dzếnh's poem, contains these lines: "Love is only beautiful when it is unfulfilled / Life ceases to be happy when promises are completed."[62] When I taught at the University of Huế in the late 1960s and early 1970s, students loved to recite these lines from Xuân Diệu's poem and from the song "Love is Only Beautiful."

Given his audience's love for sad love songs, one can say that Trịnh Công Sơn was lucky to have had some real experiences of unfulfilled love to draw on when he wrote his songs. Sơn's challenge was to breathe new life into this tradition, and one way he did this was by using certain "defamiliarizing" devices that I describe in Chapter 19. These devices no doubt helped make his songs appear fresh and new.

It seems likely, too, that Sơn's depictions of the heart wrenching sadness of unfulfilled love moved listeners because they were based on personal experience, and therefore came across as sincere. It is interesting to compare Trịnh Công Sơn's situation with that of Phạm Duy, an older and very talented composer whose songs were still popular in the 1960s. Phạm Duy did not suffer from unfulfilled love, at least not in the sexual sense. In his memoirs he does not give the precise number of his lovers,

---

61. Compare these lines from Trịnh Công Sơn's song "Tình sầu" [Sad Love]: "Love is like death / a long illness."
62. One website identifies Thủy Tiên as the composer of "Love is Only Beautiful"; another lists Vinh Sử. See Karaoke Lyrics Database, http://lyric.tkaraoke.com/17571/tinh_chi_dep.html and Nhạc Của Túi, http://www.nhaccuatui.com/bai-hat/tinh-chi-dep-huong-lan.dw5rpHG3t6.html (Both accessed July 9, 2017).

but he describes relationships with twenty-five women.[63] Phạm Duy married in 1949, but this did not slow him down. He had numerous adulterous affairs, including one with a 17-year-old French cellist and one with Lan Nam, an actress who was married to his wife' younger brother. It is interesting, however, that some of his most popular love songs were inspired by a non-carnal love affair with Alice, a young girl just entering puberty who was twenty years his junior.[64] She has an English name because her mother, Hélène Defrosse, was the daughter of a Protestant missionary from Great Britain and a Vietnamese woman. Alice inspired famous songs like "On That Day the Two of Us" [Ngày đó chúng mình] and "A Thousand Leagues Apart" [Nghìn trùng xa cách]. Phạm Duy wrote this last song to say good-bye to his beloved Alice. Phạm Duy explains that he confessed his love to Alice but received a non-committal response so, he says, "I exerted myself to avoid any carnal involvement in this relationship." The payoff for Phạm Duy that resulted from Alice's cool response and his hesitation came in the form of some very successful love songs about unfulfilled love. Songs derived from his affairs with his "carnal lovers" [người tình xác thịt], which, in his memoirs, Phạm Duy makes clear were very fulfilling—songs like "Red Summer" [Hà hồng] and "Summer Days and Months" [Ngày tháng hạ]—were less successful. Phạm Duy explains that he "had absorbed lessons in love while still a child and had been involved in love affairs that unfolded effortlessly as I grew up."[65] Trịnh Công Sơn was not so fortunate but effortless success in love may be a problem for a composer whose audience expects and loves sad songs of unrequited love. In any event, Trịnh Công Sơn, who had several experiences of unrequited love, suffered from no such handicap.

---

63. Phạm Duy's memoirs include the following volumes: Vol. I.: *Thời thơ ấu-vào đời* [Childhood and Young Adulthood] (1990); Vol. II: *Thời cách mạng-kháng chiến* [The Revolution and Resistance Periods] (1989); Vol. III: *Thời phân chia quốc-cộng* [The Period of Nationalist-Communist Division] (1991); and Vol. IV: *Thời hải ngoại* [My Sojourn Abroad] (2001). The first three volumes were published by Phạm Duy Cường Musical Productions in Midway City, CA. The last volume, to my knowledge, has not been published in print form but has been available on various websites. I found it at https://web.archive.org/web/20070525092710/http://www.saigonline.com/phamduy/2005/pdf/ (accessed 11 June 2009). All four volumes have been expertly translated into English by Eric Henry but have not yet been published. For more information on Phạm Duy and his memoirs, see John C. Schafer, "The Curious Memoirs of the Vietnamese Composer Phạm Duy," *Journal of Southeast Asian Studies* 43 (1) (Feb., 2012).
64. Alice was either 14 or 16 when he began seeing her in Saigon in 1956. Phạm Duy suggests both possibilities in his memoirs.
65. Phạm Duy, *Thời phân chia quốc-cộng* [The Period of Nationalist-Communist Division] (Midway City, CA: Phạm Duy Cường Musical Productions, 1991), 56.

Trịnh Công Sơn's good friend Sâm Thương says that Sơn "greatly valued beautiful women but that was not love. The women that Sơn loved were not real."[66] Khuất Đầu agrees with Sâm Thương: "No woman left a deep impression on his life," he says. In speaking of Ngô Vũ Bích Diễm, the inspiration for his famous song "Diễm of the Past" [Diễm xưa]*, Khuất Đầu says that Diễm "was not anyone at all. Diễm was beauty [đẹp], feminine beauty [nhan sắc]"[67]; and the woman in "Flower of Impermance" [Đóa hoa vô thường] is not a real woman but rather a representation of the ephemeral quality of life, an embodiment of a Buddhist concept; and the mothers in his anti-war songs who sing lullabies to their children while bombs fall represent the traditional Vietnamese virtues of patience and sacrifice.[68] "In Vietnamese literature," Khuất Đầu says, "there has not been an author who loved women so deeply, subtly, and generously and cherished them to the point of worship like Trịnh Công Sơn."[69]

Sâm Thương and Khuất Đầu's point is that the women in Trịnh Công Sơn's songs were not real flesh-and-blood women but idealized abstractions. I believe this is true to a certain extent, but Ngô Vũ Bích Diễm was certainly a real person. Sơn's sister Trịnh Vĩnh Trinh remembers that before Diễm left Huế to study in Saigon, she placed a large bouquet of hyacinths near the door of their home. In the bouquet was a note saying good-bye to Sơn. Later Sơn fell deeply in love with her younger sister, Dao Ánh.[70] In his essay "A Recollection" [Hồi Ức]* Sơn talks about the girl named Diễm who inspired "Diễm of the Past." He describes the "surreal" atmosphere of Huế, how the city with its camphor trees, its royal tombs, and the Perfume River blew "a pure romantic mist" into the souls of girls in Huế.[71] Cao Huy Thuần suggests that Trịnh Công Sơn was affected by that romantic mist as well. He points out that no word in "Diễm of the Past" indicates that Huế is the setting for the song. Instead of referring to Huế's famous royal tombs, Sơn speaks more generally about "old towers" [tháp cổ].[72] What makes this song about Huế, Cao Huy Thuần suggests,

---

66. Sâm Thương, "Những ngày cuối của Sơn ở cõi tạm."
67. Khuất Đầu, "Người nữ trong nhạc Trịnh Công Sơn," 61-62.
68. Ibid., 65-66.
69. Ibid., 66.
70. Trịnh Vĩnh Trinh, Interview with Giao Hương and Dạ Ly.
71. Trịnh Công Sơn, "Hồi Ức" [A Recollection]. This essay originally appeared in *Thế Giới Âm Nhạc* [Music World] (March, 1997). It can be found in *Trịnh Công Sơn, Tôi là ai, là ai...*, eds. Nguyễn Minh Nhựt et al.154–157. See Appendix E for an English translation of this essay.
72. Cao Huy Thuần, introductory remarks at a concert titled "Đêm hoài niệm Trịnh Công Sơn" [An Evening to Remember Trịnh Công Sơn], May 26, 2001. The event took place in Paris.

is the way the young woman, Diễm, is portrayed. Descriptive phrases like "your long arms, your pale eyes" and "soft steps" indicate that Diễm is not a country girl but a sophisticated young woman. Huế was the capital of the country, the home of emperors, and many people in Huế are proud of being descended from kings and queens. Cao Huy Thuần says that although he does not know how much royal blood Trịnh Công Sơn has in his veins, the images and language in his songs are "elegant, sophisticated, and cultivated" and the women portrayed in them are delicate and regal. In this sense, I agree that one could say that the women in his love songs are idealized abstractions.[73]

TRỊNH CÔNG SƠN AND KHÁNH LY AND HỒNG NHUNG

Though he never married, Trịnh Công Sơn had close friendships with women including Khánh Ly and Hồng Nhung, who both became famous singing his songs. Both women have spoken about Trịnh Công Sơn's character. Both of their careers were enhanced by their relationship with Sơn, and thus it is perhaps not surprising that they have good things to say about him. It is worth noting, however, that they, like his male friends, found Sơn to be kind and generous. Both have made clear that Sơn was a close and valued friend, not just a pathway to fame, though he was that as well. Other singers have sung his songs, but Khánh Ly and Hồng Nhung will forever be linked to Trịnh Công Sơn because they sang and continue to sing his songs so well and because they were such close friends of the composer.[74] His sister Trịnh Vĩnh Trinh is also a fine singer of his songs despite the fact that, as Sơn once said, "she has wavered between the life of a singer and an ordinary life."[75]

Because they sang together many people thought Khánh Ly and Trịnh Công Sơn were lovers, but they both have explained that they were only good friends. They had different backgrounds. Khánh Ly, whose real name is Nguyễn Thị Lệ Mai, was born in 1945 in Hanoi. She chose her stage name in 1962 when she was seventeen and about to sing in a Saigon nightclub. She derived it from two characters (Khánh Kỵ and Yêu Ly) who appear in the classic Chinese historical novel *Chronicles of the Eastern Zhou*

---

73. Ibid.
74. See Appendix I for links to videos of Khánh Ly and Hồng Nhung performing Trịnh Công Sơn's songs.
75. Trịnh Công Sơn, "Khánh Ly, Vĩnh Trinh, Hồng Nhung," in *Trịnh Công Sơn: Một người thơ ca một cõi đi về* [Trịnh Công Sơn: A Singer-poet, a Place for Leaving and Returning], eds. Nguyễn Trọng Tạo et al., 203. This is an excerpt from an article Trịnh Công Sơn wrote in 1995.

Kingdoms written by Feng Menglong in the late Ming Dynasty. Apparently this was her favorite novel.[76] She attended a Catholic elementary school in Hanoi and wanted to become a nun because she thought "the image of a nun was so beautiful."[77] She was baptized a Catholic when she was eighteen, and has been very devout all her life. Khánh Ly says that her father was a member of the anti-French resistance and died in a prison called Đầm Đùn in 1954 or 1955 after being incarcerated there for four years.[78] Đầm Đùn, however, was a communist prison and reeducation center run by the Việt Minh. I have not been able to determine what side her father was on in the First Indochina War.

Her father, Khánh Ly says, instilled in her a love of music and singing. He loved music and played the mandolin and would hold her in his arms and sing pre-war songs to her, songs like Nguyễn Văn Khánh's "Golden Afternoon" [Chiều vàng] and Đặng Thế Phong's "A Boat Without a Dock" [Con thuyền không bến].[79] Pre-war songs were still popular in the 1960s, and Trịnh Công Sơn's songs, as I explain in Chapter Eighteen, resemble them in some ways and differ from them in others.

When the Geneva Accords ended the First Indochina War in 1954, Khánh Ly and her mother, like many Catholic families in the North, moved to the South. She was nine years old. After her father died, Khánh Ly's life became harder. Her mother remarried and, she says, both her mother and stepfather disciplined her severely, though she admits that she was an "unmanageable and fearless child."[80] "I didn't have the love of my father," she says, "and didn't get along with my mother. Except for liking to sing, I didn't know what I should do."[81] Her stepfather, a policeman in Đà Lạt, was, she says, a heavy drinker. Speaking of her life in Đà Lạt in the late 1950s and early 1960s, she says that "there was nothing remarkable

76. See T. Van, "Vietnamese Singer Khánh Ly to perform in Hanoi," VietNamNet, Apr. 10, 2014, https://web.archive.org/web/20140902061713/http://english.vietnamnet.vn/fms/art-entertainment/99543/veteran-singer-khanh-ly-to-perform-in-hanoi.html (accessed May 11, 2014).
77. Khánh Ly, Interview with Bùi Văn Phú, "Khánh Ly nói về đời mình, về Trịnh Công Sơn" [Khánh Ly Talks about Her Own Life and about Trịnh Công Sơn], *Văn* [Literature] 92 (2004), 82.
78. Khánh Ly, "Huế, Tình Yêu Tôi" [Huế, My Love], *Tiếng Sông Hương* [Voice of the Perfume River] (1988), 16.
79. Khánh Ly, *Đằng Sau Những Nụ Cười* [Behind the Smiles] (HCMC: Văn Học, 2015), 15-16.
80. Ibid., 15.
81. Khánh Ly, "Huế, Tình Yêu Tôi," 16.

about it except every night my stepfather was drunk and my mother after complaining about him would scold her children."[82]

Khánh Ly was from Hanoi and a devout Catholic and Trịnh Công Sơn was from Huế and a Buddhist, but their backgrounds were similar in some ways. Both lost their fathers when they were young. Sơn's father died in 1955 when he crashed his Vespa motorcycle, and Khánh Ly's father died in prison around the same time. Partly because of the war and their losing their fathers when they were young, both Trịnh Công Sơn and Khánh Ly lived relatively free of parental supervision.

Sơn and Khánh Ly first met when she was around eighteen years old and singing at a nightclub in Đà Lạt, and Sơn was teaching in Bảo Lộc, a town about 70 miles south of Đà Lạt. Khánh Ly had been in Đà Lạt since 1962. She already had two children at this time, a fact that few fans in the early 1960s were aware of. She does not discuss her first husband in her autobiographies, but in her interview with Bùi Văn Phú she says that her first marriage was "a spur of the moment decision, a mistake."[83] Khánh Ly's first husband, whose given name was Quang, was the manager of a radio station in Đà Lạt.[84] In his book about Trịnh Công Sơn's time in Bảo Lộc, Nguyễn Thanh Ty, one of Sơn's roommates when they both taught elementary school there, retells a story about Khánh Ly and her husband that he says Sơn told him when he returned to Bảo Lộc after a night in Đà Lạt. I retell it here because it reveals the nature of Khánh Ly's relationship with her first husband and with Sơn. Sơn prefaces his story by explaining to Nguyễn Thanh Ty that Khánh Ly's lifestyle was "broad-minded like that of Westerners" and that her "intimate gestures worried him." But, Sơn says, she told him "Don't worry, Sơn, my husband and I live very freely, we're very broad-minded. He understands me. There's no problem."[85]

Apparently, however, there was a problem one night in Đà Lạt when Khánh Ly and Sơn decided to go dancing after performing together in a nightclub. As they left the club Khánh Ly said to her husband, "Tonight Sơn and I are going to go have some fun. If we're late, don't wait for us. You can go home and watch the children." Later, however, while they were

---

82. Khánh Ly, Chapter 1, *Chuyện kể sau 40 năm* [Stories Told after 40 Years], 4 Phuong.Net, https://web.archive.org/web/20170924021848/http://4phuong.net/ebook/12182147/chuyen-ke-sau-40-nam.html (accessed Aug. 8, 2017).

83. Khánh Ly, Interview with Bùi Văn Phú, "Khánh Ly nói về đời mình, về Trịnh Công Sơn," 82.

84. I have not been able to determine his family name.

85. Nguyễn Thanh Ty, *Về một quãng đời Trịnh Công Sơn* [On a Period of Trịnh Công Sơn's Life] (Place of publication and publisher not listed: 2001), 95.

dancing, someone told Sơn that Khánh Ly's husband had a gun and was looking for him. He escaped out the backdoor of the dance hall and stayed at a friend's house in Đà Lạt. Early the next morning he returned to Bảo Lộc.[86]

Khánh Ly, it seems, is not eager to talk about her first husband. In *Stories Told after 40 Years* [Chuyện kể sau 40 năm] she says that she and her two children and her mother and stepfather lived with her paternal grandparents in their home in Đà Lạt. She speaks proudly of making enough as a dancer and singer at a dance club called "Night Club" to pay someone to take care of her children while she was working. She explains that in the 1960s, dancing [*khiêu vũ*] was an art and that the dancers and customers treated each other courteously. The dancers, she says, did not sleep with their customers.[87]

In 1964 Sơn asked Khánh Ly to come to Saigon to sing with him. She declined but joined him later in 1967. Their performances together at the Literature Café [Quán Văn] on the grounds of the University of Saigon helped to make them both famous. Hoàng Xuân Sơn, who helped to establish this Café, has explained that it was established by some university students involved in social action projects.[88] They contributed the supplies and money to build it so it had a "pure artistic character." "To speak plainly," he says, "it was a little '*bụi đời*,' [dust of life]," an expression that suggests it resembled a homeless encampment.[89] Khánh Ly would sing barefoot and so came to be called "the barefoot queen" [*nữ hoàng chân đất*]. Trịnh Công Sơn was dodging the draft at this time and they both were camping out near the Café. Khánh Ly has described how she and Trịnh Công Sơn were living at the time. "We shared one plate of rice," she says, "smoked one cigarette, shared one cup of coffee. We slept together on the ground near the Café on crumpled up dirty newspapers. Friendship, brother-sister love sprouted there."[90]

---

86. Ibid.
87. Khánh Ly, Chapter 1, *Chuyện kể sau 40 năm*.
88. The Quán Văn became the "unofficial headquarters" of an organization called A Program to Develop Student Activities [Chương trình Phát triển sinh hoạt Thanh niên học đường] which was administered by the Ministry of Education of the Republic of Vietnam. See *Trịnh Công Sơn: Thư tình gửi một người*, 262, note 103.
89. Hoàng Xuân Sơn, Interview with Bùi Văn Phú, "Hoàng Xuân Sơn: nơi tôi sinh sống thì hát nhạc Trịnh cũng nên dè dặt."
90. Khánh Ly, "Bên Đời Hiu Quạnh" [Next to a Desolate Life], in Nguyễn Trọng Tạo et al., eds., *Trịnh Công Sơn: Một người thơ ca một cõi đi về* [Trịnh Công Sơn: A Singer-poet, a Place for Leaving and Returning], 57.

In the late 1980s an article by Khánh Ly appeared, in which she apparently suggested that her relationship with Sơn was deeper than friendship. I have not been able to find that article, but Sơn discussed it when interviewed in 1989. He praises the article but says that Khánh Ly's "heartfelt lines about him were for someone else, someone who has died. Khánh Ly and I were just friends. We loved each other as friends." He ends the interview in this way: "We had a time when we shared each bite of food, each drink. That experience gave birth to a love not like other love. We were like two male friends. . . . Who has the courage to deny a happy period during which Khánh Ly and I benefited from emotions as humane as any person can enjoy."[91] It seems that Khánh Ly was influenced by Sơn's philosophy of life. In an article about Trịnh Công Sơn and Huế, she says she once asked Sơn what one needed in life. Sơn's answer, which he had already suggested in a song written in 1971,[92] was "a good heart." "To do what with?" she asked. "To let the wind blow it away," he replied. Khánh Ly says she tried to live by that philosophy.[93] In her autobiography *Behind the Smiles* she describes the "lesson of love" that Sơn left behind for future generations, a lesson about the importance of avoiding hate. Sơn teaches us, she says, that "pretty flowers and trees full of sweet fruit cannot sprout from a hateful heart. Hate only makes people smaller and uglier and life darker. It makes the soul poorer and inferior."[94]

Khánh Ly's personal life has not been easy. She calls her first marriage a mistake and explained in 2004 that she and her husband, Nguyễn Hoàng Đoan, whom she married in 1975, have each lived a life of several spouses and many lovers.[95] She left Saigon by boat on April 29, 1975, the day before Saigon fell. She and her two-year-old child went with three brothers and a sister. Her parents and two sisters remained in Vietnam. Eventually Khánh Ly settled in Cerritos, California, a suburb of Los Angeles. She has four children, two boys and two girls. She says that she and Nguyễn Hoàng Đoan, who had been a journalist in Vietnam, lived happily in Cerritos. They were, she says, "an extended family [*đại gia đình*] and we

---

91. Trịnh Công Sơn, interview by Lữ Quỳnh, titled "Tôi Đã Tận Hưởng Những Tình Cảm Nhân Loại" [I Have Benefited from Humane Emotions], in *Trịnh Công Sơn: Một người thơ ca một cõi đi về*, eds. Nguyễn Trọng Tạo et al., 215.
92. "Let the Wind Blow It Away" [Để gió cuốn đi].
93. Khánh Ly, "Huế, Tình Yêu Tôi," 16.
94. Khánh Ly, *Đằng Sau Những Nụ Cười*, 58.
95. Khánh Ly, interview by Bùi Văn Phú, 84.

did not pay attention to whose children were his and whose were mine."[96] Nguyễn Hoàng Đoan died in 2015.

Before Trịnh Công Sơn died, Khánh Ly visited him in Montreal where he had gone to visit relatives. She also visited him twice in Hồ Chí Minh City. On both visits to Vietnam she spent most of her time with Sơn.[97] In May, 2014, she returned to her native Hanoi to sing his songs at a concert called "Khánh Ly Live Concert." She was seventy years old and had not been in Hanoi since she was nine. Before going to Hanoi for the concert, however, she visited Sơn's grave in Thủ Đức near Hồ Chí Minh City where she left some yellow roses and poured a little of Sơn's favorite whiskey on his grave. She chose yellow roses, not red, she explained to a reporter, because red roses, the flowers of love, would not be appropriate given the "special feeling" that they had for each other; and because, she added, "I love yellow flowers the most."[98]

Many other singers, including Sơn's sister, Trịnh Vĩnh Trinh, have sung his songs publicly and released popular albums of his songs, but after 1975 the most successful has been Hồng Nhung. She and Sơn were also very close friends. Sơn credits her with making his songs "new again." "Some like it [her way of singing], some don't," he wrote in 1995. "Of course, I like it because it is a new way of performing that fits the rhythm of the present—a new romanticism. It has helped me have a place in the present and not just be a guy one remembers from the past."[99] Others agree with the composer. A reporter praises Hồng Nhung for "singing Trịnh music in a modern way, without the sad mood associated with Khánh Ly."[100]

Hồng Nhung was, like Khánh Ly, born in the north. She grew up in Hanoi in an artistic and intellectual family. Her paternal grandfather was an artist and her maternal grandfather was a linguist. Her father was a translator. Her parents separated before she was two years old and although she lived with her father and her paternal grandparents, she

---

96. Ibid.
97. Ibid., 86.
98. Hương Bùi, "Khánh Ly lặng lẽ viếng mộ Trịnh Công Sơn" [Khánh Ly Quietly visits Trịnh Công Sơn's Grave], 24h.com.vn, May 2, 2014, https://web.archive.org/web/20140507031225/http://us.24h.com.vn:80/ca-nhac-mtv/khanh-ly-lang-le-vieng-mo-trinh-cong-son-c73a627448.html (accessed May 26, 2014).
99. Trịnh Công Sơn, "Khánh Ly, Vĩnh Trinh, Hồng Nhung," 203.
100. No author listed, "Trịnh Công Sơn – Hồng Nhung: Những ngày 'không ngày tháng'" [Trịnh Công Sơn – Hồng Nhung: Days without Days or Months], Người Đưa Tin [Person Who Delivers News], http://www.ngkuoiduatin.vn/trinh-cong-son-hong-nhung-ngung-ngay-khong https://ngoisao.vn/am-nhac/tin-tuc/trinh-cong-son-hong-nhung-nhung-ngay-khong-ngay-thang-66725.htm (accessed Apr. 13, 2012).

continued to see her mother on weekends. When she was twenty years old her father married again. From all reports, she gets along well with her stepmother, who is only ten years older than she is. They are reported to have a sisterly relationship. She drives Hồng Nhung to her events and helps her concentrate on her singing career.[101]

Hồng Nhung was a very good student before she became a singer. In 1983 she was one of the best students in Hanoi and received a certificate from Premier Phạm Văn Đồng for her achievement. In 1991 she moved to Hồ Chí Minh City with her father and stepmother primarily to advance her singing career, but she continued her studies there. English was her major but she was required to study French as a second language as well. Trịnh Công Sơn, she says, helped her with her French lessons.[102] Eventually she graduated from the Hồ Chí Minh City University of Social Sciences and Humanities.

She met Trịnh Công Sơn the first time at the home of a pop music composer named Thanh Tùng, and they became close friends. She had won singing contests and received awards in the North, but her career really began to take off after she moved to Hồ Chí Minh City and began singing the songs of Trịnh Công Sơn. People struggle for the right word to describe their relationship. Once, when asked about it, Sơn smiled and said: "Hồng Nhung is a person very close to me whom I don't know how to address."[103] They spent a lot of time together. "Sometimes we would be with his friends and play the guitar and sing," Hồng Nhung says. "And sometimes we would go to art exhibits and sometimes the two of us would sit in his house, look out at the gravel yard and talk about this and that."[104] And sometimes, she says, Trịnh Công Sơn would teach her how to sing his songs. "How can a person so small sing so powerfully?" she says he once asked her. Toward the end of the week she and Sơn would go to sing at the musicians' café [*quán nhạc sĩ*].[105]

101. "Ca sĩ Hồng Nhung và câu chuyện về người mẹ kế đặc biệt" [The Singer Hồng Nhung and Stories about Her Special Stepmother], Báo Mới, http://www.baomoi.com/ca-si-hong-nhung-va-cau-chuyen-ve-nguoi-me-ke-dac-biet/c/6819031.epi (accessed Aug. 22, 2016).

102. Hồng Nhung, "Xuất xứ 'Bống bồng ơi'" [How "Bống bồng ơi" Came to Be], Trịnh Công Sơn – Articles, http://www.comp.nus.edu.sg/-nguyenvu/Artists/TC_Son/TCS_articles/About_TCS/TCSon (accessed Feb. 7, 2005).

103. "Trịnh Công Sơn – Hồng Nhung: Những ngày 'không ngày tháng.'"

104. Hồng Nhung, "Hồng Nhung & Trịnh Công Sơn những ngày đầu quen nhau" [Hoàng Nhung & Trịnh Công Sơn—First Days Together], Trịnh Công Sơn—Articles, http://wwwcomp.nus.edu.sg/--nguyenvu/artists/TC_Son/TCS_articles/About_TCS/TCSon (accessed Feb. 7, 2005).

105. "Trịnh Công Sơn – Hồng Nhung: Những ngày 'không ngày tháng.'"

One writer says that "they were friends but more than friends; they were student and teacher but more than student and teacher."[106] "There was love," Hồng Nhung herself once said of her relationship to Sơn, "but the kind of love it was I will keep to myself."[107] Hồng Nhung credits Trịnh Công Sơn with teaching her about life as well as music. "He showed me," she says, "that happiness is living truthfully with one's emotions. It is loving and caring for beautiful things. And he showed me that the most beautiful things in life are people and their need for each other in their lives."[108]

The cover of a video recording of a 2006 Hồng Nhung performance named for the Trịnh Công Sơn song Như cánh vạc bay *[Like the Wing of a Flying Heron].*

When Trịnh Công Sơn said Hồng Nhung "made his songs new again" he was probably suggesting that she sang his old songs in a new and fresh way. But he also wrote new songs inspired by his relationship with her, the most famous being the following three songs which all have "*bống*" in the title: "Bống bồng ơi" [Calling Bống] (1993), "Bống không là bống" [Bống Is not Bống] (1995), and "Thuở bống là người" [When Bống Was a Person] (1998). "Bống," which in Vietnamese means "goby" (a very small fish), was also Hồng Nhung's nickname within her family. "Calling Bống"

---

106. Ibid.
107. Ibid. (The writer quotes Hồng Nhung.)
108. Hồng Nhung, "Hồng Nhung & Trịnh Công Sơn những ngày đầu quen nhau."

appeared in a collection titled *K7 Trịnh Công Sơn và Hồng Nhung* which was released in 1993. In a preface to "Calling Bống," Trịnh Công Sơn provides this information:

> *Bống* is the name of a small fish. In a Vietnamese legend a fairy magically transforms a *bống* into a beautiful girl. Bống is also the informal and intimate name that Hồng Nhung's family members called her at home. This is a love song that gently borrows the golden afternoon sunlight to speak of a nostalgic memory.[109]

Hồng Nhung has explained how she first received this song from Trịnh Công Sơn.[110] She had gone to Hanoi without telling him and he didn't know where she was until he met a friend of hers. The next day a close friend of Sơn's brought a bunch of red roses to her home along with a folded-up paper. When she opened it up she saw Sơn's handwritten words and music for "Calling Bống." Hồng Nhung says Sơn was upset that she didn't tell him she was leaving. His mood is reflected in the opening lines: "Golden sunshine where did you go so quick / So quick golden sunshine golden sunshine." Note Sơn's inclusion, in the second stanza, of Hồng Nhung's name, which is also the name of a rose.

> *One day your mother held you light as a thread of silk*
> *Rocking* bống bồng bông
> *Rocking softly the* hồng nhung *flower*

The untranslated words in the second line have these meanings: *bống* means "goby fish," *bồng* means "to hold a child," and *bông* can mean "flower," "cotton," or "to kid or jest." But in this song these words—at least the last two—are just rhyming[111] nonsense words which are there for the sound more than the meaning, functioning something like "diddle diddle" in the English nursery rhyme about the cat and the fiddle. The entire song evokes Vietnamese folk tales and folk lullabies. All Vietnamese know a folktale called "Tấm Cám" in which the goby fish plays a prominent role. Tấm and Cám are young girls who have the same father but different mothers. First Tấm's mother died, and then her father, and so Tấm lives with Cám's mother, definitely an evil stepmother. One day when Tấm is sad and forlorn the Buddha appears and tells her that if she puts a goby

---

109. "Thư mục ca khúc Trịnh Công Sơn" [Trịnh Công Sơn Song Catalogue], TCS Forum, https://www.tcs-home.org/ban-be/articles/thu-muc-ca-khuc-trinh-cong-son/(accessed Aug. 15, 2017).
110. See Hồng Nhung, "Xuất Xứ 'Bống bồng ơi.'"
111. Each of these three words differ only in tone. The word "*bống*" has a rising tone, "*bồng*" a falling tone, and "*bông*" a level tone.

fish in the well and feeds him, her troubles will cease. To call the goby fish at feeding time Tấm should, the Buddha tells her, chant the following:

Bống bống bang bang
Come up and eat our home's gold and silver rice
Don't eat other people's stale rice and bad porridge

Words similar to the rhyming words Tấm uses to call the goby fish appear in folk lullabies, usually composed in traditional six-eight verse (*lục bát*), that mothers sing to their children. Here is a stanza from one lullaby:

Oh oh bống bống bông bông
When you grow up try hard to learn to be a person
Learning is to study ethics, study life
Don't loiter about or people will laugh at you

When Hồng Nhung sings "Calling Bống" it sounds a little like a lullaby, a little like a love song, a little like a song a father or mother would sing to a grown-up daughter leaving home for the first time, a way to say "Not so long ago I cradled you in my arms and now, so quick, you're gone."[112] In her comments on this song Hồng Nhung suggests how it has encouraged other people to love her as her parents do: "In a natural and simple way," she says, "he took the name my mother called me, a common word for the goby fish, and put it into music and since then not only close family members but everyone can affectionately call me Bống. Isn't that enough—to live one's whole life and have people love you in this way?"[113]

In 2011 Hồng Nhung married an American businessman named Kevin Gilmore. On April 8, 2012, when she was forty-two, she gave birth to twins, a boy and a girl. Their official names are Aiden and Lea but their names in the family are Tôm (shrimp) and Tép (small shrimp). In naming their children after water creatures, the singer, whom many fans call "Cô Bống" (Miss Goby Fish), and her husband kept alive the tradition in Hồng Nhung's family of naming children after water creatures. In June, 2018, Hồng Nhung announced that she and her husband were separating. Six months after they were publicly divorced, Kevin married a woman from Myanmar.

---

112. It is easy to find YouTube film clips of Hồng Nhung singing this song. In one clip, titled "Bống bống ơi (Trịnh Công Sơn) - Hồng Nhung," Trịnh Công Sơn introduces Hồng Nhung. See https://www.youtube.com/watch?v=Xn4BNlkFAFM (accessed Aug. 24, 2016).
113. Hồng Nhung, "Xuất xứ 'Bống bống' ơi."

In searching to understand the character of Trịnh Công Sơn I have discussed his unfulfilled love life, his love of drinking with his male friends, and his close friendships with two women who sang his songs. What do these windows into his life tell us? Probably in all cultures people, especially friends of the deceased, are reluctant to speak ill of the dead. For the above portrait I rely heavily on reports by friends written after Trịnh Công Sơn's death. His friends may exaggerate his virtues and minimize his faults, but even if we allow for some exaggeration these reports suggest that Trịnh Công Sơn was a gentle and kind man and also, during much of his life, a very lonely and sad man. He yearned, as he sings in "Sad Sacred Words" [Lời buồn thánh],* for someone with angel hands to pierce that loneliness, but he never found that person.

9

PERSONAS &
PERSONALITIES:
BOB DYLAN

Most books about Dylan quote people, both friends and acquaintances, who say that although he could be funny and entertaining,
he could also be mean-spirited and insensitive in social interactions. No
one suggests that gentle tolerance and boundless generosity—qualities
Vietnamese ascribe to Trịnh Công Sơn—were core parts of Dylan's personality. But before talking about his personality, we must consider his
persona. Dylan was more of an actor than Trịnh Công Sơn was. Sơn pretty
much played himself in his songs. He appears in them as a soft-spoken
and kind man who was saddened by both the war and unrequited love.
Dylan, however, played different parts. The speakers in his true love songs
are different from those in his anti-love songs. In a 1985 interview with
Cameron Crowe, he attacked unnamed writers who said his song "You're a
Big Girl Now" was about his wife. "I mean," Dylan told Crowe, "it couldn't
be about anybody else but my wife, right? Stupid and misleading jerks,
these interpreters sometimes are . . . . I don't write confessional songs.
Emotions got nothing to do with it. It only seems so, like it seems that
Lawrence Olivier is Hamlet."[1] Dylan may protest too much. "You're a
Big Girl Now" was released on Dylan's 1975 album *Blood on the Tracks*, an

---

1. Bob Dylan, interview with Cameron Crowe. This interview accompanied Dylan's
boxed set *Biograph*, released in 1985. Chris Willman discusses Cameron Crowe's interview in "Dylan's Bloody-Best Album: 40 Facts About the 40-Year Old 'Blood on
the Tracks,'" *Rolling Stone* (Jan. 21, 2015), https://www.rollingstone.com/music/
news/dylans-bloody-best-album-40-facts-about-the-40-year-old-blood-on-the-
tracks-20150121 (accessed June 29, 2018).

album that most friends and critics, and his son Jakob, say was about his failing marriage to Sara Lowndes.[2] As I argued in the previous chapter, speakers in lyric poems and songs may exist in "some remove," to use M. H. Abrams' phrase, from the author, but there is a connection.[3] Here is how Paul Williams describes that "remove" in "You're a Big Girl Now": "Let's just say, then, that it's a song sung by an imaginary person whose present relationship with the person he's singing to is not altogether unlike the performer's relationship with his own estranged spouse."[4]

It is difficult to separate the persona Dylan strove to create from the "authentic Dylan." When Dylan arrived in Greenwich Village in the early 1960s he created a fictitious past, telling people he was abandoned by his parents at an early age and went on the road for a while with a traveling circus. He wanted to be like and sing like Woody Guthrie. Like Lawrence Olivier on the stage and in film, Dylan played different parts in his live performances and in his songs, but rarely that of a kind and gentle man.

Throughout most of his career Dylan's typical on-stage persona has been cold and distant, but occasionally he could be angry and antagonist as he was, for example, in his 1966 world tour with The Hawks. British fans loved his folk songs and resented the fact that he had abandoned his acoustic guitar and "gone electric." At a show at the Royal Albert Hall in London on May 27, 1966, Dylan's argument with his audience became intense with fans shouting "Judas!" at Dylan and the Hawks. William McKeen reports that Dylan reacted by telling The Hawks they should play louder.[5] "During the 1974 tour with The Band," William McKeen says, "he rarely spoke. He might mutter a couple of dozen words, but rarely did he say anything by way of greeting or patter between songs: That was not the Dylan way."[6] During his so-called "Alimony Tour" in 1978, after his divorce from Sara, however, he became gregarious, bantering with the crowd between songs;[7] and on his "Gospel Tour" (1979-1980) after

2. See Chris Willman, "Dylan's Bloody-Best Album,"; see also Howard Sounes, *Down the Highway: The Life of Bob Dylan* (New York: Grove Press, 2001), 283-284; Clinton Heylin, *Bob Dylan: Behind the Shades* (New York: Summit Books, 1991), 240-241.
3. M. H. Abrams, *A Glossary of Literary Terms* (Fort Worth, TX: Harcourt Brace Jovanovic, 1985), 136.
4. Paul Williams, *Bob Dylan, Performing Artist: The Middle Years, 1974-1986* (New York: Omnibus Press, 2004), 31.
5. William McKeen, *Bob Dylan: A Bio-Bibliography* (Westport, CT: Greenwood Press, 1993), 267, 292.
6. Ibid., 267.
7. Ibid., 275.

becoming a born-again Christian he gave long sermons between songs.[8] These sermons and his refusal to sing his old songs, only Christian songs, annoyed hecklers who would shout "Rock 'n' roll!" or "Everyone must get stoned!"

Dylan's gregariousness on his Alimony and Gospel tours, however, was a departure from his usual practice. On his "Never Ending Tour"[9] that he has been on for over fifty years, he has rarely interacted with the audience. Vietnamese who attended Dylan's concert in Hồ Chí Minh City in 2011 can find some comfort in knowing that he treated them as he treats most of his audiences. They got the "Dylan way" like audiences everywhere. Tim Russell, who was at the concert in Hồ Chí Minh City in 2011, provides this running account of Dylan's onstage demeanor: "He may be here in body but he could have stayed home and phoned it in, and we'd scarcely have been any the wiser. He barely looks at the audience, standing behind keyboards and facing the band."[10] This was the concert I described in my Introduction, which featured performances of Trịnh Công Sơn's songs to mark the tenth anniversary of the singer-songwriter's death. When my son and I attended a "Bob Dylan and His Band" concert in San Francisco on October 17, 2012, we experienced the Dylan way firsthand. We knew where he was as he moved from keyboard to guitar because he wore a white wide-brimmed hat to distinguish himself from other band members, and we heard him sing, but he never said a word to the crowd.

When a tour is never-ending and the performer is old, he or she may find it difficult to be lively. Sheer fatigue may be one reason for Dylan's cold and distant on-stage persona. Dylan has been touring for most of his adult life. A concert on April 19, 2019, in Innsbruck, Austria, was his 3,000th show. He planned to continue touring in 2020 but, according to one report, stopped because of the COVID-19 pandemic.[11] Instead,

---

8. See Clinton Heylin, ed., *Saved! The Gospel Speeches of Bob Dylan* (Madras and New York: Hanuman Books, 1990).
9. The phrase "Never Ending Tour" sometimes refers to Dylan's long, still continuing, tour schedule, which is the meaning I intend here, but it also is used to refer to specific tours. William McKeen uses it to refer to Dylan's tours in 1988, 1989, 1990, 1991, and 1992. See William McKeen, *Bob Dylan: A Bio-Bibliography*, 280-284.
10. Tim Russell, "Sub Par Homesick Blues: Bob Dylan Live in Vietnam," http://thequietus.com/articles/06062-bob-dylan-live-in-vietnam-review (accessed Apr. 13, 2011).
11. David Bauder, "Ending 18-month hiatus, Bob Dylan returns to the (online) stage," *The Times of Israel*, July 19, 2021, https://www.timesofisrael.com/after-2-year-hiatus-bob-dylan-returns-to-the-online-stage (accessed Sept., 21, 2021).

he produced a video that fans could pay $25 to watch online. According to David Bauder, "It was less a concert than a stylized black-and-white film, with the 80-year-old singer fronting a four-piece band in a juke joint before audience members who smoked a lot and paid little attention to him."[12]

Why has he kept going? In 2018 Bill Wyman, a music critic (not to be confused with Bill Wyman, the bass guitarist for the Rolling Stones), suggested that Dylan and other stars had continued to tour because ticket prices went up. In the 1970s and 1980s, he says, lots of big bands did not tour regularly, but they began to when they realized they could make four, five, or six million dollars a night.[13] Dylan doesn't like the name "Never-Ending Tour." "Critics should know," he told Douglas Brinkley in a 2009 interview, "that there's no such thing as forever. You never heard about Oral Roberts and Bill Graham being on some Never-Ending Preacher tour."[14] Other aging superstars in their seventies and eighties have continued to tour. Joan Baez began a "Fare Thee Well" tour in 2018 when she was seventy-seven. When it was about to end she extended it into 2019 with shows in France, Germany, Italy, and Spain. Willie Nelson, who is eighty-eight years old and still on the road, suggests why he keeps touring in his song "On the Road Again":

> On the road again
> I just can't wait to get on the road again
> The life I love is makin' music with my friends
> And I can't wait to get on the road again

What makes Dylan different is that unlike other aging performers he doesn't seem to be enjoying himself.

Greil Marcus provides a capsule summary of the persona Dylan created for himself. It caught, he says, "Charlie Chaplin, James Dean, and Lenny Bruce in talk and gesture, Woody Guthrie and the French symbolists in writing, and perhaps most deeply such nearly forgotten 1920s stylists as mountain balladeer Dock Boggs and New Orleans blues singer Rabbit

---

12. Ibid.
13. Bill Wyman, "10 Things You Didn't Know about Bob Dylan's Never-Ending Tour." *Vulture*, Dec. 19, 2018, https://www.vulture.com/2018/12/10-things-to-know-about-bob-dylans-never-ending-tour.html (accessed Aug. 8, 2019).
14. Bob Dylan, interview with Douglas Brinkley, "Bob Dylan's Late-Era, Old-Style American Individualism," *Rolling Stone*, May 14, 2019. I read it online. See https://www.rollingstone.com/music/music-news/bob-dylans-late-era-old-style-american-individ-ualism-90298/ (accessed Nov. 23, 2021).

Brown in voice."[15] It does seem likely that Dylan modeled his voice—his nasal twang, his gravelly sound—after singers like Dock Boggs and Rabbit Brown, and also Clarence Ashley and Blind Willie Johnson. Songs sung by these four singers and by many others are on Harry Smith's *Anthology of American Folk Music*, a collection of six long playing records that were made from 1927 to 1932 and were released in 1952. As I explain in Chapter Twenty-One, "Dylan's Musical Roots," Dylan loved these records so much that he stole them from a friend named Jan Pankake, a student at Minnesota University.[16]

Perhaps not just his voice but his entire persona should be seen as an imitation of these singers. Elizabeth Brake describes Dylan's "outlaw persona." "Over and over," she says, "Dylan casts himself as an outlaw, as the negation of whatever society expects or requires, as judge and satirist of the status quo." "The outlaw," she says, "rejects possessive love, a fixed abode, regular work, social niceties, and the authority of law."[17] We see this outlaw spirit in Dylan's anti-love songs "It Ain't Me Babe," "Don't Think Twice It's All Right," and "To Ramona."[18] In this last song, the speaker tells Ramona that her sorrow is the result of letting society "hype" and "type" her—push her into some predefined category. In constructing his outlaw persona, Dylan very likely drew on the unconventional lives of traditional singers and the lawless characters in their songs. One senses he admired their independence, their refusal to let society define them or possessive lovers tame them. Dylan expresses his admiration for the outlaw life in his liner notes for his album *World Gone Wrong*, a collection of traditional songs released in 1993. Here is how he describes Stack A Lee, a character in the traditional song "Stack A Lee," one of the songs on this album. Stack A Lee ends up in jail after killing Billy for stealing his Stetson hat.

---

15. Greil Marcus, *The Old Weird America: The World of Bob Dylan's Basement Tapes* (New York: Picador, 2011), 19.
16. Howard Sounes, *Down the Highway*, 57-60.
17. Elizabeth Brake, "'To Live Outside the Law, You Must Be Honest': Freedom in Dylan's Lyrics," in *Bob Dylan and Philosophy*, eds., Peter Vernezze and Carl J. Porter (Chicago, IL: Open Court, 2006), 79.
18. Daniel Wolff argues that "Like a Rolling Stone" also promotes the outlaw spirit. According to Wolff the question in the first line of the chorus—"How does it feel?"—is directed not just at the woman described in the song but at us also; and the answer to this question is, "It feels good. It feels great," to shake off previous entanglements, to be "invisible" with "no secrets to conceal." See Daniel Wolff, *Grown-Up Anger* (New York: Harper, 2017), 246-248.

Stack's in a cell, no wall phone. He's not some egotistical degraded existentialist dionysian idiot. Neither does he represent any alternative lifestyle scam . . . . Billy didn't have an insurance plan, didn't get airsick, yet his ghost is more real and genuine than all the dead souls on the boob tube.[19]

If you listen to some Dylan songs and then to songs from Harry Smith's anthology—songs like Clarence Ashley's "The House Carpenter" you will notice similarities in voice. Listen to Blind Willy Johnson's "John the Revelator" and you will hear the gravelly, raspy voice which Dylan uses in many of his songs, a voice that Anthony Scaduto says one "folkie" described as "the sound of a prairie dog caught on a barbed wire fence."[20] Scaduto himself says Dylan's voice early in his career had a nasal quality that made him "sound like a man from a chain gang whose nose had been broken by a guard's rifle butt."[21] He points out, however, that on some early albums, Dylan employs a more natural voice. (He mentions the albums *John Wesley Harding* and *Nashville Skyline*.)[22]

In 2015 at the Grammy's annual charity awards dinner, Dylan was given an award by MusiCares, a charity organization that aids musicians in need. After former President Jimmy Carter introduced him, Dylan gave a speech that lasted over thirty minutes.[23] In this speech he complains about critics who say he sounds like a frog and asks why they don't say the same thing about Tom Waits. Actually, critics do say the same thing about Tom Waits, a younger singer-songwriter who admired Bob Dylan. Gary Graff and Daniel Durchholz say Waits' voice sounds "as if it was soaked in a vat of bourbon, left hanging in the smokehouse for a few months, and then taken outside and run over with a car."[24] Critics no doubt enjoy coming up with these colorful descriptions. Personally I do not find his nasal twang pleasing, but I agree with the film critic Jon Landau who argues that Dylan's "singing style" is his "most intensely personal quality."

---

19. Bob Dylan, liner notes for Dylan's album *World Gone Wrong*.
20. Anthony Scaduto, *Bob Dylan* (London: Helter Skelter Publishing, 1996), 259.
21. Ibid., 275.
22. Ibid., 248, 259.
23. I quote from a transcript of the event prepared by Randall L. Roberts. "Grammys 2015: Transcript of Bob Dylan's MusiCares Person of Year Speech," *LA Times* (Feb. 7, 2015) http://www.latimes.com/entertainment/music/posts/la-et-ms-grammys-2015-transcript-of-bob-dylans-musicares-person-of-year-speech-20150207-story.html (accessed Sept. 9, 2018).
24. Gary Graff and Daniel Durchholz, *MusicHound Rock: The Essential Album Guide.* (London: Omnibus Press, 1996), ISBN 0-8256-7256-2. See also Pop Matters, "The Fifteen Best Tom Waits Songs," https://www.popmatters.com/15-best-tom-waits-songs-2495787321.html (accessed Mar. 16, 2019).

Dylan's songs, he says, "are ultimately a mixed bag, with images chasing images straight into oblivion that not even Dylan could understand. But even at their most extreme, Bob's voice is there to organize and direct them, to make them speak directly even when they only want to speak abstractly."[25] Daniel Wolff makes a similar point when he describes Dylan's performance in concerts in 1964. The lyrics of the songs he sang at these concerts, he says, were "long, loaded with words, and often hard to follow, never mind understand," but by that point, early in his career, "his singing and playing, his ability to inhabit a song," had, Wolff says, "gotten to the point where he can bring listeners on board almost no matter how difficult the ride."[26]

The power of Dylan's voice and his talent as a performer are revealed in two films, both of which include footage from live performances. The first, *Trouble No More*, directed by Jennifer Lebeau, was released in 2017 and is included in a deluxe edition of the album *Bob Dylan: Trouble No More— The Bootleg Series Vol. 13, 1979-81*. The second film, *Rolling Thunder Revue: A Bob Dylan Story*, directed by Martin Scorsese, was released in 2019. I discuss Lebeau's film in Chapter Twenty-Six but mention it here because it includes some powerful footage of Dylan and gospel singers performing songs on his Gospel Tour in 1980. Dylan's passion is on full display in this film. "He puts his message across as fervently as a tent-revivalist," says John DeFore, who reviewed the film *Trouble No More* for *The Guardian*.[27]

Martin Scorsese's film *Rolling Thunder Revue* is about the most legendary of all Dylan's tours. There were two Rolling Thunder Revue tours, one in 1975 and one in 1976.[28] Scorsese's film contains footage from the first tour, which began in Plymouth, Massachusetts at the end of October 1975 and concluded with two performances, one at the Clinton Correctional Facility in New Jersey on December 7 (where the

25. Jon Landau, *It's Too Late to Stop Now: A Rock and Roll Journal* (San Francisco, CA: Straight Arrow Books, 1972), 61.
26. Daniel Wolff, *Grown-up Anger*, 176.
27. John Defore, "'Trouble No More': Film Review," *Hollywood Reporter*, Oct. 4, 2017. https://www.hollywoodreporter.com/review/trouble-no-more-1045663 (accessed July 2, 2019).
28. One could say there were three Rolling Thunder Revue tours, because after the concert in Madison Square Garden on December 8, 1975, the band rested for the holidays and then resumed in Jan. 1976, with shows in Los Angeles, Houston, and Austin. William McKeen refers to this post-holiday part of the tour as "The Rolling Thunder Revue, Part I (Continued)." The Rolling Thunder Review Part II began in Lakeland, Florida on April 18, 1976, and ended in Salt Lake City. See William McKeen, *Bob Dylan: A Bio-Bibliography*, 273-274.

prize fighter Rubin "Hurricane" Carter was incarcerated), and another at Madison Square Garden on December 8. This final show of his first Rolling Thunder Revue tour was a benefit for Carter who was in prison for killing three people in a tavern in New Jersey in 1966. In 1974, two key witnesses, Alfred Bello and Arthur Dexter Bradley, recanted their testimony and in 1975 Carter published his autobiography, *The Sixteenth Round*. Dylan was so moved by the book that he visited Carter in prison and later wrote his song "Hurricane" in which he argues that the authorities blamed Carter "for somethin' that he never done." Scorsese includes Dylan's performance of "Hurricane" at the Clinton Correctional Facility in his movie and it is one of the highlights of the documentary. Dylan's song helped generate pressure for Carter's release, which finally occurred in 1985 after Carter had spent 19 years in prison. In November 1985, Judge H. Lee Sarokin of the Federal District Court in Newark concluded that previous convictions of Carter were based on "an appeal to racism rather than reason, concealment rather than disclosure."[29]

When I watched Scorsese's film I was surprised by the intensity of the Dylan performances that are included in it. Instead of the cold and distant onstage persona he displays on his Never-Ending Tour we see a passionate and completely engaged singer pouring his heart out in his songs. After watching this film I was curious about what reviewers would say about it. They had a similar reaction. Alan Light says Dylan's performances of "Isis," "A Hard Rain's A-Gonna Fall," and "The Lonesome Death of Hattie Carroll" were "searing and riveting." They reveal, he says, "how energized Dylan was, how he had recommitted to his material at a time when music was in a phase of safe, corporate bloat."[30] Andy Greene talks about the "fiery passion" that Dylan displays in songs included in the movie.[31] Joel Selvin observes that in Scorsese's film Dylan, "who can be quite indifferent in the performance of his own songs, is captured singing with uncommon passion and a jazz soloist's sense of nuance."[32]

---

29. Selwyn Raab, "Reversal Is Won by Rubin Carter in Murder Case," *New York Times*, Nov. 8, 1985.

30. Alan Light, "'In 'Rolling Thunder Revue,' Scorsese Tries to Capture a Wild Dylan Tour," *New York Times*, June 12, 2019.

31. Andy Greene, "The Inside Story of Bob Dylan and Martin Scorsese's New 'Rolling Thunder Revue' Doc," *Rolling Stone*, June 10, 2019, https://www.rollingstone.com/movies/movie-features/the-inside-story-of-bob-dylan-martin-scorseses-rolling-thunder-revue-doc-844268/ (accessed July 11, 2019).

32. Joel Selvin, "Scorsese is 'Rolling' with Dylan," *San Francisco Chronicle*, June 14, 2019, Section E, 1, 7.

Rarely has Dylan been as animated as he was in performances on his Gospel Tour and the first part of his Rolling Thunder Revue tour. The animated and passionate singing on his Gospel Tour that we see in the film *Trouble No More* appears to be a result of Dylan having had the born-again experience that I describe in Chapter Twenty Six. In songs like "Solid Rock" and "Saved" Dylan is overcome with joy and gratitude. "I've been saved," Dylan sings in "Saved": "And I'm so glad / Yes, I'm so glad / I'm so glad, so glad." Probably, too, Dylan was influenced by the joy and enthusiasm of the talented back-up singers who performed with him.[33]

His animation on the first part of The Rolling Thunder Revue tour seems to be the result of two things: First, the tour was relaxing and fun because Dylan was touring with old friends from the early 1960s who, it seems, were also enjoying themselves. "In many ways, the rest of my life has been downhill since then," T Bone Burnett told Alan Light in a phone interview after Scorsese's film was released.[34] Second, during the tour Dylan was filming a movie called *Renaldo and Clara* and had hired Sam Shepard to be the screenwriter.

I need to explain these two possible causes for Dylan's uncharacteristically impassioned performances on this tour. In January 1975, Dylan's album *Blood on the Tracks* was released and highly praised by critics. This is the album that critics and Dylan's son Jakob agree was about the breakup of Dylan's marriage to Sara. In 1975 Dylan and his wife were attempting a reconciliation but living separately. Sara was in Malibu and Dylan, after a trip to France, went to New York where he reconnected with old friends from the 1960s, including Ramblin' Jack Elliot and Bobby Neuwirth, who were performing at a nightclub called the Bitter End where Dylan began to make guest appearances.[35] Dylan later invited both these old friends to join The Rolling Thunder Revue, during which they played some songs solo, some with Dylan.

While in Greenwich Village Dylan also met Rob Stoner, a younger musician who, Paul Williams says, became the "de facto leader" of the band for both Dylan's album *Desire* and his Rolling Thunder Review Tour.[36] He also reconnected with Jacques Levy, a theater director and lyricist

33. Clyde King, Mona Lisa Young, Mary Elizabeth Bridges, Gwen Evans, and Regina Mc-Crary.
34. T Bone Burnett, in Alan Light, "In 'Rolling Thunder Revue' Scorsese Tries to Capture a Wild Dylan Tour."
35. Howard Sounes, *Down the Highway: The Life of Bob Dylan*, 286.
36. Paul Williams, *Bob Dylan, Performing Artist: The Middle Years, 1974-1986*, 41.

whom Dylan knew but not well; and he discovered a talented violin player named Scarlet Rivera while he was driving along 13th Street in New York.[37] Dylan was bursting with new material at this time and the people just mentioned—especially Bob Neuwirth, Jacques Levy, and Scarlet Rivera— helped him develop it into the songs that appeared on his album *Desire,* which was released in January 1976. Apparently Levy's and Rivera's con- tributions were substantial. Paul Williams says that Dylan and Levy "spent several weeks in mid-July [1975] holed up in East Hampton, Long Island writing a dozen songs" for the album.[38] Howard Sounes says that "Rivera's violin helped define the sound of the record."[39] Songs that later appeared on this album were hits on the Rolling Thunder Revue tour—songs like "Isis," "One More Cup of Coffee (Valley Below)," and "Hurricane." Both Levy and Rivera were on the Rolling Thunder Revue tour.

Reuniting with old friends and traveling with them apparently energized Dylan and led him to abandon his typical cold and distant on-stage persona and replace it with one that was more lively and friendly and more dramatic—dramatic in the literal sense of the word. Dylan had decided to make a film about the tour—not a documentary but a fictional drama called *Renaldo and Clara* with tour participants playing different characters. Dylan played Renaldo, his wife Sara (who joined the tour) played a prostitute named Clara, Scarlet Rivera played the Queen of Swords, Bobby Neuwirth was "the Masked Tortilla," etc. Dylan hired Sam Shepard to write the script and two camera crews to do the filming. According to Howard Sounes, however, no script was ever written. Participants just improvised.[40] When the film, a four-hour-long bizarre combination of documentary footage and improvised scenes, was released in 1978, it was dismissed by critics as an unwatchable mess. In an article in Rolling Stone Andy Greene, who talked to "a source close to the Dylan Camp," explains that the negatives of the film, which were stored at Iron Mountain, a company that protects—or at least is supposed to protect— data and assets, were lost but a "work print," a copy used to edit a film, was found. This work print, which had been used to make the movie, was in bad shape. Scorsese and his team restored it as best they could.[41]

---

37. Howard Sounes, *Down the Highway: The Life of Bob Dylan*, 288-289.
38. Paul Williams, *Bob Dylan, Performing Artist: The Middle Years, 1974-1986*, 41.
39. Howard Sounes, *Down the Highway: The Life of Bob Dylan*, 289.
40. Ibid., 293.
41. Andy Greene, "The Inside Story of Bob Dylan and Martin Scorsese's New 'Rolling Thunder Revue' Doc," *Rolling Stone*, June 10, 2019, https://www.rollingstone.com/mov-

All singers adopt an onstage persona and so are, in a sense, actors. The singers and band members on the Rolling Thunder Revue tour, however, knew that they were being filmed for a movie. Wearing make-up and dressed in colorful costumes they played colorful characters in improvised scenes during the tour. Dylan performed in white face for some songs. The pressure on everyone to be dramatic must have been intense. Dylan, the leading actor in this drama, had to have felt this pressure himself. He must have realized that his usual cold and distant onstage persona would not work on this tour, so he abandoned it and the result was some impassioned performances of his songs.

BOB DYLAN'S PERSONALITY

> I believe in his genius, he is an extraordinary writer but I don't think of him as an honorable person. He doesn't necessarily do the right thing. But where is it written that this must be so in order to do great work in the world?
>
> Suze Rotolo[42]

Dylan's early loves and love songs, which I have described in previous chapters, provide clues to his personality. In this chapter, to understand him better, I will first discuss his relationship to two singer-songwriters, Dave Van Ronk and Phil Ochs, who both knew Dylan when he came to Greenwich Village in 1961. Comparing Trịnh Công Sơn to Bob Dylan provides an international and cross-cultural perspective; comparing Dylan to two American singer-songwriters helps us understand the artistic and political choices that Dylan made early in his career. I will end this chapter by summarizing some key events and relationships in his life after he had become famous, including what is perhaps his crowning achievement: winning the 2016 Nobel Prize for literature.

DAVE VAN RONK

When Dylan arrived in New York in the early 1960s, Dave Van Ronk was the most important singer-songwriter in Greenwich Village. Because he was a gifted singer and performed at the Gaslight Café on MacDougal Street, the most prestigious folk music venue in New York City at that

---

ies/movie-features/the-inside-story-of-bob-dylan-martin-scorseses-rolling-thunder-revue-doc-844268 (accessed Apr. 17, 2022).

42. Suze Rotolo, *A Freewheelin' Time: A Memoir of Greenwich Village in the Sixties* (New York: Broadway Books, 2008), 277.

time, he was known as the Mayor of MacDougal Street. At the Gaslight singers were paid by the owners but at other places, called "basket houses," singers had to pass a basket around after they performed. Dylan started out in the basket houses but then performed at more prestigious places including the Gaslight and another folk music venue, Gerde's Folk City, which was owned by a businessman named Mike Porco. Previously the place had been a saloon called Gerde's, but in 1959 Izzy Young, the director of a music shop called the Folklore Center, convinced Porco to change the name to Gerde's Folk City and turn it into a venue for folk singers.[43] In his autobiography, *Chronicles*, published in 2004, Dylan says he first met Van Ronk in Izzy Young's Folklore Center. He explains that he had listened to some of Ronk's records back in the Midwest before he came east and "thought they were pretty great." He said that he "copied some of his recordings phrase for phrase."[44] Van Ronk, he adds, "could howl and whisper, turn blues into ballads and ballads into blues. I loved his style."[45] At the Folklore Center, Dylan says, Van Ronk asked him if he did janitor work. Dylan said no, he wasn't a janitor, he was a singer, and asked Ronk if he could sing a song for him. Dylan sang "Nobody Knows You When You're Down and Out," a blues song written by Jimmy Cox in 1923. Van Ronk was impressed and invited Dylan to come to the Gaslight and sing some songs in his set.[46]

Van Ronk, however, says he first heard Dylan sing at the Café Wha? on the corner of MacDougal and Minetta. Dylan was, Van Ronk says, "the scruffiest-looking fugitive from a cornfield" he had ever seen, but the older singer was impressed by Dylan's harmonica playing and his "take-no-prisoners delivery."[47] He and his wife Terri became, Ronk says, "probably Bobby's biggest boosters."[48] Dylan sometimes slept on a couch at their place. Terri Ronk, who helped manage other singers, became Dylan's manager for a while. According to Van Ronk, he and Terri convinced Mike Porco, the owner of Gerde's Folk City, to book Dylan. Robert Shelton says it was some friends of Dylan's, Eve and Mac MacKenzie, who did

---

43. Dave Van Ronk with Elijah Wald, *The Mayor of MacDougal Street* (Philadelphia, PA: Da Capo Press, 2005), 141; Robert Shelton, *No Direction Home: The Life and Music of Bob Dylan* (Milwaukee, WI: Backbeat Books, 2011), 76.
44. Bob Dylan, *Chronicles: Volume One* (New York: Simon and Schuster, 2004), 15.
45. Ibid.
46. Bob Dylan, *Chronicles*, 21-22.
47. Dave Van Ronk, *The Mayor of MacDougal Street*, 158.
48. Ibid., 163.

the convincing, but in any event Dylan began performing at Gerde's Folk City and after Shelton's glowing review in the *New York Times* of a Dylan performance there, Dylan's career took off.[49]

Van Ronk's career never took off. At least, he never was a big success commercially. He was known more for helping other singer-songwriters than for his own singing and composing. After he died in 2002 of cancer at the age of 65, he began to receive some recognition. In 2005 a memoir, *The Mayor of MacDougal Street*, was published. Before Van Ronk died a musician and writer named Elijah Wald began helping him write a book. Wald was a good friend of Van Ronk. According to a note on the back cover, he "spent much of his youth sleeping on Dave's couch." This book was not originally intended to be an autobiography. Wald explains that Van Ronk wanted to talk about the "writers, comedians, painters, crooks, and all the uncategorizable denizens of the streets and bars," but they could not find a publisher, and then Van Ronk was hospitalized.[50] The memoir is told by Van Ronk in the first person and is based on some sections Van Ronk wrote and on the many interviews he gave over the years. In December 2013 *Inside Llewyn Davis*, a movie directed by Joel and Ethan Coen that is very loosely based on Van Ronk's memoir, came out. (The title comes from a record of Van Ronk's, *Inside Dave Van Ronk*, released in 1964.) A three-CD (54 tracks) retrospective collection of Van Ronk's was released by Smithsonian Folkways before the film came out. This film by the Coen brothers may have gotten Van Ronk some publicity, but the main character, Llewyn Davis, played by Oscar Isaac, resembles Bob Dylan more than Van Ronk. Like Dylan he has an agent whose last name is Grossman; like Dylan, he can be mean to his friends and admirers; and like Dylan he gets a girl pregnant and arranges for her to get an abortion.

Why did Dave Van Ronk never become better known and more successful financially? T Bone Burnett, a record producer, song writer, and musician, says "his age worked against him, for one, and there just wasn't a tour infrastructure when he started out."[51] One senses, too, that plain old bad luck played a role. Van Ronk sang a highly praised version of "House of the Rising Sun" but it never became a hit until the Animals

---

49. Ibid., 64. See also Robert Shelton, *No Direction Home: The Life and Music of Bob Dylan*, 76.
50. Elijah Wald, "Afterword," in Dave Van Ronk with Elijah Wald, *The Mayor of MacDougal Street*, 228.
51. Larry Rohter quotes T Bone Burnett in "For a Village Troubadour, a Late Encore," *New York Times*, Dec. 8, 2013.

and Dylan recorded it using Van Ronk's arrangement. "I always knew this song, but never really learned it until Dave Van Ronk sang it," Dylan told Robert Shelton.[52] Albert Grossman, who became Dylan's manager, once asked Van Ronk if he wanted to be part of a trio he was forming. He had Peter Yarrow and Mary Travers and wanted Van Ronk to be the third member. Van Ronk turned him down, explaining in his memoir that he "would have stood out like a sore thumb, vocally, visually, you name it."[53] So Grossman found Noel Paul Stookey and the group was Peter, Paul, and Mary not Peter, Dave, and Mary. (It was decided to use Stookey's middle name.) In his memoir, Van Ronk says he made the right choice but had second thoughts every time he looked at his bank balance.[54]

A third possible reason for his lack of commercial success may have been his rigid beliefs regarding what made a good song. Van Ronk was a confirmed leftist, a Trotskyist, but he did not like political "topical" songs. Dylan wrote and sang them, and Phil Ochs made them his specialty, but not Ronk. "I don't think anyone was ever converted with a song," he told Robert Shelton.[55] When you write political songs, he says in his memoir, you don't change anyone's mind: You're just "preaching to the choir."[56] Topical songs, however, like Dylan's "Only a Pawn in the Game" about the death of Medgar Evers, were popular when the folk revival first began. Dylan eventually concluded, as we saw in Chapter Six, that topical songs, or "message songs" as he called them, were "a drag,"[57] and moved on to songs that were more poetic and artistic but much more obscure. This avenue was not open to Van Ronk because he disliked songs that were obscure or unintelligible. "That whole artistic mystique," he says in his memoir, "is one of the great traps of this business because down that road lies unintelligibility."[58] Dylan, he says, fell into this trap when "he discovered that he could get away with anything—he was Bob Dylan and people would take whatever he wrote on faith."[59] Van Ronk admits, however, in his memoir that his own rigid theories about what made a

---

52. Robert Shelton, *No Direction Home*, 93.
53. Dave Van Ronk, *The Mayor of MacDougal Street*, 168.
54. Ibid.
55. Robert Shelton, *No Direction Home*, 79.
56. Dave Van Ronk, *The Mayor of MacDougal Street*, 200.
57. Bob Dylan, "Interview with Nat Hentoff, *Playboy*," in *Bob Dylan: The Essential Interviews*, ed. Jonathan Cott (New York: Wenner Books, 2006), 100. This is a reprint of an interview that first appeared in *Playboy*, March 1966.
58. Dave Van Ronk, *The Mayor of MacDougal Street*, 207-208.
59. Ibid., 208.

good song "served as cover for an absolutely, immutable, self-imposed writer's block."[60]

A fourth possible reason Van Ronk never became as rich and famous as other singers is his politics. He was a Trotskyist who, during the Cuban missile crisis in October 1962, ended a performance at the Gaslight by singing the left-wing anthem "The International."[61] During this crisis he also demonstrated in support of Cuba at the United Nations. He explains in his memoir that he felt that if the US could put missiles in Turkey,[62] then Khrushchev had the right to put them in Cuba.[63] He was never blacklisted like Pete Seeger who, during the era of McCarthyism, had to appear before the House Un-American Activities Committee, but it seems likely that some record companies were reluctant to offer a contract to such an avowed leftist.

Dave Van Ronk was more than a singer. He was a nurturer of new talent and a community builder. "He nurtured a lot of people onto the repertoire, people who went on to record those songs and became better known than he was," says Jeff Place, the music archivist at the Smithsonian Institution who assembled the CD package *Down in Washington Square.*[64] In his obituary for the singer-songwriter, Jon Pareles, a music critic for the *New York Times*, mentions three essential qualities that made Van Ronk a leader of the folk revival: "a sense of history, a sense of humor and a gift for making fellow musicians feel at home."[65]

Perhaps no one was more indebted to Dave Van Ronk than Bob Dylan. Robert Shelton, the journalist for the New York Times who helped launch Dylan's career with his review of Dylan's performance in 1961 at Gerdes Folk City, says that Dylan's most important debt to the older singer was in "style, perception, and interpretation. . . . Dylan picked up some of Dave's guitar ideas, but a lot more of his special showmanship, the ability

---

60. Ibid., 209.
61. Suze Rotolo says that when Van Ronk found out that her parents had been communists, "he felt it his duty, as a Trotskyite, to work on my politics." See Suze Rotolo, *A Free-wheelin' Time: A Memoir of Greenwich Village in the Sixties,* 114.
62. American nuclear weapons were deployed in Turkey in 1959. During the Cuban missile crisis in 1962 President Kennedy secretly agreed to remove these missiles if Russia would remove its nuclear missiles from Cuba.
63. Dave Van Ronk, *The Mayor of MacDougal Street,* 199.
64. Larry Rohter quotes Jeff Place in "For a Village Troubadour, a Late Encore," *New York Times,* Dec. 8, 2013.
65. Jon Pareles, "Dave Van Ronk, Folk Singer and Iconoclast, Dies at 65," *New York Times,* Feb. 12, 2002.

to space sound and silences into a whole that compelled attention."[66] Perhaps the best proof of Van Ronk's influence on Dylan is the fact that half of the songs on Dylan's first album were, as Dylan says in his memoir, "renditions of songs that Van Ronk did."[67]

Van Ronk and Dylan say nice things about each other in their memoirs, which were both published over two decades after the folk revival began. For example, as I mentioned in discussing Dylan's persona, some people have laughed at Dylan for adopting, both on and off the stage, a hobo persona when he came to New York City in the early 1960s. But not Van Ronk who says Dylan's "romantic hobo thing," his "Guthriesque persona," helped to make him popular. In those days, Van Ronk says, "We were all inventing characters for ourselves."[68] Van Ronk also praises Dylan for his genuine respect for Woody Guthrie. When Dylan came to New York Guthrie was dying of Huntington's chorea in a hospital in New Jersey. Dylan would visit him in his hospital room and sing for him. "We all admired Woody and considered him a legend," Van Ronk says, "but none of us was trucking out to see him and play for him. In that regard, Dylan was as stand-up a cat as I have ever known."[69]

In his memoir Van Ronk also makes light of the fact that Dylan recorded his version of "The House of the Rising Sun" for his first album without first asking his permission. In the early 1960s it had become one of Van Ronk's signature songs. Van Ronk says that when he learned what Dylan had done, he flew into "a Donald Duck rage" and had to be calmed down by his friend, the singer Dave Cohen.[70] After Dylan started singing it, Van Ronk says, people in the audience when he performed would ask him to sing "that Dylan song" ("House of the Rising Sun") so he dropped it from his repertoire. Then in 1964, he says, Eric Burdon and The Animals released the song, also with his arrangement. When it became number one on the charts, Van Ronk says, fans would ask Dylan to sing "that Animals song" and so Dylan dropped it from his repertoire.[71] In his memoir he refers to this squabble over "House of the Rising Sun" as a "tempest in a teapot."[72] His account of it is light and humorous, and there is no suggestion of any lingering anger or resentment.

---

66. Robert Shelton, *No Direction Home*, 79.
67. Bob Dylan, *Chronicles*, 262.
68. Dave Van Ronk, *The Mayor of MacDougal Street*, 162.
69. Ibid., 159.
70. Ibid., 177.
71. Ibid., 177.
72. Ibid., 178.

In his memoir Van Ronk also does not criticize Dylan for moving away from protest songs. He was, he says, "dubious about Bobby's contrived primitivism and his later obscurantism" but praises him for expanding his repertoire, for resisting the view that protest songs were the only kind of songs one should write.[73] When Dylan stopped writing them and instead wrote "Like a Rolling Stone" and other rock and roll songs, the folk community was angry. Irwin Silber, the editor of *Sing Out!*, wrote Dylan a letter chastising Dylan for abandoning the struggle. Van Ronk, however, defended Dylan. Using language far from politically correct, he accused "the folk community of acting like a Jewish mother." Van Ronk thought that Dylan's "Positively Fourth Street," assumed to be an attack on this "folk community," was a "great song." "It was high time," Van Ronk told Robert Shelton, that "Bobby turned around and said something to Irwin Silber and all those Jewish mothers."[74]

Dylan praises Van Ronk in his memoir, Chronicles, released in 2004. His praise for the older singer is, in fact, more effusive than Van Ronk's praise of Dylan. He calls Van Ronk "the one performer I burned to learn particulars from." Dylan emphasizes Van Ronk's talent as a performer, his ability to enthrall the audience. If you were on MacDougal Street in the evening, Dylan says, "he'd be the first and last vital choice of the night." Dylan mentions the special feeling he had for the older singer-songwriter. "I felt different towards Van Ronk," he says, "because it was him who brought me into the fold."[75]

Clearly Van Ronk's feelings about Dylan changed over time. Robert Shelton, who knew both men before Dylan became famous, says that Dylan "outgrew" his friendship with Van Ronk and his wife, Terri Thal. People like Van Ronk and Izzy Young, owner of the Folklore Center in Greenwich Village, and others who befriended and helped Dylan early in his career, suggest that Dylan was a taker who failed to show appreciation for the help they had given him. "The part of Dylan that was the sponge could function on all four cylinders," Van Ronk told Robert Shelton. "He gets what he can and then discards it. This is why Terri and I are not Bob's best friends anymore. He got what he could absorb here, and he moved on."[76] "He knew exactly what he wanted, knew how to use people," Izzy

\

73. Ibid., 197-198.
74. Robert Shelton, *No Direction Home*, 78.
75. Bob Dylan, *Chronicles*, pp. 261-263.
76. Robert Shelton quotes Van Ronk in *No Direction Home*, 78.

Young told Anthony Scaduto. "And when the point came that he didn't have to use them anymore he dropped them."[77]

Others suggest that Dylan was not just ungrateful but also mean, even cruel. S. David Cohen, a singer, songwriter, and actor who hung out with Dylan in Greenwich Village in the 1960s, says that Dylan was "a mean cat, very cruel to people."[78] "Sweetness wasn't a part of his personality, and neither was compassion," says Mikki Isaacson, whose apartment on Sheridan Square in Greenwich Village became a home and meeting place for Dylan and other stray folk singers. "He was," Isaacson says, "a bit of a terror."[79] Some friends and biographers have suggested that fame, which made it difficult for him to lead a normal life, made him mean. Fame certainly changed his life in drastic ways but it seems that Dylan, even before fame descended on him, rubbed a lot of people the wrong way. Anthony Scaduto interviewed Kevin McCosh, who owned a bookstore in Dinkytown and knew Dylan and the people he hung out with there in 1959 and 1960. "There was something about his personality," McCosh told Scaduto. "Basically nobody liked him very much. He was arrogant, boorish, aggressive."[80]

PHIL OCHS

One person in Dylan's group of friends and acquaintances that he is said to have treated harshly in the 1960s and early 1970s was Phil Ochs, a singer-songwriter whose specialty was the topical or protest song. When these songs were popular in the early sixties, he was considered the master of the genre. No one has argued that Ochs was as talented as Dylan, musically. His guitar playing was only so-so, his voice unexceptional, and his songs were not as poetic as many of Dylan's songs. What is most impressive about Phil Ochs was his never-ending commitment to bring peace and social justice to the peoples of the world. In the course of his career he wrote songs about most of the major issues of his time. For the civil rights struggle he co-wrote (with Bob Gibson) "Too Many Martyrs," about the murder of Medgar Evers, and "Talking Birmingham Jam" about the desegregation battle in Alabama in spring 1963, during which Bull Connor,

---

77. Anthony Scaduto quotes Izzy Young in *Bob Dylan*, 72.
78. S. David Cohen's stage name was David Blue. Anthony Scaduto quotes him in *Bob Dylan*, 227.
79. Anthony Scaduto quotes Mikki Isaacson in *Bob Dylan*, 101.
80. Anthony Scaduto quotes Kevin McCosh in *Bob Dylan*, 47.

Birmingham's Chief of Police, turned dogs lose on unarmed protesters. In his song Ochs imagines a conversation he had with these dogs:

> Well, I said, "There must be some man around,
> There can't be only you dogs in town."
> They said, "Sure, we have Old Bull Connor,
> There he goes, walkin' yonder,
> Throwin' some raw meat to the Mayor,
> Feedin' bones to the City Council!"

"Here's to the State of Mississippi," another civil rights song and one of Ochs' most controversial works, was written after he returned from a trip to the South with the Mississippi Caravan of Music, a group promoting voter registration. It was the summer of 1964. Soon after he arrived in Mississippi, he learned that the bodies of three young civil rights workers—James E. Chaney, Michael Schwerner, and Andrew Goodman—had been found in a swamp. The three men, who were associated with the Congress of Racial Equality, or CORE, had disappeared on June 21, 1964. Chaney was an African American from Mississippi and Schwerner and Goodman, who were white, were from New York. The song was controversial because it singled out one state. Each of the eight stanzas ends with the lines: "Oh, here's to the land you've torn out the heart of / Mississippi find yourself another country to be part of." Michael Schumacher, in his biography of Ochs, says that even some of Ochs' friends pointed out that the problem was much more widespread. Also, some African Americans in Mississippi, Schumacher reports, "appreciated Phil's involvement with the cause" but insisted that "they were as much a part of Mississippi as their prosecutors."[81]

In 1964 Ochs wrote an anti-Vietnam war song, "Talking Vietnam," which was, Mike Marqusee says, "the first musical protest against the embryonic war."[82] In 1964 the United States had military advisors in Vietnam, but the first American combat troops did not arrive in Vietnam until March 1965. In "Talking Vietnam" the speaker in the song is a US soldier who is "Sailing over to Vietnam / Southeast Asian Birmingham" where he will be "Training a million Vietnamese / To fight for the wrong government and the American Way." In the jungle he meets the head of

---

81. Michael Schumacher, *There But for Fortune: The Life of Phil Ochs* (New York: Hyperion, 1996), 88.
82. Mike Marqusee, *Chimes of Freedom: The Politics of Bob Dylan's Art* (New York: The New Press, 2003), 102.

that wrong government, President Diem, who tells the soldier that he will be "fighting to keep Vietnam free / For Good old de-em-moc-ra-cy [Diem-ocracy]. De-em-moc-ra-cy, Diem explains, "means rule by one family / And 15,000 American troops."

Ochs wrote another anti-war song,"The War is Over," to perform at a large antiwar demonstration in Los Angeles on June 23, 1967. The demonstration was planned to correspond with President Johnson's appearance at a campaign fundraiser at the Century Plaza Hotel. "The War Is Over" was inspired by a poem titled "Wichita Vortex Sutra," written by Allen Ginsberg in 1966, in which he declares the war is over: "I lift my voice aloud, / make Mantra of American language now, / I here declare the end of the War!"[83] The idea of fighting an absurd war with more absurdity—declaring that a war still raging was over—appealed to Ochs.[84] At the rally Ochs led an impromptu parade and then stood on the back of a flatbed truck and sang "The War Is Over," which ends with these lines:

> One-legged veterans will greet the dawn
> And they're whistling marches as they mow the lawn
> And the gargoyles only sit and grieve
> The gypsy fortune teller told me that we'd been deceived
> You only are what you believe
> I believe the war is over
> It's over, it's over

After Ochs had finished singing the police announced on a bullhorn that people needed to disperse. When they didn't, the police moved in and started beating demonstrators with billy clubs.[85] The rally turned even more violent later when 15,000 (estimates vary) protesters began moving from Cheviot Hills Park to the Century Plaza Hotel where President Johnson was to speak.[86] According to the permit they were not supposed to stop marching. When the march stalled in front of the hotel, the police attacked with billy clubs. People interviewed for a report by the American Civil Liberties Union testify that they saw police beating

---

83. Allen Ginsberg, "Wichita Vortex Sutra," in *Planet News* (San Francisco, CA: City Lights Books, 1974), 127.
84. Michael Schumacher, *There But for Fortune*, 139.
85. Ibid., 145.
86. A headline in the *Los Angeles Times* for June 24, 1967, said 10,000; a report by the American Civil Liberties Union (ACLU) put the number of protestors at 15,000. See ACLU of Southern California, *Day of Protest, Night of Violence* (Los Angeles, CA: Sawyer Press, 1967).

defenseless marchers, some of them elderly, who, because the crowd was compressed in a small space, had nowhere to go.[87] The violent police response shocked many people and infuriated and energized those in the anti-war movement.

In November 1967, Ochs organized another The War Is Over Rally in New York City. Unlike the rally in Chicago, this one was joyful and peaceful. Allen Ginsberg was there, as were Paul Krassner, Jerry Rubin, Stew Albert, and Rennie Davis of the The Yippies, short for The Youth International Party, an anti-war and flamboyantly theatrical radical group. The rally began in Washington Square Park where Ochs sang "The War Is Over," and then he led participants on a march through the streets of New York. Michael Shumacher describes a pre-event press conference in which Ochs, when asked by a policeman what would happen at the march, said that there would be "a lot of hugging and kissing."[88] Reports suggest it was a festive and fun event.

The next The War Is Over Rally, which occurred a little over a year later, in August 1968, was anything but festive. Anti-war protesters of all types, including the Yippies led by Jerry Rubin and Abbie Hoffman, flocked to Chicago to protest what most people believed was a foregone conclusion: the nomination of then-Vice President Herbert Humphrey to run for president. Humphrey supported the war in Vietnam. Ochs, like many in the anti-war movement, had pinned his hopes on Robert Kennedy and then, when he was killed, on Senator Gene McCarthy. Those opposed to the war feared Humphrey would continue Johnson's pro-war agenda. This rally too, like the one in June 1967 in Los Angeles, ended in violence—what some people called a police riot—when Chicago police on the orders of Mayor Richard Daley brutally attacked the war protestors. August 27, the day before Humphrey was to be nominated, was President Johnson's birthday, so the Yippies organized an "un-birthday" for him in the Chicago Coliseum. Ochs sang several songs at this rally, including "I Ain't Marching Anymore," Ochs' most famous anti-war song. Mike Marqusee calls it Ochs' "most successful anthem."[89] Ochs never mentions the Vietnam War in his song. The speaker in the song is a universal American soldier who has marched in many wars, from the war

---

87. ACLU of Southern California, *Day of Protest, Night of Violence.*
88. Michael Schumacher, *There But for Fortune*, 172.
89. Mike Marqusee, *Chimes of Freedom*, 251.

of independence to the second World War, but has decided he has had enough of war:

> For I marched to the battles of the German trench
> In a war that was bound to end all wars
> Oh I must have killed a million men
> And now they want me back again
> But I ain't marchin' anymore

When Ochs began singing "I Ain't Marching Anymore" at the Chicago Coliseum, a man stood up and started burning his draft card. Then, Michael Schumacher says, "others followed suit, and before long the Coliseum twinkled from draft cards burning like votive candles."[90] The next day Ochs received an impressive ovation—and prompted more young men to burn their draft cards—when he again sang "I Ain't Marching Anymore" at a rally held at a bandshell in Grant Park.[91] After the rally the plan was to march peacefully to the Democratic Convention, but the police would not let them out and viciously beat some who tried to get out of the park. The event shocked many people who saw it on television.

Ochs was much more of an internationalist than Dylan and was moved by injustice wherever it occurred. "Every newspaper headline is a potential song," he argued, in a 1963 article about the need for topical songs.[92] Ochs, Mike Marqusee says, was "a much keener reader of the newspapers than Dylan, and, unlike Dylan, had a genuine intellectual curiosity about politics."[93] In his article about topical songs Ochs regrets that songwriters in America seem moved to write only about two causes: "the Negro struggle for civil rights and the peace movement."[94] Ochs was interested in a variety of movements and struggles in the United States and around the world. In 1971 he became fascinated with Chile after reading that Salvador Allende had been elected President of Chile—the first Marxist in Latin America to be elected in a free election. Ochs was intrigued and visited Chile with two founders of the Yippies, Jerry Rubin and Stew Albert. They traveled all over Chile and met a lot of interesting people, including a popular folksinger and political activist named Victor Jara, who fascinated and inspired Ochs. They traveled around the

---

90. Michael Schumacher, *There But for Fortune*, 200.
91. Michael Schumacher, *There But for Fortune*, 201; Mike Marqusee, *Chimes of Freedom*, 251.
92. Phil Ochs, "The Need for Topical Music," *Broadside* no. 22 (March, 1963), 2.
93. Mike Marqusee, *Chimes of Freedom*, 102.
94. Phil Ochs, "The Need for Topical Music," 1.

country, sang together at the halftime of a basketball game, and appeared together on national television. In her biography of her husband, Joan Jara describes a day "two hippy-looking gringos" (Phil Ochs and Jerry Rubin) went to a copper mine where Victor was singing in support of striking mine workers. Her husband let them sing a few songs, she says, and Victor translated them for the miners and then all three of them sang Pete Seeger's "If I Had a Hammer."[95]

On September 11, 1973, Chilean troops commanded by General Augusto Pinochet mounted a coup, with assistance from the CIA, against the Allende government. Military officials in Chile have maintained that Allende committed suicide during the coup. Others, including Michael Schumacher, say he was murdered by the military after the coup.[96] In 2011 a British ballistics expert conducted an autopsy and concluded that Allende did commit suicide—by shooting himself using an AK-47 given him by Fidel Castro.[97]

A few days after the coup, Victor Jara was seized and taken to the Santiago Stadium, where he was tortured and killed. When he heard the news, Ochs began organizing a concert featuring popular singers to make people aware of what was happening in Chile and to raise funds for charitable work there. He exhausted himself recruiting singers to perform at the concert and singing himself at a variety of venues to raise funds. After he finally succeeded in persuading Dylan, who was reluctant at first, to sing at the concert, ticket sales increased. According to Michael Schumacher the performances at the concert, which took place May 9, 1974, at the Felt Forum in Madison Square Garden, were uneven, apparently in part because many singers, including Ochs and Dylan, were drunk.[98]

Phil Ochs was at the height of his popularity in 1964. He was the hero at Newport Folk Festival in July, where he outshined Dylan. This festival occurred when topical songs, Ochs' specialty, were never more popular

95. Joan Jara, *The Unfinished Song: The Life of Victor Jara* (New York: Ticknor & Fields, 1984), 213.
96. Michael Schumacher, *There But for Fortune*, 287.
97. "Chilean President Salvador Allende Committed Suicide, Autopsy Confirms," *The Guardian*, July 19, 2011, https://www.theguardian.com/world/2011/jul/20/salvador-allende-committed-suicide-autopsy (accessed Mar. 20, 2019).
98. Michael Schumacher, *There But for Fortune*, 4, 295; "Tag Archives: Bob Dylan Live 'Friends for Chile' Benefit," The Amazing Kornyfone Label https://theamazingkornyfonelabel.wordpress.com/tag/bob-dylan-live-friends-for-chile-benefit-1974-carnegie-hall-1962/ (accessed Mar. 21, 2019).

and when Dylan was growing tired of what he called "finger pointing songs," songs that Dylan in a 1964 interview said "point to all the things that are wrong."[99] Writing an article that appeared in the December 1964 issue of *Broadside*, Paul Wolfe says that this Festival's "most significant achievement was specific and twofold: It marked the emergence of Phil Ochs as the most important voice in the movement, simultaneous with the renunciation of topical music by its major prophet, Bob Dylan."[100] At a topical song workshop held on Friday at this Festival, Dylan sang "It Ain't Me Babe" and "Tambourine Man," two non-topical songs, and on Sunday night he sang other non-political songs that would be featured on his album *Another Side of Bob Dylan*: "All I Really Want to Do," "To Ramona," and "Chimes of Freedom." According to Michael Schumacher, his performance "left people grumbling that they hadn't ventured to Newport to hear Dylan sing about his love life."[101]

In his article in *Broadside*, Paul Wolfe says Ochs' and Dylan's performances at the Newport Folk Festival in 1964 revealed these differences between the two singer-songwriters: "meaning vs. innocuousness, sincerity vs. utter disregard for the tastes of the audience, idealistic principles vs. self-conscious egotism."[102] Wolfe calls Dylan's decision to stop writing topical songs "a defection," which is strong language, but it highlights a key difference between the two singer-songwriters: For Ochs the cause—politics—was more important than art. For himself he could not adopt an "art for art's sake" philosophy, but he understood and accepted Dylan's position. In a letter in *Broadside* he objected to the attacks on Dylan by Wolfe and others. "To cater to an audience's taste," he wrote, "is not to respect them, and if the audience doesn't understand that they don't deserve respect."[103] Dylan was not so kind about Ochs' topical songs. "The stuff you're writing is bullshit," he told Ochs, "because politics is bullshit. It's all unreal. The only thing that's real is inside you. Your feelings."[104] "Dylan despised what I write," Ochs said in an interview. "He can't accept what I'm doing. It's political in his mind and therefore bullshit." Instead

---

99. Bob Dylan, interview by Nat Hentoff. See "The Crackin', Shakin', Breakin', Sounds" in *Bob Dylan: The Essential Interviews*, ed. Jonathan Cott (New York: Wenner Books, 2006), 16. This interview appeared in The *New Yorker*, Oct. 24, 1964.
100. Paul Wolfe, untitled essay in *Broadside* 53 (December, 1964), no page numbers listed.
101. Michael Schumacher, *There But for Fortune*, 84.
102. Paul Wolfe, untitled essay in *Broadside* 53, no page numbers listed.
103. Phil Ochs, "An Open Letter from Phil Ochs to Irwin Silber, Paul Wolfe, and Joseph E. Levine," *Broadside* 54 (1965).
104. Anthony Scaduto quotes Dylan in *Bob Dylan*, 176.

of resenting Dylan's harshness, Ochs considered it constructive criticism. Dylan feels, he said, that "I'm not writing about myself and my deepest emotions. He thinks that I could be much more honest with myself."[105]

An incident described by Anthony Scaduto reveals how badly Dylan treated Ochs. One night in 1965 Dylan played a new single, "Can You Please Crawl Out Your Window," for Ochs and David Cohen and asked them what they thought. Cohen said he liked it; Ochs said, "It's okay, but it's not going to be a hit." Dylan exploded in anger and later, still angry, pushed him out of a limousine taking them to discos uptown. "Get out, Ochs," Dylan ordered. "You're not a folk singer. You're just a journalist."[106] It turned out that Ochs was right: "Can You Please Crawl Out Your Window" never became a hit. Sam Hood, the manager of the Gaslight where Ochs and Dylan performed, says Ochs was "so vulnerable" to Dylan who "would play with him the way a cruel person might when you know you have the full affection of someone else and you toy with it and that went on over and over again with Phil and Dylan." Dylan was, Hood says, "such a prick."[107] "Ochs worshiped the ground Bobby walked on—it actually became a sort of fixation," Dave Van Ronk says, and it "did him a lot of harm."[108]

It is difficult to understand Dylan's meanness to Phil Ochs. Dylan's friends and acquaintances suggest that fame made Dylan mean. It started, they suggest, at the Newport Folk Festival in 1963. Dave Van Ronk, who was with Dylan at the festival, talks about groups of fans running after Dylan and how they piled into a car to escape them. Van Ronk says that Dylan was "paranoid to start" and didn't like people "pulling at his coat and picking his brain" and now five million people were after him.[109] He was a "street cat," David Cohen says, and liked to hang out in bars, but when fame came he lost his freedom.[110] Suze Rotolo says that "the paranoia and secrecy that were a part of his personality early on were essential for his survival later on. He was becoming prey. Either people wanted to devour him or they offered themselves up for him to consume."[111] It became more

---

105. This interview is included in *There but for Fortune*, a documentary film about Ochs by Kenneth Bowser that was released in 2011.

106. Anthony Scaduto, *Bob Dylan*, 229. An account by Ochs of this incident also appears in Clinton Heylin, *Bob Dylan: Behind the Shades Revisited*, 234.

107. Sam Hood in the film *There but for Fortune*.

108. Dave Van Ronk, *The Mayor of MacDougal Street*, 207.

109. Anthony Scaduto quotes Van Ronk in *Dylan*, 149.

110. Anthony Scaduto quotes David Cohen in *Bob Dylan*, 227.

111. Suze Rotolo, *A Freewheelin' Time*, 274.

troubling after his motorcycle accident in Woodstock, New York, on July 29, 1966. He and his wife Sara had bought a place in Woodstock to achieve some privacy, and for a while it was, Dylan says in *Chronicles*, the "quiet refuge" he wanted for himself and his family, but then "moochers" from California and "rogue radicals looking for the Prince of Protest began to arrive" and shattered the privacy he was seeking.[112] He had to learn what he says the actor Tony Curtis told him: that fame is an occupation.[113] Fame, Dylan argues in *Chronicles*, is a difficult occupation for a creative artist because creativity "has much to do with experience, observation, and imagination, and if any one of those key elements is missing, it doesn't work." After he became famous, he says, "it was impossible for me to observe anything without being observed."[114]

But why did he treat friends like Phil Ochs so badly? Some who knew him suggest that Dylan's nastiness and cruelty were a defense mechanism adopted to protect himself, and later his family, from fans. Ochs, always eager to say good things about Dylan, suggests as much. He told Anthony Scaduto that Dylan was "basically a very human person and wanted to keep human relationships from souring. And I think he felt that slipping away because of his fame, in the way people reacted to him."[115] It seems, however, that certain aspects of his personality have made it difficult for Dylan to deal with and enjoy his fame. Suze Rotolo, Dave Van Ronk and others say Dylan was paranoid, a term used to describe someone who intensely distrusts and suspects others.[116] Dylan has been concerned about protecting his privacy and that is understandable, but other singer-composers as famous if not more famous than Dylan—one thinks of Paul McCartney, Willie Nelson, and Leonard Cohen, for example—have handled fame more graciously. Joan Baez, in an interview with Anthony Scaduto, says that Dylan did not have "the stage fright kind of fear." He did not, Baez says, suffer from diarrhea or feel nauseated before a concert as she did. "He seemed to submerge that [his stage fright]," Baez says, "and it came out in paranoia about people afterwards."[117] She describes how after one concert two girls appeared, yelling "There's Bobby," and he wanted to

---

112. Bob Dylan, *Chronicles*, 116.
113. Ibid., 123.
114. Ibid., 121.
115. Anthony Scaduto quotes Ochs in *Dylan*, 154.
116. Suze Rotolo, *A Freewheelin' Time*, 95; Anthony Scaduto quotes Dave Van Ronk in *Bob Dylan*, 149.
117. Anthony Scaduto quotes Joan Baez in *Dylan*, 192.

run. Baez convinced him to calm down, talk to them a minute, and give them his autograph, and it turned out to be a pleasant encounter. Baez told Scaduto that she believes that Dylan was genuinely terrified of people like these fans.[118] One shouldn't discount the danger of being trampled by crazed fans, but perhaps Dylan has been afflicted by agoraphobia as well as paranoia.

Clinton Heylin, the author of several fine books about Dylan, argues that in 1966 "drugs, especially methamphetamine, played a major role in sending his worldview spiraling down into an all-embracing paranoia."[119] Heylin mentions prescriptions from a Dr. Rothschild written for Dylan in 1966 for "a quantity of methamphetamine" and also for the "downers" Desbutal and Pentobarbital, which can be used to soften the aftereffects of taking meth.[120] Heylin does not indicate how he obtained these prescriptions.

Phil Ochs was possessed by demons much more self-destructive than whatever caused Dylan's nastiness. In Kenneth Bowser's film about Phil Ochs, *There but for Fortune*, his brother, Michael Ochs, explains that their father was manic depressive, and that both he and Phil had inherited this affliction. They had, Michael says, made a vow that neither would commit the other to an institution. In the summer of 1975 Phil had a complete mental breakdown. He announced that he had been murdered by John Train, whose identity he was assuming, and began drinking heavily in bars in Greenwich Village. His drinking drove him deeper into depression. On April 9, 1976, he hung himself in his sister Sonny's apartment in Far Rockaway, a neighborhood in Queens.[121]

In Kenneth Bowser's film, the late Christopher Hitchens, a well-known Anglo-American[122] journalist and literary critic, praises Ochs for his "very tough, grainy songs," citing as examples "Santo Domingo," "Love Me I'm a Liberal," and "Here's to the State of Mississippi." These songs, Hitchens says, "were far more political and much more tough-minded than the more generalized and accessible 'Blowin' in the Wind."[123] In an interview just before his film was released, Bowser says that "there is no one more important—as an entertainer—to the political movement of the 60s than

---

118. Ibid., 192-193.
119. Clinton Heylin, *Bob Dylan: Behind the Shades Revisited*, 231.
120. Ibid., 231-232.
121. Michael Shumacher, *There but for Fortune*, 351-352.
122. He was born in Portsmouth, England and moved to the United States in 1981.
123. Christopher Hitchens, speaking in Kenneth Bowser's film *Phil Ochs: There But for Fortune*.

Phil Ochs. He's more important than Bob Dylan .... He wrote more songs, he was at more of those rallies, and he's been written out of history and you kind of have to ask why."[124] Bowser suggests it was Ochs' "personal issues"—his mental illness, his problem with alcoholism. No doubt these problems are part of the answer. They led to Ochs' early death when he was only thirty-five years old and so, unlike Dylan, he has not been around to keep his name in the news. Meanwhile, Dylan, who was thirty-four when Ochs died, is still touring, winning awards, advertising products, and granting the occasional interview when he wishes to promote a new album or a new product. Kenneth Bowser suggests another reason why Ochs is not well-known. Ochs, he says, wanted to be as famous as Dylan but "he would always choose the political benefit over the politically astute entertainment move."[125] Because Ochs was passionate about politics he wrote mostly topical songs, works which, because they were about current and historical events, tended to have a relatively short shelf life. More "generalized" songs like Dylan's "Blowin' in the Wind," however, could be sung to protest any catastrophe or injustice. Kenneth Bowser also points out that Ochs sometimes attacked the left, which may have lessened the enthusiasm of some of his fans. He did not hesitate, Bowser says, to attack the choir he was singing to.[126] In songs like "Love Me, I'm a Liberal" Ochs chides liberals for being too timid and cautious to solve the nation's problems. Here's the third stanza:

> *I cheered when Humphrey was chosen*
> *My faith in the system restored*
> *I'm glad the commies were thrown out*
> *Of the A.F.L. C.I.O. board*
> *I love Puerto Ricans and negroes*
> *As long as they don't move next door*
> *So love me, love me, love me, I'm a liberal*

In many ways Trịnh Công Sơn is the Phil Ochs, not the Bob Dylan, of Vietnam. Like Phil Ochs he was kind to his friends, and like Phil Ochs he was known for his anti-war songs. Dylan, on the other hand, wrote only two or three anti-war songs and by 1966 had stopped writing political and

---

124. Kenneth Bowser, interview for PBS's American Masters, 22, 2012. http://www.pbs.org/wnet/americanmasters/phil-ochs-but-there-for-fortune-interview-director-kenneth-bowser/1960/ (accessed Aug. 31, 2018).
125. Ibid.
126. Ibid.

social protest songs. He did not protest the Vietnam War, though Joan Baez begged him to in her song "To Bobby":

> *Do you hear the voices in the night, Bobby?*
> *They're crying for you*
> *See the children in the morning light, Bobby*
> *They're dying*

Trịnh Công Sơn wrote anti-war songs that resemble Ochs' "protest" or "topical" anti-war songs in some ways, but they are written from a different perspective. Sơn wrote about one war, the war that was raging in his homeland, whereas Ochs, a citizen of a superpower with troops and interests around the world, wrote about wars and clashes that took place in various hot spots around the globe—Cuba, the Dominican Republic, Chile, Vietnam.

Another difference between Trịnh Công Sơn's and Ochs' anti-war songs involves tone. The tone of some of Ochs' anti-war songs is purposely jaunty and humorous. It's hard not to laugh while listening to his "Draft Dodger Rag." Here is the chorus, which is what the speaker, a young man about to be inducted, told his draft board:

> *Yes, I'm only eighteen, I got a ruptured spleen*
> *And I always carry a purse*
> *I got eyes like a bat, and my feet are flat, and my asthma's getting worse*
> *Yes, think of my career, my sweetheart dear, and my poor old invalid aunt*
> *Besides, I ain't no fool, I'm a-goin' to school*
> *And I'm working in a defense plant*

Ochs' "Talking Vietnam," at least on the surface, also has a humorous tone. It is designed to make listeners first smile, then cry, when some of the absurdities of American policy in the war are exposed. "Threw all the people in relocation camps," the speaker in "Talking Vietnam" says. "Under lock and key, made damn sure they're free." Trịnh Công Sơn's anti-war songs were not humorous. It is easier to be humorous when the war you are opposing is taking place in a foreign land.

Phil Ochs differed from both Dylan and Trịnh Công Sơn in another respect: He did not write love songs. Throughout his short life he was always protesting. He seemed unable to step away from his anger at injustice to talk about love's pains and pleasures.

I agree with Mike Marqusee, who admires and praises Ochs, but says that "Ochs' songs were never as multilayered as Dylan's, and always more reliant on topical references for their impact."[127] As I will explain in Chapter Nineteen, "Understanding Trịnh Công Sơn's Obscurity," Trịnh Công Sơn's anti-war songs [*nhạc phản chiến*] are less obscure than his love songs [*tình ca*] and songs about the human condition [*ca khúc về thân phận*] but they are not topical songs; they are not journalistic but rather sad and poetic expressions of the sadness of war. In "Blowin' in the Wind" Dylan sings "Yes 'n' how many times must the cannonballs fly / Before they're forever banned?" In "Lullaby of Cannons for the Night"* Trịnh Công Sơn asks how many nights must cannons rain destruction down on Vietnamese cities and towns. Phil Ochs was a passionate fighter for social justice and peace but did not, in his short life, succeed in writing songs as "multilayered" and poetic as these and other songs by Dylan and Trịnh Công Sơn. He comes close, however, in "There but for Fortune," a song in which he reveals his ability, despite his own mental suffering, to empathize with the suffering of others. Ochs wrote "There but for Fortune" in 1963, but it was not recorded until 1964 when it was included on Vanguard's compilation *New Folks Volume 2*. After hearing Jack Landron sing it in Club 47 in Cambridge, Massachusetts, Joan Baez recorded it for her album *Joan Baez/5* and also released it as a single.[128] It was never a big hit in the US but was very popular in England, where it reached 13 on the charts.[129] Here are the closing lines:

> *Show me the country where bombs had to fall*
> *Show me the ruins of buildings once so tall*
> *And I'll show you a young land with so many reasons why*
> *There but for fortune, go you or go I—you and I*
> *You and I*
> *There but for fortune, go you or go I—you and I*

Both Dylan and Trịnh Công Sơn were famous for writing obscure songs. Biographers and music critics talk about the obscurity of songs like Dylan's "Gates of Eden" which are packed with what Allen Ginsberg called "chains of flashing images"—images which are powerful and provocative and seem designed to steer the listener away from a quick interpretation

---

127. Mike Marqusee, *Chimes of Freedom*, 103.
128. Michael Shumacher, *There but for Fortune*, 95.
129. Ibid.

of meaning.[130] Trịnh Công Sơn's fans, the singers who sing his songs, and scholars who write about him all comment on the obscurity of his lyrics. One scholar describes the language in some of Trịnh Công Sơn's songs as "word-less" moving toward "word-destroying"[131] (See Chapter Nineteen). Most of Ochs' song lyrics, however, are not obscure at all. They are perhaps too clear to be poetic. The meaning may be too obvious to hold a listener's attention for long. Using Roland Barthes' terms that I discussed in my introduction, we can say that Ochs' songs are "readerly works" not "writerly texts."[132] Their meaning is stable, unambiguous, and so we process them quickly and somewhat passively.[133]

Ochs' great strength, one he shared with Trịnh Công Sơn, was empathy, the ability to understand and feel the suffering of others, in Ochs' case not just of people in his own country but of people around the globe. Ochs was tortured by his own personal demons but they did not close his mind to the suffering of others. In each of the first three stanzas of "There but for Fortune" he describes someone suffering: a prisoner "whose life has gone stale," a hobo "who sleeps out in the rain," and a drunkard who "stumbles out the door." In the last stanza he talks about the suffering of an entire country "where bombs had to fall."

Ochs wrote "There but for Fortune" in 1963 before the US began heavy bombing in Vietnam, so when he wrote it he may not have had Vietnam in mind, but other songs of his are unquestionably about Vietnam. Ochs was passionately opposed to the war in Vietnam and unlike Dylan wrote songs specifically about it, which he performed at anti-Vietnam War demonstrations. As explained in Chapter One, songs people refer to as Dylan's anti-war songs—"Blowin' in the Wind," "With God on Our Side," and

---

130. Allen Ginsberg, interview by Peter Barry Chowka, Modern American Poetry, 1995. See "Online Interviews with Allen Ginsberg," https://web.archive.org/web/20090212153234/http://www.english.illinois.edu:80/maps/poets/g_l/ginsberg/interviews.htm (accessed July 27, 2019). See also David S. Wills, "Allen Ginsberg and Bob Dylan," *Beatdom*, http://www.beatdom.com/allen-ginsberg-and-bob-dylan/ (accessed Mar. 24, 2019).
131. Trần Hữu Thục, "Một cái nhìn về ca từ Trịnh Công Sơn" (One View of Trịnh Công Sơn's Lyrics), *Văn học* [Literary Studies] 186 & 187 (Oct.-Nov., 2001), 60.
132. Roland Barthes, "From Work to Text," in *Image – Music – Text* (New York: Hill and Wang, 1977), 155-164.
133. Victor Shklovsky argued in 1917 that the "technique of art is . . . to increase the difficulty and length of perception because the process of perception is an aesthetic end in itself and must be prolonged." See Victor Shklovsky, "Art as Technique," in *Russian Formalist Criticism: Four Essays*, trans. and ed. by Lee T. Lemon and Marion J. Reis (Lincoln, NE: University of Nebraska Press, 1965), 12. I will discuss Shklovsky's views in Chapter Nineteen, "Understanding Trịnh Công Sơn's Obscurity."

"The Times They Are A-Changin'"—were not specifically about the war in Vietnam. To my knowledge Dylan never attended an anti-Vietnam War protest. In "To Bobby" Joan Baez sang about the cries of dying children and begged him to join her and other protestors, but her appeal fell on deaf ears.

Ochs, however, wrote songs about the Vietnam war and performed them at anti-war protests—songs like "Talking Vietnam" and "The War Is Over," which I have already discussed, as well as "White Boots Marching in a Yellow Land" and "We Seek No Wider War." In "White Boots Marching in a Yellow Land" Ochs brings up the issue of race: the fact that majority-white American soldiers are helping yellow Vietnamese soldiers kill other yellow Vietnamese soldiers. In the fourth stanza the speaker says that Americans are involved in a civil war between people of the same race, and that race loyalty will eventually trump other allegiances:

> Train them well, the men who will be fighting by your side
> And never turn your back if the battle turns the tide
> For the colors of a civil war are louder than commands
> When you're white boots marching in a yellow land

In the next stanza the speaker says "We're fighting in a war we lost before the war began" because "We're the white boots marching in a yellow land." In other words, there is no way those in the white boots are going to win this war. As explained in Chapter One, Trịnh Công Sơn also called the Vietnam War a civil war: "Twenty years of civil war," he sings in "A Mother's Legacy" [Gia tài của mẹ]*; and he also talks about race, emphasizing that in this civil war "golden-skinned" Vietnamese were killing other golden-skinned Vietnamese. In another song, "Who Is Still Vietnamese?" [Những ai còn là Việt Nam] he sings "Open your eyes and turn over the corpse of an enemy soldier / On it you'll see a Vietnamese face."

The title of Ochs' song "We Seek No Wider War" is a familiar refrain repeated often by President Lyndon Johnson and other people in his administration in speeches announcing some major escalation of the war, perhaps most notably on August 4, 1964, when Johnson approved the first bombing of North Vietnam after two US destroyers, the Maddox and the C. Turner Joy, were allegedly attacked in the Gulf of Tonkin by North Vietnamese torpedo boats. It came to light later that the second destroyer was never attacked. Apparently freak weather conditions affected the radar and caused overeager sonar operators to file false reports. This Gulf of Tonkin incident helped persuade members of Congress to pass the Gulf of

Tonkin Resolution, which became the legal justification for the Vietnam War. In announcing the bombing, President Johnson said "We seek no wider war."[134] In his song Ochs describes the "civilized soldiers" who, after committing various acts of destruction and violence, tell Vietnamese to "please be assured, we seek no wider war."

When the war finally did end after the North Vietnamese troops entered Saigon on April 30, 1975, a coalition of anti-war groups organized an End of War Rally in New York. In Sheep Meadow in Central Park on May 11, an estimated 50,000 people attended, many of them veterans of years of anti-Vietnam war rallies.[135] This would be Ochs' third "The War Is Over" rally. He had performed his song "The War is Over" on many other occasions, but the title was no longer an absurdist phrase: Now the war truly was over. Ochs and Cora Weiss, a leader in the anti-war movement, were co-chairs of the organizing committee. According to Michael Schumacher, Ochs "oversaw every detail of the event's planning, staying up for days on end, eschewing alcohol and running on raw energy alone."[136] The performers at the rally included Pete Seeger, Joan Baez, Peter Yarrow, Paul Simon and Odetta. Ochs and Joan Baez sang a duet of "There but for Fortune," and Ochs sang "The War is Over" one more time.[137]

Trịnh Công Sơn was not the Bob Dylan or the Phil Ochs of Vietnam. But Phil Ochs, in his fervent opposition to the war in Vietnam and perhaps in demeanor, resembles Trịnh Công Sơn more than Bob Dylan.

DYLAN IN HIS OLDER YEARS

Dylan's personal life has been complicated and bizarre. Dylan is obsessed with secrecy and so the general public did not know just how bizarre his love life was until Howard Sounes published his book *Down the Highway* in 2001. Sounes interviewed many people who knew Dylan well—band members, other singers, and girlfriends. Sounes concludes that Dylan became "an inveterate womanizer in young adulthood and would remain so throughout most of his life."[138] I have already explained that in the early 1960s he was seeing Suze Rotolo, Joan Baez, and Sara Lownds at the same time. While married to Lownds, he arranged for another

134. Geoffrey C. Ward and Ken Burns, *The Vietnam War: An Intimate History* (New York: Alfred A. Knopf, 2017), 105.
135. Paul L. Montgomery, "End-of-War Rally Brings Out 50,000," *New York Times*, May 12, 1975.
136. Michael Shumacher, *There but for Fortune*, 395.
137. Ibid., 305.
138. Howard Sounes, *Down the Highway*, 128.

girlfriend, a woman named Malka Marom, to live on his estate with them.[139] Her arrival hastened the collapse of Dylan's marriage to Lownds, which was already deteriorating as Dylan, according to Lownds, became "continuously quarrelsome." "I was in such fear of him," she says, "that I locked doors in the home to protect myself from his violent outbursts and temper tantrums. . . . He has struck me in the face, injuring my jaw. . . My five children are greatly disturbed by my husband's behavior and his bizarre lifestyle."[140] Immediately after the divorce in 1977, he had an affair with an art teacher that Lownds had hired to take care of their children, a woman named Faridi McFree.[141]

Sounes reveals that Dylan secretly married a backup singer named Carolyn Dennis in 1986 and kept this marriage a secret for years. He married her, it seems, because she gave birth in 1986 to his daughter, Desiree, and he wanted to give her a stable home life. At the time, however, he was dating an executive with Atlantic Records named Carole Childs, who didn't learn about this secret marriage until years later.[142]

NOBEL PRIZE FOR LITERATURE

In October 2016 Dylan received the Nobel Prize in Literature, perhaps the most prestigious award that a writer or singer-songwriter can win. The way he reacted to this great honor struck many fans and journalists, at least those not familiar with the Dylan way, as strange. In an article in the New York *Times*, Ben Sisario described Dylan's "tumultuous relationship with the Swedish Academy since he was awarded the Nobel Prize last fall."[143] After the award was announced, Dylan issued no response for two weeks, behavior which Per Wästberg, a member of the Academy, called "impolite and arrogant."[144] Finally, however, in November Dylan informed the Academy that "pre-existing conditions" prevented him from attending the award ceremony, which is always held on December

---

139. Ibid., 306-307.
140. These statements by Sara Lownds were made in court proceedings when she requested a restraining order against Dylan. See Clinton Heylin, *Bob Dylan: Behind the Shades*, 286. See also Heylin's footnotes to Chapter 25, page 449.
141. Clinton Heylin, *Bob Dylan: Behind the Shades*, 287.
142. Howard Sounes, *Down the Highway: The Life of Bob Dylan*, 372.
143. Ben Sisario, "Bob Dylan Delivers His Nobel Prize Lecture, Just in Time," *New York Times*, June 5, 2017. https://www.nytimes.com/2017/06/05/arts/music/bob-dylan-nobel-prize-lecture-literature.html (accessed Apr. 15, 2019).
144. Per Wästberg is quoted by Liam Stack in "Bob Dylan's Silence on Nobel Prize Is Called 'Impolite and Arrogant' by Academy Member," *New York Times*, Oct. 22, 2016. https://www.nytimes.com/2016/10/23/arts/music/bob-dylan-nobel-prize-arrogant-impolite.html (accessed Apr. 15, 2019).

10, the anniversary of the death of Alfred Nobel, the Swedish inventor and philanthropist for whom the prize is named.[145] He did, however, send the Academy a long letter which was read at the ceremony by the United States Ambassador to Sweden, Azita Raji. In his letter Dylan apologizes for not being present in person but says that he is with them in spirit. He talks about reading the works of previous Nobel Prize winners—Rudyard Kipling, George Bernard Shaw, Thomas Mann, Pearl Buck, Albert Camus, and Earnest Hemingway. "That I now join the names on such a list," Dylan told the Academy, "is truly beyond words." "Not once have I ever had the time to ask myself, 'Are my songs literature?'" Dylan says in his closing paragraph. "So I do thank the Swedish Academy, both for taking the time to consider that very question, and, ultimately, for providing such a wonderful answer."[146]

Bob Dylan was not present at the ceremony but as a result of a strange coincidence, people attending the ceremony in Stockholm felt as if he were there, if not in body at least in spirit. In September 2016—before it was announced that Dylan would receive a Nobel Prize—the Swedish Academy had invited Patti Smith, the well-known American singer-songwriter, to perform at the Nobel Prize ceremony. She accepted the invitation and had chosen one of her own songs to sing, but after she learned that Dylan would be receiving an award she decided that it would not be appropriate for her to sing one of her songs and chose instead to sing Dylan's song "A Hard Rain's A-Gonna Fall." She explains that she had loved this song since she was a teenager and that it was one of her late husband's favorite songs. Her performance was remarkable for several reasons. After singing the first verse she was overcome by emotion and the solemnity of the occasion and simply could not continue. "I hadn't forgotten the words," she explains. "I was simply unable to draw them out."[147] She finally pulled herself together, completed the song and received loud applause.

Dylan finally picked up his Nobel medal in a private meeting with members of the Academy, when he was in Stockholm in April 2017 on his Never-Ending Tour. When he arrived, Alexandra Schwartz reports in an

---

145. Ben Sisario, "Bob Dylan Will Not Attend Nobel Ceremony," *New York Times*, Nov. 16, 2016. https://www.nytimes.com/2016/11/17/books/bob-dylan-not-attending-nobel-prize-ceremony-stockholm.html (accessed Apr. 15, 2019).
146. Bob Dylan, "Banquet Speech," The Nobel Prize, https://www.nobelprize.org/prizes/literature/2016/dylan/25424-bob-dylan-banquet-speech-2016 (accessed July 7, 2019).
147. Patti Smith, "How Does It Feel," *The New Yorker*, Dec. 14, 2016, https://www.newyorker.com/culture/cultural-comment/patti-smith-on-singing-at-bob-dylans-nobel-prize-ceremony (accessed June 9, 2019).

article in the New Yorker, "he looked more like a cat burglar than a laureate, sneaking into the private prize hand-off through a service door, wearing a hoodie, leather jacket, and gloves."[148] To receive his Nobel Prize officially, however, and to obtain the $900,000 award that came with it, Dylan had to deliver a lecture within six months of the official ceremony. He made the deadline but just barely, turning in a written and an oral recorded version just five days before the cutoff. In his lecture, Dylan explains how his reading of famous Anglo-American literary works inspired him to tell similar tales in his songs. I discuss his speech in Chapter Twenty: "Dylan and the Anglo-American Literary Tradition.

---

148. Alexandra Schwartz, "The Rambling Glory of Bob Dylan's Nobel Speech," *The New Yorker*, June 6, 2017. https://www.newyorker.com/culture/culture-desk/the-rambling-glory-of-bob-dylans-nobel-speech (accessed Aug. 8, 2019).

II

LITERARY & MUSICAL
TRADITIONS

W hy is Bob Dylan so often angry and accusatory, not only in his political finger-pointing songs, but also in many of his love songs?
Why is Trịnh Công Sơn so sad and forgiving in both his anti-war and love
songs? In attempting to answer these questions, I will emphasize religious
differences, but clearly other factors are involved. The two songwriters
come from countries that differ not just in religion but in a host of other ways. Vietnam and the US have different histories, climates, levels of
economic development, child-rearing practices, courtship and marriage
customs, and literary and musical traditions. One can't possibly talk about
all these differences. I emphasize religious differences because I believe
exploring them is the best way to understand these two singers and their
songs. Literary and musical traditions are also important, however, and
so before taking up religious differences I will discuss them. One needs
to know the traditions that Trịnh Công Sơn and Bob Dylan were reacting
to—furthering in some ways, opposing in others.

10

TRỊNH CÔNG SƠN'S EARLY YEARS & FRENCH SCHOOLING

EARLY YEARS

Trịnh Công Sơn was born in 1939 in Đắk Lắc Province in the Central Highlands but his home village was Minh Hương, on the northern edge of the city of Huế.[1] Minh Hương is in Hương Vinh Commune, Hương Trà District. "Minh" refers to the "Ming," the name of the Chinese Dynasty who ruled in China from 1368 to 1644. "Hương" means "village." So "Minh Hương" means "village of the Ming." When the Manchu took over China, many Ming loyalists came to Vietnam and they and their descendents were called "Minh Hương." Trịnh Công Sơn's father was descended from these Chinese immigrants who came to central Vietnam in the seventeenth century. Many Vietnamese have a Chinese ancestor in their family tree, so Sơn is not unusual in this regard.

Sơn's father, Trịnh Xuân Thanh, was a patriot and was involved in secret activities to support the resistance to colonial rule. The secret police

---

1. My account of Sơn's early years in this section and his French education in the next section is based on the following sources: Bửu Ý, *TCS: Một nhạc sĩ thiên tài* [TCS: A Genius of a Musician] (HCMC: Trẻ, 2003); Hoàng Phủ Ngọc Tường, *Trịnh Công Sơn và cây đàn lya của hoàng tử bé* [Trịnh Công Sơn and the Lyre of the Little Prince] (HCMC: Trẻ, 2004); Nguyễn Đắc Xuân, *Trịnh Công Sơn: Có một thời như thế* [Trịnh Công Sơn: There Was Such a Time], (HCMC: Văn Học, 2003); Sâm Thương, "Đi tìm thời gian đã mất" [In Search of Lost Times], https://www.sachhiem.net/VANHOC/Samthuong.php (accessed Apr. 27, 2022); email exchanges involving Sâm Thương, Phạm Văn Đình, Thái Kim Lan, and the author in February and December, 2005.

in Huế were watching him and making his life difficult, so in 1937 he quietly took his family to Đắk Lắc where he established a tailor shop in Buôn Mê Thuột, the largest town in the province. After Sơn was born in 1939 his mother gave birth to another boy, Trịnh Quang Hà, in 1941. In 1943 the family moved back to Huế and lived in a part of Huế called Bến Ngự, or Royal Wharf, because kings of the Nguyễn Dynasty going by boat up the An Cư River used to dock their boats there. The family grew and by 1956, when his last sibling was born—a girl named Trịnh Vĩnh Trinh— Trịnh Công Sơn had seven siblings—two brothers and five sisters.[2]

The decade of the 1940s was a tumultuous time for the world and for Vietnam.[3] When the decade began, Vietnam was ruled by France but different modes of control were applied depending on the region. The six southernmost provinces were an outright colony of France called Cochin China. The northern and central provinces, referred to as Tonkin and Annam[4] respectively, were protectorates. Nominally Bảo Đại, Vietnam's last emperor, ruled Tonkin and Annam, but his power was only theoretical. Emperor Bảo Đại had ceremonial duties, but the French Résident Supérieur in each protectorate made all the important decisions. In March of 1940, Japan occupied Vietnam. Then in May Germany occupied France and set up Marshall Philippe Pétain as head of a French puppet regime in Vichy. Because Japan left intact—until 1945—the French colonial administration in Vietnam, the French were not yet forced to relinquish completely their power over Vietnam.

At mid-decade, however, more momentous events occurred. Germany surrendered on May 8, 1945, and, after the Americans bombed Hiroshima and Nagasaki, Japan capitulated on August 15. At the Potsdam Conference that had taken place only a few weeks before (July 17-August 2, 1945), US President Harry Truman, British Prime Minister Winston

---

2. Sơn was not the firstborn but he ended up being the oldest son because Trịnh Xuân Dương, born in 1936, died soon after he was born. See Nguyễn Đắc Xuân, *Trịnh Công Sơn: Có một thời như thế*, 19.
3. In preparing this summary I have consulted the following: Joseph Buttinger, *Vietnam: A Dragon Embattled*, vol. 2, *Vietnam at War* (New York: Frederick A. Praeger, 1967); Stanley Karnow, *Vietnam: A History* (New York: Viking Press, 1983); and Robert Shaplen, *The Lost Revolution* (New York: Harper Colophon Books, 1955).
4. Vietnamese object to the term "Annam," from a Chinese term meaning "pacified south," and it was not used after the French were defeated. The French used it, and the related term Annamese, in confusing fashion. Annam referred to central Vietnam but also to Vietnam as a whole and "Annamese" could refer to all Vietnamese, not simply to those who lived in central Vietnam.

Churchill (later Clement Attlee),[5] and Soviet Premier Joseph Stalin had already decided that British troops would disarm the Japanese south of the 17th parallel, which cuts across Vietnam sixty miles north of Huế, and Chinese Nationalist troops would have this responsibility north of this line. Taking advantage of the political uncertainty following the Japanese surrender, popular forces inspired by Hồ Chí Minh and led by Võ Nguyên Giáp seized control of towns and cities throughout the country. This "August Revolution" (Cách Mạng Tháng Tám) culminated in Hồ Chí Minh declaring the independence of Vietnam on September 2, 1945.

Hồ Chí Minh's declaration of independence did not, however, end France's power in Vietnam. The British commander of the British forces sent to south Vietnam to disarm the Japanese was a dyed-in-the-wool colonialist named Douglas Gracey. His orders from Lord Louis Mountbatten, the Allied commander for Southeast Asia, were to disarm the Japanese and not get involved in internal problems. He did not follow orders. When he arrived in Saigon on September 12, government buildings in Saigon were occupied by Hồ Chí Minh's Việt Minh forces.[6] Gracey rearmed the French and threw the Việt Minh authorities out, an action which set the stage for the First Indochina War. After French warships bombed the northern city of Hải Phòng on November 23, 1946, the war began.

From 1946 to 1949 Võ Nguyên Giáp's Việt Minh troops used guerilla tactics, mounting small operations to harass French forces. Large scale operations began in 1950 after Chinese communists reached the Vietnamese border and began supplying the Việt Minh with automatic weapons, mortars, howitzers, and trucks.[7] The Việt Minh's pre-1950 operations may have been small, but they were effective. By 1947 Việt Minh forces controlled about a half to two-thirds of the entire country.[8] The French firmly controlled only what the Việt Minh called "occupied zones," which consisted of Hanoi, Huế, the Saigon-Cho Lon area, the valley of the Lower Mekong, the rubber-producing areas of Cochin China, and the industrialized north (Nam Định, Hải Phòng, Hòn Gay). Việt Minh officials divided the rest of the country into three zones based on

<hr>

5. Attlee won a general election and became Prime Minister during the conference.
6. Robert Shaplen, *The Lost Revolution*, 6.
7. Stanley Karnow, *Vietnam: A History*, 184.
8. Joseph Buttinger says "at least half." See *Vietnam: A Dragon Embattled*, 739. Jean Chesneaux says "about two-thirds." See *The Vietnamese Nation: Contribution to a History*, trans. Malcolm Salmon (Sydney, Australia: Current Book Distributors, 1966), 185.

the degree of control they exerted over the zone. "Free zones" were areas under their control that were subject to French air raids and paratrooper landings; "guerilla bases" were areas in which they had outposts inside the lines of the French Expeditionary Corps; "guerilla zones" were contested areas where military operations were occurring.[9]

Việt Minh control was particularly strong in the north and central regions. According to Joseph Buttinger, they controlled "close to eighty percent of both the land and people of northern and central Annam [Vietnam]" and they retained this control at the end of the First Indochina War in 1954.[10] The Việt Minh did not control Huế but they were firmly entrenched in the surrounding countryside of Thừa Thiên Province. In fact, they were entrenched in all the coastal provinces of central Vietnam— Quảng Trị, Thừa Thiên, Quảng Nam, and Bình Định. These provinces in the narrow middle of Vietnam offered limited incentives for colonial exploitation, and the French never established a firm presence in them. According to the Việt Minh classification just described, Huế, occupied by the French, was in an "occupied" zone, but most of the coastal provinces were a "free zone" under Việt Minh control.[11] In fact, between the coastal cities of Vinh in Nghệ An Province and Quy Nhơn in Bình Định Province, the Việt Minh controlled all but a narrow coastal strip from Đà Nẵng to Quảng Trị, a stretch that included the city of Huế. But French control of even this strip was shaky. From a string of fortified villages built on coastal sand dunes, Việt Minh forces would attack French forces on Highway 1. The section of this highway between Huế and Quang Tri was attacked so often that French soldiers called it "*la rue sans joie*," the street without joy.[12]

In an essay, "A Childhood Obsession," Trịnh Công Sơn says that when he was young he was obsessed with death. He would dream, he says, about the death of his father.[13] His obsession stems, at least in part, from the fact that although Huế did not become a battleground until the Tết Offensive of 1968, death and suffering were never far away. According to his close friend Sâm Thương, Trịnh Công Sơn would often talk about two places

---

9. Jean Chesneaux, *The Vietnamese Nation*, 185-90.
10. Joseph Buttinger, *Vietnam: A Dragon Embattled*, 740.
11. Ibid., 185.
12. See Bernard Fall, *Street Without Joy: Indochina at War* (Harrisburg, PA: Telegraph Press, 1961).
13. Trịnh Công Sơn, "Nỗi ám ảnh thời thơ ấu" [A Childhood Obsession] in *Trịnh Công Sơn: Tôi là ai là ai …* [Trịnh Công Sơn: Who Am I?], ed. Nguyễn Minh Nhựt (HCMC: Trẻ, 2011), 133-134. The original date and source are not given.

near his childhood home in Bến Ngự. One was a French garrison near the bridge over the An Cựu River. Walking by this garrison Trịnh Công Sơn heard the screams of detainees being tortured. The other place was a tall, ancient almond tree [*cây bàng*]. Sâm Thương describes what Trịnh Công Sơn would see when he walked by this tree on the way to school:

> Early in the morning distraught people, French and Vietnamese alike, would gather in front of this almond tree to view corpses hanging from the branches, their heads thrown back, their bodies slashed. Written in blood in large letters on their shirts or on banners were the words: "Punishment for Vietnamese traitors" or "Invaders must pay for their crimes." These words and images always attracted the nervous attention of those living in this area, including young students like Sơn. On these occasions, Sơn, before he went to school, would go with some friends to sneak a look at these scenes, and then they would disperse, each one reflecting, in a no doubt undefined way, on what they had seen.[14]

Huế may have been occupied by the French, but Việt Minh cadres were able to enter at night and kill those they considered "Việt gian"—traitors to the nation. In the two places Trịnh Công Sơn remembers as a young child, the French Garrison and the almond tree, Vietnamese—on both sides of the conflict—were being tortured and killed in gruesome ways.

For Trịnh Công Sơn the suffering was very close to home. In "A Childhood Obsession," Sơn says that his worries about his father's death "probably resulted from his father having been imprisoned and tortured until he died and came back to life again when he was active in the resistance against the French. During the last years of the decade of the 1940s it was as if my father's primary residence was the prison."[15] He and his mother took turns visiting his father in Thừa Phủ Prison, and in 1949 Sơn was allowed to spend some time in prison with his father. This had been a French prison and famous revolutionaries, including General Võ Nguyên Giáp and the poet Tố Hữu, spent time there.[16] Later in 1949 Sơn's father took him and his brother Hà to Saigon to open a new family business: selling parts for bicycles and motorcycles. No doubt Sơn's father decided he had to get out of Hue to avoid being tortured and imprisoned. The next year the entire family joined them in Saigon. After the Geneva Accords were signed in 1954, the family moved back to Huế. In 1955, just

---

14. Sâm Thương, "Đi tìm thời gian đã mất."
15. Trịnh Công Sơn, "Nỗi ám ảnh thời thơ ấu," 133.
16. The prison no longer exists. It was destroyed when the International Hospital [Bệnh Viện Quốc Tế] was built.

after Sơn turned 15, his father went to Quảng Trị, about fifty miles north of Huế. He was killed on his way back to Huế.

Mystery surrounds Sơn's father's death. Two of Sơn's friends, Nguyễn Đắc Xuân and Sâm Thương, provide different accounts. In Nguyễn Đắc Xuân's account, on June 17, 1955, Sơn's father went to Quảng Trị by Vespa to set up an underground network for the Việt Minh. On his return to Huế he was turning off the road to avoid military vehicles belonging to the Ngô Đình Diệm regime when he lost control of his Vespa and crashed, hitting his head on a rock. His friends got him to the hospital in Huế but he died a few hours later. In Sâm Thương's account Sơn's father and two other men, one of them his brother-in-law, were traveling to Quảng Trị on motorcycles to investigate business prospects there. There is no mention of it being a secret trip to assist the Việt Minh. On their return trip to Huế Sơn's father tried to swerve out of the way of a truck coming from the opposite direction but failed and was struck. He died in a hospital in Huế soon after the accident—on June 17, 1955.

Obviously, before 1975 Sơn and his family would not have wanted to talk about his father's revolutionary activities. This would not be wise when intensely anti-communist regimes controlled South Vietnam. Perhaps Sâm Thương's version is based on a very guarded account that Sơn told him before 1975. Nguyễn Đắc Xuân says that Trịnh Công Sơn told him in 1977 that his father was on a mission for the Việt Minh when the accident occurred. (Nguyễn Đắc Xuân puts "accident" [*tai nạn*] in quotes, hinting that his death was not an accident.) Surprised, and probably desiring to improve Trịnh Công Sơn's relations with the new government, Nguyễn Đắc Xuân immediately asked Trịnh Công Sơn why he didn't seek a paper to confirm his father's contribution to the revolution. Trịnh Công Sơn replied: "That relates to my father. As for me, my music is my confirmation."[17] This comment suggests that Trịnh Công Sơn was not as eager to ingratiate himself with the new government as Nguyễn Đắc Xuân expected him to be.

Nguyễn Đắc Xuân also reports that in another conversation, one which took place in the early 1980s, Sơn told him that he had an uncle, an older brother of his father's, who was active in the Resistance in the Đắc Lắc area. This uncle regrouped [*tập kết*] to the North in 1954, as required

---

17. Nguyễn Đắc Xuân, *Trịnh Công Sơn: Có một thời như thế*, 27.

by the Geneva Accords,[18] but returned to Đắc Lắc in 1975. As in the American Civil War, in the Vietnam War members of the same family often ended up on different sides of the conflict. In "A Mother's Legacy"* Trịnh Công Sơn sings about a mother who hopes that her children far away, children of the same race, will forget hatred.

In "A Childhood Obsession" Sơn traces the "quiet atmosphere of loss" and the "obsession with the absence of people" that pervades his songs to his father's death:

> Clearly death alarmed the extremely sensitive soul of a young boy. My father died when I had just turned fifteen. Lingering in many songs early in my life is a quiet atmosphere of loss. To a greater extent later, as I slowly progressed toward adulthood, in the midst of life's pressures, during sad and happy times, that obsession [with death] became—exactly when I do not know—the source of a long-standing worry about the absence of people.[19]

For Sơn, it seems, his father's death forced him to come to grips with impermanence, one of the most important concepts in Buddhism. After his father died, Sơn's family went to Phổ Quang Pagoda in Huế where monks chanted prayers for the dead in a ceremony called *cầu siêu*. While mourning his father's death Sơn completed the Buddhist ceremony called *quy y* which resembles, in some ways, Christian baptism. It involves taking a Buddhist name and accepting the Three Jewels of Buddhism [*Tam Bảo*]—Buddha, dharma, and sangha [*Phật, Pháp*, and *Tăng già*]. According to Thích Nhất Hạnh, who talked with Buddhist monks who knew Trịnh Công Sơn in Huế, Sơn often visited Hiếu Quang Pagoda or Phổ Quang Pagoda, which were both very near his home, and sometimes stayed at these pagodas for the night.[20] "Faced with an immense loss," Sâm Thương says, "Sơn probably turned to the Buddha for spiritual peace."[21]

---

18. The Geneva Accords, which ended the First Indochina War, divided Vietnam temporarily at the 17th parallel and called for elections in two years. It required that French forces withdraw from the North and Việt Minh forces from the South. Vietnamese say Việt Minh cadre "regrouped" (*tập kết*) to the North in 1954.

19. Trịnh Công Sơn, "Nỗi ám ảnh thời thơ ấu," 134.

20. Thích Nhất Hạnh mentions Trịnh Công Sơn's visits to pagodas in Huế in a series of dharma talks about Buddhism and Trịnh Công Sơn that he organized in 2010. The title of the series is *Thiền Sư Nhất Hạnh Pháp Thoại TCS* [Zen Monk Nhất Hạnh Leads Dharma Talk on TCS]. The talks are in Vietnamese. Youtube recordings of all ten talks are available online at multiple sites including this one: https://www.youtube.com/watch?v=LfrAeX-nM2w

21. Sâm Thương, "Đi tìm thời gian đã mất."

FRENCH SCHOOLING

Trịnh Công Sơn received his middle and high school education in French schools. In the French schools in Vietnam in the 1950s there were two levels: a primary level which began with grade eleven and ended with grade seven, and a secondary level which began with grade six and ended with grade one. Sơn attended a Vietnamese primary school and then began attending French schools, eventually finishing all but the last year of the secondary cycle. If Trịnh Công Sơn had instead gone to Vietnamese schools, he probably would have studied more works by Vietnamese writers. In explaining what was new about Sơn's songs Vietnamese scholars point out that his songs do not echo traditional verse forms—like *thất ngôn đường luật* [literally, "seven-word T'ang prosody"], a T'ang form consisting of seven words per line that Vietnamese inherited from the Chinese—as closely as songs composed by older songwriters, including Văn Cao and Phạm Duy, contemporaries of Trịnh Công Sơn who were the most famous Vietnamese song composers when Trịnh Công Sơn burst onto the scene.[22] "How did such a young man who was educated only in French schools learn to use Vietnamese so exquisitely?" the scholar Đặng Tiến asks.[23] In searching for an answer, he suggests that perhaps Trịnh Công Sơn's French schooling was an advantage. Perhaps because he didn't study Vietnamese literature intensely, Đặng Tiến hypothesizes, he "wasn't a slave to the old rules of versification and his mind wasn't full of classical, ready-made literary allusions."[24] To evaluate observations like this one by Đặng Tiến we need to know more about both Trịnh Công Sơn's educational background.

Attending French schools was prestigious. Most students attending them were from families who were, if not rich, fairly well off. Because these schools included teachers who were native speakers of French, and because the medium of instruction was French, students who attended them had the opportunity to learn how to speak French well. Because French was also the medium of instruction used in many university level courses, going to a French school facilitated further education in fields such as medicine or architecture. By 1956, the percentage of native Vietnamese

---

22. Đặng Tiến, "Trịnh Công Sơn: đời và nhạc" [Trịnh Công Sơn: Life and Music] *Văn* 53 & 54 (2001), 11-13; Văn Ngọc, "Trịnh Công Sơn, Khánh Ly và những khúc tình ca một thời" [Trịnh Công Sơn, Khánh Ly and the Love Songs of an Era], *Diễn đàn* [Forum] 110 (Sept. 2001), 27-28.
23. Ibid., 11.
24. Ibid.

in French secondary schools was 81% but there were French and Eurasian students at these schools as well.[25] Students like Trịnh Công Sơn who attended French schools were therefore more immersed in modern international culture than were students who attended Vietnamese schools. In these French schools Sơn was exposed to works by Alfred de Musset, Alphonse Daudet, Anatole France, Antoine de Saint-Exupéry, and other French writers.[26]

Figuring out exactly which secondary schools Sơn attended and when he attended them is difficult because his friends—in books, articles, and emails to me—do not agree on all points. I contacted some of Trịnh Công Sơn's brothers and sisters, but in emails they explained that they were young and busy with their own lives when Sơn, the oldest in the family, was in school and so couldn't say exactly when he attended which French school. I will present what I think is a correct account but will also mention points of disagreement in footnotes.[27] First, however, some background information on French schools in Vietnam. The goal of French colonialists in the nineteenth century was to make Vietnam a monolingual French-speaking state. Their goal was not bilingualism but something resembling linguistic genocide. In 1890 Monsignor Puginier, head of Catholic missionaries in North Vietnam, spoke of establishing "a little France of the Far East."[28] Etienne Aymonier, Director of the École Coloniale, an elite training school for colonial administrators, foresaw "an Asiatic France solidly tied to European France by this community of ideas and sentiments which alone will enable the metropolis to benefit directly from the future progress of the colony." The "surest and most efficacious means to obtain this supreme result," Aymonier added, was "the diffusion of the French language in the Far East."[29] The only argument among French colonialists was whether to achieve this goal by a direct or indirect approach—by teaching French immediately or by first teaching the Vietnamese writing system, the so-called National Script

---

25. Thaveeporn Vasavakul, "Schools and Politics in South and North Viet Nam: A Comparative Study of State Apparatus, State Policy, and State Power (1945-1965)," PhD diss., (Cornell University: 1994), 116.
26. Sâm Thương, "Đi tìm thời gian đã mất" [In Search of Lost Times].
27. See note 1 for the sources on which this account of Sơn's schooling is based.
28. Puginier is quoted by John DeFrancis in *Colonialism and Language Policy in Viet Nam* (The Hague: Mouton Publishers, 1977), 140.
29. Etienne Aymonier, *La langue française et l'enseignement en Indochine* (Paris: Armand Colin et Cie 1880), 7. John DeFrancis summarizes the views of Puginier and Aymonier in *Colonialism and Language Policy in Viet Nam*, 131-142.

[Quốc Ngữ] which the French missionary Alexandre de Rhodes, working with Vietnamese scholars, had devised in the seventeenth century. Quốc Ngữ was, like most Western European writing systems, a Romanized system using Latin characters, and some administrators realized it could therefore be used to transition students to French.

World War II, and then France's defeat in the First Indochina War, led to changes in Vietnam's educational system. To regain control after World War II the French made concessions in an attempt to head off nationalist opposition to their continuing presence.[30] One concession, granted in 1948, was to make Vietnamese the language of instruction in Vietnamese primary and secondary schools while retaining French as a "second language."[31] A series of decrees issued by the Ministry of Education in 1953 reaffirmed that Vietnamese would be the medium of instruction. In these decrees French was listed as a "compulsory" foreign language whereas English and Chinese could be taken as electives.[32]

The reforms described above, however, affected only Vietnamese schools, not French schools. A Cultural Convention signed in 1949 by Bảo Đại, the Head of State, and Léon Pignon, French High Commissioner in Indochina, allowed France to maintain a cultural presence in Vietnam. This "presence" could include the maintenance of public and private primary and secondary schools based on the French educational model.[33] This agreement privileged the French language by considering it as occupying some middle ground between "national" language and "foreign" language.[34] Bảo Đại probably could not have objected to French schools even if he had wanted to: The Élysée Agreement between French representatives and the new Associated State of Vietnam, which was signed in March, 1949, acceded him only inconsequential powers. But even after South Vietnam became an independent republic after 1954, the French government still retained control of its French schools which were administered by the French Cultural and Educational Mission in Viet Nam.[35] There were both public and private French schools. Tuition was lower at the public French schools than it was at the private schools, most of which were run by the Catholic Church. There were three private

---

30. John DeFrancis, *Colonialism and Language Policy in Viet Nam*, 228.
31. Thaveeporn Vasuvakul, "Schools and Politics in South and North Viet Nam," 97-98.
32. Ibid., 101-102.
33. Ibid., 107-108.
34. Ibid., 101.
35. Ibid., 114.

secondary schools in Huế: the École Pellerin, which was run by the Brothers of Christian Schools [Frères des écoles chrétiennes]; the Institution de la Providence [Trường Thiên Hựu], run by the Catholic diocese in Huế; and the Lycée Jeanne D'Arc, a secondary school for girls.

Trịnh Công Sơn went to Vietnamese primary schools in Huế, but when the family moved to Saigon in 1950 he began studying at the Lycée Chasseloup-Laubat, a public French school. Prosper de Chasseloup-Laubat was an arch colonialist—Minister of the Navy under Napoleon III when France attacked Saigon in 1861—and so when the First Indochina War ended in 1954 and South Vietnam became an independent state (the Republic of Vietnam), the school was re-named Lycée Jean Jacques Rousseau.[36] After the family moved from Saigon back to Huế in 1954, Sơn studied for one year at the Lycée Français de Huế, also a public French school. When this school closed in 1955, Sơn moved to the Institution de la Providence, or Trường Thiên Hựu, a private French school run by the Catholic diocese in Huế.[37] He remained at this school until he received his First Baccalaureate [Tú tài bán phần] in 1956 and then returned to his old school in Saigon, the Lycée Jean Jacques Rousseau, to study for his Second Baccalaureate.[38] He never attained this goal. An accident pushed him in a different direction. Sơn liked sports—running, lifting weights,

---

36. The Geneva Accords of 1954 divided Vietnam into two countries, the Republic of Vietnam in the South and the North Vietnam, or Democratic Republic of Vietnam, in the North. The Accords stipulated that free elections be held in 1956 to reunify the country.

37. Let me point out here some confusing discrepancies in accounts of Sơn's schooling. Nguyễn Đắc Xuân quotes Sơn himself as saying he studied also at another French school in Huế, École Pellerin, a private French school in Huế which was run by the Brothers of Christian Schools [Frères des écoles chrétiennes]. Other friends of Sơn do not say he attended École Pellerin. See Nguyễn Đắc Xuân, *Trịnh Công Sơn: Có một thời như thế* [Trịnh Công Sơn: There Was Such a Time], 28. Nguyễn Đắc Xuân and Bửu Ý say that Sơn returned to Saigon in 1958—not 1956—to study philosophy and prepare for his second Baccalaureate exam at Lycée Chasseloup-Laubat. Sâm Thương, however, argues for the 1956 date. In an essay Sơn talks about being alone in Saigon in 1956-1957. This is the essay in which he mentions sleepless nights and his decision that he wanted to express himself and reach out to other people through song. It seems, therefore, that he returned to Saigon in 1956, not 1958. See Nguyễn Đắc Xuân, *Trịnh Công Sơn: Có một thời như thế* [Trịnh Công Sơn: There Was Such a Time], 25; Bửu Ý, *TCS: Một nhạc sĩ thiên tài* [TCS: A Genius of a Musician], 20; Sâm Thương, email to author, Feb. 24, 2005; Trịnh Công Sơn, "Phác thảo chân dung tôi" [Sketching a Self-Portrait], in *TCS: Tôi là ai là ai . . .* [TCS: Who Am I, Am I . . .], eds. Nguyễn Minh Nhựt et al. (HCMC: Trẻ, 2011), 13-14. Sơn's essay originally appeared in *Phụ san Thơ-Văn Nghệ* [Poetry and Art], No. III (2003).

38. Bửu Ý says that Sơn passed his Baccalaureate I exam in Đà Nẵng in 1958, but Sâm Thương argues that he must have passed it earlier, before he began to study for his Baccalaureate II exam at Lycée Chasseloup Laubat, because one has to have a Bac I to study for a Bac II. See Bửu Ý, *TCS: Một nhạc sĩ thiên tài* [TCS: A Genius of a Musician], 20; Sâm Thương, email to the author, Feb. 24, 2005.

and martial arts. While back in Huế on vacation in 1957, he injured himself while practicing Judo with his brother Hà. His brother's elbow struck Sơn's chest, piercing an artery in his lung, and it took him two years to recover.[39] This accident was, as both he and his friends attest, a turning point in his life. He never returned to the Lycée Jean Jacques Rousseau but instead remained in Huế where he hung out with some close friends and began writing songs. "Wet Eyelashes" [Ướt mi], his first song to be publicly released, first appeared in 1957.

---

39. Trịnh Công Sơn, "Để bắt đầu một hồi ức" [To Begin a Recollection], *Âm Nhạc* [Music] (1997); reprinted in Nguyễn Trọng Tạo et al., ed., *Trịnh Công Sơn: Một người thơ ca một cõi đi về* [Trịnh Công Sơn: A Singer-poet, a Place for Leaving and Returning] (Hanoi: Âm Nhạc, 2001), 202.

11

TRỊNH CÔNG SƠN'S INFORMAL EDUCATION IN HUẾ

Sơn studied philosophy during his last year in secondary school, but it seems he learned more about philosophy and the world from the reading he did on his own and from conversations with his sophisticated friends. In this respect he resembled Bob Dylan, who enrolled at the University of Minnesota but soon left for Greenwich Village where he read books on his own and learned much from well-informed friends. After the Geneva Accords ended the First Indochina War in 1954, intellectual and artistic activity flourished in South Vietnam as students and teachers returned from studies abroad bringing new ideas home with them. Northern refugees, many of them Catholics, also moved to the south and added their talents to the mix.

Huế in the mid-1950s was a small city of around 100,000 people. Because it had been home to Vietnam's emperors, who had a vested interest in preserving old customs, and because it lacked a seaport and had little industry, it was more insular and conservative than Đà Nẵng or Saigon. But after 1954 the city began to change. In 1957 the Huế School of Fine Arts [Trường Mỹ thuật Huế] was established. Saigon had a similar school, the National School of Fine Art [Trường Quốc gia Cao đẳng Mỹ thuật Sài Gòn], but according to Hoàng Phủ Ngọc Tường the Huế school was a livelier place, primarily because it was able to attract young teachers recently returned from France. These teachers, he says, with their "brand new ideas about Western post-war painting," were able to attract students from the Saigon area, including Trịnh Công Sơn's close friend Đinh Cường.[1]

Huế became a university town when the University of Huế was also founded in 1957, the same year the new art school opened its doors. In 1958 the first issue of a scholarly journal called *University: A Research Journal of the University of Huế* [Đại Học: Tạp Chí Nghiên Cứu Viện Đại Học Huế] was published. It was edited by a northern Catholic intellectual named Nguyễn Văn Trung, who had recently returned from study in Belgium. Well-read, passionate about philosophy, and a skillful writer, Professor Trung became, Sơn's friend Bửu Ý says, the leader of philosophical discussions in Huế.[2]

The journal *University* contained many articles on existential philosophy, many written by Professor Trung himself. His article "The Problem of Human Liberation in Buddhism and in the Thought of J.P. Sartre" [Vấn đề giải thoát con người trong Phật Giáo và tư tưởng J. P. Sartre], appeared in the second issue published in May 1958. Another article, "Some Reflections on the Absurd Condition of the Exile," primarily a discussion of Camus' *The Myth of Sisyphus*, appeared two years later in an issue memorializing the Nobel prize-winning author, who died in an auto accident on January 4, 1960. In the November 1960 issue of *University*, there appeared articles—written by other scholars—on Merleau-Ponty, Gabriel Marcel, Karl Jaspers, and Martin Heidegger. In his book *Twenty Years of Literature in South Vietnam—1954-1975* [Hai mươi năm văn học miền nam—1954-1975] the writer Võ Phiến, who grew up in central Vietnam, says that in the mid- and late 1950s, young people were tired of the old "-ism's"—nationalism, communism, capitalism, Marxism, Confucianism, Buddhism. "They were waiting for something new, a way out, some kind of escape. There was a vague but pressing expectation. A thirst for philosophy—the thirst of the age." Professor Trung, Võ Phiến

---

1. Hoàng Phủ Ngọc Tường, *Trịnh Công Sơn và cây đàn lya của hoàng tử bé* [Trịnh Công Sơn and the Lyre of the Little Prince] (HCMC: Trẻ, 2004), 23.
2. Bửu Ý, *TCS: Một nhạc sĩ thiên tài* [TCS: A Genius of a Musician] (HCMC: Trẻ, 2003), 19.

says, "responded to this expectation and he was warmly received. His 'comments' were read, distributed, and discussed by young people."[3]

These young people surely included Trịnh Công Sơn. His close friend Hoàng Phủ Ngọc Tường, who taught philosophy at the National Secondary School [Trường Quốc Học], had written his thesis under Nguyễn Văn Trung's direction at the University of Saigon where Professor Trung taught before moving to the University of Huế. Another friend of Sơn's, a woman named Thái Thị Kim Lan, a student at Huế University, describes "movements in the West" that intrigued her and her friends, including Sơn: "The existentialism of Heidegger, Sartre, and Camus; the movement in film of Jean Luc Godard, the approach to 'Chanson' of Juliette Greco, F. Hardy." These movements, she continues, "came to us young people in the 60s like an ill wind blowing through the city of Huế, a small city insulated from the outside world and very traditional in its way of thinking and acting."[4]

Like many young Vietnamese in South Vietnam at this time, Sơn was fascinated by philosophy, especially existentialism. It was an interest that he apparently pursued out of school more than in. For his final year of secondary school Trịnh Công Sơn did choose track C, the philosophy path,[5] but he never finished the year, and, according to Sâm Thương, the philosophy courses he took did not emphasize individual philosophers but rather were general introductions to logic, morality, and psychology. Sâm Thương says that Sơn read philosophers on his own, especially while he was recovering from the Judo accident. His out-of-school reading included works by Friedrich Nietzsche, Albert Camus, Jean Paul Sartre, Martin Heidegger, Merleau-Ponty, and Rabindranath Tagore. Sơn was also interested in works by French poets, novelists, screenwriters, and filmmakers. Sâm Thương mentions Guillaume Apollinaire, Marcel Pagnol, Jacques Prevert, and Marcel Proust.[6] How deeply any of these

3. Võ Phiến, *Văn học miền nam tổng quan: 1954-1975* [Literature in South Vietnam: 1954-1975] (Westminster, CA: Văn Nghệ, 1986), 192.
4. Thái Thị Kim Lan, "TCS, Nơi vùng ưu tư thành tiếng du ca" [Trịnh Công Sơn: Where Sorrow Becomes a Folk Song], in *Trịnh Công Sơn: Cuộc đời, âm nhạc, thơ, hội họa và suy tưởng* [TCS: Life, Music, Poetry, Painting, Reflections], ed. Trịnh Cung and Nguyễn Quốc Thái (HCMC: Văn Nghệ, 2001), 84.
5. French secondary schools offered three tracks: math (track A), experimental sciences (track B), and philosophy (track C). When Sơn went to Saigon to study for his Baccalaureate II at Lycée Jean Jacques Rousseau he chose track C.
6. Sâm Thương, "Đi tìm thời gian đã mất [In Search of Lost Times], https://web.archive.org/web/20100621125353/http://www.tcs-home.org/ban-be/sam-thuong/DiTimThoiGianDaMat1 (accessed January 15, 2014).

works affected Sơn is difficult to determine. It is clear that he admired the poems of Apollinaire and was intrigued by Albert Camus' *The Myth of Sisyphus*.

Tuấn Huy, a friend of the singer's, reports meeting Sơn at a party in Saigon in the 1960s. When they raised their drink glasses, filled with "strong amber whiskey," Sơn quoted these lines from Apollinaire's poem "Zone": *E tu bois cet alcool brûlant comme ta vie / Ta vie que tu bois comme une eau-de-vie* [And you drink this burning alcohol / Burning like your life]. "Apollinaire," Tuấn Huy said. "Wonderful. Drinking whisky and reciting a poem by Apollinaire. I love Apollinaire." "I do, too," Sơn replied. "When I was still in school, I would take a book of poems by Apollinaire with me and murmur to myself each word of his outstanding poems and gaze dreamily out at the white clouds drifting by the window. I especially like these two lines: '*Jeunesse adieu jasmin du temps / J'ai respiré ton frais parfum*' [Farewell youth jasmine of time / I breathed your fresh perfume]."[7] In a short article written in 1974 Sơn reminisces about his friend Đinh Cường who, he says, was nostalgic— "passionate about memories." Sơn fondly remembers former times with friends like Đinh Cường. Then he quotes the first two lines from Apollinaire's five-line poem "L'Adieu": *J'ai cueilli ce brin de bruyère / L'Automne est morte, souviens-t'en* [I gathered a sprig of heather / The autumn is dead, remember].[8]

Phạm Duy, older than Trịnh Công Sơn and already famous in the 1950s, wrote a song in 1965 based on "L'Adieu" titled "Dead Autumn" [Mùa thu chết]. Phạm Duy's song became very popular in the 1970s after famous singers, including Khánh Ly, sang it in tea houses in Saigon.[9] Phạm Duy's lyrics are a loose translation of Apollinaire's poem. Here are the opening lines:

> *I pick a wisp of heather—*
> *Remember, dear, autumn now is dead!*
> *Autumn has died, remember this,*
> *Autumn has died, has died*

---

7. Trịnh Công Sơn quotes lines from Apollinaire's "Les Collines" [The Hills]. See Tuấn Huy, "Trịnh Công Sơn, có sót xa người" [Trịnh Công Sơn: Painful Memories of Someone], *Văn học* [Literary Studies] 186 & 187 (Oct.-Nov., 2001), 31.
8. Trịnh Công Sơn, "Đinh Cường," in *TCS: Tôi là ai là ai...*, eds. Nguyễn Minh Nhựt et al. (HCMC: Trẻ, 2011), 43. No information is provided regarding where this short essay was first published in 1974.
9. Phạm Duy, *Hồi ký* [Memoirs], Vol. III, *Thời phân chia quốc-cộng* [The Period of Nationalist-Communist Division] (Midway City, CA: Phạm Duy Cường Musical Productions, 1991), 255.

Remember this; the two of us
Will never look upon each other further in this world[10]

Ta ngắt đi một cụm hoa thạch thảo
Em nhớ cho: Mùa thu đã chết rồi
Mùa Thu đã chết, em nhớ cho
Mùa Thu đã chết, đã chết rồi
Em nhớ cho, đôi chúng ta
Sẽ chẳng còn nhìn nhau nữa trên cõi đời này!

In his memoirs Phạm Duy says that in this song he "extended the tradition of 'autumn music' [*nhạc mùa thu*] of romantic composers of former times."[11] This is a rich tradition that probably goes back at least as far as seventh and eighth century T'ang poems.[12] The "romantic composers of former times" that Phạm Duy mentions are probably composers of pre-war songs [nhạc tiền chiến] such as Văn Cao, Đặng Thế Phong, and Đoàn Chuẩn and Từ Linh (see Chapter Eighteen). Open up any collection of pre-war songs and you will find many sad songs about autumn, songs like Văn Cao's "Sadness as Autumn Fades" [Buồn tàn thu]; Đặng Thế Phong's "Autumn Night" [Đêm thu] and "Autumn Raindrops" [Giọt mưa thu]*; and Đoàn Chuẩn and Từ Linh's "Leaves Fall in All Directions" [Lá đổ muôn chiều]. Sơn wrote his first publicly released song "Wet Eyelashes" [Ướt mi] after listening to Đặng Thế Phong's "Autumn Raindrops"* in 1954. Sơn continued this "autumn tradition" in songs like "Watching Autumn Pass" [Nhìn những mùa thu đi] (1961) and "An Autumn Leaf Fades" [Chiếc lá thu phai] (1973). The former song begins:

Watching autumn pass
You hear sadness rise in sunshine
And leaves fall beyond the window
You hear my name fall into forgetfulness
You hear months and days die in golden autumn

Here are the closing lines:

---

10. Translated by Eric Henry in his as yet unpublished translation of Phạm Duy's memoirs. Eric Henry kindly sent me a copy of his translation of these memoirs.
11. Phạm Duy, *Hồi ký* [Memoirs], Vol. III, *Thời phân chia quốc-cộng*, 255.
12. The tradition continues. Nguyễn Trọng Tạo reports that 50 of the 100 top-rated songs composed after Renovation (Đổi mới), the move from a socialist to a market economy that began in 1986, talk about falling autumn leaves. He mentions examples by composers Vũ Quang Trung, Bảo Chấn, Bằng Kiều, and Thanh Tùng. See "Chatting about Lyrics and Music," *Vietnam Cultural Window* 47 (February, 2002), 13.

Autumn has come many times
In the park the afternoon passes quickly
Our story in days gone by
I record with many leaves of gold
This autumn comes and the dream has faded

Both the East and the West have a "tradition of autumn music" and Trịnh Công Sơn surely was aware of songs from both traditions when he wrote "Watching Autumn Pass" and other songs about autumn. The fall season, when leaves die and drift to the ground, when colder weather is imminent, evokes nostalgia, sadness, and reflections on mortality in composers from many cultures. "Autumn Leaves," a song covered by many American singers, including Nat King Cole, Frank Sinatra, and Andy Williams, was originally a French song, "Les feuilles mortes" [The Dead Leaves] with music by the Hungarian-French composer Joseph Kosma and lyrics by the French poet Jacques Prévert, a poet whose work Trịnh Công Sơn and his friends apparently admired.[13] Phạm Duy turned Apollinaire's poem "L'Adieu" into a song, "Dead Autumn" [Mùa thu chết]. Trịnh Công Sơn didn't put any of Apollinaire's poems to music. The voice of this forebear of surrealism probably echoed in Trịnh Công Sơn's mind, but if so it certainly echoed much more faintly than did a host of famous pre-war poems and songs about autumn by Vietnamese songwriters.

In "Where Sorrow Becomes a Folk Song," Thái Thị Kim Lan has some interesting things to say about Trịnh Công Sơn's song "Watching Autumns Pass."[14] She and other students in Huế sang this song when they and other anti-Diệm protestors were locked up by the police after demonstrating against President Diệm's suppression of Buddhists. The music of "Watching Autumn Pass," she writes, was not complex and the subject, the autumn season, was so common that it was difficult to write a song about it without falling into clichés. Lưu Trọng Lư's famous poem "Golden Autumn" [Tiếng thu] and pre-war songs like Đặng Thế Phong's "Autumn Raindrops" [Giọt mưa thu] and Cung Tiến's "Golden Autumn" [Thu Vàng] were so well-known, she says that it was difficult to write an autumn song that would not be viewed as an inferior echo of these old favorites. According to Thái Kim Lan, however, in "Watching Autumns Pass" Trịnh

---

13. Đặng Tiến, "Trịnh Công Sơn: đời và nhạc" [Trịnh Công Sơn: Life and Music], *Văn* [Literature] 53 & 54 (2001), 14. Sâm Thương, "Đi tìm thời gian đã mất,"; Bửu Ý. *Trịnh Công Sơn: Một nhạc sĩ thiên tài...*, 87-89.
14. Thái Thị Kim Lan, "Trịnh Công Sơn: Nơi vùng ưu tư thành tiếng du ca," 87-91.

Công Sơn succeeded in writing a song that captured the thinking and hopes and fears of his own generation and of the next generation as well. She feels that it was this song, written in 1961, that truly launched Sơn's songwriting career, not "Wet Eyelashes," which was written in 1958, and publicly distributed in 1959. In "Pre-War Songs" (Chapter Eighteen) and "Understanding Trịnh Công Sơn's Obscurity" (Chapter Nineteen) I discuss some ways that Sơn made songs about old and familiar topics—autumn, the sadness of love, the cruelty of fate—seem new.

Trịnh Công Sơn's long song, "The Song of the Sand Crab" [Dã tràng ca], which was written to be performed chorally, reveals the influence of Albert Camus' *The Myth of Sisyphus*,[15] a work that he was reportedly reading when he composed it.[16] Different voices are heard in this song—the voice of the sea and the crab and also a disembodied voice from the sky—but the main speaker is a youth in his twenties. This youth compares his sad life to that of the sand crab. For Vietnamese the sand crab, which is seen as working endlessly to fill up the Eastern Sea, or South China Sea, is a symbol of ceaseless and useless toil—roughly equivalent to the image of Sisyphus pushing a rock up a hill. "The Sand Crab" begins with the voice of the sea:

> *The sand crab moves sand to the Eastern Sea*
> *The sand crab, the sand crab moves sand to the Eastern Sea*
> *The sand crab, the sand crab moves sand in useless toil*
> *Oh the oceans for thousands of years*
> *Call endlessly for the tide waves to rise*
> *Forgetting the sand crab day and night moving sand*

Later in this long song the sand crab speaks, lamenting its sad fate and blaming the oceans for sending waves to smash its work. In the second section the youth speaks and acknowledges that he has heard and been affected by the sand crab's story of wasted effort. He fears he will suffer a similar fate.

> *When I hear life calling I walk forward with no hesitation*
> *When I hear the long night my heart hopes for light*
> *When I'm twenty I sit burning the midnight oil*

---

15. Another song, "Quiet Imprint" [Vết lăn trầm], which was written in 1963, a year after "The Song of the Sand Crab," contains images of a rolling stone and of a tired exile far from home. Very likely it too was inspired by Camus' *Myth of Sisyphus*.
16. Nguyễn Đắc Xuân, *Trịnh Công Sơn: Có một thời như thế* [Trịnh Công Sơn: There Was Such a Time] (HCMC: *Văn Học*, 2003), 32-33; 45-46.

Suddenly there's darkness, suddenly my soul hears the sand crab's voice
The sand crab, the sand crab moves sand to the Eastern Sea
The sand crab, the sand crab moves sand in useless toil

The song ends with the youth identifying love as the only effective solution to the futile, sad life that the sand crab symbolizes. In printed versions each section of this song has a title. In the next to last section, "Revealing Intentions," the youth sings: "Loneliness comes like mountain clouds / What's left, what's left if we don't love each other?" The last section, titled "The Final Refuge: Love Puts on Angel Wings," ends with a plea for love: "Calling for love, calling for love, calling for love / I search for a thousand ways to call for love."

This song was never officially released. Sơn wrote it in 1962 when he was at the School of Education in Quy Nhơn. It was intended to be sung by a chorus of around thirty fellow education students, a chorus that Sơn conducted when they performed his song at a school concert in 1962.[17] In "Song of the Sand Crab," Trịnh Công Sơn, like Camus in *The Myth of Sisyphus*, presents a powerful image of the absurdity of life—the sand crab's futile attempts to fill the sea. Camus, however, sees the endless rock pushing of Sisyphus as a glorious act of defiance whereas the speaker in Sơn's song seems to pity the poor sand crab and—because he identifies his plight with the crab's—to pity himself as well.

Nguyễn Đắc Xuân suggests that when Sơn was in Quy Nhơn he had a lot on his mind: He was worried about being drafted, concerned about his family's deteriorating financial situation, upset because Phương Thảo in Huế had not returned his affections (See Chapter Five) and disappointed that a woman he liked in Quy Nhơn, a fellow student from Nha Trang named Tôn Nữ Bích Khê, had "not yet shown any sign of returning his love."[18] Sâm Thương and Đinh Cường, however, paint a different picture of Sơn's life in Quy Nhơn. Sâm Thương says that Sơn's family was not suffering economically at this time and that if Sơn were depressed it was because he wasn't enthusiastic about being at the School of Education, an institution that he was attending to avoid the draft, not because he wanted to be a grade school teacher.[19] Đinh Cường visited Sơn in Quy Nhơn

---

17. Nguyễn Đắc Xuân, while investigating Trịnh Công Sơn's life in Quy Nhơn, talked to people who sang in this chorus and found a photo of them performing, with Sơn directing. He includes it in *Trịnh Công Sơn: Có một thời như thế*, 42.
18. Ibid., 45, 50.
19. Sâm Thương, email message to the author, August 6, 2006.

during the summer of 1962 and reports that he, Sơn, and Bích Khê would spend a lot of time at the beach, talking late into the night and drinking coffee under the latania roof of a hut.[20] Sơn's song "The Sea Remembers," written in 1962, is generally assumed to be inspired by Bích Khê and his time with her in Quy Nhơn. Here are stanzas one and six:

> *Tomorrow you leave*
> *The sea remembers your name*
> *Calls the spirit of long drooping willows*
> *Calls the white sand late at night*
> *Tomorrow you leave*
> *The sea remembers your name*
> *The tide drenches dreams*
> *The sky pulls at mountain* [sơn] *streams* [khê]

Đinh Cường and others believe that Sơn evokes his relationship to Bích Khê by ending his sixth stanza with the words "sơn khê," a phrase which means "mountain stream" but also contains his name and (Bích) Khê's.

In parts of his chapter on Trịnh Công Sơn's "The Song of the Sand Crab," Nguyễn Đắc Xuân suggests this song is about Sơn's unrequited— or insufficiently requited—romantic relationships with Phương Thảo and Bích Khê, but in other places he suggests it has deeper, more philosophical meanings. He and others see this song as an "archive" of themes that Sơn would continue to develop throughout his life. Nguyễn Đắc Xuân says that it "forecasts the genius of Trịnh music," that it "realizes most completely the style and method of Trịnh Công Sơn music."[21] In researching this song, which most people never knew or had forgotten about, he interviewed the musician Phan Văn Bình, who studied with Sơn at the School of Education.

"'Song of the Sand Crab,'" he told Nguyễn Đắc Xuân, "is an archive of the concerns that we usually find in later songs by Trịnh Công Sơn, in, for example, 'Sad Sacred Words' [Lời buồn thánh]* and 'Impermanence' [Đóa hoa vô thường]."[22] Nguyễn Đắc Xuân says the ideas in "Song of the Sand Crab" come from different sources: "from the actual situation of his family, from the influence of Buddhism since he was young, from books

---

20. Đinh Cường, "Gửi Sơn, Những đoàn ghi rời của người bạn ở xa" [For Sơn, Scattered Notes from Friend Far Away], in *Trịnh Công Sơn: Cuộc đời, âm nhạc, thơ, hội họa, suy tưởng*, eds. Trịnh Cung and Nguyễn Quốc Thái, 61.
21. Nguyễn Đắc Xuân, *Trịnh Công Sơn: Có một thời như thế*, 51.
22. Ibid.

and music that entered South Vietnam at the time." He summarizes the song's philosophy in this way: "A person's life is meaningless and full of suffering and only love can decrease suffering."[23]

Đặng Tiến, the writer and critic, argues that "the songs of Trịnh Công Sơn provoked reflection; they satisfied the legitimate intellectual needs of a minority and the faddish intellectual illusions of the majority."[24] One of the ways Sơn made his songs appealing to both true and wannabe intellectuals was by dressing old concepts, many of them Buddhist, in a language that struck young people as fresh and new. Thái Kim Lan, a friend of Sơn's and a philosophy student in Huế in the early 1960s, explains Trịnh Công Sơn's appeal in this way:

> In this lively atmosphere [in Huế in the early 60s] with young people passionate about metaphysics, Sơn began to sing instead of arguing. Instead of engaging in lengthy debates with his friends, or with those in the world at large, Sơn sang 'for fun' [cho vui], as he often said, with his friends. . . . It's true Sơn was moved by the most secret anxieties of those of us in our twenties, and by the thinking of our generation, by our way of 'presenting the problem' [đặt vấn đề], using the jargon of metaphysical philosophy that was popular at that time, and this made him different from musicians who had come before him.[25]

How deeply was Sơn immersed in Western, primarily French, culture? His letters to Dao Ánh are full of French phrases and quotations and references to French novels and songs. On February 16, 1965, he sent Dao Ánh a poem which begins "*Ex nihilo nihil fit / Du rien rien ne se fait*" [Nothing comes from nothing] and ends with the line "*Déjà le néant se dévoile dans l'angoisse*" [Nothing reveals itself in anxiety].[26] In this same poem he refers to Dao Ánh, the girl he loves, as "the nothingness of spring" [*Ánh-hư-vô của mùa Xuân*]. In his thirteen-line poem/letter he uses the Vietnamese word "*hư vô*" [nothingness or emptiness] five times. This letter seems full of the faddish jargon that Đặng Tiến and Thái Kim Lan refer to, jargon that Sơn could have acquired without careful study of any of the possible sources for his references: Lucretius' poem "On the Nature of Things," René Descartes' *Principia philosophiae*, Martin Heidegger's *Introduction to Metaphysics*, Shakespeare's *King Lear*.

---

23. Ibid.
24. Đặng Tiến, "TCS: đời và nhạc," 14.
25. Thái Kim Lan, "Trịnh Công Sơn, nơi vùng ưu tư thành tiếng du ca," 85.
26. See *Trịnh Công Sơn: Thư tình gửi một người* [Trịnh Công Sơn: Love Letters for Someone] (HCMC: Trẻ, 2011), 143.

Lovers, of course, say crazy things in love letters, which aren't written for public consumption. Both Bob Dylan and Trịnh Công Sơn, however, put images and metaphors drawn from their reading in their songs. How important is it to consider the source and ponder the original meanings of these images and metaphors? Michael Gilmour raises this issue in regard to Dylan's biblical allusions and concludes that some are just pretty metaphors but others have specific meanings that require one to consider their source. We need only accept "she was the rose of Sharon" in Dylan's "Caribbean Wind" as a "beautiful expression," Gilmour says: We do not need to recognize it as an allusion to the Song of Solomon.[27] But if we don't know who Judas Iscariot was, the "punch" of Dylan's song "With God on Our Side" is "diminished."[28]

A similar problem arises when Trịnh Công Sơn uses words that have Buddhist meanings, or that can have Buddhist meanings in certain contexts. The word "hư vô," which Sơn repeats five times in his poem/letter to Dao Ánh, and "hư không," a close synonym, can refer to the Buddhist concept of emptiness, or *shunyata*, but in his songs Sơn sometimes appears to use these words to refer to a more general emptiness or nothingness, not the Buddhist concept. For example, when in "I Hear Life Leaning" [Có nghe đời nghiêng], he sings "Do heaven and earth know I've returned? / A street that's pink, a street that's empty [hư không]" most Vietnamese would not—my Vietnamese friends tell me—understand "hư không" to be referring to the Buddhist notion of emptiness (*shunyata*).

In other songs, however—"Age of Stony Sadness" [Tuổi đá buồn],* "What Age Left for You?" [Còn tuổi nào cho em], and "Words of the River's Current" [Lời của dòng sông], for example—"hư vô" [nothingness, emptiness] seems to be used to suggest a deep sadness, a sadness with metaphysical implications, a sadness that is not a mood but a fact of the human condition, something to be expected when one moves from youthful innocence to adulthood. "Emptiness [hư vô]," Sơn sings in "Words of the River's Current," "smothers the fragile age of youth and innocence." I will say more about emptiness in later chapters.

In some songs, however, Sơn uses words with undeniable Buddhist meanings and it is difficult to appreciate these songs fully if one isn't aware

---

27. "I am the rose of Sharon, and the lily of the valleys / As the lily among thorns, so is my love among the daughters," Song of Solomon, 2:1.
28. Michael J. Gilmour. *Tangled Up in the Bible: Bob Dylan and Scripture* (New York: Continuum, 2004), 10.

of the concepts these words refer to. Examples include the phrase "*Vô thường*" [impermanence] in Sơn's song "Flower of Impermanence" [Đóa hoa vô thường]; and the phrase "*từ bi*" [loving-kindness and compassion] in Sơn's song "Lullaby for You" [Ru em].* I discuss these songs in later chapters.

Through his reading of Western works and his association with avant-garde friends in Huế, Sơn was exposed to European modernism. The notorious obscurity of his songs, which I discuss in Chapter Nineteen, no doubt stems in part from this exposure. Western critics of art and literature use the term "modernism" to describe a new approach to art that developed after two world wars shattered people's faith that life was coherent and comprehensible. Responding to an uncertain world, artists and writers produced works that lacked the realism and coherence of traditional paintings and literary texts. Cubism and surrealism reflected this "modernist" tendency in art. French Literature became surreal as well in, for example, the poems of Jacques Prévert, Paul Eluard, and Louis Aragon—all poets whose works, Sơn's friend the French teacher Bửu Ý suggests, were read by Sơn and his coterie of friends. This reading, Bửu Ý says, influenced Sơn's approach to songwriting. "Under Trịnh Công Sơn's pen," he maintains, "things, people, and life sparkle in a surrealistic light."[29] Sơn's friend Ngô Kha was famous for writing surreal poems and his friend Đinh Cường painted surreal works, many of which appeared on the covers of his song books or within them on separate pages between songs. Sơn himself was a painter, and included abstract, surrealistic paintings of his own in his songbook *Love Songs* [Tự tình khúc]. The juxtaposition in Sơn's songbooks of songs with obscure, unconventional lyrics and paintings, some that he himself painted, that are equally obscure and hard to decipher strengthens the possibility that Sơn was influenced by modernism generally and surrealism in particular.

It is important, however, not to overemphasize the influence of Euro-American modernism on Trịnh Công Sơn. His friend Thái Kim Lan, who later taught philosophy in Germany, says that terms popularized by Søren Kierkegaard, Jean Paul Sartre, and Albert Camus—terms like "angst," "nausea," "the wasted effort of Sisyphus"— "were mysterious knocks on the doors of our young souls, invitations to wander in strange regions of the intellect." But now, decades later, "as I reflect I realize that we were

---

29. Bửu Ý, *Trịnh Công Sơn: Một nhạc sĩ thiên tài*, 87-89.

dumb, because none of those ideas were new, they all could be found in Buddhism, but at that time, in the tranquil setting of Huế, a stronghold of old-fashioned ideas and behavior, they had a strange appeal."[30] Thái Kim Lan argues—convincingly, in my view—that "Sơn understood Buddhism better than Western philosophy, but he created a 'singing philosophy' that harmonized East and West. Western thought in Trịnh Công Sơn songs lies in the area of external form, but the essence is Eastern. That was the unique creation of Trịnh Công Sơn: He caught the rhythm of thought of the era and of the young generation of Vietnam."[31]

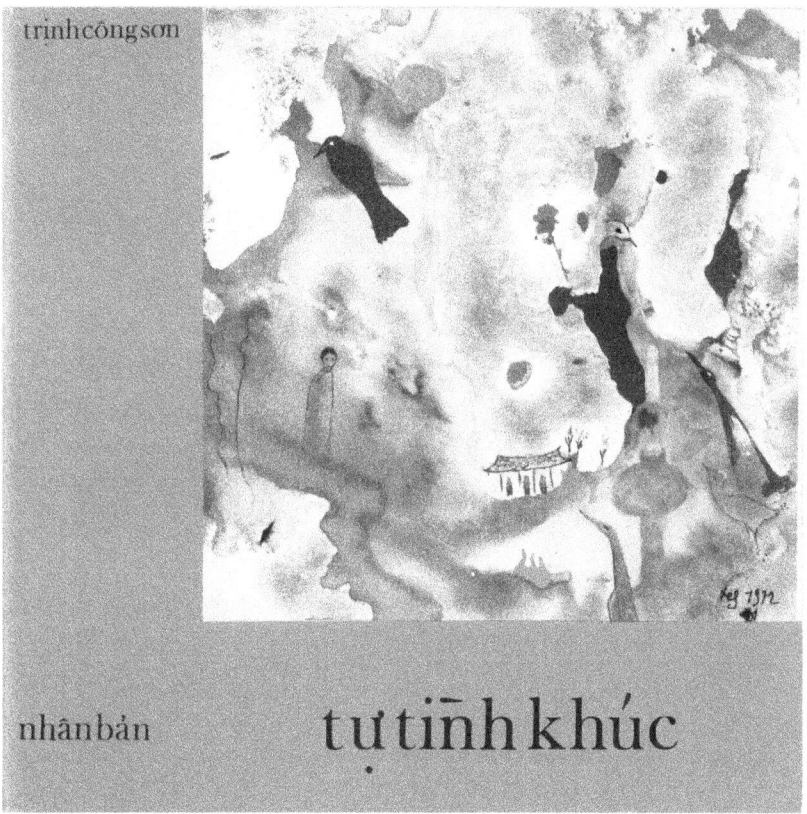

Trịnh Công Sơn's cover for his 1972 songbook Love Songs [Tự tình khúc].

30. Thái Kim Lan, "Trịnh Công Sơn, nơi vùng ưu tư thành tiếng du ca," 84.
31. Thái Kim Lan, email message to the author, December 15, 2005.

A painting by Trịnh Công Sơn included on page four of Tự tình khúc.

12

CHRISTIAN IMAGES IN TRỊNH CÔNG SƠN'S SONGS

In discussing how Westernized Trịnh Công Sơn was I need to address the fact that he does include Christian references in a few songs, or, more accurately, he uses expressions that some people perceive as having Christian connotations. According to Bùi Bảo Trúc, Sơn was breaking new ground in using such expressions. People noticed them because, Bùi Bảo Trúc says, "this was the first time words of this kind were used in songs that did not project a church atmosphere. Trịnh Công Sơn brought these words outside the church and changed them, made them more familiar and agreeable."[1] Bùi Bảo Trúc mentions the words "*Chiều chủ nhật*" [Sunday evening], "*thiên thần*" [angel], and "*ăn năn*" [repent]—words which, he says, made people think of church bells and organs. He also mentions a song with a title that evokes Christianity—"Phúc âm buồn" [Sad reply]—because "*Phúc âm*," which means "reply" or "to return news," is the term Vietnamese Christians use for "gospel" and "glad tidings."

Here are some songs that contain the expressions that Bùi Bảo Trúc mentions. In "Age of Stony Sadness" [Tuổi đá buồn]* Sơn describes a girl

---

1. Bùi Bảo Trúc, "Về Trịnh Công Sơn" [About Trịnh Công Sơn], *Văn* [Literature] 53 & 54 (May and June, 2001), 50.

walking to church on a "sad Sunday" [*ngày chủ nhật buồn*] with a rose pinned to her hair:

> *It's still raining, rain falls everywhere*
> *Your sad fingers you bring, you bring*
> *Going to church on a sad Sunday*
> *No one's there except a girl with a rose pinned in her hair*
> *Oh, the road is long*
> *Calming words for a thousand years, a thousand years*
> *A lullaby for your warmth, a lullaby for your warmth*

The action of another song, "Sad Sacred Words" [Lời buồn thánh],* also takes place on a sad Sunday. This song may echo Rezso Seress' "Sombre Dimanche," or "Gloomy Sunday," a song popular in Europe and America in the 1940s, a song so sad it is said to have driven some people to suicide. Here are the opening lines of Sơn's song:

> *A sad Sunday evening*
> *Lying in a lonely room*
> *Oh, the pale, sad singing of an afternoon*
> *Rain, rain without end*
> *Oh, how lonely I still am*

In the third stanza he talks about his loved one's "angel hand" [*tay em thiên thần*] and of "a region of repentance" [vùng ăn năn]:

> *Please give me the five fingers of your angel hand*
> *In a region of repentance*
> *Through fits of sulking*
> *I ask the five fingers of your hand to lead me to loneliness*

The title of "Sad Reply" [Phúc âm buồn] sounds Christian because "*Phúc âm*" can, as I mentioned, mean glad tidings or gospel but the song itself has no obvious Christian meaning. It certainly does not convey "glad tidings." According to the writer Hoàng Diệp Lạc the original title was simply "Phúc âm." Khánh Ly, he says, "added 'sadness' [*buồn*] to the title because '*phúc âm*' suggests good news, but the tune and the words in the song are very sad."[2] Khánh Ly was herself a Catholic and therefore perhaps more eager than Sơn to make the title fit the song. The speaker in the

---

2. Hoàng Diệp Lạc, "Âm hưởng Kinh Thánh trong âm nhạc Trịnh Công Sơn" ["Biblical Echoes in the Music of Trịnh Công Sơn"]. Giáo Phận Qui Nhơn [Diocese of Qui Nhơn], https://web.archive.org/web/20140414212023/http://gpquinhon.org/qn/news/tap-chi-muon-phuong/Am-huong-Kinh-Thanh-trong-am-nhac-Trinh-Cong-Son-2209/#. U0xRJEfLeUk (accessed September 21, 2014).

song is a sad exile figure who lies curled up like an animal in winter and bemoans his exile existence:

> *How much longer will my body be exiled in this place*
> *How much longer before eternity descends on this body*
> *How much longer before black clouds over human souls dissolve*
> *How much longer will I be far from you* [em], *from you* [anh],[3]
> *from myself*

Another song, "Speck of Dust" [Cát bụi], is not mentioned by Bùi Bảo Trúc but comes up frequently in discussions of Christian elements in Sơn's songs, probably because it reminds them of the prayer spoken at Christian funerals—the prayer from the *Book of Common Prayer* (based on Genesis 3:19) which contains the phrases "earth to earth, ashes to ashes, dust to dust." In an essay written in 1998 Sơn explains that he wrote this song after experiencing two works of art in one afternoon. First he saw a Japanese samurai film, one of a famous series featuring a blind swordsman called Zatoichi; and then he read Kazantzakis' *Zorba the Greek* in a French translation. "There was something like a chemical reaction that occurred that afternoon," he explains. "A sadness or something related to being far away was stirring within me."[4] Sơn's story illustrates the mystery of inspiration but it does not suggest that "Speck of Dust" was motivated by an interest in Christianity. In fact the speaker in "Speck of Dust" seems to have Buddhist reincarnation, not Christian rebirth, on his mind. He wonders what speck of dust he was reincarnated from and laments how quickly life passes—how soon he will return to dust, which will begin another cycle of birth and death. Here are the second and third stanzas:

> *What speck of dust have I been reincarnated from*
> *So one day I return to dust*
> *Oh, speck of dust weary and exhausted*
> *What sound beats without end*
>
> *Many years it takes to live a life*
> *Then suddenly my hair turns as white as lime*

---

3. The words *"em"* and *"anh"* are pronouns with uses too complicated to explain fully here. In this line they are used as second-person pronouns. *"Em"* refers to people (of either sex) younger than the speaker and *"anh"* refers to boys or men older than the speaker. *"Em,"* however, is also the pronoun men use to address their lover or wife.
4. Trịnh Công Sơn, "Cát bụi" [Speck of Dust], in *Trịnh Công Sơn: Tôi là ai, là ai*, eds. Nguyễn Minh Nhựt, Phạm Sỹ Sáu, Nguyễn Duy and Nguyễn Trọng Chức (Hồ Chí Minh City: Trẻ, 2011), 163-164. The article originally appeared in *Thế Giới Âm Nhạc* [The World of Music] No. 1 (1998).

> *Leaves on trees turn yellow and fall*
> *A hundred years die in a day*

Like Bùi Bảo Trúc, Đặng Tiến also argues that one should not conclude, based on some Christian phrases and images found in a few songs, that Trịnh Công Sơn was expressing Christian ideas. Sơn used Christian images, Bùi Bảo Trúc says, as a device to "present his romantic emotions." Đặng Tiến says that words like *"giáo đường"* [church], *"lời buồn thánh"* [sad sacred words], *"vùng ăn năn"* [region of repentance], and *"cát bụi"* [speck of dust] are, for Trịnh Công Sơn, "literary words, not words to stir religious emotions. You could call them clichés, expressions used to make a song line sound 'modern.'"[5] Then Đặng Tiến makes a point about these Christian elements that no one else to my knowledge has made, though it is perhaps the most important: namely, that they reflect Sơn's inclusiveness, his desire to bring people together, most urgently his "golden-skinned" people but eventually all people, golden-skinned or white-skinned, Buddhist or Christian. Sơn didn't belong to any religious sect or political party, Đặng Tiến says. Though he was raised in a Buddhist family, he distanced himself from Buddhist-led political demonstrations in 1963 and 1966. But, Đặng Tiến argues, "when he wanted to affirm his political attitude in the midst of banners and sticks and stones he chose clearly: 'Waiting for love upon the cross / Waiting to wipe out anger in the shade of the bodhi tree.'"[6] Đặng Tiến quotes the first two lines of Sơn's "Waiting for a Day" [Đợi có một ngày]. The song continues in this way:

> *Waiting for vultures on a branch shedding tears*
> *Waiting for smiles in the midst of worry*
> *Waiting to walk around the world*
> *To see the world's heart petty and mean*
> *Waiting to hear the return of humanity's conscience*
> *Waiting till worn and exhausted before the morning's gone*

To appreciate fully the open-mindedness, tolerance, and peacefulness of this song and of many songs by Trịnh Công Sơn one must understand the role Catholicism has played in Vietnam. Stanley Karnow argues that the Catholic Church "left a deeper imprint on Vietnam than on any other Asian country apart from the Philippines."[7] Catholic priests from the West

---

5. Đặng Tiến, "Trịnh Công Sơn: Tiếng hát hòa bình" [Trịnh Công Sơn: Voice of Peace], 187.
6. Ibid.
7. Stanley Karnow, *Vietnam: A History* (New York: Viking Press, 1983), 58.

began missionary work in Vietnam in 1533. The Latin writing system that Vietnamese now use to write their language was developed by Alexandre de Rhodes, a Jesuit from Avignon, France, who arrived in Vietnam in 1627. Assisted by Vietnamese scholars, he devised what is now called the "National Script" [*Quốc ngữ*] to facilitate the propagation of Catholicism. In 1682 a French missionary named Langlois built a grass and bamboo church near the bank of An Cựu River very near where Trịnh Công Sơn and his family lived in Huế.[8] Rebuilt many times and eventually moved to a higher elevation on Nguyễn Trường Tộ Street, this church, Phủ Cam, is the highest building in the area.[9]

The authority of Vietnamese rulers was buttressed by Confucianism, which stresses filial piety and loyalty to the king. They worried about Catholicism, fearing it would erode their authority by getting people to seek individual salvation instead of obeying their edicts, and so they fought and persecuted missionaries, insufficiently aware that by mistreating them they were providing a pretext for the French to colonize their country. From 1833 to 1840 Emperor Minh Mạng executed ten foreign missionaries. In 1848 Emperor Tự Đức issued seven anti-Christian decrees but could not stem the spread of Catholicism or slow the invasion of the French, who took Saigon in 1861 and by the end of the nineteenth century controlled the entire country.[10]

After the French defeat at Điện Biên Phủ in 1954 the French presence in Vietnam diminished greatly. Soon American military advisors replaced the French, and American culture, including Hollywood films, began to permeate Vietnamese cities, including Huế. Sơn particularly admired James Dean and had a large photograph of him on the stairwell of his home.[11] But in the late 1950s Catholicism was still a dominant presence in all of South and Central Vietnam, especially in Huế. The pagodas Sơn visited, Hiếu Quang and Phổ Quang, were tucked away off busy streets but the Phủ Cam and Redemptorist cathedrals dominated the skyline in the area of the city where Sơn lived. The offices of the archbishop were across the street from Sơn's house on Nguyễn Trường Tộ Street. In the 1950s and

---

8. Trần Ngọc Bảo, *Từ Điển ngôn ngữ văn hóa du lịch Huế xưa* [A Tourist Language and Culture Dictionary about Huế in the Past] (Gia Định, Việt Nam: Thuận Hóa, 2005), 234.
9. Nguyễn Trường Tộ (1828-1871) was a Catholic who received a Western education and urged Emperor Tự Đức to modernize education, mining, agriculture, and industry. Vietnamese historians, communist and non-communist, praise him for his reform efforts.
10. Stanley Karnow, *Vietnam: A History*, 67-77.
11. Hoàng Phủ Ngọc Tường, *Trịnh Công Sơn và cây đàn lya của hoàng tử bé* [Trịnh Công Sơn and the Lyre of the Little Prince] (HCMC: Trẻ, 2004), 24.

1960s many parents, like Sơn's, still sent their children to schools run by Catholic religious orders.

From 1955 to 1963 the country was ruled by President Ngô Đình Diệm, a fervent Catholic, with help from his brothers Ngô Đình Nhu, Ngô Đình Thục, and Ngô Đình Cẩn. President Diệm made Nhu Minister of the Interior and organizer of his secret Cần Lao Party. Fearing that Central Vietnam, especially the very Buddhist city of Huế, could become a center of resistance to his regime, he put Cẩn in charge of an area stretching from Phan Thiết in the South to the 17th parallel. Cẩn ruled the region like a warlord. In 1961, Thục, the oldest of the brothers, a Catholic priest, became archbishop of Central Vietnam. The president of the University of Huế, Father Cao Văn Luận, was also a Catholic priest. The result was an overwhelming Catholic presence in a region where most of the people were Buddhists.

Buddhists in Huế resented this Catholic presence.[12] In 1963 government officials in Huế refused to let Buddhists in Huế display Buddhist flags at a celebration commemorating Buddha's birthday, despite the fact that recently the streets had been filled with Vatican flags for the anniversary of Ngô Đình Thục's investiture as Archbishop. Buddhists wanted the government radio station to broadcast speeches of Buddhist leaders. When Ngô Đình Cẩn refused, Buddhist demonstrators gathered on May 8, 1963 at the radio station near the bank of the Perfume River. When the demonstrators refused to disperse, the deputy province chief ordered his troops to fire and eight people, seven children and one woman, were killed. This event, which was followed by demonstrations

---

12. Most American historians adopt what has come to be called an "orthodox" view of President Diệm and the Buddhist Struggle Movement but there is also a "revisionist" view championed most vociferously by Mark Moyar, a former professor at Marine Corps University. Orthodox historians argue that the US erred in supporting Diệm, a leader who, they argue, was hopelessly out of touch with political reality. They argue that Buddhists had legitimate reasons to fear that their faith was threatened under his rule. The revisionist Moyar, however, argues that communist agents manipulated the Buddhist Struggle Movement and that the decision by US leaders, when they grew disenchanted with him, to support the coup that overthrew him was a terrible mistake. I find the "orthodox" view more persuasive and my brief account here of the Buddhist movement is based on orthodox sources, primarily the following: George McT. Kahin, *Intervention: How America Became Involved in Vietnam* (New York: Alfred A. Knopf, 1986); and Robert J. Topmiller, *The Lotus Unleashed* (Lexington, KY: University Press of Kentucky, 2002). I have also considered Vietnamese accounts like, for example, documents collected by the Vietnamese journalist Thanh Thương Hoàng (pen name: Quốc Oai), *Phật Giáo Tranh Đấu* [The Buddhist Struggle], (Saigon: Tân Sanh, 1963). For the revisionist view, see Mark Moyar, *Triumph Forsaken: The Vietnam War, 1954-1965* (Cambridge: Cambridge University Press, 2006).

in Huế and Saigon, convinced US officials that President Diệm must go. His oppression of Buddhists was increasing resistance to his rule in South Vietnam and causing more Americans to oppose the war. On November 1 he and his brother Nhu were removed from power in a coup that was encouraged and approved by Washington and US Ambassador Henry Cabot Lodge. Diệm and Nhu were later shot by army officers.

In a 2011 interview, Cao Huy Thuần, who was a teacher in Huế in the early 1960s, explains that in the beginning Buddhists did not oppose Diệm specifically; they opposed his policy of religious discrimination. Their struggle in its early stages, he says, had a moral and cultural quality. The aim was not to overthrow Diệm, and it certainly was not to establish a Buddhist State like that which existed in Vietnam during the Lý and Trần dynasties. Buddhist leaders believed, however, that "Buddhism, which had been the religion of the Vietnamese people since olden times, formed the basis of Vietnamese culture," and they feared that President Diệm's policies threatened the survival of this culture.[13] They opposed religious discrimination, including the elevation of Catholicism to a national religion. They resented the fact that Diệm had left in place a French decree—Decree #10—which classified Buddhism as an association rather than a religion.[14] And they resented having to sing at flag ceremonies and in movie theaters a song called "Venerating President Ngô" [Suy Tôn Ngô Tổng Thống], which contained these lines:

> *All the people of Vietnam are grateful to President Ngô*
> *President Ngô, long live President Ngô*
> *All the people of Vietnam are grateful to President Ngô*
> *Please God convey Your blessings upon him*

Buddhist leaders wondered, Cao Huy Thuần says:

> ... why Diệm was now forcing all the people to sing a song venerating him, a song with the line 'Please God convey Your blessings upon him.' Traditional Vietnamese culture has no concept of 'God,' no

---

13. Cao Huy Thuần, "Vài điều căn bản về phong trào Phật giáo" [Some Fundamental Aspects of the Buddhist Movement], *Thời đại mới* [New Era] 21 (May 2011), available at Thời đại mới, http://www.tapchithoidai.org/ThoiDai21/201121_CaoHuyThuan.htm (accessed September 23, 2014). Thiên Đo explains that "the infamous *Decree No. 10* put all religious organizations, except the Catholic and Protestant missions, in the category of public associations. Article 7 of the decree stipulates that 'permission to establish an association can be refused without any explanation given.'" See "The Quest for Enlightenment and Cultural Identity: Buddhism in Contemporary Vietnam," in *Buddhism and Politics in Twentieth-Century Asia*, ed. Ian Harris (London: Pinter, 1999), 270-271.
14. Ibid. See also Robert J. Topmiller, *The Lotus Unleashed*, 2, 18.

phrase 'convey Your blessings.' Let those who believe in these things request such blessings but why make every single person request them, especially in front of the sacred symbol of the national flag? God and the flag are one? The government and the [Catholic] church are one? Is that cultural or political humiliation? Anger at such insults accumulated for nine years, not because Mr. Diệm believed in a particular religion, but because he was such a fanatical believer that he humiliated a cultural legacy the primary element of which was Buddhism.[15]

In 1966 Buddhists in Huế and Đà Nẵng took to the streets again. What provoked them this time was Prime Minister Nguyễn Cao Kỳ's decision, approved and encouraged by US Ambassador Lodge, to remove General Nguyễn Chánh Thi, who was the military commander of First Corps, or I-Corps, a region that included the five northernmost provinces of South Vietnam. Huế and Đà Nẵng were the largest cities in I-Corps. The problem with General Thi, from the point of view of Kỳ and his American backers, was that he was popular in the region and had developed a good relationship with Thích Trí Quang, a charismatic monk, and other Buddhist leaders. In 1963 US leaders wanted to stop President Diệm from oppressing the Buddhists; in 1966 they wanted a Vietnamese general in I-Corps who was willing to squash the Buddhist Struggle Movement because it was destabilizing the Saigon military regime. General Thi was removed from power on March 12, 1966, which provoked more demonstrations in Huế and Đà Nẵng, as well as in Saigon.

These demonstrations led to what Stanley Karnow calls a "civil war within a civil war": a confrontation between different units of the South Vietnamese army.[16] Many soldiers in the ARVN 1st Division, which was stationed in Huế and the surrounding area, sympathized with the Buddhist Struggle Movement and refused to squash it. Fearing the collapse of the Kỳ regime, Ambassador Henry Cabot Lodge ordered that US planes be made available to Kỳ so he could transport paratroopers and tanks to Huế and Đà Nẵng to put down the rebellion. On April 5, ten C-130 transports piloted by Americans began flights to move soldiers loyal to Kỳ from Saigon to the Đà Nẵng Airport. Soon four thousand troops and armored personnel carriers and tanks were transported to Đà Nẵng by US and South Vietnamese planes. On May 21 Kỳ sent his troops and tanks out into the city of Đà Nẵng. Thousands of Buddhist families placed family

---

15. Cao Huy Thuần, "Vài điều căn bản về phong trào Phật giáo."
16. Stanley Karnow, *Vietnam: A History*, 445.

altars in the streets to block the advance of Kỳ's troops but by May 24, after several days of heavy fighting, the battle for Đà Nẵng was over. Kỳ's troops then moved to Huế where students supporting the Struggle Movement, angry at US support for Kỳ's troops, had burned down the US Consulate and the library of the United States Information Service. By June 19, however, Kỳ's forces had taken control of Huế. Thích Trí Quang, the monk considered to be the leader of the struggle, was arrested and flown to Saigon where he was imprisoned but released when he began a fast. The Buddhist Struggle Movement was essentially over. "The middle ground that the Buddhists had been building up between the Saigon military and the NLF," the historian George McTurnan Kahin says, "was cut away and prospects destroyed for anything resembling a viable 'third force.'"[17]

Trịnh Công Sơn's friends Nguyễn Đắc Xuân, Hoàng Phủ Ngọc Tường, and Ngô Kha participated in the Struggle Movement in Huế. Nguyễn Đắc Xuân and Hoàng Phủ Ngọc Tường both left Huế to join the NLF shortly after Kỳ's troops put down the rebellion in Huế, probably because they knew they would be imprisoned if they stayed. Ngô Kha stayed and, as explained in Chapter Four, was arrested and imprisoned on Phú Quốc Island. Ngô Kha was on the violent fringe of the Struggle Movement. He was for burning American vehicles and throwing stones at police.[18] In 1966 he organized ARVN soldiers on leave in Huế to confront Kỳ's troops in a futile attempt to prevent them from entering Huế. Buddhists led by the determined Thích Trí Quang were the most visible faction but the demonstrators included students, civil servants, and even soldiers.[19] Hoàng Phủ Ngọc Tường reports that Ngô Kha did succeed in drawing Sơn into one demonstration but Sơn clearly preferred other ways of opposing the war. Sơn's anti-war songs—works like "Waiting for a Day," described above—indicate that he was a pacifist more in the style of Thích Nhất Hạnh than Thích Trí Quang, a point I shall return to in Chapter Twenty-Four. He never turned his back on his more politically active friends, and respected the decisions they made, but he was reluctant to become involved in demonstrations and political machinations. He felt he could best contribute by writing songs that emphasized the importance of inner peace, compassion, and the ending of hatred.

---

17. George McT. Kahin, *Intervention*, 432.
18. Hoàng Phủ Ngọc Tường, *Trịnh Công Sơn và cây đàn lya của hoàng tử bé*, 41.
19. Don Luce and John Sommer, *Vietnam—The Unheard Voices* (Ithaca, NY: Cornell University Press, 1969), 126.

The Christian references that appear in a few of Sơn's songs are there, I suggest, for three reasons. First, because Catholic churches, schools, and language were a part of the world in which he lived. Second, because he sensed that using Christian terms was one of many devices to make his songs sound fresh and new. Third, because he wanted to be inclusive. Bob Dylan in the high tide of his Christian period said that he wouldn't be "talkin' about no mysticism, no meditation, none of them Eastern religions,"[20] but Sơn talked about Christianity, and talked about it kindly. He was waiting for both religions, Christianity and Buddhism, to end the suffering in his homeland: "Waiting for love upon the cross / Waiting to wipe out anger in the shade of the bodhi tree."

20. See Clinton Heylin, ed., *Saved! The Gospel Speeches of Bob Dylan* (Madras and New York: Hanuman Books, 1990), 100.

13

CA DAO (FOLK VERSES)
& *DÂN CA* (FOLK SONGS)

Tomorrow night no more sounds of guns in the sky
Mothers will sing ca dao *in the fields*

Đêm mai này trời im tiếng súng
Cho mẹ hát ca dao trên đồng[1]

The ultimate source of most verbal art in Vietnam lies in folk verses called *ca dao*. The compound word *ca dao* refers to verses that for centuries have been passed down from one generation to the next. Both "*ca*" and "*dao*" are Sino-Vietnamese terms that were used by Confucian scholars when they began to collect folk verses that had been a part of Vietnam's oral culture for generations. "*Ca*" originally meant "a song with a melody" and "*dao*" a song that circulated among the people. Vietnamese use the word "*dân ca*" to refer to folk songs (*dân* means "people"). Now, however, both terms—*ca dao* and *dân ca*—may refer to folk songs.[2] After discussing this problem of terminology, the famous singer and musicologist Phạm Duy says "We can speak simply and say '*ca dao* is *dân ca.*' . . . If there is a distinction it is that when we speak of *ca dao* we think of a poem of the masses, the common people. When we speak of *dân ca* we think of a kind of music."[3]

---

1. Lines from Trịnh Công Sơn's "Night Now, Night Tomorrow" [Đêm bay giờ đêm mai], composed in 1967.
2. Lê Bá Hán, Trần Đình Sử, and Nguyễn Khắc Phi, *Từ Điển Thuật Ngữ Văn Học* [Dictionary of Literary Terms] (HCMC: Giáo Dục, 2006), 31. See also Chu Xuân Diên, "Ca Dao" [Folk Verses], in *Từ Điển Văn Học* [Cultural Dictionary], eds. Đỗ Đức Hiểu, Nguyễn Huệ Chi, Phùng Văn Tửu, and Trần Hữu Tá, (Hà nội: Thế giới, 2003), 180-182.
3. Phạm Duy, *Đường về Dân Ca* [The Road Back to Folk Songs] (Los Alamitos CA: Xuân Thu), 6, 19.

I translate *ca dao* as "folk verses," not "folk songs," because when *ca dao* are sung they are usually called *"dân ca"*—folk songs. Vietnamese folklorists today use the term *ca dao* when they refer to the poetic aspects of a *dân ca*—to artistic features that are apparent when a *ca dao* is recited, not sung; they use the term *dân ca* when describing artistic features (melody, filler sounds, etc.) that become apparent when a folk poem [*ca dao*] has been transformed into a folk song [*dân ca*]. The fact that when Vietnamese recite the verses of a *ca dao* they typically chant or declaim them [*ngâm*] in a manner that resembles singing complicates the issue. Vietnamese scholars conclude that there really is no sharp border between *ca dao* and *dân ca*. As Phạm Duy says, "In the traditional culture and art of the common people, poetry cannot be separated from music. The first poem was very likely the first song. And so between *dân ca* [folk song] and *ca dao* [folk verse] there is no border."[4] *Ca dao* are woven so deeply into the language and culture of Vietnam that all Vietnamese know many verses and can recite them from memory. They are the source, the bedrock, from which Vietnamese verbal art—proverbs, poetry, and song—emerges.

Because these poems, and many poems composed much more recently, are performed in a way that approaches song—because they are recited or chanted, not read—it is not always easy to separate Vietnamese literature from Vietnamese songs. The first Vietnamese prose novel did not emerge in Vietnam until around 1910.[5] Throughout the nineteenth century Vietnamese preferred to tell their stories in verse. The most famous and most beloved literary work in Vietnam is Nguyễn Du's *Truyện Kiều* [*The Tale of Kiều*], which I discuss in Chapter Fifteen. This verse narrative, composed around 1800, is read by students and scholars, but to appreciate it fully one should hear it recited using a special style of reciting called *kể Kiều* (*"kể"* means to declaim or recite; "Kiều" is the name of the main character).

In an interview with Vĩnh Xương published in a Vietnamese language journal in Canada in 1986 Trịnh Công Sơn mentions some types of songs that intrigued him early in his career.

> When I was young I really liked pre-war songs and listened also to some foreign music. In the 60s I listened to Blues music about the

---

4. Ibid., 19.
5. See John C. Schafer and Thế Uyên, "The Novel Emerges in Cochinchina," *Journal of Asian Studies* 52, no. 4 (Nov. 1993).

fate of blacks in America. I really liked the music of Louis Armstrong and Duke Ellington. I felt close to this kind of music and thought I could use this music to express my feelings. . . . In the 64-66 period my songs had a Blues quality; during the 67-72 period they had a strong folk song quality [*chất dân ca*].[6]

Pre-war songs are Vietnamese sentimental love songs written from the late 1930s to the mid-1950s. I will discuss them in Chapter Eighteen. Here I focus on Sơn's comment about his songs having a "folk song quality." Đặng Tiến, who discusses Vĩnh Xương's interview in an article published in 2001, says that Sơn has in mind "the folk songs of Bob Dylan and Joan Baez that were popular at that time," not Vietnamese folk songs, not *dân ca*. "Sơn was not influenced much by the [folk] music of the people," Đặng Tiến says.[7]

I am not sure, however, that when Sơn talks about "a folk song quality" [*chất dân ca*] in his songs he is referring to the folk songs that Baez and Dylan sang. During the revival of folk songs in the mid-sixties both Baez and Dylan did, of course, sing folk songs, many of them revivals of old Scottish and English ballads—including murder ballads. We know Sơn listened to some of these songs. In a letter to Dao Ánh he mentions listening to a recording of Baez singing "Black is the Color of My True Love's Hair," "I Still Miss Someone," "It Ain't Me Babe," "I'm Gonna Leave You," and "With God on Our Side."[8] Trịnh Công Sơn, however, was not trying to revive traditional Vietnamese folk songs in the same way that Pete Seeger, Bob Dylan, and Joan Baez were trying to revive American folk songs performed in the 1920s. I agree with Đặng Tiến that when Sơn speaks of a "folk song quality" in his works he is not referring to folk songs like traditional Vietnamese work songs called "*hò*" which were sung by men and women when pounding rice, pulling wood, or rowing boats. And I agree with him when he states that Trịnh Công Sơn's lullabies, which I discuss in the next chapter, do not *in form* resemble traditional lullabies. But I can't agree with his comment that "the music of the people [*nhạc dân tộc*] did not influence Trịnh Công Sơn much."[9] What Sơn wanted to revive was not the form of old Vietnamese folk songs but the more

---

6. Trịnh Công Sơn, interview with Vĩnh Xương in the journal *Đất Việt* [Vietnamese Land], June 6, 1986, 21-22.
7. Đặng Tiến, "Trịnh Công Sơn: đời và nhạc" [Trịnh Công Sơn: Life and Music] *Văn* 53 & 54 (2001), 15.
8. *Trịnh Công Sơn: Thư tình gửi một người* [Trịnh Công Sơn: Love Letters for Someone] (HCMC: Trẻ, 2011), 229.
9. Đặng Tiến, "Trịnh Công Sơn: đời và nhạc," 15.

peaceful world that the mere mention of *ca dao* (folk verse) or *dân ca* (folk song) evokes in the minds of Vietnamese. When Sơn speaks of a "folk song quality" in his songs he expresses a nostalgic yearning for a more peaceful Vietnam.

Trịnh Công Sơn's relationship to folk songs was different from Bob Dylan's. Dylan covers and rewrites old English ballads and American folk, blues, gospel and country songs of the 1920s. He was one of the leaders of the folk revival that swept America in the 1950s and 1960s. Sơn did not cover and rewrite Vietnamese folk songs, but he clearly was inspired by them. He too wanted to contribute to a folk revival, a revival not of the folk song form but of the cultural world represented in *ca dao*, a world of peace and kindness, a world filled with the simple pleasures of rural life. This world, if revived, would not be free of pain—many *ca dao* talk about the heartbreak of unrequited love—but the dramas, happy or sad, of courtship and romance would unfold in a peaceful setting. In "I Shall go Visiting" [Tôi sẽ đi thăm] and "Night Now, Night Tomorrow" [Đêm bây giờ đêm mai], both from the collection *Songs of Golden Skin*, Sơn associates the end of war with the return of folk songs. "When we no longer kill each other in my country," he sings, in the first song, "Children will sing folk songs [*đồng dao*] in the street." (A "*đồng dao*" is a folk song for children.) In "Night Now, Night Tomorrow" Sơn contrasts nights now, during the war, with peaceful nights to come when the war ends. Here is the first verse:

> *Oh the long nights and the storms that fall*
> *On a parched and barren native land*
> *Oh the bombs that plow up corpses*
> *On today's abandoned fields of rice*
> *Oh Vietnam's golden skin broken and crushed*
> *That flesh and bone that is so sacred*

And here is the third verse:

> *Tomorrow night no more sound of guns in the sky*
> *Mothers will sing folk songs [ca dao] in the fields*
> *Tomorrow night no flares will glare*
> *And mothers will see a future for their children*
> *A radiant night with falling rain*
> *That will sound like paradise*

In 1968 after the Paris Peace Talks began, Sơn wrote a folk song for children—and adults—to sing when peace comes, appropriately titled

"A Children's Folksong of Peace" [Đồng dao hòa bình]. This song, which describes love bursting out at the prospect of peace, does not resemble a traditional folk song in form, but it has a sprightly rhythm that appeals to young people. It suggests that the past twenty years have been a terrible, unnatural interlude in which Vietnamese have been separated from the traditional values encapsulated in folk songs:

> Twenty years of hatred have passed
> Today we see the faces of people have changed
> We love the earth, we love each other, we love you
> We love the peaceful sun that's just come up

Sơn also can be said to have been involved in a folk revival because he wanted to encourage a sense of common identity among Vietnamese. He wanted to remind them that they were all the same "folk"—all golden-skinned people, all descendants of "Lạc-Hồng," the original Vietnamese who, according to legend, lived in 2000 B.C. in a kingdom called Văn Lang. "Mother hopes her children won't forget the color of their skin," he sings in "A Mother's Legacy," the skin color "of the old Vietnam." In "Marching Song" [Hành ca] Sơn sings:

> The group enters a native village
> Bright torches in their hands
> Searching for the old land of the golden-skinned race of fairies and
> dragons

According to the Vietnamese creation myth, Vietnamese are children of a fairy princess named Âu Cơ and a dragon lord called Lạc Long Quân. Hence the reference to "race of fairies and dragons."

Nguyễn Thanh Ty, one of Sơn's roommates when he was teaching primary school in Bảo Lộc, claims that Sơn was unfamiliar with *ca dao*. One day, he says, Sơn recited some lyrics from a song called "Nụ Tầm Xuân" [A Rosehip Flower] by Phạm Duy and marveled at how great they were. According to Nguyễn Thanh Ty, Sơn thought Phạm Duy had written the lyrics, which surprised him because they were words from a well-known *ca dao*.[10] Nguyễn Thanh Ty recites other verses from other songs inspired by *ca dao* and Sơn is again amazed at how good they are; and Nguyễn Thanh Ty is again surprised that Sơn had never heard of them. Every student, he says, learns *ca dao* in elementary and junior high school. Nguyễn Thanh Ty

---

10. Nguyễn Thanh Ty, *Về một quãng đời Trịnh Công Sơn* [On a Period of Trịnh Công Sơn's Life] (Place of publication and publisher not listed: 2001), 100.

says Sơn told him that he didn't know anything about *ca dao* or proverbs because he had studied in French schools. "You're kidding!" Nguyễn Thanh Ty says. "Well at least you learned 'Our ancestors were the Gauls,' right?" "That was our first lesson," Sơn says.[11] Many Vietnamese of Sơn's generation who studied in French schools have complained about learning only the history of France, not their own history.

Nguyễn Thanh Ty may exaggerate Sơn's lack of knowledge of *ca dao*. They had very different views of the war, as I've explained in Chapter Two. In his book he seems eager to present a negative portrait of Sơn. Phạm Duy's song based on the *ca dao* "Nụ Tầm Xuân" was well known and so it's not surprising that Sơn thought Phạm Duy was the author of the lines he remembers. Nguyễn Thanh Ty does, however, say that after this conversation "Sơn became infatuated with *ca dao* and proverbs and collected materials to read about them."[12] One can imagine Sơn studying *ca dao* just as Dylan listened again and again to the songs on Harry Smith's *Anthology of American Folk Music*.

In a 1997 article Sơn says that "he came to music because he loved life" but that a "twist of fate," the injury he suffered in 1957 while practicing Judo with his brother, also played a part. After recovering from this injury, he says, "I suddenly wanted to express some things that were on my mind. I had always liked philosophy and wanted to put philosophy into my songs, a soft philosophy that everyone could understand, like a *ca dao* or a lullaby [*lời ru con*] a mother sings to her child. Vietnamese philosophy is always there but it hasn't been systemized because it is found everywhere in the life of the people."[13] Sơn's friend Sâm Thương suggests that Sơn read Western philosophers while recuperating from his Judo accident— Nietzsche, Albert Camus, Jean Paul Sartre, Merleau-Ponty, etc.[14]—but in this essay Sơn confirms that while recuperating he realized that he was interested in philosophy, but that the philosophy he wanted to put in his songs was a Vietnamese, not a Western philosophy; and he suggests that the songs he wanted to write to express that philosophy would resemble

---

11. Ibid., 101.
12. Ibid., 101-102.
13. Trịnh Công Sơn, "Để bắt đầu một hồi ức" [To Begin a Recollection], *Âm Nhạc* [Music] (January 1997); reprinted in *Trịnh Công Sơn: Một người thơ ca một cõi đi về* [Trịnh Công Sơn: A Singer-poet, a Place for Leaving and Returning], eds. Nguyễn Trọng Tạo, Nguyễn Thụy Kha, and Đoàn Tử Huyến (Hanoi: Âm Nhạc, 2001), 202.
14. Sâm Thương, "Đi tìm thời gian đã mất" [In Search of Lost Times], https://web.ar-chive.org/web/20100621125353/https://www.tcs-home.org/ban-be/sam-thuong/DiTimThoiGianDaMat1/ (accessed January 15, 2014).

Vietnamese *ca dao* and lullabies. So we need to talk more about *ca dao* and also lullabies, which are not different things because when Vietnamese sing lullabies they are, in most cases, singing *ca dao* in a particular style called "ru." I will discuss lullabies in the next chapter.

Some Vietnamese may not know the longer *ca dao* verses cited by Nguyễn Thanh Ty but it would be hard to find a Vietnamese who did not know the following *ca dao*:

> Ca Dao #1
> *In ponds nothing's more beautiful than the lotus*
> *Green leaf, white flower with gold pistel*
> *Gold pistel, white flower, green leaf*
> *Near mud but exudes no scent of mud*
> Trong đầm gì đẹp bằng sen
> Lá xanh bông trắng lại chen nhụy vàng
> Nhụy vàng bông trắng lá xanh
> Gần bùn mà chẳng hôi tanh mùi bùn

> Ca Dao #2
> *A head of hair has short and long strands*
> *We can't be married so our feelings last a thousand years*
> Tóc mai sợi vắn sợi dài
> Lấy nhau chẳng đặng, thương hoài ngàn năm

> Ca Dao #3
> *We return and bathe in our pond*
> *Pure or muddy our pond's still better*
> Ta về ta tắm ao ta
> Dù trong dù đục ao nhà vẫn hơn

> Ca Dao #4
> *Yesterday bailing water by the town hall*
> *I left my shirt on a lotus flower*
> *If you found it, please give it back to me*
> *Unless you wish to keep it as a pledge*
> *My shirt is unstitched at the edges*
> *I have no wife, and my old mom has not yet sewn it*
> *The seam has long been burst*
> *Tomorrow can I ask you to mend it for me?*[15]

---

15. Translated by Nguyễn Đình Hòa in *Vietnamese Literature: A Brief Survey* (San Diego, CA: San Diego State University, 1994), 19.

Hôm qua tát nước đầu đình
Bỏ quên cái áo trên cành hoa sen
Em được thì cho anh xin
Hay là em để làm tin trong nhà
Áo anh sứt chỉ đường tà
Vợ anh chưa có, mẹ già chưa khâu
Áo anh sứt chỉ đã lâu
Mai mượn cô ấy vào khâu cho cung

Ca Dao #5
You bailing water by the roadside
Why do you scoop out the golden moonlight and pour it away?
Hỡi cô tát nước bên đàng
Sao cô múc ánh trăng vàng đổ đi?

Not all but most *ca dao* are written in a poetic meter called "six eight" [*lục bát*], so named because it requires couplets consisting of a six-syllable line followed by an eight-syllable line. Vietnamese have adopted many Chinese verse forms but *lục bát* is a uniquely Vietnamese form, one not found in other Asian prosody.[16] Most traditional Chinese poems have an odd number of syllables—five or seven—in each line. The rules for the *lục bát* verse form are elaborate. Vietnamese, like Chinese, is a tonal language. In a tonal language a word can have a different meaning depending on the pitch in which it is pronounced. Here are words that differ only by tone which is indicated by the symbol above the vowel (except for the level tone which is unmarked):

1. *ma* (ghost)—level tone, unmarked (flat)

2. *má* (cheek)—high rising (sharp)

3. *mà* (but)—low falling (flat)

4. *mả* (grave, tomb)—low rising (sharp)[17]

5. *mã* (horse)—high rising, broken (sharp)

6. *mạ* (rice seedling) low broken or constricted (sharp)

---

16. John Ballaban, *Ca Dao Việt Nam: Vietnamese Folk Poetry* (Greensboro, NC: Unicorn Press, 1980), 18.
17. Speakers in Huế do not distinguish tone 4 from tone 5, so for them *mả* and *mã* are homonyms.

Phạm Duy illustrates the musical quality of ordinary spoken Vietnamese by putting the six tones on a musical scale. The diacritical marks above the "a" in "*ma*" indicate the tone.[18]

The Vietnamese six-eight form may not be as complicated as the Chinese "regulated poem" [*lu shih*] form, which I shall discuss in Chapter Fifteen, but it has its complexities. One complexity involves the placement of flat and sharp tones. Of the six tones listed above, number 1 and number 4 are "flat" [*bằng*] tones and the other four are "sharp" [*trắc*] tones. Words with certain tones must be placed in certain places in a line. The second and sixth word in the six-syllable line and the second, sixth, and eighth word in the eight-syllable line should be a word with a flat tone. The fourth word in both the six-syllable and eight-syllable line should be a word with a sharp tone. I will use the *ca dao* verse about the lotus (Ca Dao #1 above) to illustrate this pattern. Words with flat tones are written in large bold unitalicized type; words with sharp tones are written in large italicized type.

> Trong **đầm** gì *đẹp* bằng **sen**
> Lá **xanh** bông *trắng* lại **chen** nhụy **vàng**
> Nguỵ **vàng** bông *trắng* lá **xanh**
> Gần **bùn** mà *chẳng* hôi **tanh** mùi **bùn**

Note how Nguyễn Du observes these same rules for flat and sharp tones in the opening lines of *The Tale of Kiều*:

> Trăm **năm** trong *cõi* người **ta,**
> Chữ **tài,** chữ *mệnh,* khéo **là** ghét **nhau**
> Trải **qua** một *cuộc* bể-**dâu**
> Những **điều** trông *thấy* mà **đau** đớn long

> *A hundred years—in this life span on earth*
> *Talent and destiny are apt to feud*
> *You must go through a play of ebb and flow*
> *And watch such things as make you sick at heart*[19]

---

18. Phạm Duy, *Đường về Dân Ca*, 21.
19. Translated by Huỳnh Sanh Thông. See Nguyễn Du, *The Tale of Kiều, A Bilingual Edition of Truyện Kiều* (New Haven CT: Yale University Press, 1983), 3.

Matching words with flat tones or words with sharp tones is not rhyming. The words *đầm* and *sen* in the first line of the *ca dao* about the lotus flower both have flat tones but they do not rhyme. *Cõi* and *mệnh* in the opening lines of the *Tale of Kiều* both have sharp tones but they do not rhyme.

Rhyme does, however, play a key role in six-eight verse. It is used within a couplet to tie the first line to the second. Note that *sen* [lotus], the last word in the first line of the *ca dao* about the lotus, rhymes with *chen* [mixed with], the sixth word in the next line. Below, in bold, are the words that rhyme. Note that *vàng* [gold], the last word in the second line, only partially rhymes with *xanh* [green], the sixth word in the third line. In the *lục bát* form the rhyme need not be perfect and often assonance is a better word than rhyme to describe the similarity of sound.

> *In ponds nothing's more beautiful than the lotus*
> *Green leaf, white flower with gold pistel*
> *Gold pistel, white flower, green leaf*
> *Near mud but exudes no scent of mud*

> Trong đầm gì đẹp bằng **sen**
> Lá xanh bông trắng lại chen nhụy vàng
> Nhụy vàng bông trắng lá **xanh**
> Gần bùn mà chẳng hôi tanh mùi bùn

The result of these rules for rhyme, Huỳnh Sanh Thông explains, is that "each line rhymes with the next, but a new, different rhyme appears in every other line, in every couplet."[20]

Huỳnh Sanh Thông points out that the two features just described, the required alternation of flat and sharp tones and rhyming between lines in a couplet and between adjoining couplets, enabled Nguyễn Du and other poets to tell long stories without creating a tedious structure of sound. These features, he says, provided "adequate diversity within the predictable continuum."[21] One of the advantages of *lục bát* is that it works well for short, haiku-like two-line poems but also for long narrative poems like Nguyen Du's *The Tale of Kieu*, the most famous literary work in the Vietnamese language, which is 3,254 lines long; and Nguyễn Đình Chiểu's *Lục Vân Tiên*, which is 2,076 lines long.

Vietnamese have a variety of terms for ways of performing both *ca dao*, most of which are very short and of anonymous authorship, and long

---

20. Huỳnh Sanh Thông, *An Anthology of Vietnamese Poems* (New Haven, CT: Yale University Press, 1996), 10.
21. Ibid., 11.

poems like *The Tale of Kiều,* which were written by known authors. In the North and Central regions the general term for performing poetry is "*ngâm*" whereas in the South it is called "*nói thơ*" (literally, "to speak a poem" but here "*nói*" does not refer to ordinary speaking). When one performs the *The Tale of Kieu,* however, which is not a *ca dao* but is written in the same *lục bát* verse form used for *ca dao,* one is said to "*kể Kiều.*" Performing a lullaby is called "*ru.*" These terms for performing poetry are sometimes translated as ways of "declaiming" or "reciting," but perhaps "chanting" would be a more accurate translation. To Western ears the performing of *ca dao* sounds like chanting: It is song-like but not quite singing.

Because Vietnamese is a tonal language in which a change in the pitch of a word changes its meaning, when you speak Vietnamese or read a prose passage out loud it already sounds musical to speakers of English. If you read, not chant, a *ca dao* verse it will, of course, sound more musical than, say, a line from a newspaper because *ca dao* are poems with other musical features besides sharp and flat tones. They have rhyme and rhythm, for example. Most *ca dao* verses follow the rules for six-eight [*lục bát*] verse, and these rules—for placement of rhyming words and for the distribution of tones—guarantee that the poem will have rhythm. But when Vietnamese chant [*ngâm*] a *ca dao,* as opposed to reading it, they push it much further toward song. The next step is to sing the *ca dao* verse and turn it into a *dân ca* [folk song].

Different kinds of folk songs result from this process of turning *ca dao* verses into folk songs. For example there are *lý* [lyrical songs], *hò* [work songs], and *ru* [lullabies]. I discuss lyrical songs and work songs in this chapter and lullabies in Chapter Fourteen. Many *lý* songs are about courtship and love but they can be about a variety of topics. According to Trần Gia Linh, in south and central Vietnam any folk song that is not a work song [*hò*] is called a *lý.*[22] He explains that "*lý,*" which means "village" in Sino-Vietnamese,[23] is a term used to distinguish songs sung in villages in the countryside from songs sung by the upper class at the royal court in Huế at coronations, official receptions, and religious events.

---

22. Trần Gia Linh, "*Lý* [Lyrical Song]," in *Từ điện Văn Học* [Literature Dictionary], Đỗ Đức Hiểu et al. (Hanoi: Thế Giớ, 2004), 907.

23. John DeFrancis explains that the term Sino-Vietnamese (*Hán Việt*) is usually applied to anything written in classical Chinese by a Vietnamese and pronounced when read aloud in the Vietnamese manner. See John DeFrancis, *Colonialism and Language Policy in Viet Nam* (The Hague: Mouton Publishers, 1977), 15.

What Phạm Duy refers to as a "pure *hò*" [*hò thuần túy*] is a song that laborers sing while they work to relieve the drudgery of the hard labor involved in activities like rowing a boat, cultivating a rice paddy, transplanting rice seedlings, or pounding rice with a pestle.[24] The tune and rhythm of work songs vary depending on the work being done. A tune and rhythm appropriate for cultivating a rice paddy is not appropriate for rowing a boat, for example. Tune and rhythm may also vary depending on the stage of the work project. Phạm Duy explains that boatmen on the River Mã in Thanh Hòa Province sing a different *hò* depending on the stage of their journey. When they leave port to go upstream they sing a "leaving the dock *hò*" [*hò rời bến*]; when they go through a shallow stretch they sing a "caught in the shallows *hò*" [*hò mắc cạn*], when they go downstream, they sing a "long run *hò*" [*hò đường trường*]. Geography may influence the tune and rhythm of a *hò* for rowing. Phạm Duy points out that because the canals and rivers in the less mountainous South are gentler than northern rivers, southern rowing songs are also gentler than rowing songs in other regions. They are so gentle, Phạm Duy says, that they resemble *hò* about the reunion of old friends [*hò hội ngộ*].[25] He calls *hò hội ngộ* and also *hò giao duyên* [songs lovers sing to each other] impure *hò* songs because they are not about work, but he includes them in the *hò* category because they involve call-and-response and are sung at public events.[26]

Most Vietnamese folk songs were originally *ca dao*. Phạm Duy, who was a musicologist and collector of traditional folk songs as well as a composer, shows what this change involves in his book *Đường về Dân Ca* [*The Way Back to Folk Songs*]. He takes *ca dao* verses and writes them in musical notation to show how they are sung when performed. One of his examples is a *ca dao* about a mynah bird performed in the manner called "*hát lý*" [sing *lý*].[27] Songs in the "*Lý*" style are sung in different tunes in different regions. Below I provide Phạm Duy's notation which indicates how "Lý Con Sáo" [Song of the Mynah Bird] is sung in the Huế style.[28] I first give the *ca dao* verse on which it is based.

---

24. Phạm Duy, *Đặc khảo về dân nhạc ở Việt Nam* [Research on the Folk Music of Vietnam] (Saigon: Hiện Đại, 1972), 57.
25. Ibid., 76.
26. Ibid., 57.
27. Phạm Duy, *Đường về dân ca*, 26.
28. Phạm Duy also provides musical notation indicating how "Song of the Blackbird" is sung in other regions. Ibid., 36-38.

Who carries the Mynah bird across the river
So the blackbird can flee its cage and fly away

Ai đem con sáo sang sông
Để cho con sáo xổ lồng bay xa?

To make the *ca dao* verse more song-like, the performer provides a tune or melody and also repeats some phrases and adds filler sounds. The *ca dao* core, however, remains clear.

I am not suggesting that Sơn wrote folk songs like "Song of the Mynah Bird"—songs based on *ca dao* verses. In fact, the only Trịnh Công Sơn song that I'm aware of that is obviously built on a *lục bát* [six-eight] prosodic framework is "To Board" [Ở trọ]. Here's the first stanza of the song which has six stanzas:

> *The bird boards on the bamboo branch*
> *The fish boards in a crevice of spring water*
> *I myself am a boarder in this world*
> *In one hundred years I'll return to the edge of the sky*
>
> Con chim ở đậu cành tre
> Con cá ở trọ trong khe nước nguồn
> Cành tre …í … a
> Dòng sông … í … a
> Tôi nay ở trọ trần gian
> Trăm năm về chốn xa xăm cuối trời
> í … a … í … à … í … à … a …

"Song of the Mynah Bird" and "To Board" share this underlying six-eight structure, but the former is based on only one *ca dao* verse couplet whereas Sơn's song consists of five stanzas each with seven lines. Another difference is that Sơn's verses are of his own creation: They are not traditional *ca dao*. Sơn's "To Board" resembles what Phạm Duy calls a "new folk song" [*dân ca mới*], which I discuss in Chapter Sixteen, as opposed to an "ancient folk song" [*dân ca cổ*] like "Song of the Mynah Bird."[29] As modern music was developing in the 1940s, Phạm Duy and other composers wrote new folk songs which can be seen as a bridge connecting traditional folk songs to modern Vietnamese songs. In "To Board" Sơn purposefully "cites" or echoes the ancient folk song genre by using a six-eight structure and adding filler sounds, but it is a modern song.

The song is modern but the philosophy is old. This song has that "soft philosophy" that Sơn said he wanted to put in his songs, that philosophy that "everyone can understand, like a *ca dao* or lullaby."[30] It is about the fact that we—like the bird on the bamboo branch and the fish in the spring water—are only boarders on this earth. Impermanence is a key Buddhist concept. The "soft philosophy" that underlies this song—and, I suggest, many Trịnh Công Sơn songs—is Buddhism.

---

29. Phạm Duy contrasts *dân ca cổ* [old folk songs] and *dân ca mới* [new folk songs] in *Đường về dân ca*, 1. The songs Phạm Duy calls "new folk songs" are songs that reflect the influence of Western music. Others call these songs *nhạc cải cách* [reformed music] or *tân nhạc* [modern music]. I discuss these modern folk songs in Chapter Sixteen.
30. Trịnh Công Sơn, "Để bắt đầu một hồi ức," 202.

14

TRỊNH CÔNG SƠN'S
LULLABIES

Each day I choose one thing to celebrate . . .
Choose a lullaby for a child slowly stepping into life

In the above lines from his song "Each Day I Choose a Piece of Happi-ness" [Mỗi ngày tôi chọn một niềm vui]* Trịnh Công Sơn expresses his fondness for lullabies. In English "lullaby" is a noun, though we do have the verb "lull." In Vietnamese the word "*ru*," which means to lull a child to sleep by singing, is usually used as a verb.[1] A song sung for this purpose is a "*bài hát ru con*," literally "a song to lull or calm a child."

"*Ru*" refers to the act of singing a lullaby but it also refers to a way of performing *ca dao* [folk verses]. In this sense "*ru*" is like "*lý*" and "*hò*" discussed in the previous chapter. It is another way of singing *ca dao* verses, in this case verses about calming people and lulling them to sleep. As with "*lý*" and "*hò*," the way one does this varies from region to region.[2] In *Research on the Folk Music of Vietnam* Phạm Duy explains the different tunes used to *ru* in North, Central, and Southern Vietnam.[3] Vietnamese poets and songwriters *ru* often but perhaps none more often than Trịnh Công Sơn, probably because he found that singing lullabies was a good

---

1. The word "*ru*" is used in the compound word "*êm ru*," which means very quiet or soft, and in the expression "*êm như ru*" [soft as a lullaby].
2. Phạm Duy defines "*ru*" as "a way of putting to music [*phổ nhạc*] six-eight *ca dao* verses, either original verses or transformed variants of original verses." See *Đặc khảo về dân nhạc ở Việt Nam* [Research on the Folk Music of Vietnam], (Saigon: Hiện Đại, 1972), 52.
3. Ibid., 52-56.

way to convey his "soft philosophy," a philosophy that he wanted to be "like a *ca dao* or a lullaby [*lời ru con*] a mother sings to her child."[4]

Sơn wrote eleven songs with "*ru*" in the title and other songs like "Sleep, My Child" [Ngủ đi con] and "Go Ahead and Sleep, My Love" [Em hãy ngủ đi] which are clearly lullabies. And he talks about lullabies in other songs. In "Age of Stony Sadness" [Tuổi đá buồn],* for example, he speaks of "Calming words [*lời ru*] for a thousand years, a thousand years / A lullaby for your warmth, a lullaby for your warmth."

The American folklorist Bess Lomax Hawes discusses difficulties in defining "lullaby." "Is a lullaby," she asks, "a song about going to sleep, or is it any song on any subject that is used to induce slumber?"[5] Many of Trịnh Công Sơn's "*ru*" songs could be sung to induce sleep. What is interesting about them is that many seem designed not to induce sleep but to soothe pain. In Trịnh Công Sơn's lullabies, Cao Huy Thuần says, "to '*ru*' is not to coax into sleep but to soothe pain. And because pain is long lasting, Trịnh Công Sơn is always singing lullabies."[6]

If one understands a lullaby to be a song that induces calmness and acceptance of pain, then many of Sơn's songs are lullabies. Cao Huy Thuần says Trịnh Công Sơn "led music into the lullaby. Lullabies for children. Lullabies for lovers. Lullabies for himself. The lullaby was his specialty, his occupation, because to sing a lullaby is to sing poetry."[7] "We can say that no musician wrote as many lullabies as Trịnh Công Sơn," writes Bùi Bảo Trúc. "He wrote at least more than twenty. He sadly sang himself lullabies. He sang lullabies to love, to life. He sang lullabies to a life that was lost. He sang a loved one to sleep on a winter morning and again on a morning in spring. He sang lullabies always, without stopping."[8]

The image of a mother singing a child a lullaby is a moving and powerful image, one that suggests peace, safety and love. It is probably found in the poems and songs of all cultures, but it is especially prevalent and powerful in Vietnam. In "Go to Sleep, Child" [Ngủ đi con] and "A

---

4. Trịnh Công Sơn, "Để bắt đầu một hồi ức" [To Begin a Recollection], *Âm Nhạc* [Music] (January 1997); reprinted in *Trịnh Công Sơn: Một người thơ ca một cõi đi về* [Trịnh Công Sơn: A Singer-poet, a Place for Leaving and Returning], eds. Nguyễn Trọng Tạo, Nguyễn Thụy Kha, and Đoàn Tử Huyến (Hanoi: Âm Nhạc, 2001), 202.

5. Bess Lomax Hawes, "Folksongs and Function: Some Thoughts on the American Lullaby," *Journal of American Folklore* 87, no. 344 (April-June 1974), 141.

6. Cao Huy Thuần, Introductory Remarks at "Đêm Trịnh Công Sơn: Hòa Bình và Tình Yêu" [An Evening of Trịnh Công Sơn: Peace and War], May 3, 2001, Paris.

7. Ibid.

8. Bùi Bảo Trúc, "Về Trịnh Công Sơn" [About Trịnh Công Sơn], *Văn* [Literature] 53 & 54 (May and June, 2001), 52.

Mother's Folk Poem" [Ca dao mẹ], both written during the war, Sơn contrasts this peaceful lullaby image with its polar opposite—war. "Go to Sleep, Child" begins as follows:[9]

> *(Hò o o ớ o o hò) Go to sleep, child*
> *Child of a mother with golden skin*
> *A lullaby for you, child, and for the bullet that reddens your*
> *wounds*
> *Twenty years*
> *A flock of children join the army*
> *They go and don't return*
>
> (Hò o o ớ o o hò) Con ngủ đi con
> Đứa con của mẹ da vàng
> Ru con ru đạn nhuộm hồng vết thương
> Hai mươi năm
> Đàn con đi lính
> Đi rồi không về

Here are the closing lines:

> *Twenty years*
> *The children grow up*
> *They go to the battlefield*
> *Golden skinned child of Lạc Hồng*[10]
> *Go to sleep, child*
> *A lullaby for your hard life*
> *Oh, what wound deeply pierces your warm skin*
> *This flesh and blood your mother cared for night and day*
> *(Hò o o ớ o o hò) why sleep at the age of twenty*
>
> Hai mươi năm
> Đàn con khôn lớn
> Ra ngoài chiến trường
> Đưa con da vàng Lạc Hồng
> Ngủ đi con

---

9. Both "Go to Sleep, Child" [Ngủ đi con] and "A Mother's Folk Poem" [Ca dao mẹ] are difficult to translate into English. For other attempts see Gigi's [no surname provided] translation of "Ngủ đi con" and Richard Fuller's translation of "Ca dao mẹ" at TCS-Home, https://www.tcs-home.org/ban-be/articles/DoiVaNhacTCS (accessed February 9, 2020).
10. Lạc Hồng refers to ancestors of the Vietnamese people who lived near the Red River. Both "Hồng" and "Hùng" refer to Vietnam's first kings who, according to legend, were descendants of Lạc Long Quân, the dragon lord of Lạc, and a fairy named Âu Cơ. The four-syllable expression "con Lạc cháu Hồng" [child of Lạc child of Hồng] is used by Vietnamese to express pride in their ancestry.

Ru con ru đã phong trần
Ôi vết thương nào đục sâu da nồng
Thịt xương này mẹ nhọc nhằn hôm mai
(Hò o o ớ o o hò) Sao ngủ tuổi hai mươi

This song became a hit record in Japan in 1970 where sales topped two million.[11] In an article titled "Trịnh Công Sơn Music Passes from Paris to Japan" Võ Quang Yến explains that in 1968 Asai Takashi, a reporter covering the Vietnam war for the Mainichi Broadcasting System, brought back to Japan a record containing twenty-three of Trịnh Công Sơn's anti-war songs. The singer Takaishi Tomoya chose two songs from that record, "Go to Sleep Child" and "I Shall go Visiting," and translated them into Japanese. According to Võ Quang Yến, to soften the song and not overemphasize its civil war quality, in the Japanese version the mother sings this lullaby to a child who has lost his father, not to a dying son.[12]

Khánh Ly has sung Trịnh Công Sơn's songs in Japan both before and after the war. At a concert in Osaka in 1970 she sang "A Mother's Folk Poem" [Ca dao mẹ] in both Vietnamese and Japanese. This song, probably Sơn's most famous lullaby, begins in this way:

A mother sits singing her child a lullaby
Rocking the hammock to and fro
Rocking the hammock to and fro
A mother sits and sings her child a lullaby
Clouds drift over the pass
Pray to the heavens for rain
Pray to the heavens for rain
So the earth is soft
And the seeds sprout
A mother sits and sings her child a lullaby
Tears from tired eyes
Her heart broken

And ends in this way:

---

11. "Tiểu Sử Trịnh Công Sơn" [Biography of Trịnh Công Sơn]. This fact sheet on Trịnh Công Sơn's life was sent to me by Trịnh Vĩnh Trinh, Trịnh Công Sơn's sister, and her husband, Nguyễn Trung Trực.
12. Võ Quang Yến, "Nhạc Trịnh Công Sơn từ Paris qua Nhất Bản" [Trịnh Công Sơn Music from Paris to Japan," *Diễn Dàn* [Forum] https://www.diendan. org/sang-tac/nhac-trinh-cong-son-tu-paris-qua-nhat-ban?searchterm=N-h%E1%BA%A1c+Tr%E1%BB%8Bnh+C%C3%B4ng+S%C6%A1n+t%E1%B-B%AB+Paris (accessed February 17, 2020).

A mother sits and sings her child a lullaby
Hearing the earth's soft call
Her son has paid his debt
A mother sits for a hundred years
Like a sad statue
Left behind for the native land
Age of helplessness
A world full of hate
And war and prisons

Sơn titles his song "Ca dao mẹ" [A Mother's Folk Poem] but it is not written in *lục bát* [six-eight] or any other regulated verse form. As Đặng Tiến points out, "Trịnh Công Sơn's songs which have lullaby as their main topic do not sound [*âm hưởng*] much like Vietnamese lullabies."[13] In other words, Sơn's "lullabies" are modern songs about lullabies which he sang, and other singers still sing, in the modern style. Trịnh Công Sơn was called the Bob Dylan of Vietnam, Đặng Tiến points out, not only because the content of some of his songs was anti-war but also because his manner of performing his songs resembled Dylan's. He didn't chant them like one would *ru* a *ca dao*.[14]

Sơn's lullabies were not performed in the traditional *ru* manner used in singing *ca dao* verses but in some of his lullabies he does pay obeisance to traditional Vietnamese lullabies, which almost always included filler sounds, by including these sounds in his songs. Note the "*Hò o o ờ o o hờ*" in "Go to Sleep, Child" and the "*í . . . i . . .a*" in the following song, "A Mother's Lullaby" [Lời mẹ ru]:

A mother's lullaby extends to the garden
Singing a lullaby at noon (í . . . i . . . a)
The child smiles
Amidst sweet dreams

In his modern lullabies Sơn typically evokes not a poetic form but an image, the image of a mother singing her child to sleep. Bùi Bảo Trúc suggests that Sơn may have been more strongly drawn to this image than others because his father died when he was young. Sơn was very close to his mother and listened to her sing lullabies to his siblings.[15] In "Love

---

13. Đặng Tiến, "Trịnh Công Sơn: đời và nhạc" [Trịnh Công Sơn: Life and Music], *Văn* 53 and 54, (May and June, 2001), 15.
14. Ibid.
15. Bùi Bảo Trúc, "Về Trịnh Công Sơn," 50-51.

Found" [Tình yêu tìm thấy] Sơn sings about a mother, perhaps his own mother:

> *A lullaby mother sang in years gone by*
> *Folk poems [ca dao] forever for all the four seasons*
> *I find a memory on every leaf*
> *In the corner of every town I see my native place*

The speaker of this song is expressing gratitude for lullabies and folk songs, along with other peaceful images of his native land. These images, the speaker suggests, nourish and sustain one.

"Love Found" was written in 1983, eight years after the war ended. In songs Sơn wrote during the war, however, folk poems—including lullabies—are things that have been lost, not found, things that have no place in the violent, dangerous world of war. The song "Vietnamese Girl" [Người con gái Việt Nam]* (1965) tells the story of a young girl who "loves her native land / As she loves the fields of ripe rice." Then tragedy strikes:

> *One day the girl returns to her village*
> *She goes at night as gunshots resound*
> *The girl suddenly clutches her heart*
> *On fragrant skin the blood slowly spreads*

The girl dies, Sơn says, before experiencing the benefits of peace, including the singing of folk poems:

> *You've never known your native land at peace*
> *You've never seen the old Vietnam*
> *You've never once sung a folk song [ca dao]*
> *You only have a heart of hate*

In another song, "Lullaby of Cannons for the Night" [Đại bác ru đêm]* (1967), there are lullabies but in the terrible surreal world of war it is cannons, not mothers, that are singing them; and they are keeping children up, not lulling them to sleep:

> *Every night cannons resound in the town*
> *A street cleaner stops sweeping and listens*
> *The cannons wake up a mother*
> *The cannons disturb a young child*
> *At midnight flares shine in the mountains*
> *Every night cannons sing a lullaby for golden skin*
> *The cannons sound familiar like a prelude to a sad song*
> *And children are gone before they see their native land*

In "A Lullaby for Night" [Lời ru đêm], written five years later in 1972, a mother and her child are still being kept awake by bombs and before the song ends the mother is singing a lullaby over a cradle that holds the cold body of her son:

> *A lullaby for her departing child*
> *Singing lullabies forever*
> *Singing without hope above the cradle*
> *Singing above the cold body of her child*
> *Singing a lullaby for hatred not yet cooled*

There would appear to be several reasons for Sơn's many references to folk poems, especially lullabies, in his songs. Bùi Bảo Trúc says that probably no song has moved people as much as the following two lines from Trịnh Công Sơn's song "Vietnamese Girl" [Người con gái Việt Nam]*: "You've never once sung a folk song [*ca dao*] / You only have a heart of hate."[16] Bùi Bảo Trúc says that Trịnh Công Sơn mentions *ca dao* in his song because he wanted to remind the young generation—his generation, the twenty-year olds [*tuổi hai mười*]—of the precious things the war was taking from them. It was taking their lives, of course, the most precious thing of all, but it was also destroying their culture. Sơn talks about *ca dao*, Bùi Bảo Trúc says, "to sound a warning: Our nation is committing cultural suicide."[17] At the same time he wanted to console and calm his generation, and so the lullaby motif, present in many *ca dao*, was useful for him. "The sad fate of young people in the war became an unshakable obsession for Trịnh Công Sơn," says Bùi Bảo Trúc. "He cried for them, felt their pain, and then tried to comfort and console them."[18]

I believe Trịnh Công Sơn also sang lullabies to calm himself, to come to grips with his own sadness. Songs can soothe the singer as well the listener. In 2017, on a trip to Vietnam, I asked two of my sisters-in-law to tell me what verses they had sung to lull their children to sleep. Both mentioned the following folk poem:

> *Evenings I stand in the back doorway*
> *I look toward my mother's village and feel a heartrending pain*
>
> Chiều chiều ra đứng cửa sau
> Ngó về quê mẹ ruột đau chín chìu

---

16. Ibid., 56.
17. Ibid.
18. Ibid., 55.

Note that in this six-eight verse the speaker does not tell anyone to go to sleep. The poem is about mothers who miss *their* mothers and their native village, which they, because patrilocality was the rule, have had to leave to live with or near their husband's family. As Phạm Duy explains, "The lullaby [*ru*] has the function of lulling children to sleep but Vietnamese women often borrow the lullaby to speak of their own fate."[19] Songwriters, too, borrow the lullaby and write songs that seem designed to calm themselves, songs that are implicit if not explicit lullabies. Sơn's "Calming [*ru*] My Melancholy" [Ru ta ngậm ngùi] (1970) is a quite explicit lullaby for the self. After telling someone—presumably a loved one—to go home, he sings himself to sleep:

> *You go ahead and go home*
> *I'll drift through life*
> *The sweet smell of incense remains*
> *I'll light a stick this evening*
> *Let me sleep in a cradle*
> *I shall calm my melancholy*
> *Let me sleep under a dome of trees*

> Em về hãy về đi
> Ta phiêu du một đời
> Hương trầm có còn đây
> Ta thắp nốt chiều nay
> Xin ngủ trong vòng nôi
> Ta ru ta ngậm ngùi
> Xin ngủ dưới vòm cây

In songs like this one we see Trịnh Công Sơn longing to return to the security of childhood, to a happier time before he turned twenty—to a time before his father died, a time preceding unrequited love affairs and a terrible war. In the closing lines of "Quiet Imprint" [Vết lăn trầm], written in 1963 when the war was intensifying, Sơn comments on how the good things of one's youth—folk poems, one's native village, peaceful sleep—can suddenly vanish:

> *A folk poem [ca dao] on a rock*
> *On the gold throne of one's native village*
> *A time of sleeping the peaceful sleep of youth*
> *Then suddenly one day one sees desolation all around*

---

19. Phạm Duy, *Đặc khảo về dân nhạc ở Việt Nam*, 52.

Bài ca dao trên cồn đá
Trên ngai vàng quê nhà
Một thời ngủ yên tuổi xanh
Rồi một hôm chợt thấy hoang vu quanh mình

Finally, although I would certainly not call Trịnh Công Sơn's *ru* songs religious songs, I do believe that they reflect the high value Buddhism places on calmness and quietness and on the importance of curbing anger and hatred—a topic that I will return to in later chapters.

15

THE TALE OF KIỀU

If *The Tale of Kiều* survives, our language survives;
If our language survives, our country survives.

-Phạm Quỳnh[1]

In *Chronicles* Dylan mentions the books he was reading at the start of his career. Trịnh Công Sơn never wrote an autobiography and left behind no reading lists. In the eighty or so short essays he wrote and in his love letters to Dao Ánh he occasionally mentions a writer or literary work, but only briefly.[2] One learns very little from these sources about which literary works intrigued him and therefore perhaps influenced his song writing. Journalists and scholars, however, including some who were close friends of Sơn's, have written articles and books about him and from these sources we can learn something about his reading and the literary figures that he admired. As I mentioned in Chapter Eleven his friends say he read the works of philosophers like Albert Camus, Friedrich Nietzsche, Jean Paul Sartre, and Martin Heidegger; and poems by Guillaume Apollinaire, Jacques Prévert, and Marcel Pagnol.

---

1. Phạm Quỳnh, an influential literary figure in early twentieth century Vietnam, praised *The Tale of Kiều* in a speech he gave on August 12, 1924, to commemorate the death of Nguyễn Du who died in 1820. Phạm Quỳnh was a royalist who did not oppose the French presence in Vietnam but was a strong advocate for the use of *quốc ngữ*, the Romanized writing system. See Maurice M. Durand and Nguyen Tran Huan, *An Introduction to Vietnamese Literature*, translated from the French by D.M. Hawke (New York: Columbia University Press, 1985), 91.
2. These essays, which originally appeared in various journals or as prefaces to song collections, have been collected in *Trịnh Công Sơn: Tôi là ai là ai ...* [Trịnh Công Sơn: Who Am I?], eds. Nguyễn Minh Nhựt et al. (HCMC: Trẻ, 2011). Sơn's love letters can be found in *Trịnh Công Sơn: Thư tình gửi một người* [Trịnh Công Sơn: Love Letters for Someone] (HCMC: Trẻ, 2011).

There is no reason, however, to talk only about works that Trịnh Công Sơn or his friends have said that he read. Writing in Vietnamese for a Vietnamese audience, his friends would not mention works I discuss in this chapter and the following two chapters about the New Poets because every educated young person knew them. It went without saying that Trịnh Công Sơn knew them. When I taught English at a secondary school in Đà Nẵng and at the University of Huế in the late 60s and early 70s, I soon realized that there were some works by Vietnamese poets and novelists that almost all urban young people who had gone to school knew. These are the works that I will discuss in this chapter and the following two chapters. I do so not to suggest that they directly influenced Trịnh Công Sơn—that he echoes lines from them in his songs, for example—but rather to provide a few glimpses into the literary culture that surrounded Trịnh Công Sơn in his formative years.

Ernest Hemingway said that all American writing comes from Mark Twain's *Huckleberry Finn*. One could make a similar—and much stronger—case that all Vietnamese writing comes from *The Tale of Kiều*, a verse narrative composed in six-eight verse, the same form used for *ca dao*.[3] Composed around 1815 by Nguyễn Du, it is Vietnam's national poem. Nguyễn Đình Hòa, a Vietnamese scholar, calls it "Vietnam's literary Bible."[4] René Crayssac, a French civil servant and journalist in Vietnam, produced a French translation of *The Tale of Kieu* in 1926. In a preface, he says of Nguyễn Du: "Blessed is a poet who could in one poem make the whole soul of his race vibrate and sing."[5] Nguyễn Du took the story from a mediocre Chinese prose novel and compressed it into an exquisite and engaging narrative poem consisting of 1,627 six-eight couplets—3,254 lines. It is about a beautiful and talented young woman from a middle-class family who falls in love with a handsome scholar named Kim Trọng. They agree to marry, but soon thereafter Kiều's father is falsely accused of a crime by unscrupulous officials. Kiều agrees to sell herself into marriage to pay off the officials and keep her father out of jail. She asks her sister

---

3. This tale is sometimes called *Kim Vân Kiều*, a title made up of the names of three important characters in the story: Kim, the young man Kiều falls in love with; Vân, her sister; and Kiều, the central character. Quotations from *The Tale of Kiều* are from this bilingual edition: Huỳnh Sanh Thông, Nguyễn Du, *The Tale of Kiều: A Bilingual Edition of Truyện Kiều* (New Haven, CT: Yale University Press, 1983).
4. Nguyễn Đình Hòa, *Vietnamese Literature: A Brief Survey* (San Diego, CA: San Diego State University, 1994), 103.
5. Quoted by Trần Văn Dĩnh in "Why Every American Should Read *Kim Vân Kiều*," *The Washingtonian*, September 1968, 2.

to honor her pledge and marry Kim Trọng. The man who purchases Kiều turns out to be a pimp for the madam of a house of prostitution within which Kiều is pressed into service. This is the beginning of years of suffering.

Kiều is rescued twice from prostitution, once by the scholar Thúc Sinh and once by a rebel chief named Từ Hải. She truly loves both men but fails to find lasting peace with either of them. Thúc Sinh makes Kiều his second wife or concubine without consulting his wife, who gets back at her husband by forcing Kiều to work as a slave in their home. Fearing further mistreatment by Thúc Sinh's jealous wife, Kiều takes refuge in a Buddhist temple. A warm-hearted nun superior, Giác Duyên, arranges for her to marry her nephew but he, like Kiều's first husband, turns out to be a pimp and she again becomes a prostitute. Từ Hải, the rebel chief, rescues her and, after he conquers a large part of the empire, she becomes his queen. Five years later, however, the Emperor tricks Từ Hải into accepting a high position in return for ending his rebellion and giving up the territory he controls. Từ Hải wants to keep fighting but Kiều urges him to accept the Emperor's offer in order to save lives. Từ Hải is captured and killed and Kiều, about to be forced to marry a tribal chief, attempts suicide by jumping into a river. She is saved by fishermen sent by the nun Giác Duyên.

The story ends when Kim Trọng, who has been searching for Kiều, eventually finds her. Kiều enjoys a happy reunion with him and her parents and sister. Kim Trọng beseeches Kiều to become his lawful wife, and she agrees, but stipulates that the relationship remain platonic. A woman, she says, should bring "priceless chastity" to the wedding bed: "How dare I, boldfaced, soil with worldly filth the homespun costume of a virtuous wife" (lines 3103-3104). Her sister, Vân, becomes Kim Trọng's concubine and provides him with many heirs.

Huỳnh Sanh Thông, who has translated *The Tale of Kiều* into English, calls it "the supreme masterwork of Vietnamese literature." He mentions its "pervasive popularity, little short of adulatory worship, among both scholars and illiterates and in all spheres of life."[6] Why is it so loved? One reason, Vietnamese scholars point out, is that ordinary people, even if they were illiterate, could enjoy it. Nguyễn Du composed it in *chữ nôm*, a way of writing Vietnamese using modified Chinese characters, but because it was

---

6. Huỳnh Sanh Thông, "Introduction," in Nguyễn Du, *The Tale of Kiều: A Bilingual Edition of Truyện Kiều*, xx.

written in six-eight verse it could be memorized and recited. Thus it was enjoyed by ordinary people who could not read Chinese characters. *The Tale of Kiều* is packed with allusions to Chinese classics like the Confucian *Book of Odes*, for example, but it is also filled with proverbial expressions and *ca dao* verses. "By triumphantly rescuing Vietnamese poetry from the stranglehold of classical Chinese," Huỳnh Sanh Thông says, "Nguyễn Du performed for the vernacular what Dante had once done for Italian, liberating it from its position of subservience to Latin."[7]

The Tale of Kiều has other features that make it appealing. Vietnamese enjoy its melodramatic plot, which is full of twists and turns as Kiều suffers disasters but then is saved from death in the nick of time. They also appreciate Nguyễn Du's frank representation of the many different kinds of love, from the pure and unfulfilled love between Kiều and Kim Trọng to a coarser variety represented by Kiều's encounters with men in brothels. The specific instructions that the brothel owner, Dame Tú [Tú Bà], gives Kiều on how to please men in bed clearly lie at the latter end of the continuum (lines 1199-1216). A very moving section of the story describes a love somewhere between these extremes: Kiều's relationship to the scholar Thúc Sinh, which, as Nguyễn Du says, begins in lust but ends in love:

> *Man and girl, girl and man in fevered clasp*
> *On a spring night, how can one quell the heart*
> *Of course, when two kin spirits meet, one tie*
> *Soon binds them in a knot none can yank loose*
> *They'd tryst and cling together night or day*
> *What had begun as lust soon turned to love* (lines 1285-1290)

Probably the main reason Vietnamese love *The Tale of Kiều*, however, is because they realize—consciously or unconsciously—that it expresses and reinforces a very Vietnamese sensibility. "To the Vietnamese," the writer and former Việt Minh soldier Trần Văn Dĩnh wrote in 1968, *The Tale of Kiều* is "the heart and the mind of their nation, the mirror of their society, past and present."[8] "Peasants and scholars alike," Huỳnh Sanh Thông says, "have found in it some common denominator about their world that touches a chord in their collective psyche."[9]

---

7. Ibid., xxi.
8. Trần Văn Dĩnh, "Why Every American Should Read *Kim Vân Kiều*," 2.
9. Huỳnh Sanh Thông, "Introduction," xxxii.

What is that common denominator? One aspect is a belief in fate—that one's life will unfold according to a predestined plan that one can modify only in limited ways. Talented people can perform great deeds, but these talents themselves are a gift from heaven and so the talented have no cause to be prideful. *The Tale of Kiều* emphasizes that "cruel fate" [*bạc mệnh*] has a way of singling out the talented by afflicting them with pain and suffering. Because talent and disaster are paired, no one should expect to be both talented and lucky. Fate is a gendered concept in traditional Vietnamese culture; it is believed to be crueler to women—especially beautiful and talented women—than men, but ultimately no one can escape it.[10] Nguyễn Du states the above view of fate and talent in his opening and closing lines. It is the moral that his *Tale of Kiều* teaches us. Here are the opening lines which many Vietnamese know by heart:

> *A hundred years—in this life span on earth*
> *Talent and destiny are apt to feud*
> *You must go through a play of ebb and flow*
> *And watch such things as make you sick at heart*
> *It is so strange that losses balance gains*
> *Blue heaven's wont to strike a rose* [beautiful woman] *from spite*

The Vietnamese belief in fate stems partly from Buddhist teachings regarding *karma*, the idea that present lives are influenced by previous ones. "If I did not earn merit in past lives / Could I be blessed with you, my treasure, now?" Kim Trọng asks Kiều (lines 407-408). When disaster strikes and Kiều ends up in Dame Tú's brothel, Kiều says: "Because I badly lived an earlier life / Now in this world I must redeem past sins" (lines 1195-1196). The Vietnamese notion of fate derives not only from Buddhist texts, however. Other sources are Chinese poems, sayings and astrological texts. Reflecting on Kiều's life of woe, Thúc Sinh says: "Misfortune's never spared a single rose / The rule has held since ages out of mind" (lines 1906-1907). Thúc Sinh uses the well-known Sino-Vietnamese four syllable expression "Hồng nhan bạc mệnh," which links the "rosy faced"—beautiful girls [*hồng nhan*]—to "cruel fate" [*bạc mệnh*].

Probably people from many cultures believe that when lovers meet they meet not merely by chance, that some higher power is at work. Certainly many Vietnamese believe in some such higher power, a power

---

10. "'Since ages out of mind,' retorted Kiều / 'Harsh fate has cursed all women, sparing none,'" (*The Tale of Kiều*, lines 108-109).

suggested by the word *duyên* and the compound words *nhân duyên* and *tình duyên*, all of which mean predestined affinity—the destiny that brings lovers together.[11] After Kiều and Kim Trọng meet for the first time, Kiều asks "And who is he? Why did we chance to meet? / Does fate [*duyên*] intend some tie between us two?" (lines 181-182). The word *duyên* evokes the story of the marriage god, Ông Tơ [Mr. Spinner of Silk Threads], who sits in the shadow of the moon and plays the role of cosmic matchmaker. When he rubs two threads together, the two people represented by those threads will marry.

The Tale of Kiều suggests that some people are fated to lead sad lives. Nguyễn Du tells an almost unbearably sad story. He originally called it *A New Cry from a Broken Heart* [Đoạn trường tân thanh]. Trịnh Công Sơn's songs, too, are cries from a broken heart, a heart broken by women he loved and by a cruel war. In both his love songs and anti-war songs one may occasionally detect a flash of bitterness or anger, but a mood of acceptance and forgiveness predominates, perhaps because solace comes from recognizing that there are larger forces at work, that one cannot shape the world according to one's wishes, cannot always have the love one cherishes. The mood of forgiveness, which one finds in *The Tale of Kiều* and in Trịnh Công Sơn's songs, no doubt has many sources but one of them surely is Buddhism. William Negherbon, an American scientist who became fascinated with this poem when he lived in Hanoi in the 1950's, mentions a "haunting perfume of charity and compassion that breathes from *The Tale of Kiều*," the source of which, he says, is Buddhism.[12] A similar perfume breathes from the songs of Trịnh Công Sơn.

Vũ Hạnh, a left-leaning scholar, finds Kiều too accepting, arguing that her sacrifices uphold an unjust feudal society.[13] It is true that Nguyễn Du does not preach rebellion, but he does make clear that officials in power do not treat their people well. Huỳnh Sanh Thông argues that the presence of this theme—the abuse of the weak by the powerful—is another reason why Vietnamese love this poem. To fend off foreign invaders and peasant revolts, Vietnamese monarchs have, Huỳnh Sanh Thông says, developed

---

11. "Nhân duyên," when used in Buddhist contexts, refers to *hetu pratyaya*, the Sanskrit term for cause and effect.
12. William Negherbon, "The Story of Lady Kieu," in *Some Aspects of Vietnamese Culture: Four Lectures by Nguyễn Đình Hòa, Nguyễn Ngọc Bích, William Negherbon, and Võ Đình,* 57.
13. Vũ Hạnh, *Đọc lại Truyện Kiều* [Rereading the Tale of Kiều], (Saigon: Cảo Thơm, 1966), 18-31.

an apparatus "designed more for repression and suppression than for justice."[14] Often these monarchs had to rely on corrupt local officials, like those that falsely accused Kiều's father. It is Kiều's need to pay off these officials that triggers the chain of disasters. A feeling of being "wronged" [*oan*]—a word that occurs often in *The Tale of Kiều*—is, Huỳnh Sanh Thông says, a feeling that Vietnamese throughout the centuries have shared. Certainly many Vietnamese in Trịnh Công Sơn's time felt "wronged" by corrupt regimes in Saigon and by the inability of political and military leaders on both sides of the 17th parallel to achieve peace. Kiều, like Trịnh Công Sơn, wanted peace. "She caused one death, but saved ten thousand lives / She knew right thoughts from wrong, fair deeds from foul" (lines 2681-2686), says the prophetess Tam Hợp, a reference to Kiều's persuading of her lover and protector, the rebel chief Từ Hải, to sue for peace. "Since you rose up in arms," Kiều tells Từ Hải, "dead men's white bones / Have piled head-high along the Wayward Stream [tributary of the Yellow River]" (lines 2493-2494). Từ Hải listens to Kiều, and dies as a result, but many others were saved. Trịnh Công Sơn also pleaded for peace, which did not satisfy all Vietnamese, but few would question that he acted sincerely and morally.

When Kiều must give up Kim and sell herself into marriage, Nguyễn Du asks us to "Pity the child, so young and so naïve— / Misfortune, like a storm, swooped down on her" (lines 615-616). This couplet contains the four-syllable expression "*Vạ gió tai bay.*" Translated word for word it means "Misfortune blows calamity flies." It refers to unexpected disasters, natural disasters like floods or manmade ones like Kiều being forced into prostitution. The Vietnam War, Huỳnh Sanh Thông says, "tore asunder the warp and woof of society in South Vietnam and bred prostitution, sexual and otherwise, on a vast scale. Unseen, unheard B-52 bombers that rained death and destruction out of the blue gave a new meaning to the phrase 'disasters that come flying on the wind.'"[15] Nguyễn Du through his character Kiều expressed the feeling of *oan*, the idea that the Vietnamese were wronged by those in power. Trịnh Công Sơn in his anti-war songs expresses a similar feeling.

The historian Alexander B. Woodside calls *The Tale of Kiều* "a remarkable hymn to individual fortitude and individual moral respon-

---

14. Huỳnh Sanh Thông, "Introduction," xxxii.
15. Ibid., xxix.

sibility."[16] The two most important virtues in the Confucian moral code were filial piety [*hiếu*], or reverence for one's parents, and loyalty [*trung*], or obedience to the emperor. Kiều demonstrates *hiếu* when she sells herself to help her father. She demonstrates *trung* when she urges Từ Hải to accept the emperor's gifts and end his rebellion. If he agrees, Kiều tells Từ Hải, then she can return home, making her parents happy. Từ Hải's acceptance of the offer will enable her to demonstrate loyalty to the state and filial piety to her parents.[17]

Kiều's morality is more Confucian than Buddhist, though Buddhist figures like the nun Giác Duyên, and Buddhist ideas like *karma*, figure prominently in *The Tale of Kiều*. Kiều, seeking refuge from Thúc Sinh's cruel wife, enters a temple where she accepts the Three Jewels of Buddhism [*Tam Bảo*]—Buddha, dharma, and sangha [*Phật, Pháp, Tăng*]—and vows to follow the Five Commandments [*Ngũ giới*] (to reject murder, theft, lust, lying and drunkenness). She takes the Buddhist name Pure Spring [*Trạc Tuyền*] and begins performing routine tasks: "At Buddha's feet she buried griefs—by day / She'd copy texts, light incense up at night" (lines 1929-1930). Nguyễn Du states the moral of his tale in both his opening and closing lines, but his ending is more Buddhist than his opening. In both opening and closing Nguyễn Du says that fate, referred to as Heaven [*trời*] or destiny [*mệnh*], tends to make the talented suffer, but the ending emphasizes another idea as well, that instead of "decrying Heaven's whims and quirks" we should try to develop a good heart:

> *Does Heaven ever favor anyone*
> *Bestowing both rare talent and good luck*
> *In talent take no overweening pride*
> *For talent* [tài] *and destiny* [tai] *form a pair*[18]
> *Our karma we must carry as our lot*
> *Let's stop decrying Heaven's whims and quirks*
> *Inside ourselves* [lòng] *there lies the root of good* [thiện căn]

---

16. Alexander B. Woodside, "The Historical Background," in Huỳnh Sanh Thông, Nguyễn Du, *The Tale of Kiều: A Bilingual Edition of Truyện Kiều*, xvii.
17. Lines 2473-2486.
18. Note that in Vietnamese the words talent [*tài*] and destiny [*tai*] are paired by rhyme as well as meaning: They differ only in tone. In his translation Huỳnh Sanh Thông says only that they "form a pair" but Nguyễn Du says explicitly that they rhyme. In doing so he emphasizes the tightness of the talent-destiny relationship. Huỳnh Sanh Thông does explain in a footnote that the word for "talent" (*tài* in Vietnamese; *ts'ai* in Chinese) rhymes with the word for misfortune (*tai* in Vietnamese; *tsai* in Chinese). See Huỳnh Sanh Thông, Nguyễn Du, *The Tale of Kiều*, page 208, note 3248.

THE TALE OF KIỀU

The heart [*tâm*] outweighs all talents [*tài*] on this earth (lines 3245-3252). "Root of good" is Huỳnh Sanh Thông's English translation of the Sino-Vietnamese compound word "*thiện căn*," a Buddhist term which is itself a translation of the Sanskrit term *kusala mula*. It refers to three "roots of advantageous action": "no greed" (Skt. *alobha*), "no hate" (Skt. *advesha*), and "no delusion" (Skt. a*moha*). Buddhist teachers emphasize that these three roots of good must be nourished through practice to prevent them from developing into the Three Poisons [*Tam Độc*]—greed, hate, and delusion. Practice [*tu*] may involve mindfulness training, reciting sutras and meditating, but whatever the means adopted one should keep in mind the goal, which is "to correct your character, to eliminate bad habits, to be joyful and compassionate, to build virtue."[19]

The words "*lòng*" in line 3251 and "*tâm*" in line 3252 also have Buddhist connotations. Both words are usually translated as "heart" in English. "*Lòng*" can refer to innards like intestines but it is also used to describe a kind-hearted person. In English we say "He is a kind-hearted person." Vietnamese say "*Ông là người có lòng tốt*" [He is a person with a good heart]. "*Tâm*," which means "heart," "spirit," or "mind," is the word Vietnamese use to translate the Sanskrit word *citta*, one of the most important words in Buddhism. Vietnamese call the heart sutra, one of the most popular Buddhist sutras, the *Tâm Kinh* [Heart Sutra].

After the prologue about talent and destiny that begins Nguyễn Du's tale comes this invitation: "By lamplight turn these scented leaves and read / A tale of love recorded in old books" (lines 7-8). Nguyễn Du's version of this old tale was 150 years old when Trịnh Công Sơn began composing his songs. It may not have directly influenced those songs, but it provides a window into the culture from which they come.

---

19. Thư Viện Hoa Sen [Lotus Dictionary], http://thuvienhoasen.org/p10a11888/tu (accessed November 11, 2014).

16

THE NEW POETRY
[*THƠ MỚI*] MOVEMENT

PART I

THREE DEVELOPMENTS

During the 1930s, three developments profoundly altered Vietnamese literature and music. In 1932 a man named Phan Khôi published a poem called "Tình Già" [Old Love] that launched the New Poetry [Thơ Mới] Movement which would change Vietnamese poetry. In 1933 Nhất Linh and other leading writers founded the Self-Strength Literary Group [Tự Lực Văn Đoàn]. Though included in this group were some New Poets and writers of reportage, its core members were novelists who pioneered a more modern prose style. Finally, in 1938 at a concert in Hanoi, a musician from Huế named Nguyễn Văn Tuyên sang songs that had some features of traditional Vietnamese songs but also revealed Western influences. This concert, aided by an article about it in the magazine *Today* [*Ngày Nay*],[1] launched what came to be called "Modern Music" [Tân Nhạc] or "Reformed Music" [Nhạc Cải Cách]. These terms were used to describe songs that were influenced by Western popular songs but also contained features of Vietnamese folk songs [*dân ca*], songs sung in modern folk opera [*cải lương*], and songs performed by songstresses to entertain upper class audiences [*hát ả đào*]. Works associated with these three movements—New Poetry, the Self-Strength Literary Group, and Reformed Music—are typically called "pre-war" [tiền chiến], a vague term that generally refers to a period from the early 1930s to the end of the First Indochina War in 1954.

---

1. The article was written by Thế Lữ, a New Poet who was also a member of the Self-Strength Literary Group. See Thế Lữ, "Một hy vọng trong làng âm nhạc: Ông Nguyễn Văn Tuyên" [Something Hopeful in the Village of Music: Mr. Nguyễn Văn Tuyên], Ngày Nay [Today] 116 (26 June 1938).

These three movements shaped the cultural environment that existed in South Vietnam when Trịnh Công Sơn began composing. In this chapter and the next I will discuss the New Poetry Movement. In Chapter Eighteen I will discuss Reformed Music and songs that represented a further development of Reformed Music, songs that Vietnamese call "Pre-war Songs" [*Nhạc Tiền Chiến*]. I will not discuss the novels of the Self-Strength Literary Group because although Trịnh Công Sơn certainly read them, I believe the poems of the New Poets and pre-war songs influenced Trịnh Công Sơn more.

THE NEW POETS: SOME POEMS MY STUDENTS LOVED

When I taught English as a second language at Phan Chu Trinh High School in Đà Nẵng and later at the University of Huế in the late 1960s and early 1970s, I was struck by how much my students loved poetry. Teachers, including foreign teachers like myself, were often invited to social events at which students would recite poetry. These events would typically include singing also, usually of pre-war songs (see Chapter Eighteen) or songs by Trịnh Công Sơn. (If it were an official university event, students would sing Sơn's love songs and not his anti-war songs.) I sensed that students who were talented at reciting poetry had a social status roughly equivalent to the status of a student athlete at an American university. I was so struck by my students' love of poetry that I wrote an article about it for a journal published by the University of Huế.[2] Neil L. Jamieson, the author of *Understanding Vietnam*, a fine book, says that he too was struck by how passionate Vietnamese were about poetry. He suggests that it is hard for Americans to comprehend this love Vietnamese have for poetry because for us poetry has "connotations of elitism, obscurity, impracticality."[3]

My students would quote lines from poems by the New Poets, and when I asked them about the source they would bring me a copy of the poem and ask me to help them translate it into English. One poem they greatly admired was "To Love" [Yêu] by Xuân Diệu. Here is Huỳnh Sanh Thông's translation:

> *To love is to die a little in the heart,*
> *for when you love, can you be sure you're loved?*

---

2. John C. Schafer, "Thi ca đối với người Việt và người Mỹ" [Poetry in Regard to Vietnamese and Americans], *Đặc San Văn Khoa* [Special Issue of the Faculty of Letters] *1972-1973* (Huế: Viện Đại Học Huế), 109-113.
3. Neil L. Jamieson, *Understanding Vietnam* (Berkeley, CA: University of California Press, 1993), 108.

You give so much, so little you get back–
the other lets you down or looks away.

Together or apart, it's still the same.
The moon turns pale, blooms fade, the soul's bereaved,
for when you love, can you be sure you're loved?
To love is to die a little in the heart.

They'll lose their way within dark sorrowland,
those passionate fools who go in search of love.
And life will be a desert reft of joy,
and love will tie the knot that binds to grief.
To love is to die a little in the heart.[4]

My students loved the line "To love is to die a little in the heart" [*Yêu là chết trong lòng một ít*]. Nguyễn Vỹ suggests that this line was inspired by a similar line ("*Partir c'est mourir un peu*") in *Sur la route mandarine* [On the Mandarin Road], a work of reportage by a French writer named Roland Dorgelès.[5] Huỳnh Sanh Thông, however, says it is "closely patterned after Edmond Haraucourt's '*Partir, c'est mourir un peu.*'"[6] Vietnam was a colony of France and the New Poets were learning French in schools run by the colonial authorities so it is not surprising that echoes of French works appear in their poems.

Another favorite poem of my students' was Lưu Trọng Lư's "The Sound of Autumn" [Tiếng thu]:

Don't you hear the sound of autumn
Crying under the pale moon?
Aren't you stirred by
The image of the absent warrior
In the heart of his lonely wife?
Don't you hear the autumn forest,
The rustling of the leaves,
And a bewildered golden deer
Stepping on golden leaves?

Because Xuân Diệu was the newest and the most famous New Poet I will discuss him in some depth. I will speak more briefly about Lưu Trọng Lư

---

4. Translated by Huỳnh Sanh Thông in *An Anthology of Vietnamese Poems*, (New Haven: Yale University Press, 1996), 284.
5. Nguyễn Vỹ, *Văn thi sĩ tiền chiến* [Pre-war Poets] (Hà Nội: Hội Nhà Văn, 1994), 117.
6. Huỳnh Sanh Thông, *An Anthology of Vietnamese Poems*, 284.

and Chế Lan Viên. Most of the New Poets were men but there were some female New Poets. I will discuss two: Nguyễn Thị Manh Manh[7] and Anh Thơ.

Most of the New Poets joined the communist revolution in the 1940s. I was not aware of this when I first began teaching English in Vietnam and I am not certain whether my students knew. Probably some did and some did not. I will talk about the lives of these New Poets before and after what Hoài Thanh calls their "miraculous resurrection."[8] Neil Jamieson, citing Hoài Thanh's term, makes the case for this extraordinary rebirth or resurrection that, he argues, the New Poets and other men and women their age experienced when they joined the revolution.[9] According to Jamieson, "the revolution and its ideology symbolized their personal revitalization, their rebirth into a new identity rooted in what was for them a more congenial and succoring environment."[10] Party discipline and being part of a close-knit group, Jamieson says, enabled the New Poets to "slough off the oppressive weight of individualism."[11] Lại Nguyên Ân and Alec Holcombe, in a ninety-page research essay about Xuân Diệu, question this explanation for Xuân Diệu's embrace of communist principles, but it is, they point out, the view that "comes closest to the official view of the poet still promoted in Vietnam today."[12] After discussing Xuân Diệu and some other New Poets I will consider whether "miraculous resurrection" is too hyperbolic a term to describe how these poets changed after they joined the revolutionary forces led by Hồ Chí Minh. First, however, I will explain what was new about the New Poets.

THE NEWNESS OF THE NEW POETS

Before Vietnamese developed a national script [*Quốc ngữ*] using Roman characters Vietnamese wrote poetry in *chữ nôm*, a way of writing Vietnamese using modified Chinese characters. This was the script, for example, that Nguyễn Du used to write *The Tale of Kiều*, discussed in

---

7. Nguyễn Thị Manh Manh is a pen name. Her given name is Nguyễn Thị Kiêm.
8. Nguyễn Khắc Viện and Hữu Ngọc quote Hoài Thanh's comments about a "miraculous resurrection" in *Vietnamese Literature: Historical Background and Texts*, (Hanoi: Red River, Foreign Languages Publishing House, n.d.), 145. These authors give no source but Neil Jamieson, who quotes this same passage in *Understanding Vietnam*, provides this source on page 411 of his bibliography: Tu Sơn, "Lời Cuối Sách" [Afterward], in *Thi Nhân Việt Nam*, 1932-1941, eds. Hoài Thanh and Hoài Chân, 377-99.
9. Neil Jamieson, *Understanding Vietnam*, 208.
10. Ibid., 280.
11. Ibid., 269.
12. Lại Nguyên Ân and Alec Holcombe, "The Heart and Mind of the Poet Xuân Diệu: 1954-1958," *Journal of Vietnamese Studies* 5, No. 2 (Summer, 2010), 4.

Chapter Fifteen, and that Nguyễn Đình Chiểu used to write *The Tale of Lục Vân Tiên*, another famous verse narrative. Both these poems were written in six-eight verse [*lục bát*], the Vietnamese folk meter that I described in Chapter Thirteen. Until the arrival of New Poetry, however, the preferred model for shorter poems was the Chinese "regulated poem" or *lu-shih*. Before *Quốc ngữ* [national script], a system of writing Vietnamese using roman characters, began to be used in schools, poets wrote their regulated poems in *chữ nôm*. When the New Poets were emerging on the scene, however, poets wrote their regulated poems in *Quốc ngữ*.

Because poems written in this highly "regulated" form had to have eight lines each consisting of seven words, Vietnamese refer to this form as "seven words eight lines" [*thất ngôn bát cú*], or simply as "*thơ Đường*" [T'ang poetry] because during the T'ang Dynasty (618-907) Chinese poets such as Li Po and Du Fu produced exquisite poems in this form, turning the mid-T'ang period into a golden age of Chinese poetry. Because it is a fixed form like the English sonnet, Westerners sometimes call it an eight-line sonnet, but the regulated poem has many more intricacies than the English sonnet. Huỳnh Sanh Thông provides this list with some examples: "the use of rhymes at the end of alternate lines; syntactical and semantic parallelism in the middle couplets; fixed patterns of tonal contrast in all couplets; and the avoidance of eight specific defects, such as the 'wasp's waist,' the 'crane's knee,' and so on."[13] In Vietnam poets such as Hồ Xuân Hương (1772-1822), Cao Bá Quát (1809-1853), Nguyễn Khuyến (1835-1909), and Hàn Mặc Tử (1912-1940) wrote highly praised poems in this form.

The regulated poem was a prestigious form in part because to become a mandarin, a government official, in China and Vietnam one had to demonstrate the ability to write one. It was one of the requirements on a rigorous entrance exam that those who wished to join the mandarinate had to fulfill. Hoài Thanh and Hoài Chân, authors of a famous book about the New Poets, argue that this requirement hurt the quality and prestige of the regulated poem. Because students studied it so much, they say, even masterpieces in this form became "almost meaningless." The form, they say, became "a machine to produce thousands of candidates and thousands of bad poems."[14] These exams were discontinued in the 1860s

---

13. Huỳnh Sanh Thông, *An Anthology of Vietnamese Poems*, 3.
14. Hoài Thanh and Hoài Chân, *Thi Nhân Việt Nam* [Vietnamese Poets], 34. First published in North Vietnam in 1942. My page references refer to an edition published in South Vietnam in 1967 by Hoa Tiên.

in the French colony of Cochinchina but they continued longer in the Protectorates, ending in 1915 in Tonkin and 1918 in Annam. With the arrival of the French and the establishing of Franco-Vietnamese schools, the older regulated poem began to seem old-fashioned, out of place in the new intellectual milieu created by colonization. According to Huỳnh Sanh Thông, another problem with the regulated poem was that it was not a good fit for the Vietnamese language. It did not accurately reproduce the "common cadence of Vietnamese speech."[15]

By the 1930s Vietnamese poets realized that the rules for the regulated poem stifled personal expression. Nguyễn Khắc Viện and Hữu Ngọc point out that poems written in the old style were about potentially emotional topics—the seasons, nostalgia, the death of a friend, how to enjoy life— but in them "individual sensitivity was effaced, or at least camouflaged in favor of expressions of primary truths or typical beauty portraying not so much the thing itself but its essence."[16] If emotions were expressed, they were carefully depersonalized, probably because the strict rules regarding form made sincere expression difficult. Huỳnh Sanh Thông argues that although the regulated poems written by Vietnamese were less formal in subject matter than those written by Chinese poets, the looser form that Vietnamese New Poets adopted "encouraged a freer and fresher, less stereotypical expression of an individual's innermost feelings."[17] It was these feelings that the New Poets wanted to write about. The main issue, Nguyễn Khắc Viện and Hữu Ngọc explain, was content, not form. The New Poets were tired of literature that presented "general laws," tired of poems that described a "depersonalized joy, sadness, and despair already filtered and purified, even crystalized." They wanted poems that expressed "the intimate, quivering flesh-and-bones man.[18] . . .They wanted poetry that revealed the hidden aspects of a human being who suffers, rejoices, feels and savours the things and situations he experiences with vibrating, sharpened, almost pathological sensitivity."[19]

Young aspiring Vietnamese poets felt estranged from the old poetry in part because it differed greatly from the French poetry that they were exposed to in Franco-Vietnamese schools. Xuân Diệu, Lưu Trọng Lư,

---

15. Huỳnh Sanh Thông, *An Anthology of Vietnamese Poems*, 8.
16. Nguyễn Khắc Viện and Hữu Ngọc, *Vietnamese Literature*, 120.
17. Huỳnh Sanh Thông, *An Anthology of Vietnamese Poems*, 7, 22.
18. Nguyễn Khắc Viện and Hữu Ngọc, *Vietnamese Literature*, 120-121.
19. Ibid., 121.

Chế Lan Viên, and other New Poets were reading the French romantics—Victor Hugo, Alphonse de Lamartine, Alfred de Vigny, and Alfred de Musset.[20] An even stronger influence on this group, according to critics Hoài Thanh and Hoài Chân, were the French Symbolists, particularly Charles Baudelaire but also Arthur Rimbaud, Paul Verlaine, and Stéphane Mallarmé. Hoài Thanh and Hoài Chân comment that "during a ten-year span Vietnamese poetry drew on one-hundred years of French poetry, from romanticism to the Parnassian School,[21] from symbolism to the poets that followed the symbolists."[22]

Having grown tired of the regulated poem with its rigid rules and excited by the works of French poets, it is not surprising that the New Poets embraced a new way writing poetry that a scholar named Phan Khôi presented in *Phụ Nữ Tân Văn* [Women's News] in 1932: "Take a true idea from the bottom of one's heart and describe it in lines that have rhyme but are not at all bound by the rules of prosody and provisionally call your work 'new poetry' [*thơ mới*]."[23] Phan Khôi included with his article an example of a poem in this new style that he wrote himself, a poem called "Old Love" [Tình già]. In this poem, considered to be the first "new poem," the speaker addresses a woman he loved twenty-four years ago but could not marry because marriages were arranged by one's parents. The speaker describes a chance meeting when they both had silver hair. They only exchange glances, but, the speaker says, "There still are corners in the eyes," a line which suggests their "old love" has not been forgotten. Here is the final stanza.

> *Twenty Years Later . . .*
> *A chance encounter faraway . . .*
> *Both heads had turned to silver;*
> *Had they not known each other well,*

20. Công Huyền Tôn Nữ Nha Trang, "The Role of French Romanticism in the New Poetry Movement in Vietnam," in *Borrowings and Adaptations in Vietnamese Culture*, ed. Trương Bửu Lâm (Manoa, Hawaii: Center for Asian and Pacific Studies, University of Hawaii, 1987), 52-62.
21. According to the *Encyclopedia Britannica* the Parnassian School was "A group . . . of 19th-century French poets who stressed restraint, objectivity, technical perfection, and precise description as a reaction against the emotionalism and verbal imprecision of the Romantics. See *Encyclopedia Britannica Online Academic Edition*, s.v. "Parnassian," https://www.britannica.com/topic/Parnassian (accessed Nov. 15, 2014).
22. Hoài Thanh and Hoài Chân, *Thi Nhân Việt Nam*, 33.
23. Phan Khoi, "Một lối thơ mới trình chánh giữa làng thơ" [A New Way of Writing Poems is Presented to the Village of Poetry], *Phụ Nữ Tân Văn* [Women's News] (March 10, 1932).

> *Might they not have passed each other unknown?*
> *An old affair was recalled, no more.*
> *It was just a glance in passing!*
> *. . . There are still corners to the eyes.*[24]

It is surprising that it was Phan Khôi (1887-1960), an older scholar educated in the Confucian system, who suggested this new way of writing, not one of the younger poets who studied in schools controlled by the French, but Phan Khôi was an unusual man, a fervent patriot who spoke his mind and wasn't afraid to criticize Communist Party leaders. In the 1950s he was a key supporter of the Nhân Văn-Giai Phẩm [Humanities-Masterpieces] movement which was led by individuals who resisted the Party's strict control of writers.

One can imagine how liberated young writers must have felt when they learned about this distinguished scholar and patriot's suggestion about how to write a poem. No longer would they have to worry about semantic parallelism, rules for tonal contrasts, etc. The critics Hoài Thanh and Hoài Chân describe how young people reacted to Phan Khôi's poem and definition: "It is not clear," they write, "whether anyone liked the 'new poem' [*thơ mới*] 'Old Love' [Tình già] that he included as an example. But many young people in the country suddenly saw the sky open up because their bold feelings, which they had kept hidden, had been noticed and approved of by a senior poet."[25]

Hoài Thanh and Hoài Chân suggest that the differences between the old and new poetry can be summed up by two words "*tôi*" [I] and "*ta*" [we]: "Before was the time of 'we'; now is the time of 'I.'"[26] In traditional poetry, one did not encounter the word "I." These two critics describe its arrival:

> The first day—who can say exactly what day it was—that the word 'I' appeared in Vietnamese poetry it was truly surprised. It was as if it were lost in a strange land. This is because it brought with it a perspective that had not been seen in this country: the individual perspective. Since ancient times there was no individual in Vietnamese society. There was only the collective: a large one, the country, and a small one, the family. As for the individual, the individual aspect was submerged in the family and in the country like a drop of water in the sea.[27]

---

24. Translated by Neil Jamieson, *Understanding Vietnam*, 109-110.
25. Hoài Thanh and Hoài Chân, *Thi Nhân Việt Nam*, 16-17.
26. Ibid., 51.
27. Ibid., 51-52.

Gradually, Hoài Thanh and Hoài Chân continue, writers became accustomed to "I" and it was not long before they preferred it to "we." "The word 'we' became too big for them. Their souls fit only the framework of the word 'I.'"[28] From this perspective the New Poets wrote sad but moving poems like Xuân Diệu's "To Love" and Lưu Trọng Lư's "The Sound of Autumn," quoted above.

VIETNAMESE PRONOUNS

To understand Hoài Thanh and Hoài Chân's discussion of pronouns it helps to know that in Vietnamese, kinship terms are also pronouns. When a child addresses his father he refers to himself as "child" [con] and his father as "father" [cha or bố]. "I will go with you" becomes "Child will go with father." The pronouns change depending on the kinship relationship. Well-known non-family members are turned into fictitious relatives. A child addresses a well-known male neighbor around the age of his father as "uncle" [bác] even if there is no blood relationship. There is a first-person pronoun that can be used when one does not want to assert what David Marr refers to as "a quasi-familial relationship"—when speaking to a stranger, for example.[29] This pronoun is "tôi," the pronoun which, according to Hoài Thanh and Hoài Chân, the New Poets fit their souls into when the pronoun ta [we] became too big for them. A problem with "tôi," however, was that it could make one sound too humble and self-deprecating because it was used in compounds like tôi tớ [servant, subordinate], bề tôi [subject, vassal], and vua-tôi [king-subject]. (Vua-tôi refers to the most important of the five Confucian relationships: king-subject, parent-child, husband-wife, older sibling-younger sibling, and friend-friend.) Phan Khôi mentioned this problem with the pronoun "tôi" in 1930, two years before he wrote "Old Love" [Tình già], the work considered to be the first New Poem. Some writers, he explained, avoided "tôi" because they thought of it as the way slaves refer to themselves.[30]

Despite this limitation in the early decades of the twentieth century, tôi was, David Marr explains, "promoted to the equivalent of moi or je in French, designed to give identity to the self without reference to 'the other,' whether high or low, kin or non-kin, male or female."[31] Marr argues

---

28. Ibid., 53.
29. David G. Marr, "Concepts of 'Individual' and 'Self' in Twentieth-Century Vietnam," *Modern Asian Studies* 34, no. 4 (2000), 786.
30. Phan Khôi, "Phép làm thơ" [Rules for Writing Poetry], *Phụ-nữ Tân-văn* [Women's News] 73 (October 9, 1930), 13.
31. David Marr, "Concepts of 'Individual and 'Self'," 786-787.

that *tôi* "failed to achieve the status of *moi* and *je* in French but remains important and can still be observed as a marker of individuality in certain circumstances."[32] He suggests that *tôi* never caught on because "sociolinguistically it needed a second-person singular form, like *vous* in French, to hook up with."[33] Working against the wider use of *tôi* is the fact that in most circumstances Vietnamese are inclined to use a first person pronoun that indicates their relationship to other people. That is why the critics Hoài Thanh and Hoài Chân Chân say that when *tôi* first appeared in the New Poetry it was lost in a strange land. Its presence indicated the rise of an "individual aspect" [*quan niệm cá nhân*] and the weakening of a customary familial and communal spirit.[34]

Though this new "I" became popular because it took one out of a web of family, social, and class relationships, its emergence was inevitable, David Marr points out, because printing presses and the rise in literacy facilitated by the Roman script [*Quốc ngữ*], which was easier to learn than the modified Chinese characters of *chữ nôm*, led to a publishing explosion in the 1920s.[35] The number of journals in French and Vietnamese increased rapidly in the late 1920s and early 1930s. To write for the strangers who read their works writers needed this new impersonal and non-familial "I." What Nguyễn Khắc Viện and Hữu Ngọc refer to as the "eruption of the 'I'" in the New Poetry occurred when Vietnamese poets, influenced by French poets, began to question Confucianism, a moral system that stressed the curbing of individual desires in order to better serve family and country.[36]

In the beginning, the New Poets were enthusiastic as they began to write personal poems about their sorrows and their joys. They wrote sad poems like Xuân Diệu's "To Love" [Yêu] about unrequited love, but also some happy poems about their love of poetry. Xuân Diệu expresses his exuberance for poetry in "Feelings and Emotions" [Cảm xúc]:

> To be a poet is to hum with winds,
> To ride the moon and dream, to roam with clouds,
> To have one's soul involved in myriad ties
> And share one's heart among a hundred loves.[37]

---

32. Ibid., 788.
33. Ibid.
34. Hoài Thanh and Hoài Chân, *Thi Nhân Việt Nam*, 51-52.
35. David Marr, "Concepts of 'Individual and 'Self,'" 787.
36. Nguyễn Khắc Viện and Hữu Ngọc, *Vietnamese Literature*, 120.
37. Translated by Huỳnh Sanh Thông in *An Anthology of Vietnamese Poems*, 297-298.

Thế Lữ, another New Poet, expresses the joy he derives from writing poetry in a poem titled "The Lyre of Myriad Tunes" [Cây đàn muôn điệu] in which he compares writing a poem to playing music and painting. Here are the closing lines:

> *I echo that glad warble of a flute*
> *Or comfort with a bell's miraculous voice.*
> *The muse lends me her lyre of myriad tunes,*
> *Her brush of myriad tints—I want to play*
> *A wizard making wonders, magic tricks*
> *With all the sounds and colors of the earth.*[38]

Eventually, however, individualism, the narrow framework of the "I," proved to be too confining. It was like a powerful drug that the New Poets' upbringing had not prepared them to withstand and eventually it did them in, brought them to the brink of personal disintegration. In *Vietnamese Poets,* published in 1942, Hoài Thanh and Hoài Chân, contemporaries of the New Poets, describe what was happening to them and the New Poets that they write about. Now, they write, "Our lives lie within the sphere of 'I.' Having lost breadth, we seek depth. But the deeper we go, the colder it becomes. . . . Never before has Vietnamese poetry been so sad or in such turmoil. Along with our sense of superiority we have lost the peace of mind of previous times."[39] Neil Jamieson argues that socialization within Confucian families had "stunted the psychological independence" of the New Poets, making it difficult for them to function in the individualist society of the West that they were exposed to in school and at work. At the same time their individualism caused difficulties at home where more traditional and hierarchical values still prevailed.[40]

SADNESS, THEN MIRACULOUS RESURRECTION

Many poems of the New Poets are expressions of a deep sadness. In poems like Lưu Trọng Lưu's "When Autumn Leaves Fall" [Khi thu rụng lá] the speaker is overcome with sadness when he remembers an old love who has married someone else. The tone is wistful and romantic but still sad. Here are the first and last stanzas:

> *Do you ever speak to me*
> *Words full of the love we knew when we were young*

---

38. Ibid., 296-297.
39. Hoài Thanh and Hoài Chân, *Thi Nhân Việt Nam*, 53-54.
40. Neil Jamieson, *Understanding Vietnam*, 172.

> *When autumn leaves fell and lay in the empty yard*
> *And a flute far beyond the curtain is heard?*
>
> *Winter came to the riverbank*
> *And hurriedly you married.*
> *Do you remember the vivid summer*
> *And my love lingering in a corner of my heart?*

Sadness, however, is too weak a word to describe the mood of a poem like Chế Lan Viên's "The Graves" [Những nấm mồ] which, with its morbid images of tombs and graves, conveys a mood of deep despair. Here is the third stanza:

> *The past is one long row of tomb on tomb.*
> *The future is a row of graves unfilled.*
> *And do you know, my friend? The present, too,*
> *is silently interring all our days.*[41]

Why this relentless sadness and despair? The Marxist critic Phan Cự Đệ argues that it was capitalism that left the New Poets so depressed and "degenerate" [*tha hóa*]. As they competed individually for jobs, he argues, they became "isolated in small, separate, and selfish little worlds."[42] He quotes a passage from Friedrich Engels' *The Condition of the Working Class in England* to bolster his case. Engels, in the passage Phan Cự Đệ cites, describes people from different classes elbowing each other as they compete for jobs, forgetting that they all crave the same things. Phan Cự Đệ says this explains the loneliness and sadness of characters in works by the European romantics and also the sad "individual 'I'" in the works of the Vietnamese New Poets.[43]

Even Phan Cự Đệ, however, acknowledges that some New Poets had personal reasons for being sad. He talks about the unhappy childhood of Xuân Diệu, who was the son not of his father's primary wife but of his father's *vợ bé* [second wife or concubine]. He lived with his biological mother in her home village near Quy Nhơn the first nine years of his life and then, when he was nine, moved back with his father and stepmother. In a book published in 1958 Xuân Diệu describes sneaking back to visit his biological mother when he was nine and how sad he felt when he had to

---

41. Translated by Huỳnh Sanh Thông in *An Anthology of Vietnamese Poems*, 336.
42. Phan Cư Đệ, *Tuyển Tập* [Selected Works], vol. 3 (Huế: Giáo Dục, 2006), 95.
43. Ibid., 96.

leave her.[44] Lưu Trọng Lư also was the son of his father's concubine. Phan Cự Đệ concludes, however, that the main cause of the sadness of the New Poets "was the blocked vision, with no escape, of urban petty bourgeoisie intellectuals who separated themselves from the political struggle."[45]

Many New Poets did not stay separated from the political struggle for long. In the late 1940s Xuân Diệu, Lưu Trọng Lư, Chế Lan Viên, Huy Cận, and the critics Hoài Thanh and Hoài Chân all joined the Indochinese Communist Party. Soon the New Poets stopped writing introspective, melancholy poems about love and alienation and began writing upbeat poems praising the revolution and Uncle Hồ—poems like the following poem by Xuân Diệu from his collection *Star* [Ngôi sao], published in 1955. The title of this collection refers to the flag of the Vietnam Workers' Party which had a yellow star on a red background.

> *Whenever the struggle grows fierce,*
> *Uncle Hồ always comes to visit.*
> *As we children listen to his teachings,*
> *We want to follow in his path.*
> *We children swear a solemn oath:*
> *To be resolute in our devotion,*
> *To shed our skins from this day forth.*[46]

The phrase "To shed our skins" [lột người] is significant. Personally troubled and lacking in direction before joining the revolution, these poets recreated themselves and achieved new identities in the anti-colonial struggle. The new poets were, Neil Jamieson says, "born again" in communism.[47] They apparently experienced what Hoài Thanh called a "miraculous resurrection." The revolution saved them psychologically. "In the new atmosphere of our homeland," Hoài Thanh writes, "we, the victims of the century of individualism—victims or the guilty—we realize how little our individual life means in the immense life of the community."[48]

---

44. Xuân Diệu, *Những bước đường tư tưởng của tôi* [Stages on My Journey of Thought] (Hà Nội: Văn hóa, 1958). I found this work online. See *Quê Hương* [Native Land], http://vanhoc.quehuong.org/viewtruyen.php?ID=6741&cat=15 (accessed June 16, 2020).
45. Phan Cự Đệ, *Tuyển Tập*, vol. 3, 101.
46. Translated by Neil Jamieson in *Understanding Vietnam*, 208. His source for this poem is Kim Nhật, *Những Nhà Văn Tiền Chiến Hà Nội Hôm Nay* [Pre-war Hanoi Literary Figures Today] (Saigon: Hoa Đăng, 1972), 93-94. No title of the poem is provided by Kim Nhật in the edition of his book that Jamieson cites or in a later edition that I have.
47. Neil Jamieson, *Understanding Vietnam*, 209.
48. Nguyễn Khắc Viện and Hữu Ngọc quote Hoài Thanh's comments about a "miraculous resurrection" in *Vietnamese Literature: Historical Background and Texts*, 145.

Lưu Trọng Lư's life was in shambles in the early 1940s but then he experienced a "rebirth" of the soul when he joined the resistance after the August Revolution. He describes this rebirth in "The Sound of Autumn II" [Tiếng Thu II],* a revised version of his famous "Sound of Autumn":

> *Villages and cities echo to the sound of gongs*
> *Fledgling birds waken in their dreams,*
> *Broken destinies are born again*
> *In the rebirth of my soul, dearest one,*
> *Can you feel the changed song of yours?*[49]

In this new version the deer, no longer bewildered, "pricks up its ears / and quivers on the trail of warhorses."

Anti-communists in the South who loved the early work of these poets could not believe that the New Poets could change so quickly, that such wildly individualistic types could suddenly conform themselves to rigid communist doctrine. To join the resistance, that was understandable. Few people wish to be ruled by a foreign power. But to join the communists? That was hard for those who admired their early poems to accept. Kim Nhật describes how they reacted to Xuân Diệu's conversion:

> That Xuân Diệu would join the Communist Party, accept communist ideals—in truth this was something that no one expected or could understand. Those ideals, that regime, the narrow horizon were not the home for the romantic, free, and liberal soul of a poet. We thought that Xuân Diệu would cut the thread before going too far, that he would divorce himself from the restrictive atmosphere so painful and shameful for a poet to endure. But no.[50]

After discussing Xuân Diệu, Lưu Trọng Lư, and Chế lan Viên and two women poets, Nguyễn Thị Manh Manh and Anh Thơ, I will consider whether "miraculous resurrection" is too hyperbolic a term to describe how these poets changed after they joined the revolutionary forces led by Hồ Chí Minh.

---

49. Translated by Mary Cowan et al. in Nguyễn Khắc Viện and Hữu Ngọc, *Vietnamese Literature*, 604.
50. Kim Nhật, *Những Nhà Văn Tiền Chiến Hà Nội Hôm Nay*, 92.

17

THE NEW POETRY
[THƠ MỚI] MOVEMENT

PART II

XUÂN DIỆU (1916-1985)

Xuân Diệu is a pen name. His given name is Ngô Xuân Diệu. He was born in 1916 or 1917 (accounts differ) in Tùng Giản, a village in Tuy Phước District, Bình Định Province about five miles north of the city of Quy Nhơn. He lived with his mother, Nguyễn Thị Hiệp, who was his father's second wife, or concubine, until he was eleven. After studying in primary school in Quy Nhơn his family sent him to Hanoi to study at the Trường Trung Học Bảo Hộ [Collège du Protectorat]. After obtaining his first baccalaureate degree in Hanoi he returned to central Vietnam and studied at the Khải Định Secondary School, later called Trường Quốc Học [National Academy], where he obtained his second baccalaureate degree in 1936. While studying in Huế he met and fell in love with Huy Cận and began a relationship that lasted his entire life. In 1938 he returned to Hanoi where he studied law and taught literature at a private school called Thăng Long.[1]

In *Vietnamese Poets*, published in 1942, Hoài Thanh and Hoài Chân say that Xuân Diệu was "the newest of the New Poets" and so only people

---

1. Information on Xuân Diệu's early life and schooling comes from Hoàng Trung Thông, "Tiểu sử nhà thơ Xuân Diệu" [Life History of the Poet Xuân Diệu], in *Tuyển tập Xuân Diệu Thơ* [Selected Poems of Xuân Diệu], eds. Hoàng Trung Thông and Vũ Quần Phương (Hanoi: Văn Học, 1986), 9-13; and Hạ Vinh Thi, "Vài nét về tiểu sử Xuân Diệu [Some Comments on the Life of *Xuân Diệu*], in *Hoàng tử của thi ca Việt Nam hiện đại* [Xuân Diệu: The Crown Prince of Modern Vietnamese Poetry], ed. Hạ Vinh Thi (Hanoi: Hanoi Publishing, 2000), 8-20.

with young hearts like to read his poems. But for a poet, they add, "nothing is more precious than to be appreciated by the young."[2] His first collection, *Thơ thơ* [Poésies], appeared in 1938 and his second, *Gửi hương cho gió* [Casting Fragrance to the Wind], in 1945. Hoài Thanh and Hoài Chân say at first readers were a bit put off by his poems because, they explain, Xuân Diệu "came to us in the most modern clothing and we were initially hesitant to befriend a person whose form seemed so foreign. But we gradually grew accustomed to Xuân Diệu, realizing that he still had a deep love for his homeland."[3] After a while, Hoài Thanh and Hoài Chân say, "we started not to notice his Western sentence constructions; we even forgot the thoughtful tone he borrowed from French poetry. We realized that within the graceful elegance of his poetic style was something quintessentially Vietnamese, and we were charmed."[4] According to Kim Nhật, before the first Indochina war against the French began everyone was memorizing Xuân Diệu's poems.[5] Critics started calling him the "The Prince of Love Poetry" [*Ông Hoàng của thơ tình yêu*]. His appearance perhaps helped him earn this title. Here is how another New Poet, Thế Lữ, describes him in the introduction he wrote for Xuân Diệu's collection *Poésies* [Thơ thơ]:

> This poet is a kind and passionate young man with hair that sits on his innocent forehead like a cloud, eyes that linger lovingly on everyone, and a wide smile like a heart that is ready for love. He travels the road of poetry, picking flowers around him as he goes. The fragrance of his poems emerges from the brightness of his heart.[6]

Xuân Diệu's wavy hair, Kim Nhật says, was his most distinguishing physical feature. "You just have to see that hair," he says, "and you know it's Xuân Diệu."[7]

Xuân Diệu joined the Communist Party in 1949 after he had actively supported the revolutionary forces for several years.[8] The party leadership

---

2. Hoài Thanh and Hoài Chân, *Thi nhân Việt Nam* [Vietnamese Poets], 120. First published in North Vietnam in 1942. My page references are from an edition published in South Vietnam in 1967 by Hoa Tiên (name of publisher).
3. Ibid., 115.
4. Ibid.
5. Kim Nhật, *Những Nhà Văn Tiền Chiến Hà Nội Hôm Nay* [Pre-War Hanoi Literary Figures Today] (Los Alamitos CA: Xuân Thu, 1991), 88.
6. Thế Lữ, "Tựa tập 'Thơ Thơ'" [Preface to *Poésies*], in Mã Giang Lân, *Thơ Xuân Diệu: Những lời bình* [The Poetry of Xuân Diệu: Reviews] (Hanoi: Văn Hóa—Thông Tin, 1999), 20.
7. Kim Nhật, *Những Nhà Văn Tiền Chiến Hà Nội Hôm Nay*, 88.
8. The name of the communist party in Vietnam has changed. From 1931 to 1945 it was the Indochinese Communist Party; from 1951 to 1975 it was the Vietnamese Workers Party; and from 1976 to the present it has been the Vietnamese Communist Party.

was well aware that recruiting Xuân Diệu, the most famous of the New Poets, was a propaganda victory. In 1944 Trường Chinh, general secretary of the Indochinese Communist Party, wrote a poem, "To Be a Poet" [Là thi sĩ] which was a response to Xuân Diệu's poem "Feelings and Emotions" [Cảm xúc], the poem I mentioned in the previous chapter in which Xuân Diệu expresses the joy of being a poet. In his poem Trường Chinh quotes lines from Xuân Diệu's poem and then refutes them. To be a poet, Trường Chinh says, is not just "to hum with the wind" as Xuân Diệu says:

> To be a poet is to sing and laud
> The greatest struggle ever fought on earth,
> Resist aggressive forces in the world,
> And raise the democratic flag
>
> The time of wine and roses is long past.
> No longer moan with winds and weep with clouds—
> Along the road of progress take brisk steps.
> Make poems, and with poems shed cold light
> On social issues that fester everywhere.
> With workers sow and grow tomorrow's world—
> In Soviet Russia it has budded forth.[9]

By attacking Xuân Diệu's poem Trường Chinh revealed he was aware of the poet's influence. He must have been pleased when five years later Xuân Diệu began writing poems like the one quoted above, in which talks about shedding his skin and following the path of Hồ Chí Minh.

In 1946 Xuân Diệu became managing editor of the revolutionary magazine *Tiên Phong* [Vanguard] which was published in a part of Hanoi controlled by the Việt Minh; and he became a member of the Democratic Republic of Vietnam's newly formed National Assembly [Quốc Hội], a position he held until 1960.[10] In May 1946, Hồ Chí Minh went to Fontainebleau to negotiate with the French but failed to reach an agreement and so returned to Hanoi in October. Fighting soon broke out and Việt Minh forces were forced to leave Hanoi. Xuân Diệu and other writers moved first to Gia Điền in the northern tip of Phú Thọ Province and then in 1949 they went to Đại Từ in Thái Nguyên Province. Xuân Diệu spent the

---

9. Translated by Huỳnh Sanh Thông, *An Anthology of Vietnamese Poems* (New Haven, CT: Yale University Press, 1996), 302-305. Huỳnh Sanh Thông lists the author as Sóng Hồng [Red Wave], one of Trường Chinh's pen names.
10. Hoàng Trung Thông, "Tiểu sử nhà thơ Xuân Diệu," 10.

last five years of the war in Đại Từ.[11] This village was only a short distance from where Hồ Chí Minh and Võ Nguyên Giáp had their headquarters. Both villages—Gia Điền and ĐạiTừ—are in a region referred to as *Việt Bắc* [North Vietnam], a confusing term because it does not refer to all of North Vietnam but only to this storied region where Việt Minh leaders devised a strategy that enabled them to win the First Indochina War.

The Việt Minh were delighted to have such a famous poet join their ranks. But did Xuân Diệu completely abandon his romantic, free-wheeling self after he joined the revolutionary movement? Was he a true believer in Marxist-Leninism? Lại Nguyên Ân and Alec Holcombe take up this question in a ninety-page article in the *Journal of Vietnamese Studies*. They focus on the years 1954-1958 when the Vietnamese Workers' Party was attempting to fight off a dissident movement led by a group of writers and artists associated with two literary publications: *Nhân Văn* [Humanity] and *Giai Phẩm* [Masterworks].[12] I will refer to this movement as the NVGP movement. Some of Vietnam's most talented writers, intellectuals, and artists were involved in this push for freedom of expression. Kim N. B. Ninh says it helped to set in motion "a series of developments that comprised the only instance of widespread dissent ever to occur in North Vietnam.[13] Peter Zinoman says that although it was "not quite a mass movement NVGP's size, duration and popularity exceed, by a wide margin, that of every other domestic protest movement prior to the mid-80s."[14] The movement in the 1980s that Zinoman refers to was a major reform movement known as *Đổi Mới* [Renovation] which was launched by the Sixth National Congress in December 1986. Vietnam's Đổi Mới was influenced by the Soviet Union's perestroika led by Mikhail Gorbachev in the mid-1980s. Zinoman explains that the NVGP movement in the 1950s was also affected by events in the Soviet Union and other communist countries: Nikita Krushchev's "secret speech" in 1956 attacking Stalinism; the anti-Stalinist movements in Poland and Hungary; and China's Hundred Flowers Campaign.[15] "Let a hundred

---

11. Lại Nguyên Ân and Alec Holcombe, "The Heart and Mind of the Poet Xuân Diệu: 1954-1958," *Journal of Vietnamese Studies* 5, No. 2 (Summer, 2010), 9-10.
12. Ibid.
13. Kim N. B. Ninh, *A World Transformed: The Politics of Culture in Revolutionary Vietnam* (Ann Arbor, MI: The University of Michigan Press, 2005), 122.
14. Peter Zinoman, "Nhân Văn Giai Phẩm on Trial," *Journal of Vietnamese Studies*, Vol. 11, No. 3/4 (Summer-Fall, 2016), 192.
15. Ibid., 191.

flowers bloom, and a hundred schools of thought contend," Mao Xedong announced in 1956.

One would think that a free spirit like Xuân Diệu would support the NVGP movement and be in favor of loosening strings on writers and artists but in March 1956 he wrote an article that suggests otherwise. "For us, whether we are writers inside or outside the party," he wrote, "the most important aspect of our viewpoint regarding free literature is recognition of the Communist Party's role in every aspect of life and every aspect of literature."[16] Then in July, 1956 he wrote "Dictatorship" [Chuyên chính], a poem in which he repudiates his former poetic self, that person who in "Feelings and Emotions" [Cảm xúc] declared that "To be a poet is to hum with winds / To ride the moon and dream, to roam with clouds." That was in 1938. In 1956 he has lost his love for winds and clouds. Here is the concluding stanza of "Dictatorship":

> *I once wrote poems about winds and clouds;*
> *Tonight I write verse about ideas;*
> *Those who mock our political poems,*
> *If their form is not yet polished,*
> *How merrily they boo and jeer;*
> *Forget those lamenters of fallen leaves and wilted flowers,*
> *To the dictatorship I openly sing and cheer*[17]

Xuân Diệu wrote "Dictatorship" in July 1956, when the de-Stalini-zation movement was occurring in the Soviet bloc and affecting Party members in Vietnam, but it was not published until November 1957. Lại Nguyên Ân and Alec Holcombe suggest that Xuân Diệu delayed publishing it because it would not make sense to praise dictatorship when the notorious dictator Stalin was being condemned for crimes and for abandoning Leninist principles of party rule.[18] In December 1957, however, Xuân Diệu wrote "Ask" [Hỏi] which resembles the romantic poems collected in *Poésies* [Thơ thơ] and "Fragrances on the Wings of the Wind" [Gửi hương cho gió]. Here is the closing stanza:

---

16. Xuân Diệu, "Vai trò lãnh đạo của Đảng" [The Party's Leadership Role], *Văn Nghệ*, no. 110, March 1, 1956. Translation by Lại Nguyên Ân and Alec Holcombe, "The Heart and Mind of the Poet Xuân Diệu," 25-26.
17. Translated by Lại Nguyên Ân and Alex Holcombe, "The Heart and Mind of the Poet Xuân Diệu," 57. The poem originally appeared in *Văn* [Literature], no. 26, November 1, 1957.
18. Lại Nguyên Ân and Alec Holcombe, "The Heart and Mind of the Poet Xuân Diệu," 57.

> *Lovesick I have swallowed the bait,*
> *Walking on fire, lying in clouds*
> *If it's love, if it's fate, then let's love,*
> *No more of these endless nights and days, my sweet!*[19]

Lại Nguyên Ân and Alec Holcombe argue that Xuân Diệu was continually seeking some "aesthetic compromise" between "romantic and revolutionary themes."[20] Going against the Party's rules for literature could get a writer dismissed from important positions. Xuân Diệu was not a supporter of the NVGP movement, in fact he was often criticized by individuals involved in it. He knew, it seems, that he had to be careful because all writers were expected to toe the party line. He was, however, an incurable romantic and could not completely forswear romantic poems.

Xuân Diệu, however, had something else to worry about: his sexual orientation. He worried about it but did not try to hide it. Xuân Diệu was, Lại Nguyên Ân and Alec Holcombe say, "the least secretive homosexual celebrity Vietnam had ever seen."[21] His first poetry collection, *Poésies* [Thơ thơ], released in 1938, included a poem titled "Love of Men" [Tình trai]* which begins as follows:

> *I remember Rimbaud and Verlaine*
> *Fellow poets of dazzling bacchanal spirit*
> *Intoxicated by strange rimes, infatuated with friendship*
> *They scorned well-worn paths and forsook the usual ways.*
>
> *Their steps ran in parallel cross the miles,*
> *Their souls entwined, aglow in floral scent.*
> *They went weak arms in strong ones embracing*
> *To the tune of love amidst wind and fog.*[22]

Most readers of "Love of Men" probably thought that Xuân Diệu was simply praising Arthur Rimbaud and Paul Verlaine, two gay French symbolist poets who had a tempestuous relationship. In a quarrel Verlaine once shot Rimbaud in the arm. Scholars, as I have mentioned, stress the influence of the symbolists on the New Poets. Some fans may have thought that Xuân

---

19. Translated by Lại Nguyên Ân and Alec Holcombe in "The Heart and Mind of the Poet Xuân Diệu," 60. Xuân Diệu's poem was first published in *Văn,* no. 32, December 13, 1957.
20. Lại Nguyên Ân and Alec Holcombe, "The Heart and Mind of the Poet Xuân Diệu," 52-53.
21. Lại Nguyên Ân and Alec Holcombe, "The Heart and Mind of the Poet Xuân Diệu," 8.
22. Translated by Nguyễn Quốc Vinh, in "Love of Men: Xuân Diệu, Translations and Interview with Tô Hoài," *Việt Nam Forum* 16 (1997), 264.

Diệu in "Love of Men" was just acknowledging two poets he admired. Party leaders, however, knew about Xuân Diệu's homosexuality but for many years looked the other way because both Xuân Diệu and Huy Cận supported the revolution. The Party even found a French villa on 24 Cột Cờ Street (now Điện Biên Phủ Street) for the couple to live in. They were joined in this villa by a half-sister of Xuân Diệu's named Ngô Xuân Nhủ who was married to Huy Cận.[23]

Xuân Diệu's homosexuality, however, did come up in a "rectification" [chỉnh huấn] session in 1952. Lại Nguyên Ân and Alec Holcombe explain that *chỉnh huấn*, a Soviet and Maoist technique, "is a type of thought reform using 'criticism and self-criticism' to prepare both soldiers and political cadres for difficult revolutionary tasks."[24] We know about this rectification session and how Xuân Diệu's reacted to it because the writer Tô Hoài, who was at that session, describes it in *Dust on Whose Feet?* [Cát bụi chân ai?], a surprisingly frank and detailed memoir that he wrote in 1992. Tô Hoài, it should be mentioned, was also a lover of Xuân Diệu. The rectification session was led by Tố Hữu, a hardliner committed to Marxist-Leninist principles. For him and other accusers Xuân Diệu's homosexuality was a class issue, a type of behavior associated with the bourgeoisie. In his memoir Tô Hoài explains that at this rectification session "everybody was raising their voice against 'bourgeois ideas, which must be recanted'! Xuân Diệu was sobbing over 'my love of men . . . love of men . . .' and then his words were choked, and tears would once again stream down."[25]

Lại Nguyên Ân and Alec Holcombe suggest that Xuân Diệu's moves back and forth between romantic poems like "Ask" and poems supporting the revolution like "Dictatorship" were evidence that he was engaged in a delicate balancing act. His homosexuality, they say, probably got him expelled from his position on the Standing Committee of the Literature and Arts Association.[26] He had to produce works glorifying the revolution from time to time to stay in the Party's good graces. In 1958 Xuân Diệu married a woman named Bạch Diệp, then a reporter for *Nhân dân* [The People]. The marriage lasted only six months and was never consummated.

---

23. Huy Cận and Ngô Xuân Nhủ had one child (two children according to Tô Hoài). The couple later divorced and in 1964 Huy Cận remarried and had three more children. See Lại Nguyên Ân and Alec Holcombe, "The Heart and Mind of the Poet Xuân Diệu," 13-14; and Nguyễn Quốc Vinh, "Love of Men: Xuân Diệu," 284.
24. Lại Nguyên Ân and Alec Holcombe, "The Heart and Mind of the Poet Xuân Diệu," 11.
25. These passages from Tô Hoài's memoir are translated by Nguyễn Quốc Vinh in "Love of Men: Xuân Diệu, Translations and Interview with Tô Hoài," 284.
26. Lại Nguyên Ân and Alec Holcombe, "The Heart and Mind of the Poet Xuân Diệu," 11.

Lã Xưa, in an article based in part on an interview with Bạch Diệp herself, says that her father met with Xuân Diệu to find out what the problem was. Xuân Diệu told him that he had a congenital birth defect that made husband-wife relations impossible.[27] Lại Nguyên Ân and Alec Holcombe say it is possible that Xuân Diệu never had any "serious intentions with Bạch Diệp" and that he married her to fend off charges by both the Party and the members of the NVGP movement that he was a homosexual.[28] Bạch Diệp later remarried and became a famous film director. Tô Hoài reports that when Xuân Diệu died "she sent a wreath of white flowers in his memory."[29]

In 1994 Nguyễn Quốc Vinh, who was at that time a graduate student in the Ph.D. program in East Asian Languages and Civilizations at Harvard, went home to Vietnam. He was a Xuân Diệu fan and had read Tô Hoài's memoir and was eager to meet the author. This was arranged with the help of Dan Duffy, editor of the journal *Việt Nam Forum* at Yale. Nguyễn Quốc Vinh met with Tô Hoài in July 1994. A summary of the part of their conversation about Xuân Diệu was later published in the *Việt Nam Forum*.[30] In this interview Tô Hoài told his young interviewer that "Xuân Diệu's love poetry is about love for both men and women, and it's wrong to understand that it is only about love for women."[31] He returns to this point later in the interview when he is describing the poetry Xuân Diệu wrote later in his life. "One must understand," he says, "that its object of reference is both men and women . . . But the passion in Xuân Diệu's poetry is still largely with the love of men."[32]

I have mentioned wondering whether my students at Huế University who brought me New Poems to translate knew the authors of these poems had joined the revolutionary forces and were in North Vietnam. I now wonder whether they knew that Xuân Diệu and Huy Cận, two of the most famous of all the New Poets, were gay. The question never occurred to me when I was in Huế. I understood the two poets were friends but only learned they were lovers as I did more reading about Vietnamese literature. My wife, who went to Đồng Khánh Secondary School in Huế

---

27. Lã Xưa, "Giải mã nghi án giới tính của 'ông hoàng thơ tình' Xuân Diệu," [Solving the Case of the Sexuality of Xuân Diệu, the "Prince of Love Poetry"] Saigon Ocean, https://saigonocean.com/gocchung/html/xuandieu.htm (accessed April 8, 2020).
28. Lại Nguyên Ân and Alec Holcombe, "The Heart and Mind of the Poet Xuân Diệu," 68.
29. Tô Hoài, interview by Nguyễn Quốc Vinh, 278.
30. Ibid., 275-280.
31. Ibid., 276.
32. Ibid., 279.

and graduated from the University of Huế where she later taught, says that Xuân Diệu's sexual orientation never came up within her circle of acquaintances and friends.

In 2016 a young poet named Đặng Vương Hưng wrote an article titled "The Secrets of Xuân Diệu's 'Male Loves.'"[33] In 1983 he had received first prize in a writing contest for young people. Xuân Diệu was one of the judges of this contest and afterwards the poet suggested that Đặng Vương Hưng send him his manuscript of poems and he would critique them. They met several times to discuss his work. The young writer admired Xuân Diệu and read his works and books and articles others had written about him. He found, he explains, that almost everyone who wrote about Xuân Diệu avoided talking about what he refers to as "the delicate— some would even call the taboo—topic" of Xuân Diệu's homosexuality.[34] When he was invited to speak at a conference to commemorate Xuân Diệu, which was to be held on what would have been Xuân Diệu's 100th birthday, Đặng Vương Hưng decided to write about this "taboo" topic, Xuân Diệu's "tình trai" [male love]. He explains that he uses this term, not "male homosexual" [đồng tính nam], because "if anyone asserted that this talented poet, an iconic figure beloved by countless generations of people who love Vietnamese poetry, was a male homosexual it is certain that his fanatic fans would shout: that's crazy, that can't be!"[35] This comment suggests that in 2016 many people were just as unaware of Xuân Diệu's homosexuality as my students in Huế in the 1960s and 1970s.

While writing this chapter on the New Poets some lines from a poem by Xuân Diệu that my students loved to quote came to mind. They are from "Vì sao" [Why?], which is included in *Thơ thơ* [Poésies], published in 1938:

> *How can love be defined*
> *It's just an afternoon*
> *It fills our soul with pale sunshine*
> *With soft clouds, a light breeze*

> Làm sao cắt nghĩa được tình yêu
> Có nghĩa gì đâu, một buổi chiều

---

33. Đặng Vương Hưng, "Bí ẩn 'Những mối tình trai'của nhà thơ Xuân Diệu" [The Secrets of Xuân Diệu's 'Male Loves'"], *Việt Times*, March 15, 2016, https://viettimes.vn/bi-an-nhung-moi-tinh-trai-cua-nha-tho-xuan-dieu-post22219.html (accessed June 8, 2020).
34. Ibid.
35. Ibid.

> Nó chiếm hồn ta bằng nắng nhạt
> Bằng mây nhè nhẹ, gió hiu hiu

My university students in Huế knew and loved this poem, especially the fourth stanza quoted above. The pronoun "our" [ta] in the third line of this stanza could refer to people in general, at least to people who have loved one another, or it could refer to a single person, the person the speaker in the poem is addressing. In the first and fifth stanza of this six-stanza poem the speaker uses a feminine second person pronoun, "cô," [miss] to refer to the person being addressed, clear evidence that the speaker is talking to a woman. Below the title, "Vì sao," of the poem, however, are the words "Tặng Đoàn Phú Tứ." *Tặng* means "presented to" or "given as a gift to." Đoàn Phú Tứ was a male playwright who was seven years older than Xuân Diệu. He was born in Bắc Ninh, a province that lies east of Hanoi. In 1945 when Hồ Chí Minh announced the setting up of a provisional government he became a representative in the National Assembly. He was editor of the journal *Literature and Art* [Văn Nghệ] in the late 1940s.[36] Xuân Diệu went to Hanoi in 1935, returned to Huế in 1936, and then went back to Hanoi in 1938,[37] so there were years when they both were in Hanoi. "Why?" appears in *Poésies*, Xuân Diệu's first collection of poems, which was published in 1938. "Diệu" does not quite rhyme with but sounds like the word for whiskey [rượu]. Kim Nhật says that Đoàn Phú Tứ used to call Xuân Diệu "Xuân Rượu" [Whiskey Xuân] because for a while Xuân Diệu worked as a commissar in the customs office in charge of regulating the sale of whiskey.[38] So clearly Xuân Diệu and Đoàn Phú Tứ knew each other and perhaps were friends. Vietnamese men and women, however, do not "present" [tặng] poems or books just to lovers, they *tặng* them to people they barely know as well, so Xuân Diệu's presenting of this poem to Đoàn Phú Tứ does not indicate they were lovers. Đặng Vương Hưng examined Xuân Diệu's two famous collections of poems, *Poésies* and *Casting Fragrance to the Wind*, the collections that earned him the title "The Prince of Poetry." The total number of poems in these two collections is one hundred, and twenty-one are presented to someone. All the receivers were men.[39]

---

36. Nguyễn Khoa Điềm and Ngô Văn Phú, *Nhà văn Việt Nam hiện đại* [Modern Vietnamese Writers] (Hanoi: Hội Nhà Văn, 1997), 742.
37. Hạ Vinh Thi, "Vài nét về tiểu sử Xuân Diệu," 10-11.
38. Kim Nhật, *Những Nhà Văn Tiền Chiến Hà Nội Hôm Nay*, 88.
39. Đặng Vương Hưng, "Bí ẩn 'Những mối tình trai' của nhà thơ Xuân Diệu."

Đặng Vương Hưng discusses Xuân Diệu's "Biển" [Ocean], a well-known and highly praised poem that Xuân Diệu wrote in 1962. Most people have assumed it was addressed to a woman, a reasonable assumption because the speaker addresses his lover as "*em*," a second-person singular pronoun which, in the context of a love poem like "Ocean"—especially one with verses like the following—would be understood to refer to a girl or woman:

> *Please let me be an azure wave*
> *That forever kisses your golden sand*
> *Kisses real gently, real softly*
> *Kisses calmly forever*

In 2016, however, Hoàng Cát, a younger male poet, told Đặng Vương Hưng that "Ocean" was addressed to him, that he was the inspiration for the poem. Đặng Vương Hưng was incredulous at first but became convinced when Hoàng Cát showed him a small, faded gold notebook in which Xuân Diệu had written out his poem "Ocean." Above the poem Xuân Diệu had written "Presented to my Hoàng Cát." Beneath the inscription was his signature.[40]

This signature, however, is not proof that Hoàng Cát and Xuân Diệu were lovers, but it seems that they in fact were. In an interview with Thiên Kim, also in 2016, Hoàng Cát said that he (Hoàng Cát) was the inspiration for "Ocean." But back then, Thiên Kim said, "throughout society people were prejudiced against what was called "male love" [*tình trai*]. How could you and the poet Xuân Diệu remain calm and endure the gossip and the slings and arrows of public opinion?" "You just closed your eyes and proceeded," Hoàng Cát said. He added that fortunately Xuân Diệu wrote "Ocean" in the early 60s, before everything got posted on the Internet.[41]

Đặng Vương Hưng suggests that Xuân Diệu's homosexuality helped him become the Prince of Love Poetry. "People always thirst for what they cannot have naturally," he says, and "for Xuân Diệu that was love! And that was what he wrote poems about."[42] I believe Đặng Vương Hưng is suggesting that it is difficult for anyone to find someone to love but

---

40. Ibid.
41. Hoàng Cát, interview with Thiên Kim, "Mối 'tình trai' của nhà thơ Xuân Diệu và nhà thơ Hoàng Cát" [The 'Male Love' between Xuân Diệu and the Poet Hoàng Cát], in *An Ninh Thế Giới* [World Security], January 30, 2016, http://antg.cand.com.vn/Kinh-te-Van-hoa-The-Thao/Moi-tinh-trai-cua-nha-tho-Xuan-dieu-va-nha-tho-Hoang-Cat-381592/ (accessed June 20, 2020).
42. Đặng Vương Hưng, "Bí ẩn 'Những mối tình trai'của nhà thơ Xuân Diệu."

for homosexuals the search is even more difficult—more tortured, more anguished. Xuân Diệu was able to express the sadness of unrequited love, a common theme in Vietnamese poems and songs, because he had experienced it in an intensified form. His advances, however, were not always unrequited and so he knew about and could express the joys of love as well.

Both Xuân Diệu and his friend Tô Hoài seem prescient in raising this issue of how love is defined. They insisted that male love should be as valued and respected as heterosexual love. Xuân Diệu, who wrote "Male Love" in 1938, was way ahead of his time. He was sending clear signals regarding his sexual orientation but nobody in central and south Vietnam was getting them. Xuân Diệu's acceptance of both heterosexual and homosexual love is certainly another reason why he is the newest, the most modern, of the "New Poets."

Xuân Diệu was extremely skillful in adapting to the rules for writers promulgated by Party officials. He would push against these rules at times and write works like those published before he joined the Party, works like those in his early poetry collections *Poésies* and *Casting Fragrance to the Wind*, but he also wrote poems that supported the Party. Other writers went to prison, but not Xuân Diệu. In the late 1950s and early 1960s when writers associated with the NVGP movement were being persecuted and imprisoned, Xuân Diệu was being rewarded. One reward was a two-month long trip to New Delhi in 1958. Upon his return to Vietnam he translated the poems of Rabindranath Tagore.[43]

When Xuân Diệu died in 1985 the editors of *Literature and Arts* [Văn Nghệ], a magazine that Xuân Diệu helped establish, devoted six pages of their December edition to articles about him. On the second page is a summary of key events in Xuân Diệu's life. An entry for the 1957-1958 period includes this comment: "When those in the Humanities and Masterworks [*Nhân Văn—Giai Phẩm*] movement opposed socialism in literature and art, Xuân Diệu took up the fight against them in a series of essays included in *Những bước đường tư tưởng của tôi* [My Ideological Development]."[44] Lại Nguyên Ân and Alec Holcombe report that in these essays Xuân Diệu confesses that he and other New Poets had been, as

---

43. Hoàng Trung Thông, "Xuân Diệu: Tiểu Sử nhà thơ Xuân Diệu," 12.
44. "Tiểu sử nhà thơ Xuân Diệu" [Life History of the Poet Xuân Diệu] in *Văn Nghệ* [Literature and Arts Magazine], no. 52 (December, 1985), 2. The essays in which Xuân Diệu describes his ideological development are available online. See *Truyện Dài: Những Bước Dường Tư Tưởng Của Tôi* [A Long Story: My Ideological Development], *Văn Học*

Xuân Diệu put it, "entranced by the false halo of individualism" and had "wallowed in [their] misfortunes and lost sight of the shining path." He also expresses his appreciation for how the Party has treated him. It was, Xuân Diệu says, "a bond of gratitude as deep as the ocean, as endless as a flowing stream," a love "like touchstones when they are in contact with pure gold."[45] Vietnamese refugees who escaped from Vietnam after 1975 will never forgive Xuân Diệu for failing to support the NVGP movement. For them the suppression of this movement and a disastrous land reform program that was occurring at the same time (1955-1956), a program that Xuân Diệu and other New Poets participated in, are reminders of the evils of totalitarian governments. We need these reminders, but we also need to sympathize with the hard choices that Xuân Diệu and all the New Poets had to make. Lại Nguyên Ân and Alex Holcombe make clear that Xuân Diệu's homosexuality increased the difficulty of his choices.

Xuân Diệu remained active in his later years. He made several trips to the Soviet Union and translated Russian works into Vietnamese—works like the poems of Alexander Pushkin and Vladimir Mayakovsky's *Vladimir Ilyich Lenin*, a long epic poem about the Russian leader. In 1978 he published a book about poets in Hungary and another about poets in Bulgaria. He also gave poetry readings. Hoàng Trung Thông reports that from 1949 to 1982 he gave 400 readings. In 1981 he was invited to give a talk about Vietnamese poetry in France.[46]

Xuân Diệu died of a heart attack on December 18, 1985. At a ceremony on December 21, 1985, the funeral oration [*điếu văn*] was given by Hà Xuân Trường, the Chairman of the Central Committee in Charge of Culture, Literature, and Art. In one section of his long address he suggests how Xuân Diệu will be remembered: "What we will never forget is his friendly way of speaking, his finely crafted literary works, his openness, his sincerity, his refusal to do anything half-way, and his fervent emotions." Then, addressing the deceased poet directly, he says this about Xuân Diệu's relationship with Huy Cận and with all his friends: "The feelings between you and Huy Cận were the exemplary feelings of loyal friends, something rarely seen. And how ardent and profound were your

---

Quê Hương [Literature of the Native Land], http://vanhoc.quehuong.org/viewtruyen. php?ID=6741&cat=15 (accessed May 28, 2020).
45. Lại Nguyên Ân and Alec Holcombe, "The Heart and Mind of the Poet Xuân Diệu," 58-59. Translation by Lại Nguyên Ân and Alec Holcombe.
46. Hoàng Trung Thông, "Tiểu sử nhà thơ Xuân Diệu," 11-13.

feelings for all your literary friends!"[47] By suggesting that Xuân Diệu's relationship to Huy Cận was like his relationship to all his friends, only more ardent, Hà Xuân Trường avoids mentioning Xuân Diệu's homosexuality, the issue that caused the poet so much grief in the 1950s.

Huy Cận was in France when Xuân Diệu died. He wanted to return for the memorial service but did not arrive in time. In a letter he wrote to the Vietnamese community in France he said that Xuân Diệu's "friends and relatives had lost an artist and a close friend, someone who had shared with us his feelings for over half a century; and I myself have lost my closest lifelong friend, a dear soul that life and poetry bestowed to me."[48]

LƯU TRỌNG LƯ (1912-1991)

Lưu Trọng Lư, like Xuân Diệu, led an unconventional life. The times, of course, made it difficult for anyone to live a normal life. Lưu Trọng Lư and other New Poets grew up during a period of political and social turmoil. The revolution was gaining strength in the 1930s and the French authorities watched all intellectuals carefully, arresting or transferring those they suspected of revolutionary sympathies. Lưu Trọng Lư was also a poet and Vietnamese expect their poets to live unconventional lives. If he was even more unconventional than other literary figures it is probably because he was so completely a poet, someone with a very romantic sensibility who, at least before 1945, preferred his dreams to the reality around him. "I have never seen anyone," comments Nguyễn Vỹ, "who had more of the poet in his soul and body than Lưu Trọng Lư. Whenever I met him, Lưu Trọng Lư impressed me as a restless soul, here today, somewhere else tomorrow, like a cloud, like the wind, drifting in space."[49]

Lưu Trọng Lư was born in Quảng Bình into a family of Confucian scholars. His father was a mandarin who had passed the *cử nhân* exam, the second level in the traditional exam system, and was the chief of a district in Quảng Bình Province. Lưu Trọng Lư attended elementary school in Quảng Bình and then studied at Quốc Học School in Huế. Expelled from this school, for reasons that neither he nor others make clear, he studied

---

47. Hà Xuân Trường, "Điếu văn" [Funeral Oration], *Văn Nghệ* [Literature and Arts Magazine], no. 52 (December, 1985), 1, 15.
48. This letter, which Huy Cận called "Lá thư đưa tin thay lời điếu của Huy Cân" [A Letter in Place of a Memorial Talk], was reprinted in the issue of *Văn Nghệ* [Literature and Art] eulogizing the poet: no. 52 (December, 1985), 5.
49. Nguyễn Vỹ, *Văn thi sĩ tiền chiến* [Pre-war Poets] (Hanoi: Hội Nhà Văn, 1994), 103.

in Hà Nội for a while and then began writing for newspapers and teaching in private schools in Hà Nội, Thanh Hóa, Huế and Hội An.[50]

Lưu Trọng Lư was a key person in the New Poetry movement. He promoted it, Nguyễn Văn Long explains, by giving speeches and writing about this new way of writing poems and also by publishing poems that people loved, poems like "Tiếng thu" [The Sound of Autumn], that appeared in the journals *Women's News* [Phụ Nữ Tân Văn] and *Customs* [Phong hóa] in the early 1930s. In 1939 he published his first collection of poems, which he titled *The Sound of Autumn* [Tiếng Thu] which is also the title of his best-known poem.

According to some accounts, Lưu Trọng Lư lived a very dissolute and troubled life in Huế in the years before the August Revolution of 1945. One must be somewhat careful in drawing conclusions from these accounts, however. Some are based more on rumors than personal observation. It seems clear, however, that Lưu Trọng Lư led an unusual life, even for a poet, during these years. Nguyễn Vỹ describes an incident in Hanoi in 1939. He was staying at a friend's house when Lưu Trọng Lư arrived by rickshaw at 2 o'clock in the morning in a semi-conscious state after having smoked opium and eaten too much dog meat.[51] In his memoir *Nửa đêm sực tỉnh* [Waking Suddenly in the Middle of the Night] Lưu Trọng Lư speaks frankly about the lure of opium, which Vietnamese refer to as visiting the brown fairy, an allusion to the color of the opium mixture.

> Why, at that time, did many writers and poets follow the brown fairy? It is difficult for any of us to forget the pleasurable or painful experience of that first time we followed the brown fairy. The way a little bit of brown penetrated the lungs and the blood and brought a dreamy pleasure to the soul; the way it made one's body feel strong and affected the hands and legs. All this is difficult to forget. Those days we never thought about the terrible devil that hid behind the fairy's skirt, the devil that one day would cause pain and suffering.[52]

In 1945 the Japanese replaced the French as the administrators of the country. These were hard times for Lưu Trọng Lư. In his memoir he explains that he was having trouble making a living with his writing, and then his wife died and he decided he had no choice but to leave his two children with his wife's family in Hội An. This family, however, was also

---

50. Nguyễn Văn Long, "Tiểu sử" [Life History], in *Tuyển Tập Lưu Trọng Lư* [Lưu Trọng Lư: Selections] ed. Nguyễn Văn Long (Hanoi: Văn Học, 1987), 9-10.
51. Nguyễn Vỹ, *Văn thi sĩ tiền chiến*, 108.
52. Lưu Trọng Lư, *Nửa đêm sực tỉnh* [Waking in the Middle of the Night] (Thuận Hóa, 1989), 115. No date of publication is listed on my copy but online sources list 1989.

struggling financially and so he arranged to have his children live with his older brother, a successful contractor, who lived in Kỳ Lam, a village twenty kilometers from Hội An.[53]

Lưu Trọng Lư's memoir, however, is not all gloom and doom. It is primarily a love story, one complete with a happy ending. It is an account of his love for a woman named Tôn Lệ Minh whom he called Mừng. She was born into a noble family and lived in a section of Huế reserved for relatives of Bảo Đại, Vietnam's last king of the Nguyễn dynasty. When she was young she would go with an aunt to wait on Bà Từ Cung, the mother of Bảo Đại. Her father had taught her how to play the zither [*đàn tranh*] and she became very accomplished with this instrument, good enough to teach others how to play it. When she was seventeen one of her students was the daughter of Phạm Quỳnh, the director of Bảo Đại's cabinet.[54] Lưu Trọng Lư refers to the sound of Mừng's zither in several of his poems. Here are the first and last stanzas of "Chải lại đời anh" [You Groomed My Life], which Trần Hoàng Thiêm Kim says was one of Mừng's favorites.[55]

> *A boundless miracle*
> *Expressed clearly through your hands*
> *The music continued as time passed*
> *Echoes of the first time I heard you play remain*
>
> *You are the moon at night, the sunlight in the morning*
> *In autumns of tattered golden leaves, you groomed my life*
> *You've straightened my scarf, buttoned my shirt*
> *With the moon and stars you make our love complete*[56]

Lưu Trọng Lư and Mừng were distant relatives. Lưu Trọng Lư had the same father but different mother as a woman named Tú Ý. The mother of Tú Ý was the cousin of Mừng's father.

She called Lưu Trọng Lư "chú" [uncle] and he called her "cháu" [niece]. Only when they had fallen in love did they switch to "anh" and "em," the pronouns husbands and wives use to address each other. They met because Mừng's father and Lưu Trọng Lư were friends and would

---

53. Ibid., 54.
54. Trần Hoàng Thiêm Kim, "Bà Tôn Lệ Minh—Vợ nhà thơ Lưu Trọng Lư: 'Em chải lại đời anh'" [Mrs. Tôn Lệ Minh—Wife of the poet Lưu Trọng Lư: 'You Groom My Life'], *An ninh thế giới online* [World Security Online], February 27, 2018, http://antg.cand.com. vn/Kinh-te-Van-hoa-The-Thao/Ba-Ton-Le-Minh-vo-nha-tho-Luu-Trong-Lu-Em-chai-lai-doi-anh-479752 (accessed July 21, 2020).
55. Trần Hoàng Thiêm Kim "Bà Tôn Lệ Minh—Vợ nhà thơ Lưu Trọng Lư."
56. For the complete poem see Nguyễn Văn Long, ed., *Tuyển tập Lưu Trọng Lư* [Lưu Trọng Lư: Selections] (Hanoi: Văn Học, 1987), 152.

meet to discuss and recite poetry together. They became closer when both Mừng's father and Lưu Trọng Lư's wife died around the same time. Mừng's family was suffering economically and so Mừng and her sister asked their mother to let them go to Quảng Nam to sell lichi. On one of her trips to Quảng Nam, feeling what Trần Hoàng Thiên Kim calls a "youthful curiosity," she decided to stop in the village of Kỳ Lam, the village near Hội An where she knew Chú Lưu's children were living with their uncle, Lưu Trọng Song.[57] Finding that his children were miserable in Kỳ Lam she suggested that Chú Lưu join her and her sister on their next lichi-selling trip so he could see how unhappy his children were. He accepted this invitation and that was the beginning of their life together.[58] She pledged her love to him and promised to take care of his two children as if they were her own. In his memoir Lưu Trọng Lư describes a night, January 19, 1944, when they took a boat ride on the Perfume River in Huế. That night, he says, was a wedding night "for two people who loved each other but never knew anything called an engagement or a wedding ceremony."[59] Mừng, after her momentous decision to marry Lưu Trọng Lư, makes another bold decision: to join the revolution against the French. When he joined the resistance Mừng left Huế with him.

After the August Revolution in 1945 they were both active in the Resistance in Battlezone IV [*Chiến Khu* IV] which included the provinces of Thanh Hóa, Nghệ An, Hà Tĩnh, Quảng Bình, Quảng Trị, and Thừa Thiên.[60] After he joined the Communist Party in 1948 he became the leader of a branch of the Association for Literature and Art in Battlezone IV. His assignment was to propagandize for the Party by writing works and encouraging others to write works that aided the revolution, works like his "The Sound of Autumn II" [Tiếng Thu]*, in which, as I've mentioned, the tame doe of his original version now "pricks up its ears / And quivers on the trail of war houses"; and "O the Supply Carrier" [O tiếp tế]* about a young woman who "walked on at a steady pace" as she carried supplies for revolutionary soldiers. The kind of works New Poets who joined the Party were expected to write is succinctly described by Neil Jamieson. Their task, he said, was "to wed artistic skill and talent with propagandis-tic intent."[61] Jamieson notes that Trường Chinh, a powerful member of

---

57. Trần Hoàng Thiêm Kim, "Bà Tôn Lệ Minh—Vợ nhà thơ Lưu Trọng Lư."
58. Lưu Trọng Lư describes Mừng's trip to visit his children in *Nửa đêm sực tỉnh*, 119-120.
59. Ibid., 126.
60. Nguyễn Văn Long, "Tiểu Sử," 10.
61. Neil L. Jamieson, *Understanding Vietnam*, 212.

the Indochinese Communist Party and a key assistant to Hồ Chí Minh, describes their task more bluntly in a report he delivered in 1948 to the Second National Congress. Trường Chinh told artists and writers that they needed to produce "cultural bazookas, mortars and guns" to destroy the enemy.[62]

When the First Indochina War against the French ended in 1954 Lưu Trọng Lư went to Hanoi where he worked in the central office of the Association for Literature and Art. During the war against the Americans he returned to Battlezone IV where he continued to write and propagandize for the war effort.

Lưu Trọng Lư and Tôn Lệ Minh had seven children together, six sons and one daughter. One son, Lưu Trọng Nông, joined the army and was killed in 1975 in the Mekong Delta as communist troops began their final assault on Saigon. Lưu Trọng Lư wrote a moving poem about his son's death titled "Again, Saying Goodbye to My Son" [Lại tiễn con].[63] Two other sons, Lưu Trọng Ninh and Lưu Trọng Văn, were soldiers also but survived the war. Lưu Trọng Ninh is a successful film director and Lưu Trọng Văn is a journalist. Lưu Trọng Lư and Mừng's only daughter, Lưu Ý Nhi, has become the secretary in charge of important manuscripts in the family home on Nguyễn Thái Học Street in Hanoi.[64]

After the war ended Lưu Trọng Lư was a member of the advisory board of the Writers Association and the Association for Dramatists. (Although he was best known for his poetry Lưu Trọng Lư also wrote fiction and plays.) In 1985, six years before he died, he was one of several writers and artists who received an Independence Medal, level 3.[65]

CHẾ LAN VIÊN

Chế Lan Viên is a pseudonym for Phan Ngọc Hoan. "Chế" is a Cham name that the author chose because, though not a member of the Cham ethnic group, he sympathized with the tragic history of the Cham people who lived in a flourishing kingdom they called Champa until the eleventh century when the Vietnamese pushing southward destroyed

---

62. For the report that Neil Jamieson cites see Trường Chinh, *Selected Writings* (Hanoi: Foreign Language Publishing House, 1977).
63. This poem is included in Nguyễn Văn Long, ed., *Tuyển tập Lưu Trọng Lư*, 130-132.
64. Trần Hoàng Thiêm, "Bà Tôn Lệ Minh—Vợ nhà thơ Lưu Trọng Lư."
65. Nguyễn Văn Long, "Tiểu sử" [Life History], in *Tuyển Tập Lưu Trọng Lư* [Lưu Trọng Lư Selections], 10.

their kingdom. Chế Lan Viên expresses sympathy for the Cham in "Silk Threads of Memory" [Những sợi tơ lòng]:

> *The earth stirs my silk heartstrings as it turns.*
> *My private grief soaks in all nothingness.*
> *Cham bricks keep falling as the months flee past*
> *Cham towers keep crumbling under their wan moon.*
>
> *Creator, send me back to Champaland!*
> *Take me away, far from the world of men.*
> *All scenes of life offend and hurt my eyes.*
> *All fresh, bright hues remind me of decay.*[66]

In "On the Way Home" [Trên đường về] Chế Lan Viên takes a mental journey back in time and remembers terrible battles when Champa blood was shed but also beautiful aspects of life in Champa land. Here are the second and final stanzas:

> *Here too are placid images: hamlets at rest*
> *In evening sun, Champa girls gliding homeward,*
> *Their light chatter floating*
> *With the pink and saffron of their dresses.*
>
> *All this I saw on my way home years ago*
> *And still I am obsessed,*
> *My mind stunned, sagged with sorrow,*
> *For the race of Champa.*[67]

Chế Lan Viên speaks of the Cham but no doubt has in mind the domination of his own country by foreign powers. Huỳnh Sanh Thông says that Chế Lan Viên "apparently used the Champa metaphor to mourn the loss under the French of national independence."[68]

Chế Lan Viên was born in Quảng Trị (central Vietnam) in 1920 but grew up three hundred miles to the south in Bình Định Province, a part of the country where Cham towers and other remains of the Kingdom of Champa still existed, though they were in ruins. Not coincidentally *Điêu tàn* [In Ruins] was the title of his first collection of poems. It was published in 1937 when the author was only 17 and a secondary school student in Quy Nhơn, the capital of Bình Định Province. This collection

---

66. Translated by Huỳnh Sanh Thông, *An Anthology of Vietnamese Poems*, 336-337.
67. Translated by Nguyễn Ngọc Bích, *A Thousand Years of Vietnamese Poetry* (New York: Alfred A. Knopf, 1975) 168-169.
68. Huỳnh Sanh Thông, *An Anthology of Vietnamese Poems*, note 1, 337.

quickly made Chế Lan Viên famous. The most morbid of the new poets, Chế Lan Viên was, according to Hoài Thanh and Hoài Chân, influenced greatly by Baudelaire and Edgar Allen Poe (whom he knew through Baudelaire's translations).[69] *In Ruins* contains poems with these titles: "The Graves" [Những nấm mồ], "The Skull" [Cái sọ người], and "The Funeral Procession" [Đám ma].

In 1939 he went to Hanoi to study and then became a journalist in Saigon, then taught in secondary schools in Thanh Hóa, a province about 85 miles south of Hanoi, and in Huế. He became involved in revolutionary activities during the early 1940s. When the August Revolution occurred in 1945 he was in Quy Nhơn (Bình Định Province).[70] After the August Revolution in 1945 he joined the resistance and like Lưu Trọng Lư operated as a journalist for the Party in Interzone IV [*liên khu* IV], a region that included five provinces in central Vietnam.[71] He wrote for *Victory* [Quyết thắng], a Việt Minh newspaper. He was inducted into the Communist Party in Quảng Trị, near the home village of his mother, in 1949. A poem that he wrote celebrating this event ends with these lines:

> *I stand beneath the flag [of the Party], offering my hand for the oath,*
> *On my native land pervaded by the spirit of my mother,*
> *I feel as if I were being born for the first time,*
> *That the Party had become my birthplace.*[72]

After joining the Communist Party, Chế Lan Viên moved from morbid, haunting poems of graves and ghosts to poems supporting the Party and the resistance. A transitional collection, *Light and Silt* [Ánh sáng và phù sa], published in 1960, reveals the poet moving from personal to more public and political concerns. In poetry written during the period of the American War public concerns dominate. I myself and, I think, other Americans, even those who opposed the war in Vietnam as I did, will find his political poems difficult to read, partly because they remind us of how cruel and devastating the American bombing was, partly because we expect poetry to be lighter and gentler and less political. There are also

---

69. Hoài Thanh and Hoài Chân, *Thi nhân Vietnam*, 32-33.
70. Nguyễn Xuân Nam and Vũ Thị Thường, *Tuyển tập Chế Lan Viên* [Selections: Chế Lan Viên] (Hanoi: Văn Học, 1985), 9.
71. Nghệ An, Hà Tĩnh, Quảng Bình, Quảng Trị, and Thừa Thiên.
72. For the entire poem, titled "Kết nạp đảng trên quê mẹ" [Joining the Party in the Native Land of My Mother], see Nguyễn Xuân Nam and Vũ Thị Thường, *Tuyển tập Chế Lan Viên*, 99-101.

problems in reading translations of poems. Artistic touches that native speakers would detect, touches that might soften a poem somewhat, are often lost in translation. As we have seen, Xuân Diệu, Lưu Trọng Lư and other New Poets also moved from sad private poems about their own sorrows to more public political poems opposing the war. Chế Lan Viên, however, more strictly heeded Trường Chinh's call to produce works that were "cultural bazookas." His later poems are filled with much more hatred of the Americans, especially their leaders—Richard Nixon, for example—than are the poems of Xuân Diệu and Lưu Trọng Lư. He specialized in what Nguyễn Xuân Nam calls "attack poems" [*thơ xung kích*].[73] One of his poetry collections is entitled *Fighting Poems* [Những bài thơ đánh giặc].[74] "In his poetry," Hà Minh Đức says, "Chế Lan Viên used a painful whip to strike the ugly and cruel face of the enemy."[75] A long poem called "Reflections" [Suy Nghĩ], which was written in 1966, ends in this way:

> *So children's breasts won't be perforated with bullets,*
> *So cradles won't be burned in one-thousand-degree heat,*
> *So mothers won't give birth in air filled with hot phosphorous,*
>
> *So all these things won't be:*
> *Kill them! It's the only way. Kill them!*
> *Oh, today our hearts are like the barrel of a gun;*
> *EXTERMINATING THE AMERICANS IS THE GREATEST ACT*
> *OF LOVE!*[76]

This poem was probably a response to Nixon's bombing of Hanoi and Haiphong in June 1966. Chế Lan Viên's poems are more closely related to American military and diplomatic efforts than are those by Xuân Diệu and Lưu Trọng Lư. In them he comments on the Mỹ Lai massacre, the Nixon Doctrine, Kissinger's trip to China, and the US aerial bombing campaign of North Vietnam in 1973, referred to as "The Christmas bombing" because it was conducted from December 18 to December 29. Here are the first two stanzas of a poem entitled "In Every Heart the American Imperialists Are Our Special Enemies" [Đế quốc mỹ là kẻ thù riêng của mỗi trái tim ta]*:

---

73. Ibid., 15.
74. Chế Lan Viên, *Những bài thơ đánh giặc* [Fighting Poems] (Hà Nội: Thanh Niên, 1972).
75. Hà Minh Đức, "Chế Lan Viên," in *Nhà văn Việt Nam* [Vietnamese Writers], ed. Phan Cự Đệ and Hà Minh Đức (Hà Nội: Đại Học và Trung Học Chuyên Nghiệp, 1979), 658.
76. The capital letters in the last line are Chế Lan Viên's. Excerpts from this long poem, which is dated July 28, 1966, can be found in Nguyễn Xuân Nam and Vũ Thị Thường, *Tuyển tập Chế Lan Viên*, 171-174.

They tear up the bodies of children, they burn down houses
They kill our rice fields with chemicals
They chop down trees still young and growing
They stab through the saffron robes of monks

What's horrifying is that they still have human faces
Are molded like us from the finest gold
Woven like us in the silk of life
The face of the killers is like the face of the killed[77]

In a 1965 poem called "Thinking about Poetry" [Nghĩ về thơ] Chế Lan Viên says: "Before poems only lamented, rarely asked; / The Party teaches us: Poetry must answer."[78] In his poems about current events Chế Lan Viên is implementing the Party's directive, trying to find answers for his people. In introducing Chế Lan Viên's poems written during the American War Nguyễn Xuân Nam, a communist writer, admits that "they are hard to understand if we don't remember a period when our people were listening to political discussions and announcements with great attention and zeal."[79] He points out, however, that even during the American War "few people set off on the struggle with the poems of Chế Lan Viên ringing in their ears."[80] Chế Lan Viên wrote a sixteen-page long poem about the Nixon doctrine. Probably this long poem was not ringing in soldiers' ears when they were on the march. Some people, Nguyễn Xuân Nam says, thought that Chế Lan Viên was too concerned about national and international political events and "didn't pay enough attention to everyday life." He wanted, Nguyễn Xuân Nam says, his poems to be both "booby traps to kill the enemy" and "cooling flowers for life."[81] The phrases about traps and flowers that Nguyễn Xuân Nam quotes are from a poem by Chế Lan Viên praising Hồ Chí Minh titled "The Person Who Changed My Life, The Person Who Changed My Poetry" [Người thay đổi đời tôi, Người thay đổi thơ tôi].[82] Chế Lan Viên's poems certainly contain more booby traps than cooling flowers.

---

77. This poem is included in Nguyễn Xuân Nam and Vũ Thị Thường, *Tuyển tập Chế Lan Viên*, 145-146.
78. For excerpts from this long poem see Nguyễn Xuân Nam and Vũ Thị Thường, *Tuyển tập Chế Lan Viên*, 174-176.
79. Nguyễn Xuân Nam, "Lời giới thiệu," in Nguyễn Xuân Nam and Vũ Thị Thường, *Tuyển tập Chế Lan Viên*, 27.
80. Ibid.
81. Ibid.
82. For the complete poem, see Nguyễn Xuân Nam and Vũ Thị Thường, *Tuyển tập Chế Lan Viên* [Selections: Chế Lan Viên], 141-143.

Hà Minh Đức points out that Chế Lan Viên uses oppositions to structure his poems: us versus the enemy, nobleness versus baseness, love versus hatred, etc. He is applying, he says, "dialectical thinking," apparently suggesting that Chế Lan Viên, knowingly or unknowingly, is using Marxist dialectics to write his poems.[83] In Chế Lan Viên's collection *Fighting Poems* [Những bài thơ đánh giặc], published in 1972, the dominant opposition is between a heroic people and cruel imperialists, and the constant repetition of this opposition makes his poems more propaganda than poetry. Sometimes, however, Chế Lan Viên employs this opposition technique in a powerful way. He does so in "Child Goes to Quê Võ" [Con Lên Quê Võ], a poem that is not in *Fighting Poems* but which Hà Minh Đức mentions in his discussion of Chế Lan Viên's effective use of oppositions.[84] Here is the third stanza:

> *Oh child, how I love you,*
> *Sleeping, hugging your mother tightly.*
> *Their bombs weigh a thousand pounds,*
> *And your skin is so soft.*

That child Chế Lan Viên mentions in "Child Goes to Quê Võ" may have been one of his own children. In 1959 he married Vũ Thị Thường,[85] a woman from Hà Tây, a province in the Red River delta which is now a part of the city of Hanoi. She was twenty-nine when they were married. This was her first marriage but Chế Lan Viên had been married before and had three children. In 1959 he had just separated from his wife.[86] According to Kim Nhật the marriage pleased Party leaders. Vũ Thị Thường was from a worker-peasant background so they did not worry about Chế Lan Viên being "corrupted" [hủ hóa] and then disloyal to the Party like other cadre who had fallen for women who came from "petit bourgeois families or families of rich peasants, or landowners."[87] Vũ Thị Thường had good revolutionary credentials. She was a labor union cadre, then a member of the Women's Association in a district in Thái Bình Province.

Vũ Thị Thường was also a writer. From 1958 to 1961 she was a journalist in Kiến An, a district in the city of Hải Phòng which is about

83. Hà Minh Đức, "Chế Lan Viên" in *Nhà văn Việt Nam*, 664-665.
84. The entire poem is available in a collection edited by Chế Lan Viên's wife Vũ Thị Thường: *Chế Lan Viên toàn tập* [Chế Lan Viên, a Complete Collection].
85. Vũ Thị Thường is a pen name. Her given name is Lê Kim Nga.
86. Nguyễn Thành Long, "Hai câu chuyện về Chế Lan Viên" [Two Stories about Chế Lan Viên] *Văn Nghệ* [Literature and Art] no. 27-28 (1989), 2.
87. Kim Nhật, *Những Nhà Văn Tiền Chiến Hà Nội Hôm Nay*, 241.

75 miles from Hanoi. She also wrote short stories. In 1959 one of her stories won first prize in a national short story contest conducted by the Vietnamese Writers Association. In the 1960s she helped produce the journals *Literary Studies* [Văn nghệ] and the magazine *New Works* [Tác phẩm mới].[88] Phan Thị Vàng Anh, the youngest daughter of Chế Lan Viên and Vũ Thị Thường, who was born in 1968, has followed in her parents' footsteps. She has become a successful writer of short fiction.[89] In a tribute to her father written in 1992, three years after his death, she describes how as a child she would accompany him when he gave talks on literature. Her jobs on these trips were to tell him to stop drinking when his face started to get red, and to "make sure that he had combed his hair, that he had folded back the collar of his shirt, that he had not forgotten his eyeglasses."[90]

Chế Lan Viên's life story resembles that of other New Poets, particularly Xuân Diệu, Huy Cận, and Lưu Trọng Lư who were also from central Vietnam and who became Party members around the same time he did. He differed, it seems, by living a more conventional private life particularly after he married Vũ Thị Thường. Kim Nhật suggests another distinguishing characteristic: Chế Lan Viên's ability to operate skillfully within the communist system. Kim Nhật, who was an officer in the North Vietnamese army before he defected to the Republic of Vietnam, does not admire this skill, seeing it instead as spinelessness, but his descriptions of how Chế Lan Viên operated in this system provide clues to the poet's character. For example, here is Kim Nhật's account of how Chế Lan Viên behaved during the re-education sessions conducted by the Party in Thái Nguyên in 1952 and 1953, the same sessions at which Xuân Diệu was chastised for his homosexuality. The quotation marks are Kim Nhật's, who uses them to indicate communist jargon.

> At the "Reeducation Camp for Writers and Artists" in the forests of Thái Nguyên in 1953, the sessions at which other writers and artists took turns examining themselves, airing their grievances [tố khổ] and "zealously shedding their skins" [lột xác] Chế Lan Viên was as

---

88. Nguyễn Khoa Điềm et al., eds., *Nhà Văn Việt Nam Hiện Đại* [Contemporary Vietnamese Writers] (Hà Nội: Hội Nhà Văn, 1997), 670.
89. One of Phan Thị Vàng Anh's collections of short stories, "When We Were Young" [Khi người ta trẻ], has been translated into French: *Quand on est jeune* [When We Were Young] (Arles, France: Editions Philippe Picquier), 996.
90. Phan Thị Vàng Anh, "Chế Lan Viên: A Daughter's Memories," translated from Vietnamese by Huỳnh Sanh Thông, *Vietnam Review* (Spring-Summer, 1997), 276-281.

unruffled as a clay pot.[91] He studied documents like everyone else and came to the meeting hall and listened all morning as comrades examined their sins but he was indifferent. He never once "rushed to express his opinion" or "spoke of grievances" [kể khổ]. It was strange.[92]

Kim Nhật also says that during the Nhân Văn-Giai Phẩm controversy "Chế Lan Viên kept quiet, never writing a single word praising or insulting this or that despite orders from above to do so."[93] As a result, Kim Nhật says, he was only gently criticized whereas other writers who expressed support for the Nhân Văn-Giai Phẩm movement were treated much more harshly.

After the first Indochina War ended in 1954, Chế Lan Viên lived in Hanoi where he held important positions including member of the Association of Vietnamese Writers and representative in the National Assembly [Quốc hội].[94] Using the pen name Chàng Văn [Mister Literature] he wrote two columns for the journal Văn Học [Literary Studies], one in which he discussed the works of other writers, and another in which he provided advice for younger writers trying to make a name for themselves.[95] Like other well-known writers who supported the communist regime he was rewarded with trips to foreign lands including the Soviet Union, France, Yugoslavia, and India.[96] In 1969 during the Paris peace talks he went with Huy Cận to France to organize cultural activities in support of the positions of the Democratic Republic of Vietnam.[97]

When he died in 1989 an entire sixteen-page issue of *Literature and Art* [Văn Nghệ] was filled with tributes to him and a sampling of his poems. In his funeral oration the poet Bảo Định Giang describes Chế Lan Viên as someone who "faithfully loved the Party, the nation, and people, who intensely loved his friends, and cared deeply about nurturing young talent."[98] He also mentions that he did not hesitate to speak frankly about

---

91. The term "*tố khổ*" was used during the land reform campaign that began in 1953 and ended in 1956. Land reform cadre encouraged people to air their grievances and denounce cruel landlords.
92. Kim Nhật, *Những Nhà Văn Tiền Chiến Hà Nội Hôm Nay*, 217.
93. Ibid., 234.
94. "Chế Lan Viên, Nhà thơ" [Chế Lan Viên, Poet], in Nguyễn Khoa Điềm and Ngô Văn Phú, eds. *Nhà văn Việt Nam hiện đại* [Contemporary Vietnamese Writers] (HCMC: Hội Nhà Văn, 1997), 762.
95. Kim Nhật, *Những Nhà Văn Tiền Chiến Hà Nội Hôm Nay*, 234.
96. Nguyễn Xuân Nam and Vũ Thị Thường, "Tiểu Sử" [Biography], in *Tuyển tập*, 9.
97. Kim Nhật, *Những Nhà Văn Tiền Chiến Hà Nội Hôm Nay*, 248; Neil L. Jamieson, *Understanding Vietnam*, 283.
98. Bảo Định Giang, "Điếu Văn" [Funeral Oration], *Văn Nghệ* [Literature and Art] 26 (July 1, 1989), 15.

issues regarding literature and art, a trait which Bảo Định Giang admits annoyed some people. He also praises Chế Lan Viên for his "beautiful family life."[99] Before an operation that he sensed would not save him, Chế Lan Viên wrote some words for his family which Bảo Định Giang reads. Chế Lan Viên tells his family to cremate him and not bury him some place far away that would be difficult for them to travel to, and he urges his youngest daughter, the writer Phan Vàng Anh, to continue the profession of her parents.

WERE ANY NEW POETS WOMEN?

"Yes," is the short answer, but much less has been written about them. Of the forty-six poets that Hoài Thanh and Hoài Chân discuss in *Thi Nhân Việt Nam* only five are women, but there were many more.[100] The authors of *The Defiant Muse: Vietnamese Feminist Poems from Antiquity to the Present* don't classify women writers as new or old but they include poems by thirteen women who were writing poems when the male New Poets I have discussed were producing their "New Poetry."[101] I will briefly discuss two female poets, one from the South and one from the North. Nguyễn Thị Manh Manh (real name Nguyễn Thị Kiêm) was born in 1914 in Gò Công district in Tiền Giang, a province in the Mekong River Delta south of Hồ Chí Minh City.[102] Anh Thơ (real name Vương Kiều Ân) was born in 1921 in Hải Dương Province in northern Vietnam.[103]

NGUYỄN THỊ MANH MANH

Nguyễn Thị Manh Manh's parents were well educated and able to prepare her for the career she chose. Her father was chief of Gò Công district and a member of the City Council for the Sài Gòn and Gia Định region in South Vietnam, and her mother was well versed in both Confucian studies and French culture. Nguyễn Thị Manh Manh graduated from the Gia Long Secondary School in Saigon. Thanks to her parents, Nguyễn Huệ Chi says, she received a "complete, global" education.[104] After graduating from

---

99. Ibid.
100. Hoài Thanh and Hoài Chân, *Thi Nhân Vietnam*.
101. Nguyễn Thị Minh Hà, Nguyễn Thị Thanh Bình, and Lady Borton, eds., *The Defiant Muse: Vietnamese Feminist Poems from Antiquity to the Present: A Bilingual Anthology* (New York: The Feminist Press, 2007).
102. Nguyễn Huệ Chi, "Nguyễn Thị Manh Manh," in *Từ Điển Văn Học* [Cultural Dictionary], eds. Đỗ Đức Hiểu, Nguyễn Huệ Chi, Phùng Văn Tửu, and Trần Hữu Tá, (Hà nội: Thế giới, 2003), 1185.
103. Nguyễn Thị Minh Hà, et al., *The Defiant Muse*, 245.
104. Nguyễn Huệ Chi, "Nguyễn Thị Manh Manh," 1185.

secondary school she taught in her former school for a while and began writing for newspapers in the Saigon region: *Công luân* [Public Opinion], *Phụ nữ tân văn* [Women's News], and *Việt Nam*.

Nguyễn Thị Manh Manh wrote New Poems and also promoted them. Hoài Thanh and Hoài Chân mention that on July 26, 1933, when she was only nineteen years old, she gave a speech praising New Poetry at a meeting of the Society for Promotion of Learning in Saigon. According to Hoài Thanh and Hoài Chân this was the first time that a young woman had addressed this group and the first time such a large crowd had come to hear a speech.[105] She also read some of her own New Poems. Then she took to the road and spoke on this same topic in Quy Nhơn, Đà Nẵng, Huế, Hải Phòng and Hà Nội. In her talk, which later appeared in *Phụ nữ tân văn* [Women's News],[106] she advocated abandoning the approach of the T'ang poets and adopting the approach taken by Phan Khôi, Thế Lữ and Lưu Trọng Lư. Her speeches, according to the authors of *The Defiant Muse*, "created a vociferous debate and were a major turning point in modern Vietnamese literature."[107]

Đoàn Lê Giang argues that Nguyễn Thị Manh Manh was "the first woman in the New Poetry movement to make innovations in poetic form."[108] He identifies some of her innovations in his discussion of her poem "Viếng phòng vắng" [Visiting the Deserted Room], Nguyễn Thị Manh Manh's first "New Poem" which was published in *Phụ nữa tân văn* [Women's News] on January 1, 1933, less than ten months after the poem generally agreed to be the first New Poem, Phan Khôi's "Tình già" [Old Love], was published in the same newspaper. Here are the first and fourth stanzas of this seven-stanza poem:

> *Wind slips into the empty room,*
> *Splashing fresh air from the fields*
> *Cold as copper.*

105. Hoài Thanh and Hoài Chân, *Thi nhân Việt Nam*, 19.
106. Nguyễn Thị Manh Manh, "Về Lối thơ mới" [About the New Poetry], a speech Nguyễn Thị Manh Manh gave in Saigon on July 26, 1933, at the Society for the Promotion of Learning in Saigon [Hội Khuyến học Sài Gòn]. This speech later appeared in *Phụ nữ tân văn* [Women's News] no. 211 (Aug. 10, 1933).
107. Nguyễn Thị Minh Hà, Nguyễn Thị Thanh Bình, and Lady Borton, eds., *The Defiant Muse*, 16.
108. Đoàn Lê Giang, "Nguyễn Thị Manh Manh—nữ sĩ tiến phong trong Phong trào Thơ mới" [Nguyễn Thị Manh Manh—A Vanguard Member of the New Poetry Movement], Khoa Việt Nam Học [Faculty of Vietnamese Studies], November 10, 2018, http://www.vns.edu.vn/index.php/vi/nghien-cuu/van-hoa-viet-nam/569-nguyen-thi-manh-manh-a-nu-si-tien-phong-trong-phong-trao-tho-moi (accessed October 26, 2020).

She sits dreaming—
The old days floating by,
Gossamer threads rousing the heart[109]

Plans to meet in another time
Search for each other again
How can that happen
Though one believes
She will be reborn
In what universe will that be?[110]

Here are the innovations Đoàn Lê Giang finds in this poem: a quicker and awkward cadence, lines that run on to the next line, the use of language common at that time in the Saigon dialect, and images that were not found in the old poetry—images like "sẽ tái sinh" [shall be reborn] and "ở vũ trụ nào" [in what universe]. Nguyễn Thị Manh Manh wrote one poem that has lines containing more than twenty words. This poem, "A Letter for All People Who Love or Hate New Poetry,"[111] is unusual in subject as well as form. Here is the concluding stanza:

Now I try to encourage guests in the village of poetry
To change things around, those who love the new should look for
the bad
Those who hate it should try to find the good in the poem
By blaming and praising a new flower will blossom

Nguyễn Thị Manh Manh wished to change people's idea about what was poetic. She praised "Child in the Home of the Unemployed" [Con nhà thất nghiệp], a poem by Hồ Văn Hảo that describes the suffering that results when a father, a coolie, loses his job and he and his wife have no money to buy medicine for their sick child. Maybe, Nguyễn Thị Manh Manh says, some people think a story of a half-naked coolie is not "romantic" and therefore not a proper topic for a poem. Clearly she disagrees.[112] Nguyễn Huệ Chi explains that after the journal *Phụ Nữ Tân Văn* [Women's News] ceased publishing in 1934 Nguyễn Thị Manh Manh did not publish a lot of "New Poems" but the poems she did write included not only "lyrical"

---

109. This translation of this stanza appears in *The Defiant Muse*, Nguyễn Thị Minh Hà, Nguyễn Thị Thanh Bình, and Lady Borton, eds., 16. The translators are Xuân Oanh and Michelle Noullet.
110. This stanza is translated by Cao Thị Như Quỳnh.
111. The Vietnamese title is "Bức thư gởi cho tất cả ai ưa hay là ghét lối thơ mới."
112. Nguyễn Huệ Chi, "Nguyễn Thị Manh Manh," 1186.

poems but also poems that "argued" and "testified about" and "discussed" various topics.[113]

What is most striking about Nguyễn Thị Manh Manh is her total commitment to the liberation of women. In a series of speeches that she delivered in 1934 in cities all over the country, she talked about the patriarchal nature of Vietnamese society and argued that women should be liberated from old sexist beliefs and customs. In these speeches, which were later published in *Phụ nữ tân văn* [Women's News], she argued against polygamy and the practice of women marrying when they were underage [*tảo hôn*] and insisted on the right of women to choose whom they marry.[114] She also insisted that the notion of "the three submissions" be abolished.[115] The three submissions [*tam tòng*] specified that women must be submissive to their fathers before marriage, to their husbands when married, and to their oldest son if they outlived their husbands. She also argued that sports were not just for men, that women should play them too.[116]

Vietnam has a much longer history than the US and some of the customs that Nguyễn Thị Manh Manh says should be abandoned were established centuries ago. The doctrine of the three submissions [*tam tòng*], for example, is spelled out in *Song on Family Education* [Gia huấn ca], a work usually attributed to Nguyễn Trãi, who was born in 1380. She sounds very modern, however, when in "The Male View of Progressive Women" she objects to men who say women working to advance women's rights just want to be like men.[117]

On November 11, 1937 Nguyễn Thị Manh Manh married a man from Hà Tiên named Trương Tuấn Cảnh, a teacher in a secondary school in Saigon and also a writer whose pen name was Lư Khê. He came from a poor family but, according to Trương Minh Đạt, a younger brother of her husband, that did not bother her. In her speeches and writing, Trương

---

113. Ibid.
114. Nguyễn Thị Manh Manh, "Có nên bỏ chế độ đa thê không?" [Should We Abandon Polygamy?] *Phụ nữ tân văn* [Women's News] no. 268 (November 29, 1934); "Có nên tự do kết hôn không?" [Should We Be Free to Choose Whom We Marry?] *Phụ nữ tân văn* [Women's News] no. 267 (November 21, 1934).
115. Nguyễn Thị Manh Manh, "Một ngày của một người đàn bà tân tiến" [A Day in the Life of a Progressive Woman] *Phụ nữ tân văn* [Women's News] no. 259 (September 20, 1934).
116. Nguyễn Huệ Chi, "Nguyễn Thị Manh Manh," 1186.
117. Nguyễn Thị Manh Manh, "Dư luận nam giới đối với phụ nữ tân tiến" [The Male View of Progressive Women], *Phụ nữ tân văn* [Women's News] no. 243 (April 24, 1934).

Minh Đạt points out, she defended the poor.[118] The marriage, however, did not last long and the reason for its short duration reveals the patriarchal nature of Vietnamese society that Nguyễn Thị Manh Manh opposed in her speeches and articles. She had trouble giving birth and a baby, a girl named Mi Nu, was paralyzed from birth and lived only one year. When Mi Nu died Nguyễn Thị Manh Manh allowed her husband to marry again. He was the oldest son in his family and so needed to have a son to maintain a clear line of descent, an unbroken lineage. In 1950 Nguyễn Thị Manh Manh moved to France, married a Frenchman and remained in France for fifty-five years.[119] For many years she had no contact with people in Vietnam. In 1999, however, Thiên Mộc Lan and Thanh Việt Thanh wrote a book about her which a friend of hers, who lived in Paris, obtained on a trip to Vietnam.[120] She brought back a copy, signed by the authors, for Nguyễn Thị Manh Manh who was 85 and living in a rest home when she received it. "I never thought," she said, "that after fifty years friends of literature in the country (Vietnam) would still remember me and write about me."[121]

ANH THƠ

Vương Kiều Ân (pen name Anh Thơ) was born in 1921 in Ninh Giang, a district [*huyện*] of Hải Dương Province in the Red River Delta region of Vietnam. Her father was a Confucian scholar and official, part of the mandarinate which the French maintained in central (Annam) and north

---

118. Different people in online articles about Nguyễn Thị Manh Manh cite Trương Minh Đạt's comments about his sister-in-law but do not provide a source, perhaps because Trương Minh Đạt made them in an unpublished speech. Phan Văn Hoàng, in "Nhớ một nữ sĩ có tài và có gan" [Remembering a Woman Writer Who Was Talented] cites this speech by Trương Minh Đạt: "Những kỷ niệm sống với anh Lư Khê và chị Manh Manh [Memories of My Life with Lư Khê and Manh Manh] [speech given at the College of Social Science and Humanities, in Hồ Chí Minh City, May 26, 2006). For Phan Văn Hoàng's article see the webpage Hồn Việt, http://www.honvietquochoc.com.vn/bai-viet/2538-nho-mot-nu-si-co-tai-va-co-gan-.aspx (accessed December 26, 2020).
119. Trần Nhật Vy, "Nữ phóng viên đầu tiên" [The First Woman Reporter], Tuổi Trẻ [Youth], June 18, 2015, https://tuoitre.vn/nu-phong-vien-dau-tien-763227.htm (accessed January 7, 2021).
120. I have not been able to obtain this book by Thiên Mộc Lan and Thanh Việt Thanh but Phan Văn Hoàng mentions it in "Nhớ một nữ sĩ có tài và có gan." He cites it as follows: Thiên Mộc Lan and Thanh Việt Thanh, *Nữ sĩ Nguyễn Thị Manh Manh* [The Woman Writer Nguyễn Thị Manh Manh] (HCMC: Văn Nghệ, 1999).
121. Phan Văn Hoàng, in "Nhớ một nữ sĩ có tài và có gan" [Remembering a Woman Writer Who Was Talented and Brave], provides this source for Nguyễn Thị Manh Manh's comments about being surprised that people still remember her: Thiên Mộc Lan, "Phấn son tô điểm sơn hà" [Women Beautify the Country], *Phụ nữ tân văn* [Women's News] (2010), 260.

(Tonkin) Vietnam because it decreased the need for a large staff of French administrators. Her father, it seems, believed in the "Three Submissions" and other patriarchal practices that Nguyễn Thị Manh Manh was attacking in speeches. Anh Thơ, Nguyễn Văn Long says, turned to poetry to "liberate herself and affirm the value of women in contemporary society."[122]

Anh Thơ began writing poetry when she was thirteen. She became well known after she released a collection of her poems in 1939 called Bức tranh quê [Rural Landscapes]. When it was still in manuscript form the Self-Reliant Literary Group [Tự lực văn đoàn] presented her with a poetry encouragement prize for this collection.[123] It was published in 1941. Hoài Thanh and Hoài Chân praise Anh Thơ for her ability to portray rural life. "Scenery in poetry," they write, "doesn't have to be immense. An empty seashell is enough for us to hear ocean waves."[124] They, and other critics and fans, praise Anh Thơ for her ability to portray country life in homespun images like those in these lines from "Moving to Autumn" [Sang thu]:

> Golden melon flowers fall scattered on the ground
> The dragonfly missing the sunshine flies aimlessly

Anh Thơ's poem "Spring Afternoon" [Chiều xuân] is also packed with images of country life:

> Rain like dust motes gentles the wharf
> A lazy boat lounges on the river
> A thatched stall stands silent in the deserted village
> Floating purple flowers fall to the earth near the margose trees.
>
> Young grass spreads in a blue-green blush along the dike road
> Starlings swoop down, peck aimlessly
> Butterflies undulate in the breeze
> Cattle and buffalo graze in the soft rain.
>
> From the lush green paddies all wet and quiet
> Young egrets take off in flight
> Startling a young woman in a red halter
> Raking weeds in a rice field about to bloom.[125]

---

122. Nguyễn Văn Long, "Anh Thơ," in Từ Điển Văn Học [Cultural Dictionary], eds. Đỗ Đức Hiểu, Nguyễn Huệ Chi, Phùng Văn Tửu, and Trần Hữu Tá, (Hà nội: Thế giới, 2003), 47.
123. Nguyễn Khoa Điềm and Ngô Văn Phú, Nhà văn Việt Nam hiện đại, 648.
124. Hoài Thanh and Hoài Chân, Thi Nhân Việt Nam, 198.
125. Translated by Xuân Oanh and Lady Borton. See Nguyễn Thị Minh Hà, Nguyễn Thị Thanh Bình, and Lady Borton, eds., The Defiant Muse, 117.

Anh Thơ joined the Việt Minh in 1945 and began writing poems that Nguyễn Văn Long says "gave voice to the innermost feelings of women behind the front lines, especially female cadre who bravely overcame pain, and loss, and separation. They sacrificed quietly and contributed to the victory of the people."[126] These poems are included in her collection *Kể chuyện vũ lăng* [Telling Stories about Vũ lăng], published in 1957. During the war against the Americans, Nguyễn Văn Long says, Anh Thơ "enlarged her range of topics and expanded her emotions and wrote poems about the beauty of the new life and the heroism of the Vietnamese people, especially ordinary and simple women."[127]

Anh Thơ held various notable positions, first in Bắc Giang Province and later at the national level. In Hải Dương she was secretary of the Women's Association [Hội phụ nữ] for four districts. In 1957 she became a member of the Vietnamese Writers Association [Hội Nhà Văn Việt Nam]. From 1971 to 1975 she was a staff member for the journal *New Works* [Tác phẩm mới] and the Association for Vietnamese Literature and Art [Hội Liên hiệp Văn học nghệ thuật Việt Nam].[128] While holding these positions she continued to write poems. Anh Thơ died in 2005. In 2007 she received Vietnam's highest award: the Hồ Chí Minh Award for Literature and Art.[129]

MIRACULOUS RESURRECTION?

Did the New Poets experience a "miraculous" change when they joined the communist revolution led by Hồ Chí Minh? I have mentioned that the critic Hoài Thanh says they did and that Xuân Diệu speaks of "shedding his skin" [lột người], a phrase which suggests a complete change, in a poem in his collection *Ngôi Sao* [A Star]. Chế Lan Viên in his poem "Joining the Party in My Mother's Native Village" [Kết nạp đảng trên quê mẹ] says "I felt like being born again / The Party became my native place."[130] To indicate native place Chế Lan Viên uses the phrase "the place where one's umbilical cord was cut and one's placenta buried" [nơi cắt rốn chôn rau]. This phrase suggests loyalty and love for one's native land.

---

126. Nguyễn Văn Long, "Anh Thơ," 47.
127. Ibid.
128. Nguyễn Khoa Điềm and Ngô Văn Phú, *Nhà văn Việt Nam hiện đại*, 648.
129. Nguyễn Thị Minh Hà et al. in *The Defiant Muse*, 17.
130. For the entire poem see Lý Hải Châu et al. *Tuyển tập Chế Lan Viên*, Tập một [A Collection of Works by Chế Lan Viên, Vol. 1] (Hà Nội: Văn học 1985), 99-101.

However, to say that you were born again, that you had shed your old skin [lột xác] when you joined the Party, was what Party leaders wanted you to say. It was expected. In the 1950s many other writers made similar statements when they joined the Party or when they were criticized in "rectification" [chỉnh huấn] sessions like the one Xuân Diệu was forced to attend. Kim Nhật describes the dramatic performances of some writers who were eager to convince Party leaders that they regretted their previous literary works and were abandoning them. The poet Hoàng Cầm, he says, after repudiating his previous works and apologizing for his bourgeois background, put all his old books in a bag and burned them. This was a symbolic act designed, Kim Nhật says, to prove that he had "shed his skin" [lột xác] and become a new person. Nguyễn Tuân, a famous essayist, imitated Hoàng Cầm and burned a bag of his previous works.[131] Hoàng Cầm and Nguyễn Tuân adopted these dramatic gestures, Kim Nhật says, because if they failed to convince Party leaders they had shed their skins and become new people they would lose the protection of the Party.

Kim N. B. Ninh points out that these confessions did have "religious overtones." "Images of salvation and rebirth abounded," she says.[132] The Party and the revolution were "reified" and became a godlike presence.[133] Some of the New Poets and writers had personal problems or economic hardships which were alleviated when they joined the Party. I have mentioned that Lưu Trọng Lư was rumored to be smoking one hundred pipes of opium a day before he joined the Revolution. Images of suicide, Kim N. B. Ninh points out, appeared in Nguyễn Tuân's writing before the August Revolution.[134] Hoài Thanh used the phrase "miraculous resurrection" to describe the changes the New Poets underwent but Neil Jamieson suggests that what improved their psychological condition was their "participation in meaningful group action" to resist French imperialism.[135] In other words the changes were no doubt real but not "miraculous." After joining the Resistance they felt that their lives had purpose. Neil Jamieson discusses Chế Lan Viên's poem "When You Have Purpose" [Khi đã có hướng rồi], which was published in Văn nghệ [Literature and the Arts] in March 1958. Here is his translation of the second and third stanzas and the last two lines of the final stanza:

---

131. Kim Nhật, *Những Nhà Văn Tiền Chiến Hà Nội Hôm Nay*, 61.
132. Kim N. B. Ninh, *A World Transformed*, 116.
133. Ibid., 117.
134. Ibid., 33.
135. Ibid., 267.

When you have purpose, a common stick can slay the enemy.
Our brothers of old used their teeth to rend the flesh of opposing
troops.
One leaflet can activate an entire district.
Dirty hands and muddy feet can overturn even the throne of a king.

When you have purpose, on those morning and afternoons with-
out savor,
Which are molded by fortifications meant to protect the "self,"
In the vale of agony weapons can be found
To shatter the loneliness and mix with "people."

When there is purpose, fear not that the flame of life will end,
For when the wind blows, life will arise naturally.[136]

In a series of essays written in the 1950s Xuân Diệu, the most famous
New Poet, describes experiences that intensified his commitment to the
Revolution led by Hồ Chí Minh. In these essays he portrays his ideological
development as a gradual process that was shaped by his observations of
the suffering of his people when the French, and briefly the Japanese,
occupied his country. The story he tells suggests that what he experienced
was not a "miraculous resurrection" but rather a growing commitment to
the Revolution that deepened over time. It is, as he suggests in the title of
his collection of these essays, "a long story."[137]

By the end of the 1930s these poets were no longer called "new,"
the disappearance of the adjective proof that their poetic innovations
had been generally accepted. After the country's division in 1954 by the
Geneva Accords, people living in south Vietnam referred to these poets as
"pre-war poets" [*nhà thơ tiền chiến*], an appropriate designation in some
respects because people in the south knew little about what happened to
these poets after they joined the revolution. It was as if they had dropped
off the face of the earth, their lives suddenly terminated in 1945. In the
south, only their pre-war poems were read. These were the works that
my students in Huế were eager to share with me in the late 1960s and
early 70s. Some were put to music by Phạm Duy and other composers and
became popular "pre-war songs," a category of songs that I discuss in the

---

136. Translated by Neil L. Jamieson, *Understanding Vietnam*, 266-267.
137. Xuân Diệu, "Truyện Dài: Những Bước Đường Tư Tưởng Của Tôi" [A Long Story: My
Ideological Development], *Văn Học Quê Hương* [Literature of the Native Land], May
28, 2020, http://vanhoc.quehuong.org/viewtruyen.php?ID=6741&cat=15 (accessed
May 28, 2020).

next chapter. In the martial atmosphere of the North the weepy, romantic pre-war poems of these poets were out of place and rarely appeared in print, so readers above the 17th parallel saw only their new revolutionary poetry.

THE NEW POETS AND TRỊNH CÔNG SƠN

The New Poets helped prepare the way for Trịnh Công Sơn. He continued to do in popular songs what they had done in poetry. In the 1930s the New Poets wrote poems expressing their sadness and loneliness in a society which was changing, becoming less communal, more individualistic. They talked about being sad [*buồn*], about endless rain [*mưa*] that aggravated their sadness, and about nothingness [*hư vô, hư không*]. "Today the sky is soft and high," Xuân Diệu wrote in his poem "Afternoon" [Chiều], and "I'm sad [*buồn*] and don't know why I'm sad [*buồn*]." In "Nothingness" [Hư vô] Xuân Diệu talked about being pushed toward "the brink of nothingness":

> *Sweat soaked my brow, tears welled up in my eyes.*
> *The months and years had pushed me, hustled me*
> *Toward this, the chilly brink of nothingness [hư vô].*[138]

Lưu Trọng Lư talked about rain "Rain …Endless Rain" [Mưa…mưa mãi]:

> *Endless rain, always raining,*
> *Who is there to love?*
> *The cold wind has gone to the mountains, not to return again*
>
> *Why this rain, this endless rain?*
> *My heart is always longing*
> *For whom do I bear this pain?*[139]

Huy Cận, talked about rain and sadness in "The Sadness of a Rainy Night" [Buồn đêm mưa]:

> *I hear the rain dripping from the roof*
> *Hear the heaviness of heaven, hear my own sadness*

And in "A Dirge" [Nhạc sầu] Huy Cận described a burial service at a grave and a soul sinking into "nothingness" [*hư vô*].[140]

In the 1960s Trịnh Công Sơn used similar words and images to express his state of mind. In "Age of Stony Sadness" [Tuổi đá buồn]* rain

---

138. Translated by Huỳnh Sanh Thông in *An Anthology of Vietnamese Poems*, 324.
139. Translated by Neil Jamison in *Understanding Vietnam*, 168.
140. Huỳnh Sanh Thông has translated this poem. See *An Anthology of Vietnamese Poems*, 333-334.

is falling everywhere and the speaker laments his sad life. In "Words of the River's Current" [Lời của dòng sông], "nothingness" [*hư vô*] "smothers the fragile age of youth and innocence." "*Hư vô*" was, as I have pointed out in other chapters, a word Trịnh Công Sơn used often in conversation, letters, and songs.

Trịnh Công Sơn's sadness, however, seems to have been caused by unrequited love and a civil war in which thousands of Vietnamese died. The New Poets also wrote poems about unrequited love. In fact, in what is considered to be the first New Poem, Phan Khôi's "Old Love," the speaker describes his love for a woman he could never marry. But the New Poets were also struggling to adapt to an increasingly more individualistic society. Their lives, Hoài Thanh and Hoài Chân explain, lay "within the sphere of the 'I'" and the deeper they went into this "I" the sadder they became.[141] Most of the New Poets, however, were at least twenty years older than Trịnh Công Sơn. Lưu Trọng Lư, born in 1912, was twenty-seven years older than Trịnh Công Sơn. Xuân Diệu, born in 1917, was 22 years older. When Trịnh Công Sơn began to write his songs in late the 1950s and early 1960s people who lived in central and southern Vietnam, particularly those who lived in the larger towns, had already begun to accept a society that was becoming more tolerant of individualism, less bound by Confucian principles. Neil Jamieson describes a "profound contradiction" that "reached its apogee in the 1930s," a contradiction "between the individualism that was at the core of modern Western culture and the near total immersion of the individual in hierarchical social groups, especially the family, which constituted the basis of Vietnamese society."[142] This apogee Jamieson describes, however, was reached thirty years before Trịnh Công Sơn began to compose his songs. In central Vietnam in the late 1950s and early 1960s there were no prohibitions or worries about focusing on the "I" in poems and songs. South of the DMZ, songs that were anti-war might be banned but there was no pressure to stop composing or reading sad love poems or singing sad love songs. The love poems of the New Poets, including works by poets who had joined the communist revolution, were part of the curriculum. Students read them in their Vietnamese literature classes.

---

141. Hoài Thanh and Hoài Chân, *Thi Nhân Việt Nam*, 53-54.
142. Neil L. Jamieson, "Shattered Identities and Contested Images: Reflections of Poetry and History in 20th-Century Vietnam," *Crossroads* vol. 7, no. 2 (1992), 84.

Trịnh Công Sơn did in his anti-war songs what the New Poets, fearful of being criticized in a rectification session, did not do in their poems. In "A Mother's Legacy" [Gia tài của mẹ]* he called for an end to an internecine civil war that had been going on for twenty years and was bequeathing mothers "a forest of dry bones" and "a mountain of graves." In "A Song for the Corpses" [Bài ca dành cho những xác người] he expressed his sad reaction to the death and destruction that occurred in his beloved home city of Huế during the 1968 Tết Offensive. The speaker in this song walks around the city strewn with corpses wondering which corpse is his sister or brother. Trịnh Công Sơn also envisioned a time when people from the three regions—north, central, and south—would, he sings in "Huế Sài gòn Hà nội,"* "step away for once from extermination" and "build one common house for all."

Some of Trịnh Công Sơn's love songs, however, resemble the love poems of the New Poets. A song like Trịnh Công Sơn's "Because I Need to See You Love Life" [Vì tôi cần thấy em yêu đời] resembles Huy Cận's "Melancholy" [Ngậm ngùi].* Both Huy Cận and Trịnh Công Sơn are very solicitous of their lover's comfort. Note these lines from Huy Cận's poem:

Sleep, love, let me fan for you
My heart opens with this fan
A hundred birds bring dreams to the head of your bed
Sleep, love, and dream an ordinary dream

And these similar lines from Sơn's song:

May I be a distant tree
Standing and watching you so radiant
Let me make you a small dream
So you will sleep soundly

May I make the river flow
And quietly carry away your sadness
So you enter a season
With pink the only color

Trịnh Công Sơn also wrote a song titled "Calming My Melancholy" [Ru ta ngậm ngùi] (1970) which I discussed in Chapter Fourteen. This is a lullaby for the self not for a loved one but it may reflect the influence of Huy Cận's poem.

In 1961 Phạm Duy set to music several poems by the New Poets, including Huy Cận's "Melancholy" [Ngậm ngùi], Xuân Diệu's "Afternoon"

[Chiều],[143] and Lưu Trọng Lư's "The Sound of Autumn" [Tiếng thu].* In turning poems into songs Phạm Duy was doing what French poets like Georges Brassens and Jacques Prévert were doing in France. Brassens set to music the poems of Victor Hugo, Paul Verlaine, and Francois Villon. Some of Prévert's poems, including "Les feuilles mortes" [Autumn Leaves] and "Les bruits de la nuit" [The Sounds of the Night], were set to music by Joseph Kosma.[144] In an article describing how he set songs to music Phạm Duy explains that the setting to music in France of poems by famous French poets enhanced the prestige of songs in Vietnam. Songs, Phạm Duy says, were no longer considered a minor art form [*un art mineur*]; they were a part of literary studies [*văn học*].[145]

The songs based on poems by the New Poets that Phạm Duy released became extremely popular. Famous singers, including Phạm Duy's wife, Thái Hằng, and daughter, Thái Hiền, sang them in coffee houses in Saigon. My students at Phan Chu Trinh High School in Đà Nẵng and at the University of Huế knew them well. Phạm Duy did not change the words of the poems very much when he turned them into songs. For example, the only change he makes in Huy Cận's "Ngậm ngùi" is to repeat the line "Sleep, love, and dream an ordinary dream" three times in his song. It occurs only once in Huy Cận's poem. He changes more lines in Xuân Diệu's "Afternoon" and gives it a different title: "Late Afternoon Song" [Mộ khúc]. These poems turned into songs were so popular that Trịnh Công Sơn could not avoid hearing them when he composed his love songs.

An interesting aspect of some of the poems by the New Poets that Phạm Duy turned into songs is that they are written in either the *lục bát* [six-eight] verse form or a variation of *lục bát* called *song thất lục bát* [seven-seven-six-eight]. *Lục bát* is the verse form that Nguyễn Du used to write his masterpiece *The Tale of Kiều*. This Vietnamese verse form is not as complicated as that required for the Chinese regulated poem [*lü-shih*], the form used by poets of the T'ang Dynasty that the New Poets led by Phan Khôi rebelled against, but, as explained in Chapter Thirteen, it is a long way from free verse. For example, words with certain sharp and flat tones

---

143. Phạm Duy gives a different title for this poem turned into song. He titles it "Mộ khúc" [Song in Late Afternoon].
144. *Encyclopaedia Britannica Online*, s.v. "Jacques Prévert," https://www.britannica.com/biography/Jacques-Henri-Marie-Prevert (accessed April 25, 2021).
145. Phạm Duy, "Nói về ca khúc và thơ phổ nhạc" [Speaking about Songs and Poems Put to Music], *Văn: Tạp Chí Văn Học Nghệ Thuật* [Literature: a Journal of Literary Studies and Art] 66 and 67 (June and July, 2002), 183.

must be used in certain places and the last word in a six-syllable line must rhyme with the sixth word in the eight-syllable line. New Poets, spurred on by Hoài Thanh and Hoài Chân, agreed that it was time to abandon rigid rules for writing poems but some New Poets in some poems hung on to the old six-eight verse form.

The New Poets were focused on content, not form. They wanted to express their innermost feelings, their joys and their sorrows. Hoài Thanh and Hoài Chân explain that the term "thơ mới" [new poetry] was just a convenient term that did not specify form. It is true, they say, that many people thought it referred to poems written in free verse, but they emphasize that poems people call "new poetry" were composed in a variety of forms.[146] Phan Khôi suggested new poems should be in free verse, Hoài Thanh and Hoài Chân explain, but, they say, it is better not to accept that narrow definition. Only a small percentage of "new poems," they point out, were written in free verse [*thơ tự do*].[147] When Phạm Duy and others turned them into song these old poems were reborn: they experienced a rebirth in popularity. They became what Vietnamese call "pre-war" [*tiền chiến*] songs, which are the topic of my next chapter.

Like the New Poets, Trịnh Công Sơn wanted to express his innermost feelings, to talk about his joys and sorrows. Because he attended French schools he may not have studied the New Poets in school, but many poems of the New Poets were so well known that all educated Vietnamese knew them. It seems likely that the popularity of poems in the *lục bát* form that Phạm Duy and other composers turned into songs inspired Trịnh Công Sơn to pour out his feelings in his songs.

Huy Cận's poem "Ngậm ngùi" will remind many Vietnamese of these famous lines from Nguyễn Du's *The Tale of Kiều* in which the heroine expresses her melancholy [ngậm ngùi]:

> Buồng riêng riêng những sụt sùi,
> Nghĩ thân mà lại ngậm-ngùi cho thân

> *Alone in her own room, she sobbed and wept*
> *Brooding upon herself, she mourned her lot*

Kiều, the heroine, speaks these lines when she realizes she has been tricked by a cad named Sở Khanh who has sold her to the owner of a

---

146. Hoài Thanh and Hoài Chân, *Thi Nhân Việt Nam* [Vietnamese Poets], 47.
147. Ibid.

house of prostitution. Trịnh Công Sơn, like Kiều, brooded upon himself and mourned his lot: "Let me sleep in a cradle," he sings in "Calming My Melancholy" [Ru ta ngậm ngùi] and "calm my melancholy." In a land with a legacy of domination by foreign powers and endless war, both the New Poets and Trịnh Công Sơn had a lot of melancholy to calm.

18

PRE-WAR SONGS

In 1938 at a concert in Hanoi, a musician from Huế named Nguyễn Văn Tuyên sang songs that had some features of traditional Vietnamese songs but also revealed Western influences. This concert, aided by an article about it in the magazine Ngày Nay [*Today*],[1] launched what came to be called "modern music" [*tân nhạc*] or "reformed music" [*nhạc cải cách*], terms used to describe songs that were influenced by Western popular songs but also contained features of Vietnamese folk songs [*dân ca*], songs sung in modern folk opera [*cải lương*], and songs performed by song-stresses to entertain upper class audiences [*hát ca trù* or *hát ả đào*]. Western music came to Vietnam in various ways. In colonial times Christian hymns were a part of Catholic church services conducted by French and Vietnamese priests. In 1927 the Conservatoire Francais d'Extreme Orient opened in Hanoi and taught Western classical music. Nguyễn Xuân Khoát, an influential early composer of "reformed" songs, attended this institute. Vietnamese in cities also heard Western songs when they watched French films or attended ballroom dance parlors. 78 RPM records of French music were also available.[2]

---

1. The article was written by Thế Lữ, a New Poet who was also a member of the Self-Strength Literary Group. See Thế Lữ, "Một hy vọng trong làng âm nhạc: Ông Nguyễn Văn Tuyên," [Hope in the Village of Music], Ngày Nay [Today] 116 (June 26, 1938).
2. In preparing this discussion of the origins of modern Vietnamese music I have drawn on the following sources: Jason Gibbs, "Reform and Tradition in Early Vietnamese Popular Song," ThingsAsian, http://thingsasian.com/story/reform-and-tradition-early-vietnamese-popular-song (accessed March 17, 2015); Jason Gibbs, "Nhac Tien Chien: The Origins of Vietnamese Popular Song," ThingsAsian, http://thingsasian.com/story/nhac-tien-chien-origins-vietnamese-popular-song (accessed March 17, 2015); Phạm Duy, "Những bước đầu (trong nửa thế kỷ tân nhạc)" [First Steps (in half a centu-

Before Vietnamese songwriters composed modern Vietnamese songs, they composed what Vietnamese refer to as "our songs with Western tunes" [*bài ta theo điệu tây*]. French songs like "J'ai Deux Amours," "C'est À Capri," and "Guitare d'Amour" were sung with Vietnamese words but the tunes remained the same as in the original Western songs. Sometimes the meaning of the lyrics was changed somewhat, sometimes completely, as in this patriotic version of "Frère Jacques!":

Hời hợi đồng bào
Hời hợi đồng bào
Tỉnh dạy mau
Tỉnh dạy mau
Nước (ứ) ta đã mất rồi
Nước (ứ) ta đã mất rồi
Mau tỉnh mau
Mau tỉnh mau

Fellow countrymen
Fellow countrymen
Wake up fast!
Wake up fast!
Our land's already lost!
Our land's already lost!
Quick wake quick!
Quick wake quick![3]

These French tunes with Vietnamese words, however, failed to satisfy Vietnamese because they were not really Vietnamese songs. In the next phase of development, Vietnamese musicians composed songs that contained features of Vietnamese traditional music but resembled Western songs. These songs were later called "pre-war music," a vague term that refers to sentimental and romantic songs, many of them about unrequited love, composed from the late 1930s to the late 1950s and early 1960s. The war referred to is the First Indochina War against the French which began in 1946 and ended in 1954. The term "pre-war" is inexact: Songs composed after 1954 may be called pre-war songs. Pre-war songs were popular when Trịnh Công Sơn first began composing and they remain popular today, particularly in central and south Vietnam and in the Vietnamese diaspora.

---

ry of modern music)], *Hợp lưu* [Convergence] 17 (June & July, 1992), 23-43; and Phạm Duy, *Tân nhạc Việt Nam thuở ban đầu* [Modern Vietnamese Music in the Early Days] (Hồ Chí Minh City: Trẻ, 2006).

3. Phạm Duy, *Tân nhạc Việt Nam thuở ban đầu*, 21.

In North Vietnam during both the First and Second Indochina War these sad and sentimental pre-war songs were banned. The communist regime encouraged songs that mobilized the masses in the battle against first the French and then the Americans.

In Appendix H I include translations of five pre-war songs. I don't remember hearing "Predestined Love" [Duyên kiếp], but in the 1960s I heard the other four songs often in cafés in Sài Gòn, Đà Nẵng and Huế, and also at student concerts. Here are their titles, composers, and the dates when they were written: "Innermost Feeling" [Nỗi lòng] composed by Nguyễn Văn Khánh around 1951; "Send the Wind to Make the Clouds Fly" [Gửi gió cho mây ngàn bay]* composed by Đoàn Chuẩn and Từ Linh in 1952; and "Melancholy" [Ngậm ngùi] composed by Phạm Duy in 1961 (based on a poem with the same title by Huy Cận). Except for the fact that the singers were singing in Vietnamese, when I first heard these songs they sounded like American songs of the type called "easy listening." Before songs like these three appeared, there were what Jason Gibbs calls "musical hybrids" that contained obvious traces of traditional folk songs.[4] Gibbs gives two examples: "Dawn" [Bình minh] composed by Nguyễn Xuân Khoát in 1938, and "Night's End at the Royal Docks" [Đêm tàn bến Ngự] composed by Dương Thiệu Tước in 1946. Both these songs contain distinctive modal systems found in Vietnamese folk songs. (The *Oxford English Dictionary* defines a mode as "a type of scale, coupled with a set of characteristic melodic behaviors.") The folk modes in Vietnamese music have names, and different modes are associated with different regions. "Dawn" contains the "bắc" [northern] mode. "Night's End at the Royal Docks" evokes two "nam" [southern] modes, *nam ai* and *nam bình*. I say "evokes" because although "Night's End" reveals the influence of these two modes, Dương Thiệu Tước did not compose "Night's End at the Royal Docks" completely in these modes.[5]

These two "musical hybrids" are called pre-war songs but for Westerners they sound much more exotic and foreign than the three pre-war songs mentioned above— "Innermost Feeling," "Send the Wind to Make the Clouds Fly," and "Melancholy"—which were composed later, in the 1950s and 1960s. These hybrid songs are often sung to accompaniment

---

4. Jason Gibbs, "Reform and Tradition in Early Vietnamese Popular Song."
5. Jason Gibbs: "It would go too far to say that Dương Thiệu Tước composed his song in *nam ai* or *nam bình*, but the influence of these modes is unmistakable. Vietnamese audiences have no trouble in identifying this song as 'Hue music.'" See "Reform and Tradition in Early Vietnamese Popular Song."

provided by traditional Vietnamese instruments—the three-stringed lute [*đàn tam*], the two-stringed lute [*đàn nguyệt*], the monochord [*đàn bầu*], or the sixteen-string zither [*đàn tranh*]. Even if they are sung accompanied with Western instruments—an orchestra or a combo (guitar, keyboard, drums)—they still sound very non-Western due primarily to the presence of the distinctive modes discussed above.

When Trịnh Công Sơn began composing, people were listening to pre-war songs. Sơn wrote "Wet Eyelashes" [Ướt mi], his first song to become well-known, after hearing a sixteen-year-old singer named Thanh Thúy sing "Autumn Raindrops" [Giọt mưa thu] in the Văn Cảnh tea house[6] in Saigon in 1958. This pre-war song was composed by Đặng Thế Phong in 1939. Sơn describes his experience hearing Thanh Thúy sing "Autumn Raindrops" in an essay published in 1991. While she sang this song, Sơn says, Thanh Thúy cried because at the time her mother was lying at home sick with tuberculosis. "Those tear drops of the young singer," Sơn says, were like "a small rain shower on my fragile soul; they made me go back further to some other faraway world and made me cry."[7]

Rain, tears, and sadness are featured in both "Autumn Raindrops"* and Sơn's "Wet Eyelashes." Đặng Thế Phong's song begins "Outside on the veranda the autumn rain is gently falling / The somber sky is quieting, suspended clouds are scattering." Later in the song the speaker hears someone crying and asks: "Who's sobbing, lamenting, teardrops rushing down? / The world's immeasurably sad." Trịnh Công Sơn echoes Đặng Thế Phong's opening in "Wet Eyelashes" and, like his predecessor, talks of tears and sadness:

> *Outside on the veranda the rain falls and falls*
> *Whose heart is lost and alone*
> *Your tears have spoiled your eyelashes*

---

6. "Tea house" [*phòng trà*] should be understood as a cabaret or music café or music bar. When modern or reformed music [*tân nhạc* or *nhạc cải cách*] emerged in the late 1930s, the places where old-style literati listened to poetry recited by songstresses [*hát à đào*] gradually disappeared and tea houses became the places people in cities went to hear songs. Besides Văn Cảnh some other well-known tea houses in Saigon in the 1950s and 1960s were Tự Do [Freedom], the Ritz, the Queen Bee, and Maxims. For a summary of the tea house movement, see Phạm Duy, *Hồi ký* [Memoirs], Vol. III, *Thời phân chia quốc-cộng* [The Period of Nationalist-Communist Division] (Midway City, CA: Phạm Duy Cường Musical Productions, 1991), 248-253.

7. Trịnh Công Sơn, "Bài hát đầu tiên bài hát cuối cùng" [The First Song, the Last Song], in *Trịnh Công Sơn: Tôi là ai, là ai*, eds. Nguyễn Minh Nhựt, Phạm Sỹ Sáu, Nguyễn Duy and Nguyễn Trọng Chức (Hồ Chí Minh City: Trẻ, 2011), 69. The article originally appeared in *Lao Động Chủ Nhật* [Labor Sunday] in 1991.

Don't cry on a rainy night
Don't lament in a song line
Hello sadness in the deep of night
Hold her for me please

Trịnh Công Sơn's anti-war songs made him famous but his love songs have always been popular and remain popular today. In 1960 Sơn wrote "Diễm of the Past," which was well-received and remains one of his most famous love songs. Why were Sơn's early love songs popular? Văn Ngọc suggests it was because they resembled traditional songs and pre-war songs that Vietnamese were accustomed to. They were, Văn Ngọc says, "suited for the soul of Vietnamese who were familiar with the melody of lullabies, folk songs, and some pre-war songs. They fit with a sad and romantic mood and could move listeners who already had that 'sad melody' within them."[8] Sơn's early love songs, however, differed from pre-war songs in some important ways. Both Văn Ngọc and Đặng Tiến argue that Sơn made his songs sound fresh and new by not echoing—or by echoing much more faintly—the prosody of declaimed poetry. Văn Ngọc describes songs by Văn Cao and Phạm Duy, two composers who, before Trịnh Công Sơn burst on the scene, were the most famous Vietnamese composers. Here is how Văn Ngọc describes how these songs affected singers and their audience:

> When one sings songs like "The Sadness of Autumn Passing" [Buồn tàn thu] by Văn Cao (1940) or "Song of a Warrior's Wife" [Chinh phụ ca] by Phạm Duy (1945), one can't refrain from declaiming each line, each word, as if one were singing a songstress song [*ca trù*]. As they sound in the ears it's as if one can hear the moon lute and the singer's lute, or the drum and bamboo castanets![9]

In other words, the pre-war songs of Trịnh Công Sơn's two famous predecessors were modern songs but they echoed pre-modern *ca trù* (also called *hát ả đào*) songs which in English are referred to as "chamber music" or "songstress songs."[10] Listening to songstress songs was a diversion for

---

8. Văn Ngọc, "Trịnh Công Sơn, Khánh Ly và những khúc tình ca một thời" [Trịnh Công Sơn, Khánh Ly, and the Love Songs of an Era], *Diễn đàn* [Forum] 110 (September, 2001), 28.
9. Ibid., 27.
10. In "Nhạc tình Văn Cao" [The Love Music of Văn Cao], Phạm Duy points out how Văn Cao, Lê Thương, and he himself echoed works by T'ang poets in their songs. He points out parallels between some of Văn Cao's songs and poems by the T'ang poets Du Fu and Cui Hao and between a famous song of his, "Tiếng hát trên sông Lô" [Singing on the River Lô], and a poem by the T'ang poet Zhang Ji. The article appears in *Hợp lưu* [Convergence] 8 (December, 1993), 13.

learned men who went to songstresses' houses to hear female singers sing ancient poems or poems of their own (the men's) composition. These poems were usually written in the seven-word [*thất ngôn*] form used in T'ang poetry, the same form that the New Poets of the early 1930s rejected as too restraining.

Đặng Tiến compares the pre-war song "Send the Wind to Make the Clouds Fly"* (1952) to Trịnh Công Sơn's "Sad Love" [Tình sầu] (1965). He argues that the following lines from "Send the Wind to Make the Clouds Fly" echo the time-honored seven-word [*thất ngôn*] form:

> Lá vàng từng cánh rơi từng cánh (seven words)
> Rơi xuống âm thầm trên đất xưa (seven words)
> *One by one each golden leaf*
> *Falls silently on old ground*[11]

As I mentioned in Chapter Ten, Đặng Tiến wonders whether Trịnh Công Sơn does not echo traditional verse forms because he went to Franco-Vietnamese schools in which Vietnamese literature was rarely, if ever, taught.[12]

DEFAMILIARIZING DEVICES

Trịnh Công Sơn songs were not, however, fresh and new solely because he avoided echoing the prosody of classical Vietnamese poetry. More important, many Vietnamese scholars agree, was Trịnh Công Sơn's use of language, more specifically his fresher diction and startling word collocations, purposeful incoherence, unusual grammar, and what Bùi Vĩnh Phúc calls "encapsulated images" [*hình ảnh tỉnh lược*].[13] Some of these techniques are obvious even to a non-native speaker of Vietnamese such as myself, but native speakers are far better guides and so I will offer some examples provided by Vietnamese scholars. These techniques are important because they are the means Trịnh Công Sơn used to distinguish his songs from pre-war songs. Bùi Vĩnh Phúc, who teaches English and courses in Vietnamese language and culture at California State University in Fullerton, says these techniques enabled Trịnh Công Sơn to "defamiliarize" [*lạ hóa*] his songs. Though he does not cite them, Bùi Vĩnh Phúc probably takes the term "defamiliarize"—*ostranenie*, literally "making strange"—from the Russian Formalists, a group of literary critics who, in

---

11. Đặng Tiến, "Trịnh Công Sơn: đời và nhạc" [Trịnh Công Sơn: Life and Music] *Văn* 53 & 54 (2001), 12.
12. Ibid., 11.
13. Bùi Vĩnh Phúc, *Trịnh Công Sơn ngôn ngữ và những ám ảnh nghệ thuật* [Trịnh Công Sơn: Language and Artistic Obsessions] (Gardena, CA: Văn Mới, 2005), 137-140.

the early decades of the twentieth century, argued that defamiliarization was what distinguished poetic language from ordinary language. Defamiliarization is not a single device but a term for a variety of devices that poets use to slow up the "automatism of perception." "The technique of art," Victor Shklovsky argued in 1917, "is to make objects 'unfamiliar,' to make forms difficult, to increase the difficulty and length of perception because the process of perception is an aesthetic end in itself and must be prolonged."[14]

Note that Shklovsky says art involves making forms difficult. Trịnh Công Sơn's anti-war songs are not difficult to understand, but many of his other songs are notoriously difficult to paraphrase or to translate. If you ask Vietnamese, including those who love his songs, to explain his lyrics to these more difficult songs, most will laugh and say no one can explain them. Not even, it seems, Khánh Ly, who has been singing his songs for fifty years. "Before, when I was young, I didn't understand what he wanted to say in his lyrics," Khánh Ly says. "Even now, when I'm older, I understand them only partially."[15] Pre-war songs, including those in Appendix H that my wife and I have translated, are much easier to understand (and to translate). Their lyrics are not exactly "ordinary language": The speakers in these songs speak more poetically than people do in ordinary conversation, but they speak much more clearly than do the speakers in many Trịnh Công Sơn songs.

Here are some examples mentioned by Vietnamese scholars of what, following Bùi Vĩnh Phúc, I shall call Trịnh Công Sơn's defamiliarizing devices, starting with his fresher diction. Đặng Tiến compares four lines from the pre-war song "Send the Wind to Make the Clouds Fly"* composed by Đoàn Chuẩn and Từ Linh to some lines from Sơn's "Sad Love" [Tình sầu]. Here are the lines from the pre-war song:

> *Send the wind to make the clouds fly*
> *Send colorful butterflies to the flower*
> *Send also moonlight the pale blue of a love letter*
> *Send them here with the autumn of the world*

---

14. Victor Shklovsky, "Art as Technique," in *Russian Formalist Criticism: Four Essays*, trans. and ed. by Lee T. Lemon and Marion J. Reis (Lincoln, Nebraska: University of Nebraska Press, 1965), 12.
15. "Khánh Ly: 'Xin cho quê hương mãi bình an,'" [Please Make the Native Land Forever Peaceful], *Khampha.vn*, October 5, 2014, https://web.archive.org/web/20141019075107/http://khampha.vn:80/giai-tri/khanh-ly-xin-cho-que-huong-mai-binh-an-c6a189609.html (accessed January 7, 2015).

331

Here are the lines from Sơn's "Sad Love":

> *Love is like a burning wound on the flesh,*
> *Love is far like the sky*
> *Love is near like the mist of clouds*
> *Love is deep like a tree's shadow*
> *Love shouts with joy in the sun*
> *Love's sadness intoxicates*

According to Đặng Tiến the stanza from Sơn's "Sad Love" contains unconventional comparisons. He does not explain what makes them unconventional but clearly comparing love to a flesh wound, for example, is unusual. The song's first line—"Love is an artillery shell that blinds the heart"— also associates love with war. "Sad Love" was written in 1965 when the war began to escalate, the same year Sơn was writing his anti-war "Songs of Golden Skin." The prewar song "Send the Wind," on the other hand, Đặng Tiến points out, has conventional images and juxtapositions, like the following found in the four lines quoted above: wind-cloud, butterfly-flower, moonlight-autumn. "The only new item in this series—the image of the blue letter—doesn't stand out," Đặng Tiến says, "because it is only one link in a tight chain of conventional images that destroy the poetic quality."[16]

Unusual word choice is related to collocation. Scholars suggest that Sơn's lyrics appear new not because he chooses unusual words but because he pairs words and phrases with unusual partners. Trần Hữu Thục provides many examples, including the following:

1. "age of stony sadness" [*tuổi đá buồn*], the title of a song.

2. "your pale hand greets distress" [*bàn tay xanh xao đón ưu phiền*], a line from the song "Crystal Sunshine" [*Nắng thủy tinh*].

3. "seed of loving-kindness" [*hạt từ tâm*], a phrase which appears in the song "Lullaby for Love" [*Ru tình*]. The entire line is: "A lullaby for you, a bird holding a seed of loving-kindness in its beak" [*Ru em là cánh nhạn miệng ngọt hạt từ tâm*].

4. "your long arms many times pale eyes" [*dài tay em mấy thuở mắt xanh xao*], the second line of "Diễm of the Past."*

Trần Hữu Thục says that the italicized words in brackets in the above list "are not new or strange in the Vietnamese language. Many people

---

16. Đặng Tiến, "Trịnh Công Sơn: đời và nhạc," 12.

use them. The strangeness results from the way they are united in word clusters to create images and symbols with slightly new or completely new meanings. They also are used to create special sound effects."[17]

Another scholar, Lê Hữu, explains that before Trịnh Công Sơn arrived on the scene we had "pink spring," "red summer," and "purple or golden autumn," but now in Trịnh Công Sơn's lyrics we have "white summer," "pink rain storms," and "green rain." In other words, Trịnh Công Sơn attaches a color term to things that are not usually described as being that color.[18] The lyrics surrounding each of these strange collocations mentioned by Lê Hữu suggest a plausible explanation for Trịnh Công Sơn's word choice. In the song "White Summer" [Hạ trắng], for example, white night blooming jasmine flowers, which could be seen as turning summer white, are mentioned.[19] In the song "Pink Rain" [Mưa hồng] it is suggested that the rain appears pink because a girl is viewing it through a veil of pink blossoms falling from royal Poinciana trees [hoa phượng].[20] And in "A Limitless Age" [Tuổi đời mênh mông] the second line—"The sky makes green rain under rows of tamarind trees"—suggests the rain is colored by the leaves of trees.

Lê Hữu points out another unusual collocation involving rain in Sơn's "Diễm of the Past."* In the seventh line, translated as "In the afternoon rain I sit waiting," Sơn uses the phrase "trips of rain pass" [chuyến mưa qua] to describe the rain, an unusual use of "chuyến" [trips, flights], a word that is usually used in phrases like "plane trips," "car trips," "train trips," etc. but not to describe periods of rain.[21] Though naturalistic interpretations are sometimes possible, unusual collocations such as these create what Bùi Vĩnh Phúc calls "a mixed or hybrid world [thế giới lai], a world situated

---

17. Trần Hữu Thục, "Một cái nhìn về ca từ Trịnh Công Sơn" [One View of Trịnh Công Sơn's Lyrics], Văn Học [Literary Studies] 186 & 187 (Oct.-Nov., 2001), 58.

18. Lê Hữu, "Từ 'Diễm xưa' đến 'Một cõi đi về'," [From 'Diễm xưa' to 'Một cõi đi về'], Văn Học [Literary Studies] 186 & 187 (Oct.-Nov., 2001), 228.

19. In an essay, "Giấc mơ hạ trắng" [White Summer Dream], Trịnh Công Sơn explains that this song was written after a nap on a hot summer day. While sleeping he dreamed of being in a forest of sweet-smelling white flowers. When he woke up he found a bunch of night blooming jasmine flowers near his bed, left there by a girl. This essay was first published in Thế Giới Âm Nhạc [The World of Music] 5 (1997). It is reprinted in Trịnh Công Sơn: Tôi là ai, là ai . . . [Trịnh Công Sơn: Who Am I, Am I . . .], 152-153.

20. There are many of these trees in Huế, especially along Lê lợi Street, which parallels the Perfume River. A famous secondary school for girls, Đồng Khánh Secondary School (now Hai Bà Trưng General Secondary School), is on Lê lợi Street. A classic image of Huế is of girls in white dresses walking or riding their bikes down Lê lợi Street against a background of pink Poinciana flowers.

21. Lê Hữu, "Từ 'Diễm xưa' đến 'Một cõi đi về'," 227.

between reality and fantasy, between a present that vanishes in the wink of an eye and a dim and distant eternity."[22]

These unusual collocations along with some unusual grammar produce what seems to be a purposeful incoherence. Trịnh Công Sơn's lyrics, Văn Ngọc says, "were not restricted to the function of telling a story with a beginning and an end. They had a life completely independent, free. They could evoke beautiful images, impressions, and brief thoughts that sometimes reached the level of surrealism; and between them sometimes there was no logical relationship at all."[23] Lê Hữu provides an example of this illogicality in "Diễm of the Past."* Referring to two lines in the fourth verse, Lê Hữu asks "What does 'Please let the rain pass over this region' have to do with 'Let the wanderer forget he's a wanderer'? It sounds like 'The man talks chickens, the woman talks ducks'; as though a line from another song has been plugged into this one."[24] Though the basic situation of the song is clear—the singer is waiting in the rain for a visit from someone he loves—the song is not a coherent narrative.

Trịnh Công Sơn's unusual grammar can make a single line hard to process. A good example is found in the second line of the song just discussed, "Diễm of the Past"*: "Dài tay em mấy thuở mắt xanh xao" (Your long arms, your pale eyes). In our translation my wife and I have left out the phrase "*mấy thuở*" (many times, many periods of time) because Sơn's grammar does not enable one to know for certain how this phrase relates to the rest of the line. Referring to this same line, Trần Hữu Thục asks "What is this? Does it mean 'Your arms are often long and your eyes pale'? And if that's the case, what does *that* mean? *Nothing*. But we still sing it and what's strange is that it seems to have meaning. We sing some more and decide it really does have meaning!"[25]

In some songs Trịnh Công Sơn includes what Bùi Vĩnh Phúc calls "unfinished lines" [*câu bỏ lửng*]. These lead to unusual grammar and make comprehension of meaning difficult. Bùi Vĩnh Phúc comments on these lines from "Fly Away Quietly" [Bay đi thầm lặng]:

> *There is some worry at the moment of parting*
> *There are people who don't love because*
> *There are lives that are completely naïve*

22. Bùi Vĩnh Phúc, *Trịnh Công Sơn ngôn ngữ và những ám ảnh nghệ thuật*, 131-132.
23. Văn Ngọc, "Trịnh Công Sơn, Khánh Ly và những khúc tình ca một thời," 27.
24. Lê Hữu, "Từ 'Diễm Xưa' đến 'Một Cõi Đi Về,'" 227.
25. Trần Hữu Thục, "Một cái nhìn về ca từ Trịnh Công Sơn," 59.

Có chút bổi hổi trong phút chia ly
Có những mặt người không yêu là vì
Có những cuộc đời hết sức ngây ngô

The second line is unfinished: In Vietnamese one does not end a statement with "vì" [because].

"Who don't love because why?" Bùi Vĩnh Phúc asks. "Trịnh Công Sơn doesn't say." Maybe, Bùi Vĩnh Phúc continues, it is like in American English when you answer "Because," or "Just because," when you cannot explain exactly the reason for an action which the question refers to.[26] Bùi Vĩnh Phúc does not mention what seems to me to be another possibility, namely that this "because" refers back to the first line. Perhaps Trịnh Công Sơn is suggesting that some people do not love because they fear they cannot endure the separation that will follow.

Bùi Vĩnh Phúc gives another example from "Moon Song" [Nguyệt ca] which includes the lines:

From the time you were the moon
You gave me cool shade that really was

Từ khi em là nguyệt
Cho tôi bóng mát thật là

Is Trịnh Công Sơn saying, Bùi Vĩnh Phúc asks, "'Cool shade that really was cool'? Or 'Cool shade that made me happy'? We cannot be sure."[27]

A final defamiliarizing feature is what Bùi Vĩnh Phúc calls "encapsulated images." These are images from which elements that would make them clearer have been cut. Trịnh Công Sơn's encapsulated images are not totally incomprehensible; they are unfinished sketches that listeners, Bùi Vĩnh Phúc says, can complete and clarify.[28] Because Trịnh Công Sơn's images are encapsulated, Bùi Vĩnh Phúc says, they "lose their worn out character and become new, as a result of their being re-assembled in the imagination of the listener."[29] Encapsulated images would seem to be a common feature of poems and songs: No one expects poets or song composers to flesh out their descriptions as novelists do. Bùi Vĩnh Phúc probably emphasizes them because Trịnh Công Sơn's images are vaguer and require more unpacking by the listener than do the images

---

26. Bùi Vĩnh Phúc, *Trịnh Công Sơn: ngôn ngữ và những ám ảnh nghệ thuật*, 141.
27. Ibid.
28. Ibid., 138.
29. Ibid.

in pre-war songs. He is trying to explain Trịnh Công Sơn's extraordinary popularity. Bùi Vĩnh Phúc analyses encapsulated images in three of Sơn's most famous songs: "Pink Rain" [Mưa hồng]*, "Remembering Autumn in Hanoi" [Nhớ mùa thu Hà Nội], and "Age of Stony Sadness" [Tuổi đá buồn]*. He focuses on this line from "Pink Rain": "You go home on the bridge, the rain wets your dress." Bùi Vĩnh Phúc says the image this line evokes is "very vague, as if it were blurred in the rain," and then offers a reading of it, an account of how he has "re-assembled" this image in his imagination: "Perhaps," he says, "it constructs an image of a girl crossing a bridge, and it's raining and a rustling wind is blowing, and the girl covers her head with one arm and clutches her dress with the other to prevent the wind from blowing her hair and dress. She walks quickly and the rain comes faster. The image of the girl and the rain becomes blurred."[30] Bùi Vĩnh Phúc says listeners can add more features, that they "are free, within certain limits, to complete and clarify the image of the girl crossing a bridge in the rain."[31]

Next Bùi Vĩnh Phúc considers an image from Trịnh Công Sơn's song "Nhớ mùa thu Hà Nội" [Remembering Autumn in Hanoi]. He focuses on the following three lines, especially on the image of flying coots, migrating birds that used to be a common sight on West Lake in Hanoi:

> West Lake in autumn the water's golden surface pushes the far bank and calls
> A foggy color of memory
> A flock of small coots flap their wings [toward? under? through?] the sun

> Hồ Tây chiều thu mặt nước vàng lay bờ xa mời gọi
> Màu sương thương nhớ
> Bầy sâm cầm nhỏ vỗ cánh mặt trời

Bùi Vĩnh Phúc considers some possible meanings of the third line, sketchily indicated by the English prepositions I have added in brackets, but concludes that pursuing absolute clarity is a fool's errand. "This picture lacking features is already good because it creates a blurred effect. Drawing that image of the 'foggy color of memory' more fully, he argues, would lessen its expressive power."[32]

---

30. Ibid., 138-139.
31. Ibid., 139.
32. Ibid., 139.

Next Bùi Vĩnh Phúc turns to "Age of Stony Sadness."* This song is extremely difficult to translate for a variety of reasons. Bùi Vĩnh Phúc focuses on the closing verse, especially the line about the wilted rose:

> *It's still raining rain falls everywhere*
> *Your bare feet you forget you forget*
> *Oh, the church on a sad Sunday*
> *No one's there except a wilted rose kissing her lips* (Or, a wilted rose she is kissing?)
> *You who are slender with long fingers*
> *Calming words for a thousand years, a thousand years*
> *A lullaby for your sadness, a lullaby for your unfaithfulness*

Bùi Vĩnh Phúc explicates these lines as follows: "A young girl brings a rose, which, having been forgotten is now wilted, to her lips to kiss?" The question mark is important because, he explains, we don't know the subject of the word "kiss." Does the girl kiss the flower or is the girl kissed by the flower? It is not clear.[33] Unlike English verbs, Vietnamese verbs "do not in themselves imply a clear notion of 'voice' in the grammatical sense," explains Laurence C. Thompson, author of a highly respected book on Vietnamese grammar. "In English a (transitive) verb must be either active or passive. No such distinction is necessary in Vietnamese. As a matter of fact, the actor and the goal or object of Vietnamese verbs are regularly not formally marked."[34] Thompson goes on to explain that they are not formally marked because usually it is clear from the context what or who is the actor and what or who is the object. These relationships can be made clear, he says, but in "the vast majority of Vietnamese sentences" they are not.[35]

Thompson is talking about prose sentences, not song lyrics. I mention his comments about Vietnamese verbs not conveying voice (active or passive) because it helps us understand that it is easier to not be clear in Vietnamese than it is in English. As anyone who translates Vietnamese texts into English knows, English grammar forces the translator to formally mark actor and object—and other relationships as well—that one does not have to specify in Vietnamese. In English if one leaves these formal signals out, one will produce non-grammatical sentences. Despite

---

33. Ibid., 140.
34. Laurence C. Thompson, *A Vietnamese Reference Grammar* (Honolulu: University of Hawaii Press, 1987), 217.
35. Ibid.

337

their lack of formal markers, Vietnamese sentences may still communicate clearly to other Vietnamese because both speaker and listener share the same background knowledge. Translators who are not native speakers of Vietnamese must not be too quick to call Trịnh Công Sơn's song lyrics obscure simply because they do not understand them. Vietnamese scholars, however, also find Sơn's lyrics obscure. Bùi Vĩnh Phúc concludes that in Sơn's "Age of Stony Sadness"* the rose kisses the girl's lips, but he admits that this is his interpretation. Unclear images like this one, he says, reveal Sơn's artistry. "They are incomplete but full," he says, "because they force us to draw on our experience and aesthetic awareness and add to the picture and complete it and make it more meaningful."[36] Because the lyrics of so many Trịnh Công Sơn's songs are obscure and because obscurity has become a defining feature of "Trịnh music," particularly of his love songs, I will discuss it further in the next chapter.

---

36. Bùi Vĩnh Phúc, *Trịnh Công Sơn: ngôn ngữ và những ám ảnh nghệ thuật*, 140.

338

19

UNDERSTANDING TRỊNH CÔNG SƠN'S OBSCURITY

Vietnamese scholars and journalists typically divide Trịnh Công Sơn's songs into three categories: anti-war songs [*nhạc phản chiến*]; love songs [*tình ca*]; and songs about the human condition [*ca khúc về thân phận*]. Trần Hữu Thục points out that Trịnh Công Sơn's anti-war songs, his songs of war and peace, differ greatly from songs in the other two categories. In them, he says, one finds realistic images that are not difficult to understand. The lyrics of these songs are, he says, "very 'grammatical,' which is to say they have concrete meanings because the sentence structure is simple, easy to understand." In them, Trần Hữu Thục says, the composer "wanted to send a clear message to singers and listeners."[1] The language of Trịnh Công Sơn anti-war songs, he continues, is "ordinary, often no different from that found in war reports. It resembles the language used in stories and memoirs."[2]

The language that Trịnh Công Sơn chose for his love songs and songs of the human condition, however, is—as Trần Hữu Thục and other scholars have pointed out—very different. It was "skillful, bold, and strange," Trần Hữu Thục says, and it affected people powerfully. Here is how he describes that different language:

---

1. Trần Hữu Thục, "Một cái nhìn về ca từ Trịnh Công Sơn" (One View of Trịnh Công Sơn's Lyrics), *Văn học* [Literary Studies] 186 & 187 (Oct.-Nov., 2001), 57-58.
2. Ibid., 63.

In the process of creating rhymes appropriate for the sound and music, he 'burst out' ideas, images and language that were completely unexpected, that were new and strange and sometimes amazed us; it was as if they fell from the sky. Even after reading and singing and listening to them many times, they still had the power to amaze us: Their newness was as fresh as the first time we heard them.[3]

Trịnh Công Sơn's lyrics were fresh and intriguing, the result of his employment of the defamiliarizing features described in the previous chapter. They also were (and remain) obscure, very difficult to paraphrase. Obscurity, it seems, was one of the defamiliarizing devices that made his songs intriguing. Scholars and other song composers point out that there was nothing especially distinctive about Sơn's music in terms of theory. He wrote, for example, most of his songs in 2/4 or 3/4 time. His tunes did not sound unfamiliar to Vietnamese. It was his language that intrigued people, a language that Trần Hữu Thục describes as "word-less," moving toward "word-destroying."[4] Here is how he describes that new language:

> It was not tied to the readymade ordinary meanings that we typically assume words have. This language is designed to create images and sounds and to a certain extent can be considered a "word-less" language [*ngôn ngữ vô ngôn*]. The words in the song are there to join images and ideas; suddenly encountered [by a listener] they suddenly fall into the imagination. To put it another way, it is not absolutely necessary to attach any concrete, fixed meanings to them. Just let them dissolve in sound, let them drift along with other words. A word is pulled by another word. A sound is pulled by another sound. An image is pulled by another image.[5]

Many songs dissolve in sound because of Trịnh Công Sơn's skillful use of rhyme and off-rhyme. There are rigid rules for rhyming in classical Vietnamese poetry. Rhyming words had to share not only consonant and vowel sounds but also had to have the same type of tone. One didn't rhyme a word with a flat tone [*bằng*] to one with a sharp [*trắc*] tone. The rhyming rules for song composers are greatly relaxed, however, and, according to Vietnamese scholars, Trịnh Công Sơn took full advantage of this fact. Trần Hữu Thục argues that some of Trịnh Công Sơn's famous songs "could be called 'rhyming songs'—they contain near rhymes and off rhymes, rhymes between a flat and a sharp tone and vice versa. Perhaps that's why people

---

3. Ibid., 60.
4. Ibid.
5. Ibid., 59.

still like to sing his songs even though they are quite meaningless and difficult to understand. When people sing some songs they 'sing rhyme'; they don't 'sing ideas.'"[6]

Because the Latin script now used to write Vietnamese is quite phonetic one can get a sense for how prevalent rhymes, both near and off rhymes, are in many Trịnh Công Sơn songs by examining the Vietnamese lyrics. Note, for example, that in the second stanza of "Diễm of the Past"* the sound "a"—pronounced like the "a" in "father"—appears frequently at the end of lines, in the words "lá" (repeated twice) and in "qua" and "xa." Note also that Sơn ends three lines in the third stanza of "Pink Rain"* with the words *cao, áo,* and *vào.* These words differ in tone but end in the same vowel sound; and the words that end the other two lines in this stanza, *lâu* and *nhau,* are near rhymes.

Lyrics of popular songs in many countries are often obscure, but the way Vietnamese listeners have reacted to Trịnh Công Sơn's lyrics suggests that they consider their obscurity to be a significant departure from past practice. Trịnh Công Sơn's songs are sometimes referred to as "Trịnh Music [*Nhạc Trịnh*] which suggests they are special, a departure from what has come before. One of the distinguishing characteristics of Trịnh Music is the obscurity of Sơn's lyrics. In my introduction I mentioned that both Dylan and Trịnh Công Sơn wrote songs that are difficult to interpret. I explained Roland Barthe's distinction between "writerly" texts and "readerly" works and said that the lyrics of both composers are "writerly" texts, not "readerly" works. In other words they are not easy to understand; they require interpretation by listeners. As listeners decipher their meanings the distinction between composer/writer and listener/reader becomes blurred: Both are involved in the creation of meaning. Both Dylan and Trịnh Công Sơn wrote "writerly" lyrics, but Sơn's lyrics are more "writerly" than Dylan's.

Dylan, like Trịnh Công Sơn, was famous for his experiments with language. He was exposed to modernism through his reading of T.S. Eliot and Beat Generation writers such as Allen Ginsberg and Kenneth Patchen, and like these writers filled his songs with what his friend Allen Ginsberg called "chains of flashing images."[7] In "Stuck Inside of Mobile with

---

6. Ibid., 56.
7. Allen Ginsberg, interview by Peter Barry Chowka, *Modern American Poetry*, 1995. See "Online Interviews with Allen Ginsberg," http://www.english.illinois.edu/maps/poets/g_l/ginsberg/interviews.htm (accessed July 27, 2019).

the Memphis Blues Again," railroad men smoke eyelids and a preacher is dressed in headlines. Chains of unusual images abound in "Chimes of Freedom" and "Gates of Eden." In the latter song a "motorcycle black madonna" and "her silver-studded phantom / cause a gray flannel dwarf to scream." These are bizarre, grotesque images and I will discuss them further when I talk about Dylan's apocalyptic visions. Note, however, that although these lines and the poems in which they occur are difficult to interpret, from a grammatical perspective the statements made are clear. We have no trouble identifying the subjects and objects. We know eyelids get smoked by the railroad men, for example, and that the black Madonna and her phantom make the dwarf scream. Dylan's images flash and confuse but his grammar is conventional and clear. From my experience working with native speakers to translate Trịnh Công Sơn's songs, I sense that Sơn's obscurity is different from Dylan's. When Đặng Tiến talks about Sơn's "broken up images that penetrate the minds of listeners without requiring that they understand their exact meanings,"[8] and when Trần Hữu Thục refers to Sơn's approach in some songs as "word-less moving toward word-destroying"[9] I believe they are searching for a way to describe Sơn's obscurity, to suggest that Sơn departed further from conventional language than his predecessors did. Sơn certainly seems to have departed further from conventional Vietnamese than Dylan departs from conventional English.

Why did Trịnh Công Sơn write such obscure lyrics? I believe he did so because he was a poet and poets turn to poetry rather than to prose to convey ideas and feelings that are ineffable and cannot be expressed in prose. He wanted to reach people's hearts, not their conscious minds. He also wished to appeal to young listeners who were growing tired of pre-war songs. Vietnamese call songs that we would call "sappy," cliché-ridden, or excessively sentimental "*nhạc sến*" [*sến* music]. The term is believed to derive from *con sến* [maidservant] and is sometimes applied to pre-war songs popular among uneducated and unsophisticated working people—girls who left their home villages and came to larger towns to serve as servants for Westerners or for well-off Vietnamese, as well as operators of pedicabs, and workers on boats. To provide an example of the kind of

---

8. Đặng Tiến, "Trịnh Công Sơn: đời và nhạc" [Trịnh Công Sơn: Life and Music], *Văn* [Literature] 53 & 54 (2001), 11.
9. Trần Hữu Thục, "Một cái nhìn về ca từ Trịnh Công Sơn," 60.

song that has been called "*sến*," my wife and I have translated "Predestined Love" [Duyên kiếp] by Lam Phương (See Appendix H), a song that my wife remembers hearing often in Huế in the 60s and 70s. The pre-war songs "Innermost Feeling,"* and "Send the Wind to Make the Clouds Fly,"* discussed in Chapter Eighteen, were popular among sophisticated listeners but they were already "golden oldies" when Trịnh Công Sơn began composing and probably had acquired a *sến*-like quality—at least in the mind of young people in southern cities. Trịnh Công Sơn needed a way to distinguish his songs from *sến* songs and from other pre-war songs that resembled them. Making his songs lyrically obscure was one way to do so.

"Predestined Love" resembles Trịnh Công Sơn's love songs in some ways. Like many of Sơn's songs it describes an unfulfilled love relationship that has been blocked by "the road of life." It lacks, however, the defamiliarizing features that are characteristic of "Trịnh music." Because it lacks these features it is much easier to translate than Sơn's "Pink Rain" or "Age of Stony Sadness" but its lack of these features, many would say, makes it a less artistic work. Tastes vary, of course. In recalling "Predestined Love" and other songs that she thought of as being "sến"[10] when she was a student in Huế in the 1960s, my wife criticized herself for judging them harshly. She realized that her tastes were shaped by her social group of young, educated, and more cosmopolitan city dwellers.[11] In the beginning it was this group that embraced Sơn's songs but soon, aided by the arrival of cassette tapes, his popularity spread to smaller towns and villages and to less privileged segments of the population.

To explain Trịnh Công Sơn's preference for obscure lyrics, one must also remember that, as explained previously, he was influenced by European modernism and the avant-garde movements that flourished after the first World War. A European poet he admired, Guillaume Apollinaire, was a friend of Pablo Picasso and wrote a book about cubist painters. In his poems he set out, an article in *Encyclopedia Britannica*

---

10. The other songs were "Getting Acquainted on the Way Home" [Quen nhau trên đường về] by Thăng Long and "White Rice Clear Moon" [Gạo trắng trăng thanh] by Hoàng Thi Thơ, sung by Ngọc Cẩm and Nguyễn Hữu Thiết.
11. In a recent blog post titled "Thế nào là nhạc sến" [What Is Sến Music?], Nguyễn Duyên says that although it is generally believed that *sến* music has a "lower artistic value" than more refined music, tastes differ. Even secondary school and university students have complained to him, he says, that they like the sound of Trịnh Công Sơn's songs but they can't understand his lyrics. See VNWEBLOGSMUSIC, July 7, 2008, http://nhacviet. vnweblogs.com/post/7181/7829 (accessed May 15, 2014).

explains, "to create an effect of surprise or even astonishment by means of unusual verbal associations, and because of this he can be considered a forebear of Surrealism."[12] Trịnh Công Sơn's close friend Đinh Cường painted cubist works and Ngô Kha, another close friend, wrote surreal poems. Two songs that I will focus on to discuss the obscurity of Trịnh Công Sơn's lyrics—"Pink Rain" and "Age of Stony Sadness"—appear in song collections with abstract paintings by Đinh Cường on the cover. These paintings resemble Picasso's cubist works.

Apollinaire's collection *Calligrammes* contains poems typographically arranged to form images. Trịnh Công Sơn did not go that far, but his lyrics have a painterly quality. In describing what he calls Trịnh Công Sơn's "word-less language," Trần Hữu Thục argues that Trịnh Công Sơn doesn't use words to create meanings; he uses them to create "collages" like those found in modern painting.[13]

Another reason for the obscurity of Trịnh Công Sơn's lyrics relates to lullabies. Speaking of Trịnh Công Sơn's lullabies, Cao Huy Thuần says that they "were not to soothe one into sleep but to soothe pain. . . . And because pain lasts a long time Trịnh Công Sơn was always and forever singing lullabies."[14] The idea of the lullaby figures prominently in "Age of Stony Sadness" and "Pink Rain," songs which, as I discussed in the previous chapter, contain many defamiliarizing devices. In "Age of Stony Sadness" the word "*ru*" (to sing a lullaby) occurs eight times and "Pink Rain" ends with lines that link a "long-lasting pain" to a lullaby. In these two songs the lullaby, as in many other Trịnh Công Sơn songs, suggests relief from pain. It reminds us that although we may suffer in a world that seems oblivious to our desires, there are good and gentle things that ease our pain. "Pink Rain" ends with these lines:

> *A person sits and asks for plentiful rain*
> *On two hands a long-lasting pain*
> *A person lies down and listens to a lullaby*
> *Life is too brief to be indifferent*

---

12. *Encyclopaedia Britannica Online*, s.v. "Guillaume Apollinaire," https://www.britannica.com/biography/Guillaume-Apollinaire (accessed March 17, 2015).
13. Trần Hữu Thục, "Một cái nhìn về ca từ Trịnh Công Sơn," 60.
14. Cao Huy Thuần, introductory remarks at a concert titled "Đêm hoài niệm Trịnh Công Sơn" [An Evening to Remember Trịnh Công Sơn], May 26, 2001. The event took place in Paris.

In a letter to the woman he loved, Dao Ánh, written in December 1964, Trịnh Công Sơn says this about "Pink Rain": "I sang again the song 'Pink Rain' which I wrote for the days you were angry in Huế."[15] I am not suggesting that this song is a lullaby, but anger is a kind of pain, a very dangerous kind of pain, Buddhists believe. It may not be a lullaby but Sơn suggests in his letter that it was designed to soothe, and that is the work of a lullaby.

In order to soothe, a lullaby does not have to be logical or clear. It doesn't have to make sense. Cao Huy Thuần emphasizes this point in discussing the following opening lines from Sơn's song "A Lullaby for Your Passionate Fingers" [Ru em từng ngón xuân nồng]:

For a thousand years I'll sing my lullaby
Praising the sad stream of your hair
The five fingers of your hand
I'll sing my lullaby a thousand years
In spring when leaves are green
Your fingers are slender
So I'll sing a lullaby for a thousand years more

"Why," Cao Huy Thuần asks, "do slender fingers require singing a thousand years? If the fingers were fat would it be necessary to sing for only five hundred years? No one asks mathematical questions like this about lines in a lullaby. No one insists on reasoned argument in a lullaby. To sing a lullaby is to sing vague lines that evoke vague and wavering images that have no head or tail, that appear only to disappear. By being vague and indefinite Trịnh Công Sơn reaches his goal."[16]

Finally, it is useful, I believe, to relate Trịnh Công Sơn's obscure lyrics to cultural assumptions regarding the value of clarity. Americans value it and the following French saying suggests that the French do too: "That which is not clear is not French" [*Ce qui n'est pas clair n'est pas francais*]. M. Yoshikawa, however, argues that the Japanese mistrust verbal language and value more what is not said but perceived by intuition:

What is often verbally expressed and what is actually intended are two different things. What is verbally expressed is probably important enough to maintain friendship, and it is generally called *tatemae* which means simply "in principle" but what is not verbalized counts

---

15. *Trịnh Công Sơn: Thư tình gửi một người* [Trịnh Công Sơn: Love Letters for Someone], (HCMC: Trẻ, 2011), 101.
16. Cao Huy Thuần, introductory remarks at a concert titled "Đêm hoài niệm Trịnh Công Sơn."

most—*honne* which means "true mind." Although it is not expressed verbally, you are supposed to know it by *kan*—"intuition."[17]

D. T. Suzuki maintains that Japanese authors do not like to be clear. They prefer to give vague hints. Japanese readers, he says, "anticipate with pleasure the opportunities that such writing offers them to savor this kind of 'mystification' of language."[18]

John Hinds argues that in addition to classifying languages according to word order (subject-verb-object or subject-object-verb, for example), or into subject-prominent or topic-prominent languages, we should also consider whether a language is "writer-responsible" or "reader-responsible." Speakers of a *writer*-responsible language, Hinds says, assume that it is the responsibility of the speaker (or writer) to make clear what he or she is saying (or writing). Speakers of a *reader*-responsible language, on the other hand, assume that it is the responsibility of listeners (or readers) to understand what they had intended to say (or write). Japanese and classical Chinese (but not modern Chinese), Hinds says, are reader-responsible languages; English is a writer-responsible language.[19]

Ask Vietnamese about clarity in their language and they might, jokingly, respond: "That which is clear is not Vietnamese." Vietnamese, I would argue, is a reader-responsible language. This is not to say that Vietnamese speakers cannot be clear but rather to point out that they often choose to be unclear. Nguyễn Hưng Quốc, a prominent Vietnamese writer and intellectual now living in Australia, does not discuss John Hinds' classification, but in "Writing, Culture and the Need to Create" [Viết, giữa truyền thống và nhu cầu sáng tạo] he suggests that Vietnamese is a reader-responsible language. He begins by reporting that Vietnamese high school and university students in Australia who write clearly in English write unclearly in Vietnamese. (Presumably these are students who are fluent in both languages.) Why, he asked these students, don't you write clearly in Vietnamese as you do in English? Almost all of them

---

17. M. Yoshikawa, "Some Japanese and American Cultural Characteristics," in *The Cultural Dialogue: An Introduction to Intercultural Communication,* ed. M. H. Prosser (Boston, MA: Houghton Mifflin, 1978), 228-229.
18. T. Suzuki, *Tozasareta Gengo: Nihongo no sekai* [A Bound Language: The World of Japanese] (Tokyo: Shinchosha, 1975). Qtd. by John Hinds in "Reader Versus Writer Responsibility: A New Typology," in *Writing Across Languages: Analysis of L2 Text,* ed. Ulla Connor and Robert B. Kaplan (Reading, MA: Addison-Wesley, 1987), 145.
19. John Hinds in "Reader Versus Writer Responsibility: A New Typology," 141-152.

replied: "Because if we write Vietnamese as clearly as we write English it would be bad writing."[20]

Nguyễn Hưng Quốc argues that Vietnamese highly value obscurity and vagueness over clarity because of their history. They were dominated by the Chinese for almost a thousand years and then colonized by the French. During this period they learned that loose talk could get one in trouble and that writing, because it wasn't ephemeral like speech, was even more dangerous. This fear of "the calamity of the mouth and the calamity of written words" [vạ miệng và vạ chữ] has led Vietnamese, Nguyễn Hưng Quốc, says, "to pay little attention to the relation of words to thought, to not worry whether spoken or written words describe exactly and sufficiently what they are thinking and feeling; instead, they concentrate on the power relationship between speaker and listener. They take seriously the power that lies behind the words." They know there is wisdom in proverbs like the following: "Spoken words are a bowl of blood" [Lời nói đọi máu], "The mouth of a mandarin has iron and steel" [Miệng nhà quan có gang có thép], and "A pen falls and a chicken dies" [Bút sa gà chết]. From their history of living under dictatorial regimes, Nguyễn Hưng Quốc argues, Vietnamese have learned to write defensively [rào đón]: "We express ourselves and protect ourselves at the same time, we take precautions to avoid accusations regarding what we have said." This would be bad enough, but what makes things worse, he argues, is that gradually Vietnamese began to consider this way of writing—"obscure, vague, and tortuous"—to be "not simply wise but an art." In this way, in his view, a defect was elevated into a virtue.

Nguyễn Hưng Quốc complains mostly about defects in Vietnamese prose, but poetry is implicated because, he argues, "this art [of writing prose obscurely] is strengthened by the Vietnamese people's traditional love of poetry, a tradition in which the peak of excellence involves figuring out how to present ideas that lie beyond words and can be perceived only by intuition, not by analyzing the text." Nguyễn Hưng Quốc argues, however, that the problem lies deeper than a love of poetry: It is rooted in the Vietnamese language itself. Vietnamese write obscurely, he says, not simply to avoid violent reprisals that might result if they spoke clearly

---

20. Nguyễn Hưng Quốc (real name is Nguyễn Ngọc Tuấn), "Viết, giữa truyền thống và nhu cầu sáng tạo" [Writing, Culture and the Need to Create], https://web.archive.org/web/20140716052451/http://www.tienve.org/home/literature/viewLiterature.do?action=viewArtwork&artworkId=852 (accessed March 17, 2015).

but also because of "traps" or "nets" rooted in the Vietnamese language. The result of these traps, he argues, is that "each time we pick up a pen to write Vietnamese, we—completely unconsciously—fall into this aesthetic net. There is, he says, "an expressive substance in the Vietnamese lexicon" that leads writers to write "romantically, to express themselves effusively and melodiously all with the supreme goal of getting people to praise their writing as poetic."[21]

During the war Trịnh Công Sơn wrote and distributed explicit anti-war songs knowing that by doing so he risked being imprisoned. This fact suggests that Vietnam's long history of dictatorial rule did not force him always to be obscure. He also wrote songs with very obscure meanings—songs like "Pink Rain" and "Age of Stony Sadness"—but this obscurity would seem to be motivated not by fear of censorship but by a desire to create a new language of song that would distinguish his works from pre-war songs. Nguyễn Hưng Quốc's account of why Vietnamese write obscurely and how obscurity came to be seen as a sign of artistry might, however, explain why Trịnh Công Sơn's obscure songs were so well-received. Perhaps what M. Yoshikawa says of the Japanese is also true of the Vietnamese. Perhaps for Vietnamese, as for Japanese, what counts most is that which is "not verbalized," that which is "perceived by intuition."[22]

Trịnh Công Sơn reveals that he relied on the intuition of listeners in the following comments on his song "A Place for Leaving and Returning."* He is talking about only this one song, which he calls "very unusual" [rất lạ], but I know from conversations with Vietnamese friends that many of Trịnh Công Sơn's songs both mystify and move listeners in the way the composer describes in this interview.

> This is a very unusual song. It's truly not easy to understand because it has some lines in it that even I find hard to explain. I wrote it but explaining it clearly is really difficult. I have, however, met a lot of people who are not very educated, and they like it. If you ask them if they understand it, they say that they don't, but that they feel there is something in it that, when they listen to it or when they sing it, touches their heart. I think in art the most important thing is to somehow open the shortest road from one own's heart to the hearts of other people without having to explain the meaning.[23]

21. Ibid.
22. M. Yoshikawa, "Some Japanese and American Cultural Characteristics," 145.
23. Trịnh Công Sơn, "Kiếp sau tôi vẫn là người Nghệ sĩ" [In the Next Reincarnation I'll still be an Artist], in *Trịnh Công Sơn: Một người thơ ca một cõi đi về* [Trịnh Công Sơn: A

Attention to the not-verbalized and the high value placed on intuition in Vietnam is no doubt caused by a host of factors, but very likely one of them is Buddhism. As I will explain in Chapter Twenty-Two, Vietnamese Buddhism is a blend of Pure Land, which emphasizes the recitation of Buddha's name, and Zen, which emphasizes meditation. In both these practices, which are designed to assist one in discovering one's Buddha nature, word meanings are not emphasized. Adherents of Pure Land are told that chanting the sounds "Nam mô A Di Đà Phật"[24] will lead to a quiet mind and rebirth in the Western Paradise. Trịnh Công Sơn, in an interview with a monk named Thích Tâm Thiện, explains that when he was sick his mother would ask a monk to come to their house and chant prayers and he would fall asleep listening to them. Words of Buddhist prayers, Sơn suggests, remained in his unconscious mind.[25]

In 2010 Thích Nhất Hạnh contacted some monks he knew in Huế, monks who also knew Trịnh Công Sơn, and learned from them that after Trịnh Công Sơn's father died in 1955 until he left to study in Saigon in 1958, Trịnh Công Sơn frequently visited Hiếu Quang Pagoda and Phổ Quang Pagoda, sometimes staying overnight. A monk at Hiếu Quang Pagoda, Hoà Thượng Chánh Pháp, was famous for being able to chant prayers in a beautiful and moving way. Trịnh Công Sơn joined novices in a class in prayer chanting that this monk taught and, according to the monks Thích Nhất Hạnh contacted, Trịnh Công Sơn was an excellent student. He quickly mastered the words and rhythms of Buddhist prayers.[26]

Singer-poet, a Place for Leaving and Returning], eds. Nguyễn Trọng Tạo, Nguyễn Thụy Kha, and Đoàn Tử Huyến (Hanoi: Âm Nhạc, 2001), 204-205. This is a reprint of an interview conducted by Văn Cầm Hải in Huế on March 27, 1998.

24. "Nam mô" means to return to the Buddha within oneself. "A Di Đà Phật" is the Amitabha Buddha.

25. Trịnh Công Sơn, interview with Thích Tâm Thiện which originally appeared in *Nguyệt San Giác Ngộ* [Enlightenment Monthly Review] no. 1, April 1996. I found it at Diễn Đàn Văn Hóa Học [Forum for Studies of Culture], http://www.vanhoahoc.edu.vn/dienan/viewtopic.php?f=56&t=1229 (accessed September 18, 2011). Excerpts from this interview and other comments that Trịnh Công Sơn has made about his Buddhist background can be found in "Nhạc sĩ Trịnh Công Sơn: 'Phải biết sống hết mình trong mỗi sát na của hiện tại'" [The Musician Trịnh Công Sơn: "You Must Know How to Live Completely in Each Moment of Reality"], in Lê Minh Quốc, ed., *Trịnh Công Sơn: Rơi lệ ru người* [Trịnh Công Sơn: Shedding Tears, Singing Lullabies] (Hanoi: Phụ Nữ 2004), 202-204. Parts of this interview also appear in "Nghĩ về thiền" [Thinking about Zen] in *Trịnh Công Sôn: Tôi là ai, là ai . . .* [TCS: Who Am I, Am I . . .], eds. Nguyễn Minh Nhụt et al. (HCMC: Trẻ, 2011), 212-214.

26. Thích Nhất Hạnh mentions these conversations in a series of dharma talks about Buddhism and Trịnh Công Sơn that he organized in 2010. The title of the series is *Thiền Sư Nhất Hạnh Pháp Thoại Trịnh Công Sơn* [Zen Monk Nhất Hạnh Leads Dharma Talk on Trịnh Công Sơn]. The talks are in Vietnamese. Youtube recordings of all ten talks are

"It is certain," Thích Nhất Hạnh says, "that Trịnh Công Sơn listened to Thầy[27] [the monk Chánh Pháp] recite prayers many times and that the music of Buddhist prayers [*kinh*] and gathas [*kệ*] entered his bloodstream [*máu huyết*] and that is why Trịnh Công Sơn's music echoes prayers and gathas."[28]

Vietnamese monks study the Buddhist sutras and understand their meaning but many Vietnamese who chant them have only a vague idea of what the words mean, even if they have read them in the Vietnamese (Romanized) script [*Quốc ngữ*]. The texts of Buddhist prayers in Vietnam derive from Chinese versions which are not translations but sound transcriptions—attempts to capture the sounds of the original Sanskrit using Chinese characters. When Chinese chant Buddhist prayers their pronunciation is fairly close to the original Sanskrit but when Vietnamese chant them their pronunciation departs further from the Sanskrit. This is because they "Vietnamize" the Chinese and chant them in what is called "Sino-Vietnamese," a term for Chinese words and texts which when read aloud are pronounced in the Vietnamese manner. [29] Vietnamese has many borrowed words from Chinese that are well-known and familiar, just as English has many familiar words borrowed from French, Greek, and other languages. The words in many Buddhist prayers, however, are Sino-Vietnamese versions of Sanskrit words most of which are not familiar to lay Buddhists.[30] Therefore it is not surprising that when lay Buddhists *tụng kinh* [chant prayers] the words of the prayers "dissolve in sound," which is, according to Trần Hữu Thục, what happens when people sing or listen to one of Trịnh Công Sơn's obscure songs.[31]

I am not saying Trịnh Công Sơn's songs are Buddhist prayers, though Thích Nhất Hạnh says many of them can be chanted as well as sung. In one dharma session at Plum Village, Vietnamese participants first chant a Buddhist prayer in Chinese, then another prayer in Vietnamese, and then

---

available online; the first can be found here: https://www.youtube.com/watch?v=LuA-m0guxjCw&ab_channel=Tr%C3%AD%C4%90%E1%BB%A9c%28chanthienluc%29.

27. "Thầy" means "teacher." Vietnamese often address Buddhist monks as "thầy."

28. Thích Nhất Hạnh, *Thiền Sư Nhất Hạnh Pháp Thoại Trịnh Công Sơn*, Part 4.

29. John DeFrancis, *Colonialism and Language Policy in Viet Nam* (The Hague: Mouton, 1977), 15.

30. This account of how Buddhist Prayers are recited in Vietnam draws on the following article by Trần Văn Khê, a highly respected Vietnamese musicologist: "Phong Cách Tán Tụng trong Phật Giáo Việt Nam" [The Way of Recitation in Vietnamese Buddhism], Giác Ngộ Online, http://giacngo.vn/PrintView.aspx?Language=vi&ID=524658 (accessed August 17, 2015).

31. Trần Hữu Thục, "Một cái nhìn về ca từ Trịnh Công Sơn," 59.

Trịnh Công Sơn's song "Lullaby of Cannons for the Night" [Đại bác ru đêm]*.[32] It is possible that a Buddhist background prepares Vietnamese to feel comfortable listening to and chanting or singing words they do not understand. "When one chants prayers," my Buddhist Vietnamese dictionary says, "it is not necessary to try to understand the meaning, but the meaning will be absorbed naturally and will gradually become clear in the process of one's practice. Chanting involves saying the prayers with a rising and falling voice and subtle sounds so the prayers will enter our hearts and the hearts of others deeply and soothe our troubles, our worries, and our desires."[33] Many Vietnamese, I believe, listen to and sing Trịnh Công Sơn's songs in the way this Buddhist dictionary suggests one should listen to and chant a Buddhist prayer. And many Vietnamese find that his songs, like Buddhists prayers, have a soothing effect.

The Zen aspect of the Zen-Pure Land union within Vietnamese Buddhism also helps make Vietnamese open to an understanding that does not need to involve words, that can be achieved outside the scriptures. Thích Tâm Thiện, when he interviewed Trịnh Công Sơn, asked the singer to talk about his experiences with Buddhism. Sơn's answer is long but here is how it ends:

> At the end of 1995 I wrote a song that I like a lot and that my friends also like. That's the song "Where Will the Wave Go" [Sóng về đâu].* This song was inspired by the Buddhist prayer: "Gatê Gatê, Paragate, Parasamgate. Bodhi Savaha" [Gone, gone, gone beyond, gone altogether beyond, O what an awakening, all hail!] I am searching for a new way to describe things so, when I compose, I must forget the present in order to enter a reality, a drifting reality, where there are no worldly clashes of words and their meanings and no arguing that goes nowhere, that ends in a blind alley.[34]

The Buddhist prayer that Sơn refers to is the mantra that ends the Heart Sutra, probably the best known and the most chanted of all the sutras in Mahayana Buddhism. I discuss Trịnh Công Sơn's song "Where Will the Wave Go" in Chapter Twenty-Five. Here I simply want to call attention to Sơn's mention of this sutra and to his comments that immediately follow

---

32. This session is available on Youtube. See "Thiền Sư Nhất Hạnh Pháp Thoại Trịnh Công Sơn P.5 https://www.youtube.com/watch?v=6h7htuhK4Ms (accessed October 26, 2019).
33. Tâm Tuệ Hỷ, ed., *Danh từ Phật học thực dụng* [Useful Buddhist Terms] (Hà Nội: Tôn Giáo, 2004), 518.
34. Interview with Thích Tâm Thiện."

about how he is trying when he composes to enter a "drifting reality" where words and their meanings do not clash.

Scriptures like the Heart Sutra were an important ingredient of the Zen Buddhism brought to Vietnam by Chinese monks during the Lý and Trần Dynasties.[35] Cuong Tu Nguyen argues that these monks "saw the underlying unity of the scriptures in the experience of the mind of enlightenment."[36] The motto of this new Buddhism was the message that the Indian monk Bodhidharma brought from India to China: "A special transmission outside the scriptures. No dependence upon words and letters."[37] The emphasis was on "direct, personal experience and not abstract categorization." Adherents were to trust intuition and not rely on words.

Chinese histories of Buddhism in China, for example, the *Jingde chuandeng lu* [Transmission of the Lamp Composed during the Jingde Era], compiled in 1004, and Vietnamese Buddhist histories modeled on them, like the *Thiền uyển tập anh* [A Collection of Outstanding Figures of the Zen Community], composed in the third decade of the fourteenth century, contain stories of famous Zen masters assisting disciples to attain enlightenment by engaging them in what have come to be called "encounter dialogues." These dialogues do involve words but the language is unconventional. Typically before participating in these dialogues the disciple has spent years studying, meditating, and pondering koans [Vn. *công án*], paradoxes designed to get the disciple to move beyond reason and rely on intuition. The dialogue typically occurs when the Zen master is old and wishes to transfer the "mind seal"—or mental impression [Vn. *tâm ấn*]—to his disciple, a transfer which links the disciple to the master's lineage.

Histories of Vietnamese Buddhism contain many examples of these encounter dialogues. Here is one between Liễu Quán, a Vietnamese monk from central Vietnam who founded a branch of Lâm Tế (Japanese: Rinzai) Zen in Vietnam in 1708. (According to Thich Thien An, "most Buddhist monks, nuns, and laymen in Vietnam belong to the Lâm Tế Zen tradition.")[38] Liễu Quán studied with a Chinese master named Minh

---

35. The Lý Dynasty ruled from 1010-1255, the Trần Dynasty from 1225-1400.
36. Cuong Tu Nguyen, *Zen in Medieval Vietnam* (Honolulu, HI: University of Hawai'i Press, 1997), 26.
37. Ibid.
38. Thich Thien An, *Buddhism and Zen in Vietnam* (Rutland VT: Charles E. Tuttle Company, 1975), 11.

Hoàng Tử Dung who, as part of his instruction, had Liễu Quán ponder this koan: "All things return to the One, but where does the One return?" After months of meditating on this koan, Liễu Quán realized his mind had become "ripe for awakening" and so he sought out his master for confirmation.[39] Tử Dung tested him in the following exchange:

> Tử Dung: Buddhas have succeeded one after the other as have the patriarchs. So what did they transmit among them?

> Liễu Quán: Are you asking how long the bamboo sprout grows on the piece of stone, or would you like to know the weight of a turtle-feather broom?

> Tử Dung: Water flows uphill, horses race in ocean depths, a boat floats on the mountain.

> Liễu Quán: The unstrung guitar made music the whole day through; the horn-broken earthen oxen roared the night long.

Pleased by his disciple's responses, Tử Dung conveyed on him the mind seal.

In discussing the "defamiliarizing" techniques that Trịnh Công Sơn used to make his songs seem fresh and new in comparison to pre-war songs, I quoted Lê Hữu who comments that a line from Sơn's famous love song "Diễm of the Past" is so illogical that it sounds like "the man talks chickens, the woman talks ducks."[40] Trịnh Công Sơn's "Diễm of the Past," however, appears downright straightforward in comparison to this dialogue between Liễu Quán and Tử Dung. Many of Trịnh Công Sơn's songs, however, do resemble the koans and encounter dialogues of Zen masters. Like these masters he may have used unusual language to jar people out of their customary way of seeing the world. In other words, his obscurity may be more than simply a stylistic feature to distinguish his songs from pre-war music. It may reflect a deep-seated faith in his audience's ability to intuit his songs. Trịnh Công Sơn may have defamiliarized his lyrics by making them more obscure than the lyrics of pre-war songs, but he no doubt did so knowing that while he was doing something new he was harking back to something old—to a tradition of obscure

---

39. Ibid., 164.
40. Lê Hữu, "Từ 'Diễm xưa' đến 'Một cõi đi về" [From 'Diễm xưa' to 'Một Cõi Đi Về'], *Văn Học* [Literary Studies] 186 & 187 (Oct.-Nov., 2001), 227. The expression that Lê Hữu cites, "The man talks chickens, the woman talks ducks" [Ông nói gà, bà nói vịt] is a proverbial expression used when people misunderstand each other.

Buddhist texts that included prayers, Zen poems, koans, and encounter dialogues.

Nguyễn Hưng Quốc blames the inability of Vietnamese students in Australia to write clearly in Vietnamese on a poetic tradition that valorizes obscurity. He does not discuss Buddhist attitudes toward language, but I believe these attitudes should be considered. It seems likely that over the centuries these attitudes have made Vietnamese more comfortable with obscurity, more confident in their own powers of intuition. Language certainly plays a different role in Buddhism than it does in Christianity. Words play a primary role in Christianity: They create the world. According to Genesis 1:3, God said "Let there be light," and there was light. In the Old Testament, William P. Tuck points out, the word Yahweh occurs over four hundred times to describe God's revelation. It is "the word of the Lord," Tuck says, that comes to Old Testament prophets like Ezekiel (Ezek. 1:3) and Jeremiah (Jer. 1:4).[41] In the New Testament, he explains, "the 'Word' of God is not limited to words or utterances but is declared, by the Gospel of John, to be an event in the flesh and life of Jesus Christ." Words in this gospel ring with reminders of Genesis 1:1 where it is stated that, "In the beginning was the Word"; and Genesis 1:14: "And the Word became flesh and dwelt among us."[42] The theologian Paul F. Knitter argues that this belief—that "this Word that created the world became flesh in the human being Jesus the Nazarean"—is "the belief that, more than any other, has distinguished Christianity from other religions."[43]

In Buddhism words play an important role, but it is always, Knitter argues, a subordinate role. "Experience comes first—the experience of Enlightenment, the Awakening to one's existence within Interbeing" [emptiness; Skt. *sunyata*].[44] Living comes first—"living a life of compassion toward all sentient beings."[45] Knitter, a Christian whose study of Buddhism has, he says, helped him understand his own faith, points out that words for Buddhists are always "inadequate"; they are always "a means to an end, never an end in themselves." In Buddhism, Knitter says, "'mystery'

41. William P. Tuck, "Toward a Theology of the Proclaimed Word," *Review and Expositor* (Jan. 1, 1984), 293.
42. Ibid.
43. Paul F. Knitter, *Without Buddha I Could Not Be a Christian* (UK: One World Publications, 2013), 55.
44. Knitter explains that Thích Nhất Hạnh translates *sunyata* as "interbeing." See page 12 of *Without Buddha I Could Not Be a Christian*. I will discuss Thích Nhất Hạnh's term "interbeing" further in Chapter Twenty-Four.
45. Paul F. Knitter, *Without Buddha I Could Not Be a Christian*, 59.

always holds priority over words, either coming or going—that is, either in preparing for or looking back at what one 'sees' when one's eyes are truly opened."[46]

Both the koan Tử Dung presents to his disciple Liễu Quán, and the dialogue he engages him in, contain words, but the words are only a bridge to the mystery that lies beyond them. They are like the raft in perhaps the best known of all Buddhist stories. In this story the Buddha compares the *dharma* [Buddhist teachings] to a raft. A man makes a raft to get him across a river. After successfully crossing the river, instead of abandoning the raft he continues to carry it. He forgets that the raft was only a means to an end. Words are like the finger in the famous Buddhist expression: "The finger is not the moon." The finger is needed to know where to look for the moon but it is not the moon itself. If we become too involved with words, Buddhist teachers warn us, we will never reach the mystery that lies beyond them. Trịnh Công Sơn's experience chanting difficult-to-understand prayers and a perhaps primarily unconscious absorption of Buddhist attitudes toward language may have, along with the other possible causes I have described, made Trịnh Công Sơn very comfortable with obscurity.

The lyrics of many of Trịnh Công Sơn's songs may be obscure but, based on the way his fans responded to them, his confidence in their powers of intuition was not misplaced. His fans understood him. They felt he gave voice to things they could not express. Books and journal articles about his life and songs are full of testimonials like this one by Tuấn Huy:

> For his entire life Trịnh Công Sơn expressed for us our worries, torments, quandaries, pain, regrets, self-pity, hesitations, and all our despairs, all our doubts, and all our obsessions about our fate as human beings, about a divisive war, about love, about destruction and separation. This is why Trịnh Công Sơn is considered an outstanding talent, a genius. That cannot be denied but one more thing must be emphasized: Trịnh Công Sơn is the splendid Heart and Soul of Vietnam.[47]

---

46. Ibid.
47. Tuấn Huy, "Trịnh Công Sơn, cỏ xót xa người" [Trịnh Công Sơn: The Painful Grass of Humanity], *Văn Học* [Literary Studies] 186 & 187 (Oct.-Nov. 2001), 37.

DYLAN & THE ANGLO-AMERICAN LITERARY TRADITION

D ylan was an autodidact. Although he never finished his first year at the University of Minnesota, he was an avid but haphazard reader. Before he arrived in New York, Dylan says he had already read works by Voltaire, Rousseau, John Locke, Montesquieu, and Martin Luther. "It was like I knew those guys, like they'd been living in my backyard," he says in *Chronicles*.[1] In New York Dylan stayed with a couple, Ray Gooch and Chloe Kiel, who let him sleep on a sofa in their living room. The couple had a well-stocked library. Dylan comments that he wanted to read all the books in it, but, he says, "I would have to have been in a rest home or something in order to do that."[2] He says he looked at or "read some of" Machiavelli's *The Prince*, Dante's *Inferno*, William Faulkner's *The Sound and the Fury*, Albertus Magnus,[3] Sigmund Freud's *Beyond the Pleasure Principle*, Thucydides, a book on Joseph Smith (the Morman leader), and Clausewitz' *On War*. Dylan suggests that he read the following prose works more carefully: Robert Graves' *The White Goddess*; novels by the western writer Luke Short; stories by Edgar Rice Burroughs, Jules Verne, and Balzac; and Jack Kerouac's *On the Road*.[4]

Dylan says a lot of the books in Ray and Chloe's library were "too big to read, like giant shoes fitted for large-footed people," and so "he read

---

1. Bob Dylan, *Chronicles: Volume One* (New York: Simon and Schuster, 2004), 30.
2. Ibid., 37.
3. Dylan does not indicate which works by this Catholic Dominican friar and bishop he read.
4. Ibid., 36-41, 45, 56-57.

the poetry books, mostly."[5] He mentions reading John Milton's "Massacre in Piedmont," a sonnet protesting the slaughtering of a religious group in Italy by the Catholic Duke of Savoy. He reports that he also read poems by Lord Byron, Percy Shelley, Samuel Taylor Coleridge, Henry Wadsworth Longfellow, Edgar Allan Poe, T. S. Elliot and the fifteenth century French poet Francois Villon (1431-1463).[6] "I began cramming my brain with all kinds of deep poems," he writes. "It seemed like I'd been pulling an empty wagon for a long time and now I was beginning to fill it up and would have to pull harder. I felt like I was coming out of the back pasture."[7] Dylan wanted to write "deep" songs, maybe not as deep as the works of these famous writers but deeper, he hoped, than the songs he was hearing on the radio, which, he says, "came at you like you didn't have a brain."[8] Dylan read the works of famous writers to stock up his mind so he could give his songs some intellectual weight.

The English critic and writer Michael Gray, an acknowledged authority on Dylan, describes how Dylan echoes many of the great writers in the English and American literary tradition in his songs.[9] His list of the writers Dylan echoes includes John Milton, John Bunyan, John Donne, William Blake, Robert Browning, Lewis Carroll, T.S. Eliot, Ralph Waldo Emerson, Henry Wadsworth Longfellow, Edgar Allan Poe, Walt Whitman, Edward Arlington Robinson, E. E. Cummings, and the following Beat writers: Kenneth Patchen, Allan Ginsberg, Lawrence Ferlinghetti, and Jack Kerouac. Many of the echoes that Gray finds appear far-fetched to me. Take, for example, Dylan's description of his wife in these lines from "Sara":

> *Sweet virgin angel, sweet love of my life . . .*
> *Radiant jewel, mystical wife . . .*
> *Scorpio Sphinx in a calico dress . . .*
> *Glamorous nymph with an arrow and bow . . .*

Gray says that Dylan in these lines is echoing Edgar Allan Poe's poem "To Helen" and that realizing this "removes the puzzle of all those embarrassingly florid pseudo-classical phrases."[10] Gray is referring to phrases like the following that occur in Poe's famous poem:

---

5. Ibid., 37.
6. Ibid., 37-38, 56, 110, 112.
7. Ibid., 56.
8. Ibid., 33.
9. See Michael Gray, *Song and Dance Man III: The Art of Bob Dylan* (London: Continuum, 2000).
10. Ibid., 77.

Thy hyacinth hair, thy classic face,
Thy Naiad airs have brought me home
To the glory that was Greece,
And the grandeur that was Rome.

How statue-like I see thee stand,
The agate lamp within thy hand!
Ah, Psyche, from the regions which
Are Holy-Land!

It is possible that Dylan echoes Poe's poem in "Sara," but who can be sure? In speaking of possible echoes of the poems by Edward Arlington Robinson in some of Dylan's songs Gray says that "it is more in the nature of a hunch, a suggestion of a link there somehow."[11] Most literary echoes that Gray finds, however, are not presented as hunches but as inescapable conclusions. He says the echo of Poe "hangs emphatically over" songs like "Sara." Maybe Dylan does echo Poe's "To Helen" in this song, as Gray asserts, but I do not see how he can be so certain.

Gray, however, is steeped in the English literary tradition in a way that I am not and in discussing some writers he makes a fairly convincing case for their influence on Dylan. Even if we do not fully accept his argument for direct influence, we can learn much from his readings of Dylan's songs. His remarks concerning the pre-romantic poet and painter William Blake, the Victorian poet Robert Browning, and the so-called Beat writers are particularly helpful and interesting and so I will discuss them briefly here.

Gray finds the most Blake influence in Dylan's "Gates of Eden" and "Every Grain of Sand." The first song is Blakeian, he maintains, in its comparison of the temporal to the eternal—in the way it seems designed to make people conscious of an infinity beyond the everyday world. Gray lists a series of "balances of opposites" in "Gates of Eden": "of material wealth and spiritual; of earthly reality and the imaginatively real; of the body and the soul; of false gods and the true vision; of self-grat-ification and salvation," etc. These themes, he says, "could not be more Blakeian."[12] "Gates of Eden" is a difficult song—even Gray finds much of it "irrevocably obscure"[13]—but in most of the ten verses Dylan does seem to be balancing one or more of the "Blakeian" opposites that Gray enumerates. Here is the eighth verse:

---

11. Ibid., 79.
12. Ibid., 62.
13. Ibid., 63.

> *The kingdoms of Experience*
> *In the precious wind they rot*
> *While paupers change possessions*
> *Each one wishing for what the other has got*
> *And the princess and the prince*
> *Discuss what's real and what is not*
> *It doesn't matter inside the Gates of Eden*

Gray discusses "Gates of Eden" in his chapter titled "Dylan and the Literary Tradition" and takes up "Every Grain of Sand," the other song he sees as heavily influenced by Blake, in a special chapter that runs for twenty-six small-print pages. Although Gray suggests Dylan's "Gates of Eden" is Blakeian because its themes are those that interested Blake, he calls "Every Grain of Sand" Blakeian primarily because it contains Blakeian rhythms and language. This song, he points out, is composed in a poetic meter, heptameter,[14] that, he says, "is rare in English-language poetry but is one of Blake's principal trademarks."[15] It contains many—too many, in Gray's view—X of Y phrases, a grammatical structure found frequently in Blake.[16] Dylan uses twenty-three of these phrases in "Every Grain of Sand." Five occur in the third stanza:

> *Oh, the flowers of indulgence and the weeds of yesteryear*
> *Like criminals, they have choked the breath of conscience and*
> *good cheer*
> *The sun beat down upon the steps of time to light the way*
> *To ease the pain of idleness and the memory of decay*

Gray says that Dylan also indicates his "embrace of Blake" in this song by using "some commonality of theme,"[17] but he never makes this commonality clear, and, in fact, he states—in several places in his analysis—that the religious views that Dylan expresses in this song differ from those held by Blake. Both Blake and Dylan rewrite the Bible, Gray says, but "the ideas that Dylan takes from his Judeo-Christian religion are far more orthodox than Blake's."[18] "It seems to me," Gray says, "that the boundaries of Dylan's vision in his song ["Every Grain of Sand"] are smaller and rather more modest as is, always, his rewriting of the Bible."[19]

---

14. A heptameter line has seven iambic feet, or beats, per line.
15. Michael Gray, *Song and Dance Man*, 415.
16. Ibid., 415-420.
17. Ibid., 415.
18. Ibid., 412.
19. Ibid., 415.

In other words, when Dylan rewrites the Bible in this and other songs, he ends up expressing quite orthodox Christian views. Blake takes a biblical text and flies it to "mystical heights"; Dylan is more orthodox, less mystical.[20]

Gray contrasts the more conventionally religious Dylan with the mystical Blake by discussing the "grain of sand" image. "I can see the Master's hand," Dylan says, "In every leaf that trembles, in every grain of sand." Gray says that in these lines Dylan echoes the well-known first stanza of Blake's "Auguries of Innocence":

> To see a World in a Grain of Sand
> And a Heaven in a Wild Flower
> Hold Infinity in the palm of your hand
> And Eternity in an hour

Dylan echoes these lines, Gray says, but assigns a different meaning to that grain of sand. In Gray's interpretation, Blake is saying that if we were not so bound by our five senses we could see a world *within* a grain of sand. In other words, Blake gives the image a "visionary meaning."[21] Certainly the lines I've quoted above from Blake's "Auguries of Innocence" do sound visionary and mystical. Gray explains that in "Every Grain of Sand," however, Dylan uses this image to convey the conventional idea, supported by scripture, that God's hand is revealed in the smallest of things—in a grain of sand and also in other small things, like a trembling leaf, a hair on a person's head, and a sparrow's fall (things which Dylan also mentions in his song). According to Gray, the "founding text of the song's title theme" is Matthew 10:29-31—verses that quote Christ directly:[22]

> Are not two sparrows sold for a farthing? and one of them shall not fall on the ground without your Father. But the very hairs of your head are all numbered. Fear ye not therefore, ye are of more value than many sparrows.

This chapter is about literary traditions, not religion, but it is difficult to separate the two because many writers and composers rewrite the Bible in their works. Gray maintains that "Every Grain of Sand" is heavily influenced by Blake's poetry but the first ten pages of his analysis are about how Dylan rewrites the Bible in this song. Gray calls his analysis of this song "a long interpretative exploration" of the "scriptural signposts" that

---

20. Ibid., 412.
21. Ibid., 413-414.
22. Ibid., 414.

it contains.[23] I have already discussed one signpost, the biblical verses quoted above, but he mentions many others. Gray suggests that Dylan's confession in the first line parallels Daniel's (9:3-19). Like Daniel, who hopes God will forgive his people for worshiping false gods after he delivered them from Egypt, Dylan in "Every Grain of Sand" hopes that God will forgive him for his sins.[24] Gray argues that in stanza four Dylan evokes the parable of the sower, a parable that Christ used to explain to his disciples that the words of God are like seeds: they will have different effects depending on where they fall. Some seeds will fall nearby but will be devoured by fowls. Some will fall on stony ground and not take root. Some will fall among thorns which will choke the plant before it yields fruit; and some will fall on good ground and flourish. Dylan's narrator, Gray says, is one of the thorn people—one of those described in Mark 4:18-19 who hear the word but get distracted:

> And these are they which are sown among thorns: such as hear the word, And the cares of this world and the deceitfulness of riches, and the lusts of other things entering in, choke the word, and it becometh unfruitful.

Gray says that Dylan takes the biblical X of Y phrases—"cares of this world" and "deceitfulness of riches"—and "compresses these together into his own confession of such distractions" in phrases like "the flowers of indulgence and weeds of yesteryear" which, Dylan says, "Like criminals . . . have choked the breath of conscience and good cheer."

I will discuss Dylan and the influence of his Judeo-Christian heritage in later chapters, but before leaving "Every Grain of Sand" I want to point out that although Dylan evokes biblical texts in this song, he does not—in *this* song—evangelize but seems rather, as the first line suggests, to be making a confession.[25] The biblical verses that Dylan echoes suggest that Christ cares for all things, but values humankind most. Because he values people more, however, he will be watching them carefully, and will not be happy if they reject him. The message of Matthew 10, which contains verses that Gray says Dylan echoes, is—taken in its entirety—a

---

23. Ibid., 409.
24. I say "Dylan" not "persona," "narrator," or "speaker" because I understand this song to be an expression of Dylan's personal beliefs. Gray goes back and forth between "Dylan" and "narrator," but he understands this song to be a personal statement. He calls one of the many biblical allusions in this song "an example of how quietly and intelligently Dylan uses his biblical allusions to speak for him; to articulate his own position." See Michael Gray, *Song and Dance Man*, 402.
25. "In the time of my confession, in the hour of my deepest need."

stern warning to non-believers to accept Christ's message or face dire consequences. "Think not that I am come to send peace on earth; I came not to send peace, but a sword," Christ tells his disciples (Matthew 10: 34). Gray links this passage to Luke 21:18: "But there shall not a hair on your head perish." This passage from Luke occurs, Gray points out, in the context of warnings about the apocalypse and the second coming of Christ after which believers will be fine—not a hair on *their* heads will perish— but non-believers will be cast into everlasting punishment (Matthew 25: 41-46).[26] Dylan, as we will see in Chapter Twenty-Seven: Prophet of the Apocalypse, is fascinated by the apocalypse and has a healthy respect for the wrath of God, but these themes, although present in the biblical verses Dylan echoes, are not exploited in his song. Instead the message seems to be that God is concerned about everyone. Even in "the fury of the moment" the Master seems merciful, not wrathful. If every falling sparrow counts then, the song suggests, we must too. There is, Gray says, a "universality" of "meaning and feeling'" and a "simple humanitarianism" in Dylan's song and I believe that is why many have praised it.[27]

Gray also argues that Dylan has been influenced by the Victorian poet Robert Browning. Gray sees several "notable corridors" between the two men.[28] He mentions, for example, that both men had an "equal relish for the blatantly grotesque"; that both wrote works criticizing people who were excessively theoretical and intellectual—people who retreat to "the artificial safeness of vicarious living";[29] and that both wrote dramatic monologues. Speaking of the dramatic monologue, Gray says that Robert Browning "mastered this form as no one before him" and that "Dylan has used it as no one else since."[30] High praise indeed! I will discuss this similarity because some of Dylan's most famous poems are dramatic monologues and although I don't share Gray's certainty that Dylan was influenced by Browning, I believe comparing Dylan's use of this form to Browning's helps us understand how Dylan adapted this form to achieve his own purposes.

---

26. Michael Gray, *Song and Dance Man*, 405.
27. Ibid., 425.
28. Ibid., 69.
29. Ibid., 66. Examples are Gigadibs in Browning's "Bishop Blougram's Apology" and Mr. Jones in Dylan's "Ballad of a Thin Man."
30. Ibid., 64. T. S. Eliot's "The Love Song of J. Alfred Prufrock" (1915) is probably the most famous modern dramatic monologue.

The dramatic monologue resembles the soliloquy but differs from it in certain important respects.[31] In a soliloquy an actor in a play talks to himself or herself. It is a convention playwrights use to convey to the audience an actor's thinking and motives. A dramatic monologue is a lyric poem in which a speaker, who is not the poet, addresses one or more people. Those addressed do not speak, which is why it is a monologue. We learn that they are present and get information about them not from them but from the words of the speaker. Dramatic monologues, Michael Gray explains, are one-way conversations, "half of a dialogue in which the imagined other participant gets only an implicit hearing."[32]

As I pointed out in Chapter Six, Dylan's narrators in his anti-love songs seem to relish getting in the last word, and the dramatic monologue is a form that allows them to do so. Dylan asks "Miss Lonely" in "Like a Rolling Stone" how it feels "To be on your own / With no direction home." The form does not require that the narrator report her reply. Poems written in this form also commonly feature narrators who are mean and immoral. According to Robert Langbaum, author of a book on the dramatic monologue in the English tradition, the "most successful dramatic monologues deal with speakers who are in some way reprehensible."[33] The narrator in probably the most famous dramatic monologue in the English language, Browning's "My Last Duchess," is a cruel Italian duke who has had his wife killed and, in the poem, negotiates with an envoy to procure a dowry for a new wife. The duke describes a portrait of his late wife to the envoy in a way that suggests he considers it, much as he had regarded his late wife, to be an important object in a collection of possessions, which he hopes to add to by acquiring a new duchess. Yet, as Langbaum points out, "moral judgment does not figure importantly in our response to the duke" and, in fact, "we even identify ourselves with him."[34] "What interests us more than the duke's wickedness," Langbaum says, "is his immense attractiveness. . . . We suspend judgment of the duke because we prefer to participate in the duke's power and freedom, in his hard core of character fiercely loyal to itself. Moral judgment is in fact

---

31. For a good short definition of a dramatic monologue, see M. H. Abrams, *A Glossary of Literary Terms*, 5th ed. (Fort Worth, TX: Harcourt Brace Jovanovich, 1988), 45-46; for an extended discussion of the form in English literature, see Robert Langbaum, *The Poetry of Experience* (New York: W. W. Norton, 1957).
32. Michael Gray, *Song and Dance Man*, 64.
33. Robert Langbaum, *The Poetry of Experience*, 85.
34. Ibid., 82.

important as the thing to be suspended, as a measure of the price we pay for the privilege of appreciating to the full this extraordinary man."[35]

Something similar happens, I believe, when we listen to Dylan's anti-love songs. We become so captivated by the narrator—by his "power and freedom" and "fierce loyalty to himself"—that we suspend moral judgment and overlook the fact that he is saying mean things to women he supposedly loves or has loved. We accept his harsh judgments of his silent female interlocutors. The narrator's own character flaws—lack of sensitivity, meanness, even cruelty—do not register on our consciousness. At least they didn't register on mine when I first heard Dylan's anti-love songs in the 60s. Speaking of Browning's "My Last Duchess," Langbaum says it is the form—the dramatic monologue—that encourages us to sympathize with the villainous duke. Probably it is Dylan's adoption of this form that leads some listeners to sympathize with the narrators in his anti-love songs.

Gray mentions some ways that Dylan's dramatic monologues differ from the traditional literary form found in English poetry. Dylan's adaptations alter the form so drastically they lead one to suspect Browning's dramatic monologues may have influenced Dylan far less than Gray suggests. Two of Dylan's adaptations of the form—in my view at least—serve to make his anti-love songs more personal and spiteful. Gray points out that Browning's narrators were fictional characters, like the Italian duke in "My Last Duchess," whereas "Dylan, like other modern poets, projects himself." This is one reason why, Gray says, "it is often exceptionally difficult to distinguish the created character from the man."[36] In literary criticism one is supposed to carefully distinguish the two—to avoid assuming that the speaker or narrator in a work is identical to the writer or composer who created it. That's easy to do in Browning's "My Last Duchess," but much more difficult in Dylan's anti-love songs. I have discussed this issue in Chapter Eight: Personas and Personalities. I mention it here because I think most people, in the absence of any indication to the contrary, assume that Dylan is speaking in his anti-love songs. This makes them more personal than "My Last Duchess," perhaps *too* personal to be considered dramatic monologues if one accepts M. H. Abrams' first defining criterion of the form, namely that the person who speaks must not be the creator of the work. If "we are invited to identify

---

35. Ibid., 83.
36. Michael Gray, *Song and Dance Man*, 67-68.

the speaker with the poet himself," M. H. Abrams says, as we are, for example, in William Wordsworth's "Tintern Abbey," then the work is a dramatic lyric, but not a dramatic monologue.[37]

Another departure from the traditional dramatic monologue makes Dylan's anti-love songs more spiteful. Gray points out that the "you" in Browning's dramatic monologues, the silent interlocutor, "is not merely silent but actually unnecessary. A mere tip of the hat to Victorian expectations."[38] Browning provides little information, for example, about the envoy that the duke addresses in "My Last Duchess." In Dylan's anti-love songs, however, the person who is addressed has, Gray says, "a felt presence the exploration of which is central to the song's purpose. In his songs to women, where they are the 'silent' ones, the portrayal of their characters is a main ingredient."[39] Typically Dylan's portrayals of these silent women are far from flattering. As examples of dramatic monologues in which women have a "felt" but "silent" presence, Gray mentions "Positively 4th Street"[40] and three songs from his album *Blonde on Blonde*: "Most Likely You Go Your Way (and I'll Go Mine)," "One of Us Must Know (Sooner or Later)," and "Leopard-Skin Pill-Box Hat." Gray could also have mentioned the famous anti-love songs "It Ain't Me, Babe" and "Like a Rolling Stone." In these songs women certainly have a "felt presence," and in them the narrator spitefully and unfeelingly rejects women for alleged character flaws—possessiveness in "It Ain't Me, Babe" and a snobbish aloofness in "Like a Rollin' Stone."

Gray and other Dylanophiles, as well as Dylan biographers, maintain that Dylan was influenced by the Beat poets and writers—Allen Ginsberg, Lawrence Ferlinghetti, William Burroughs, and Jack Kerouac, for example. "In many ways," says Howard Sounes, "Bob was the spiritual heir to the beat poets. He knew their work, he had a similar sensibility, and he was excited to meet them."[41] Dylan and Ginsberg first met in 1963 and were friends until Ginsberg's death in 1997. In 1965, when Dylan was performing in San Francisco and Berkeley, he invited Ginsberg and beat poet and playwright Michael McClure to join him on the Southern

---

37. M. H. Abrams, *A Glossary of Literary Terms*, 46.
38. Michael Gray, *Song and Dance Man*, 68.
39. Ibid.
40. Dylan may have been addressing a woman in this song—some people think he had Joan Baez in mind—but it is generally interpreted as an attack on the folk song purists who resented his move to rock and roll.
41. Howard Sounes, *Down the Highway: The Life of Bob Dylan* (New York: Grove Press, 2001), 148.

California part of their tour. According to Howard Sounes, they traveled in Ginsberg's Volkswagen camper van, driven by Ginsberg's lover, the poet Peter Orlovsky.[42] Ginsberg also accompanied Dylan on his Rolling Thunder Revue tour in 1975 (for more on the Revue, see Chapter Nine). During this tour Dylan, aided by Sam Shepard, was filming *Renaldo and Clara*, which turned out to be a financial disaster. Ginsberg was on the set, "screaming for attention," Sounes says, "anxious to get as much of his poetry on film as possible."[43]

Dylan read the beat writers when he was still in Minnesota. He suggests in his autobiography that he had grown less enchanted with them after moving to New York. He comments specifically on Jack Kerouac's *On the Road*:

> Within the first months that I was in New York, I'd lost my interest in the 'hungry for kicks' hipster vision that Kerouac illustrates so well in his book *On the Road*. That book had been like a bible for me. Not anymore, though. I still loved the breathless, dynamic bop poetry phrases that flowed from Jack's pen, but now, that character Moriarty seemed out of place, purposeless—seemed like a character who inspired idiocy.[44]

Nevertheless, on liner notes for his 1985 compilation album *Biograph*, Dylan speaks fondly of "the beat scene, the Bohemian, BeBop crowd" that, he says, he "just naturally fell in with" when he was in New York.[45] Poems were always recited at gatherings, Dylan says, and not just works by the beat writers. He quotes lines from T. S. Eliot's "Love Song of J. Alfred Prufrock" and e.e. cummings' untitled poem about Buffalo Bill.[46] But most of the people he memorializes in these liner notes were beat writers: Allen Ginsberg, Jack Kerouac, Gregory Corso, Lawrence Ferlinghetti, William Burroughs, and Gary Snyder. Ginsberg gets special attention. Dylan quotes part of the opening of Ginsberg's long poem "Howl": "I saw the best minds of my generation destroyed by madness." That, Dylan says, "said more to me than any of the stuff I'd been raised on."[47] Michael Gray maintains that "there is not one line from this huge sprawling poem that cannot claim

42. Ibid., 197.
43. Ibid., 293.
44. Bob Dylan, *Chronicles*, 57-58.
45. Bob Dylan, liner notes accompanying *Biograph*.
46. The lines from Eliot's "Love Song" that Dylan's quotes are "In the room the people come and go / Talking of Michelangelo" and "I have measured out my life with coffee spoons." The lines that he quotes from the cummings poem are "and what I want to know is / how do you like your blueeyed boy / Mister Death."
47. Bob Dylan, liner notes accompanying *Biograph*.

to be the deranged, inspired midwife of the Dylan of the mid-1960s, the Dylan of 'the motor cycle black Madonna two-wheel gypsy queen' and the rest."[48] Gray refers to characters in "Gates of Eden," a song released in 1965 on Dylan's album *Bringing It All Back Home*. "The Dylan of 1965-66," Gray says, "swims in a [literary] milieu" composed of the beat writers. "In a way all Dylan did was to put it on stage with a guitar."[49] This sounds more than a little hyperbolic to me, but clearly Dylan read and admired the beat writers. Probably their voices—their "bop poetry phrases"—were murmuring in his unconscious when he composed many of his songs.

These beat writers, especially Allen Ginsberg and Jack Kerouac, could also have helped Dylan obtain his Nobel Prize in literature, which he was awarded in October 2016. Quite a few people were surprised that Dylan, a singer-songwriter, received an award for literature. "If Dylan's a poet," Norman Mailer, author of *The Naked and the Dead*, commented, "then I'm a basketball player."[50] Probably anticipating such a reaction, in a speech announcing the award Professor Horace Engdahl, a member of the Nobel Committee for Literature, said that "It ought not to be a sensation that a singer/songwriter now stands recipient of the literary Nobel Prize. In a distant past, all poetry was sung or tunefully recited, poets were bards, troubadours; the word 'lyrics' comes from 'lyre' [harp]."[51] Luc Sante, a writer for the *New York Review of Books*, approved of the Academy's choice. In an article titled "Dylan's Time" he mentions that for the Elizabethans song lyrics and poetry were "interchangeable concepts," but by the middle of the twentieth century "an air of frivolity" pervaded songwriting. Popular songs—he mentions works by Cole Porter and Smokey Robinson—exhibited "verbal dexterity" but also "rapid evaporation." The lyrics were clever but not poetic. Dylan changed popular song writing, Sante argues, by creating "a climate in which lyrics were taken seriously" and he did that, he says, "through his ambiguity, his ability to throw down puzzles that continue to echo and to generate interpretations."[52]

---

48. Michael Gray, *Song and Dance Man III*, 83.
49. Ibid., 80.
50. Quoted by Johan Sennaro and Alistair Scrutton in "'Greatest Living Poet' Bob Dylan Wins Nobel Prize for Literature," Reuters, October 13, 2016, https://www.reuters.com/article/us-nobel-prize-literature-idUSKCN12D1A1 (accessed June 9, 2019).
51. Horace Engdahl, "Presentation Speech for the 2016 Nobel Prize in Literature," Nobel Prize.org, https://www.nobelprize.org/prizes/literature/2016/ceremony-speech/ (accessed July 15, 2018).
52. Luc Sante, "Dylan's Time," The *New York Review of Books*, October 13, 2016, https://www.nybooks.com/daily/2016/10/13/bob-dylan-nobel-prize (accessed July 19, 2019).

One way Dylan threw down puzzles was by filling his songs with what Allen Ginsberg, in an interview in 1995 with Peter Barry Chowka, calls "chains of flashing images."[53] In this interview Ginsberg describes a visit that Dylan and he made to Jack Kerouac's grave in Lowell, Massachusetts in early November 1975 during the Rolling Thunder Review Tour. This scene is included in *Renaldo and Clara,* Dylan's unsuccessful film, and in Martin Scorsese's 2019 film *Rolling Thunder Revue: A Bob Dylan Story*, which was assembled from editing proofs from Dylan's film. While standing at Kerouac's grave, Ginsberg says, Dylan took his (Ginsberg's) copy of Kerouac's book *Mexico City Blues* and began reading passages from it. When Ginsberg asked him "What do you know about that?" Dylan told him that someone had given it to him in 1959 in St. Paul and "it blew my mind." It was, Dylan told Ginsberg, "the first poetry that spoke to me in my own language." "So," concludes Ginsberg, "those chains of flashing images you get in Dylan, like 'the motorcycle black Madonna two-wheeled gypsy queen and her silver studded phantom lover,' they're influenced by Kerouac's chains of flashing images and spontaneous writing."[54]

The lines Ginsberg quotes here are again from Dylan's "Gates of Eden." Mike Marqusee argues that Dylan's "Chimes of Freedom," released a year before "Gates of Eden," was "both his last protest song and the first of those songs comprised of 'chains of flashing images' that make up the heart of his sixties canon."[55] Marqusee suggests it reveals the influence of Kenneth Patchen, a fervent pacifist during World War II who experimented with different forms of poetry and was a favorite of the beat writers. But he also sees the influence of Rimbaud and the French symbolists whom Dylan was reading at the time. He points out that the first four lines of each verse in "Chimes of Freedom" begin with convoluted images of thunder, lightning, and church bells. Dylan's use of these images, he says, is "a self-conscious exercise in the 'disarrangement of the senses' recommended by Rimbaud and the French Symbolists."[56] Rimbaud explained what he meant by "disarrangement of the senses" [*dérèglement de tous les sens*] in a letter to Paul Demeny:

---

53. Allen Ginsberg, interview by Peter Barry Chowka, Modern American Poetry, 1995. See "Online Interviews with Allen Ginsberg," http://www.english.illinois.edu/maps/poets/g_l/ginsberg/interviews.htm (accessed July 27, 2019).
54. Ibid.
55. Mike Marqusee, *Chimes of Freedom* (New York: The New Press, 2003), 93.
56. Ibid.

I say you have to be a visionary, make yourself a visionary. A Poet makes himself a visionary through a long, boundless, and systematized disarrangement of all the senses. All forms of love, of suffering, of madness; he searches himself, he exhausts within himself all poisons, and preserves their quintessences.[57]

Clinton Heylin also sees a Rimbaudian derangement of the senses in "Chimes of Freedom," and he finds this same feature also in "Mr. Tambourine Man."[58] (According to the Bob Dylan website, both songs were first played on the same day: May 17, 1964.) Heylin argues that "Chimes of Freedom" "reflected an important shift in Dylan's perception, a move toward the intensely poetic songs he would write later in the year."[59] Mike Marqusee, who titles his book *Chimes of Freedom*, makes a similar point twelve years later. He sees this song as marking a shift that Dylan made from "the plain-spoken rigors of the protest songs" to works that are more poetic.[60]

"Chimes of Freedom" is a wonderful song, the kind of song that would, it seems to me, impress members of the Nobel Prize selection committee. Its poetic chains of flashing images make it literary and its sentiments, its sympathy for all the downtrodden and suffering people of the world, give it a religious flavor. It is the "clinging of the church bells" that sends out poetic messages of tolerance, and so religion and poetry join forces to relieve the suffering of "each' an' ev'ry underdog soldier," for the "mistreated, mateless mother," for "the lonesome-hearted lovers with too personal a tale," etc. This song is, Dave Van Ronk says, Dylan's version of an old Irish song called "The Chimes of Trinity." Here is the chorus from this Irish song:

> *Tolling for the out-cast, tolling for the gay*
> *Tolling for the million-aire and friends long pass'd away*
> *But my heart is light and gay as I stroll down old Broadway*
> *And I listen to the chimes of Trin-i-ty[61]*

---

57. C. A. Hackett discusses Rimbaud's "disarrangement of the senses" in *Rimbaud: A Critical Introduction* (Cambridge: Cambridge University Press, 1981). See Chapter 6, "Illuminations," 48-84.
58. Clinton Heylin, *Bob Dylan: Behind the Shades* (New York: Simon & Schuster, 1991), 100-101.
59. Ibid., 100.
60. Mike Marqusee, *Chimes of Freedom*, 93.
61. "The Chimes of Trinity" was composed by M. J. Fitzpatrick in 1895. See "A Song to Charm All. The Chimes of Trinity: Song and Chorus," John Hopkins Sheridan Library, The Lester S. Levy Sheet Music Collection, https://levysheetmusic.mse.jhu.edu/collection/140/076 (accessed August 5, 2019).

In his memoir Dave Van Ronk talks about his Brooklyn Irish mother who all day long would sing songs that she had learned from her mother in Ireland. One day, he explains, Dylan heard him playing "Chimes of Trinity," a song Van Ronk's mother had sung. "He made me sing it for him a few times," Van Ronk says, "until he had the gist of it, then he reworked it into 'Chimes of Freedom.'"[62]

In 1988 Bruce Springsteen with the E-Street Band performed "Chimes of Freedom" on Amnesty International's "Human Rights Now" tour. It was an appropriate choice because Dylan includes falsely accused prisoners in his list of people for whom the church bells toll. They toll, he says in the fifth stanza, "for each unharmful, gentle soul misplaced inside a jail." Sting, The Police, Peter Gabriel, Youssou N'Dour, Joan Baez and U2 were also part of Springsteen's Amnesty tour. In his autobiography *Born to Run,* Springsteen describes performing "Chimes of Freedom" in concerts around the world, including England, Zimbabwe, the Ivory Coast, and Hungary.[63] A video of "The Boss" singing a rendition of "Chimes of Freedom" at the end of a sold-out concert at RFK Stadium in Philadelphia on September 19, 1988, is available online.[64] Springsteen leaves out the third and fourth stanzas. It's a moving performance, one I prefer to Dylan's performance on his album *Another Side of Bob Dylan,* perhaps because the setting was more dramatic. Dylan was singing in a studio whereas Springsteen was performing outdoors for thousands of fans while supporting Amnesty International. Also, for me, Dylan's nasalized voice is off-putting.

In order to officially receive the Nobel Prize for Literature (and $900,000), Dylan had to deliver a lecture, which he submitted on June 5, 2017. Dylan begins his speech with a comment that suggests that he, being a singer-songwriter, was surprised to receive this literary award. "I got to wondering," he says, "exactly how my songs related to literature."[65] In his talk he tries to answer this question but before doing so he talks about Buddy Holly, Dylan's inspiration when he was still in high school, who died in a plane crash in 1959; and about Leadbelly's "Cotton Fields," a song

62. Dave Van Ronk with Elijah Wald, *The Mayor of MacDougal Street: A Memoir* (Philadelphia: De Capo Press, 2006), 4.
63. Bruce Springsteen, *Born to Run* (New York: Simon & Schuster, 2016), 353-356.
64. Setlist.fm, "Bruce Springsteen: September 19 1988 Setlist," https://www.setlist.fm/setlist/bruce-springsteen/1988/john-f-kennedy-stadium-philadelphia-pa-13d7adf5.html (accessed August 5, 2019).
65. Ibid., 1.

he loved. In one long paragraph he mentions folk songs sung in the 1920's and 1930's: "Stagger Lee" (also known as Stackalee), "John the Revelator," "Frankie," "Lord Donald," and "When the Great Ship Went Down." (I discuss these songs and their influence on Dylan in the next chapter.) When he started writing his own songs, the "folk lingo" he picked up from listening to these songs was, Dylan says, "the only vocabulary that I knew, and I used it."[66]

But, he continues, he had something else as well: "principles and sensibilities and an informed view of the world" that he acquired in "grammar school" by reading canonical works in the Anglo-American literary tradition. He mentions *Don Quixote*, *Ivanhoe*, *Robinson Crusoe*, *Gulliver's Travels*, and *The Tale of Two Cities* before talking at greater length about three works: *Moby Dick*, *All Quiet on the Western Front*, and *The Odyssey*.[67] In an article for the *New Yorker* magazine about Dylan's Nobel lecture Alexandra Schwartz says that Dylan's "plainspoken descriptions" of these books "glow with an unexpected beauty and power." The books, she says, "are alive in him, and as he talks about them we, too, begin to see them afresh."[68] I had a similar reaction. I am the same age as Dylan and remember reading these works in junior high and high school and being moved by them in the same ways Dylan describes. Schwartz says Dylan writes about them "with a passion stripped of any pretense."[69] Stripped away, too, are any concerns about critical method: He simply explains how these works moved him and inspired him to tell similar tales in his songs. He is much more concerned about how these literary works made him feel than about what they mean. Dylan wanted to write songs that made people feel the way he felt when he read these great books in grammar school. He guesses that he got a Nobel prize in literature because members of the academy thought that he had succeeded in this endeavor. That is, I think, the "connection" between his songs and literature that he was searching for, the connection that he explains in an admittedly "roundabout way" in his Nobel prize lecture.

---

66. Ibid., 5.
67. Ibid., 6-20.
68. Alexandra Schwartz, "The Rambling Glory of Bob Dylan's Nobel Speech," *The New Yorker*, June 6, 2017, https://www.newyorker.com/culture/culture-desk/the-rambling-glory-of-bob-dylans-nobel-speech (accessed August 8, 2019).
69. Ibid.

21

DYLAN'S MUSICAL ROOTS: THE BASEMENT TAPES

D ylan's musical roots were in the folk tradition, not rock and roll. He liked folk songs because they did not sugarcoat life in America. Instead they talked about its violence and its weirdness and highlighted the tribulations of those who lived through difficult lives far removed from America's comfortable suburbs. Dylan explains in his autobiography that he did not want to write or sing gentle songs about gentle people because such songs reflected a "mainstream culture" that he thought was "lame as hell and a big trick."[1] He was attracted to the underbelly of American life. Folk songs were for him the underground story that, he says, he wanted to tell—"Songs about debauched bootleggers, mothers that drowned their own children, Cadillacs that only got five miles to the gallon, floods, union hall fires, darkness and cadavers at the bottom of rivers."[2] The folk songs he sang, presumably both the traditional songs he covered and those he wrote himself, were not, he says, "friendly or ripe with mellowness. They didn't come gently to the shore . . . They were not light entertainment."[3] The rock and roll songs he heard on the radio, however, were *not* the kind of songs he wanted to sing. He regarded them all, except those sung by Roy Orbison, as "strictly dullsville . . . gutless and flabby. It all came at you like you didn't have a brain." He kept turning the radio on, he explains, but

---

1. Bob Dylan, *Chronicles* (New York: Simon & Schuster, 2004), 35.
2. Ibid., 34.
3. Ibid.

"sadly, whatever it played reflected nothing but milk and sugar and not the real Jekyll and Hyde themes of the times."[4]

Many—perhaps most—popular love songs in the 1950s *were* insipid and silly. There were songs like "How Much Is That Doggie in the Window," in which a woman buys a dog for her sweetheart so he won't be lonely when she's on a trip to California. Sung by Patti Page, it was number one on the charts in 1953. Elvis Presley's "Let Me Be Your Teddy Bear," number one in 1957, contains these cute but rather silly lyrics:

> *I don't wanna be a tiger*
> *Cause tigers play too rough*
> *I don't wanna be a lion*
> *Cause lions ain't the kind*
> *You love enough.*
> *Just wanna be, your teddy bear*
> *Put a chain around my neck*
> *And lead me anywhere*
> *Oh let me be*
> *Your teddy bear.*

Dylan did compose rock and roll songs but the term "folk rock" is more accurate because in these songs, including his anti-love songs, Dylan was trying to express the honest and gritty truths of folk songs using the rock rhythms of popular music. "In the past," says Robert Shelton, "pop had dealt almost exclusively with sophomoric love." Dylan "matured the form."[5] "It was he," J. J. Goldberg says, "who showed us that pop songs could be about something."[6]

Dylan's hero and model was Woody Guthrie, sometimes referred to as the father of American folk music.[7] Dylan says that the first song "of any substantial importance" that he wrote, "Song to Woody," was a tribute to him.[8] "I'm a-singin' you the song, but I can't sing enough," Dylan tells Woody in this song. "Cause there's not many men that done the things that you've done." Guthrie traveled with migrant workers during the dust bowl years and sang about the people he met—buffalo skinners, prostitutes,

---

4. Ibid., 33-34.
5. Robert Shelton, *No Direction Home: The Life and Music of Bob Dylan* (Milwaukee, WI: Backbeat Books, 2011), 192.
6. J. J. Goldberg, "Bob Dylan at 60: 'We Used to be Young Together'; A Musical Seer Who Disdained Role of Prophet," *Forward*, May 18, 2001.
7. Dylan had a chance to meet his idol in New York in 1961 when Guthrie was very sick with Huntington's chorea. He died in 1967. See Robert Shelton, *No Direction Home*, 80.
8. Bob Dylan, *Chronicles*, 54.

hobos, miners, and steel workers. Here's a stanza from Guthrie's "Hard Travelin'":

> *I've been hittin' some hard harvestin', I thought you knowed*
> *North Dakota to Kansas City, way down the road*
> *Cuttin' that wheat, stackin' that hay, and I'm tryin' make about a*
> *dollar a day*
> *And I've been havin' some hard travelin', lord*

In this "hard-travelin'" tradition the speaker is often moving on to some new adventure. There's no time for self-pity. Sometimes he has to leave a woman he loves behind, but the compensation is the freedom represented by the open road ahead. Dylan had other heroes, however, besides Woody Guthrie. He was influenced by a host of singers and songwriters, quite a few of them older than Guthrie, who were rediscovered during the folk revival of the 1950s. They are the artists who sang the folk songs that helped Dylan connect with what Greil Marcus calls "the old weird America," a phrase which became the title of a book he wrote about Dylan's basement tapes.[9] A reviewer of Marcus's book describes this world as "the playground of God, Satan, tricksters, Puritans, confidence men, Illuminati, braggarts, preachers, anonymous poets of all stripes."[10]

Dylan began his career in the midst of the folk revival and the "founding document" of that revival, Greil Marcus argues, was Harry Smith's *Anthology of American Folk Music*.[11] Released in 1952, it is a collection of six LPs on which are found 84 American folk, blues, gospel, and country songs that were originally recorded from 1927 to 1932. The songs on the *Anthology* were, David Janssen and Edward Whitelock say, "artifacts from a world that was disappearing at the very moment they were being recorded. Past was being made into permanent present via the scratching of a stylus on wax."[12] The folk singers on Smith's *Anthology*— people like Dock Boggs, Clarence Ashley, Blind Lemon Jefferson, Blind Willie Johnson, Cannon's Jug Stompers, Elders McIntorsh and the Edwards Sanctified Singers—appeared in the 1950s, Greil Marcus says, "like visitors from another world, like passengers on a ship that had drifted into the

---

9. Greil Marcus, *The Old, Weird America* (New York: Picador, 2011).
10. This description by Luc Sante appears on the back cover of *The Old, Weird America*. Sante's review appeared in *New York* magazine.
11. Greil Marcus, *The Old, Weird America*, 85.
12. David Janssen and Edward Whitelock, *Apocalypse Jukebox: The End of the World in American Popular Music* (Brooklyn, NY: Soft Skull Press, 2009), 77.

sea of the unwritten."[13] Some folk song enthusiasts thought the singers on the *Anthology* were all dead, but many were still living and singing and as the folk revival gained momentum, they were invited to perform. At the 1963 Newport Jazz Festival the following singers, all represented on the *Anthology*, shared the stage with Bob Dylan and Joan Baez and other younger folk singers: Dock Boggs, Mississippi John Hurt, Clarence Ashley, Buell Kazee, and Sara and Maybelle Carter.[14]

Smith's *Anthology* was tremendously influential. For folk singers in Greenwich Village in the 1950s, Dave Van Ronk has written, "The *Anthology* was our bible. We all knew every word of every song on it, including the ones we hated."[15] Dylan listened to the *Anthology* LP's in 1959-1960 when he was still in Minnesota. His hunger to listen to and learn from these records was so intense that he stole them, along with some other folk records, from a friend named Jan Pankake, a university student and banjo player. Pankake confronted Dylan, they fought, and eventually Dylan returned most of the records.[16] Smith's *Anthology* became, Greil Marcus says, Dylan's "first true map of a republic that was still a hunch to him."[17] "The old, weird America" is Marcus's name for this republic—for the "territory that opens up out of the *Anthology*."[18] The title of Marcus's first edition was "Invisible Republic," a title chosen by both his publisher in the United Kingdom and Henry, Holt and Company in New York. ("The Old, Weird America" *was*, however, used as a title of Chapter Four.) Editors at Picador, which published his second edition in 2011, agreed to call it "The Old, Weird America," the title that Marcus says he always preferred. In his note to his updated edition published in 2011, he explains that the title "Invisible Republic" was so vague and forgettable that people commenting on the book avoided it and used "The Old, Weird America" instead. Marcus was delighted when the publishers of his second edition agreed to use the title he preferred. This new edition is essentially the same book but with an updated discography section—a more complete catalogue of all the songs referred to as "basement tapes."[19]

---

13. Greil Marcus, *The Old, Weird America*, 92.
14. Ibid., 188.
15. Greil Marcus quotes Dave Van Ronk in *The Old, Weird America*, 85-86.
16. Howard Sounes, *Down the Highway: The Life of Bob Dylan* (New York: Grove Press, 2001) 57-60.
17. Greil Marcus, *The Old, Weird America*, 86.
18. Ibid., 87.
19. Ibid., xiv, xv.

In his book Marcus calls the world revealed in the *Anthology of American Folk Music* "Smithville," a name which recognizes the work of Harry Smith, the compiler of this important collection. By whatever name it is known, this "world" is similar to the world evoked in many of Dylan's songs, particularly those recorded on his "basement songs."

Dylan and the Band—known at the time as the Hawks—began recording these basement songs in the spring of 1967 and sessions continued into the following year. The songs—over 100 in all—were recorded first in the Red Room at Dylan's place in Woodstock, New York, where Dylan was recovering from a motorcycle accident. Later they were recorded in the basement—hence the term "basement tapes"—of a house in West Saugerties, near Woodstock that they called the Big Pink (because it had pink siding). The atmosphere of the recording sessions was casual and somewhat haphazard. "The procedure," Clinton Heylin says, "was to work up an arrangement of a song, either an original or a cover, and, if they liked it, record it on a basic reel-to-reel using just three microphones."[20]

According to Robbie Robertson, the Band's lead guitarist, Dylan "would pull these songs out of nowhere. We didn't know if he wrote them or if he remembered them. When he sang them, you couldn't tell."[21] He would find an old song and say "Maybe there's a *new* song to be had here."[22] Garth Hudson, the Band's organ and piano player, says that some of the songs were "old ballads and traditional songs, some were written by Bob, but others would be songs Bob made up as he went along. We'd play the melody [and] he'd sing a few words he'd written or else just mouth sounds or syllables. It was a pretty good way to write songs."[23]

What music historians call "The Basement Tapes" are tapes of songs recorded by Dylan and the Band in Woodstock in 1967. In August 1967 Dylan had Dwarf Music, a music publisher jointly owned by Dylan and his manager, Albert Grossman, send out ten songs as demos for other artists to cover. Among the artists who responded were Peter, Paul and Mary, who recorded the basement song, "Too Much of Nothing," and Manfred Mann, who released a version of "The Mighty Quinn."[24] In 1968 Dwarf Music released a fourteen-song acetate of publishing demos

---

20. Clinton Heylin, *Bob Dylan: Behind the Shades* (New York: Summit Books, 1991), 181.
21. Greil Marcus quotes Robbie Robertson in *The Old, Weird America*, xxiv.
22. Greil Marcus quotes Robbie Robertson in *The Old, Weird America*, 234.
23. Sid Griffin quotes Hudson in *Million Dollar Bash: Bob Dylan, The Band, and The Basement Tapes* (London: Jawbone Press, 2007), 104.
24. Clinton Heylin, *Bob Dylan: Behind the Shades*, 182.

of basement songs. The first official appearance of the basement songs was in 1975 when Columbia released twenty-four songs on an album called *The Basement Tapes*. These basement tapes, however, are perhaps the most bootlegged recordings of all time. According to Greil Marcus there has been "more than thirty years of scattershot bootlegging," He says they appear "most definitively, regarding both sound and performances," on *A Tree with Roots: The Genuine Basement Tape Remasters/The Genuine Tapes Revisited*. This four-cd set was released in 2001 by Wild Wolf bootleg, a name that doesn't suggest attention to detail, but Greil Marcus says it includes "all circulating basement performances with Dylan leading."[25]

In the early 1990s Dylan released two albums of traditional songs, *Good as I Been to You* (1992) and *World Gone Wrong* (1993). Songs on these albums were not, strictly speaking, basement songs—they were not recorded at the Big Pink—but they resemble them. These albums, Greil Marcus says, "were a continuation of the story the basement tapes told, or an unlocking of their laboratory."[26] Almost all the songs on these two albums are covers of traditional blues, folk, and country songs. Their appearance twenty-five years after Dylan began recording the basement tapes suggests that Dylan's fascination with old songs—those collected on Henry Smith's *Anthology* and others like them—was no passing fancy.

One can, in fact, detect the influence of Smith's *Anthology* in many Dylan albums, not just those released during the folk revival in the early 1960s. On his first album, *Bob Dylan* (1962), Dylan sings a song by Blind Lemon Jefferson, "See That My Grave Is Kept Clean," that is included on the *Anthology*; and the title track on his 2012 album *Tempest* seems to be inspired by William and Versey Smith's "When That Great Ship Went Down," also on the *Anthology*.[27] Dylan's idol, Woody Guthrie, also sang this song. Greil Marcus, however, whose *Old, Weird America* is about the influence of Smith's *Anthology* on Dylan, is not really interested in tracing a specific basement song back to a song that Harry Smith included in his *Anthology*, though he does that occasionally. None of the songs on the official album, *The Basement Tapes* (released in 1975, recorded in 1967), appear to be a cover or close imitation of a song on the *Anthology*.

---

25. Greil Marcus, *The Old, Weird America*, 235.
26. Ibid., xxiv.
27. Richard Rabbit Brown's "The Sinking of the Titanic" may also have inspired Dylan. It's not on the *Anthology* but another song by Brown is— "James Alley Blues," a song that Dylan covered in the early 1960s. Dylan's version of "James Alley Blues" appears on the bootleg album *The Minnesota Tapes*.

Robert Shelton describes the songs on this album as a "catalogue of chanteys, old blues, early rock, and truck-driver, hoedown, gospel, and folk songs."[28] Members of Dylan's band make clear that Dylan had all kinds of songs running through his head when he composed the so-called basement songs. What Greil Marcus *does* argue is that the "old, weird America" portrayed in the basement tapes resembles "Smithville," the world portrayed in the songs Harry Smith collected in his *Anthology of American Folk Music*.

What are the similarities? One, according to Marcus, is that the Bible is everywhere in both places.[29] Fifteen of the songs in Harry Smith's *Anthology* are explicitly Christian songs. There is, for example, a 1927 recording of Sister Mary Nelson singing "Judgment":

> *The gamblers, the drunkards, the liars*
> *And the adulterers, too*
> *Well, all these false pretenders*
> *And all them hypocrites, too*
>
> *Better get ready for judgment!*
> *You better get ready for judgment morning!*
> *You better get ready for judgment!*
> *My God is coming down*[30]

The *Anthology* also contains a 1930 recording of Blind Willie Johnson's "John the Revelator" (1930), a song that sums up the entire Christian narrative—Adam's sin, Christ's sacrifice, and the resurrection. "John the Revelator" is a call and response song about John of Patmos, the writer of the Book of Revelation, which was Dylan's favorite part of the Bible. In his gravelly voice Blind Willie Johnson calls out "Well who's that writin'?" and a female voice responds "John the Revelator." "What's John writin'?," asks Blind Willie, and then he and the female singer together reply, "A book of the seven seals."[31]

Some of Dylan's basement songs are explicitly Christian songs—"Sign of the Cross" and "I Shall Be Released," for example. In the first song, the speaker worries about the "old sign of the cross," the "key to the kingdom."

---

28. Robert Shelton, *No Direction Home*, 266.
29. Greil Marcus, *The Old, Weird America*, 124-125.
30. Dylan sounds a similar warning in two songs he wrote after his conversion, "When You Gonna Wake Up?" (1979) and "Are You Ready?" (1980).
31. The seven seals, described in Revelation, chapters 5-8, are the seals on the scroll that John of Patmos saw. The scroll is an apocalyptic document describing terrible events that will occur before Christ returns.

I may not see you again, the speaker says, and so I want to tell you "one time" that "the sign on the cross is what you need the most." In "I Shall Be Released"—probably the most famous basement tape song, a work that has been covered by 164 singers[32]—Dylan sees the "light come shining / From the west unto the east," a reference to Matthew 24:27.[33] Other basement songs are not so obviously Christian, but many are, like the songs in Smith's *Anthology*, very moralistic. Smith's *Anthology*, Janssen and Whitelock argue, is "a radically moral collection of songs reflecting the strong thread of moral righteousness that runs through America's history and people."[34] One detects this same thread in Dylan's basement songs (and, some argue, in his entire oeuvre).[35]

The presence of violence is another similarity between the songs in Smith's *Anthology* and Dylan's basement songs. Songs in the *Anthology* may be "radically moral," as Janssen and Whitelock argue, but many tell stories of violent crimes. More violence ensues when the guilty—and sometimes the innocent—are punished. The radical morality of many songs is a quick and crude frontier justice. Crimes—not petty thievery but gruesome acts of passion and revenge—are committed in both "Smithville" and Dylan's "old, weird America." Greil Marcus refers to both Smithville and Dylan's world as Kill Devil Hills, the name of a real town in North Carolina where, in 1995, a father killed three of his children before committing suicide. By linking Dylan's world to Kill Devil Hills Marcus, in my opinion, exaggerates the amount of violence in the basement songs, but perhaps not by much if one considers, as Marcus does, the songs on the albums *Good as I Been to You* and *World Gone Wrong* as a "continuation" of the basement tape story.[36] Because the topic of murder is so pervasive in *World Gone Wrong* this album could have been titled *Murder Ballads*.

Acts of violence are described in 15 of the 27 songs in the first volume of Smith's *Anthology*. Some are variants of old ballads listed in Francis James Child's collection *English and Scottish Popular Ballads* (1882-1898).

---

32. Sid Griffith lists all the covers in *Million Dollar Bash*.
33. "For as the lightning cometh out of the east, and shineth even unto the west; so shall also the coming of the Son of man be."
34. David Janssen and Edward Whitelock, *Apocalypse Jukebox*, 66.
35. Francis J. Beckwith, for example, argues that Dylan is judgmental and moralistic in all his songs, not just his explicitly Christian works, a point I will return to in Chapter Twenty-Five. See "Busy Being Born Again: Bob Dylan's Christian Philosophy," in *Bob Dylan and Philosophy*, ed. Peter Vernezze and Carl J. Porter (Chicago: Open Court, 2006), 145-155.
36. Greil Marcus, *The Old, Weird America*, xxiv.

Murder ballads originally were, Paul Slade explains, "tabloid newspapers set to music, carrying news of all the latest horrible murders to an insatiable public."[37] They were written and sold on the streets soon after the crimes were committed. Women as well as men commit violent acts in *Anthology* songs. Dick Justice's "Henry Lee" (1932), the first song on the *Anthology*, is a variant of "Lady Isabel and the Elf Knight," an old English ballad. The song is about a girl who lures a man to bed and then kills him with a pen knife. She wants a bird, who witnesses the act, to land on her knee so she can hush it forever, but the wise bird declines: "I can't fly down, or I won't fly down, and alight on your right knee / A girl would murder her own true love would kill a little bird like me." Dylan's version of this song, "Love Henry," is included on *World Gone Wrong*.

In "Frankie," sung by Mississippi John Hurt, Frankie shoots Albert, her lover, three times in a saloon because he had another woman on his arm. The narrator and one of the two bartenders in the song agree that she had a right to shoot him because Albert "did her wrong." Dylan's version of this song, "Frankie and Albert," appears on *Good as I Been to You*. A killing in another *Anthology* song would appear to be far less justified. In "Stackalee," recorded by Frank Hutchison, Stackalee shoots a father of three children because he stole his John B. Stetson hat! Dylan's cover of this song appears on *World Gone Wrong*.

Why did Smith, Dylan, Pete Seeger, Joan Baez, and many other singers become fascinated with these old traditional songs? Why were famous folk singers and their fans, including privileged college students like myself, singing songs like "Tom Dooley," an old song first recorded in 1929 that tells the story of a man who stabs the woman he loves and is later hanged?[38] How, in other words, does one explain the folk revival of the late 50s and 60s? This was a tumultuous period in American history, a period that included worries about nuclear war, racial tensions, the Tết Offensive in Vietnam, and the assassinations of Martin Luther King, Jr., President John F. Kennedy, and Senator Robert Kennedy. Greil Marcus suggests that young people were looking for "peace and home in the midst of noise and upheaval," and they found it in these old songs. "It was this purity, this glimpse of a democratic oasis unsullied by commerce or greed,

---

37. Paul Slade, "Murder Ballads: An Introduction," http://www.planetslade.com/murder. html (accessed November 18, 2013).
38. "Tom Dooley" is not in Smith's *Anthology*, but it easily could have been because it was first recorded by G. B. Grayson and Henry Whitter in 1929. G. B. Grayson's recording of a similar murder ballad, "Ommie Wise," *is* included in Smith's *Anthology*.

that in the late 1950s and early 1960s so many young people began to hear in the blues and ballads first recorded in the 1920s and 1930s, by people mostly from small towns and tiny settlements in the South. . . . It was the sound of another country—a country that, once glimpsed from afar, could be felt within oneself. That was the folk revival."[39]

Marcus's point about young people being tired of commerce and greed sounds plausible, but why the fascination with old songs about gruesome crimes? One can understand why people were singing, along with Pete Seeger and Peter, Paul, and Mary: "If I Had a Hammer / I'd hammer out love between my brothers and my sisters / All over this land." But why were old English murder ballads suddenly popular? David Janssen and Edward Whitelock suggest that it is because people feared the apocalypse was near. "Smith's collection," they argue, "is a patently American apocalyptic text," because in their view Smith was worried about an "Atomic apocalypse" and so collected traditional songs "to submerge his listeners into an alternate vision/version of America in all its diversity, beauty, ugliness, and violence." He wanted to invoke "a new collective consciousness, one that will not be so fast with a finger on the button."[40] Greil Marcus suggests Dylan's basement tapes were similarly motivated. The primal dramas enacted in the songs Smith collected appealed to Dylan, Marcus says, because the language in vogue in the 1960s—"the political languages of right and left, the aesthetic languages of corruption and purity"—were, "in comparison to those Smith gathered, impoverished" and therefore incapable of describing the violence and crimes that were occurring in the world.[41] Dylan, Marcus says, wanted to begin a dialogue between the old voices and the new. As you revived and sang these old songs, Marcus says, "you might find yourself less impressed by the crimes of your own time than you once were, and [be] drawn to the possibility of fashioning a country of your own—a country where both you and the old voices that spoke to you might converse and feel at home."[42]

But how would these old songs keep people's fingers off the nuclear trigger? Quite a few of the characters who appear in these old songs have itchy trigger fingers. Frankie, Tom Dooley, Stackalee, for example—are quick to shoot (or stab, or drown) people who, in their view, have wronged

---

39. Greil Marcus, *The Old, Weird America*, 20-21.
40. David Janssen and Edward Whitelock, *Apocalypse Jukebox*, 65-66.
41. Greil Marcus, *The Old, Weird America*, 131.
42. Ibid., 132.

them. "Violence is as American as apple pie," H. Rapp Brown, leader of the Student Nonviolent Coordinating Committee, said in 1967, the year the basement tapes were recorded. These old American songs support his contention. It seems possible that both Smith and Dylan wanted to face up to the violence at the heart of the American experience. Janssen and Whitelock say that Harry Smith wanted to avert an "atomic future" by "singing it down." "Sing it down! This is what his text [the *Anthology*] sets out to do," they argue.[43] Singing songs of violence, like those included in volume one of the *Anthology*, can, they suggest, provide "a safe cathartic release of pent-up urges and impure thoughts. Sometimes we turn to music to uphold our moral longings, at others we turn to music to play out the fantasies of our immoral desires. In these songs, listeners get to take a walk on the wild side without leaving the turntable's side."[44] As they revived these old songs in the 1960s, perhaps Dylan in that basement at the Big Pink and many other folksingers—and the fans like me who sang along with them—were trying to sing down the violence, not only the violence we saw in the world around us, but that which lay deep in our own hearts and minds.

In February 2015, Dylan received a "Person of the Year" award from MusiCares, a charity to help musicians who are suffering financially or in bad health. In his acceptance speech he touches on different topics. He thanks people who had helped him along the way, including John Hammond, a producer at Columbia Records; the Staple Singers, Johnny Cash, and Joan Baez. He also attacks critics for singling him out, for saying that he had various defects—that he had a bad voice and croaked like a frog, that he couldn't carry a tune and talked through his songs, that he slurred his words. Other singers had these same defects, he argues, but have not been criticized. In this speech Dylan also talks about his musical roots—about where his songs came from, and in doing so he opens up a window into his composing process. "These songs," he says, "didn't come out of thin air. I didn't make them up out of whole cloth . . . It all came out of traditional music: traditional folk music, traditional rock 'n' roll and traditional big-band swing orchestra music."[45]

---

43. David Janssen and Edward Whitelock, *Apocalypse Jukebox*, 66.
44. Ibid., 67.
45. Bob Dylan, "MusiCares Person of Year Speech." Randall Roberts has transcribed Bob Dylan's speech. See "Grammys 2015: Transcript of Bob Dylan's MusiCares Person of Year Speech," Pop & Hiss: The L.A. Times Music Blog, http://www.latimes.com/enter-

Before mentioning some rock and roll and band music that he admires, Dylan provides six interesting examples of how traditional folk songs— works from that "old weird America" that Greil Marcus describes— inspired songs that he wrote. The composing process in general is complex, and how one song inspires a songwriter to write another is mysterious, but Dylan offers some hints in this speech. He mentions six traditional songs that inspired him to write a song of his own. For example, Dylan suggests a link between "Key to the Highway," a song by Big Bill Broonzy, and his own "Highway 61 Revisited." Big Bill Broonzy was an African American blues singer and songwriter who began his career in the 1920s. Dylan mentions the opening lines of "Key to the Highway," saying that he sang that song a lot, and tells the audience if they had too they "just might write" lines like these from "Highway 61 Revisited": "Georgia Sam he had a bloody nose / Welfare Department they wouldn't give him no clothes," etc. (In his speech he reads the entire second stanza of "Highway 61 Revisited.") Except for the fact that in both Broonzy's song and Dylan's events happen on a highway, there is no obvious link between these two songs.

Dylan mentions a link between traditional "Come all you" songs and his "Masters of War" that is less obscure but not at all obvious. Dylan quotes the opening lines of some of the "Come all you" songs that he has sung: "The Old Chisholm Trail," "The Death of Floyd Collins," "Come All Ye Fair and Tender Ladies," and "Pretty Boy Floyd." If you had sung all these songs, Dylan says, then you would be writing "Masters of War," a song which begins "Come you masters of war / You that build all the guns." During the folk revival of the 1960s some people might have noticed this link but I suspect it went unnoticed by most fans. Dylan borrowed the melody of this song from "Fair Nottamun Town," a very old folk song. He borrowed his arrangement from Jean Ritchie, a singer, songwriter, and dulcimer player from Kentucky. According to Howard Sounes, Ritchie sued Dylan, whose lawyers paid her $5,000.[46]

Another link between a traditional song and one of his own that Dylan mentions is between the traditional song "John Henry" and his "Blowin' in the Wind." John Henry, an African American and an ex-slave, was a legendary character in the South. He was a "steel-driving man" whose job

---

tainment/music/posts/la-et-ms-grammys-2015-transcript-of-bob-dylans-musicares-person-of-year-speech-20150207-story.html (accessed February 8, 2015).
46. Howard Sounes, *Down the Highway*, 132.

was to hammer a drill into rocks to make a hole for explosives that would blow up the rocks and enable railroad tunnels to be built. Dylan took his tune for "Blowin' in the Wind" from "No More Auction Block for Me," an old spiritual that Dylan sang at the Gaslight Café in Greenwich Village in 1962. A recording of him singing this spiritual at the Gaslight appears on *The Bootleg Series Volumes 1-3* (1991). Lots of songs with similar lyrics have been written about John Henry. Lines Dylan quotes in his MusiCares award speech suggest that the version Dylan sang was the same, or very similar to, the version Pete Seeger sang which appears on his *Favorite Ballads, Vol. 1* released in 1957.

"If you sang 'John Henry' as many times as I did," Dylan says in his speech, "you'd have written 'How many roads must a man walk down?' too." The theme that links this old ballad to Dylan's "Blowin' in the Wind," it seems to me, is human dignity and indignity. How accomplished and hardworking does a person have to be before you recognize his or her worth? "How many roads must a man walk down / Before you call him a man?" And why were dignified hardworking people like John Henry ever subjected to the indignity and cruelty of slavery? And why are so many people around the world still deprived of basic freedoms? "Yes, 'n' how many years can some people exist / Before they're allowed to be free?"

Dylan suggests a link between "Sail Away Ladies" and his "Boots of Spanish Leather." Dylan does not explain the link. The earliest known recording of "Sail Away Ladies," which is included on Harry Smith's *Anthology of American Folk Music*, is a solo fiddle tune. Few versions have the same lyrics but most of the versions I could find, including Odetta's, begin with the lines "It ain't no use to sit and cry / You'll be an angel by and by," lines that probably were running around in Dylan's head when he wrote "Don't Think Twice, It's All Right," which begins "It ain't no use to sit and wonder why, babe / It don't matter anyhow." The link between "Sail Away Ladies" and "Boots of Spanish Leather" is probably the image of a lady (singular, in Dylan's song) sailing away. Robert Shelton says Dylan's song was "probably sparked by" Suze Rotolo's leaving on a boat for a long stay in Italy in 1962.[47]

After giving these examples of traditional songs that inspired him, Dylan suggests that we could have written these songs too. "There's nothing secret about it," he told his audience. "You just do it subliminally

---

47. Robert Shelton, *No Direction Home*, 153.

and unconsciously, because that's all enough, and that's all I sang. That was all that was dear to me. They were the only kinds of songs that made sense." Dylan is being modest, not mentioning the talent it takes to write so many songs that so many people love, but I think in this speech he helps us understand how important his total immersion in songs from that old, weird America that Marcus describes was to his success. Dylan's speech reminded me of Stephen Krashen's views of language acquisition. Krashen talks about the "input hypothesis"—the idea that to learn to read and write a first or second language one must find "comprehensible input" and immerse oneself in it.[48] Dylan immersed himself in American folk, blues, gospel, and country songs and the result of that input, mixed with talent, led to some amazing contributions to the American songbook.

---

48. Stephen D. Krashen, *The Input Hypothesis: Issues and Implications* (New York: Longman, 1985).

III

TWO VERY DIFFERENT RELIGIOUS TRADITIONS

22

BUDDHISM IN VIETNAM

BUDDHISM: ONE OF THE "THREE TEACHINGS" [*TAM GIÁO*]
Vietnam borders China, but it is also not far from India and is close to other Southeast Asian countries where a variety of religions have flourished. As a result of its location, Vietnam has been home to followers of Buddhism, Taoism, Confucianism, Christianity, Hinduism, and Islam. All these religions still have followers today in the Socialist Republic of Vietnam, where, according to Philip Taylor, people are becoming "re-enchanted" with religion.[1] The faith of most Vietnamese, however, can be described as an amalgamation of Confucianism, Buddhism and Taoism [Nho Giáo, Phật Giáo, Lão Giáo], a combination summed up in the Sino-Vietnamese expression "Tam giáo đồng nguyên" [The three teachings are one]. Spirit worship and ancestor worship are also important parts of the religious life of Vietnamese. Because I believe that for Trịnh Công Sơn Buddhism was the most important element in this amalgamation and continues to be the most important element for most citizens of Huế, I emphasize it in this and coming chapters. In this first chapter, however, I will first comment briefly on spirit worship, ancestor worship and Taoism. Then, drawing on Cuong Tu Nguyen's book Zen in Medieval Vietnam and works by other

---

1. Philip Taylor, "Modernity and Re-enchantment in Post-Revolutionary Vietnam," in Modernity and Re-enchantment: Religion in Post-revolutionary Vietnam, ed. Philip Taylor (Singapore: Institute of Southeast Asian Studies, 2007), 2-56. Taylor's introduction to his collection of articles has nearly the same title as the complete collection.

scholars, I will discuss how Buddhism and Confucianism have co-existed throughout much of Vietnam's history.

SPIRIT WORSHIP, ANCESTOR WORSHIP AND TAOISM

Philip Taylor describes spirit worship, sometimes called animism, as a "Southeast Asian cultural substrate, an 'endemic religion' tied to place and enduring through time."[2] It is difficult to distinguish spirit worship from ancestor worship. The Vietnamese believe that the dead are living with them, that they are invisible but present—close to them "like sunlight," in the words of a Vietnamese scholar.[3] At Tết, the lunar new year, ancestors are invited back to join their living descendants and celebrate the transition to a new year with them. In death anniversaries, referred to as "kỵ" or "*giỗ*," food is placed on the family altar for the deceased relative. Relatives of the deceased bow [*vái*] and prostrate themselves [*lạy*] in front of the altar and then, after the ancestors have enjoyed the food, it is taken from the altar and eaten by family members.

But Vietnamese believe in many spirits besides ancestral spirits. Most villages have a patron deity that is supposed to watch over and protect it. Sometimes these deities are animals but they may also be the village founder or a famous historical figure. There are bad spirits and good spirits. In some families children are given unattractive nicknames, or "house names" [*tên ở nhà*], to prevent their being seized by a ghost [*bị ma bắt*]. A boy, for example, might be named "penis" [*cu*]. Within the family Vietnamese children are often identified by indicating their family ranking—as "second sister" [*chị hai*] or "third brother" [*anh ba*], for example. In the South, however, the all-important first son is never called "first brother." Instead he is called "second brother" [*anh hai*]. The first son's true ranking in the family is disguised to protect him from evil spirits.

When I lived with a family in Huế, I'd wash my clothes and would sometimes forget to bring them in before nightfall. Someone in the family would always remind me to take my clothes in, or else spirits or ghosts would inhabit them. Clearly, for Vietnamese, departed ancestors and spirits of all kinds are nearer and more numerous than they are for most Americans. As Philip Taylor, a scholar who has written extensively about

---

2. Ibid., 16.
3. Trần Văn Chương, *Essai sur l'esprit du droit sino-annamite* (Paris: 1922). Nguyen Van Huyen quotes this scholar in *The Ancient Civilization of Vietnam* (Hanoi: Thế Giới, 1995), 61.

religion in Vietnam, puts it, "Among the most pervasive beliefs in Vietnam is the view that spirits [*thần thánh*] co-inhabit alongside the living."[4]

It is difficult, Hue-Tam Ho Tai says, to distinguish Taoism in Vietnam from spirit worship. Hue-Tam Ho Tai explains that when Taoism came to Vietnam during the Chinese occupation (111 BC to 939 CE) "it had lost its original identity as the philosophy of Lao Tzu and his disciples, and had come to refer to magic practices, animist beliefs, and popular religion in general. Geomancers, horoscope-casters, I-ching diviners, fortune-tellers, spirit-mediums, faith-healers, and all sorts of wonder-workers . . . were labeled as Taoist priests" even though in many cases they had, she says, "scant understanding of the teachings of Lao Tzu."[5] Mark W. McLeod and Nguyen Thi Dieu suggest that these Taoist priests were accepted because "they must have looked like sophisticated practitioners of the same magical or spirit-worshipping arts that Yueh [Việt] peoples had known since pre-Chinese times." The "Taoist pantheon's deities," these scholars say, "blended easily into the Vietnamese spiritual universe."[6]

One Taoist belief that survives in Vietnam involves the Kitchen God, referred to as Ông Táo, Ông Vua Bếp, or Thần Bếp.[7] Belief in a Kitchen God is common in China and other East Asian countries, but beliefs regarding him differ. In Vietnam stories about this god involve two men and a woman and he is thought to be a three-person god, the three persons linked to the three stones or tripod on which a cooking pot is placed. He is generally referred to in the singular, however—as Ông Táo.

According to popular belief, on the twenty-third day of the twelfth month in the lunar calendar, the Ông Táo of each household goes up to heaven to present a report on the family to the Jade Emperor [Ngọc Hoàng], the Taoist supreme being. Ông Táo is therefore frequently depicted as an old man reading a scroll. If Ông Táo's report is positive the Jade Emperor may bestow blessings on the family in the coming year. Kitchens in Huế often contain a small altar, complete with incense sticks and a candle, which are burned to encourage Ông Táo to look after the family. The kitchen is important in Vietnamese families, Huỳnh Ngọc

4. Philip Taylor, "Modernity and Re-enchantment," 15.
5. Hue-Tam Ho Tai, "Religion in Vietnam: A World of Gods and Spirits," *The Vietnam Forum* 10 (Summer-Fall, 1987), 121.
6. Mark W. McLeod and Nguyen Thi Dieu, *Culture and Customs of Vietnam* (Westport, CT: Greenwood Press, 2001), 48.
7. See Patrick McCallister and Thi Cam Tu Luckman, "The Kitchen God Returns to Heaven [Ông Táo Về Trời]: Popular Culture, Social Knowledge, and Folk Beliefs in Vietnam," *Journal of Vietnamese Studies* 10 (Winter 2015), 110-150.

Trảng explains, because it "symbolizes life together, the family's warm roof, the relationship between men and women, and the love, cooperation and sustenance of the fire" that it provides.[8] Sometimes at Lunar New Year parties a worker in a government office or a business, or a high school or university student, will dress up as the Kitchen God and present a partly humorous, partly serious report, written in verse, to the Jade Emperor.

BUDDHISM

Let me now turn to Buddhism, which, for Trịnh Công Sơn, was the most important "teaching" of the aforementioned "Three Teachings" (Confucianism, Buddhism, and Taoism). Some people say all three teachings came to Vietnam from China, but Buddhism was first introduced to the Red River delta by Indian monks who arrived by sea or overland from the north in the first or second century AD.[9] Under Chinese rule this delta area was called *Giao Chỉ* [Ch. *Jiaozhi*]. Later it became a district within Giao Province, or *Giao Châu* [Ch. *Jiaozhou*]. Thích Nhất Hạnh says that Giao Châu in the second century A.D. was "a rest station for Buddhist missionaries traveling by sea between India and China and vice versa."[10] Giao Chỉ, particularly its administrative center, Luy Lâu, was, Keith Weller Taylor says, "a center for the diffusion of Buddhism into China."[11] According to Minh Chi et al., it was at Luy Lâu that what is thought to be one of the first books about Buddhism in the Chinese script was written.[12]

Buddhism was founded in what is now Nepal toward the end of the sixth century BCE by a man named Siddhartha Gautama. His father was head of the Sakya clan, and he could have led a comfortable, privileged life, but at the age of twenty-nine he left home, renounced his inheritance, and went into the wilderness to search for a way to end people's suffering. For six years he traveled and studied and practiced harsh disciplines with a band of five ascetics. Then one day after a long night of meditation under a Bodhi tree in the state of Bihar, India, he achieved Nirvana and

---

8. Huỳnh Ngọc Trảng, "The Kitchen God Returns to the Heavens," *Vietnam Heritage* 1, no. 4 (2014), 7.

9. Keith Weller Taylor says that Buddhist influence from India continued in later centuries. "As late as the T'ang times [618-906 CE]," he says, "the primary Buddhist influence" came from India, not from China, "in spite of Vietnam's political attachment to the Chinese empire." See Keith Weller Taylor, *The Birth of Vietnam* (Berkeley, CA: University of California Press, 1983), 83.

10. Thích Nhất Hạnh, *Lotus in a Sea of Fire* (New York: Hill and Wang, 1967), 4.

11. Keith Weller Taylor, *The Birth of Vietnam*, 80.

12. Minh Chi et al. are referring to *Lý Hoặc Luận* [Truth Illusion Metaphysics] by Mâu Tử. See Minh Chi, Ha Van Tan, and Nguyen Tai Thu, *Buddhism in Vietnam* (Hanoi: The Gioi, 1993), 16.

discovered a method to help others liberate themselves from suffering. He explained his method to the five ascetics in the Deer Park near Benares, India. He called it the Middle Way because it avoided the extremes of sensual pleasure and excessive asceticism. At the heart of his method are the Four Noble Truths. The first truth is that life involves *dukkha*, which is usually translated as "suffering" but that translation, Jack Maguire argues, "reflects only the most negative aspect of what the root term means." It also includes, he says, "notions of unsatisfactoriness, imperfection, bothersomeness, incoherence, and, most critical, impermanence."[13] The second truth is that the cause of this suffering is desire or craving. The third truth is that suffering can be ended by abandoning craving. The fourth truth is the Eightfold Path, a plan for moving from the suffering of *samsara*, the endless cycle of birth and death, to a liberated state called *nirvana*.

After the death of the Buddha, various Buddhist doctrines, rituals, and practices have evolved. One of the first rituals involved taking refuge in the Three Jewels: the Buddha, the *dharma* (Buddhist teachings), and the *sangha* (the Buddhist community). In a ceremony called *sarana* [Vn. *quy y*], lay followers of Buddhism pledge to take refuge in these Three Jewels and to obey the Five Precepts (Skt. *pañcaśīla*): to refrain from killing, stealing, sexual misconduct, lying, and taking intoxicants. Following the making of these pledges they will receive a Buddhist name.

From India Buddhist doctrine spread to other countries in Asia. An older form of Buddhism, called Theravada, which means "the way of the elders," took root in Sri Lanka, Burma, Thailand, Cambodia, Laos, Malaysia, and Indonesia. A newer form, called Mahayana, which began to emerge around 100 CE, was accepted in China, Korea, Japan, and Vietnam. Vajrayana, or tantric Buddhism, sometimes considered an extension of Mahayana, developed in Tibet and Nepal. These three traditions are sometimes called vehicles—*yanas* in Sanskrit—because they are seen as carrying people from *samsara*, the cycle of birth and death, to Nirvana. In Sanskrit "Mahayana" means "Great Vehicle," Hinayana, another name for Theravada Buddhism, means "Little Vehicle,"[14] and "Vajrayana" means "Diamond Vehicle."

---

13. Jack Maguire, *Essential Buddhism: A Complete Guide to Beliefs and Practices* (New York: Pocket Books, 2001), 86. See also Peter Harvey, *An Introduction to Buddhism* (Cambridge: Cambridge University Press, 1990), 47-48.
14. "Hinayana," is rarely used now because it is seen as pejorative. Similarly, in Vietnamese the polite way to refer to Theravada Buddhism is *đạo Phật nguyên thủy* [original Buddhism], not *đạo Phật tiểu thừa* [Lesser Wheel Buddhism].

There are followers of Theravada Buddhism in Vietnam. They are more numerous in South Vietnam than in the central or northern regions. Most Vietnamese Buddhists are Mahayana Buddhists but from what I have observed the distinction is not emphasized either by monks and nuns or lay Buddhists. The relationship between followers of the two "vehicles" seems to be one of tolerance and mutual respect. Thich Thien-An argues that "generally speaking Vietnamese Buddhists have no sect discrimination. According to them the sutras and disciplines of all sects in Buddhism were taught by the Buddha or developed by the patriarchs and are therefore worthy of study."[15] There are, however, some differences. The ideal figure of Theravada Buddhism is the Arhat [Vn. *A la hán*] or "worthy one" who has extinguished the Three Poisons (greed, hate, and delusion), achieved Nirvana, and escaped from the cycle of birth and death. This image emphasizes the personal achievement of the Arhat but not his assistance to others. In Mahayana Buddhism the ideal figure is not the Arahat but the Bodhisattva, a person who has achieved enlightenment but postpones entering Nirvana in order to help others achieve enlightenment.

Vietnamese Buddhism is a mixture of Zen and Pure Land. In an article about Zen [Ch. *chàn*] and Pure Land in China David Chappell explains these "two major poles of Buddhist practice in East Asia":

> Pure Land devotees emphasize the inadequacies of their own capacities and the futility of their times; salvation can only be achieved at another time (in the next rebirth), in another place (the Western Pure Land) and through another power (Amitabha Buddha). By contrast, Ch'an affirms the completeness of the present moment and human capacities, collapsing the space-time distinctions of Pure Land symbolism into an existential challenge by arguing for the nonduality of oneself and the Buddha, as well as the identity of this realm and the Pure Land. Whereas Pure Land devotionalism calls up an external power, Ch'an affirms self-reliance and rejects dependence upon external religious objects.[16]

Perhaps because Zen appeals to intellectuals who write books, most histories of Buddhism in Vietnam emphasize Zen. The devotional practices of Pure Land, however, have great appeal for many Vietnamese.

---

15. Thich Thien-An, *Buddhism and Zen in Vietnam in Relation to the Development of Buddhism in Asia* (Rutland, VT: Charles E. Tuttle, 1975), 23-24.
16. David W. Chappell, "From Dispute to Dual Cultivation: Pure Land Responses to Ch'an Critics," in *Traditions of Meditation in Chinese Buddhism*, ed. Peter N. Gregory (Honolulu: University of Hawai'i Press, 1986), 163.

Zen schools encourage silent meditation whereas a key practice of Pure Land is the chanting of Buddha's name, or *niệm Phật* [Jp. *nembutsu*]. One repeats the six syllables *"Nam mô A Di Đà Phật"* again and again.[17] Repeating Buddha's name [*niệm Phật*], and chanting Buddhist sutras [*tụng kinh*] have been and still are important Vietnamese Buddhist practices, as anyone who visits a Vietnamese pagoda soon learns. Cuong Tu Nguyen argues against the notion that Zen is the essence of Vietnamese Buddhism. "In fact," he says, "Zen in Vietnam has never been a 'school' in the sense of a recognizable social institution with an identifiable set of scriptures, doctrines, and practices. For the ordinary Vietnamese Buddhists, Zen was (and probably still is) merely 'a rumor from the monasteries.' They never actually embraced it as they did the devotional, ritualistic Buddhism that bears more resemblance to Pure Land Buddhism."[18]

I will summarize Cuong Tu Nguyen's views because it is important to know that the history of Vietnamese Buddhism is not a settled topic— that a scholarly debate about whether Vietnamese Buddhism throughout its history has been more Zen or more Pure Land continues. This debate need not concern us too much, however. Clearly Vietnamese Buddhism when Trịnh Công Sơn was growing up in Huế was a combination of the two and remains so today. It is important to listen to Cuong Tu Nguyen, however, because Zen has become so popular in the West that many Westerners have assumed "Buddhism" equals Zen concepts plus meditation. Cuong Tu Nguyen faults both Thích Nhất Hạnh and D. T. Suzuki for misleading both Westerners and Vietnamese.[19] When Suzuki's works appeared in Vietnam in modern Vietnamese translation, Cuong Tu Nguyen says, they "confirmed and convinced the Vietnamese

---

17. "Nam mô" means to return to the Buddha within oneself. "A Di Đà Phật" is the Amitabha Buddha. As Thiên Đỗ explains, "Pure Land, or Amidist groups, who hold that salvation comes from outside oneself, focus on Amitabha." See Thiên Đỗ, "The Quest for Enlightenment and Cultural Identity: Buddhism in Contemporary Vietnam," in *Buddhism and Politics in Twentieth-Century Asia*, ed. Ian Harris (London and New York: Pinter, 1999).

18. Cuong Tu Nguyen, *Zen in Medieval Vietnam: A Study and Translation of the Thiền Uyển Tập Anh* (Honolulu: University of Hawai'i Press, 1997), 99.

19. For Thích Nhất Hạnh, Cuong Tu Nguyen has in mind a two-volume history that this Vietnamese monk and scholar wrote using the pen name Nguyễn Lang: *Việt Nam Phật Giáo Sử Luận* [Essay on the History of Vietnamese Buddhism], vol. I (Saigon: Lá Bối, 1974). Volume II was published by the same publisher in Paris in 1978. Cuong Tu Nguyen does not mention specific works by D. T. Suzuki but presumably he is thinking of *Essays in Zen Buddhism* (1949), *Essays in Zen Buddhism* (1950), and *Studies in Zen* (1953).

Buddhists that Zen is the 'essence' of Buddhism, the supreme teaching of the Buddha."[20]

Cuong Tu Nguyen describes an "old" Buddhism that prevailed for ten centuries in Vietnam, from the first or second centuries of the CE until the later Lý Dynasty (1010-1225 CE). This old Buddhism was, he says, "composite in character, included Tantrism, ritual and devotional practices, and magic, blended together with elements from Indian and Cham Buddhism[21] and Hinduism, Chinese Buddhism, and indigenous popular religions."[22] This old, composite Buddhism, Cuong Tu Nguyen says, "appeared to share the same characteristics with the Buddhist world of Southeast Asia in general."[23] This old Buddhism was not Zen, Cuong Tu Nguyen argues, but as early as the eleventh century Vietnamese Buddhist scholars began what he calls a "Zenification" of Buddhist history, a practice that he sees as continuing into the twentieth century in histories written by well-known Buddhist scholars such as Thích Thien-An and Thích Nhất Hạnh.

Why would Vietnamese Buddhist scholars in medieval times and today want to Zen-ify the history of Vietnamese Buddhism? Because, Cuong Tu Nguyen says, Zen was and is more prestigious. Cuong Tu Nguyen explains that during the Tang and Song Dynasties Zen became popular among Buddhist intellectuals in China. Their writing, including some fine Zen poems, poured into Vietnam and inspired Vietnamese monks, including Vạn Hạnh (938-1025), one of the most famous and revered monks in Vietnam.[24] Here is one of his poems:

> *The body is like lightning: it's there and then it's not,*
> *It is like myriad plants and trees—fresh in the spring*
> *but fading in autumn.*
> *Trust in your destiny unafraid of ups and downs,*

---

20. Cuong Tu Nguyen, *Zen in Medieval Vietnam*, 343-344.
21. The Cham, who speak a Malayo-Polynesian language and have an Indianized culture, lived in Champa, an ancient kingdom in the central and coastal region of Vietnam. This kingdom existed from the 2nd to the 17th century. Estimates of how many Cham live in Vietnam today range from 50,000 to 99,000.
22. Cuong Tu Nguyen, *Zen in Medieval Vietnam*,19.
23. Ibid., 33, 339.
24. Vạn Hạnh was revered by Thích Nhất Hạnh who chose his Buddhist name—Nhất Hạnh—to express his admiration for this famous Vietnamese monk. "Vạn Hạnh" means "a thousand actions." "Nhất Hạnh" means "a single action." "Thích" does not mean "venerable" or "reverend" as many people assume. It is the name given to Buddhist monks or nuns and replaces their family name. It is the Vietnamese transliteration of "Sakya" [Vn. *Thích ca*], the name of the Lord Buddha's clan. One of the names for the Buddha is "Sakyamuni," or "Sage of the Sakyka clan."

> *Because ups and downs are [as evanescent] as drops of dew*
> *on a blade of grass.*[25]

Vietnamese monks were inspired to emulate Chinese Buddhist histories as well as the Zen poems of Chinese monks. Cuong Tu Nguyen argues that they were very much influenced by a Chinese history titled *Chuandeng lu* [The Records of the Transmission of the Lamp] which was compiled around 1004 CE. The lamp in the title refers to the *dharma*, the teachings of the Buddha. The *Chuandeng lu* describes the history of Buddhism in India and includes biographies of famous Chinese Buddhist patriarchs beginning with Bodhidharma, the Indian monk credited with introducing Buddhism to China. He is regarded as the first patriarch of Zen Buddhism in China. Cuong Tu Nguyen claims that Vietnamese "transmission of the lamp" works were inspired by the *Chuandeng lu*. He mentions an eleventh century work by Thông Biện and a thirteenth century work by Thường Chiếu but focuses on the *Thiền Uyển Tập Anh* (A Collection of Outstanding Figures of the Vietnamese Zen Community), a fourteenth century work written in Chinese by an unknown author, because he believes that it is the work that contemporary Buddhist historians like Thich Thien-An and Thích Nhất Hạnh have relied on to write their histories. The gist of Cuong Tu Nguyen's argument is that the author or authors of the *Thiền Uyển Tập Anh*, overcome by an eagerness to connect Vietnamese Buddhism to the glories of Chinese Zen, falsified or exaggerated this connection and as a result presented Vietnamese Buddhism as more Zen-influenced than it really was. And contemporary Buddhist historians, who rely on this work, have, Cuong Tu Nguyen argues, compounded the error.

Let me give an example of this alleged falsification and exaggeration, one related to a Vietnamese Zen Buddhist school begun in the sixth century CE by Vinitaruci (Vn. *Tỳ ni da lưu chi*), an Indian monk. According to Thich Thien-An, Vinitaruci arrived in Vietnam in 580 CE and took up residence at the Pháp Vân temple in Luy Lâu, the administrative capital of Giao Chỉ which, as mentioned previously, was a center of Buddhist studies beginning in the second century. Thich Thien-An argues that the "Vinitaruci School" descends from the Zen of Bodhidharma, the Indian monk famous for introducing Zen to China. Drawing on Buddhist

---

25. Translated by Cuong Tu Nguyen in *Zen in Medieval Vietnam*, 60.

histories,[26] he says that before coming to Vietnam Vinitaruci had studied with Sengcan, the third patriarch of Zen in China, and that Sengcan had transferred the "mind-seal" to him and told him to go south to teach the *dharma*. "Mind-seal," or "mental impression"—*tâm ấn* in Vietnamese— refers to the passing on of enlightenment from a Zen master to a disciple, a transfer which links the disciple to the master's lineage. I have included "The Lineage of Chinese and Vietnamese Zen" from Thich Thien-An's book. Note how he connects Vinitaruci to Sengcan (transliterated as "Sêng-ts'an") and eventually to Bodhidharma.

In Thich Thien-An's account, Vinitaruci obeyed his master and went south, first to Guangzhou and then to Vietnam. At Pháp Vân Temple in North Vietnam Vinitaruci met a Vietnamese monk, Pháp Hiền, who became his student. Before Vinitaruci died he passed the "mind-seal" to Pháp Hiền and so, according to Thich Thien-An, Pháp Hiền becomes the first Vietnamese patriarch of the Vinitaruci Zen School.[27] Because the "Founding Patriarch" of this school was Vinitaruci, who received the "mind-seal" directly from Sengan, the third patriarch of Chinese Zen (Bodhidharma was the first), the Vinitaruci School, in Thich Thien-An's account, one very similar to those by other Vietnamese historians, Vietnamese Buddhism has a glorious history.

Cuong Tu Nguyen, however, maintains that "the Vinitaruci Zen school is a mere fiction."[28] Vietnamese authors, he says, "eager to connect Vietnamese Buddhism to Chinese Zen erroneously related [Vinitaruci] to the legendary Third Patriarch Sencan."[29] Cuong Tu Nguyen also questions the veracity of descriptions one finds in Vietnamese histories of other Vietnamese schools—for example, the Vô Ngôn Thông [Speechless Understanding] School which was founded in the tenth century by a Chinese monk (Vô Ngôn Thông);[30] and the Thảo Đường School, which

---

26. Thich Thien-An's account of Vinitaruci is based primarily on two sources. He cites the *Thiền Uyển Tập Anh*, which he refers to by a different title: *Đại Nam Thuyền Uyển Truyền Đăng Tập lục* [A Record of Transmission of the Lamp in the Zen Community of Đại Nam]. (This title was used for later editions of *Thiền Uyển Tập Anh* published in 1715 and 1858.) Cuong Tu Nguyen explains the different titles in *Zen in Medieval Vietnam*, 209. Thich Thien-An also cites the following fourteenth century Buddhist history: *Cổ Châu Pháp Vân Phật Bản Hạnh Ngữ Lục* [Recorded Sayings of the Pháp Vân Buddha at Cổ Châu].
27. Thich Thien-An, *Buddhism and Zen in Vietnam*, 32-36.
28. Cuong Tu Nguyen in *Zen in Medieval Vietnam*, 43.
29. Ibid., 41.
30. Thich Thien-An translates "Vô Ngôn Thông," the name of the founder of this school and for the school itself, as "the one who neither learned nor spoke but fully understood." See *Buddhism and Zen in Vietnam*, 53.

was, according to most histories, founded in the eleventh century by a Chinese monk (Thảo Đường) whom Emperor Lý Thánh Tông brought to Vietnam (then called Đại Việt) as a prisoner after a battle with Champa. Later, impressed with his wisdom, the Emperor gave him the title *Quốc sư* [National Teacher] and put him in charge of teaching Buddhism in the royal palace.[31] Cuong Tu Nguyen questions this story about Thảo Đường but Thich Thien-An and other scholars accept it, citing a fourteenth century work by Lê Trắc[32] titled *An Nam Chí Lược* [Brief Records An Nam],[33] a work that, Cuong Tu Nguyen says, "has been accepted uncritically by scholars in the history of Vietnamese Buddhism."[34] But even Cuong Tu Nguyen admits there could have been a monk named Thảo Đường. He simply points out some inconsistencies in Lê Trắc's account.

It seems true that Zen elements have been overemphasized in many histories of Vietnamese Buddhism, but it is important to remember that the goal of Zen meditation and Pure Land recitation is the same: enlightenment. Thich Thien-An, accused—too harshly, in my view—of Zenifying the history of Vietnamese Buddhism, makes this point clearly. "Even the distinctions 'Ch'an' [Zen] and 'Pure Land,'" Thich Thien-An says, "vanish in Vietnamese Buddhism where all ways are Buddha-ways and are one in the communal quest of enlightenment through *Thiền Tịnh Nhất trí*, the unification of meditation and recitation."[35] Zen and Pure Land are unified by the Buddhist concept of "skill in means" [Vn. *phương tiện*; Skt. *upaya*]. *Upaya* refers to the idea that because people differ in their abilities and education Buddhist teachers should adjust their method to fit their audience. Distinguishing between difficult and easy practices goes back at least as far as Nāgārjuna (150 CE - 250 CE), an Indian and one of the most important Buddhist philosophers.[36] The Zen methods of contemplation and meditation are considered most effective for educated people and Pure Land's method of Buddha name recitation more effective for the less-educated. Buddhist scholars relate Zen and Pure Land and their

---

31. Ibid., 75.
32. Other scholars refer to the author as Lê Tắc.
33. *An Nam Chí Lược* [Brief Records An Nam], (Huế: Huế University Press, 1961).
34. Cuong Tu Nguyen, *Zen in Medieval Vietnam*, 51.
35. This Sino-Vietnamese four-syllable expression could also be translated as "Zen Pure Land one mind." Thich Thien-An translates this expression into Chinese [*Ch'an-ching I-chih*] and Japanese [*Zenjo itchi*]. See *Buddhism and Zen in Vietnam*, 102. Another four-syllable expression, "*Thiền Tịnh song tu*" ["Zen and Pure Land parallel each other"], also expresses the idea that the two forms of Buddhist practice are compatible.
36. Thich Thien-An, *Buddhism and Zen in Vietnam*, 89.

respective teaching approaches to the two pillars of Buddhism, wisdom [Skt. *prajna*; Vn. *trí tuệ*] and compassion [Skt. *karuna*; Vn. *từ bi*], with wisdom being associated with the former, and compassion with the latter. Thich Thien-An celebrates this union, which he says was achieved in Vietnam by the Thảo Đường School in the eleventh century. In this union, he says, differences disappear and instead "there is oneness and togetherness within the Karuna-Prajna [Compassion-Wisdom] mind which is indeed the meeting place of all sects in Buddhism."[37]

Zen, with its emphasis on meditation, however, has long been considered a higher path than the practices associated with Pure Land. Alexander Soucy points out that "this primacy placed on Zen has been assumed by Buddhists and academics alike in colonial and communist Vietnam because it fits the rhetorical requirements of the nationalist elite who continue to disparage 'folk' beliefs and practices."[38] Soucy argues that most Vietnamese Buddhists who pray to the Amitabha Buddha "do not give much serious thought, or speak about, attaining a Pure Land." They are concentrating on "more mundane goals, such as having a successful career, a male child or a healthy family."[39] When in 2014 my wife and I visited Hiếu Quang pagoda in Huế, the pagoda Trịnh Công Sơn frequently visited, we noticed a tree in the courtyard with handwritten messages attached to the branches. In these messages people asked for things like those Soucy mentions. One woman requested that her husband's stomach troubles be ended. Soucy argues that Pure Land has become a label for "normative practices" such as these, practices not approved of by some educated Vietnamese Buddhists who are attracted to the "self-power" of Zen, not the "other-power" emphasized in Pure Land. Thích Nhất Hạnh emphasizes this self-power by pointing out that "the practice of Zen is by no means easy. It requires a profound and powerful inner life, long and persistent training, and a strong, firm will."[40]

There are signs that the recent popularity of Buddhism in the West is contributing to a Zenification of Buddhism in Vietnam. American converts to Buddhism, Charles S. Prebish says, "treat Buddhism as if

---

37. Ibid., 102-103.
38. Alexander Soucy, "Nationalism, Globalism and the Re-establishment of the Trúc Lâm Thiền Buddhist Sect in Northern Vietnam," in *Modernity and Re-enchantment: Religion in Post-revolutionary Vietnam*, ed. Philip Taylor (Singapore: Institute of Southeast Asian Studies, 2007), 344.
39. Ibid., 357.
40. Thích Nhất Hạnh, *Lotus in a Sea of Fire*, 4.

it were a 'onefold path' [i.e., not Buddha's eightfold path] focusing on meditation and little, if anything, else."[41] Soucy describes how Thích Thanh Từ, a Vietnamese monk from from Cần Thơ in the Mekong Delta, is trying to revive Zen at the Sùng Phúc Meditation Center [Sùng Phúc Thiền Tự] in Hanoi. Soucy observes that the Zen Buddhism that this monk is teaching resembles "Western forms of Buddhism that accentuate the individual aspects of Zen meditation, such as Thích Nhất Hạnh's Order of interbeing."[42] Soucy found that under Thích Thanh Từ's instruction a lay Buddhist woman whom he calls Cô Tuyết had abandoned folk beliefs and devotional practices associated with Pure Land and had taken up meditation. In other words émigré monks like Thích Nhất Hạnh and Thích Thanh Từ from Central and South Vietnam are repatriating within Vietnam a form of Buddhism that emphasizes meditation much more than it has been emphasized in traditional Vietnamese Buddhism.

THE BAMBOO GROVE ZEN SCHOOL

The Zen School that Thích Thanh Từ is trying to revive in Hanoi is the Trúc Lâm Thiền Tông (Bamboo Grove Zen School). This school is revered in Vietnam because it was founded by a Vietnamese, King Trần Nhân Tông, a devout Buddhist who rallied his people to defeat troops of the Mongol Yuan Dynasty in 1287-1288. Kublai Khan, the grandson of Genghis Khan, was the Mogol emperor at this time. In a climactic battle on the Bạch Đằng River in North Vietnam, Vietnamese troops defeated over three hundred thousand Mongol troops. In 1293 Trần Nhân Tông turned over power to his eldest son, Trần Anh Tông, and he became a monk, wandering from place to place teaching the *dharma*. Later he went to Mount Yên Tử, where he established the Bamboo Grove School.

When his son, Trần Anh Tông (reign: 1293-1314), took over the throne the battles with the Cham were over. He ruled in a more peaceful time. In 1306 King Trần Anh Tông and Chế Mân agreed on an important exchange, one that placed a large section of present-day central Vietnam within the southward expanding Vietnamese empire. Chế Mân wished to marry princess Huyền Trân, the daughter of Trần Nhân Tông, who reigned from 1278 to 1293, and sister of King Trần Anh Tông. In return Chế Mân agreed to cede two Cham provinces, Châu Ô and Châu Lý, to

---

41. Charles S. Prebish, *Luminous Passage: The Practice and Study of Buddhism in America* (Berkeley: University of California, 1999), 63.
42. Alexander Soucy, "Nationalism, Globalism and the Re-establishment of the Trúc Lâm Thiền Buddhist Sect," 362.

Vietnam (then known as Đại Việt or Great Việt). The deal was made and the Cham king and the Vietnamese princess lived happily together and had a child. Before a year had elapsed, however, Chế Mân died. According to Cham custom, the queen of a deceased king must be cremated when her husband dies. Hearing of this, her brother King Trần Anh Tông sent an expedition to Champa ostensibly to mourn Chế Mân's passing but actually to rescue Huyền Trân from death. The mission was successful. The princess was brought back to Great Việt and became a nun.

Princess Huyền Trân is a famous figure and many poems have been written about her, some of which compare her to the famous Chinese beauty Chiêu Quân [Ch. Wang Zhaojun] whom a Han emperor sent to be a tribute wife of a barbarian king. She is especially famous in Huế because her willingness to marry a Cham king resulted in the Huế region becoming part of Great Việt. In Huế today an elaborate shrine has been built to memorialize her (and attract tourists)—the The Princess Huyền Trân Cultural Center. The ceded provinces, Châu Ô and Châu Lý, now the provinces of Quảng Trị and Thừa Thiên, became known as Thuận Hóa after King Trần Anh Tông gave the Cham provinces the Vietnamese names Thuận and Hóa. In the middle of the 16th century, the Nguyễn lords set up a separate state in Thuận Hóa and maintained only loose ties to the state of Đại Việt. I will have more to say in the next chapter about these Nguyễn lords because they played a key role in the history of Buddhism in the city of Huế.

Trần Nhân Tông was the third king of the Trần Dynasty. He was not the only fervent Buddhist leader belonging to this Dynasty. Trần Nhân Tông's grandfather, Trần Thái Tông (r: 1225-1258) had previously set a model for his grandson by skillfully handling affairs of state while remaining a devout Buddhist. He negotiated a temporary peace with Champa and when the Mongol forces of Kublai Khan threatened Vietnam in 1257 he rapidly mobilized forces to resist them. He also found time to write learned books on Buddhism, including *Khóa hư lục* [Instructions on Emptiness], *Thiền tông Chỉ nam* [A Guide to Zen Buddhism], and *Kim cang Kinh Sớ* [A Commentary on the Diamond Sutra].[43]

Both Trần Thái Tông and his grandson, Trần Nhân Tông, wrote some fine Zen poems which are still cited and reprinted in Vietnam. Here are two, one by Trần Thái Tông and one by Trần Nhân Tông, from a bilingual

---

43. Thich Thien-An, *Buddhism and Zen in Vietnam*, 125.

edition (Sino-Vietnamese and English) published in Hồ Chí Minh City in 2005:[44]

"To the Monk Đức Sơn at Thanh Phong Shrine" by Trần Thái Tông

Winds at a pine door, moonlight on an empty yard
Clear and calm. Heart and landscape one.
This bliss. And no one knows.
A monk on his peak alone until dawn.

"Joyful Practice" by Trần Nhân Tông

Living in the world, practice quietly with joy.
When hungry eat. When tired sleep.
Don't look for it elsewhere, the jewel lies within.
An empty mind facing the world, what use is Zen?

Why would a devotee of Zen suggest there is no need for Zen? Trần Nhân Tông seems to be saying that everyone has a Buddha nature [Skt. *sabhava*; Vn. *Phật tánh*] within them and so, although devotional practices, including meditation (Zen), are important, they should be pursued joyfully. If they are, one will achieve a quiet mind and become aware of the jewel within, one's Buddha nature.

Beginning during the Lý but especially during the Trần dynasty there was a merging of religious and national interests. "By the time of the Trần Dynasty," Thich Thien-An writes, "Vietnamese Buddhism and Vietnamese nationalism were one and the same, not two."[45] Historians seem to agree that during the Lý Dynasty, and most of the Trần, Buddhism was the state religion. What seems less clear is whether the kings of these dynasties should be considered "divine kings" or "god kings" [Skt. *devarāja*] like the kings who ruled the more heavily Indianized countries of Cambodia and Thailand. From 802 to 1432, Peter Harvey explains, the Khmer king "was seen as an incarnation of Siva and the great Bodhisattva."[46] Nguyễn Thế Anh says that the Vietnamese King Lý Cao Tông (r: 1176-1210) considered himself to be a *devarāja* and "ordered that he was to be looked upon as identical with the Buddha, seemingly in imitation of his contemporary

---

44. These are poetic translations by Kevin Bowen and Nguyễn Ba Chung, who also provide more literal English translations. The original Chinese versions and the translations from Chinese to Vietnamese were prepared by Nguyễn Huệ Chi and Nguyễn Duy. See *Tuyển tập Thơ Thiền Lý – Trần* [English title: Zen Poems from Early Vietnam (900 – 1400 CE)] (HCMC: Văn Hóa Sài Gòn, 2005), 91-93 and 103-105.
45. Thich Thien-An, *Buddhism and Zen in Vietnam*, 111.
46. Peter Harvey, *An Introduction to Buddhism*, 143-144.

at Angkor, Jayavarman VII."[47] Cuong Tu Nguyen, however, argues that this Hindu concept of divine king never developed in Vietnam because "contemporaneous with the development of the monarchical states and the concept of Buddhist kingship in Southeast Asia, Vietnam circumstantially and voluntarily moved into the scope of Chinese culture."[48] "When the Trần succeeded the Lý," Cuong Tu Nguyen observes, "Confucianism began to replace Buddhism as the official state ideology."[49]

When this replacement occurred a division of labor emerged: Governmental affairs began more and more to be conducted following Confucian principles, but for personal affairs—for help in dealing with sickness, suffering, and death—people turned to Buddhism. At the court Confucian officials, who were also Buddhists, began to fear that the Buddhist approach to government was too relaxed. For example, there were no strict rules for royal succession. Buddhism reached its "apogee," Nguyễn Thế Anh says, under the Lý Dynasty (1009-1225), but toward the end of this dynasty Buddhism was, he says, "becoming increasingly Vietnamized, associated with magic and medicine and miracles, with dreams and dragons, derived from traditional beliefs." And "criticism began to be voiced against the monks' supposed dissoluteness."[50] Beginning in the Trần period Vietnamese officials turned to Confucianism to combat what John Whitmore calls "Southeast Asian-style flexibilities."[51]

Trần rulers accepted this division of labor between Buddhism and Confucianism. In his *Guide to Zen* [Thiền Tông Chi Nam], King Trần Thái Tông (r. 1226-1258) says:

> Buddhism is the guide of the ignorant and the lens to scrutinize the problem of birth and death in the most crystal-clear fashion, which is the doctrine of Buddha. On the other hand, the doctrine of the Saint Confucius bears the heavy responsibility of preserving the balance of discipline for future generations. The sixth Patriarch[52] said: "There exists no difference between Buddha and the Saint Confucius."

---

47. Nguyễn Thế Anh, "Buddhism and Vietnamese Society throughout History," *South East Asia Research* 1 No. 5 (March 1993), 103.
48. Cuong Tu Nguyen adds that "a lack of exposure to Pali Buddhist literature" may be another reason why the concept of Buddhist kingship did not develop in Vietnam. See note 33 in *Zen in Medieval Vietnam*, 339-340.
49. Ibid., 83.
50. Nguyễn Thế Anh, "Buddhism and Vietnamese Society throughout History," 102, 104.
51. John K. Whitmore, "Social Organization and Confucian Thought in Vietnam," *Journal of Southeast Asian Studies* 15, No. 2 (Sept., 1984), 305.
52. Huệ Năng [Ch. Huineng] is viewed as the sixth and last patriarch of Chan Buddhism.

This shows that the doctrine of Buddha needs Confucianism for its perpetuation in the future.[53]

All Vietnamese revere the Trần rulers, especially Trần Thái Tông and Trần Nhân Tông. They admire them for embodying the humanistic values of Buddhism and for their patriotism, military skill, and literary talent. They admire them because after leading the country through perilous times—the Mongol invasions—they gave up the throne and led quiet lives teaching the *dharma*. Trần Nhân Tông is also greatly respected for having established the Bamboo Grove Zen School. Buddhism came to Vietnam from India and China but two schools, the Bamboo Grove and the Liễu Quán, are considered Vietnamese schools because they were founded by Vietnamese. (I will have more to say about the Liễu Quán School, the dominant school in Central and South Vietnam, in the next chapter.) Because these two schools have Vietnamese founders, their philosophy and methods of practice derive from the culture, thought, and character of the Vietnamese people." A nationalist pride is detectable when Vietnamese Buddhist scholars describe Trần Nhân Tông and Liễu Quán. India, China, and Japan have their famous monks who have established sects with long lineages of patriarchs, they seem to be suggesting, but Vietnam, too, has its own exemplary leaders and its own schools of Buddhism.

---

53. Quoted by Thích Nhất Hạnh in *Lotus in a Sea of Fire* (New York: Hill and Wang, 1967), 10.

23

BUDDHISM IN HUẾ

In terms of beliefs and practice Buddhism in Huế is similar to Buddhism in other parts of the country, but because Huế for several centuries was located outside the boundaries of Đại Việt (Great Viet), the land ruled by the kings of the Lê Dynasty during the 15th and 16th centuries, Huế Buddhism has a special history which is a source of pride for Huế citizens. Tourists visiting Huế today will usually be shown the Imperial City, or *Đại Nội*, the area within the Citadel [*Thành Nội*] where Vietnam's kings of the Nguyễn Dynasty lived. Most tours also include short trips to the royal tombs where, in scenic locales outside the city, these kings have been buried. Lists of the kings of the Nguyễn Dynasty typically include thirteen individuals who occupied the throne from 1802 to 1945.[1] To understand the history of Huế, however, one has to know about the Nguyễn lords [*chúa Nguyễn*] who from the middle of the 15th through the late 18th century ruled a region called by the people who lived there Đàng Trong (Inner Region) to distinguish it from Đàng Ngoài (Outer

---

1. These kings occupied the throne but after 1862 their power was greatly reduced. The French seized Saigon in 1858 and by 1862 they controlled six southern provinces. By 1883 Southern Vietnam was a French colony (called Cochin China) and Central Vietnam and North Vietnam were "protectorates" (called Annam and Tonkin respectively) over which Nguyễn rulers presided but had little real power. Bảo Đại, the last Nguyễn ruler, was more of a figurehead than a ruler. When the Japanese took control of Vietnam in March 1945 he declared independence for Vietnam within Japan's Great East Asian Co-Prosperity Sphere. On August 23, 1945, after Japan surrendered, he abdicated his throne, turning over his (limited) power to Hồ Chí Minh's Việt Minh forces. When the French and their Vietnamese supporters were fighting communist forces during the First Indochina War, Bảo Đại had the title Chief of State of Vietnam but spent much of his time abroad. After the war ended and the country was divided at the 17th parallel, he was defeated by Ngô Đình Diệm in a referendum in 1955. Ngô Đình Diệm then became President of the Republic of Vietnam.

Region). In 1600 Đàng Trong included the present-day provinces Quảng Bình, Quảng Trị, Thừa Thiên, and Quảng Nam. The southern border of Đàng Trong, however, continued to move southward as the Nguyễn lords conquered land controlled by the Cham, a people of Malayo-Polynesian ancestry with a heavily Indianized and Hinduized culture. Vietnamese refer to their movement southward as "Nam Tiến" (March to the South). By 1700 all the former Cham lands had been annexed and the Mekong Delta, including Saigon—previously controlled by Cambodian princes—was under Vietnamese control.

What was the relationship of Đàng Trong to Đàng Ngoài—the land to the north called Đại Việt? This northern territory was ruled by kings of the Lê Dynasty after Lê Lợi in 1428 drove out Chinese troops of the Ming Dynasty who had invaded Vietnam in 1406 and turned the country into a Chinese colony for roughly two decades. In the 1520s members of the Mạc family usurped the throne and then feudal clans led by members of the Trịnh and Nguyễn families opposed the Mạc but also fought each other. Both the Trịnh and the Nguyễn supported the Lê, at least in principle. The lords of both clans wished to lead the country but hesitated to confront the Lê rulers directly because the Lê Dynasty remained popular. When the Trịnh defeated the Mạc in 1593 they ruled the North but allowed the Lê monarchy to persist. This history becomes quite complicated and has been discussed by others.[2] Here I focus on the Nguyễn lords because they played a crucial role in Đàng Trong. They, not the Trịnh lords, were the leaders of the southward movement described above that enlarged the territory of Đàng Trong. From 1620 until 1788 the conflict between the two clans created two different territories with the border at the Gianh River in northern Quảng Bình Province. By learning about these Nguyễn lords and their relationship to Buddhism we can learn much about the history of Buddhism in central Vietnam.

In 1558 Nguyễn Hoàng became military commander of Thuận Hóa, then the southern part of Đàng Trong. Nguyễn Hoàng wanted this appointment and was able to secure it because at this time the Trịnh and Nguyễn families were still allies and the leader of the Trịnh, Trịnh Kiểm, was married to Nguyễn Hoàng's sister. (Fierce battles between the Trịnh and the Nguyễn occurred later, during the period 1627 to 1672.) In some ways the Trịnh had an easier time ruling Đàng Ngoài than the Nguyễn

---

2. See, for example, Jean Chesneaux, *The Vietnamese Nation: Contribution to a History* (Sydney: Current Book Distributors, 1966), 31-46.

lords had ruling Đàng Trong. Their subjects in the Red River Delta were mostly Vietnamese who had lived there for centuries. Scholars debate the relative influence of Buddhism and Neo-Confucianism in different periods of Vietnamese history, but most agree that in the fifteenth century kings of the Lê Dynasty followed the Chinese model and ruled according to Neo-Confucian principles. Though often called a religion, Confucianism is also—perhaps primarily—a method of governing. Nguyễn Hoàng, however, and the Nguyễn lords who succeeded him had to administer what was, from the Vietnamese point of view, a frontier region, a region that had been ruled by the Cham. "When the Nguyễn governors of Thuận Hóa and Quảng Nam rejected the Trịnh-dominated Lê court in the early seventeenth century," Nolo Cooke explains, "they took their stand in former Cham lands that had always been beyond the Neo-Confucian frontier of Lê Vietnam."[3]

The Nguyễn lords did not, of course, come alone to Thuận Hóa. They brought settlers from the North with them, and they needed a way to make these settlers, immigrants in a strange land, feel comfortable.[4] "Chinese political theory and Neo-Confucian philosophy," Li Tana explains, "if studied in any depth, would not serve Nguyễn needs. They would have potentially focused attention northward to the captive Lê emperor, instead of inwards and southwards, onto the expanding separatist state itself."[5] The Nguyễn lords also needed to ingratiate themselves with the Cham population. The solution, Li Tana says, was Mahayana Buddhism which was familiar and therefore comforting to Vietnamese immigrants. In addition, Buddhism's "syncretic nature allowed room to incorporate local spirits and deities" worshiped by the Cham.[6] Nguyễn lords respected

---

3. Nolo Cooke, "The Myth of the Restoration: Dang-Trong Influences in the Spiritual Life of the Early Nguyen Dynasty (1802-47)," in *The Last Stand of Asian Autonomies: Responses to Modernity in the Diverse States of Southeast Asia and Korea, 1750-1900*, ed. Anthony Reid (New York: St. Martin's Press, 1997), 279.
4. Some Vietnamese had already settled in Đàng Trong before 1558. Thích Hải Ấn and Hà Xuân Liêm explain that the people living in Thuận Hóa in 1558 included Vietnamese from Thanh Hóa and Nghệ An who had moved south before Nguyễn Hoàng arrived; some Cham people who had become Vietnamized and had Vietnamese family names; some Cham who had retained their Cham family names; and some families with a Chinese family name (Vương, Tạ, and Bạch, for example) because the father was a Chinese immigrant who had married a Vietnamese woman. See Thích Hải Ấn and Hà Xuân Liêm, *Lịch sử Phật giáo xứ Huế* [A History of Huế Buddhism] (HCMC: 2001), 74-75.
5. Li Tana, *Nguyễn Cochinchina: Southern Vietnam in the Seventeenth and Eighteenth Centuries* (Ithaca, NY: Southeast Asia Program Publications, Cornell University, 1998), 103.
6. Ibid., 104.

Cham temples and did not tear them down but instead deliberately built Buddhist pagodas near them.

The most famous example of this combining of Buddhist and Cham elements is Thiên Mụ Pagoda [Pagoda of the Celestial Mother]. This pagoda, one of Huế's most famous, is on a hill above the Perfume River about three miles west of Huế.[7] An important Cham temple honoring the Cham earth goddess Po Nagar existed on this same hill. According to legend, before Nguyễn Hoàng arrived, a woman in a red dress and blue trousers had appeared on this hill and announced that spirits with benign supernatural powers existed in this area, and if a lord arrived and built a Buddhist pagoda there and prayed to those spirits, then things would go well for the people and the country. Historians suggest that Nguyễn Hoàng, after learning from residents of the spiritual potency of this spot, decided to build Thiên Mụ pagoda there in 1601.[8]

A word about Po Nagar. She was a Cham mother goddess with the power to provide rain or destroy crops and so one can understand why Nguyễn Hoàng and the lords that succeeded him wanted to be associated with her. By the 19th century this Cham goddess was Vietnamized, becoming a Vietnamese deity called Thien Y-A-Na. Nguyễn Thế Anh suggests Vietnamese may have accepted Po Nagar because they considered her "an avatar of the other celestial queen mother they had long been familiar with, the Taoistic Saint Mother of the Fairies."[9]

Were the Nguyễn lords devout Buddhists or did they support Buddhism simply for political reasons? It seems they were devout believers. Cao Huy Thuấn compares Nguyễn Hoàng to King Lý Thái Tổ (r. 1010-1028) who grew up in a pagoda and was taught by the famous monk Vạn Hạnh. "Although Nguyễn Hoàng was not a Buddhist like King Lý Thái Tổ," Cao Huy Thuấn says, "when he began to administer a mixed population [in Đàng Trong], he immediately thought about building pagodas and after he built Thiên Mụ pagoda, he opened a Dharma Association where

7. It is the pagoda that Trịnh Công Sơn mentions in his essay about his famous love song "Diễm of the Past."* "That was also a time [late 1950s, early 1960s]," Sơn says, "when on each pure morning, each afternoon, each evening, the bell at Linh Mụ Pagoda echoed above the river to arrive at each partially shuttered or closed in house. A translation of this essay, "A Recollection" [Hồi Ức], appears in Appendix E. For a Vietnamese version, see *Trịnh Công Sơn, Tôi là ai là ai . . .*, eds. Nguyễn Minh Nhựt et al. (HCMC: Trẻ, 2011), 154-157. This essay originally appeared in *Thế Giới Âm Nhạc* [Music World] (March, 1997).
8. Thích Hải Ấn and Hà Xuân Liêm, *Lịch Sử Phật Giáo Xứ Huế*, 77-78.
9. Nguyễn Thế Anh, "The Vietnamization of the Cham Deity Pô Nagar," in *Essays into Vietnamese Pasts*, ed. K.W. Taylor and John K. Whitmore (Ithaca, NY: Southeast Asia Program, Cornell University), 44.

prayers were chanted and Buddhist teachings explained."[10] Perhaps the most devout of all the Nguyễn lords was Nguyễn Phúc Chu (r. 1691-1725). He took a Buddhist name and vowed to follow the commandments for Bodhisattvas and monks (Vn. bồ tát giới; Skt. bodhisattva sila).[11] Taking a Buddhist name involves accepting the Three Jewels and obeying the Five Precepts.[12] It is quite common for Buddhists to take a Buddhist name. Accepting the commandments of a Bodhisattva, which number fifty-eight in all, however, represents a deeper commitment to Buddhist principles.[13] It means one agrees to live by the same principles Buddhist monks vow to live by. Li Tana, citing Chinese sources, says that a Chinese monk named Da Shan, also known as Thạch Liêm, inducted Nguyễn Phúc Chu and his family and some high court officials into the Lâm Tế (Ch. Linji; Jp. Rinzai) school of Buddhism.[14] This is more proof that Cao Huy Thuần is correct when he argues that Nguyễn Hoàng and the lords that followed him "developed Buddhism because their hearts were Buddhist not because they only wanted to use Buddhism as a political tool. For these lords building the nation and building Buddhism went together; they were one."[15] Citing Li Tana's research, another scholar, Shawn McHale, concludes that "the early Nguyễn lords led what was, in many ways, a militarized Mahayana Buddhist state where Confucian influence was weak."[16]

Cao Huy Thuần and Shawn McHale are referring to the Nguyễn lords who ruled Đàng Trong from 1558 to 1777, not to the kings of the Nguyễn Dynasty who were forced to cede power and land to the French colonialists in the 19th century. Between these two sets of rulers, both

---

10. Cao Huy Thuần, "Phật giáo Huế trong dòng chảy của lịch sử" [Huế Buddhism in the Flow of History], *Liễu Quán* 1 (January 2014), 5-6.
11. Ibid., 5.
12. The Three Jewels are Buddha, Dharma, and Sangha. The Five Precepts are to refrain from killing, stealing, sexual misconduct, and lying.
13. There are fewer commandments for bodhisattvas who practice at home [*Bồ tát giới tại gia*] and so perhaps Nguyễn Phúc Chu did not vow to accept all fifty-eight commandments.
14. Li Tana, *Nguyễn Cochinchina*, 108. Thạch Liêm came to Huế from China after the Manchu defeated the rulers of the Ming Dynasty. He came with another Chinese monk, Nguyên Thiều. Vietnamese consider a Vietnamese monk, Liễu Quán, to be the founder of the Liễu Quán School in the Huế area though they acknowledge the influence of these monks from China. The lines of influence are clear: Liễu Quán became a disciple of Minh Hoàng Tử Dung, who was a disciple of Nguyên Thiều. See Thich Thien-Ân, *Buddhism and Zen in Vietnam in Relation to the Development of Buddhism in Asia* (Rutland, VT: Charles E. Tuttle, 1975), ch. 6 & 7.
15. Cao Huy Thuần, "Phật giáo Huế trong dòng chảy của lịch sử," 6.
16. Shawn Frederick McHale, *Print and Power: Confucianism, Communism, and Buddhism in the Making of Modern Vietnam* (Honolulu: University of Hawai'i Press, 2004), 71.

involving members of the Nguyễn clan, was the Tây Sơn rebellion. In 1771 three brothers from the village of Tây Sơn [Western Mountain] in what is now Bình Định Province organized a revolt—referred to now as the Tây Sơn rebellion—against the Nguyễn lords. The three brothers—Nguyễn Nhạc, Nguyễn Huệ, and Nguyễn Lữ—were merchants, but the revolt was fueled by peasants angry at the harsh way local mandarins treated them. The rebels eventually defeated the Nguyễn lords in the South, the Trịnh lords in the North, and in 1788 deposed the last ruler of the Lê dynasty. Nguyễn Huệ, the most accomplished of the three brothers, declared himself Emperor, taking the name Quang Trung. By 1802, as a result of the efforts of the three brothers, Đàng Ngoài and Đàng Trong were unified into a single Vietnamese state stretching from the Mekong Delta to the Chinese border.[17]

Nguyễn Huệ died in 1792, and a relative of the deposed Nguyễn lords,[18] Nguyễn Phúc Ánh, known as Nguyễn Ánh, attacked the Tây Sơn regime and eventually, with assistance from a French priest and diplomat named Pigneau de Béhaine, took over the entire country which he renamed Đại Nam.[19] (Under the Lê dynasty rulers it was known as Đại Việt.) Nguyễn Ánh took the dynastic name Gia Long and began a dynasty that lasted until 1945 when Bảo Đại abdicated the throne. The Imperial City in Huế, a walled series of enclosures along the Perfume River that included palaces for the royal family and government buildings, was built by members of this dynasty. Before the French colonialists arrived, Hue was the capital [*kinh đô*] of the country but in 1862 the six southern provinces became the French colony of Cochinchina and by 1883 Tonkin (North Vietnam) and Annam (Central Vietnam) had become French protectorates. The powers and functions that the Nguyễn rulers retained were mostly honorific and ceremonial.

---

17. Jean Chesneaux, *The Vietnamese Nation: Contribution to a History*, 43. See also Stanley Karnow, *Vietnam: A History* (New York: Viking Press, 1983), 62.
18. Nguyễn Ánh was the grandson of Nguyễn Phúc Khoát, the second to last of the Nguyễn lords who ruled Đàng Trong before the Tây Sơn rebellion.
19. In 1765 Pigneau de Behaine went to Cochinchina to establish a Catholic seminary. During the Tây Sơn rebellion he provided a refuge on a French-held island called Kah Kuk for the young Nguyễn Ánh (later King Gia Long). In 1787, after failing to convince King Louis XVI to assist Nguyễn Ánh, Pigneau obtained armaments, ships, and ammunition from French merchants. This assistance helped Nguyễn Ánh defeat the Tây Sơn rebels. Nguyễn Ánh, Stanley Karnow writes, "realized that he owed an 'eternal debt' to Pigneau rather than to France, and he discharged the obligation to his late mentor by tolerating Christianity." See Stanley Karnow, *Vietnam: A History*, 65-66.

The kings of this 19th century Nguyễn Dynasty modeled their Imperial City on the Forbidden City in Beijing. Did they follow the Chinese model in other ways? This question has been debated by historians. Nolo Cooke explains that "English-language historiography conventionally portrays the 19th century as the apogee of Neo-Confucian political influence in traditional Vietnam, and the new Nguyễn dynasty as perhaps the most Sinic ruling house in Vietnamese history."[20] Nolo Cooke herself, however, and other scholars provide a more nuanced view of Confucianism and Buddhism under the Nguyễn dynasty. Cooke argues that Gia Long "did not see himself as the founder of a new dynasty but rather as the worthy successor of those earlier sainted kings, the Nguyễn rulers of the south," by which she means the Nguyễn lords.[21] These eighteenth century lords were, as we have seen, more Buddhist than Neo-Confucian. Instead of applying the label "Neo-Confucian" to all the kings of the Nguyễn Dynasty, Nolo Cooke and other scholars describe how they used both teachings— Buddhism and Confucianism—to govern.

Some kings supported Buddhism more than others. Scholars disagree about Gia Long. Cao Huy Thuần lists the projects Gia Long launched to please his Buddhist subjects and bring order to the land after the Tây Sơn rebellion: "He restored large pagodas in Huế that the Tây Sơn had destroyed, built new pagodas, assembled Buddhist monks and nuns, established Buddhist organizations, held dharma talks, and large ceremonies [đại giới đàn] during which monks accept precepts. As a result Huế Buddhism raised its head after the war had destroyed it, both its pagodas and its monks."[22] Minh Chi et al., however, suggest that Gia Long's zeal for repairing pagodas had its limits. They quote this pronouncement by Gia Long from the Đại Nam Thực Lục (True Chronicles of Vietnam), a collection of annual records of the Nguyễn Dynasty written in Chinese: "Of late, Buddhists have constructed pagodas that are too many stories high and are too imposing . . . . From now on, I will allow only the repair of pagodas in a state of ruin and forbid all construction of new pagodas, all casting of statues and bells and all Buddhist ceremonies and festivals."[23]

Gia Long was the king of the entire country, however, and so Gia Long may have been addressing problems that existed in certain regions.

20. Nolo Cooke, "The Myth of the Restoration," 269.
21. Ibid., 275.
22. Cao Huy Thuần, "Phật giáo Huế trong dòng chảy của lịch sử."
23. Minh Chi, Ha Van Tan, and Nguyen Tai Thu, Buddhism in Vietnam (HCMC: The Gioi, 1993), 184.

Thiên Đô argues against the view that Buddhism declined in 19th century Vietnam. He mentions a recent study of sacred places of worship established from the sixth century up to 1900. According to this study, which was conducted by researchers at the Hán Nôm Research Institute in Hanoi,[24] the ruling elite of the Nguyễn Dynasty assisted with the building of two-thirds of the 228 Buddhist pagodas mentioned in the 19th century documents the researchers studied. With this assistance, Thiên Đô explains, pagodas "may have been built anew, repaired, refurbished, or have been provided with a building converted from a different type of temple, or given crown land to supplement income, or a new name plaque, ornaments, and furniture as a sign of royal recognition."[25]

Thích Hải Ấn and Hà Xuân Liêm say that during Gia Long's reign Buddhism was "revived" [*phục hưng*] but under the next two kings, Minh Mạng (r. 1820-1840) and Thiệu Trị (r. 1841-1847) Buddhism "began to develop" [*khởi sự phát triển*].[26] Scholars agree that these two kings who followed Gia Long did a great deal to support Buddhism. Thích Hải Ấn and Hà Xuân Liêm describe in detail the many pagodas built during Minh Mạng's reign and mention that he organized five ceremonies, called *đại trai đàn*, at Thiên Mụ Pagoda in which monks and nuns pray for the dead who died without a proper funeral.[27] Thiệu Trị also repaired and rebuilt pagodas. In 1844 he constructed the seven-floor Phước Duyên tower in front of Thiên Mụ Pagoda. In this same year he also built Diệu đế Pagoda on the banks of the Gia hội River in the place where he was born. (*Diệu đế* [Skt. *arya satya*] refers to the Four Noble Truths of Buddhism.) Inscribed on a stele outside this pagoda is a couplet by Thiệu Trị that suggests that he believed Buddhism and Confucianism were not opposed. It begins: "Good words are precious, good deeds can be inherited. How can meditating on goodness [a Buddhist practice] harm the royal way [Confucianism]?"[28] According to Nola Cooke, "Only with the accession of the doctrinaire Confucian Tự Đức did Buddhism begin to suffer Confucian-inspired

---

24. "*Hán-Nôm*" refers to premodern written materials in *Hán* (classical Chinese) and *Nôm* (the vernacular logographic Vietnamese script). Scholars connected with the Institute conduct linguist, literary, and historical research related to works stored in the Institute's library.
25. Thiên Đô, "The Quest for Enlightenment and Cultural Identity: Buddhism in Contemporary Vietnam," in *Buddhism and Politics in Twentieth-Century Asia*, ed. Ian Harris (London and New York: Pinter, 199), 258.
26. Thích Hải Ấn and Hà Xuân Liêm, *Lịch sử Phật giáo xứ Huế*, 269.
27. Ibid., 269-282.
28. Translated by Nolo Cooke in "The Myth of the Restoration," 290.

restrictions, as the king sought to diminish its place in state and society by, for example, five times reducing the ranks of monks and nuns and four times restricting pagoda construction."[29]

To sum up, from the mid-sixteenth through the eighteenth century Buddhism flourished in Đàng Trong. Cooke says under the Nguyễn lords Buddhism was the "state religion."[30] That may be an exaggeration, but clearly it seems to have reached that status when Nguyễn Phúc Chu ruled (1691-1725). Thạch Liêm, a Chinese monk living in Vietnam, observed that Nguyễn Phúc Chu's palace was decorated just like a Buddhist pagoda with Buddhist flags, wooden fish, and inverted bells.[31] The Nguyễn lords drew on Confucian principles to tighten their control over the population but, as Cooke points out, they never "institutionalized" Confucianism. The first three kings of the Nguyễn Dynasty—Gia Long, Minh Mạng, and Thiệu Trị—were all enthusiastic supporters of Buddhism. King Tự Đức (r. 1847-1883), who stated in 1878 that he never believed in Buddhism,[32] promoted Confucianism but during his reign Vietnam was colonized by the French and so he and the kings that followed him were kings in name only; they performed ceremonial functions but had little real power. In describing Tự Đức and his successors, Cao Huy Thuần says, there is no point in talking about Buddhist kings [*vua Phật*] or Confucian kings [*vua Nho*] because all the kings were puppet kings [*vua bù nhìn*].[33]

During the reign of these puppet kings, however, the majority of Vietnamese continued to be devout Buddhists. Shawn McHale, in his study of Confucianism, Buddhism, and communism during the years 1920-1945, argues against a "rhetoric of decline"—the view put forth, he says, by French administrators, Marxist critics, and Buddhist intellectuals that "twentieth century Buddhism had degenerated from a golden age."[34] He emphasizes the role that printed matter played in fostering the Buddhist Revival that began in the 1920s. This revival began when more and more

---

29. Ibid., 290.
30. Ibid., 279.
31. Li Tana Nguyễn, *Cochinchina*, 109. Li Tana uses Thạch Liêm's Chinese name, Da Shan. She found his description of Nguyễn Phúc Chu's palace in a journal the monk kept. For full citation, see Li Tana Nguyễn, *Cochinchina*, 186.
32. Nolo Cooke, "The Myth of the Restoration," 286. Cooke cites the *Đại Nam Thực Lục* [True Chronicles of Vietnam], a collection of annual records of the Nguyễn Dynasty.
33. Cao Huy Thuần, "Phật giáo Huế trong dòng chảy của lịch sử," 8.
34. McHale mentions Thích Mật Thể, a Buddhist monk from Huế, and Nguyễn An Ninh, a leading journalist and anti-French activist in the 1920s and 1930s who collaborated with Marxists. See Shawn Frederick McHale, *Print and Power: Confucianism, Communism, and Buddhism in the Making of Modern Vietnam*, 144-145.

Vietnamese could read, thanks to the spread of the National Script, *Quốc ngữ*, a way of writing Vietnamese using the Latin alphabet. The Buddhist Revival was primarily a movement of intellectuals but it included, Shawn McHale says, the printing of "simple catechisms, poetry on Buddhist themes, and fragments of the basic texts of Vietnamese Buddhism (such as the Amitabha sutra)." Thus the revival affected a broad span of the population, reaching the highly literate as well as the barely literate. In Huế the Buddhist Revival was spearheaded by an organization founded in 1932 called the Society for the Study and Practice of Buddhism in An Nam [*An Nam Phật Học Hội*]. This organization founded a journal called *Viên Âm Nguyệt San* [Perfect Sound Monthly] which included articles on the Buddhist sutras, poems on Buddhist themes, and news of Buddhist activities in the region. This journal appeared in Huế, Cao Huy Thuần explains, when Confucianism was becoming old-fashioned, Catholicism was being spread by French missionaries, and modern education in the National Script was just beginning. This journal was useful, he suggests, in reminding students and intellectuals not to overlook Buddhism in their search for "a stable morality and philosophy" to guide their lives.[35]

The three periods when there were Buddhist kings, Confucian kings, and then puppet kings are, Cao Huy Thuần says, rather far in the past but worth remembering. Then, he says, came "King Ngô"—Ngô Đình Diệm— who was president of the Republic of Vietnam when the Buddhist demonstrations which I have discussed in Chapter Twelve took place. Understanding how deeply Buddhism is embedded in Huế's history and culture helps us understand why these demonstrations began in Huế, sometimes called the "The Capital of Buddhism" [*Kinh đô của Phật Giáo*].

LIỄU QUÁN AND THE LÂM TẾ SCHOOL[36]

Beginning around the end of the Lý Dynasty (1010-1225), Chinese monks belonging to the Linji and Caodong schools brought Zen Buddhism to

---

35. Cao Huy Thuần, "Phật giáo Huế trong dòng chảy của lịch sử," 8-9.
36. "School," "lineage," and "sect" are used loosely in discussions of Buddhism. The Chinese word *tsung* and the Sino-Vietnamese equivalent *tông* can refer to either a lineage or a school. In translating *tsung* into English, T. Griffith Foulk suggests that "we use 'lineage' whenever it refers to a spiritual clan conceived as a group of individuals related by virtue of their inheritance of some sort of Dharma from a common ancestor"; and that we "reserve the English word 'school' for movements or groups within Chinese Buddhism that were made up of real persons united in a self-conscious manner by a common set of beliefs, practices, and/or social structures." Griffith Foulk points out that "lineages" may be "semi-mythological entities"—not based on historical fact; he wants to reserve the word "school" for entities that historians, following rules for "critical historiography," can

Vietnam.[37] According to Phúc Điền, a 19th century Buddhist leader and author, members of the Trần aristocracy, including the kings of the Trần Dynasty, became disciples of monks belonging to the Linji school.[38] In other words, the Bamboo Grove Zen School founded by Trần Nhân Tông at Mount Yên tử could be considered a Linji school but it is known in Vietnam as the Bamboo Grove School. It is one of two Zen schools that Vietnamese consider to be Vietnamese Zen schools because their founders were Vietnamese. The other is the Liễu Quán School founded in Vietnam by Liễu Quán who was born in the village of Bạch Mã in Phú Yên Province in Central Vietnam.[39]

In the seventeenth century, Zen Buddhism in Central Vietnam was reinvigorated by the arrival from China of talented Zen monks of the Linji School who were fleeing the Manchu invaders who in 1644 defeated the ethnic Han rulers of the Ming Dynasty.[40] These monks came to Central Vietnam where they were welcomed by the Nguyễn lords. Thich Thien-An sums up the history of the Lâm Tế School (hereafter I will use the Vietnamese name for this school) in this way: It was a tradition, he says, that was "introduced by Nguyên Thiều, propagated by Tử Dung, and institutionalized by Liễu Quán."[41] Nguyên Thiều and Tử Dung were Chinese monks. Nguyên Thiều arrived in Vietnam in 1665, residing first in Bình Định Province before coming to the Huế area where he became the head monk at Thiên Mụ Pagoda. Tử Dung, the chief disciple of Nguyên Thiều, became an important teacher of Liễu Quán but he was not his first teacher. Liễu Quán's mother died when he was six, and his father placed him in a pagoda to be cared for and taught. Later as a young novice Liễu Quán served and studied with Chinese masters at Báo Quốc Pagoda and Thiên

prove to have existed. See T. Griffith Foulk, "The Ch'an *Tsung* in Medieval China: School, Lineage, or What?" *The Pacific World* New Series, No. 8 (1992), 19-20; and Cuong Tu Nguyen, *Zen in Medieval Vietnam* (Honolulu: University of Hawai'i Press, 1997), 30-32.

37. The Linji and Caodong schools were two of the Five Houses of Zen that originated in China during the Tang Dynasty.
38. Cuong Tu Nguyen, *Zen in Medieval Vietnam*, 21.
39. Vietnamese scholars sometimes refer to the Buddhism that Liễu Quán is credited with establishing in central Vietnam as the Lâm Tế (Ch. Linji; Jp. Rinzai) School but sometimes—probably to distinguish it from Rinzai Zen in Japan—they call it the "Liễu Quán School" or the "Liễu Quán branch or arm of Lâm Tế" when they write in English, and the Liễu Quán sect [*thiền phái Liễu Quán* or *dòng thiền Liễu Quán*] when they write in Vietnamese.
40. As mentioned in Chapter Ten, Trịnh Công Sơn's father is descended from Chinese immigrants who, like these Zen monks, came to Vietnam after the Manchu came to power in China. That is why Sơn's home village on the outskirts of Huế city is "Minh Hương"—Village of the Ming. Residents of Vietnam of Chinese descent were called "Minh Hương."
41. Thich Thien-An, *Buddhism and Zen in Vietnam*, 157.

Mụ Pagoda in Huế. Tử Dung taught Liễu Quán when he was in his early twenties. In around 1690 Tử Dung had founded Từ Đàm Pagoda, one of the best known pagodas in Huế.[42] (Thích Trí Quang, who spearheaded the Buddhist demonstrations in 1963 and 1966, resided there.) Tử Dung taught Liễu Quán at Từ Đàm Pagoda and guided him toward enlightenment by having him ponder koans like this one: "All things return to the One, but where does the One return?"[43] Later Liễu Quán founded Thuyền Tôn Pagoda on Mount Thiên Thai on the outskirts of Huế city. He is considered the founder [tổ] of the Liễu Quán School and there is a founder's tower or stupa honoring him called Tháp Tổ Liễu Quán on the grounds of this pagoda.

According to Thich Thien-An the Linji Zen that Chinese monks taught Liễu Quán was not pure Zen but a mixture of Zen and Pure Land. This mixed quality made it appealing to Vietnamese, Thich Thien-An suggests, but he also praises Liễu Quán who, he says, adapted the teachings of these Chinese monks "to fit with the contour of Vietnamese practice and tradition." He gave, Thich Thien-An, says, "a large choice to monks and laymen (sic) as to the practices they could pursue." This "stability without dogmatism," he says, "enabled the Vietnamese Zen spirit to continue its transmission outside the scriptures in spite of the resurgence of Confucianism in the 19th century, the Catholic interests propagated by the French, and later difficulties presented by the political division of the country in 1954."[44]

Most Buddhist monks and nuns today belong to the Lâm Tế school, but Vietnamese scholars emphasize that Buddhism in Vietnam is less rigid in its doctrine and practices than Linji in China or Rinzai in Japan. "Present-day Vietnamese Buddhism still claims an affiliation to Linji Zen," Cuong Tu Nguyen says, "but in reality it practices a kind of easygoing, emotionally reassuring, composite Buddhism that scarcely reflects the uncompromising abstractness and iconoclasm associated with the Linji spirit."[45] As for Rinzai, Thich Thien-An says that Lâm Tế shares only a "nominal bond" with this Japanese Zen school. It "bears little resemblance to Rinzai in actual practice," he says.[46] Liễu Quán is credited with fostering

---

42. Ibid., 162-176. See also Nguyễn Hữu Thông, Trần Đại Vinh, and Lê Văn Sách, *Danh Lam Xứ Huế* [The Celebrated Pagodas of Huế] (Huế: Hội Nhà Văn, 1993), 172.
43. Thich Thien-An, *Buddhism and Zen in Vietnam*, 163-164.
44. Ibid., 156-157.
45. Cuong Tu Nguyen, *Zen in Medieval Vietnam*, 50-51.
46. Thich Thien-An, *Buddhism and Zen in Vietnam*, 259, note 9.

this more easygoing Buddhism known as Lâm Tế. In fact, Lâm Tế Buddhism in Central and South Vietnam is sometimes called the Liễu Quán Zen sect [thiền phái Liễu Quán]. According to Minh Chi et al., "Today, most Buddhists in southern Vietnam, from Huế to the southernmost regions," belong to this sect or branch of Lâm Tế Buddhism.[47]

In the view of people from the Huế area, Nguyễn Hoàng and Liễu Quán are extremely important figures. They have inspired an intense regional pride. They receive less attention from Vietnamese historians who themselves are not from Central Vietnam. Nguyễn Hoàng, Keith Taylor says, "has been ignored by modern Vietnamese historians because he does not exemplify the theme of national unity and resistance to foreign aggression that has been central to the modern experience."[48] Liễu Quán is always mentioned in histories of Vietnamese Buddhism but in most accounts he is overshadowed by Trần Nhân Tông, a northerner who was both king of the country, then known as Đại Việt, and the founder of the Bamboo Grove Zen School.

Some historians writing in English, however, consider Nguyễn Hoàng to be a seminal figure. He was significant, Keith Tayor suggests, because "in him we see the beginning of a southern version of being Vietnamese."[49] "[H]is encounter with the larger world of Southeast Asia [in Đàng Trong] bestowed a new experience of freedom. He dared to risk being pronounced a rebel because he had found a place where such pronouncements no longer mattered."[50] Li Tana also argues for the importance of Nguyễn Hoàng and the lords that succeeded him. The rise of these lords in Đàng Trong, Li Tana points out, meant that "from the seventeenth century onward the Red River delta ceased to be the only center of Vietnamese civilization; . . . Another center—Huế—appeared in addition to Thăng Long [Hanoi]; another economic area, Thuận Quảng [Thuận Hóa plus Quảng Nam],[51] emerged in addition to the Red River delta." Li Tana agrees with Keith Taylor that after the rise of Nguyễn lords

47. Minh Chi, Ha Van Tan, and Nguyen Tai Thu, *Buddhism in Vietnam*, 163.
48. Keith Taylor, "Nguyen Hoang and the Beginning of Vietnam's Southward Expansion," in *Southeast Asia in the Early Modern Era: Trade, Power, and Belief*, ed. Anthony Reid (Ithaca, NY: Cornell University Press, 1993), 45.
49. Ibid.
50. Ibid., 64.
51. Nguyễn Hoàng took control of Quảng Nam in 1602 and put one of his sons in charge of a garrison there. See Keith Taylor, "Nguyen Hoang and the Beginning of Vietnam's Southward Expansion," 63.

in Đàng Trong "clear differences now existed that marked two different ways of being Vietnamese."[52]

These differences have persisted. After the French were defeated in 1954, the Geneva Accords divided Vietnam into two countries, the Democratic Republic of Vietnam in the North and the Republic of Vietnam in the South. The line separating these two countries was set at the Bến Hải River on the 17th parallel which is not too far—only about 280 miles—from the Gianh River in Quảng Trị which separated Đàng Trong from Đàng Ngoài in the seventeenth century. In his anti-war songs Trịnh Công Sơn emphasizes that Vietnamese, no matter their home region, are all the golden-skinned children of Lạc Hồng, all descendents of a dragon king and a fairy queen [*con rồng; cháu tiên*], as their creation myth explains. This myth, however, not only obscures the fact that over fifty different ethnic groups live in Vietnam but also ignores some regional differences within the dominant ethnic group, the *kinh* Vietnamese. Vietnamese in the three regions speak distinctly different dialects: They not only pronounce words differently; they have different words for the same thing. What are known in the West as "spring rolls" are *nem* in the North, *ram* in the Huế area, and *chả giò* in the South. As we saw in Chapter Thirteen singers from different regions typically sing folk songs in different tunes. These linguistic and cultural differences enrich the culture and Vietnamese enjoy pointing them out to visitors.

Vietnamese, however, cling to unflattering stereotypes regarding people in other regions. People in Huế consider northerners to be formal and showy in speech and manner but not sincere—in a word, deceitful [*giả dối*]. In commenting on this perception they may say "*đất chật người khôn*" [little land, shrewd people], the implication being that the high people-to-land ratio in the North has forced people there to be clever and deceitful—and a little tight-fisted—to survive. Central Vietnamese tend to view southerners more favorably than northerners though they sound more than a little condescending when they use words like *mộc mạc* [simple, unaffected] and *chất phác* [sincere, simple-mannered] to describe them. In the minds of Vietnamese from other regions, southerners have had it easy. They live in the fertile Mekong Delta where rice and fruit—mangoes, custard apples, papaya, etc.—are bountiful. This easy life has dulled their ambition a bit, some Vietnamese from other regions believe,

---

52. Li Tana Nguyễn, *Cochinchina*, 12.

and that is why the South has produced fewer great political leaders and writers.

The Huế region is a special place with a unique history and, as I've shown, Buddhism was an important part of that history. To administer and develop what was then a frontier region the Nguyễn lords drew on different peoples and cultures—Vietnamese, Chinese, and Cham. Shawn McHale suggests that Huế "is quintessentially Vietnamese because, paradoxically, it draws on multiple streams of Vietnamese and non-Vietnamese influences."[53] In the seventeenth century Huế welcomed monks from China who taught the novice Liễu Quán, who later, with their help, established the Lâm Tế School in Central Vietnam. Vietnamese from Huế are proud of this history. In a recent article on Buddhism in Huế, Cao Huy Thuần compares Nguyễn Hoàng to Lý Thái Tổ, founder of the Later Lý Dynasty, who reigned from 1010 to 1028 CE. According to a well-known legend, while traveling in 1010 on the royal barge on the Red River, Lý Thái Tổ saw a golden dragon soaring in the sky. He took this as a good omen and moved the capital to that spot. He named the new capital Thăng Long, City of the Soaring Dragon. "Like Lý Thái Tổ, who dreamed he saw a dragon flying above the land of Thăng Long," Cao Huy Thuần says, "Nguyễn Hoàng also has said that a spirit waited on Hà Khê for him to build Thiên Mụ Pagoda."[54] In the same article Cao Huy Thuần associates Liễu Quán with the illustrious Trần Nhân Tông, the founder of the Bamboo Grove Zen School near Mount Yên Tử. "No one dares to compare Liễu Quán to the Buddhist king Trần Nhân Tông," he says, "but if Yên Tử is the place that gave birth to the Bamboo Grove School, I think one can boldly say that Thuận Hóa is the place where Founder Liễu Quán succeeded."[55]

Like most people from Huế Trịnh Công Sơn was proud of his hometown and familiar with its history. When Văn Cẩm Hải interviewed Sơn in 1998 he prefaced a question with an observation. "If you divide your music into parts," he said, "it sounds very simple—like a folk song; but if you string the parts together it sounds like Zen songs [*thiền ca*]."[56]

---

53. Shawn Frederick McHale, *Print and Power*, 66.
54. Cao Huy Thuần, "Phật giáo Huế trong dòng chảy của lịch sử," 5.
55. Ibid., 6.
56. Trịnh Công Sơn, interview by Văn Cẩm Hải in Huế on March 27, 1998. See "Kiếp sau tôi vẫn là người Nghệ sĩ" [In the Next Reincarnation I'll still be an Artist], in *Trịnh Công Sơn: Một người thơ ca một cõi đi về* [Trịnh Công Sơn: A Singer-poet, a Place for Leaving and Returning], eds. Nguyễn Trọng Tạo, Nguyễn Thụy Kha, and Đoàn Tử Huyến (Hanoi: Âm Nhạc, 2001), 206.

Then he asked Sơn if Huế was responsible for this effect. In his answer, Sơn does not say his songs are Zen songs, but he acknowledges the influence of his hometown:

> Our souls are nourished either a little or a lot by some special region which breathes into our souls something strange and original. Each region has a different way of talking, a different intonation, so certainly the same is true for music and art. Many people complain and criticize me. They ask why I live in Huế but never write anything about Huế. I tell them every song I write is about Huế. Because I am not from Hanoi, in a song like "Remembering Autumn in Hanoi" [Nhớ Mùa Thu Hà Nội] I must use the word "Hanoi" so people know I'm writing about that region. Just like people who are not a child of Huế often use the word "Huế" a lot in their songs. I don't say "Huế" but all my songs are "Huế."[57]

I argue that Trịnh Công Sơn's songs are "Huế" because Huế is a very Buddhist city and Trịnh Công Sơn expresses Buddhist themes in his songs, but these songs are also "Huế" in other ways. In "A Recollection" [Hồi Ức],* Sơn's essay about the inspiration for his famous love song, "Diễm of the Past," he describes how the atmosphere of Huế can affect a young girl like Diễm—and inspire a young composer:

> Camphor, almond, red royal Poinciana, sumac, laurel—and also the Perfume River that flows around the city—all mix together in a young girl's soul and become a pure romantic mist. That's why Huế never ceases to be a source of inspiration. An ancient citadel, temples and palaces, imperial tombs—all these things make people long for the past and help free them from the troubles of this world.[58] As a result Huế becomes a private space, a private world. It's not as enticing as a large metropolis but it is the source of gentle personal emotions which suddenly turn people into dreamers who wish for worlds that are not completely real.[59]

Time passes so quietly in Huế, Sơn continues, that "people do not have a perception of time. . . . Only when old people die in the coldness of winter does one wake up and suddenly become aware of the whisperings of tombs and graves in the surrounding hills and mountains."

---

57. Ibid.
58. Trịnh Công Sơn refers to the walled fortress and palace in Huế where in the 19th century emperors of the Nguyễn Dynasty resided. When they died they were buried in elaborate tombs outside of the city. These tombs, located in very scenic areas, are now tourist attractions.
59. For the original essay in Vietnamese, see Trịnh Công Sơn, "Hồi ức" in *Trịnh Công Sơn: Một người thơ ca một cõi đi về,*178-180, See Appendix E for an English translation of Trịnh Công Sơn's essay.

In Chapter Ten I mentioned Sơn's obsession with death, which he describes in his essay "A Childhood Obsession."[60] In that essay he traces this obsession to the early death of his father. Sơn also talks about that obsession in his 1998 interview with Văn Cầm Hải:

> My largest obsession, one that has pursued me from the time I was a child and still pursues me now, is an obsession with death. The problem of life and death has loomed large in my emotional life. Reflection leads me to the conclusion that I probably have this obsession because I love life so much I'm afraid of losing it. It is difficult to lose something that one once had in life, like love. It is so beautiful that it leaves you afraid that one day you will lose it. This is the biggest obsession in my life—loss and death.[61]

One senses that the atmosphere of Huế contributed to this obsession. In his interview with Văn Cầm Hải Sơn mentions the royal tombs that surround the city and the endless rain. "Rain in Huế," he says, "is terrible: It can upset the order of normal life."[62] Trịnh Công Sơn's songs are very "Huế" in part because it is raining in so many of them. Then he sings some lines from a sad song, "Listening to Sounds from Afar" [Nghe tiếng muôn trùng], in which he talks about the rain:

> *At night listen to the wind pouring out its feelings*
> *At night listen to the earth turning over in the rain*
> *And also the royal tombs in Huế:*
> *Listen to a hundred sounds of grief*
> *Listen to the royal tombs around us*

Clearly Trịnh Công Sơn was affected by many aspects of Huế, not just Buddhism. For Trịnh Công Sơn and for many Vietnamese, however, Huế and Buddhism are so deeply intertwined it is difficult to separate one from the other. "Huế and Buddhism," Sơn said in another interview, "deeply influenced my youthful emotions."[63]

---

60. Trịnh Công Sơn, "Nỗi ám ảnh thời thơ ấu" [A Childhood Obsession], in *Trịnh Công Sơn: Tôi là ai, là ai. . .* [Trịnh Công Sơn: Who Am I?], 133-134. The original date and source are not given. See Nguyễn Minh Nhụt et al., *Trịnh Công Sơn: Tôi là ai, là ai. . .* [Trịnh Công Sơn: Who Am I?] (Hà Nội: Nhà Xuất Bản Trẻ, 2011).
61. Trịnh Công Sơn, "Kiếp sau tôi vẫn là người Nghệ sĩ," 205.
62. Ibid., 206.
63. This undated interview is reprinted as "Chữ tài chữ mệnh cũng là bể dâu" [Talent and Destiny Both Lead to Disaster], in *Trịnh Công Sơn: Một người thơ ca một cõi đi về* [Trịnh Công Sơn: A Singer-poet, a Place for Leaving and Returning], 221-225.

24

TRỊNH CÔNG SƠN'S BUDDHISM

(& THÍCH NHẤT HẠNH'S DHARMA TALKS ABOUT IT)

Religion is a personal matter and so it is not easy to know about an individual's beliefs and practices. Trịnh Công Sơn is no exception but drawing on interviews the singer has given and aided by comments by friends and scholars, one can make some educated guesses about Sơn's Buddhism. In addition, in 2004 the well-known monk Thích Nhất Hạnh gave a series of dharma talks based on the life and songs of Trịnh Công Sơn. These talks, given in Vietnamese to novices at Plum Village, the Buddhist community that Thích Nhất Hạnh founded in France, are a useful source and I will discuss them in some detail. Videos of these talks, thirteen in all, are available online. Each talk has the title "Thiền Sư Nhất Hạnh Pháp Thoại Trịnh Công Sơn" [The Monk Thích Nhất Hạnh Gives a Dharma Talk about Trịnh Công Sơn].[1] In addition a transcript, in Vietnamese, of these dharma talks is available on the Làng Mai [Plum Village] website.[2] These talks were not all talk—they included the chanting and

---

1. See "Thiền Sư Nhất Hạnh Pháp Thoại Trịnh Công Sơn 9" [The Monk Thích Nhất Hạnh Gives a Dharma Talk about Trịnh Công Sơn: Part 9], https://www.youtube.com/watch?v=JQcqtK6gmsk (accessed November 17, 2018).
2. Trịnh Công Sơn, "Thông điệp thương yêu của Trịnh Công Sơn" [Trịnh Công Sơn's Message of Love], Làng Mai [Plum Village], https://langmai.org/phapduong/binh-tho-nhac/(accessed September 3, 2015).

425

singing of Trịnh Công Sơn's songs. This transcript, which is fifteen sin-
gle-spaced pages long, does not, of course, include the singing and chanting—one has to go to the videos to hear these performances—but it is a
very good summary of Thích Nhất Hạnh's remarks. Because it appears to
be a carefully considered and edited version of his talks, most of my translations of Thích Nhất Hạnh's remarks are based on this transcript.

Thích Nhất Hạnh's dharma talks are useful because few people know
more about Vietnamese Buddhism than Thích Nhất Hạnh. He was born
in 1926 in Trung Xá village in Quảng Trị Province, which is only forty
miles from Huế. He knew monks in Huế who knew Sơn when Sơn was
young and attending Hiếu Quang and Phổ Quang pagodas in Huế. When
Thích Nhất Hạnh was sixteen he entered Từ Hiếu pagoda as a novice and
in 1966, also at Từ Hiếu, he received the transmission of the dharma from
a monk named Thích Chân Thật, who represented the ninth generation
of the Liễu Quán branch of the Lâm Tế Zen school [Ch. *Lin Chi*; Jp.
Rinzai].[3]

In late 2014 he suffered a stroke which left him unable to talk. After
seeking treatment in the United States and Thailand he returned to Từ
Hiếu Pagoda on October 28, 2018 where he spent his final days.[4] He
passed away on January 22, 2022.

Thích Nhất Hạnh, before receiving a transmission of the dharma
from Thích Chân Thật, had visited the United States. In 1961 he studied
comparative religion at Princeton University and in 1962 he taught
contemporary Buddhism at Cornell. After the coup d'etat in 1963
that ended the Ngô Đình Diệm regime, Thích Trí Quang, a prominent
Buddhist leader in Huế, asked him to return to Vietnam to help him and
other Buddhist leaders strengthen Buddhism in Vietnam.

From 1964 to 1966 Thích Nhất Hạnh played a pivotal role in making
Vietnamese Buddhism more "engaged," a term which he is credited with

---

3. John Chapman says Thích Chân Thật represented the ninth generation of the Liễu
   Quán branch but Sallie B. King says it was the eighth. See John Chapman, "The 2005
   Pilgrimage and Return to Vietnam of Exiled Zen Master Thích Nhất Hạnh," in *Mo-
   dernity and Re-enchantment: Religion in Post-revolutionary Vietnam*, ed. Philip Taylor
   (Singapore: Institute of Southeast Asian Studies, 2007), 299; and Sallie B. King, "Thich
   Nhat Hanh and the Unified Buddhist Church of Vietnam: Nondualism in Action," in
   Engaged Buddhism: Buddhist Liberation Movements in Asia, eds. Christopher S. Queen
   and Sallie B. King (Albany, NY: State University of New York Press), 322.
4. Plum Village, "Official Announcement," https://plumvillage.org/news/thich-nhat-
   hanh-returns-to-vietnam/ (accessed February 5, 2019).

coining.[5] It is used now as an accepted term for a Buddhism which maintains a dual focus on inner peace and world peace.[6] Thích Nhất Hạnh founded the Order of Interbeing [*Tiếp Hiện*], a new branch of the Lâm Tế school, in Vietnam in 1965. Chân Không, one of the first six members to be inducted into this Order, explains that it "was created by Thầy[7] [Thích Nhất Hạnh] to help bring Buddhism directly into the arena of social concerns during a time when the war was escalating and the teachings of the Buddha were most sorely needed."[8] I bring up engaged Buddhism because one way to clarify Trịnh Công Sơn's Buddhism is to relate it to Thích Nhất Hạnh's "engaged" Buddhism, which I will do after commenting more generally about Trịnh Công Sơn's Buddhism.

Cao Huy Hóa, a devout Buddhist and long-time resident of Huế, suggests a way to classify followers of Buddhism in Vietnam, and so we can begin by considering where Trịnh Công Sơn might fit into his scheme.[9] He suggests we think of three concentric circles. In the innermost and smallest circle—the nucleus—are nuns and monks [*tỳ kheo ni* and *tỳ kheo tăng*] who have "left home and family" [Vn. *xuất gia*; Skt. *pravraj*] and vowed to live a monastic life and follow precepts much more numerous and rigorous than the Five Precepts that lay Buddhists pledge to follow. In the next circle, which lies near this nucleus, are the lay Buddhists, whom Vietnamese call "cư sĩ" [Skt. *upasaka* or *upasika*].[10] Unlike monks and

---

5. In two dharma talks that Thích Nhất Hạnh gave at Plum Village on May 6 and 7, 2008, he explains that in 1964 he put together some articles he had written and published them in a book called *Engaged Buddhism*. See Thích Nhất Hạnh, "Dharma Talk: History of Engaged Buddhism," The Mindfulness Bell, http://www.mindfulnessbell.org/wp/2015/02/dharma-talk-history-of-engaged-buddhism-2/ (accessed March 12, 2016). This book, *Engaged Buddhism*, is apparently the book that Kenneth Kraft cites in "Prospects of a Socially Engaged Buddhism," in *Inner Peace, World Peace: Essays on Buddhism and Nonviolence*, ed. Kenneth Kraft (Albany, NY: State University of New York Press, 1992), 18. I have not been able to find this book. Christopher S. Queen, who says Kraft's citation to this book is the only one he has seen, suggests the term may derive from the French term *engagé*. According to Queen, this term, "meaning politically outspoken or involved, was common among activist intellectuals in French Indochina long before the 1960s." See Christopher S. Queen, "Introduction: The Shapes and Sources of Engaged Buddhism," in *Engaged Buddhism: Buddhist Liberation Movements in Asia*, eds. Christopher S. Queen and Sallie B. King (Albany, NY: State University of New York Press), 2, 34 (note 6).
6. In Vietnamese "engaged Buddhism" is called "*Phật giáo dấn thân*." "*Phật giáo*" means Buddhism and "*dấn thân*" means to throw oneself into something, to plunge into life.
7. "Thầy," the Vietnamese word for "teacher," is the term Thích Nhất Hạnh's followers use to address him.
8. Chân Không (Cao Ngọc Phương), *Learning True Love: How I Learned and Practiced Social Change in Vietnam* (Berkeley, CA: Parallax Press, 1993), 79.
9. Cao Huy Hóa, "Cư sĩ giữa dòng đời" [Lay Buddhists in the Flow of Life], in Cao Huy Hóa, *Thiền một chút* [A Little Zen] (HCMC: Phương Đông, 2014), 26-35.
10. "Upasaka" is a male lay Buddhist; "upasika" a female lay Buddhist.

Unlike monks and

nuns, *cư sĩ* do not *xuất gia*: They *tu tại gia*[practice Buddhism at home]. *Cư sĩ* must pledge to accept the Three Treasures [Vn. *Tam bảo*]—Buddha, Dharma, and Sangha—and follow the Five Precepts. In the outer circle, the one furthest from the nucleus, are people who are called simply "Buddhists" [*Phật tử*] or "Buddhist people" [*Người Phật tử*]. People in this third category are nominal Buddhists, people who have made no vows or pledges and have never completed a *quy y* ceremony.

Trịnh Công Sơn did complete a *quy y* ceremony, in which one vows to accept the Three Treasures, but he was not a *cư sĩ*. This term refers to Buddhists who do more than simply accept the Three Treasures and pledge to obey the Five Precepts. According to my Buddhist dictionary, *cư sĩ* are disciples who practice the way of a Bodhisattva and work to benefit sentient beings. It refers to Buddhists "who, although they still dwell in this impure earthly realm, have heart-minds [Vn. *tâm*] that are pure, unstained by earthly dust. Actually most of us should only consider ourselves Buddhists at home [*tại gia*] and reserve the term '*cư sĩ*' for those who have advanced further on the religious path."[11] A *cư sĩ*, Cao Huy Hóa explains, "works for Buddhism in various ways, for example, by doing charitable work, by making offerings, by chanting prayers, by helping to build pagodas, casting statues, or printing prayer books."[12] Clearly Trịnh Công Sơn should be placed in the outer circle in Cao Huy Hóa's scheme: He was a Buddhist, a *người Phật tử*, not a *cư sĩ*. As he told an interviewer, "I am a Buddhist [*Phật tử*] from a family whose primary religion is Buddhism."[13] Trịnh Công Sơn never claimed to have a heart-mind as clear as a Bodhisattva's. He knew he was "stained by earthly dust." "Who

---

11. Tâm Tuệ Hỷ, ed., *Danh từ Phật học thực dụng* [Useful Buddhist Terms] (Hà Nội: Tôn Giáo, 2004), 111.

12. Cao Huy Hóa, "Cư sĩ giữa dòng đời," 33.

13. Trịnh Công Sơn, interview with Thích Tâm Thiện. This interview, titled "Theo Đạo Phật trong Âm nhạc Trịnh Công Sơn" [Buddhism in the Music of Trịnh Công Sơn] first appeared in *Nguyệt San Giác Ngộ* [Enlightenment Monthly Review] No. 1 (April 4, 1996). I found it at Diễn Đàn Văn Hóa Học [Forum for Studies of Culture], http://www.van-hoahoc.edu.vn/dienan/viewtopic.php?f=56&t=1229 (accessed September 18, 2100). Excerpts from this interview and other comments that Trịnh Công Sơn has made about his Buddhist background can be found in "Nhạc sĩ Trịnh Công Sơn: 'Phải biết sống hết mình trong mỗi sát na của hiện tại'" [The Musician Trịnh Công Sơn: "You Must Know How to Live Completely in Each Moment of Reality"], in Lê Minh Quốc, ed., *Trịnh Công Sơn: Rơi lệ ru người* [Trịnh Công Sơn: Shedding Tears, Singing Lullabies] (Phụ Nữ: Hanoi, 2004), 202-204. Parts of this interview also appear in Trịnh Công Sơn, "Nghĩ về thiền" [Thinking about Zen] in *Trịnh Công Sơn: Tôi là ai, là ai . . .* [Trịnh Công Sơn: Who Am I, Am I?], eds. Nguyễn Minh Nhựt et al. (HCMC: Trẻ, 2011), 212-214.

am I," he asks in his song "Don't Despair, I Tell Myself" [Tôi ơi đừng tuyệt vọng],* "to be so of this world? / Who am I who loves this world so much?"

The Buddhist name [*Pháp danh*] that Trịnh Công Sơn took at his *quy y* ceremony after his father's death in 1955 was Nguyên Thọ, which Thích Nhất Hạnh, in his dharma talk about Trịnh Công Sơn, says means "transmission from the source." According to Thích Nhất Hạnh, Sơn's religious name suggests the transmission of benevolence or humaneness [*lòng nhân ái*], loving-kindness and compassion [*từ bi*], and courage [*dũng cảm*].[14] Sơn himself suggests that before his father died and before his *quy y* ceremony Buddhism was already an important part of his life. "Huế and Buddhism deeply influenced my emotions when I was young," he says in an interview.[15] When he was sick, he says, his mother would invite monks to their home and he would fall asleep listening to their prayers. In this same interview he talks about studying and memorizing Buddhist prayers.[16] At Phổ Quang Pagoda, which was very near his home, Sơn was taught how to chant Buddhist prayers by a monk named Chánh Pháp who was well-known for his chanting ability. In one of his dharma talks on Trịnh Công Sơn, Thích Nhất Hạnh emphasizes that Sơn reached a skill level appropriate for chanting in a pagoda.[17] In other words, he was not an amateur.

How about meditation? Sơn, it appears, had a rather unorthodox approach to meditation. When Thích Tâm Thiện asked him if he meditated, he replied in this way:

> I have my own way of practicing meditation. I don't have a fixed time and I don't even feel as if I am meditating. It's just a way of living, of living Buddhism in each moment. It's like when I'm sitting in front of a glass of whisky or a beautiful woman. This violates the rules of Buddhism a little but I'm a worldly person [*kẻ trần tục*] and so I give myself permission in this way. Besides, there are many roads leading to Buddha, like clapping a *mõ* [a wooden bell] and reciting prayers and lighting incense. Why should I not use a method that's familiar and the closest to me—a glass of whisky? Also, I'm not of the view that one searches for Buddha nature anywhere else; it resides

---

14. Thích Nhất Hạnh "Thông điệp thương yêu của Trịnh Công Sơn."

15. Trịnh Công Sơn interview.This interview is undated and the interviewer is not identified. It is reprinted with the title "Chữ tài chữ mệnh cũng là bể dâu" [Talent and Destiny Both Lead to Disaster] in Nguyễn Trọng Tạo et al., *Trịnh Công Sơn: Một người thơ ca một cõi đi về* [Trịnh Công Sơn: A Singer-poet, a Place for Leaving and Returning], eds. Nguyễn Trọng Tạo, Nguyễn Thụy Kha, and Đoàn Tử Huyến (Hanoi: Âm Nhạc, 2001), 221-225.

16. Trịnh Công Sơn, interview with Thích Tâm Thiện.

17. Thích Nhất Hạnh, "Thông điệp yêu thương của Trịnh Công Sơn."

within oneself. That is my native village, the throne of Buddhism. I sit. Buddhism flows over me and I flow over Buddhism.[18]

I don't know of any Zen masters who recommend practicing meditation while drinking whisky and looking at a beautiful woman! The fusion of meditation with daily activities, however, as opposed to meditating only when sitting in the lotus position, is indeed a part of Zen and has been since the seventh century. In *Zen Philosophy, Zen Practice* Thich Thien-An describes how this fusion came about.[19] In India, he explains, one meditated by sitting in the lotus position but this changed in China. Zen Buddhism is believed to have been transmitted to China in the sixth century by Bodhidharma, a monk from India. Bodhidharma is considered to be the first Chinese Zen master, or patriarch. In one of many apocryphal tales about him he seeks enlightenment by staring at a wall for seven years. By the seventh century Zen and meditating had become extremely popular in China and disciples packed the monasteries to practice sitting meditation. With everyone sitting and meditating, however, there was no one to do the everyday chores—cleaning rooms, gardening, cooking, etc. The fifth patriarch of Chinese Zen, Hung-Jen (601-674), however, came up with a solution: Disciples would meditate as they did daily chores. In the seventh century, Thich Thien-An explains, meditation became "meditation in action, an extension of the principles of inward contemplation into the chores and routines of day-to-day existence."[20] When Hui-Neng (638-713), a disciple of Hung-Jen, became the sixth patriarch of Zen Buddhism he continued to promote the idea that if one were mindful one did not have to sit to meditate. One could meditate while performing daily chores and activities.

Thich Thien-An describes if not the birth at least a key development of mindfulness, one of the most important concepts in modern Zen Buddhism. In California my grandchildren learn about and practice mindfulness in their elementary school classrooms. In 2015 Headspace, a smartphone app which teaches mindfulness, had been downloaded by three million people.[21] Mindfulness has been embraced in the West by educators and business tycoons including the following: the late Steve Jobs of Apple; Richard Branson, the owner of Virgin Airlines; Mark T.

---

18. Trịnh Công Sơn, Interview with Thích Tâm Thiện.
19. Thich Thien-An, *Zen Philosophy, Zen Practice* (Berkeley, CA: Dharma Publishing, 1975), 27-28; 34-35.
20. Ibid., 28.
21. Lizzie Widdicombe, "The Higher Life," *The New Yorker*, July 6 & 13, 2015, 40.

Bertolini, the chief executive of Aetna; Eileen Fisher, the clothing designer; and Marc Benioff, the chief executive of Salesforce, a cloud-based software company. Benioff installed meditation rooms in the Salesforce Tower, the tallest building in San Francisco, and often invites Buddhist monks to his home.[22] Dan Harris has promoted meditation in books like *10% Happier* and *Meditation for Fidgety Skeptics* and in popular podcasts in which he interviews Buddhist scholars and researchers who believe in the value of meditation.[23]

The patriarchs Hung-Jen and Hui-Neng did not talk about meditating while drinking whisky: They probably were thinking of activities like carrying water and gardening. Buddhist teachers, however, emphasize that, as Sơn says, "There are many roads leading to enlightenment." In fact they say there are "Eighty-four thousand dharma gates" [*Tám vạn bốn ngàn pháp môn*]. It is worth noting that Sơn does not regard meditation as the only acceptable practice. He also accepts reciting prayers and lighting incense. He seems to accept the "other power" recognized within Pure Land Buddhism that I discussed in Chapter Twenty-Two.

In two different interviews Sơn reveals that he is aware of the Buddhist principle that one must learn to enjoy each moment of life. When Thích Tâm Thiện asks about his experience with Buddhism, Sơn says:

> I don't know why but in recent years I have begun to think of Buddhism as the religion that has the most existential character. You begin with the word "moment" [*sát na*], a small unit of time. You must know how to live completely in each moment of reality. Eating, drinking, walking, standing, lying down, sitting. Don't do one thing and think of something else. To me that is Zen, a way to live authentically. I zealously practice this way of living every day.[24]

When Văn Cẩm Hải, who interviewed Trịnh Công Sơn in 1998, told the singer that he detected existentialism in his songs Sơn responded in this way:

> Authentic existentialism is not bad. The supreme master of existentialism was the Buddha because he taught us that we must be mindful of each moment of our lives. When you, Hải, and I drink this beer we should enjoy it completely. When we are hungry a bowl of rice will

---

22. David Gelles, "Talking Mindfulness on the C.E.O. Beat," *New York Times*, November 28, 2018, https://www.nytimes.com/2018/11/28/reader-center/ceos-mindfulness-meditation.html (accessed December 5, 2018).
23. Dan Harris, *10% Happier* (New York: Harper Collins, 2019); Dan Harris, *Meditation for Fidgety Skeptics* (New York: Spiegel & Grau, 2017).
24. Interview with Thích Tâm Thiện.

only be delicious if we concentrate while eating. I say sincerely that when people are aware in each moment of their lives then existentialism is easy, nothing at all. People with this awareness live calmly in each moment; they don't live the ordinary, hurried way.[25]

Thích Nhất Hạnh, in one of his dharma talks about Trịnh Công Sơn, reads Sơn's comment from the above interview about being mindful of each moment, and exclaims "Here is a dharma teacher [Vn. *giáo thọ*; Skt. *acarya*]!" Although it sounds like Sơn is talking about mindfulness, something that Thích Nhất Hạnh emphasizes in his teaching, what he reveals in this interview, Thích Nhất Hạnh says, is his awareness of a Buddhist teaching called *drsta dharma sukha vihara* in Sanskrit and *hiện pháp lạc trú* in Vietnamese. In his talk Thích Nhất Hạnh provides this English translation: "living happily in the present moment, deeply." Mindfulness [Skt. *samyak smriti*; Vn. *chánh niệm*] involves becoming aware of all forms of feelings and sensations whereas "living happily in the present moment" refers to the Buddhist teaching that through practice one can achieve happiness in the present moment; one need not wait for it to arrive in the future. Thích Nhất Hạnh says that Trịnh Công Sơn reveals that he is aware of this teaching in his song "Each Day I Choose a Little Happiness"* [Mỗi ngày tôi chọn một niềm vui]. Here are the first and fourth verses:

> *Each day I choose a little happiness*
> *Choose flowers and smiles*
> *I pick wind from sky and invite you to take it*
> *So your eyes will smile like flying leaves*
>
> *Each day I choose one time only*
> *Choose a lullaby for a child softly stepping into life*
> *I choose full sunshine, choose a rainstorm*
> *So rice plants cry joyfully and wave like hands*

Thích Nhất Hạnh says, however, that although Sơn had acquired "wisdom" [*tuệ giác*][26] regarding the importance of living happily in the

---

25. Trịnh Công Sơn, interview with Văn Cầm Hải, "Kiếp sau tôi vẫn là người nghệ sĩ" [In the Next Reincarnation I'll still be an Artist], in *Trịnh Công Sơn: Một người thơ ca một cõi đi về* [Trịnh Công Sơn: A Singer-poet, a Place for Leaving and Returning], eds. Nguyễn Trọng Tạo, Nguyễn Thụy Kha, and Đoàn Tử Huyến (Hanoi: Âm Nhạc, 2001), 211. This is a reprint of an interview conducted by Văn Cầm Hải in Huế on March 27, 1998.

26. Thích Nhất Hạnh uses this compound word several times to describe Trịnh Công Sơn. Usually translated as "wisdom," it consists of two Sino-Vietnamese words: *tuệ* [intelligence] and *giác* [to feel, sense, perceive, be conscious of].

present moment, he could not live according to that wisdom because he lacked a "*tăng thân*," or support group. A *tăng thân* differs from a *sangha* [Vn. *tăng già*], which is the third of the Three Treasures. Thích Nhất Hạnh probably uses the term *tăng thân* instead of *tăng già* because although now, particularly in the West, a *sangha* may include anyone interested in Buddhism, in traditional use it refers only to those who have "left home" [*xuất gia*] to become nuns or monks. A *tăng thân*, however, refers to "a group that practices and studies the dharma together with no distinction made between monks and nuns and lay Buddhists."[27] Thích Nhất Hạnh tells his audience—novices, monks and nuns, and lay Buddhists—that we are lucky because, although we are not supermen or superwomen, we can do what Trịnh Công Sơn wanted to do but couldn't because we have a *tăng thân* and he did not.[28]

Using two Buddhist terms to describe how far Trịnh Công Sơn has progressed along the Buddhist path, Thích Nhất Hạnh says that he has achieved *kiến đạo* but not *chứng đạo*.[29] *Kiến đạo*, literally "to see the path," refers to a stage in which one has seen the truth and *chứng đạo*, literally "to confirm the path," refers to a later stage when one has understood the truth more clearly. "*Kiến đạo*," Thích Nhất Hạnh says, "is to see the path, see the road in order to return to a life of living deeply each moment of everyday life. After *kiến đạo* we must practice more so we can *chứng đạo*."[30] Because he did not have a support group—a *tăng thân*—Trịnh Công Sơn, Thích Nhất Hạnh says, never achieved this second stage, but reaching this first stage is no mean accomplishment. He suggests that because Trịnh Công Sơn reached *Kiến đạo* he could write songs like "Each Day I Choose a Piece of Happiness."[31]

Thích Nhất Hạnh frequently uses the compound word "*tuệ giác*" to describe Trịnh Công Sơn. Usually translated as "wisdom," it consists of two Sino-Vietnamese words: "*tuệ*" [intelligence] and "*giác*" [to feel, sense, perceive, be conscious of]. This word has Buddhist connotations. It is similar to the Sanskrit word *prajna* [wisdom; Vn. *trí tuệ*] that occurs in the Perfection of Wisdom [Prajna Paramita] sutras, the most famous being the Heart Sutra and the Diamond Sutra. One dictionary defines *tuệ*

---

27. Tâm Tuệ Hỷ, ed., *Danh từ Phật học thực dụng*, 427.
28. Thích Nhất Hạnh, "Thông điệp thương yêu của Trịnh Công Sơn."
29. These Vietnamese terms are translations of the Pali terms *ditthi magga* and *magga sacchikaranam*.
30. Thích Nhất Hạnh, "Thông điệp thương yêu của Trịnh Công Sơn."
31. Ibid.

giác this way: "the clear-sighted understanding, possessed by Sakyamuni Buddha, of all phenomena in the universe."[32] "Trịnh Công Sơn had a lot of Buddhist wisdom [*tuệ giác của đạo Bụt*]," Thích Nhất Hạnh says. "If we listen carefully, we can recognize that wisdom [*tuệ giác*] in his music."[33]

But he did not have a *tăng thân* [support group]. What he had instead, Thích Nhất Hạnh says, was a group of drinking buddies. Thích Nhất Hạnh reports that once Trịnh Vĩnh Trinh, Trịnh Công Sơn's sister, asked one of these buddies of Sơn's to advise Sơn not to drink so much. "My brother drinks too much," she told this friend. "From this morning up to now he's drunk three bottles already." But, Thích Nhất Hạnh says, that friend could not advise Sơn because he also drank.[34] "A person who has a realization [*tuệ giác*]," Thích Nhất Hạnh continues, "and wishes to live according to that realization, must return to the *tăng thân*, must have a *tăng thân* to follow. Anyone who doesn't have a *tăng thân* will remain an orphan."[35]

Thích Nhất Hạnh points out that Trịnh Công Sơn had good friends, including some who were famous, and many fans who adored him, but still he was lonely. Thích Nhất Hạnh admires Sơn for the friendships he formed and suggests that the quiet moments that he experienced with them brought him close to an escape from loneliness and suffering. He reads the following excerpt from an article Sơn wrote and then builds a dharma lesson around it:

> There are times when friends are present that are like the quiet spaces in music. That presence usually can bring us a comfort and ease that resembles pleasure. In these instances we don't need to deal with anything. We don't need to try to fill the empty spaces with talk that is forced and insipid.[36]

Thích Nhất Hạnh says we need friends and quiet moments like those Sơn mentions but points out that Sơn could not capitalize on those quiet moments because he "had not studied how to sit alone to enjoy quiet so Trịnh Công Sơn needed a friend next to him so he could enjoy the

---

32. Lê Văn Đức, *Tự điển Việt Nam* [Vietnamese Dictionary] (Saigon: Khai Trí), 1456.
33. Thích Nhất Hạnh, "Thông điệp thương yêu của Trịnh Công Sơn."
34. Ibid.
35. Ibid.
36. Trịnh Công Sơn, "Đò đưa" [A Boat that Carries Us], in *Trịnh Công Sơn: người hát rong qua nhiều thế hệ* [A Troubadour Who Sang for Many Generations], ed. Trần Thanh Phương et al. (HCMC: Trẻ, 2004), 62. This is one of a series of short essays or columns, all titled "Đò đưa," that Trịnh Công Sơn wrote in the late 1990s for a magazine called *Tạp chí Sóng Nhạc* [Music Waves]. Five essays, including the one from which this quotation is taken, appear in *Trịnh Công Sơn: Người hát rong qua nhiều thế hệ*.

quietness. We are also like that. We learn to sit and meditate but feel it is not much fun. Sitting is not talking. But sitting with three or four people is more fun. When we sit together we support each other." Trịnh Công Sơn's problem, he says, is that his friends didn't know how to sit, they knew only how to drink whisky, and so his quiet moments were "no longer precious."[37]

Thích Nhất Hạnh argues that meditation, especially *vipassana* [Vn. *thiền quán*] meditation, could have cured Trịnh Công Sơn's obsession with death, an obsession which the singer clearly struggled to overcome.[38] *Vipassana* meditation, or insight meditation, is often preceded by *samatha* [Vn. *thiền chỉ*], or calming meditation. Thích Nhất Hạnh does not explain *samatha* meditation in his dharma talks about Trịnh Công Sơn, but he does in a dharma talk given at Plum Village in 1996. In this talk he explains that *samatha* means "stopping" and *vipassana* means "looking." "Calming" or "stopping" meditation prepares one for insight or "looking" meditation. Our mind can heal itself, Thích Nhất Hạnh says, if we give it a chance; if we learn *samatha*, "the deep art of stopping."[39]

Vipassana meditation is the meditation that Thích Nhất Hạnh suggests could have cured Trịnh Công Sơn's obsession with death: "Although Trịnh Công Sơn received the seed of love from his mother and from the pagoda," Thích Nhất Hạnh says, "he never had an opportunity to study and practice the *vipassana* method in order to perceive his own everlasting non-birth [Skt. *anutpatti*; Vn. *vô sinh*]. Therefore Trịnh Công Sơn had not yet escaped an obsession with death." Then, turning to his own situation, Thích Nhất Hạnh says: "I am not obsessed with death because I have wisdom [*tuệ giác*] regarding life and death and I have practiced *vipassana* and I have perceived my own everlasting non-birth."[40] The phrase "everlasting non-birth" [Vn. *vô sinh bất diệt*] refers to a state beyond birth and death, which is Nirvana. Thích Nhất Hạnh appears to be saying that although he has perceived Nirvana, like a true bodhisattva he has delayed attaining it so he can help other suffering beings like Trịnh Công Sơn.

37. Thích Nhất Hạnh, "Thông điệp thương yêu của Trịnh Công Sơn."
38. Trịnh Công Sơn talks about this obsession in "Nỗi ám ảnh thời thơ ấu" [A Childhood Obsession] in *Trịnh Công Sơn: Tôi là ai, là ai...* [TCS: Who Am I?], eds. Nguyễn Minh Nhựt et al. (HCMC: Trẻ, 2011), 133-134. The original date and source are not given.
39. Thích Nhất Hạnh, "Returning to Our True Home." This is a transcription in English of a dharma talk that Thích Nhất Hạnh gave at Plum Village, France, on July 16, 1996. See Plum Village: Mindfulness Practice Centre, http://plumvillage.org/transcriptions/returning-to-our-true-home (accessed January 1, 2016).
40. Thích Nhất Hạnh, "Thông điệp thương yêu của Trịnh Công Sơn."

In his dharma talks Thích Nhất Hạnh often portrays Trịnh Công Sơn as a failed Buddhist, as someone who, thanks to his mother's guidance and his visits to pagodas, started out on the right path but then lost his way. He spent too much time with his drinking buddies, not enough time in a Buddhist support group. And he never learned to meditate. He also faults Trịnh Công Sơn for misrepresenting Buddhist concepts. For example, he adamantly objects to a comment that Trịnh Công Sơn made in a 1998 interview.[41] Văn Cầm Hải, the interviewer, asked Sơn: "From a philosophical perspective, what song of yours expresses new ways of looking at the destiny of human beings, at love for life, at death and liberation?"[42] Though this would seem a lot for any song to do, Sơn suggests his song "A Place for Leaving and Returning."* He adds that this is a difficult song, one that he himself has difficulty explaining. (I mention it in discussing Trịnh Công Sơn's obscure lyrics in Chapter Nineteen.) But, Sơn continues, "the main idea of the song is that everyone has a place for returning. From emptiness we enter life and after wandering through life for a while we return to emptiness."[43] Thích Nhất Hạnh adamantly objects to this view. "Trịnh Công Sơn says that we come from emptiness and we shall return to emptiness. By speaking in this way he demonstrates that he does not yet have the wisdom [*tuệ giác*] of a person who practices Zen. We do not come from emptiness and we do not return to emptiness."[44]

Thích Nhất Hạnh also objects to the following lines in Sơn's song "Speck of Dust"* [*Cát bụi*]: "What speck of dust have I been reincarnated from / So one day I return to dust?" "Speck of Dust" is one of several songs by Trịnh Công Sơn which contain Christian references. (I discuss others in Chapter Twelve.) The reference in "Speck of Dust" is to words from the *Book of Common Prayer*, based on Genesis 3:19, that are spoken at Christian burials: "We commit this body to the ground, earth to earth, ashes to ashes, dust to dust." Thích Nhất Hạnh mentions that Sơn echoes the Bible in these lines, and then firmly objects to the view regarding the origin of life that Sơn's lyrics suggest:

---

41. Trịnh Công Sơn, interview by Văn Cầm Hải, "Kiếp sau tôi vẫn là người Nghệ sĩ."
42. Ibid., 204.
43. Ibid., 205.
44. Here Thích Nhất Hạnh says that Trịnh Công Sơn does not have wisdom [*tuệ giác*] but he has also said the singer "had a lot of Buddhist wisdom [*tuệ giác*]." (See Trịnh Công Sơn, "Thông điệp thương yêu của Trịnh Công Sơn" [Trịnh Công Sơn's Message of Love].) I do not think that he is contradicting himself. He is suggesting that Sơn had insight regarding certain Buddhist concepts but lacked insight regarding others.

The Bible says that we come from dust and will return to dust. Trịnh Công Sơn also holds that view. [He quotes the relevant lines from Sơn's song "Speck of Dust."] A speck of dust is not emptiness [*hư vô*]. Dust is also not enough to be reincarnated from. Many direct causes [*nhân*] and many indirect causes [*duyên*] must combine before I appear. With only one direct cause or one indirect cause there is no way I could appear. In Christianity God is the direct cause and the sole cause of existence but in Buddhism the idea of single cause is nonsensical. There is no thing that is created from a single cause.[45]

The Sanskrit terms for the Buddhist concept of direct and indirect causes that Thích Nhất Hạnh describes are *hetu-pratyaya* [Vn. *nhân duyên*] and *pratītyasamutpāda* [Vn. *duyên khởi*]. Both terms refer to the concept of multiple causes. A seed, for example, is a direct or primary cause of a flower; rain and sunlight are secondary or indirect causes. Thích Nhất Hạnh uses this flower example to refute Sơn's single cause view of his creation: "Take this flower," he says. "There must be a seed. There must be soil, fertilizer, sunshine. There must be clouds that turn into rainwater. In other words many direct causes, many indirect causes before this flower can appear. Therefore the idea of a single cause is not compatible with the truth. The truth is multiple direct causes [*nhân*], multiple indirect causes [*duyên*]—'coinciding dependent origination' [*trùng trùng duyên khởi*]."[46]

Although it may seem unfair, even bizarre, for a famous Zen teacher to object to two lines in a popular song, actually a lot is at stake. Thích Nhất Hạnh feels these lines reveal Sơn's ignorance of a core Buddhist concept. The Buddha's chief disciple, Sariputta, emphasizes its importance: "Whoever sees interdependent co-arising sees *dharma*," he said, and "whoever sees *dharma* sees interdependent co-arising."[47] Giving a dharma talk to monks, nuns, novices, and fellow Buddhists Thích Nhất Hạnh feels he must correct Sơn's misperception. To emphasize this core concept, he named his Zen Buddhist order the Order of Interdependent Co-arising [Vn. *Dòng Tu Tiếp Hiện*] and coined the English word "interbeing" to translate *tiếp hiện*. "In early Buddhism," he explains, "we speak of interdependent co-rising. In late Buddhism, we use the words interbeing and interpenetration. The terminology is different, but the meaning is the same."[48]

45. Thích Nhất Hạnh, "Thông điệp thương yêu của Trịnh Công Sơn."
46. Ibid. "*Trùng trùng duyên khởi*" is another Vietnamese term for *pratītyasamutpāda* [interdependent co-arising].
47. Peter Harvey, *An Introduction to Buddhism* (Cambridge: Cambridge University Press, 1990), 54.
48. Thích Nhất Hạnh, *The Heart of Buddha's Teaching* (New York: Broadway Books, 1999), 225.

The implications of this core concept are many. If everything is dependent on conditions to arise, then there can be nothing that is self-creating or independent. This principle applies not only to lifeless things but to sentient beings as well. If one accepts the Buddhist principle of interdependent co-arising, one must deny that there is such a thing as an independent self. "All psychological and physical phenomena constituting individual existence," says one Buddhist dictionary, "are interdependent and mutually condition each other. This is the twelve-link chain which entangles sentient beings in *samsara*."[49] *Samsara* is the cycle of birth and death—the earthly world in which we live. The twelve links of interdependent co-arising [Skt. *pratityasamutpada*; Vn. *thập nhị nhân duyên*] are links in a chain of cause and effect. The first link is ignorance [Skt. *avida*; Vn. *vô minh*], especially ignorance of the Four Noble Truths: That life is suffering, that suffering is caused by craving, that suffering can be ended by abandoning craving, and that the Eightfold Path is the way to move from *samsara* to *nirvana*. One can gain control of this chain of cause and effect by reversing the order of the Four Noble Truths. One should begin with the Fourth Truth, the Eightfold Path, which Buddhists believe leads to "the cessation of each of the twelve links, and thus of *dukkha* [suffering]."[50] Following this path will eventually lead to Nirvana.

Despite his criticisms of Trịnh Công Sơn, Thích Nhất Hạnh clearly admires and respects the singer. If he did not he would not have given a dozen or so dharma talks about him. In some talks he faults Sơn for his failings but in others he praises him, sometimes effusively. "I began to love Trịnh Công Sơn," Thích Nhất Hạnh says, "when I heard Khánh Ly sing "Love Song of a Mad Person" [Tình ca của người mất trí].* Written in 1967, this is perhaps Sơn's best-known anti-war song. Thích Nhất Hạnh's ninth dharma talk about Trịnh Công Sơn begins with a woman singing "Love Song of a Mad Person." One can listen to her performance.[51] Here are the first and third stanzas:

> *I love someone killed in the Battle of Pleime*[52]
> *I love someone killed in Battlezone D*

49. *Thư Viện Hoa Sen* [Lotus Library], an online Vietnamese-English Buddhist Dictionary. See "Thập Nhị Nhân Duyên [The Twelve Dependent Originations]," http://thuvienhoa-sen.org/p10a11878/thap (accessed February 23, 2016).
50. Peter Harvey, *An Introduction to Buddhism*, 55.
51. See "Thiền Sư Nhất Hạnh Pháp Thoại Trịnh Công Sơn Part 9."
52. In this song Trịnh Công Sơn mentions battles which resulted in significant casualties on both sides. For example, Plei Me, a town in the central highlands 40 kilometers southwest of Pleiku, was the site of a battle in October 1965. The Battle of Đồng Xoài,

Killed at Đồng Xoài, killed in Hà Nội
Killed suddenly near the border

I want to love you, to love Vietnam
In the storm my lips whisper your name
And the name Vietnam
Bound together by our golden-skin tongue

I have always admired this song for the way it evokes the long tradition of sad love songs of unfulfilled love, but redirects this tradition so the song becomes not a romantic song but an anti-war song. Here is how Thích Nhất Hạnh describes that redirection:

> Who is that lover, that girl? It's a southerner, it's someone from central Vietnam. They are all my lovers and when they die I lose my mind. I want to love you, love Vietnam, and this love is love for one person and also a general love for the entire Vietnamese race and nation. The lover is all Vietnamese men,[53] those born in North, South, and Central Vietnam. Because war causes mutual destruction those people must die, so we love all those people because they all are our lovers.[54]

In one dharma talk Thích Nhất Hạnh reads the following two quotations from essays Sơn wrote: First he recites, "When I stand next to a corpse I don't think about whether it is one of us or one of the enemy; I think only that that someone has suffered from a meaningless war." Next he recites the following passage:

> We are people, not gods. We don't have the power to decide the fate of others. We can't say this person should live, that person should be killed. We don't have the power to let anyone die. We should even reflect before we break a blade of grass or pick a flower by the side of the road. We certainly do not have the right to decide the fate of a human being.[55]

---

a town about 100 kilometers north of Saigon, took place in June 1965. It was a victory for troops of the National Liberation Front. Đồng Xoài is now the capital of Bình Phước Province. The "battle of Chu Prong," mentioned in the second stanza, refers to battles in and around the Chu Prong (or Chu Pong in English-language accounts) massif, a 1,491-foot-high outcropping above the Ia Drang River near the Cambodia-Vietnam border in the central highlands. In October 1965, the People's Army of Vietnam launched attacks near this massif and intense fighting ensued. Americans refer to this engagement as the Battle of the Ia Drang Valley.

53. Thích Nhất Hạnh says "men" [*người con trai*] because most, though not all, soldiers were men.

54. Thích Nhất Hạnh, "Thông điệp thương yêu của Trịnh Công Sơn."

55. Ibid. Thích Nhất Hạnh appears to quote Trịnh Công Sơn: In the transcript of his dharma talks Sơn's words are enclosed in quotation marks, but he cites no source for Sơn's remarks.

Thích Nhất Hạnh says that in these remarks Trịnh Công Sơn is stating the first of the Five Precepts: don't kill. These remarks, he says, "are the words of the Buddha. In saying them he represents the Buddha."[56]

Thích Nhất Hạnh mentions several time in his dharma talks that Trịnh Công Sơn's mother passed on to her son a seed [*hạt giống*] of benevolence [*nhân ái*] and loving-kindness and compassion [*từ bi*].[57] *Từ bi* [Skt. *matri karuna*], a compound word, refers to the first two of what are called the Four Immeasurable Minds [Skt. *apramana*; Vn. *Tứ vô lượng tâm*].[58] We can see this seed of benevolence and kindness, Thích Nhất Hạnh says, in Sơn's songs, and so we can sing his songs "to water that seed and to destroy hatred within us. Trịnh Công Sơn's songs that talk about human love resemble Buddhist prayers and so we can chant them."[59] At Thích Nhất Hạnh's fifth dharma talk some monks and nuns perform Trịnh Công Sơn's song "Lullaby of Cannons for the Night" [Đại Bác Ru Đêm]* in a way that is part chant, part song.[60]

At Thích Nhất Hạnh's ninth dharma talk, after listening to a woman sing "Love Song of a Mad Person,"* Thích Nhất Hạnh talks about Sơn's obsession with death. He suggests that this obsession was caused by the war, and says to his Vietnamese audience that we also suffer from that obsession because we have seen "many friends, young people, and fellow countrymen and women die." He mentions that when an interviewer asked Sơn about his plans for the future, Sơn replied that in the days ahead he had to work harder to escape an obsession with death. Trịnh Công Sơn had a mission, he says, which was "to convey a message to those who loved him, to his fans—a message of love, of benevolence. That was the vow he made." Thích Nhất Hạnh seems to be suggesting that Sơn's obsession with death was caused by his seeing so much death around him, and so to rid himself of that obsession he vowed to encourage all Vietnamese to abandon hate and be more peaceful and benevolent. Thích Nhất Hạnh's praise reaches a crescendo when he compares Sơn to the

---

56. Thích Nhất Hạnh, "Thông điệp thương yêu của Trịnh Công Sơn."
57. Trịnh Công Sơn's religious name, Nguyễn Thọ [transmission from the source], suggests the transmission of these very same virtues, along with courage [*dũng cảm*].
58. The other two are *hỷ* [sympathetic joy; Skt. *mudita*] and *xả* [equanimity; Skt. *upeksa*]. I discuss the Four Immeasurable Minds in the next chapter.
59. Thích Nhất Hạnh, "Thông điệp thương yêu của Trịnh Công Sơn."
60. "Thiền Sư Nhất Hạnh Pháp Thoại Trịnh Công Sơn P.5" [The Monk Thích Nhất Hạnh Gives a Dharma Talk about Trịnh Công Sơn: Part 5], https://www.youtube.com/watch?v=6h7htuhK4Ms (accessed November 17, 2018). The performance of "Lullaby of Cannons for the Night" occurs in the second half of the recording.

two most respected Bodhisattvas in the Mahayana Buddhist pantheon: "If the vow of the Bodhisattva Ksitigarbha [Vn. Địa Tạng; Ch. Dizang]," Thích Nhất Hạnh says, "was to go to hell to save sentient beings, if the vow of the Bodhisattva Avalokitesvara [Vn. Quan Thế Âm; Ch. Guanyin] was to listen to the painful cry of sentient beings and rescue them from sorrow and distress, the vow that Trịnh Công Sơn sent to his listeners was a message of love. It was water to nourish the seed of love and forgiveness in all people."[61]

Ksitigarbha is the second most popular Bodhisattva. He vowed never to stop his labors until he had saved the souls of all those condemned to hell. He is known as a protector of all departed souls, but particularly the souls of children. Buddhists believe that he helps children who die young to cross a dangerous river and achieve reincarnation. Peter Harvey explains that in Japan, where Ksitigarbha is known as Jizo, statues of him are placed on country roads and in graveyards "as prayer-offerings for the good rebirth of dead children."[62] Avalokitesvara, the most popular of all the heavenly bodhisattvas, is the bodhisattva of mercy and compassion. Prior to the Song dynasty Avalokitesvara was represented as a man. Since the 11th century, however, in China, Vietnam, Korea, and Japan this bodhisattva has usually been portrayed as a beautiful woman. She exemplifies the vow of all bodhisattvas to postpone entering Nirvana until they have helped all sentient beings achieve release from suffering. One finds a statue of Avalokitesvara in almost every pagoda in Vietnam, either in the pagoda itself or nearby.

Although by comparing Sơn's vow to the vows of the two most popular bodhisattvas in Buddhism Thích Nhất Hạnh may be indulging in hyperbole, his comparison is not completely preposterous. In his songs Trịnh Công Sơn, like Ksitigarbha, reveals his love and respect for departed souls. In "Love Song of a Mad Person,"* "A Lullaby of Cannons for the Night,"* "Tears for the Native Land,"* "A Song for the Corpses," "A Morning in Spring,"* and other songs he pays his respect to the dead souls left behind in bombed cities and distant battlefields. In these songs, like Ksitigarbha, he seems especially moved by the death of children. "A Song for the Corpses," written after Sơn surveyed the death and destruction in Huế after the Tết Offensive in 1968, contains these stanzas:

---

61. Thích Nhất Hạnh, "Thông điệp thương yêu của Trịnh Công Sơn."
62. Peter Harvey, *An Introduction to Buddhism*, 133.

> *Corpses floating in rivers and lying in the fields*
> *On rooftops in the towns and on the winding roads*
> *Corpses lying helpless under a pagoda's porch*
> *In churches in the towns and on porches of abandoned homes*
>
> *Corpses lying all around in the cold and rain*
> *Corpses of the old and weak near those of the young and innocent*
> *Which corpse is my love lying in that trench*
> *In the burning fields, among those potato vines?*

In "A Morning in Spring"* Sơn mourns the death of a young student who stepped on a landmine. Here are the concluding stanzas:

> *On a morning in spring*
> *A child lies quiet and still*
> *Grasping wild flowers*
> *Fragile petals of gold*
> *On a morning in spring*
> *A child lies quiet and still*
> *His lips form a question*
> *"Is there a paradise?"*

And in his lullabies, discussed in Chapter Fourteen, Sơn tries to soothe the pain of children and their mothers.

Thích Nhất Hạnh's comparison of Trịnh Công Sơn's vow to Avalokitesvara's is also not unreasonable. Like this bodhisattva of mercy and compassion, Trịnh Công Sơn also wanted to rescue people from sorrow. He wanted to be merciful and compassionate himself and to spread these virtues to others. He wanted, as he sings in "Let the Wind Blow It Away,"* to "have a good heart" and make others good-hearted as well. Sơn explains his intentions in his essay "A Childhood Obsession":

> I am not a person who nurtures sadness and wants to cry about people's fate, but through songs I want to ring the morning bell and the evening bell,[63] to borrow the sunshine of the earth to illuminate that fate so people can see themselves and others more clearly and attentively and the time will come when everything is good and love will encourage us to see that the way to treat other people on this earth is not with cruelty but with a heart of boundless benevolence [*lòng nhân ái vô biên*].[64]

---

63. Bells in pagodas are used to gather people for communal activities, but the expression "to ring a bell to awaken people" [*đánh một tiếng chuông để thức tỉnh lòng người*] is used in non-religious contexts. You ring a bell to get people to wake up and return to common sense and humane behavior.

64. Trịnh Công Sơn, "Nỗi ám ảnh thời thơ ấu," 134.

ZEN AS ART AND ETHICAL STYLE

In Chapter Twenty-Two I presented Cuong Tu Nguyen's argument that ordinary Vietnamese throughout history have never embraced Zen Buddhism as enthusiastically as the authors of some histories of Vietnamese Buddhism suggest. Intellectuals and monks, he argues, were fascinated with Zen but ordinary people preferred instead a more "devotional" and "ritualistic" Buddhism known as Pure Land. "We can observe," he says, "that Zen has never been a tradition or school in Vietnam the same way it has been in China, Japan, or Korea."[65] Agreeing with Cuong Tu Nguyen, Alexander Soucy argues that the claim made by many Buddhist scholars, including Thích Nhất Hạnh and Thich Thien-An, that Zen has always been the core of Vietnamese Buddhism is a "cultural invention."[66] Now, however, that invention, Soucy says, is becoming a reality as Thích Nhất Hạnh and other "Zen masters" teach Vietnamese living abroad a form of Buddhism that emphasizes meditation and mindfulness and strives to avoid any rituals and practices that might be deemed superstitious. And now Vietnamese monks trained in the West are bringing this intellectualized and very Zen approach to Buddhism to Vietnam. As Alexander Soucy puts it, "the transformations of Buddhism in the West . . . are now changing Buddhist practice in Vietnam."[67]

I refer to Cuong Tu Nguyen and Alexander Soucy's views here because I think they help us put Thích Nhất Hạnh's assessment of Trịnh Công Sơn's Buddhism in a wider perspective. Thích Nhất Hạnh says that Trịnh Công Sơn could not conquer his obsession with death because he did not understand non-birth [Skt. *anutpatti*; Vn. *vô sanh*] and conditioned arising [Skt. *pratitya samutpada*; Vn. *duyên khởi*], but these are difficult concepts that few Vietnamese Buddhists, even those who are very devout, understand clearly. According to Peter Harvey, the Buddha himself referred to conditioned arising, along with Nirvana, as the "profound difficult to see" dharma which he—the Buddha—did not understand until his enlightenment![68]

---

65. Cuong Tu Nguyen, *Zen in Medieval Vietnam: A Study and Translation of the Thiền Uyển Tập Anh* (Honolulu: University of Hawai'i Press, 1997), 99.
66. Alexander Soucy, "Nationalism, Globalism and the Re-establishment of the Trúc Lâm Thiền Buddhist Sect in Northern Vietnam," in *Modernity and Re-enchantment: Religion in Post-revolutionary Vietnam*, ed. Philip Taylor (Singapore: Institute of Southeast Asian Studies, 2007), 349.
67. Ibid., 350.
68. Peter Harvey, *An Introduction to Buddhism*, 54. Harvey lists the *Majjhima Nikaya* [Collection of Middle-length Discourses], one of the "three baskets" that compose the Pali Tipitaka of Theravada Buddhism, as the source for this comment by the Buddha.

Trịnh Công Sơn was not a Zen scholar but I do believe his knowledge of Zen, however unsophisticated, helped shape his art and his "style of ethical behavior." The phrase "style of ethical behavior" is Cuong Tu Nguyen's. In Vietnam, he argues, "Zen Buddhism manifests itself, ever so vaguely but perennially, in philosophical attitudes, styles of ethical behavior, and artistic sentiments." Zen in Vietnam, he says, is "scattered across religious and cultural life" but not "as a cohesive system of thought."[69] Cuong Tu Nguyen believes that Zen Buddhism in Vietnam "is as much a literary fascination as a religious development." Vietnamese are drawn, he says, to the "romantic and heroic atmosphere in Zen literature."[70] He mentions the story of Hueneng [Vn. Huệ Năng] (638-713), the illiterate woodcutter who became the Sixth Patriarch of Zen Buddhism in China, but I believe he also has in mind the probing and intellectually clever encounter dialogues between master and disciple that lead the disciple to enlightenment, and also the beautiful Zen poems written by monks and kings of the Trần Dynasty.

Giving a dharma talk to Buddhist novices Thích Nhất Hạnh feels duty-bound to point out that Trịnh Công Sơn reveals his ignorance of Buddhist doctrine when he attempts to explain his song "A Place for Leaving and Returning"* by saying it means we enter life from emptiness and then return to emptiness. Ban Mai, however, the author of a book and numerous articles about Trịnh Công Sơn, finds the lyrics of this song to be "weighted down with Zen."[71] She points out that the song comforts people because it emphasizes a shared experience, the fact that we all arrive in and depart from this world. The song, she says, softens our fears of death. She mentions that the writer Nguyễn Quang Sáng told Sơn that after listening to this song he didn't fear death anymore.[72] What makes this poem Zen, in Ban Mai's view, is its emphasis on impermanence, a key Buddhist concept. Impermanence [Skt. *annica*; Vn. *vô thường*] is the first of the Three Dharma Seals, also known as the Three Marks of Existence [Skt. *Trilaksana*; Vn. *Tam Pháp Ấn*]. (The other two are non-self [Skt. *anatman*; Vn. *vô ngã*] and Nirvana [Skt. *nirvana*; Vn. *niết bàn*].) Like

69. Cuong Tu Nguyen, *Zen in Medieval Vietnam*, 99.
70. Ibid., 98.
71. Ban Mai, "Trịnh Công Sơn, người tình của cuộc sống" [Trịnh Công Sơn, A Lover of Life, Part 1], tcs-home, http://www.tcs-home.org/ban-be/articles/trinh-cong-son-nguoi-tinh-cua-cuoc-song-phan-1 (accessed February 19, 2016).
72. Trịnh Công Sơn made this comment when interviewed by Văn Cầm Hải. See "Kiếp sau tôi vẫn là người Nghệ sĩ," 205.

the Three Noble Truths these "marks" or "seals" are seen as presenting in succinct form Buddhism's answers to the important questions of human existence. Ban Mai says that Sơn's song "A Time for Leaving and Returning," like many poems written by famous Buddhist monks and Buddhist kings of the Lý and Trần dynasties, emphasizes the first mark: impermanence. For example, she sees similarities between "A Place for Leaving and Returning"* and a poem by emperor Trần Thái Tông who ruled Vietnam in the thirteenth century. The poem contains these lines:

> Old age arrives, no matter if wise or foolish
> Death in old times is just like it is now
> Impermanence can't be avoided when it comes
> One can't escape when death approaches
> Everyone should practice the right path
> To avoid falling into a forest of wrong[73]

Ban Mai also discusses Sơn's song "A Speck of Dust,"* the song that Thích Nhất Hạnh says reveals Sơn's lack of knowledge of Buddhist concepts, particularly conditioned arising and dependent origination. I have noted that he objects strongly to the lines "What speck of dust have I been reincarnated from / So one day I return to dust." Ban Mai, on the other hand, finds no problems with these lines and cites them to argue that the song "Speck of Dust" is about *samsara*, the infinitely repeated cycles of birth, misery, and death caused by *karma*.

Bùi Vĩnh Phúc, another scholar who, like Ban Mai, has written extensively about Trịnh Công Sơn, argues that impermanence was one of the singer's obsessions.[74] He also calls attention to Sơn's interest in "fading time." In many Trịnh Công Sơn songs, he points out, youth is fading, leaves are turning yellow, one season is passing into the next. He offers as an example the third stanza of "Speck of Dust" [Cát bụi].[75]

> Many years it takes to live a life
> Then suddenly my hair turns as white as lime
> Leaves on trees turn yellow and fall
> A hundred years die in a day

---

73. These lines come from a *kệ*, or *gatha*, titled "Thử thời vô thường kệ" (Gatha on Impermanence). A *gatha* is a short verse designed to capture or teach a spiritual concept. Some monks, including Thích Nhất Hạnh, suggest composing them helps one practice mindfulness.
74. Bùi Vĩnh Phúc, *Trịnh Công Sơn ngôn ngữ và những ám ảnh nghệ thuật* [Trịnh Công Sơn: Language and Artistic Obsessions] (Gardena, CA: Văn Mới, 2005), 56-60.
75. Ibid., 68.

Ban Mai and Bùi Vĩnh Phúc approach Trịnh Công Sơn's songs as scholars, not simply as fans, but I believe they understand "A Place for Leaving and Returning"* and "Speck of Dust" the way ordinary fans understand these songs. They perceive Zen-like sentiments and attitudes in them but are not interested in considering whether they are completely correct expressions of Buddhist doctrine.

Trịnh Công Sơn's songs are not dharma lessons and they are not "Zen songs" [thiền ca], a type of song which Thích Nhất Hạnh promoted at Plum Village to attract more young people to Buddhism. According to a Vietnamese saying, "When young, one's happy at home; when old, one's happy at the pagoda" [Trẻ vui nhà; già vui chùa]. The leaders of Plum Village, an article on its webpage explains, wish to oppose this stereotype, to counter the view that Buddhism has nothing to offer young people. Thiền ca will appeal, the article suggests, to young people who are tired of chanting in the traditional way. The lyrics for thiền ca songs should come from Buddhist texts or from the poems and other writing of elders who talk about the joy of practicing Buddhism, but the music should consist of "melodies that are pure and light, and happy and liberating; it should not be the maudlin music about relationships that ordinary people are fond of." The poems and music of Plum Village, the article on thiền ca emphasizes, "are not about being enmeshed in sorrow and pain or world weariness."[76]

Plum Village's plan to promote thiền ca and Thích Nhất Hạnh's dharma talks about Trịnh Công Sơn have the same aim: to attract young people to Buddhism by making practicing Buddhism a happy experience. Sơn's songs are no longer new but they remain popular. He is one of the most famous modern singer-songwriters in Vietnam and in the Vietnamese diaspora. In my introduction I mentioned that Buddhists talk about the "Eighty-four thousand gates to Buddhism," and I explained that Trịnh Công Sơn's songs were one such gate for me. Thích Nhất Hạnh and the monks and nuns at Plum Village promote thiền ca and Trịnh Công Sơn in the hope that they will be gates [pháp môn] for others to enter Buddhism. In Thích Nhất Hạnh's opinion, however, some of Trịnh Công Sơn's song are imperfect "gates" and he addresses these problems in his dharma talks, carefully pointing out which of his songs are proper to chant or sing, applying criteria similar to, but not as rigid as, the criteria at Plum Village

---

76. "Thực tập thiền ca" [Practicing Zen Songs], Làng Mai [Plum Village], http://langmai. org/dai-may-tim/thien-ca (accessed November 11, 2015).

for a proper *thiền ca*. Trịnh Công Sơn wrote some happy and light songs, but not many, so if the criteria for *thiền ca* were rigidly applied only a selected few of Trịnh Công Sơn songs would qualify. Thích Nhất Hạnh mentions once writing Trịnh Công Sơn a letter asking him to put to music some Buddhist prayers, but he says the letter was lost, and when Trịnh Công Sơn finally did receive it he was too ill to respond. "I know that if Trịnh Công Sơn had put those prayers to music," he says, "then Buddhists could have read them, and chanted them, and sung them and it would have been very interesting, very beneficial."[77]

Trịnh Công Sơn songs are not *thiền ca*, but Zen Buddhism manifests itself in them in much the same way Cuong Tu Nguyen says Zen manifests itself in Vietnam—in "philosophical attitudes, styles of ethical behavior, and artistic sentiments." The philosophy and ethical behavior that Sơn recommends is simple: benevolent love and compassion. That, Thích Nhất Hạnh says, is the message Sơn wanted to send in his songs. The artistic sentiments are similar to those presented in Zen poems throughout Vietnam's long history. Notice how Nguyễn Huệ Chi, a respected Hanoi scholar, describes the poetry of King Trần Nhân Tông (r. 1279-1293):

> Of course Trần Nhân Tông's ways of thinking about art were deeply imbued with Zen ideas and therefore he sees the fragile and changeable quality of life when gazing at the budding of a flower or a ray of evening sun or when hearing the flapping of an egret's wings. The poet used these artistic images cleverly in many poems to create a world that is part imaginary, part real, and very beautiful, but which, it seems, can easily disappear.[78]

Nguyễn Huệ Chi could be describing Trịnh Công Sơn's songs.

TRỊNH CÔNG SƠN, THÍCH NHẤT HẠNH,
AND ENGAGED BUDDHISM

Cao Ngọc Phượng is a Buddhist nun who was always at Thích Nhất Hạnh's side after she was inducted into his Order of Interbeing in 1966. She is known by her Buddhist name, Chân Không, which means "True Emptiness." In 1957 when she was a student at the prestigious Marie Curie French High School in Saigon she returned to Bến Tre to visit her family. Her parents encouraged her to accept the Five Precepts and receive a Buddhist name from a young monk they respected. Chân Không, who

---

77. Thích Nhất Hạnh, "Thông điệp thương yêu của Trịnh Công Sơn."
78. Nguyễn Huệ Chi, "Trần Khâm" (the given name of Trần Nhân Tông) in *Từ điển Văn Học* [Dictionary of Literature], ed. Đỗ Đức Hiểu et al. (Hanoi: Thế Giới, 2004), 1791.

was already working to help the poor in Bến Tre, asked this monk why the Buddhists did not do anything to help the poor and hungry. "Even though Catholics are in the minority in our country," she told the young monk, "they take care of orphans, the elderly, and the poor." The monk told her that "Buddhism changes people's hearts so they can help each other in the deepest, most effective ways, even without charitable institutions."[79]

This answer did not satisfy Chân Không. She was looking for a Buddhism in which spiritual practice for inner peace and political and social practice for world peace were combined. When Thích Nhất Hạnh returned to Vietnam in 1964 after studying and lecturing in the US, he began working to make his vision of an engaged Buddhism a reality. He and other monks founded Vạn Hạnh Buddhist University and the School of Youth for Social Service, a relief organization to help the poor.[80] In 1965 he founded the Order of Interbeing, an order that promoted an "engaged Buddhism," and in 1966 Chân Không was one of six people inducted into the Order.

Chân Không's exchange with the young monk in Bến Tre raises an important issue. Does Buddhism have something equivalent to the "social gospel" of Christianity? Nelson Foster believes it does not. "Compassion and generosity are the principal thrust of Zen practice," he says. "This being the case, it is remarkable that Zen lacks a clear tradition of social action. One searches in vain for a body of teaching equivalent to the 'social gospel' of Christianity."[81] Fred Eppsteiner, the editor of a collection of essays on engaged Buddhism, agrees. "In Western scholarship since Weber," he says "there has been an implicit (and sometimes explicit) understanding that Buddhism shuns the worldly arena."[82] In 1916 Max Weber, the German sociologist, criticized Buddhism for portraying salvation as a "solely personal act of the single individual."[83] Christopher S. Queen, in his introduction to *Engaged Buddhism: Buddhist Liberation Movements in Asia* (1996), says that eighty years later many specialists

79. Chân Không, *Learning True Love: How I Learned and Practiced Social Change in Vietnam*, 15.
80. Sallie B. King, "Thich Nhat Hanh and the Unified Buddhist Church of Vietnam: Non-dualism in Action," 323; and Chân Không, *Learning True Love*, 70-72.
81. Nelson Foster, "To Enter the Marketplace," in *The Path of Compassion: Writings on Socially Engaged Buddhism*, ed. Fred Eppsteiner (Berkeley, CA: Parallax Press, 1988), 48.
82. Fred Eppsteiner, "Editor's Preface," in *The Path of Compassion: Writings on Socially Engaged Buddhism*, ix.
83. Max Weber, *The Religion of India: The Sociology of Hinduism and Buddhism*, trans. and ed. by Hans H. Gerth and Don Martindale (Glencoe, IL: The Free Press, 1958), 206.

agree with Weber that "in its essence, primitive Buddhism was not based on service to others, but on the quest for individual enlightenment."[84] Buddhist ethics, these specialists conclude, are too egoistic.

Other scholars, including Thích Nhất Hạnh, point out that this conclusion reveals a misunderstanding of Buddhist concepts about the relation of self to others. If you believe that we all are connected, that we all "interare," to use Thích Nhất Hạnh's word, then there is no separation between self and other.[85] Thích Nhất Hạnh emphasizes interdependent co-arising in his dharma talks about Trịnh Công Sơn because this concept and others—non-duality and no-self, for example—underlie Buddhist ethics. "The Buddhist doctrines of dependent co-arising and no-self," Cynthia Eller says, "establish a framework in which the advancement of the true needs of the self cannot possibly detract from the true needs of the other. In fact, the fundamental interests of self and other are so intimately tied together that one can conveniently concentrate on the true needs of the self as the best means for advancing those of the other."[86] Being peace, Thích Nhất Hạnh emphasizes, is also making peace: "It is not by going out for a demonstration against nuclear missiles that we can bring about peace," he writes. "It is with our capacity of smiling, breathing, and being peace that we can make peace."[87]

In another section of his book *Being Peace*—in discussing the Buddhist precept "Do not kill"—Thích Nhất Hạnh says that this precept "means not killing, and also not letting other people kill." It is difficult, he says. "Those who try to observe this precept have to be working for peace in order to have peace in themselves."[88] In Thích Nhất Hạnh's view, however, one has to begin by cultivating inner peace. The difference between Buddhist and Christian ethics, Cynthia Eller says, "is primarily one of emphasis, of picking up the fabric of individual and social life from different ends. For Buddhists, the other will be served if the self is transformed; for Christians, the self will be transformed if the other is served."[89]

---

84. Christopher S. Queen, "Introduction," in *Engaged Buddhism*, 17.
85. Thích Nhất Hạnh, *Being Peace* (Berkeley, CA: Parallax Press, 1996), 115. "Interare" is the verb form of the noun "interbeing," which, as explained above, is the name Thích Nhất Hạnh chose for the order he founded.
86. Cynthia Eller, "The Impact of Christianity on Buddhist Nonviolence in the West," in *Inner Peace, World Peace: Essays on Buddhism and Nonviolence*, ed. Kenneth Kraft, 94.
87. Thích Nhất Hạnh, *Being Peace*, 12.
88. Ibid., 130.
89. Cynthia Eller, "The Impact of Christianity on Buddhist Nonviolence in the West," 97.

Cynthia Eller describes two models of Buddhist non-violence: an "action meditation" model and a "compassion-based" model.[90] Both models are grounded in Buddhist principles, but the action meditation model allows more room for political action—for demonstrating and other forms of political activism. When involved in political activities, however, participants must maintain self-control and not succumb to the Three Poisons of greed, hate, and delusion. They should approach political activity as an exercise in self-awareness. Though self-control and self-awareness are emphasized, the action mediation model allows more flexibility in terms of means than the compassion model, which, Eller says, has been "promoted most prominently" by Thích Nhất Hạnh. Although Thích Nhất Hạnh does talk about not letting other people kill, he emphasizes self-cultivation, not political activism. He firmly believes in the non-duality of serving the self and serving the other: "The kind of suffering that you carry in your heart, that is society itself," he writes in *Being Peace*. "You bring that with you, you bring society with you. You bring all of us with you. When you meditate, it is not just for yourself, you do it for the whole society. You seek solutions to your problems not only for yourself, but for all of us."[91]

Trịnh Công Sơn's approach to ending the war was more compassion-based than action-based. He wrote and sang anti-war songs but did not join public demonstrations. As explained in Chapter Two, some of his close friends urged him to become involved in demonstrations and some hoped that he would join the National Liberation Front, but he declined. In Vietnam in the 1960s Thích Trí Quang, another monk from Central Vietnam, was much better known than Thích Nhất Hạnh. Thích Trí Quang exemplified a more action-based model of engaged Buddhism than did Thích Nhất Hạnh. He orchestrated street demonstrations that led to the fall of Ngô Đình Diệm in 1963 and helped topple several post-Diệm regimes. He met frequently with US officials, including the US ambassador.[92] Trịnh Công Sơn's approach was closer to Thích Nhất

---

90. Ibid., 104-106.
91. Thích Nhất Hạnh, *Being Peace*, 63-64.
92. The assessments by American historians of Thích Trí Quang differ greatly. Mark Moyer argues that he was a communist agent. James McAllister maintains that he was intensely anti-communist, so much so that he favored American bombing of North Vietnam. Robert Topmiller, however, argues that the Buddhist movement that he led was devoted to neutralism and free elections. See Mark Moyar, "Political Monks: The Militant Buddhist Movement during the Vietnam War," *Modern Asian Studies* 38, no. 4 (2004), 749-784; James McAllister, "'Only Religions Count in Vietnam': Thich Tri Quang and the

Hạnh's. One senses that, like Thích Nhất Hạnh, Sơn believed that by being peace one was making peace, which is why during the war he wrote songs like "Let the Wind Blow It Away"* and "Love Each Other" [Hãy yêu nhau đi] in which he talks about the importance of having a good heart and of loving each other, "Though the night brings bullets / Though the morning brings bombs."[93] As his friend Hoàng Phủ Ngọc Tường says, Sơn's "gentle generosity and boundless tolerance were not simply aspects of his personality; they were his solution to the problems of war and hatred."[94]

Sơn's choice of this compassion-based model of engaged Buddhism was no doubt an instinctive choice, not one based on contact with Thích Nhất Hạnh, who was abroad during most of the war years.[95] Sally B. King identifies two principles for opposing war that can be derived from Thích Nhất Hạnh's engaged Buddhism. The first is to try to stop the killing and suffering, and the second is to avoid taking sides in the conflict.[96] Trịnh Công Sơn followed these principles. He did not take sides but instead wrote songs that described the suffering war was causing and urged both sides to seek peace.

Sally B. King says that Thích Nhất Hạnh's notion of non-duality prevented him from "one-sided blaming." It seems likely that Trịnh Công Sơn internalized this Buddhist concept, perhaps without being aware of it. "The influence of Buddhism in the lives of the Vietnamese," Thich Thien-An says, "is so thoroughly an inner experience that much remains inexpressible."[97] In any event, Trịnh Công Sơn did not engage in one-sided blaming. The "lovers" [người yêu] he mourns in "Love Song of a Mad Person"* include people from all over the country, from all three

---

Vietnam War," *Modern Asian Studies* 42, no. 4 (2008), 751-782; and Robert J. Topmiller, *The Lotus Unleashed* (Lexington, KY: University Press of Kentucky, 2002).

93. These lines are from "Love Each Other" [Hãy yêu nhau đi].
94. Hoàng Phủ Ngọc Tường, "Hành tinh yêu thương của Hoàng tử Bé" [The Little Prince's Planet of Love], in *Trịnh Công Sơn: Một người thơ ca một cõi đi về* [Trịnh Công Sơn: A Singer-poet, a Place for Leaving and Returning], eds. Nguyễn Trọng Tạo, Nguyễn Thụy Kha, and Đoàn Tử Huyến (Hanoi: Âm Nhạc, 2001), 26. Originally published as a column, "Nhàn đàm" [Idle Conversation], in the journal *Thanh Niên* [Youth].
95. Thích Nhất Hạnh left Vietnam for the US in September 1961; returned to Vietnam in December 1963; and went to the US again in May 1966. After the war ended, the new Vietnamese government did not allow him to visit Vietnam until 2005. See John Chapman, "The 2005 Pilgrimage and Return to Vietnam of Exiled Zen Master Thích Nhất Hạnh," 299-306.
96. Sallie B. King, "Thich Nhat Hanh and the Unified Buddhist Church of Vietnam: Non-dualism in Action," 342-346.
97. Thich Thien-An, *Buddhism and Zen in Relation to the Development of Buddhism in Asia*, 185.

regions: the North, the central region, and the South. He loves all "golden skinned" people regardless of their political affiliation.

The internalization of this concept of non-duality may also explain why it is so difficult in his songs to separate the speaker's private sadness— about the end of a love relationship, for example—from his sadness about the state of the world, particularly that part of the world he knew best: Vietnam. In reading articles about engaged Buddhism, I came across this passage in an article by Christopher Titmuss, a Buddhist scholar, teacher of *vipassana* meditation, and advocate for an engaged Buddhism:

> People are beginning to see that personal pain and global pain are not two separate factors, but very much interrelated. Some people experience inside of themselves what they conceive of as being the pain of the world, but in a way it is the pain of themselves. There are others who experience inside of themselves what they conceive of as being purely personal pain. In a way, it is the pain of the world.[98]

For Trịnh Công Sơn, it seems, personal pain and pain for the world were always intertwined. Vietnamese talk about Trịnh Công Sơn's love songs, his anti-war songs, and his songs about the fate of people [*thân phận con người*] but it seems to me all his songs could be put in this last category. In his songs sadness related to his own fate, including unsuccessful love relationships, and sadness for the human condition are difficult to separate; one is always turning into the other. If being an engaged Buddhist means seeing the connection between inner peace and world peace, then Trịnh Công Sơn was an engaged Buddhist. His Buddhism was, like Thích Nhất Hạnh's, compassion-based. Trịnh Công Sơn vowed, Thích Nhất Hạnh says, "to water the seed of love and forgiveness in all people." This is why this famous Buddhist teacher and scholar does not hesitate to compare him to Avalokitesvara, the bodhisattva of infinite compassion.

---

98. Christopher Titmuss, "Interactivity: Sitting for Peace and Standing for Parliament," in *The Path of Compassion: Writings on Socially Engaged Buddhism*, ed. Fred Eppsteiner (Berkeley, CA: Parallax Press, 1988), 184.

25

BUDDHIST THEMES IN TRỊNH CÔNG SƠN'S SONGS

In his dharma talks about Trịnh Công Sơn Thích Nhất Hạnh discusses Buddhist themes in his songs, but most writers and scholars who write about the singer do not. If they mention Buddhist themes they do so only in passing before quickly moving on to other aspects of his music. In this chapter I discuss some songs that, in my view, become much more understandable if one is aware of Buddhist concepts, particularly patience [Vn. *nhẫn nhục*; Skt. *Khanti*], loving-kindness and compassion [Vn. *từ bi*; Skt. *matri karuna*], emptiness [Vn. *không, hư không, hư vô*; Skt. *Sunyata*], and non-dualism [Vn. *bất nhị*; Skt. *advaita*]. But first, some comments on why very few Vietnamese writers and scholars call attention to Buddhist themes in Sơn's songs.

There are several possible reasons. First, most Vietnamese, including those who do not consider themselves Buddhists, have absorbed Buddhist ideas as a result of growing up in a country that is predominantly Buddhist. These ideas are so familiar to most Vietnamese that writers see no need to mention them. If they did, they might bore their readers. Second, Trịnh Công Sơn did not see himself as a spokesman for Buddhism. Many of his songs contain Buddhist themes and some listeners find them comforting, but they were not written to proselytize or to teach Buddhism. They are not Zen songs like those advocated by the monks and nuns at Thích Nhất Hạnh's Plum Village that I discussed in the previous chapter. No doubt Vietnamese critics shy away from over-emphasizing the Buddhist quality of Sơn's songs because they do not want to label him a "Buddhist musician." Much of the writing about Trịnh Công Sơn has appeared after he died and has been done to memorialize Trịnh Công Sơn, to fondly remember a singer-composer who is a national treasure, not the private property of one group. One does not memorialize a singer who wanted all Vietnamese to "join hands in a great circle" [*nối vòng tay lớn*][1] by suggesting that he was speaking primarily to some subgroup of the general population. As discussed in Chapter Twenty-Two, Vietnamese have interiorized a religion that is a blend of Confucianism, Taoism, and Buddhism. Many Vietnamese Buddhists have no doubt been influenced by other faiths as well. Vietnamese writers may not emphasize Buddhist themes in Trịnh Công Sơn songs for fear of giving too much weight to only one strand in this complex weave of religious influences.

Finally, like Bob Dylan, Trịnh Công Sơn wrote songs for oral performance—to appeal primarily to the ear and the heart, not to the eye and the brain. People listening to Trịnh Công Sơn's songs, Cao Huy Thuần says, "heard the poetic mood [*giọng thơ*] more than they heard the ideas."[2] In the early 1960s my friends and I listened to Dylan's songs in the same way. We did not analyze them and so did not notice that his early songs—songs from Dylan's first "folklore" phase (1961-1966)—were loaded with biblical echoes and images. Perhaps the biblical language was so familiar, so much a part of the English language, that we didn't recognize it as Christian. Or perhaps we were carried away by the "poetic mood" of the songs. Only relatively recently have scholars carefully examined biblical themes and imagery in Bob Dylan's songs. In a book published in 1985 Bert Cartwright described five phases in Dylan's career and explained the different ways Dylan used biblical language in each phase.[3] In the next chapter I will summarize Cartwright's five phases and also discuss Michael Gilmore's book *Tangled up in the Bible* in which he describes how Dylan has integrated the Bible into his poetry and

---

1. The title of a song that Trịnh Công Sơn wrote in 1968.
2. Cao Huy Thuần, "Buồn bã với những môi hôn" [Sadness with the Kisses], in Cao Huy Thuần, *Nắng và hoa* [Sunshine and Flowers] (HCMC: Văn hóa Sài gòn, 2006), 194.
3. Bert Cartwright, *The Bible in the Lyrics of Bob Dylan* (Bury, Lancashire, England: Wanted Man, 1992).

lyrics.[4] It seems likely that as time passes, more Vietnamese scholars will join the monk Thích Nhất Hạnh and a small group of Vietnamese writers who do discuss Buddhist themes in his songs.

LOVING-KINDNESS, COMPASSION AND THE IMPORTANCE OF PRACTICE

When Trịnh Công Sơn talks about political calamities and personal disappointments he speaks in a much softer voice than Dylan. Whether he is speaking of war or the end of a romantic relationship, there is no finger-pointing. He reacts not with anger but with kindness. In "The Eyes of This World" [Những con mắt trần gian] he contrasts the warm eyes of love with the cold eyes of hate:

> *The eyes of a lover*
> *Help us know warmth*
> *The eyes of hate*
> *Make our life cold*

Compressed into the final stanza of this song are themes one often encounters in a Trịnh Công Sơn song: sadness, loving-kindness, and the possibility of happiness—of finding "sweetness in the shadows":

> *Worried eyes looking at each other*
> *Please comfort a thousand loves*
> *Look at each other and soften the pain*
> *Search for sweetness in the shadows*

As the love letters collected in *Trịnh Công Sơn: Love Letters for Someone*, discussed in Chapter Five, confirm, the love of Trịnh Công Sơn's life was a woman from Huế named Dao Ánh.[5] When Dao Ánh married someone else and later came to the US, Trịnh Công Sơn felt betrayed, but still found a way to be forgiving. "Lullaby for You" [Ru em],* a song probably inspired by this breakup, contains these lines:

> *A lullaby for each drop of sweetness in the past*
> *A lullaby for those with hard and withered lives*
> *Loving you I also love betrayal*
> *Loving you, suddenly kindness and compassion* [từ bi] *fill my heart*

---

4. Michael J. Gilmour, *Tangled up in the Bible: Bob Dylan & Scripture* (New York: Continuum, 2004).
5. See *Trịnh Công Sơn: Thư tình gửi một người* [Trịnh Công Sơn: Love Letters for Someone] (HCMC: Trẻ, 2011).

Knowing that Trịnh Công Sơn was raised in a Buddhist family and learned to chant Buddhist prayers helps us understand this kindness, this refusal to give in to anger and resentment. What would he have learned from Buddhist prayers and from conversations with monks and nuns at the pagoda or from other Buddhist family and community members? We can only speculate but it seems quite certain that he would have learned that anger is to be avoided. Anger [*sân*] is one of the three Three Poisons [Vn. *Tam Độc*; Skt. *trivisa*].[6] (Greed [*tham*] and Delusion [*si*] are the other two.) Buddhists in Huế are familiar with the expression "*tham sân si*" and are aware that it is a shorthand expression for things that must be avoided if one is to escape suffering and achieve happiness. My Vietnamese Buddhist dictionary defines *sân* [anger], the second poison, as feeling "resentment, anger, and hatred when one is not satisfied."[7] In many songs Trịnh Công Sơn urges his listeners and himself to avoid this second poison.

If the Lotus Sutra were one of the Buddhist prayers that Trịnh Công Sơn listened to or heard discussed, he would have learned about the importance of "*nhẫn nhục*," *ksanti* in Sanskrit, variously translated as patience, forbearance, tolerance, or acceptance.[8] *Nhẫn nhục* is one of the Six Perfections [Skt. *paramitas*; Vn. *Lục Độ*][9] which Thích Nhất Hạnh refers to as "crossing-overs"[10] because they assist one in "crossing over" from a life of suffering to the other shore of well-being and enlight-

---

6. The Three Poisons are the most important poisons or defilements (Vn. *phiền não*, Skt. *klesa*) but there are others, including conceit [*mạn*] and doubt [*nghi*].

7. Tâm Tuệ Hỷ, ed., *Danh từ Phật học thực dụng* [Useful Buddhist Terms] (Hà Nội: Tôn Giáo, 2004), 402.

8. According to Cuong Tu Nguyen, among the sutras "still widely studied and read in modern Vietnamese Buddhism," the Lotus Sutra "has definitely been the most read, studied, and recited in Vietnam." See Cuong Tu Nguyen, *Zen in Medieval Vietnam: A Study and Translation of the Thiền Uyển Tập Anh* (Honolulu: University of Hawai'i Press, 1997), 92.

9. The other five are generosity [Vn. *Bố thí ba la mật*; Skt. *dana paramita*], virtue or discipline [Vn. *trì giới ba la mật*; Skt. *sila paramita*], diligence [Vn. *tinh tấn ba la mật*; Skt. *virya paramita*], one-pointed concentration [Vn. *thiền định ba la mật*; Skt. *dhyana paramita*], and wisdom [Vn. *Trí tuệ ba la mật*; Skt. *prajna paramita*].

10. In Sanskrit, *prajna* means wisdom. As David S. Lopez explains, "The term '*paramita*' has two etymologies. The first derives it from the word *parama*, meaning 'highest,' 'most distant,' and hence, 'chief,' 'primary,' 'most excellent.' Hence, the substantive can be rendered 'excellence' or 'perfection.' . . . A more creative yet widely reported etymology divides *paramita* into *para* and *mita*, with *para* meaning 'beyond,' 'the further bank, shore or boundary,' and *mita*, meaning 'that which has arrived,' or *ita* meaning 'that which goes.' *Paramita* then means 'that which has gone beyond,' 'that which goes beyond,' or 'transcendent.'" See *The Heart Sutra Explained: Indian and Tibetan Commentaries* (Albany, New York: State University of New York Press, 1988), 21-22.

enment.[11] Not everyone achieves enlightenment but it is important to journey toward it, and Buddhists believe that practicing *nhẫn nhục* and the other five perfections is a good way to begin.[12] Buddhists point out that *nhẫn nhục* should not be confused with weakness or excessive humility because in practicing it one establishes self-control, which is a strength, not a weakness.

In "Lullaby for You"* Trịnh Công Sơn sings "Loving you, suddenly kindness and compassion [*từ bi*] fill my heart." "*Từ bi*," a compound word, refers to the first two of what are called the Four Immeasurable Minds [*Tứ vô lượng tâm; Skt. apramana*][13]: *từ tâm* [loving-kindness; Skt. *maitri*], *tâm bi* [compassion; Skt. *karuna*], *hỷ* [sympathetic joy; Skt. *mudita*] and *xả* [equanimity; Skt. *upeksa*]. Some Western scholars translate *maitri* as compassion. Because other scholars translate *karuna*, the second Immeasurable Mind, as compassion, confusion results.[14] *Maitri* and *karuna* are related but not the same. Thích Nhất Hạnh explains that *maitri* "is the intention and capacity to offer joy and happiness"; karuna "is the capacity to relieve and transform suffering and lighten sorrows."[15] Vietnamese, who are fond of four-syllable expressions, refer to the Four Immeasurable Minds as "*từ bi hỷ xả*" and sometimes will use this expression to calm someone who is feeling angry or resentful. In Buddhist texts anger [*sân*], patience [*nhẫn nhục*], and the Four Immeasurable Minds, especially the first two (loving-kindness and compassion), are closely related.[16] Anger is described as the most dangerous of the poisons because it destroys loving-kindness and compassion. Practicing patience is a way to achieve these desirable states of mind/heart, and practicing the Four Immeasurable Minds is a good way to achieve patience.

---

11. Vietnamese refer to a life of suffering as "*sinh lão bịnh tử*" [birth, old age, sickness, death] or "*vòng luân hồi*" [The wheel of life; Skt. *samsara*].
12. Thích Nhất Hạnh also says that "if you practice one deeply, you practice all six." See *The Heart of Buddha's Teaching* (New York: Broadway Books, 1998), 212.
13. From the Sanskrit *apramana citta*. "Apramana" means boundless, immeasurable. Peter Harvey explains that *citta* [Vn. *tâm*] "can be seen as 'mind,' 'heart,' or 'thought.'" See *An Introduction to Buddhism* (Cambridge: Cambridge University Press, 1990), 50.
14. To avoid confusion I will always refer to *maitri* as loving-kindness and *karuna* as compassion, and in quoting Western scholars I will include the Sanskrit term in brackets to make clear which Immeasurable Mind they are referring to.
15. Thích Nhất Hạnh, *The Heart of Buddha's Teaching*, 170, 172.
16. Nagarjuna, a leading figure in Mahayana Buddhism, emphasizes the close relationship between anger, patience, and loving-kindness and compassion in chapter 14 of *The Treatise of the Great Virtue of Wisdom* [Skt. *Maha Prajna Paramita*; Vn. *Luận Đại Trí Độ*]. I found a Vietnamese translation at Quang Duc Homepage—Vietnamese-English Buddhist Library, http://www.quangduc.com/luan34daitrido 1-14.html (accessed Oct. 23, 2011).

Loving-kindness and compassion are particularly important in Mahayana Buddhism. As explained in Chapter Twenty-Two, the ideal figure in Mahayana Buddhism, the figure presented for inspiration and emulation, is the Bodhisattva. The defining qualities of a Bodhisattva, who has achieved enlightenment but postpones entering Nirvana in order to help others become enlightened, are loving-kindness and compassion. It should come therefore as no surprise that Trịnh Công Sơn's songs are imbued with loving-kindness and compassion. These virtues lie at the heart of the religious tradition that shaped Trịnh Công Sơn's world view. The Dalai Lama, a follower of a form of Buddhism referred to as Vajrayana, which derived from Mahayana, once said: "My religion is simple. My religion is kindness." One can say that kindness was Trịnh Công Sơn's religion as well.

Patience and loving-kindness and compassion are not simply given. One has to make an effort. In his discussion of the Six Perfections, Thích Nhất Hạnh quotes the Buddha: "Don't just hope for the other shore to come to you. If you want to cross over to the other shore, . . . you have to swim or row across. You have to make an effort."[17] In other words one has to "*tu Phật*" or "*tu hành*"—practice Buddhism. Practicing Buddhism, as Vietnamese Buddhist teachers describe it, is "primarily the fixing of one's heart-mind [*tâm*]."[18] "Tâm" is the Vietnamese translation of Sanskrit "*citta*," which Peter Harvey says, "can be seen as 'mind,' 'heart,' or 'thought.'"[19] The aim of Buddhist practice is to overcome the "Three Poisons" of greed, anger, and delusion not by repressing them but by transforming them into elements that create happiness. Practice, in other words, is "developing the ability to be happy."[20]

Thích Nhất Hạnh translates "*nhẫn nhục*," the third Perfection, as "inclusiveness," not "patience," because he believes it better captures Buddha's teaching concerning the third Perfection. Inclusiveness, Thích Nhất Hạnh says, means having a large enough heart so that harsh words and deeds will not make one suffer. The Four Immeasurable Minds are important in developing patience/inclusiveness because they are believed to enlarge the heart-mind—to make it "immeasurable."[21] The Buddha, Thích Nhất Hạnh explains, used the image of throwing salt into a river. If the river

---

17. Thích Nhất Hạnh, *The Heart of Buddha's Teaching*, 192.
18. Tâm Tuệ Hỷ, ed., *Danh từ Phật học thực dụng*, 511-516.
19. Peter Harvey, *An Introduction to Buddhism*, 50.
20. Tâm Tuệ Hỷ, *Danh từ Phật học thực dụng*, 512.
21. Peter Harvey, *An Introduction to Buddhism*, 209.

is small, the water will taste salty, but if it is large the water won't be too salty to drink. Similarly, Thích Nhất Hạnh says, "If your heart is small, one unjust word or act will make you suffer. But if your heart is large, if you have understanding and compassion, that word or deed will not have the power to make you suffer."[22]

In some essays and in many of his songs, Trịnh Công Sơn appears to be "practicing" [*tu hành*] in the manner just described: He appears to be striving to enlarge his own heart and the hearts of those who listen to his songs. In an essay published in 1997, Trịnh Công Sơn explains why he tries to keep a resentful attitude toward life from developing in his heart: "Although sometimes deceitful people will treat us badly, and people will betray and abandon us," he says, "life is immense and we are only specks of dust in the world. What's the point of getting angry, blaming people when life will wash away the bruises on our souls if our hearts are kind and gentle?"[23] In an article he reveals his awareness that effort or "practice" is required:

> I try not to think of Buddhism as a religion. I like to think of it as a liberating philosophy that everyone should study, even people who follow other religions. Each person has to work to build a calm and quiet pagoda within his or her own heart and nourish the Buddha nature [Skt. *Buddhata*; Vn. *Phật tính*][24] within them so it becomes firm and stable. This will help us look at the world and life differently.[25]

Trịnh Công Sơn's songs, as we have seen, are pervaded by a gentle tolerance. In some he seems particularly aware of the importance of fixing his own heart-mind—of purging it of anger and resentment and filling it with loving-kindness. One of these songs is "Each Day I Choose a Little

22. Thích Nhất Hạnh, *The Heart of Buddha's Teaching*, 198.
23. Trịnh Công Sơn, "Để bắt đầu một hồi ức" [To Begin a Recollection], *Âm Nhạc* [Music] (January 1997); reprinted in *Trịnh Công Sơn: Một người thơ ca một cõi đi về* [Trịnh Công Sơn: A Singer-poet, a Place for Leaving and Returning], eds. Nguyễn Trọng Tạo, Nguyễn Thụy Kha, and Đoàn Tử Huyến (Hanoi: Âm Nhạc, 2001), 201.
24. The idea of a Buddha nature is very important in Mahayana Buddhism. As Jack Maguire explains, Buddha nature should not be considered a separate self or soul. It is rather "an identity with all other sentient beings as well as with the absolute." Enlightenment entails realizing this Buddha nature that lies within all of us. See Jack Maguire, *Essential Buddhism: A Complete Guide to Beliefs and Practices* (New York: Pocket Books, 2001), 53-54.
25. Trịnh Công Sơn: "Phải biết sống hết mình trong mỗi sát na của hiện tại" [Trịnh Công Sơn: "You Must Know How to Live Completely in Each Moment of Reality"], in Lê Minh Quốc, ed., *Trịnh Công Sơn: Rơi lệ ru người* [Trịnh Công Sơn: Shedding Tears, Singing Lullabies] (Phụ Nữ: Hanoi, 2004), 203. A preface explains that these and other comments that Trịnh Công Sơn made about Buddhism appeared previously in the journal *Nguyệt San Giác Ngộ* [Monthly Review Enlightenment] (April 2001).

Happiness" [Mỗi ngày tôi chọn một niềm vui]. I discussed this song briefly in Chapter Six, "Love Songs and Anti-love Songs," because it is a love song, one of several Trịnh Công Sơn songs in which both romantic love for a woman and love for his country are expressed. Trịnh Công Sơn wrote "Each Day" in 1977, a time when he was still adjusting to the new communist regime and had to work especially hard to be happy. It was the first song that the communist regime allowed Sơn to sing on television after it reclaimed Saigon and renamed it Hồ Chí Minh City. Here is the first stanza:

> Each day I choose happiness
> Choose flowers and smiles
> I pick wind from sky and invite you to take it
> So your eyes will smile like flying leaves

According to Cổ Ngư, who grew up in Saigon and now lives in France, journalists at home and abroad immediately attacked it. Journalists in Vietnam, he says, objected to its "petty bourgeois images" like those in the first stanza about "picking wind from sky," and those in the second stanza about "waiting for those familiar footsteps crossing a golden carpet of tamarind leaves." There was no way, Cổ Ngư says, that in 1977 people in Vietnam could accept images like these when the whole country was engaged in productive labor projects and fighting both the Khmer Rouge [Red (communist) Cambodians] and the "expansionist Chinese."[26] During the war the Khmer Rouge had been allies of the North Vietnamese and the Viet Cong, but by 1977 they had become enemies. By December 1978 the Vietnamese had captured most of Cambodia and the Khmer Rouge, led by Pol Pot, had retreated into jungle hideouts from which they engaged in guerilla warfare.

Communists have no love for the petty bourgeois. In 1977 journalists in Saigon (recently renamed Hồ Chí Minh City) who objected to Sơn's bourgeois images were no doubt following the party line. Vietnamese journalists who had fled the country in 1975 and now lived abroad, Cổ Ngư says, emphasized suffering caused by the new communist government. These journalists wanted to know, he says, where happiness was coming from "when the native land was suffering, millions of people had left the country, or had been imprisoned in reeducation camps, or

---

26. Cổ Ngư, "Đôi dòng về Trịnh Công Sơn" [Some Lines about Trịnh Công Sơn], *Văn Học* [Literary Studies] special edition (October 10 & 11, 2001), 9.

faced dangers searching for a way to cross the sea in boats."[27] Though the lyrics of this song are seemingly innocuous, one can understand why they would upset prisoners in reeducation camps or refugees in the US, Thailand or the Philippines. Staunchly anti-communist Vietnamese both in Vietnam and abroad had not forgiven Trịnh Công Sơn for singing "Join Hands in a Great Circle" [Nối vòng tay lớn] on a Saigon radio station on April 30, 1975, the day communist troops took over the city. Written in 1968 and included in Sơn's collection *Prayer for Vietnam* [*Kinh Việt Nam*] "Join Hands in a Great Circle," like other songs in this collection, presents an optimistic view of a peaceful Vietnam, the optimism stemming from the opening of the Paris Peace Talks in May 1968. It has become a rough equivalent of "America the Beautiful" in the United States: a song sung to glorify the unity of the Vietnamese people.

Thái Thị Kim Lan, an old friend of Sơn's from Huế, heard him sing "Each Day I Choose a Little Happiness" in 1977 when she made her first visit back to Vietnam after the war ended. In 1965 she had obtained a scholarship from the Goethe Institute in Huế to study German and eleven years later, in 1976, she graduated from Ludwig-Maximilian University with a degree in philosophy. She was teaching comparative philosophy in Munich when she returned to Huế in 1977. On this visit she saw Sơn often. When she left he gave her handwritten copies of three songs, all of them written on cheap paper because at the time, she says, good paper was hard to find. One of the songs was "Each Day I Choose a Little Happiness."[28] Of all the songs Trịnh Công Sơn wrote, Thái Thị Kim Lan says, she dislikes hearing or singing this song the most, not because it has a sad tune or the lyrics aren't good but because it reminds her of her visit with Sơn in 1977.[29] "That 'little happiness' [*một niềm vui*]," she says, "like a tear too dry to fall, broke my heart."[30]

---

27. Ibid.
28. The other two songs were "To Board" [Ở trọ] and "Unknown Source" [Biết đâu nguồn cội]. See Thái Thị Kim Lan, "Trịnh Công Sơn, nơi vùng ưu tư thành tiếng du ca" [Where Sorrow Becomes a Folk Song], in *Trịnh Công Sơn: Cuộc đời, âm nhạc, thơ, hội họa, suy tưởng* [Trịnh Công Sơn: Life, Music, Poetry, Painting, Reflections], eds. Trịnh Cung and Nguyễn Quốc Thái (HCMC: Văn Nghệ, 2001), 102. "*Du ca*" in the title refers to songs sung in South Vietnam in the mid-1960s. These songs were sung by young people who participated in social work projects. See Phong Trào Du ca Việt Nam [The *Du ca* Movement in Vietnam], *Wikipedia*, July 7, https://vi.wikipedia.org/wiki/Phong_tr%C3%A0o_Du_ca_Vi%E1%BB%87tNam (accessed July 7, 2022).
29. See Thái Thị Kim Lan, "Trịnh Công Sơn, nơi vùng ưu tư thành tiếng du ca," 100-101.
30. Ibid., 102.

Four years later, however, in what appears to be an expanded version of this article, one written in 2001 after Sơn died, Thái Thị Kim Lan revises her view of "Each Day I Choose a Little Happiness." People who understand this song to be a simple song about being happy haven't, she says, listened carefully to the lyrics:

> Who says Sơn praises a little happiness in this song when everyone is sad and hungry? Whoever it is has listened too quickly, hearing only the word "happiness" and not hearing the word "choose" [chọn] that comes before it. Someone who is happy would say "I'm happy," as in the song "If You're Happy Sing" [Vui Ca Lên], but a person who sits and "chooses" a piece of happiness is not yet happy because, at the time of choosing, that happiness is something outside him or her. It's not an internal happiness; it's a happiness mixed with tears and sobbing, only a halfway happiness.[31]

Thái Thị Kim Lan compares Sơn's mood in this song to the happiness of Thúy Kiều, the heroine in Nguyễn Du's *The Tale of Kiều*, a work one Vietnamese scholar calls "Vietnam's literary Bible."[32] (See Chapter Fifteen for more on *The Tale of Kiều*.) To save her father, the main character, Kiều, agrees to marry a man who sells her to a brothel where, to cheer herself up, she would write verses, paint, or play the lute. "But such delights she feigned and did not feel," Nguyễn Du writes. Thái Kim Lan quotes this line and says it describes Sơn's mood in "Each Day I Choose a Little Happiness."

Happiness was definitely hard to find in Huế in 1977, though, Thái Kim Lan says, "Huế radio stations every day were broadcasting thousands of happy stories." When my wife and I visited family in Huế in 2011, my sister-in-law described what life was like for her and her family in Huế after the war ended.[33] Both she and her husband were teachers and received a small salary as well as five kilograms of rice and eight kilograms of a grain Vietnamese call *bo bo*.[34] *Bo bo*, she said, was hard to digest and had to be simmered for hours before you could eat it. To buy grain or flour, she explained, one had to go to a *cửa hàng lương thực* [state store for cereals]. To buy things like meat, eggs or fish sauce one had to go to

---

31. Thái Thị Kim Lan, "Trịnh Công Sơn, nơi vùng ưu tư thành tiếng du ca" [Where Sorrow Becomes a Folk Song], Giao Điểm [Point of Intersection] http////64.87.105/doithoaiIII/klan-tcson.hem (accessed December 13, 2005).
32. Nguyễn Đình Hòa, *Vietnamese Literature: A Brief Survey* (San Diego, CA: San Diego State University, 1994), 103.
33. After a series of interviews with my sister-in-law, I wrote a summary of her life which I shared with her and her family.
34. My wife and I are not certain what "*bo bo*" is, but we believe it is sorghum or maybe Job's tears (*Coix lacryma-jobi*).

another state store called a *cửa hàng thực phẩm* [state grocery store]. Meat was available but scarce. No lean meat was available. To buy meat one had to get up at 3:00 a.m. and wait in line until the store opened at 7 a.m. There was a lot of pushing and shoving, my sister-in-law said. One had to form brief alliances with the person ahead and behind you so you could push forward as a group, or you might be pushed aside. Some people suffered from a rash people called *ghẻ bộ đội* [communist soldier rash] because many soldiers in the conquering army suffered from it.

How could Trịnh Công Sơn write such a happy song during this difficult time? Because, Thái Thị Kim Lan says, he *chose* to. It was a choice that may reflect his Buddhist background. In Chapter Twenty-Four I mentioned that Thích Nhất Hạnh cites "Each Day I Choose a Little Happiness" as evidence that the singer was aware of the Buddhist concept of "living happily in the present moment" (Vn. *hiện pháp lạc trú*; Skt. *drstadharma sukhavihari*). This song also suggests the emphasis in Buddhism on practice. As Stephen Batchelor points out, "Awakening is not a thing but a process—and this process is the path itself."[35] Buddhist dharma, he explains, "is not something to believe in but something to do."[36] At this difficult juncture in Vietnam's history Trịnh Công Sơn decided what his country needed was a "good heart," and the best way to develop that good heart in himself and others was to call attention to the features of Vietnamese life that made people happy: meeting and laughing and singing with friends, singing a lullaby to a newborn baby, gazing at green rice fields. As Thái Thị Kim Lan suggests, this paean about traditional joys was Sơn's response to the political messages the government radio stations were broadcasting throughout the city in 1977.[37]

After the war ended, everyone in Huế struggled to adapt to new political and economic systems. Songwriters like Trịnh Công Sơn had to adjust to a new set of rules regarding artistic production. Immediately after the war ended the leaders of the new regime set out to eradicate all vestiges of neocolonialism that persisted in the land they had just conquered: Vietnam, south of the demilitarized zone. As explained in Chapter Three, weepy sentimental love songs, which communist authorities called "yellow music," were thought to be a corrupting influence on revolution-

---

35. Stephen Batchelor, *Buddhism Without Beliefs: A Contemporary Guide to Awakening* (New York: Riverhead Books, 1998), 10.
36. Ibid., 17.
37. Thái Thị Kim Lan, "Trịnh Công Sơn—nơi vùng ưu tư thành tiếng du ca."

ary soldiers and cadre. Sơn's supporters Nguyễn Đắc Xuân and Hoàng Phủ Ngọc Tường had to convince the new arbitrators of cultural production in Huế that Trịnh Công Sơn's songs, particularly those in his more recent collections, *Prayer for Vietnam* and *We Must See the Sun*, were not yellow music.

In the late 1970s and late early 1980s songwriters were expected to write songs glorifying manual labor and agricultural production. This was difficult for Sơn but he tried. In the late 1970s, around the same time he wrote "Each Day I Choose a Little Happiness," he wrote two very forgettable songs, "Carrying Vegetables to Market" [Gánh rau ra chợ] and "The Tractor at the State Farm" [Máy kéo nông trường]. After hearing these songs sung by another singer at a concert in Saigon organized by the Association of Patriotic Intellectuals [Hội Trí thức Yêu Nước] a friend of Sơn's, a woman named Trần Tuyết Hoa, advised him to return to writing songs about love between people and let others write songs glorifying socialist labor.[38] "Each Day I Choose a Little Happiness," with its Buddhist themes and its emphasis on having a good heart, no doubt pleased some of his old fans; and although it did not glorify manual labor or agricultural production it was too upbeat and positive to be labeled yellow music.

In "Each Day I Choose a Little Happiness" and other songs, Trịnh Công Sơn talks about the importance of having a heart. In English there is a similar expression. English speakers say "That guy has a good heart" or "She's a good-hearted person." Vietnamese speakers sometimes use the Vietnamese word for heart, *trái tim*, in a similar way. Sơn ends "I Choose a Little Happiness" with these lines: "I suddenly realize why I live / Because the country needs a good heart [*trái tim*]." Sơn just says "heart" not "good heart." The "good" is implied as it is in English expressions like "Have a heart" or "He's got a lot of heart." I've added the word "good" to make the meaning clear. My Vietnamese relatives and friends tell me that *trái tim* usually does not have Buddhist connotations; it does not, for example, evoke the heart sutra. Another word for heart, however, *Tấm lòng*, may have Buddhist connotations, as it does, for example, in these lines from a scroll I saw several years ago at a gift shop in Từ Đàm Pagoda in Huế:

---

38. Trần Tuyết Hoa, "40 Năm Hành Trình Âm Nhạc Trịnh Công Sơn, Thái Hòa và Tôi" [A 40 Year Musical Journey with Trịnh Công Sơn, Thái Hòa and I], Tcs-home, https://www.tcs-home.org/ban-be/articles/40-nam-hanh-trinh-am-nhac-trinh-cong-son-thai-hoa-va-toi (accessed July 18, 2022).

> *A hundred years ago we did not yet exist*
> *A hundred years later existence is like nothingness*
> *Life is existence existence nothingness nothingness*
> *In the hundred years remaining only a good heart* [tấm lòng]
> *matters.*

> Trăm năm trước thì ta chưa có
> Trăm năm sau có cũng như không
> Cuộc đời có có không không
> Trăm năm còn lại tấm lòng mà thôi

Note also these lines at the end of Nguyễn Du's *The Tale of Kiều*:

> *Inside ourselves there lies the root of good:*
> *The heart outweighs all talents on this earth*

> Thiện-căn ở tại lòng ta,
> Chữ tâm kia mới bằng ba chữ tài.

Although these lines do not contain the phrase *tấm lòng* [good heart], the words *thiện-căn* and *lòng ta* evoke the same concept.

In his song "Let the Wind Blow It Away" [Để gió cuốn đi]* Trịnh Công Sơn, like the author of this Buddhist poem and like Nguyễn Du in the final lines of *The Tale of Kiều*, talks about the importance of having a good heart. In this song the term he uses for heart, *tấm lòng*, is the one with Buddhist connotations. Here is the opening stanza:

> *To live in this life*
> *One needs a good heart* [tấm lòng],
> *To do what, do you know?*
> *To let the wind blow it away,*
> *To let the wind blow it away.*

EMPTINESS AND SADNESS AND HAPPINESS

Dylan's songs, as we have seen, are "Bible soaked"—full of allusions to and echoes of biblical verses. In his so-called Christian songs, which are explicit statements of his faith, Dylan talks about being "saved by the blood of the lamb," about a "man on a cross" who has been "crucified," and about how he wants the Lord to take him in his "time of dyin'." Trịnh Công Sơn's songs are not as "sutra-soaked" as Dylan's are "Bible-soaked"; and he wrote no songs as overtly religious as the songs on Dylan's Christian albums. Buddhism has no single book equivalent to the Bible in Christianity, the

465

Qur'an in Islam, or the Torah in Judaism, or the Vedas in Hinduism.[39] The Buddhist scriptures fill many volumes and have been written in various languages. Most Vietnamese Buddhist sutras and prayers are translations of Chinese translations of Pali or Sanskrit texts, and so when Vietnamese chant these prayers and sutras they chant them in Sino-Vietnamese [*Hán Việt*], a literary variant of Vietnamese that is difficult for ordinary people to understand. Trịnh Công Sơn composed popular songs for a mass audience and therefore could not overload his songs with Buddhist terminology. His songs are infused with Buddhist ideas but not weighted down with Buddhist terms.

Many of Sơn's songs, however, contain words that Vietnamese would identify as referring to Buddhist concepts. In "Ru em" [Lullaby for You] Sơn sings about "loving-kindness and compassion" [*từ bi*] filling his heart. *Từ bi* [Skt. *matri karuna*], a compound word, refers to the first two of the Four Immeasurable Minds [Skt. *apramana*; Vn. *Tứ vô thượng tâm*]. In "Này em có nhớ" [Now Do You Remember?] Sơn says in life distant "*kiếp*" are common. *Kiếp*, a Sino-Vietnamese word meaning "period of a person's life," appears alone or in phrases like "*kiếp người*" [the life of a person] and "*tiền kiếp*" [former life]. Vietnamese recognize "*kiếp*" as referring to the idea of karma and rebirth. A *kiếp* is a very long time. It refers, one dictionary of Buddhist terms says, to "a period of time between the creation and recreation of a world or universe."[40] The title of another Trịnh Công Sơn song is "Đóa hoa vô thường" [Flowers of Impermanence]. "*Vô thường*" [impermanence] is a name for one of the most important concepts in Buddhism—the impermanence of all things.

More commonly, however, a Trịnh Công Sơn song will convey Buddhist ideas in colloquial language that is free of Buddhist terminology. Here, for example, is how he talks about impermanence in "To Board" [Ở trọ]:

> *The bird boards on the bamboo branch*
> *The fish boards in a crevice of spring water*
> *I myself am a boarder in this world*
> *In one hundred years I'll return to the edge of the sky*

Another Buddhist concept that is evoked often in Trịnh Công Sơn's songs is the concept of emptiness [Skt. *sunyata*], perhaps the most

---

39. Jack Maguire, *Essential Buddhism: A Complete Guide to Buddhist Beliefs and Practices*, 34.
40. *Thư Viện Hoa Sen* [Lotus Library], an online Vietnamese-English Buddhist Dictionary, s.v. "kiếp," https://thuvienhoasen.org/p10a11844/k (accessed July 14, 2022).

important concept in Mahayana Buddhism. Emptiness is addressed in the Diamond Sutra and Heart Sutra, the two sutras that are the best known of the roughly forty Perfection of Wisdom [Skt. *Prajna Paramita*] sutras.[41] Vietnamese refer to emptiness as *không, hư vô* or *hư không* and all these terms appear in Trịnh Công Sơn's songs. In "Còn có bao ngày" [How Many More Days], for example, Trịnh Công Sơn says "At night we hear the heavens shout and moan / We hear life as fullness, as emptiness" [*Đêm nghe trời như hú như than / Ta nghe đời như có như không*]. In Buddhist texts "fullness" is discussed with "emptiness" but the point is not to contrast the two but to realize that there is no difference between them. Note that Trịnh Công Sơn does not contrast them in his song: the speaker hears life as both full *and* empty. The following famous lines in the Heart Sutra make a similar point: "Form [all phenomena][42] is emptiness and the very emptiness is form; emptiness does not differ from form, form does not differ from emptiness; whatever is form, that is emptiness, whatever is emptiness, that is form."[43] The emptiness of the Heart Sutra, Edward Conze explains, is "not empty of that which it excludes, but it includes it, is identical with it, is full of it. It is therefore a 'Full Emptiness.'"[44]

When one achieves a realization of "Full Emptiness" one has grasped the wisdom of the Wisdom Sutras. It is a wisdom that is not easy for Westerners, who assume the rightness of Aristotle's principle of non-contradiction, namely, that two contradictory statements cannot both be true at the same time.[45] According to this principle, the statements "A is B" and "A is not B" cannot both be true. Without this principle, Aristotle argued, we could not know anything that we do know. We would not be able to make distinctions—to distinguish a man from a rabbit, for example. We would arrive at the absurd conclusion that all things are one.[46] For Buddhists, however, realizing that all things are one is, as Edward Conze

---

41. In Sanskrit *prajna* means wisdom. Depending on which etymology one uses, the term *paramita* can mean either "perfect," "highest" or "most excellent"; or it can mean "that which has gone beyond" or "that which has gone to the further bank or shore." See David S. Lopez, *The Heart Sutra Explained*, 21-22.
42. "Form" in Sanskrit is *rupa*; in Vietnamese, *sắc*.
43. This is Edward Conze's translation, which is included in his book *Buddhist Wisdom: The Diamond Sutra and the Heart Sutra* (New York: Vintage Books, 2001), 86.
44. Ibid., 91.
45. Aristotle discusses the principle of non-contradiction in *Metaphysics* IV, 3–6.
46. This explanation is based on "Aristotle on Non-contradiction," Stanford Encyclopedia of Philosophy, https://web.archive.org/web/20160318122648/https://plato.stanford. edu/entries/aristotle-noncontradiction/ (accessed May 23, 2016).

says, the "great goal";[47] it is the wisdom talked about in the sutras, the wisdom that is achieved by overcoming apparent contradictions and becoming aware of the interconnectedness of all things.[48]

Emptiness is directly related to loving-kindness and compassion. "If all beings are inextricably connected," Judith Simmer-Brown explains, "then the most meaningful thing to do is to dedicate oneself to the benefit of all beings. For this reason the arising of unconditioned compassion is said to be the mark of a true realization of emptiness."[49] When we realize that we all are one, that "self" and "others" are equally empty, this wisdom strengthens our feelings of solidarity with others.[50]

The spiritual journey of the Bodhisattva, the importance of compassion, the awareness of emptiness—all these themes come together in concentrated form (about 350 English words) in the Heart Sutra.[51] In this sutra the Buddha inspires a disciple, Sariputra, to request that the Bodhisattva of compassion, Avalokitesvara, instruct him in *prajna paramita*, the perfection of wisdom.[52] The core of this instruction has to do with emptiness. The Heart Sutra is chanted daily in Buddhist pagodas in Vietnam and around the world. Trịnh Công Sơn certainly knew it, and he wrote a song, "Where Will the Wave Go"* [Sóng về đâu] which he says was inspired by the mantra that concludes the Heart Sutra: "Gone, gone, gone beyond, gone altogether beyond, O what an awakening, all hail!"[53]

---

47. Edward Conze, *Buddhist Wisdom: The Diamond Sutra and the Heart Sutra*, 90-91.
48. Some scholars have argued that the Buddhist view of reality is supported by modern science. Fritjof Capra, for example, says that both Buddhists and scientists exploring quantum field theory share "a conception of physical things and phenomena as transient manifestations of an underlying fundamental entity." See Fritof Capra, *The Tao of Physics* (Boston: Shambhala, 1991), 197-198. See also Jack Maguire, *Essential Buddhism*, 80-81; and Mu Soeng, *The Diamond Sutra* (Boston: Wisdom Publications, 2000), 41-49.
49. Judith Simmer-Brown, "Preface," in Edward Conze, *Buddhist Wisdom: The Diamond Sutra and the Heart Sutra*, xix.
50. Some Christian scholars argue that the rejection of an independent self in Buddhism makes loving-kindness and compassion impossible. I will discuss this issue in my final chapter.
51. The Heart Sutra in Sanskrit contains 448 syllables; in English it is composed of sixteen sentences; in Chinese, it is 260 characters; in Vietnamese around 400 words.
52. As we have seen, *Prajna Paramita*, according to which etymology one uses, can be understood as the "Perfection of Wisdom" or "Wisdom that Takes One to the Other Shore." See David S. Lopez, *The Heart Sutra Explained*, 21-22.
53. Trịnh Công Sơn, "Phải biết sống hết mình trong mỗi sát na của hiện tại.," See Trịnh Công Sơn, interview with Thích Tâm Thiện which originally appeared in *Nguyệt San Giác Ngộ* [Enlightment Monthy Review] no. 1, April 1996. I found it at Diễn Đàn Văn Hóa Học [Forum for Studies of Culture], http://www.vanhoahoc.edu.vn/dienan/view-topic.php?f=56&t=1229 (accessed September 18, 2011.Excerpts from this interview and other comments that Trịnh Công Sơn has made about his Buddhist background can be found in "Nhạc sĩ Trịnh Công Sơn: 'Phải biết sống hết mình trong mỗi sát na của

[*Gate gate paragate parasamgate bodhi svaha*]. The Bodhisattva Avalokita offers this mantra as a condensed version of the wisdom taught in the entire sutra. In Sanskrit *gate* means "gone" and *para* means "beyond," but *para* also conveys the idea of moving to the further bank, shore, or boundary.[54] *Parasamgate* means "completely" or "altogether." *Bodhi* [Vn. *bồ đề*] refers to enlightenment and *svaha* means "All hail!".

Trịnh Công Sơn's song "Where Will the Wave Go?" does not, at first glance, appear to be inspired by the Heart Sutra, or any other sutra. The words of the song are common everyday words. It contains no Sino-Vietnamese words associated with Buddhist texts. In this song the speaker tells the sea and the wave not to push him and not to push each other:

> *Sea and wave sea and wave don't push me*
> *Don't push me against a person's leg*
> *Sea and wave sea and wave don't push each other*
> *If I push the sea back where will the wave go*

The question that ends this first stanza is partially answered in the second line of the third stanza: "If I push the sea back the wave will lie hurt." As the song progresses the speaker stops asking questions. The song doesn't end with clear-cut answers to the questions posed earlier in the song. The last stanza, however, suggests that the physical act of pushing is an outward manifestation of sadness [*âm u*] and a hateful heart [*trái tim thù*]. Here are the last three lines of the song:

> *Sea and wave sea and wave don't be sad*
> *Don't nurture a hating heart*
> *Sea and wave don't push each other*

What does this song have to do with Heart Sutra? Poetic inspiration is complex and we can only speculate. The Heart Sutra, however, is Buddhism's most profound exposition of emptiness and those who become aware of emptiness are believed to be marked by feelings of compassion for all sentient beings. Waves and sea are not different from one another. There is sea in the waves and waves in the sea. Even things seemingly more different are not really opposed so why should sea and wave, which share so much, oppose each other? "In the Heart Sutra," my Vietnamese

---

hiện tại'" [The Musician Trịnh Công Sơn: "You Must Know How to Live Completely in Each Moment of Reality"]

54. David Lopez, *The Heart Sutra Explained: Indian and Tibetan Commentaries*, 114.

Buddhist dictionary explains, "emptiness is considered the shared feature [*cái chung*] of all seemingly opposed phenomena; in it all contradictions are wiped away, Emptiness and Fullness are not different."[55] In "Sóng về đâu?" Trịnh Công Sơn seems to be saying that we should realize that all things are connected and that we are connected to all things. When we realize this, loving-kindness and compassion will emerge.

In "The Eye That Remains" [Con mắt còn lại]* Trịnh Công Sơn relates emptiness to compassion more explicitly. In this song he uses the common terms for these concepts—*không* and *hư vô* for emptiness, and *từ tâm* for loving-kindness. Here are four lines from the last stanza:

> *There's still two eyes and one eye cries for people*
> *The eye that remains looks at life as nothingness*[56] [không]
> *Looks at you as emptiness* [hư vô], *looks at you as sun and shade*
> *The eye that remains is gentle and loving* [từ tâm]

This is a difficult song, perhaps in part because it was inspired by a poem by Bùi Giáng,[57] a poet who wrote obscure poems, some of them on Buddhist themes. It has a Zen-like quality. I will have more to say about this song at the end of this chapter. I bring up this song here because it relates emptiness to loving-kindness. In his discussion of "The Eye that Remains," Nguyễn Hoàn talks about the Buddhist notion of "Full Emptiness" and quotes the famous lines from the Heart Sutra about form being emptiness and emptiness being form. He concludes by saying that when a person realizes that "fullness and emptiness are one, that we and others are one," then "loving-kindness and compassion [Skt. *maitri* and *karuna*; Vn. *từ bi*] will arise from that realization: 'The eye that remains is gentle and loving' [*Con mắt còn lại nhẹ nhàng từ tâm*]."[58] In other words, in Nguyễn Hoàn's view "The Eye That Remains" is about becoming aware of emptiness, and the resulting feeling of loving-kindness and compassion that emerges from that awareness.

---

55. Tâm Tuệ Hỷ, *Danh từ Phật học thực dụng*, 203-204.
56. "*Không*" is translated as "nothingness" here, but it could be translated as "emptiness." Two different words are used for this concept in this English translation because Trịnh Công Sơn uses different words for emptiness in his song.
57. This is the poem titled "Mắt buồn" [Sad Eyes] that I discuss later in this chapter.
58. Nguyễn Hoàn, "Con người minh triết trong nhạc Trịnh Công Sơn" [The Wise Person in the Music of Trịnh Công Sơn], *tcs-home*, https://www.tcs-home.org/ban-be/articles/con-nguoi-minh-triet-trong-nhac-trinh-cong-son (accessed July 19, 2022).

SADNESS AND HAPPINESS

Some Americans and Europeans I've known find Vietnamese songs to be too sentimental, too full of weeping over doomed love affairs. The songs are too dark, they feel; there's too little sunshine. I myself grew tired of some very sad pre-war songs that were played over and over again in cafés I visited in the late 1960s. Composers of pre-war songs, the authors of New Poetry [*Thơ mới*] of the 1930s and 1940s, and novelists like Hoàng Ngọc Phách tended to sentimentalize sadness: They suggested that it was sweet and beautiful to be sad.[59] Although Trịnh Công Sơn was influenced by this romantic tradition, his sadness is more philosophical than romantic and too deep and heart-wrenching to be labeled sentimental. An interesting aspect of Trịnh Công Sơn's sadness is that it appears to be closely related to happiness. Trịnh Công Sơn is always finding sadness in happiness. This is, says Cao Huy Thuần, a "special feature" of the composer: "There is no happiness in Trịnh Công Sơn that is not followed immediately by sadness," he says. "Happiness/sadness go with each other and make a couple closer than lovers."[60] Trịnh Công Sơn never seems to trust happiness because he senses sadness lurks around the corner: "There's sadness with the kisses," he says in "The Fragrance of the Quỳnh Flower" [Quỳnh hương]; "There's some tears at the moment of kissing" he says in "Fly Away Quietly" [Bay đi thầm lặng]; "Under the cradle grave mounds grow" he says in "Troubled Grass Swaying" [Cỏ xót xa đưa]; "In the spring of life a desolate wind blows" he says in "A Place for Leaving and Returning"* [Một cõi đi về]; "Your lips are red like emptiness" he says in "Close to Despair" [Gần như niềm tuyệt vọng]; "Love rises very high / like a bird with tired wings" he says in "Sad Love" [Tình sầu].

There is nothing uniquely Buddhist about thinking, when in the midst of a pleasant experience, that it probably won't last, and, as a result of that thought, to feel a tinge of sadness. Regardless of our religious beliefs we all know that nothing is forever. Flowers wilt, love affairs end, et cetera,

---

59. I discuss pre-war songs in Chapter Eighteen and the new poets in Chapters Sixteen and Seventeen. Hoàng Ngọc Phách was the author of *Tố Tâm* [Pure Heart], a very sentimental novel published in 1925. For more information on this novel, see Cao Thị Như-Quỳnh and John C. Schafer, "From Verse Narrative to Novel: The Development of Prose Fiction in Vietnam," *Journal of Asian Studies* 47, no. 4 (November 1988), 756-777.
60. Cao Huy Thuần, "Chiến tranh trong Trịnh Công Sơn" [The War in Trịnh Công Sơn], in Cao Huy Thuần, *Khi tựa gối khi cúi đầu* [He'd Hug His Knees, Hang Down His Head] (Hanoi: Văn Học, 2011), 73. The title of Cao Huy Thuần's book is a quotation from *The Tale of Kiều*. It describes Kim Trọng's reaction when he heard Kiều play sad songs on her lute. See Chapter Fifteen: *The Tale of Kiều*.

and the thought of that prospect makes us sad. But to link happiness and sadness so closely and so persistently, as Trịnh Công Sơn does, and to suggest, as he does more than once, that they are one and the same—that, it seems to me, is unusual and worth discussing. My focus in this section is on emptiness, but at least two other Buddhist notions are helpful in understanding Trịnh Công Sơn's approach to happiness and sadness: the idea of impermanence (Vn. *vô thường*; Skt. *anicca*) and "suffering" or "un-satisfactoriness" (Vn. *khổ*, Skt. *dukkha*). "Impermanence" and "suffering" are related. We feel dissatisfied and suffer because things do not last. "It is because of the fact that things are impermanent," Peter Harvey explains, "that they are also *dukkha*: potentially painful and frustrating."[61] Jack Maquire, a Buddhist teacher, points out that suffering is related to our mortality, to "the fact that we age, get sick, and die." But, he says, "it also refers to more subtle matters: the transitory nature of our pleasures; the fragility of our possessions; the instability of our relationships, fortunes, moods, thoughts, and convictions."[62]

We are all—Buddhists and non-Buddhist alike—aware, at least inter-mittently, of the "transitory nature of our pleasures," but Buddhists are more persistently aware of them because impermanence and suffering are basic Buddhist concepts. Buddhists emphasize these concepts because they believe to become happy one must accept the fact that life is impermanent and full of suffering. Accepting this truth, which Buddhists believe is a fundamental truth of human existence, is what one strives to do by "practicing Buddhism" [*tu Phật*], an activity which is sometimes defined as "developing the ability to be happy." In other words, Buddhists believe that to achieve a peaceful and happy mind one must accept the reality of suffering; one should not avoid thinking about it—or singing about it.

To explain why Trịnh Công Sơn frequently links happiness and sadness, we also, I believe, have to return to the Buddhist notion of emptiness. We especially need to understand that emptiness for Buddhists is a full emptiness: It includes what would appear to be its opposite. All phenomena lack a self-nature and nothing is completely different from something else. Becoming enlightened involves grasping the intercon-nectedness of all phenomena, reaching a point at which one realizes that

---

61. Peter Harvey, *An Introduction to Buddhism*, 50.
62. Jack Maguire, *Essential Buddhism: A Complete Guide to Beliefs and Practices*, 86-87.

happiness is sadness and sadness is happiness. "Sadness is happiness" is another way of stating Buddhism's grandest paradox, which is that "Samsara, the phenomenal world, is Nirvana" (Vn. *Sanh tử tức Niết bàn*).[63] Mu Soeng explains this paradox in commenting on the path of the bodhisattva. Somewhere along this path, he explains, the bodhisattva gains insight into emptiness and realizes that all things in the phenomenal world lack self-nature (Vn. *tự tánh* or *thể tánh*, Skt. *svabhava*). This insight leads the bodhisattva to see Samsara (the phenomenal world) and Nirvana (the transcendent world) as "bipolar aspects of the same reality rather than as two exclusive realities."[64]

Another way to state this grand paradox is to say "Suffering is Enlightenment" (Vn. *Phiền não tức Bồ đề*). The phrase "*Phiền não tức Bồ đề*," roughly translated here as "Suffering is Enlightenment," suggests something else besides the idea that the two states are two different aspects of the same reality: It suggests also that one has to begin with suffering to reach happiness and enlightenment. In understanding this meaning of the phrase it helps to understand that "*phiền não*," *klesa* in Sanskrit, refers to certain "defilements" that cloud the mind and prevent one from achieving happiness. Chief among these are the Three Poisons: greed, anger, and delusion. In Mahayana Buddhism one achieves happiness by liberating oneself from these "defilements," by purifying one's mind of these pollutants. My Vietnamese Buddhist dictionary explains it this way: "We are accustomed to run after liberation apart from delusions, to search for happiness apart from suffering. But that is not right. When delusions are gone, enlightenment comes; when suffering ends there is happiness; when we know how to stop defilements [*Phiền não*], then enlightenment [*Bồ Đề*] comes."[65] Trịnh Công Sơn, it seems to me, was aware that the road to happiness proceeds through, not around, our weaknesses and troubles and that is why he does not avoid talking about sadness and loneliness in his songs.

This is not to say that Trịnh Công Sơn traveled the path of a bodhisattva and realized "Suffering is Enlightenment." He was not a bodhisattva. I believe, however, that one reason Trịnh Công Sơn's songs were so popular, and remain popular, is because he did not shirk the problem of suffering.

---

63. *Sanh tử* means "life death" and is a short way of referring to "*sanh tử luân hồi*," the cycle of birth and death from which, Buddhists believe, one must achieve Nirvana to escape.
64. Mu Soeng, *The Diamond Sutra*, (Boston MA: Wisdom Publications 2000) 34.
65. Tâm Tuệ Hỷ, ed., *Danh từ Phật học thực dụng*, 364.

"Trịnh Công Sơn was not the first to think of the suffering [*phiền não*] of this world, suffering that begins with cries in the cradle," says Nguyễn Hoàn. "But in his music that 'sings prayers' about people's fate he seeks a way to soften the crying and relieve the suffering. This is his unique contribution; it is what explains the powerful artistic effect created by Trịnh music."[66]

One way Trịnh Công Sơn "softens the crying" is by including rays of hope and reminders about the good things of life in and around expressions of sadness and loneliness. Only a few of his post-war songs are unrelentingly sad; few are sad from start to finish. Take "Thanks" [Tạ ơn], for example, which has some sad lines but also lines like these:

> *Though you came, then left, I still thank people*
> *Thank life, thank whoever gave me*
> *Love bright like a star that's fallen from the sky.*

And "Let the Wind Blow It Away" [Để gió cuốn đi], a song that has some sad lines but also encourages us to have a good heart, to smile at the end of the day, and "as long as life remains, be happy." In 2012, while my wife and I were visiting family in Huế, around a dozen former students of mine invited me for lunch at a restaurant. After the meal one former student said she would sing a song that was a favorite of hers, "Let the Wind Blow It Away." She sang it very beautifully. Her life has included some misfortune and I sensed, as she sang, that the song "softened her crying and relieved her suffering." In other words, it affected her the way Nguyễn Hoàn says that Trịnh Công Sơn wanted his songs to affect people.

"Moon Song" [Nguyệt ca] provides a good example of how Trịnh Công Sơn brings together notions of emptiness and sadness and happiness. In the section of my Introduction explaining my approach, I discussed this song in arguing that to understand a text it helps to know the prior texts evoked in it. I pointed out that Vietnamese language has two words for moon—*trăng* and *nguyệt*. "*Trăng*" is a pure Vietnamese word which is not used as a girl's given name. *Nguyệt*, a word borrowed from Chinese, is a more literary way of referring to the moon and is a quite common girl's name. As I understand this song, "Moon Song" is about a love relationship that has ended. Trịnh Công Sơn uses these two different words for moon to contrast stages in this relationship. When *trăng* was *nguyệt*, the relationship was going well and the speaker in the song was

---

66. Nguyễn Hoàn, "Con người minh triết trong nhạc Trịnh Công Sơn."

happy. Then *trăng* stopped being *nguyệt* and the speaker becomes sad. The song ends with some sad images—of rocks too tired to roll, of a tree bereft of branches. In the concluding lines of the song the speaker stands alone: "From the time you stopped being *nguyệt* / I stand alone." In the middle of the song, however, the speaker describes "hearing" something:

> *One day I suddenly heard*
> *That sadness and happiness are one*
> *Like forgetting in remembering*
> *From the time* trăng *stopped being* nguyệt
> *I'm like that drop of sunshine over there*
> *Since* trăng *stopped being* nguyệt
> *Consider that moment a coincidence*

I do not want to force a Buddhist interpretation of this song, to see emptiness everywhere, but earlier in the song the speaker has spoken about "prayers having entered his life" [*Câu kinh đã bước vào đời*]. And then a few lines later the speaker "hears" that "sadness and happiness are one," a phrase which suggests the "full emptiness" described in the Heart Sutra: the oneness of all things, even apparent opposites. I believe the speaker in this poem receives a vision of emptiness. He cannot hold on to this vision. Sadness returns in the next verse. Holding on to the vision requires constant Buddhist practice.

THE DHARMA GATE OF NON-DUALISM

Buddhists speak of "Eighty four thousand dharma gates," or ways to enter enlightenment [*Tám vạn bốn ngàn pháp môn*]. One of the best known is the non-dual dharma gate [*Pháp môn bất nhị*]. Although non-dualism is a synonym or near-synonym for emptiness, which I have already attempted to explain, I will discuss non-dualism as well because I believe it is a useful concept to use in understanding Trịnh Công Sơn songs. Buddhists speak of "skillful means" [Vn. *phương tiện thiện xảo*; Skt. *upaya kusala*]— appropriate methods of explaining the dharma to make it easy for others to understand. Non-dualism is a "skillful means" for understanding Buddhism and, I'm suggesting, many of Trịnh Công Sơn's songs.

I think Cao Huy Thuần would agree that non-dualism is a useful idea to have in mind as one considers many Trịnh Công Sơn songs. In two thoughtful articles about Trịnh Công Sơn, Cao Huy Thuần never mentions the term "non-dualism," but he does talk about something he calls "oppositional symmetry" [*đối nghịch*] and explains how, in Trịnh Công

Sơn songs, this oppositional symmetry often dissolves into "harmonious symmetry" [đối hợp].[67] Cao Huy Thuần's harmonious symmetry, I would like to suggest, is another way—a more literary, less Buddhist way—to speak of non-dualism. Cao Huy Thuần refers to oppositional symmetry as "the primary feature in Trịnh Công Sơn's music" and argues that it is found in songs that Trịnh Công Sơn wrote throughout his career, "from the first to the last, from those he wrote when he was twenty, to those he wrote when he lay sick."[68]

As examples of oppositional symmetry Cao Huy Thuần cites lines like those I have quoted above in my section on emptiness—"In the spring of life a desolate wind blows," for example, from Trịnh Công Sơn's song "A Place for Leaving and Returning" and "There's sadness with the kisses" from his song "The Fragrance of the Quỳnh Flower." Here's another example, from "Watching Autumns Pass" [Nhìn những mùa thu đi], a song Trịnh Công Sơn wrote at the start of his songwriting career:

> *Watching autumns pass*
> *You hear sadness in the sunshine*

Here's another example, from "This Quiet Place" [Lặng lẽ nơi này], a song he wrote in 1987:

> *Love is like a sea*
> *A sea with wide shoulders*
> *Love is like a sea*
> *A sea that narrows people's arms*

Cao Huy Thuần gives many more examples as he ponders this question: Why does Trịnh Công Sơn continually juxtapose something that has positive connotations, something that makes people feel good— like sunshine or wide shoulders—with something that has negative connotations, that makes people feel bad—like sadness or narrow arms?

Cao Huy Thuần does not suggest—at least not immediately—that the answer to this question lies in Trịnh Công Sơn's Buddhist beliefs. He does not want to "encase Trịnh Công Sơn within any philosophical theory," he says.[69] His approach is more literary than philosophical or religious. The terms his uses, oppositional symmetry and harmonious symmetry,

---

67. The first article is "Buồn bã với những môi hôn." The second article is "Chiến tranh trong Trịnh Công Sơn," [The War in Trịnh Công Sơn] in Cao Huy Thuần, *Khi tựa gối khi cúi đầu* [He'd Hug His Knees, Hang Down His Head] (Hanoi: Văn Học, 2011).
68. Cao Huy Thuần, "Chiến tranh trong Trịnh Công Sơn," 71.
69. Cao Huy Thuần, "Buồn bã với những môi hôn," 195.

are terms Vietnamese literary scholars use to describe the prosody of classical poetry, *câu đối* [parallel sentences], and proverbial expressions. For example, Phan Thị Đào explains that a four-syllable expression like "*Tiền phú hậu bần*" [Before rich, afterwards poor], which suggests wealth can be fleeting, has oppositional symmetry because each word in the first half of the expression is an antonym of one of the words in the second half. An expression like "*Tiền trao cháo múc*" [Money given, porridge scooped], which suggests how transactions should proceed, has harmonious symmetry because although all the words that are paralleled are different in meaning, none are diametrically opposite in meaning; in other words, they are not antonyms.[70]

It is appropriate for Cao Huy Thuần to adopt a literary approach and use terms like oppositional symmetry because he wants to suggest that the oppositions in Trịnh Công Sơn's songs reflect internal oppositions in the composer's heart and mind and that he decided "the only way to make them disappear was to 'sublimate' [*thăng hoa*] them into art."[71] "A war was taking place in Trịnh Công Sơn's heart when he decided to oppose the war," and "artillery shells were exploding inside him," Cao Huy Thuần says, "when he sang contradictory lines like these" from his song "Singing above the Corpses" [Hát trên những xác người]:[72]

> *A mother claps her hands and cheers for war*
> *A sister claps her hands and shouts for peace*
> *Some clap their hands to increase the hate*
> *Some clap their hands to avoid blame.*

In Cao Huy Thuần's view, writing songs like "Singing above the Corpses" was Trịnh Công Sơn's way to deal with the madness of war and his own inner turmoil. He argues that Trịnh Công Sơn "sublimated in this way all his life" not only in songs about war but in songs about life and love as well.

But both Trịnh Công Sơn and Cao Huy Thuần realize that art cannot end conflicts within society or within one's own mind. The Sino-Vietnamese word "*thăng hoa*," like its English equivalent "sublimate," does not mean to make something go away; it means to change its form, to make it more beautiful, or more socially acceptable. In "The Sea Will Remain

---

70. Phan Thị Đào, *Tìm hiểu thi pháp tục ngữ Việt Nam* [Understanding the Prosody of Proverbs] (Huế: Thuận Hóa, 2001).
71. Cao Huy Thuần, "Chiến tranh trong Trịnh Công Sơn," 78.
72. Ibid., 75.

Forever" [Biển nghìn thu ở lại], the last song Trịnh Công Sơn wrote, he sings "The sea hits the shore / Upset, the shore hits the sea / Don't hit each other . . ." "Don't hit each other" was, Cao Huy Thuần says, "Trịnh Công Sơn's order before he bid life good-bye. But he knew all too well that contradictions never listen to orders."[73]

I believe Trịnh Công Sơn realized that to resolve contradictions and oppositions he had to learn a new way of seeing things. He had to learn to see things not as "two" and not as "one" but as "not two" [bất nhị]. In other words, he had to enter the dharma gate of non-dualism. "To say 'one' is not correct, only temporarily satisfactory," my Buddhist dictionary explains, "because saying 'one' suggests that there is something else that is not one, like two, three, four etc." Language forces us to make distinctions, but this leads to problems because "Distinguishing of necessity involves extremes, like big as opposed to small, right as opposed to wrong, full as opposed to empty."[74] Therefore one must learn a different, non-dualistic way of seeing things, and ultimately one must leave language behind, as Burton Watson explains in his introduction to the *Vimalakirti Sutra*, one of the most important Mahayana Buddhist texts:

Seen from the point of differentiation, things fall into numberless different categories. But looked at from the point of view of emptiness, they are seen to have one quality they all share: that of forming a single entity, one that is beyond the power of language to describe because language can only deal with distinctions, a point that Vimalakirti dramatically emphasizes at the end of chapter nine.[75]

Here is how that chapter of the sutra ends. Vimalakirti was a rich layman from northeastern India who lived at the time of Shakyamuni Buddha. He was also a paragon of Buddhist enlightenment and so Shakyamuni Buddha sends a bodhisattva named Manjushri to visit him and learn from him. Dozens of other bodhisattvas are also present and Vimalakirti asks all of them to explain their understanding of how one enters the gate of non-dualism. When his turn comes, Manjushri says that he thinks all of Buddha's teachings are "without words" and "removed from all questions and answers." "In this way," he says, "one may enter the gate of nondualism."[76] Then he turns and asks Vimalakirti how a

---

73. Ibid., 78.
74. Tâm Tuệ Hỷ, ed., *Danh từ Phật học thực dụng*, 48-49.
75. *The Vimalakirti Sutra*, trans. Burton Watson (New York: Columbia University Press, 1997), 10.
76. Ibid., 110.

bodhisattva enters the gate of non-dualism. Vimalakirti remains silent and his silence is interpreted to mean that to enter this gate one must leave language behind.

Trịnh Công Sơn does not leave language behind but he often refuses to make sharp distinctions; he carefully avoids creating rigid categories. In "Like Words of Good-bye"* [Như một lời chia tay] he says "Love's not far but not real near." In "Fly Away Quietly" [Bay đi thầm lặng] he says "There are tears at the moment of kissing," and observes that "Old eyes exist under innocent foreheads." In "Life Gives Us These Things" [Đời cho ta thế] we see Trịnh Công Sơn pulling back from sharp distinctions in the first two and the last two lines of each of the three stanzas. In these twelve lines the speaker locates himself in some vague intermediate mental or physical space between something with good connotations and something with bad connotations—between melancholy and a smile, between life and a grave, between splendor and misery, between love and hate, between passion and coldness, between home and jail. Here's how the second stanza begins and ends:

> Not far from people and also not far from the sun
> Not far from complete love and also not far from being lost
>
> Not far from love and also not far from hatred
> Not far from passion and also not far from coldness

As Cao Huy Thuần points out, in Trịnh Công Sơn songs we don't just see "a little bit of this *and* a little bit of that"; we often see "a little bit of this *in* that."[77] We see oppositional symmetry [*đối nghịch*] sliding into harmonious symmetry [*đối hợp*], songs in which "there is still opposition like that between sky and earth but an immense fog joins earth to sky and all that remains is a cloudy mist."[78]

It is not easy to reach this state of cloudy mist in which the restless mind quiets—stops its persistent discriminating and categorizing. One wouldn't want to stop discriminating completely. Carried to extremes, Burton Watson points out, non-dualism would lead to an inability to distinguish right from wrong or a green light from a red light. "But the non-dualistic outlook," Burton Watson suggests, "can be used to leaven and enlarge our everyday ways of thinking, to warn us away from excessive emotional involvement in our undertakings, from excessive pride in our

---

77. Cao Huy Thuần, "Buồn bã với những môi hôn," 190.
78. Ibid., 191.

achievements, or to help us resign ourselves to ills that are beyond our control."[79]

Another song, "Advance or Retreat: Caught in a Dilemma," ends with the speaker in a more harmonious, less contradictory mood. The Vietnamese title, "Tiến thoái lưỡng nan," is a Sino-Vietnamese four-syllable expression which literally means "advance retreat both difficult" and conveys the idea of being caught in a dilemma, of not knowing whether to go forward or back. It suggests that there are no easy choices, no easy way out. This is a very sad poem. The word "*lận đận*," which means "hard" or "hardship," occurs six times in this short song. When performed this word—*lận đận*—sounds like a stone falling with a thud on one's heart. Here are the concluding lines:

> Caught in a dilemma
> Going or coming is hardship
> Former times were hard
> Didn't know where to return
> Return to the end of the lane?
> Return to the edge of the sky?
> Far off I sit
> I search again for myself
> Caught in a dilemma
> Going or coming is hardship
> Today hardship
> Is . . . a drop of emptiness.

These lines sound terribly bleak but not if one believes that that drop of emptiness is a full emptiness that contains happiness and sadness, or—more accurately—moves one to a state of mind beyond both these opposites. Cao Huy Thuần says that emptiness appears at the end of this song "as the final answer to all things, all activities, all disputes, all oppositional symmetries, all contradictions, all accusations. *Today hardship is a drop of emptiness . . .*"[80]

The biggest dualism of all, for most people, is that between life and death. For Christians, René Muller says—even for those who believe in an afterlife—"life into death is a discontinuity with a hard edge."[81] It certainly has a hard edge for Dylan who, as I will explain in coming

---

79. *The Vimalakirti Sutra*, trans. Burton Watson, 12.
80. Cao Huy Thuần, "Chiến tranh trong Trịnh Công Sơn," 80.
81. René Muller, *Beyond Marginality: Constructing a Self in the Twilight of Western Culture* (Westport, CT: Praeger, 1998), 121.

chapters, believes that, as stated in Matthew 24:31, the world will end in an apocalyptic event, the second coming of Christ. Lighting will flash in the east and the west, trumpets will sound, and Christ will return to judge both the living and the dead.[82] In songs like "Gonna Change My Way of Thinking," "Are You Ready," "When You Gonna Wake Up?" Dylan worries about being ready. Anxiety is increased because, as Dylan explains, you don't know when the end will come:

> *Jesus said, "Be ready*
> *For you know not the hour in which I come."*
> - Gonna Change My Way of Thinking

> *Am I ready, hope I'm ready*
> *When destruction cometh swiftly*
> *And there's no time to say a fare-thee-well*
> *Have you decided whether you want to be*
> *In heaven or in hell?*
> -Are You Ready?

For Buddhists, however, at least for Buddhists who enter the dharma gate of non-dualism, the boundary between life and death is blurred because death is seen as a return to a state that is beyond both life and death. In the Vimalakirti Sutra, when Vimalakirti asks a bodhisattva to explain how one enters the gate of non-dualism, the bodhisattva replies as follows:

> The realm of birth and death and that of nirvana form a dualism but if one sees the true nature of birth and death, one sees that there is no birth or death, no binding, no unbinding, no birth, no extinction. One who understands in this way may thereby enter the gate of nondualism.[83]

According to Buddhist teaching, there is no permanent, independent self. What we consider to be an individual self emerges due the presence of certain conditions, just as a wave arises in the ocean as result of various factors—wind, temperature, etc. By accepting these notions of non-dualism and non-self, Buddhist teachers suggest, one can soften the boundary between life and death. If you practice well, Thích Nhất Hạnh says, "You will touch the no-birth, no-death, no-coming, no-going nature

---

82. "For as the lightning comes from the east and flashes to the west, so also will the coming of the Son of Man be." —Matthew 24:27
"And He will send His angels with a great sound of a trumpet, and they will gather together His elect from the four winds, from one end of heaven to the other." —Matthew 24:31
83. *The Vimalakirti Sutra*, trans. Burton Watson, 106.

of reality. This can liberate you from your fear, from your anxiety and your sorrow."[84]

As explained in Chapter Ten, Trịnh Công Sơn was obsessed with death. He traces this obsession to the early death of his father when the singer was only fifteen, and he has said that "the quiet atmosphere of loss" found in many of his early songs is a result of that obsession.[85] As I mentioned in Chapter Twenty-Four, Thích Nhất Hạnh believes that Trịnh Công Sơn could not conquer his obsession with death because he did not understand and accept certain Buddhist concepts—no birth, conditioned arising, and dependent origination. Although this may be true, many practicing Buddhists find these concepts difficult to accept, no doubt because they love life so much—as did Trịnh Công Sơn. "People may think about death because life is full of unlucky events and disappointments," Trịnh Công Sơn said in an interview in 2001, "but in the end people think about death a lot because they love life so much."[86] "Who am I, who am I, who am I / To love this life so much?" he sings in "Don't Despair I Tell Myself."*

The "life into death discontinuity," has, as René Muller says, "a hard edge" for Christians.[87] For Trịnh Công Sơn the edge is softer and gentler. In some of his songs he uses "edge of the sky" to refer to death. In "To Board" [Ở trọ] he sings "Now I am a boarder in this world / In one hundred years I'll return to a place far off at the edge of the sky." In his song "Like Words of Goodbye" [Như một lời chia tay]* this edge is strewn with delicate golden flowers:

> All my rendezvous now closed
> I'm light as a cloud
>
> Delicate golden flowers at the edge of the sky
> Like words of goodbye

---

84. Thích Nhất Hạnh, *No Death, No Fear* (New York: Riverhead Books, 2002), 24.
85. Trịnh Công Sơn, "Nỗi ám ảnh thời thơ ấu" [A Childhood Obsession], in *Trịnh Công Sơn: Tôi là ai, là ai. . .* [Trịnh Công Sơn: Who Am I?], ed. Nguyễn Minh Nhựt (HCMC: Trẻ, 2011),133-134, This is a reprint of a previously published article. The original date and source are not given.
86. Trịnh Công Sơn, interview by Văn Cầm Hải, "Kiếp sau tôi vẫn là người Nghệ sĩ" [In the Next Reincarnation I'll still be an Artist], in *Trịnh Công Sơn: Một người thơ ca một cõi đi về* [Trịnh Công Sơn: A Singer-poet, a Place for Leaving and Returning], eds. Nguyễn Trọng Tạo, Nguyễn Thụy Kha, and Đoàn Tử Huyến (Hanoi: Âm Nhạc, 2001), 207-211. This is a reprint of an interview conducted by Văn Cầm Hải in Huế on March 27, 1998.
87. René Muller, *Beyond Marginality*, 121.

THE EYE THAT REMAINS

Some Vietnamese writers suggest that Trịnh Công Sơn's song "The Eye That Remains"* should be understood, at least in part, as being about non-dualism. This song evokes other Buddhist concepts as well. I mentioned this song briefly in my previous section on emptiness and loving-kindness and compassion because references to these Buddhist concepts—to *hư vô* [emptiness] and *từ bi* [loving-kindness and compassion]—appear in it. This is one of Trịnh Công Sơn's most obscure songs. I discuss it at the end of this chapter because it provokes questions raised by many Trịnh Công Sơn songs—questions like the following: How "Buddhist" is this song? Should we understand references in it to Buddhist concepts as primarily atmospheric—as literary devices to create a mood and feeling? Or should we hear them as referring to specific Buddhist ideas? Or should we, in typical non-dualistic fashion, hear them as a little bit of both—partly atmospheric, partly religious? For example, when Trịnh Công Sơn sings about "emptiness" [*hư vô, không*] in "The Eye that Remains," should we think only of "sadness" or "bleakness" or "despair"? Or should we think of the "full emptiness" described in the Perfection of Wisdom sutras? Or both?

First, I will summarize a thoroughly Buddhist interpretation of "The Eye That Remains" by Thích Giác Tâm, a monk from Pleiku who argues that one should understand "The Eye That Remains" as a discussion of the Buddhist concept of Five Eyes [Vn. *Ngũ nhãn*, Skt. *cakshus*].[88] Then I will present other interpretations that suggest that in this song Trịnh Công Sơn certainly evokes Buddhist concepts but does not base his song on the idea of the Five Eyes.

The eye and vision are very important in Buddhism. In many Buddha statues and paintings, the Buddha is depicted as having a third eye in the middle of his forehead. This third eye suggests a way of seeing that allows one to perceive a reality that lies beyond the power of ordinary vision. The first step of the Eightfold Path, which is the last of the Four Noble Truths, also relates to vision and seeing. This is the path that Buddhists believe one must take to relieve suffering. The first step involves obtaining a "right view" [Skt. *Samyak-drsti*; Vn. *chánh kiến*]. In this stage one learns to see things objectively, not in a prejudiced manner, and one becomes aware of

---

88. Thích Giác Tâm, "Con mắt còn lại" [The Eye That Remains], Giác Ngộ Online, https://giacngo.vn/con-mat-con-lai-post11286.html (accessed December 12m 2022).

the path that leads to liberation. In the previous chapter I mentioned that in a dharma talk about Trịnh Công Sơn at Plum Village Thích Nhất Hạnh refers to vision in explaining Sơn's Buddhism. Sơn, he says, could "see the path" [*kiến đạo*] but he needed to practice more and needed a support group [*tăng thân*] to enable him to "confirm the path" [*chứng đạo*].

The third eye found in depictions of the Buddha symbolizes the heart-mind eye, or the eye of *citta* [Vn. *tâm*].[89] (Peter Harvey defines *citta* as "the central focus of personality which can be seen as 'mind,' heart' or 'thought'"; I have referred to it as "heart-mind.")[90] For Buddhist scholars this third eye found in Buddhist iconography suggests the Buddhist concept of Five Eyes, the idea that in addition to the physical eye there are four other kinds of eyes, and altogether the five eyes represent different stages in one's path toward enlightenment. The Buddha discusses the five eyes in the Diamond Sutra: the physical eye, the heavenly eye, the wisdom eye, the dharma eye, and the Buddha eye. The physical eye is the weakest eye, the eye of an ordinary person who does not practice Buddhism. The heavenly eye can be achieved by meditation. The wisdom eye is achieved by the arhat, the high saint of Theravada Buddhism, who has either attained Nirvana or is very far advanced on a path leading to it. The dharma eye is the eye of the Bodhisattva, the ideal figure in Mahayana Buddhism, who, like the arhat, has advanced far on the path of enlightenment but chooses not to enter Nirvana, preferring to stay in this world to help others achieve release from suffering. Finally, there is the Buddha eye, the all-seeing eye of the Buddha, who, because he has achieved perfect enlightenment, can see all things with no limitations.[91]

Did Trịnh Công Sơn have the Buddhist idea of the Five Eyes in mind when he wrote "The Eye That Remains"? Thích Giác Tâm suggests that he did. The Five Eyes represent different ways of seeing. Thích Giác Tâm's method of analysis consists of explaining which "eye"—which way of seeing—the speaker is employing in different lines of the song. For example, according to Thích Giác Tâm, in the first and second lines of the first stanza the speaker is seeing through the physical eye, but how

---

89. "The Third Eye," Token Rock Inspiration Center, https://www.tokenrock.com/subjects/third-eye (accessed December 17, 2022).
90. Peter Harvey, *An Introduction to Buddhism*, 50.
91. For a discussion of the Five Eyes see C.T. Shen, "The Five Eyes," The Buddhist Association of the United States, http://www.baus.org/en/publications/dr-Shens-collections/the-five-eyes/ (accessed December 17, 2022).

Thích Giác Tâm determines this is not clear.[92] In the third and fourth lines the speaker is seeing through the wisdom eye because, Thích Giác Tâm explains, "Only if you have the wisdom eye can you look at oneself, sit cross-legged, and contemplate the things of the world and the essence of truth." In other words, in Thích Giác Tâm's analysis, lines three and four suggest that the speaker is seeing through the wisdom eye because he has learned the value of meditation. In lines five and six he suggests the speaker is seeing through the wisdom eye because in these lines the speaker reveals his or her awareness of impermanence. He quotes these lines and then comments on them as follows: "Do you notice this enlightenment about impermanence? We believe that our husband, our wife, our property will belong to us forever. We always grasp these things tightly in our hands, but then suddenly they are gone." But not the speaker in Trịnh Công Sơn's song. He is wiser. He knows that love fades, that a love once grasped in "two hands" will one day vanish.

Thích Giác Tâm suggests that this awareness of impermanence leads to an outpouring of loving-kindness. Here are his comments on the last two lines of the first stanza:

> Suddenly there is a beam of light and in that beam of light an eye of loving-kindness and compassion looks at us, calls to us. Whose eye is that? Are you still not clear, do you still not recognize whose eye that is? It's the eye of Buddha [*mắt Phật*], of course. That's whose eye it is [*Từ nhãn thị chúng sinh*].[93] That is who takes the eye of loving-kindness and compassion and looks at sentient beings. He loves so much and so looks at me, at sisters, at children . . . and sighs. "The eye that remains, whose eye is it / The eye that remains looks at me sighing"[94] [ellipsis in original].

According to Thích Giác Tâm the following lines from the second stanza are about non-dualism—the problem of seeing two when one should see one:

> *The eye that remains looks at one becoming two*
> *Looks at you as loving, looks at you as fierce*

---

92. It is not clear to me or to my wife, Cao Thị Như-Quỳnh.
93. Thích Giác Tâm puts "*Từ nhãn thị chúng sanh*" in parentheses because it is in Sino-Vietnamese. He then explains it in Vietnamese by saying it means "to take the eye of loving-kindness and compassion and look at sentient beings." This is a quotation from a famous section of the Lotus Sutra in which the Buddha praises the Bodhisattva Avalokitesvara [Vn. *Quan Thế Âm*; Skt. Ch. *Guanyin*] for her compassionate concern for all sentient beings. See Nikkyo Niwano, *Buddhism for Today: A Modern Interpretation of the Threefold Lotus Sutra* (New York: Weatherhill/Kosei, 1976), 377-388.
94. Thích Giác Tâm, "Con mắt còn lại."

> *The eye that remains suspects my love*
> *Loves like crazy and misses like crazy*

In his analysis Thích Giác Tâm does not use the term non-dualism [Vn. *bất nhị*, Skt. *advaita*] but instead talks about a related idea—the importance of developing a non-discriminative wisdom [Vn. *vô phân biệt trí*, Skt. *nirvikalpajnana*]. A baby, Thích Giác Tâm says, at first does not distinguish between people: young babies smile at everyone and let everyone carry them. As one grows older, however, one learns to discriminate. "If you do not live with a non-discriminative wisdom," Thích Giác Tâm says, "then you will see one become two and you will sometimes look at 'you as loving' and sometimes look at 'you as fierce.'"[95] In these lines the speaker is, according to Thích Giác Tâm, looking through a discriminating or dualistic physical eye.

Đỗ Hồng Ngọc also evokes the framework of the Five Eyes (along with other Buddhist concepts) in his discussion of this obscure song.[96] He quotes the following lines from the last stanza: "The eye that remains looks at life as nothingness [*không*] / Looks at you as emptiness [*hư vô*], looks at you as sun and shade [*bóng nắng*]." He links these lines to the opening lines of the Heart Sutra about form [Skt. *rupa*; Vn. *sắc*] being emptiness [Skt. *sunyata*; Vn. *không, hư vô*] and emptiness being form. Then he offers this interpretation: "To summarize, there are two eyes. 'The eye that cries for people' is the eye of compassion [Skt. *karuna*; Vn. *bi*]. 'The eye that remains and looks at life as nothingness' [Skt. *sunyata*] is the eye of wisdom [Skt. *prajna*; Vn. *tuệ*]. If one has compassion but no wisdom one will cry forever. Therefore one needs the eye of wisdom to achieve liberation, liberation, of course, for oneself and for other people."[97]

Sơn probably was aware of Buddhist conceptions of the third eye and knew about the Five Eyes mentioned in the Diamond Sutra, but I find it hard to believe that his song was intended to be an exposition of these Buddhist concepts. It does, however, have a koan-like quality, like the famous koan about the sound of one hand clapping. It sounds like a Zen poem and in its obscurity resembles the encounter dialogues that Buddhist masters engage their disciples in to enable them to achieve insights that lie beyond words.

---

95. Ibid.
96. Đỗ Hồng Ngọc, "Con mắt còn lại" [The Eye That Remains], Tạp *Chí Văn Hóa Phật Giáo* [Journal of Buddhist Culture] no. 57, http://tapchivanhoaphatgiao.com/blog/tan-man/con-mat-con-lai.html (accessed June 23, 2014).
97. Ibid.

Most Vietnamese are aware that "The Eye That Remains" was inspired by or at least is clearly related to a poem by a poet named Bùi Giáng (1926-1998), a friend of the singer. The line which begins each stanza in Trịnh Công Sơn's song, "*Còn hai con mắt khóc người một con*" [There's still two eyes and for people one eye cries], is the last line in a poem by Bùi Giáng titled "Sad Eyes" [Mắt buồn] from a collection published in 1963 called *Mưa nguồn* [Rain Storm].[98] Bùi Giáng, however, mentions eyes and seeing in only the final line of his poem whereas Sơn mentions these things in almost every line of his song. Bùi Giáng's poem is as difficult to interpret—if not more difficult—than Trịnh Công Sơn's song and I will not attempt to explicate it. It is one of Bùi Giáng's best known poems, in part because Trịnh Công Sơn made it famous by featuring its last line in his song. I will have more to say about this last line, but first some comments about the eccentric poet who wrote it.

Bùi Giáng came from a prosperous family in Quảng Nam Province and graduated from secondary school but never attended a university, preferring instead to study on his own. Over the course of his life he not only published dozens of poetry collections but also wrote and published books about Nguyễn Du's *The Tale of Kiều* and Nguyễn Đình Chiểu's *Lục Vân Tiên*, studies of Albert Camus and Martin Heidegger, and translations of Shakespeares's *Hamlet* and *Othello*.[99] Bùi Giáng was a character. His literary accomplishments were hard to understand, Tâm Nhiên says, because "day and night the Bùi Giáng we saw was a playful wanderer dancing in the streets. He would chant poems, go on whiskey drinking sprees with the common people, and sleep on the sidewalk, or in some corner of a market stall, or under the porch of a pagoda."[100] He loved poetry and would, if asked, write a poem on a scrap of paper and give it to you. People called him the crazy poet [*nhà thơ điên*] but he also was known as the Bodhisattva poet [*thi sĩ Bồ tát*].[101] Vietnamese compare Bùi Giáng to the Chinese monk known as Ji Gong [Vn. Tế điên] whose

---

98. Translated literally, *mưa nguồn* is "rain source," but the phrase evokes a four-syllable expression, *Chớp bể mưa nguồn*, which refers to terrible weather.

99. A list of Bùi Giáng's publications can be found in *Từ điển Tác giả Văn học Việt Nam* [Dictionary of Authors of Twentieth Century Literary Works] (Hanoi: Hội Nhà Văn, 2003), 48-49.

100. Tâm Nhiên, "Thế giới thi ca tư tưởng Bùi Giáng" [Bùi Giáng's World: His Poetry, Song and Thought], Thư Viện Hoa Sen, http://thuvienhoasen.org/a17034/the-gioi-thi-ca-tu-tuong-bui-giang (accessed June 13, 2016).

101. Lưu Kường, "Còn hai con mắt, khóc người" [There's still two eyes, crying for people], 2011*).], Công An Nhân Dân*, http://www.baomoi.com/Home/SachBaoVanTho/antget. cand.com.vn/Con-hai-con-mat-kh. . . (accessed November 7, 2011).

nickname was "Ji the Crazy Monk." Ji Gong, who lived in the early Song Dynasty (960-1279), loved to drink and eat dog meat but was also known for his loving-kindness and compassion.

Bùi Giáng was not, it seems, within the inner circle of Sơn's close friends, but he was a friend and sometimes a drinking buddy. Sơn's friends, the artists Đinh Cường and Bửu Chỉ, and the writer Bửu Ý, also knew Bùi Giáng. Both Đinh Cường and Bửu Chỉ painted portraits of him.

In an article about the Trịnh Công Sơn-Bùi Giáng relationship, the poet Ngô Văn Tao, who knew both men, says that in 1988 Bùi Giáng would often come to Sơn's home in Saigon to eat lunch and drink wine. He mentions that Sơn invited the poet to a "vodka dinner" that same year. Bùi Giáng died of a stroke in 1998 and at his funeral Sơn, standing in front of his coffin, sang "A Place for Leaving and Returning."*[102] In an article mourning his passing, Sơn speaks about Bùi Giáng's "aimlessly magical exuberance" but also his despair. "Into this world he came," Sơn says, "and he lived and fell into a never-ending dreamlike existence. He joked and conversed in a strange and otherworldly language which resulted in him being misunderstood. This misunderstanding caused him pain and as a result of this pain he became like a shipwrecked person who carried with him an unfathomable despair."[103]

Many people have speculated about the meaning of the last line in Bùi Giáng's poem: "There's still two eyes and for people one eye cries" [Còn hai con mắt khóc người một con]. This is the line which becomes the first line in each stanza of Trịnh Công Sơn's song. Trần Từ Duy, for example, says that Bùi Giáng was playing with words when he wrote "There's still two eyes and for people one eye cries." The words he was playing with, according to Trần Từ Duy, were those in a well-known Vietnamese proverb that conveys the Vietnamese belief that a woman becomes extremely beautiful after she has her first child. The expression is *"Gái một con trông mòn con mắt"* [You can wear out your eyes looking at a girl with one child]. It is a catchy expression in part because the word *"con"* is both a homophone and a homograph, that is, exactly the same as another in sound and spelling but different in meaning. In the phrase *một con* [one child] *"con"* means "child"; in the phrase *con mắt*, *"con"* is what

---

102. Ngô Văn Tao, "Bùi Giáng và Trịnh Công Sơn," https://www.tcs-hCông An Nhân Dân, http://ww.baomoi.com/Home/SachBaoVanTho/antget.cand.com.vn/Con-hai-con-mat-kh. . ome.org/ban-be/articles/bui-giang-va-trinh-cong-son (accessed July 21, 2022).
103. *Từ điển Tác giả Văn học Việt Nam* [Dictionary of Vietnamese Literary Writers], 50. I have not been able to find this source again to provide a complete citation.

linguists call a classifier, a word used to mark a specific semantic class, in this case one that includes small objects like an eye. According to Trần Từ Duy, Bùi Giáng himself has paraphrased the last line of his poem as follows: "The person with two eyes cries when seeing a beautiful girl with one child because 'You can wear out your eyes looking at a girl with one child.'" [104] If one accepts this interpretation the line should be translated as "There's still two eyes and they cry for a person with one child."

Writing on the blog site Nhà Gom Lá Bàng, an anonymous writer says this girl with one child was a beauty queen, film star, writer, and professor named Công Thị Nghĩa whose pen and stage name was Thu Trang.[105] Citing her memoir, this writer explains that Công Thị Nghĩa had a child out of wedlock after sleeping with a film director on a trip to a film festival in Japan in 1957.[106] In 1961 she left Vietnam for France. In this writer's view Bùi Giáng was enamored of this film star. The writer maintains that she was the beautiful girl with one child who inspired his poem "Sad Eyes." This unidentified blogger is not the only person to suggest that the film star was the inspiration for his poem. Lê Minh Quốc, a journalist and writer, maintains that Bùi Giáng wrote "Sad Eyes" to present to Công Thị Nghĩa.[107]

Công Thị Nghĩa herself does not claim that Bùi Giáng wrote "Sad Eyes" with her in mind, but she discusses Bùi Giáng at some length (seven pages) in her memoir.[108] She mentions meeting him in Saigon in 1959 or 1960 at gatherings organized by the writers who contributed to the journal *Bách Khoa* [Encyclopedic]. At first she found him strange but later came to appreciate his talent. It seems clear that Bùi Giáng was indeed captivated by the actress. She explains that he came to her home to say

---

104. Hoàng Nhân quotes Trần Từ Duy in " 'Con mắt còn lại'—gợi hứng từ đâu?" [The Eye that Remains—From Where Does the Inspiration come?, Thể Thao Văn Hóa [Cultural Sports], December 15. 2022, http://thethaovanhoa.vn/van-hoa-giai-tri/con-mat-con-goi-hung-tu-dau-n20110415083246950.htm (accessed December 15, 2022.

105. Blog *Nhà Gom Lá Bàng* [House to Gather Leaves of the Indian-Almond Tree], No author listed., "Tại sao 'còn hai con mắt khóc người một con'?" [Why are 'There still two eyes and for people one eye cries'?], http://nhagomlabang.blogspot.com/2012/12/tai-sao-con-hai-con-mat-khoc-nguoi-mot.html (accessed June 24, 2016).

106. Her memoir was published in 2010. See Thu Trang (Công Thị Nghĩa's pen name), *Một thời để nhớ, hồi ký* [A Time to Remember, A Memoir] (Hanoi: Văn Học, 2010).

107. Lê Minh Quốc, "Bùi Giáng—thi sĩ tinh quái của nền thi ca Việt Nam hiện đại" [Bùi Giáng—The Mischievous Poet of Modern Vietnamese Poetry and Song], [Webpage of] Lê Minh Quốc, https://leminhquoc.vn/the-loai-khac/tac-pham-cua-ban-be/1610-toa-dam-%20khoa-hoc-ve-thi-si-bui-giang.html?start=4 (accessed June 6, 2016).

108. Thu Trang herself describes her affair in her memoir, which was published in 2010. See *Một thời để nhớ, hồi ký* [A Time to Remember, a Memoir], 276-283.

goodbye to her before she left for France. He acted strangely during this meeting, which ended when he snatched up a pair of her sandals lying on the floor and left. After reading his two collections of poems, *Mưa nguồn* [Rainstorm] and *Thi ca tư tưởng* [Thought Poems], however, she realized he might be odd but he was also a talented poet. Later, on a visit to Huế, she met Bửu Ý and learned that Bùi Giáng had written a poem titled "Thu Trang" (her pen and stage name). Bửu Ý wrote it out for her and she includes it in her memoir.[109] When she was in Paris she read Bùi Giáng's poems and sent him some of her own.[110]

It seems possible that Bùi Giáng's poem "Sad Eyes" was inspired by Công Thị Nghĩa, the girl with one child. He prefaces his poem with a line from *The Tale of Kiều*: "A road that stretched far off in hushed still night."[111] The road referred to is the road that Kiều takes when she leaves home to join her husband who has just deflowered her, a husband she did not love and married only to save her father from going to prison (see Chapter Fifteen). Perhaps Bùi Giáng chose this preface because he associates the beautiful actress with the heroine of Nguyễn Du's famous poem.

Lê Minh Quốc doesn't equivocate. Bùi Giáng, he says, wrote "Sad Eyes" to "present to" [*tặng*] this actress. He does not think, however, that the poet—in his concluding line—was playing with the words from the proverb about women with one child. He prefers another interpretation. He reminds us that Bùi Giáng liked to joke and clown around, and concludes that in this line, the one that Trịnh Công Sơn borrowed, "the speaker is crying with only one eye, which leaves the other eye free to look at life happily."[112] In other words, one eye cries but the other eye doesn't. Lê Minh Quốc does not suggest that Trịnh Công Sơn's song is a continuation of or a rebuttal to Bùi Giáng's poem. He says it may have just been a way for him to acknowledge his friendship with the poet.

How should we interpret Trịnh Công Sơn's "The Eye That Remains"? I would say that in this song Sơn is trying—but not quite succeeding—to look at life the way the four-line stanza that concludes the *Diamond Sutra* says we should look at all things of this world:

---

109. Ibid., 281.
110. Ibid., 283.
111. This is Huỳnh Sanh Thông's translation. See his bilingual edition of this poem: Nguyễn Du, *The Tale of Kiều: A Bilingual Edition of Truyện Kiều* (New Haven, CT: Yale University Press, 1983), 49.
112. Lê Minh Quốc, "Bùi Giáng—thi sĩ tinh quái của nền thi ca Việt Nam hiện đại."

> *So you should view all the fleeting world:*
> *A star at dawn, a bubble in the stream;*
> *A flash of lightning in a summer cloud;*
> *A flickering lamp, a phantom, and a dream.*[113]

Note the many suggestions of impermanence packed into these four lines: Stars disappear when the sun comes out, bubbles burst, lightning is only a quick flash, a lamp flickers out, etc. Now let's look again at lines three through five of the last stanza of Sơn's song:

> *The eye that remains looks at life as emptiness* [hư không]
> *Looks at you as emptiness* [hư vô], *looks at you as sun and shade* [bóng nắng]
> *The eye that remains is gentle and loving* [từ tâm]

Vietnamese would understand "sun and shade" [*bóng nắng*] as an allusion to the stanza that concludes the Diamond Sutra.[114] "*Bóng nắng*" is a compound word that Vietnamese use to describe the dappling effect created when the sun shines through leaves. Some spots are in the sun, some in shade. It suggests impermanence because when the sun moves, or clouds arrive, the effect disappears. The stanza at the end of the Diamond Sutra, Mu Soeng explains, is not as famous as the mantra that concludes the Heart Sutra, but "it captures the urgency that the [Diamond] sutra is trying to convey: that the world of appearances is fleeting, ephemeral, transitory, and lacking in self-essence."[115] The core question in Buddhism, Mu Soeng says, is what gets transformed when one accepts the teachings of emptiness and no-self. The answer, encapsulated in this stanza, is "that what gets transformed is one's perception or way of looking at the world and at oneself."[116]

Trịnh Công Sơn writes about eyes and looking and seeing because he is trying to transform his vision. In the middle of this last stanza of "The Eye That Remains" he seems to be making progress. He accepts the emptiness and impermanence of the world, an acceptance that leads to feelings of loving-kindness and compassion. The last three lines, however,

---

113. This is Mu Soeng's translation, which, he says (on p. ix), is based on the original Sanskrit text as edited by Max Muller. See Mu Soeng, *The Diamond Sutra*, 155.
114. To my knowledge English has no word that is exactly equivalent to the Vietnamese compound word *bóng nắng*. *Bóng nắng* does not appear in Vietnamese translations that I have seen of this four-line stanza. Vietnamese friends assure me, however, that when used in Buddhist contexts it evokes the concluding verses of the Diamond Sutra.
115. Mu Soeng, *The Diamond Sutra*, 136.
116. Ibid., 137.

suggest that he is still struggling to accept calmly the end of a relationship. The eye that remains, Trịnh Công Sơn sings,

Watches you leave, your heart far away
The eye that remains is a dark night
The eye that remains is a passionate night

In this ending we see Trịnh Công Sơn's typical tendency to juxtapose positive and negative words and images and to see a little bit of this in something but also a little bit of that. Here the night is dark [*tối tăm*], a negative image, but also passionate [*nồng nàn*], a positive image.[117] The eye that remains has darkness in it but also passion. Is this oppositional symmetry or harmonious symmetry? Coming after a line in which leaving and separation are mentioned, it seems more oppositional than harmonious. The speaker is still seeing one as two, still trying to pass through the dharma gate of non-dualism.

---

117. *Nồng nàn* could also be translated as "friendly" or "warm" or "ardent."

26

BOB DYLAN: FROM JEWISH ROOTS TO BORN-AGAIN CHRISTIAN

Bob Dylan was born Robert Allen Zimmerman. Both his parents were descendants of Eastern European Jews who came to the United States in the early 1900s to escape anti-Jewish pogroms in the Russian Empire. His maternal great-grandfather, a man named B'chezer Edelstein, left Covina, Lithuania with his wife, Lyba, and three children in 1902 and eventually settled in North Hibbing, Minnesota. According to Laurence A. Schlesinger, B'chezer Edelstein, or Benjamin Harold (his anglicized name), "regarded his Jewish faith as the primary guiding force in his life."[1] Harold and Lyba's oldest daughter, Florence, who was born in Europe before the family moved to North Hibbing, married a man from Wisconsin named Ben D. Stone, a Russian Jewish intellectual. Their third child, Beatrice—known as Beatty—eventually became Bob Dylan's mother. Beatty married Abram Zimmerman, Dylan's father, in 1934.

Abram's parents, Bob Dylan's paternal grandparents, were Jewish immigrants from Odessa in Ukraine. Dylan's grandfather, Zigman Zimmerman, was a shoemaker and his grandmother, Amy, was a seamstress. When they immigrated to Duluth in the early 1900s his grandfather bought a pushcart and began peddling his wares, just as he had done in Odessa.[2] Later he opened a shoe store. Dylan used to visit

---

1. Lawrence A. Schlesinger, "Bob Dylan's Conversion: A Noteworthy Case in Point," *Journal of Reformed Judaism* (Winter, 1991), 32.
2. Ibid., 33.

his grandmother in Duluth when he was growing up and he describes her briefly in his memoir *Chronicles: Volume One*:

> My grandmother had only one leg and had been a seamstress. Sometimes on weekends my parents would drive down from the Iron Range to Duluth and drop me off at her place for a couple of days. She was a dark lady, smoked a pipe. . . My grandmother's voice possessed a haunting accent—face always set in a half-despairing expression. Life for her hadn't been easy.[3]

As a young boy Dylan enjoyed a comfortable middle-class life. His father was first an office manager at Standard Oil and then went into the furniture and appliance business with his brothers, Bob's uncles. Apparently, however, life was far from ideal for Jews in Hibbing. There were only thirty or forty Jewish families in the town. Ninety-two percent of residents were Catholic and the rest were Protestant or Unitarian. Clinton Heylin reports that "from an early age Jews [in Hibbing] were aware of an undercurrent of antisemitism."[4] Dylan's father couldn't get into the Mesabi Country Club and had to play golf at a public course.[5] Though a minority, the Zimmermans and other Jews in Hibbing were, however, able to observe their faith. There was a synagogue, the Agudath Achim Synagogue, and this is where, when he was 13, his bar mitzvah was held. To prepare for the ceremony Dylan studied Hebrew with Rabbi Reuben Maier. He had to learn how to chant Hebrew prayers using a way of chanting called "cantillation." Dylan's good ear for music must have helped him. Robert Shelton reports that at Friday night meetings before the ceremony Rabbi Maier "showed off his prodigy, wishing all his students were as bright and dutiful."[6] Someone who attended Dylan's bar mitzvah, which took place on May 22, 1954, told Stephen Pickering that "Dylan conducted the ceremony beautifully."[7]

What role has Dylan's Jewish heritage played in shaping his life and work? This question comes up in many books and articles about Dylan. On one side are some Jewish Dylanophiles who argue that it has played a crucial part. Stephen Pickering, for example, insists that "Bob Dylan is a post-Holocaust Jewish voice, searching for and rediscovering the mani-

---

3. Bob Dylan, *Chronicles: Volume One* (New York: Simon and Schuster, 2004), 92.
4. Clinton Heylin, *Bob Dylan: Behind the Shades* (New York: Summit Books, 1991), 22.
5. Robert Shelton, *No Direction Home: The Life and Music of Bob Dylan* (Milwaukee, WI: Backbeat Books, 2011), 37.
6. Ibid., 36.
7. Stephen Pickering, *Bob Dylan Approximately: A Portrait of the Jewish Poet in Search of God: A Midrash* (New York: David McKay Corporation, 1975), 17.

festations of God." In his "richly symbolic poetry," Pickering argues, there are "specific Jewish themes, root experiences consistent with centuries of thought and tradition."[8] Pickering was only one of many Jewish Americans who were convinced, or at least hoped, that Dylan spoke for them. "Dylan, né Zimmerman," J. J. Goldberg writes, "touched off rhapsodies of expectation among Jewish baby-boomers." They wanted him "to help them sort out the confusion of their Jewish souls."[9] For Jewish Dylanophiles Dylan's embrace of Evangelical Christianity at the end of 1978 is a major problem. Rabbi Laurence Schlesinger argues that Dylan's conversion to Christianity was "an extreme act of desperation—a cry for help, if you will—that was precipitated by an overwhelming avalanche of personal and professional setbacks."[10] The gratification that Christianity provided him was, however, "transitory," Rabbi Schlesinger says, and later "his own devotion to Christian fundamentalism evaporated and a return to, and reaffirmation of, Judaism ensued."[11]

I do not believe that Dylan's devotion to Christianity evaporated, but before I present my views let me summarize, in list form, some facts and events that suggest Dylan had a lifelong interest in Judaism. Jewish Dylanophiles point to items on this list to emphasize Dylan's Jewishness and deny the importance of his "Christian period," but I (and others) believe the list suggests something different.

1. Dylan's parents were Jewish and he had a bar mitzvah ceremony.

2. He attended Camp Herzl, a Zionist camp in Wisconsin, every summer from 1954-1958.[12]

3. Dylan visited Israel in 1969, 1970, 1971, and 1973.[13] He tried, unsuccessfully, to keep his May 1971 visit a secret. On May 24, the day Dylan turned 30, he and his wife Sara visited the Wailing Wall. A UPI photographer, who was taking photos of tourists, took his photo and it later appeared in newspapers around the world.[14]

8. Stephen Pickering, *Bob Dylan Approximately*, 11.
9. J. J. Goldberg, "Bob Dylan at 60: 'We Used to be Young Together'; A Musical Seer Who Disdained Role of Prophet" *Forward*, May 18, 2001. Electronic copy retrieved November 10, 2012.
10. Lawrence A. Schlesinger, "Bob Dylan's Conversion," 43.
11. Ibid., 46.
12. Lawrence A. Schlesinger, "Bob Dylan's Conversion," 34.
13. Scott M. Marshall with Marcia Ford, *Restless Pilgrim: The Spiritual Journey of Bob Dylan* (Relevant Books: Orlando, FL, 2004), 13-14; Robert Shelton, *No Direction Home*, 284; Lawrence A. Schlesinger, "Bob Dylan's Conversion," 39.
14. Scott M. Marshall with Marcia Ford, *Restless Pilgrim*, 14.

4. Dylan's first wife, Sara Lowndes, the mother of five of his six children, is Jewish and she and Dylan arranged bar mitzvahs for four of their children and gave them what some people consider to be Jewish names—Jesse, Anna, Samuel, and Jakob.[15] The Dylans sent their children to a Hebrew school in Beverly Hills.[16]

5. Dylan's brother, David, has mentioned that at their father's funeral in 1968 he was struck by his brother's knowledge of Jewish ritual, including Kaddish, a Hebrew prayer of mourning.[17]

6. In late 1972 Dylan looked into the possibility of taking his family to Israel to live on a kibbutz for an extended stay.[18]

7. Dylan is believed to have made contributions to the Jewish Defense League, a Jewish far-right organization founded by Rabbi Meir Kahane in New York City in 1968. Stephen Pickering told Robert Shelton that Rabbi Kahane asked Dylan to contribute to his Soviet Jewry Fund, but whether Dylan ever made a contribution is unclear. Pickering told Shelton that "Dylan's brief relationship with the Jewish Defense League has been blown out of proportion."[19]

8. In January and February of 1974 Dylan was touring with the Band. The Arab-Israeli War had only recently ended. This war began with a sudden—and successful—surprise attack on Israel by a coalition of Arab states led by Egypt and Syria. It is sometimes called the Yom Kippur War because it began on Yom Kippur, the holiest day in Judaism. During this 1974 tour rumors persisted that Dylan was giving part of the tour's proceeds to Israel, presumably to help Israelis recover from the war. When reporters covering his 1974 tour asked him about these rumors, he gave evasive answers.[20]

---

15. Before Sara married Dylan she had a daughter, Maria, from a previous marriage. In 1986 Dylan secretly married Carolyn Dennis and had a daughter named Desiree.
16. Scott M. Marshall with Marcia Ford, *Restless Pilgrim*, 157.
17. Robert Shelton, *No Direction Home*, 51.
18. J. J. Goldberg reports that Dylan was told that a kibbutz rule "barred families with children from extended kibbutz visits unless they declared an intention to stay." The New York placement office of the Israel kibbutz movement was willing to search for a kibbutz that would bend the rules, but Dylan's plans changed and he never pursued the matter further. See "Bob Dylan at 60: We Used to be Young Together."
19. Robert Shelton, *No Direction Home*, 284.
20. See reports of this tour by Paul West and Ben Fong-Torres that appear in *Knockin' on Dylan's Door: On the Road in '74* (New York: Pocket Books, 1974), 56.

9. In the fall of 1983, while Dylan was recording his album *Infidels*, his seventeen-year-old son Jesse had another bar mitzvah at the Wailing Wall in Jerusalem. Jesse was traveling in Israel with his grandmother and they learned that a bar mitzvah could be easily arranged. Dylan flew to Israel for the ceremony and was photographed wearing a yarmulke.[21] Dylan's album *Infidels* was released in November, 1983. On the inner sleeve of the album cover there is a photo of Dylan kneeling on the Mount of Olives with the old city of Jerusalem in the background.[22] A song on the album, "Neighborhood Bully," is a defense of Israel. Mike Marqusee, who calls the song "a Zionist apologia," says it was motivated by the criticism Israel received after it attacked a nuclear reactor in Iraq in 1981.[23] In his song Dylan argues that it is Israel's neighbors who are the bullies, not Israel. Those bombs made in the factory that Israel destroyed were meant for him (Israel), the speaker in the song says, but of course "He was supposed to feel bad /He's the neighborhood bully."

10. In the spring of 1983 Dylan began studies at the Brooklyn center of an Orthodox Jewish Movement known as Chabad-Lubavitch. The Lubavitchers, as they are called, are a Hasidic sect—the best known in the U.S. They get their name from Lyubavichi, Russia, the seat of a famous school of Hasidism. Dylan participated in several of Chabad-Lubavitch's annual telethons to raise money for their drug rehabilitation and education programs.[24]

When I listened to Dylan in the 1960s, I was only vaguely aware that he had Jewish roots. It did not seem important. I was very surprised, however, as many people were, when he became an evangelical Christian in 1978 and began writing songs like "When You Gonna Wake Up?" which closes with these lines:

---

21. Howard Sounes, *Down the Highway: The Life of Bob Dylan* (New York: Grove Press, 2001), 356.

22. Mount of Olives is a sacred place for Jews and Christians, and so his visit should not be taken as proof of his return to Judaism. At the foot of the Mount of Olives is the Garden of Gethsemane where, according to the four gospels of the New Testament, Jesus was arrested the night before his crucifixion. Dylan sings about this garden in his very Christian song "In the Garden."

23. Mike Marqusee, *Chimes of Freedom: The Politics of Bob Dylan's Art* (New York: The New Press, 2003), 280; see also Larry Yudelson, "Dylan: Tangled Up in Jews," in *The Bob Dylan Companion*, ed. Carl Benson (New York: Schirmer Books, 1998), 174.

24. Scott Marshall says that Dylan participated in Chabad telethons in 1986, 1989, and 1991. See Scott M. Marshall with Marcia Ford, *Restless Pilgrim*, 87-88, 95, 109.

There's a Man up on a cross and He's been crucified
Do you have any idea why or for who He died?
When you gonna wake up, when you gonna wake up
When you gonna wake up and strengthen the things that re-
main?[25]

His Jewish supporters were, of course, aghast. His pro-Jewish activities, like those I've just listed, had convinced them that he would never abandon his Jewish roots. Larry Yuddelson says Dylan became "perhaps the most famous Jewish apostate in American history."[26] In fact, it seems that Dylan never did deny his Jewish heritage, but it is also true that he did a lot more than flirt with Christian Messianism. To understand the role of religion in Dylan's life we need to remember that he loved gospel music as a young high school kid in Hibbing. He especially liked the Staple Sisters. "At midnight the gospel stuff would start," Dylan told an interviewer. "I got to be acquainted with the Swan Silvertones and the Dixie Hummingbirds, the Highway QC's and all that. But the Staple Singers came on . . . and they were so different."[27]

We need to realize, too, that he was an avid reader of the Bible—both the Old and New Testament—and filled his songs with biblical references long before he became a born-again Christian. We also have to understand the Vineyard Fellowship. Pastors belonging to the Vineyard were Dylan's teachers in a Bible class Dylan took in 1979. We need to consider why this particular church group appealed to him. But first some comments on when and how Dylan came to Jesus.

DYLAN IS BORN AGAIN

In a 1980 interview Dylan told Robert Hilburn that he had accepted Christ in 1978. Here is what Hilburn wrote: "Bob Dylan has finally confirmed in an interview what he's been saying in his music for 18 months: He's a born-again Christian. Dylan said he accepted Jesus Christ in his heart in 1978 after a 'vision and feeling' during which the room moved: 'There

---

25. This line echoes Revelations 3:2: "Be watchful, and strengthen the things which remain, that are ready to die; for I have not found thy works perfect before God." According to *Barnes' Notes on the Bible*, "the things that remain" refers to "the true piety that still lives and lingers among you," and "that are ready to die" means "that seem just ready to become extinct."
26. Larry Yudelson, "Dylan: Tangled Up in Jews," 173.
27. Scott M. Marshall quotes Dylan in Scott M. Marshall with Marcia Ford, *Restless Pilgrim*, 6. Dylan appeared on a Westinghouse TV special with the Staple Singers in 1962 or 1963. See Robert Shelton, *No Direction Home*, 114.

was a presence in the room,' Dylan said, 'that couldn't have been anybody but Jesus.'" Later in the interview Dylan told Hilburn that he "truly had a born-again experience."[28] In an interview with Karen Hughes, also in 1980, Dylan gives an even more graphic description of his experience. "Jesus put his hand on me," Dylan explains. "It was a physical thing. I felt it. I felt it all over me. I felt my whole body tremble. The glory of the Lord knocked me down and picked me up."[29] Clinton Heylin says the experience Dylan describes took place in a hotel room in Tucson, Arizona, when Dylan was nearing the end of his World Tour, a long tour which began in Japan in February 1978, and ended in Florida in December.[30]

After this World Tour ended, Dylan began a three-month Bible course organized by the Vineyard Fellowship, an evangelical church in southern California. In January 1979 Dylan's girlfriend was an actress named Mary Alice Artes. She had recently become born-again and knew people at the Vineyard. She contacted Kenn Gulliksen, the founder of the Vineyard, and told him that her boyfriend was interested in joining his church. Gulliksen dispatched two of his associates, Paul Emond[31] and Larry Myers, to meet with Dylan. Emond and Myers later became Dylan's teachers at the Vineyard's School of Discipleship. Sometime in winter or spring of 1979 Dylan was baptized. Reports in the press said he was baptized in Pat Boone's swimming pool. According to Scott M. Marshall and Marcia Ford, the Vineyard pastor Larry Myers confirmed to them that Dylan was baptized, but that it wasn't in Boone's pool.[32] No one has disclosed who baptized him and where he was baptized. After his conversion, Dylan released three very Christian albums: *Slow Train Coming* (1979), *Saved* (1980), and *Shot of Love* (1981).

What led Dylan to become a Christian? Most biographers suggest that Dylan's painful divorce from his wife, Sara, in 1977 was a key factor. The breakup and custody battle that followed left him depressed. Sara hired Marvin M. Michelson, a famous and shrewd divorce lawyer, and so it cost Dylan millions to settle. Howard Sounes says Sara's share reached

---

28. Bob Dylan, Interview with Robert Hilburn The *Los Angeles Times*, November 23, 1980. Reprinted in *Bob Dylan: The Essential Interviews*, ed. Jonathan Cott (New York: Wenner Books, 2006), 279 and 281.
29. Bob Dylan, Interview with Karen Hughes, *The Dominion* (Wellington, New Zealand). Reprinted in *The Essential Interviews*, ed. Jonathan Cott, 276.
30. Clinton Heylin, *Bob Dylan: Behind the Shades*, 315-316.
31. Clinton Heylin calls this Vineyard pastor "Esmond" but others call him "Emond."
32. Scott M. Marshall with Marcia Ford, *Restless Pilgrim*, 63.

$36 million.[33] He and Sara had also built an expensive mansion in Point Dume, California. And he had contributed $1.25 million of his own funds to make *Renaldo and Clara*, a four-hour film that Dylan directed. This film, co-written by Dylan with Sam Shepard, was a critical and financial failure. The World Tour just described, on which he had his born-again experience, was dubbed the Alimony Tour because it occurred when Dylan admitted he needed funds. "I've got a few debts to pay off," he told a journalist when the tour reached Los Angeles. "I had a couple of bad years. I put a lot of money into the movie, built a big house . . . and there's the divorce. It costs a lot to get divorced in California."[34]

Howard Sounes comments that Dylan's World Tour or Alimony Tour "consisted of a year of frenetic and hedonistic activity, a diversion from Dylan's failed marriage and wrecked home life."[35] Female backing singers were an important part of this tour and Dylan had affairs with two of them—Helena Springs and Carolyn Dennis. (Dylan later secretly married Dennis on June 4, 1986, about four months after their daughter, Desiree Gabrielle Dennis-Dylan, was born.[36])The third backing singer, Jo Ann Harris, told Sounes that during this tour Springs and Dennis were fighting fiercely over Bob. Harris' usual spot when the three of them stood on stage was on the end, but Bob told her to stand between Springs and Dennis to keep them from tearing each other apart.[37] Later Mary Alice Artes joined the tour and so at one point three present or former girlfriends were part of Dylan's entourage on his World/Alimony Tour. Clinton Heylin says that in this period of his life "it would appear that his soul-searching was primarily motivated by 'woman trouble.'"[38] It does seem that keeping his past and present girlfriends happy would have caused stress.

Helena Springs, Carolyn Dennis, and Mary Alice Artes were all African American. Maria Muldaur, a folk-blues singer and friend of Dylan since his Greenwich Village days, says that Dylan liked Black women because they didn't "idolize" or "worship" him. She says his African American backing singers did not know who he was until they began

---

33. Howard Sounes, *Down the Highway: The Life of Bob Dylan*, 308.
34. Howard Sounes quotes what Dylan told a reporter for the *Los Angeles Times*. The interview appeared in The *Los Angeles Times* on May 28, 1978. See Howard Sounes, *Down the Highway: The Life of Bob Dylan*, 314.
35. Howard Sounes, *Down the Highway: The Life of Bob Dylan*, 323.
36. Ibid., 371-372.
37. Ibid., 322.
38. Clinton Heylin, *Bob Dylan: Behind the Shades*, 316.

touring with him.[39] These three girlfriends were all, it seems, Christians. Artes, as previously mentioned, had recently been born-again, Dennis was a former gospel singer, and Springs urged Dylan to pray.[40] Howard Sounes says Dylan "took comfort in the strong personalities and clearly defined culture of his African-American, Christian girl-friends."[41] These strong women apparently steered Dylan toward Jesus, and Artes then introduced him to the Vineyard Fellowship. But it seems possible, too, that after a "hedonistic" tour he was becoming aware of his own sins and was looking for help. This is the view of Kenn Gulliksen, a singing pastor who founded the Vineyard Fellowship in 1971. "He was apparently ready to ask for God's forgiveness for sin," Pastor Gulliksen told Sounes.[42]

In understanding Dylan's conversion it is important to remember that Dylan was not the only musician who converted to Christianity in the late 1960s. Multiple musicians who had been in Dylan's band for a series of concerts in 1975-1976 called the Rolling Thunder Revue converted to Christianity before he did—T. Bone Burnett, David Mansfield and Steven Soles. Howard Sounes says that "there was something of a vogue for Christianity in the music business at the time, perhaps partly as a reaction to the excess of the 1960s and early 1970s." Burnett, Mansfield, and Soles were all Americans, but non-Americans were involved as well. "Beginning in 1976, something happened all across the world," Burnett told Howard Sounes. "It happened to Bono and Edge and Larry Mullens [of U2] in Ireland. It happened to Michael Hutchence [of INXS] in Australia, and it happened here in Los Angeles: There was a spiritual movement."[43]

THE GOSPEL TOUR BEGINS

Dylan opened his first Gospel Tour on Thursday, November 1, 1979, at the Warfield, a former Vaudeville theater on Market Street in San Francisco.[44] The show opened with three female backing singers who sang

---

39. Maria Muldaur, Interview with Howard Sounes reported in Howard Sounes, *Down the Highway: The Life of Bob Dylan*, 370.
40. Howard Sounes, *Down the Highway: The Life of Bob Dylan*, 323; Clinton Heylin, *Bob Dylan: Behind the Shades*, 316.
41. Howard Sounes, *Down the Highway: The Life of Bob Dylan*, 317.
42. Ibid., 325.
43. Howard Sounes, *Down the Highway: The Life of Bob Dylan*, 323. Bono (Paul David Hewson) was U2's lead singer and guitarist; the Edge (David Howell Evans) was a guitarist and backing vocalist; and Larry Mullens was a drummer. Hutchence was the lead singer and lyricist for the rock band INXS.
44. Many writers have described the opening of Dylan's Gospel Tour at the Warfield. I base my comments on press reports written at the time, and accounts by Clinton Heylin in

traditional gospel songs, including "This Train (Is Bound for Glory)." One of the backing singers was Helena Springs, who had been one of Dylan's girlfriends on the Alimony Tour. By mid-winter, after she and Dylan fought, she left and was replaced by another former girlfriend, Carolyn Dennis.[45] After six songs by the backing singers, Dylan took over and began his set, all Christian songs, most of them from his recently released album, *Slow Train Coming*, but also some not-yet-recorded songs that would later appear on his next Christian album, *Saved*. There was an encore, for which Dylan sang "Pressing On," a song in which the speaker talks about "pressing on" to "the higher calling of my Lord."[46] Clinton Heylin describes the concert closing: "Dylan walked to the piano, where unaccompanied by the band, he began to sing 'Pressing On.' After one verse he got up from the piano, walked to the front of the stage and, with no guitar between him and the audience, picked up the mike and sang the remainder of the song."[47]

Reports of how the audience reacted to his first shows at the Warfield vary. Local reviewers reacted negatively, as their headlines indicate: "Born-Again Dylan Bombs!" (Philip Elwood in the *San Francisco Examiner*) and "Bob Dylan's God-Awful Gospel!" (Joel Selvin in the *San Francisco Chronicle*). According to Selvin, the audience, surprised and angry when they realized Dylan was not going to sing any of his old songs, reacted with "catcalls and boos" and requests for old standards—"Like a Rolling Stone" and "Blowin' in the Wind."[48] A placard carried by one protestor outside the theater read "Jesus Loves Your Old Songs, Too."[49] Larry Myers, the Vineyard Pastor who helped teach the Bible course Dylan took, tried to persuade Dylan to sing at least one or two old songs. Your old songs, Myers told him, are not "anti-God."[50] The Vineyard released

---

Bob Dylan: Behind the Shades, 331-336 and by Scott M. Marshall and Marcia Ford in *Restless Pilgrim*, 35-43.

45. Both Dennis and Springs had been with Dylan on his Alimony Tour. The other two backing singers were Regina Havis and Monalisa Young. See William McKeen, *Bob Dylan: A Bio-Bibliography* (Westport, CT: Greenwood Press, 1993), 275.

46. Bert Cartwright suggests this song is based on St. Paul's words found in Philippians 3:14. See Bert Cartwright *The Bible in the Lyrics of Bob Dylan* (Fort Worth, Texas: Self-published, 1992). This edition of his book, Cartwright explains on page 17, is "a revised and amplified edition of a monograph by the same title published in *The Wanted Man Study Series* in 1985."

47. Clinton Heylin, *Bob Dylan: Behind the Shades*, 332.

48. Joel Selvin, "Bob Dylan's God-Awful Gospel," *San Francisco Chronicle*, November 3, 1979. See also "Dylan Tour Off to Shaky Start," *Rolling Stone*, December 13, 1979.

49. Scott M. Marshall with Marcia Ford, *Restless Pilgrim*, 37.

50. Clinton Heylin, *Bob Dylan: Behind the Shades*, 329.

Myers to travel with Dylan and sometimes he led the prayers that Dylan and band members said before each concert. Bill Graham, the tour's promoter, also begged Dylan to include some oldies. But Dylan refused to alter his setlist.[51]

Some people walked out of his opening night concert. Members of Dylan's entourage called it "Newport Revisited," a reference to Dylan's performance at the 1965 Newport Folk Festival where Dylan was booed for going electric.[52] But both journalists and members of Dylan's group agree that by the third performance on Saturday night the atmosphere had changed, probably because by then those attending knew that Dylan wasn't on a nostalgia tour. They knew beforehand they weren't going to hear any golden oldies. According to Robert Hilburn, this performance ended with "an uproarious standing ovation."[53]

In November 2017, *Trouble No More*, a film based on rare footage of Dylan performing his Christian songs in 1980 was put together by Jennifer LeBeau. It was released in November 2017 along with a "deluxe edition" of his Christian songs: *Trouble No More: The Bootleg Series Vol. 13/1979-1981*. The film includes Dylan singing his Christian songs aided by a talented group of backup singers.[54] LeBeau, the producer and director, moves back and forth from Dylan's performances of Christian songs to old-time sermons which were written by Luc Sante, a writer and music critic, and are delivered by actor Michael Shannon. These homilies, Sante says, were inspired by the recordings of African American preachers of the 1920s. I found these between-song sermons to be jarring and rather odd. In them the preacher covers various topics. In one sermon he paraphrases Matthew 7:5 and talks about the need to "First cast the beam out of thine own eye and then thou shalt see clearly to cast the mote out of thy brother's eye." In another he preaches about the evils of junk food. He has, he says, seen members of his congregation "skulking around downtown" carrying greasy paper bags of fried chicken and "sugary sweet soda water" in "cups just about big enough to stand umbrellas in." The Bible tells us, he says, that your body is the temple of God. By eating this "imitation food" you are, he says, "spitting in the temple." Luc Sante says that Dylan told him

---

51. Scott M. Marshall with Marcia Ford, *Restless Pilgrim*, 37-38.
52. "Dylan Tour Off to Shaky Start," *Rolling Stone*, December 13, 1979.
53. Robert Hilburn, "Latest Dylan Tour 'Most Radical,'" *Sarasota Journal*, November 7, 1979.
54. Clyde King, Mona Lisa Young, Mary Elizabeth Bridges, Gwen Evans, and Regina McCrary.

to "go easy on the fire and brimstone," so perhaps that is why we get these more gentle but rather odd homilies.[55]

Some who view this film may find, as I did, the inclusion of sermons to be an odd choice, but there is no denying the power of the singing. *Trouble No More* reminds us of how superb a performer Dylan could be. They also suggest the depth, sincerity, and intensity of Dylan's Christian faith at this time. The negative reviews of his opening show at the Warwick in San Francisco in 1979 were all about the antagonistic crowd which booed and yelled "rock & roll" because fans wanted to hear his old songs. Three days later, as I mentioned, he got a standing ovation, but then the crowds became antagonistic again during his second week in San Francisco when Dylan started giving long sermons between songs. The film *Trouble No More* is worth watching because it reveals Dylan performing in 1980 when less rowdy crowds allowed Dylan's religious conviction and his talent—and the talent of his choir of backup singers—to take center stage. The movie closes with Mona Lisa Young and Dylan sitting at the piano singing "Abraham, Martin and John," written by Richard Holler. Then, as the credits roll, Dylan stands alone on the stage and sings "Every Grain of Sand."

USING THE BIBLE IN DIFFERENT WAYS

By refusing to sing any old songs at the beginning of his Gospel Tour, Dylan emphasized his break with the past. His pre-conversion songs, however, were also "Bible-soaked"—full of references to both the Hebrew Scriptures of the Old Testament and the New Testament. According to Bert Cartwright, a Protestant minister, there are 387 "individual biblical allusions" in the 246 songs Dylan composed before his conversion and 459 allusions in the 88 songs written after his conversion.[56] He stops counting after Dylan's album *Under the Red Sky* was released in 1990. In a similar study that includes works from later albums, Michael Gilmour looks at 143 songs and finds 511 examples of "biblical imagery" in them.[57]

---

55. Richard Williams quotes Luc Sante in a review of *Trouble No More*. See Richard Williams, "Bob Dylan's Controversial Born-Again Phase Explored in New Film," *The Guardian*, March 16, 2018 https://www.theguardian.com/music/2018/mar/16/fire-and-brimstone-new-compilation-resurrects-bob-dylans-born-again-phase (accessed February 10, 2019).
56. Bert Cartwright, *The Bible in the Lyrics of Bob Dylan*, 108, 118.
57. Michael J. Gilmour's "A Selective Index of Biblical Imagery in Bob Dylan's Lyrics" is based on songs included on albums up to and including *Love and Theft*, which was released in 2001. See Michael J. Gilmour, *Tangled Up in the Bible: Bob Dylan and Scripture* (New York: Continuum, 2004), 109-136.

These researchers use different terms for what they are counting and discussing—"examples of biblical imagery," "biblical allusions," "biblical references," "biblical echoes," etc. What they identify are words, phrases, or entire lines that evoke a passage, a character, or a story from the Bible.

There is nothing surprising about an American songwriter, particularly a writer of folk songs, using biblical language in his works. The Bible is the founding book of mainstream American culture and the English language is full of expressions based on biblical verses. It is difficult to speak or write English without echoing the Bible. We speak of "writing on the wall," of "prophets honored everywhere but in their own country," of not being able to "serve two masters," of someone being a "doubting Thomas," of a place being a "land of milk and honey," of someone "being of little faith," of "girding our loins" for a difficult task ahead. All these common expressions and many hundreds more have their origin in the Bible. Bert Cartwright points out that the Bible was the "common denominator" for the music of poor whites and African Americans—two groups whose concerns and afflictions Dylan wanted to address in his early "protest" songs. Dylan's genius, he points out, was "his remarkable ability to meld into artistic expression" the music of these two groups.[58] One way he did this melding was by echoing the language of the Bible in his songs. Dylan wanted to become "a folk bard of the common people," Cartwright says, and so it is not surprising that he "took to himself the people's book—the Bible."[59]

As his career developed Dylan used biblical language in different ways. Cartwright identifies five phases. First, from 1961 to 1966, was a "folklore phase" in which biblical allusions were a natural result of Dylan's immersion in folk and gospel music. In this first phase, Cartwright argues, "the Bible is not an issue of faith; it is a given part of the culture he is making his own. The Bible is not so much to be believed as to be used by him for expressing feeling and thought."[60] One of the examples that Cartwright offers of a first phase song is "Let Me Die in My Footsteps." The first line of the second stanza—"There's been rumors of war and wars that have been"—alludes, he suggests, to Matthew 24:6: "And you will hear of wars and rumors of wars."[61] This song, released in 1963, is about the fear

---

58. Bert Cartwright, *The Bible in the Lyrics of Bob Dylan*, 11.
59. Ibid., 24.
60. Ibid., 29.
61. Ibid.

of nuclear war and the underground fallout shelters built in the 1950s. All the stanzas except the last end with the lines "Let me die in my footsteps / Before I go down under the ground"; the last stanza ends "And you'll die in your footsteps / Before you go down under the ground." Cartwright's point is that in this song Dylan alludes to the verse from the Book of Matthew not to express his Christian beliefs, but to talk about the danger of nuclear war.

In his second phase, from 1967 to 1974, Cartwright says Dylan does not simply allude to the Bible; he makes God and biblical figures central characters in his songs. Phase two begins, Cartwright says, with Dylan's album *John Wesley Harding*.[62] The song "I Pity the Poor Immigrant" is typical of this phase. According to Cartwright, God is the "I" (and "me") in this song who pities the immigrant "who falls in love with wealth itself / and turns his back on me." The "dominant theme," Cartwright says, is taken from Leviticus 26 in which the Lord tells his people what will happen to them if they break his laws.[63] In this second phase Dylan writes about Christ and reveals his growing knowledge of the Bible. Cartwright quotes the following lines from Dylan's "I Shall Be Released":

> *I see my light come shining*
> *From the west unto the east*
> *Any day now, any day now*
> *I shall be released*

According to Cartwright, Dylan is referring to Jesus' "apocalyptic words": "For as the lightning cometh out of the east, and shineth even unto the west; so shall the coming of the Son of man be" (Matthew 24:27).[64] Cartwright suggests that the next stanza, which begins "They say ev'ry man needs protection," touches on St. Paul's doctrine of the Fall as expressed in Romans 3:23: "They say ev'ry man must fall."[65]

In Cartwright's phase three (1974-1978) Dylan continues to use biblical allusions to reflect common people's understanding of the Bible (as in phase one) but now weaves these allusions into his songs more

---

62. Ibid., 37.
63. Ibid., 39. Others interpret this song differently and Cartwright himself says the song "does not rule out the possibility" that "Dylan himself is the persona, decrying America's turning its 'back on me.' America betrayed him in giving him a false vision." See Bert Cartwright, *The Bible in the Lyrics of Bob Dylan*, 40.
64. Ibid., 33.
65. Ibid.

"consciously and calculatingly."[66] In this third phase references to the Bible become vaguer and more sophisticated than they were in stage two. Cartwright says that "Forever Young," a beautiful song that Dylan told Robert Hillburn he wrote with one of his sons in mind, is a good example of this phase.[67] The opening lines of "Forever Young" vaguely echo the Judeo-Christian blessing or benediction derived from Numbers 6:24: "The Lord bless thee, and keep thee."[68]

> *May God bless and keep you always*
> *May your wishes all come true*
> *May you always do for others*
> *And let others do for you*
> *May you build a ladder to the stars*
> *And climb on every rung*
> *May you stay forever young*
> *Forever young, forever young*
> *May you stay forever young*

Bert Cartwright's first three stages are not easy to distinguish. Stage one is difficult to distinguish from stage two because it is sometimes impossible to determine whether a biblical character in a song is an "allusion" or "a central character." Stage three is difficult to distinguish from stages one and two because it is impossible to know for sure whether what sounds like a biblical allusion in a song is simply a result of Dylan's immersion in folk and gospel music or whether he has, as Cartwright says, "consciously and calculatingly" placed it there to achieve a particular artistic effect.[69] Phase four (late 1978 to 1983), however, clearly represents a sharp break with the past. In this phase, Dylan continues to employ biblical references, but now he uses these references to express his born-again experience and, in some songs, to proselytize. This phase, Cartwright says, ends when Dylan retreats from an evangelical approach and releases his album *Infidels* in 1983. In this fifth phase, Cartwright says, Dylan is not so interested in pressing his beliefs on others. His Christian beliefs have been "sufficiently internalized" and so have become "the natural context of his thought."[70]

---

66. Ibid., 47.
67. See Robert Hilburn, "Bob Dylan: Still A-Changin,'" in Carl Benson, ed., *The Bob Dylan Companion*, 204.
68. The blessing continues as follows: The Lord make his face shine upon thee, and be gracious unto thee: The Lord lift up his countenance upon thee, and give thee peace (Numbers 6: 25-26).
69. Bert Cartwright, *The Bible in the Lyrics of Bob Dylan*, 47.
70. Ibid., 75.

DYLAN AND THE VINEYARD FELLOWSHIP

In phase four Dylan unapologetically preaches his faith in songs and urges people to accept Christ as their savior. In his songs Trịnh Công Sơn often evokes Buddhist themes and mentions Buddhist virtues, but his songs are not designed to proselytize. Because in phase four Dylan writes songs that differ greatly from Trịnh Công Sơn's songs, and also from his own previous songs, it is necessary to consider this phase more carefully.

"I had always read the Bible," Dylan told an interviewer in 1980, "but only looked at it as literature. I was never really instructed in it in a way that was meaningful to me."[71] In his classes at the Vineyard Fellowship, however, he read the Bible as a believer. The songs Dylan composed during his conversion phase do not, however, simply summarize what he has learned. They also urge others to accept the Bible's teachings. In other words, they are songs designed to proselytize and convert non-believers. They are not only evangelical songs—songs which preach the views of Evangelical Christians: Some are also evangelistic songs, songs designed to bring more believers into the fold. Songs like "Are You Ready?" and "When You Gonna Wake Up?" have what Howard Sounes calls a "hectoring" tone.[72] Their message is very direct: Accept Jesus Christ as your savior. For Dylan, during this phase at least, "Ya either got faith or ya got unbelief and there ain't no neutral ground," as he puts it in "Precious Angel."

In a review of Dylan's first Christian album, *Slow Train Coming*, Greil Marcus argues that what is new in this album is Dylan's "use of religious imagery, not to discover and shape a vision of what's at stake in the world, but to sell a prepackaged doctrine he's received from someone else."[73] Marcus also objects to the bigoted attitude toward other cultures and religions that is revealed in songs on this album, songs which, he says "have nothing of the sanctified quest in them: they're arrogant, intolerant (listen to the racist, America-first attack on Arabs in 'Slow Train.')"[74] Marcus is referring to the third stanza of the title track on the album *Slow Train Coming* in which the speaker talks about "foreign oil" controlling America and "Sheiks walkin' around like kings." Marcus also mentions a stanza in

---

71. Bob Dylan, Interview with Robert Hilburn, The *Los Angeles Times*, November 23, 1980, 282.
72. Howard Sounes, *Down the Highway*, 328.
73. Greil Marcus, "Amazing Chutzpah," in *The Bob Dylan Companion*, ed. Elizabeth Thomson and David Gutman (San Bernardino, CA: Da Capo Press, 2000), 238. This article originally appeared in *New West*, September 24, 1979.
74. Ibid.

"Precious Angel," another song on the same album, in which the speaker criticizes a wife who talks to her husband about Buddha and Mohammed but fails to mention "the man who came and died a criminal's death."[75]

On his Gospel Tour Dylan preached his faith not only in song but also in between-song speeches, or "raps." These gospel speeches began at the Warfield Theater in San Francisco during the second week of his performances there. Dylan continued to sermonize between songs throughout this nationwide Gospel Tour, though he delivered them less often and shortened them as the tour proceeded.[76] Clinton Heylin reports that Dylan became "positively verbose" during his second week at the Warfield in San Francisco, where he gave thirteen performances in November 1979. Before he sang "Slow Train Coming" and "Solid Rock" he would launch into sermons like the following:

> Satan is called the god of this world. Anyone here who knows that? [Someone shouts: "He sucks!"] That's right! He does! But anyhow, we know he's been defeated at the cross. I'm curious to know how many of you all know that?[77]

"If the dictionary definition of to *evangelize*," Clinton says, "is 'to make acquainted with the Gospel . . . to preach the Gospel from place to place,' that's exactly what he was doing."[78]

Some audiences tolerated Dylan's mini-sermons better than others. His worst reception was on November 28, 1979 at the second concert he performed in Tempe, Arizona. At this performance on his Gospel Tour Dylan started his first sermon earlier than usual, after his second song. It wasn't well-received. The crowd kept yelling "rock 'n' roll," Clinton Heylin reports, "until he spat words of damnation at the nonbelievers."[79] Here is an excerpt from Dylan's sermon:

> Hmmm. Pretty rude bunch tonight, huh? You all know how to be real rude! You know about the spirit of the Antichrist? Does anyone here know about that? Ah, the spirit of the Antichrist is loose right now. [Crowd keeps yelling "rock 'n' roll."] You *still* wanna rock and roll? I'll tell you what the two kinds of people are. . . There's saved people and there's lost people. Yeah. Remember that I told you that. You may never see me again. You may not see me, but sometime

---

75. Ibid., 239.
76. For a collection of all the speeches Dylan delivered on his gospel tour see Clinton Heylin, *Saved! The Gospel Speeches of Bob Dylan* (Madras & New York: Hanuman Books, 1990).
77. Clinton Heylin, *Bob Dylan: Behind the Shades*, 334-335.
78. Ibid., 334.
79. Clinton Heylin, *Bob Dylan: Behind the Shades*, 337.

down the line you remember you heard it here, that Jesus is Lord. Every knee shall bow![80]

When we look at the songs he sang on his Gospel Tour and the sermons he preached in between them, it seems clear that Dylan's aim at this stage of his career was to bring more people to Jesus. This was also the aim of the Vineyard Fellowship, whose pastors taught him his Bible course and were with him on his Gospel Tour. According to Helena Springs, a backing singer both on Dylan's Alimony Tour and his Gospel Tour, there were a lot of Vineyard people backstage at the Warfield "pressuring him about a lot of things . . . they were not allowing him to live."[81]

Why would Dylan be attracted to an evangelical church like the Vineyard Fellowship? To ask this question in the 2020s is different from asking it in 1979. Today people are wondering if "liberal Christianity," represented by well-known denominations—Episcopal, Presbyterian, Methodist, Lutheran, etc.—can survive. By 1996, 39 percent of Americans reported that they were born-again.[82] In 2005 Garry Dorrien, a liberal Protestant Scholar, observed that the growth of evangelical churches had produced a need to "redefine the sociological meaning of 'mainline Protestantism.'"[83] In 2012 Ross Douthat, a columnist for the *New York Times*, observed that Sunday attendance at Episcopal churches dropped 23 percent from 2000 to 2010.[84] In an article in *The New Yorker* the same year Kelefa Sanneh reported that "thirty per cent of white Americans are evangelicals—more than all the mainline Protestant denominations combined."[85] A Religious Landscape Study conducted by the Pew Research Center in 2014 found that 70.6% of Americans identified themselves as Christian. "Evangelical Protestant" represented the largest Christian group—25.4%; Catholics composed 20.8%; and Mainline Protestants represented 14.7%.[86]

---

80. Clinton Heylin quotes this sermon in *Bob Dylan: Behind the Shades*, 337-338.
81. Clinton Heylin quotes Helena Springs in *Bob Dylan: Behind the Shades*, 333.
82. T. M. Luhrmann, *When God Talks Back: Understanding the American Evangelical Relationship with God* (New York: Alfred A. Knopf, 212), 15. Luhrmann cites George Gallup and D. Michael Lindsay, *Surveying the Religious Landscape* (Harrisburg, PA: Morehouse, 1999), 68.
83. Gary Dorrien, "American Liberal Theology: Crisis, Irony, Decline, Renewal, Ambiguity," *Cross Currents* 55, No. 4 (Winter, 2005-06), https://web.archive.org/web/20221105090228/http://www.crosscurrents.org/dorrien200506.htm (accessed November 5, 2012).
84. Ross Douthat, "Can Liberal Christianity Be Saved?," The New York *Times*, July 14, 2012.
85. Kelefa Sanneh, "The Hell-Raiser," The *New Yorker* (November 26, 2012), 59.
86. Pew Research Center, "Religious Landscape Study," 2014, http://www.pewforum.org/religious-landscape-study (accessed November 30, 2018).

With the advantage of hindsight, one can see Dylan's conversion to evangelical Christianity as part of a larger trend. The mainline churches have emphasized the social gospel but slighted the personal gospel. They have, Ross Douthat suggests, stressed "social reform"—he mentions the Episcopal church's decision to bless same-sex unions—but they have slighted "personal conversion." As a result, he says, they "often don't seem to be offering anything you can't already get from a purely secular liberalism."[87] They have become so concerned about institutional sinfulness that they have paid too little attention to the sinfulness of individuals and their need for forgiveness and redemption. Liberal theology, Gary Dorrien argues, has "broken out of its academic base only when it speaks with spiritual conviction about God's holy and gracious presence, the way of Christ, and the transformative mission of Christianity."[88] In 1978 the pastors of the Vineyard Fellowship *were* speaking of these things and it seems that Dylan, at the close of his frenetic Alimony Tour, was willing to listen.

Some journalists and Dylan biographers refer to the Vineyard as a "fundamentalist" church or "sect," but I call it "evangelical" because that is how Vineyard followers refer to it and because it is slightly—very slightly—more liberal on some issues than fundamentalist churches. For example, it is more willing to reach out to other Christian churches. I explain, in Appendix C, my understanding of the terms used to describe the different strands of Protestant Christianity—fundamentalist, evangelical, and liberal. Vineyard followers call themselves "Empowered Evangelicals" to emphasize that they occupy a "radical middle" between "evangelism" and "Pentecostalism." They share with Pentecostals a belief in the "supreme authority of the Bible" and the "Lordship of the Holy Spirit" but unlike Pentecostals they do not believe that one has to experience a second "baptism of the Spirit" and speak in tongues before one can receive the "gifts of the Spirit": Being "born again" and water baptism are sufficient to enable one to heal the sick, cast out demons, receive prophecies, and speak in tongues.[89]

The Vineyard Fellowship has deep roots in the Jesus Movement of the 1960s and 1970s. In his history of the Vineyard, Bill Jackson, himself

---

87. Ross Douthat, "Can Liberal Christianity Be Saved?"
88. Gary Dorrien, "American Liberal Theology."
89. See Rich Nathan and Ken Wilson, *Empowered Evangelicals* (Boise, Idaho: Ampelon Publishing, 2009), 5-8 and 25-42; and Bill Jackson, *The Quest for the Radical Middle* (Cape Town, South Africa: Vineyard International Publishing, 1999), 12-21.

a Vineyard pastor and "planter" of Vineyard churches, explains that in the late 1960s "the Holy Spirit moved in an incredible way on a new generation of young people . . . . Thousands upon thousands of young people were saved from drugs, sex and rock 'n roll between 1967 and the mid-1970s."[90] These young people were disenchanted with the establishment churches but found a home first in the Calvary Chapel and then in the Vineyard which was, as Bill Jackson explains, "birthed out of Calvary."[91] The most prominent of the "Jesus Freaks," as these young converts were called, was a man named Lonnie Frisbee, a fascinating and tragic character who died of AIDS on March 12, 1993.[92] According to Jackson, Frisbee "played a crucial role in the rocketing advance of both Calvary Chapel and the Vineyard."[93] To ensure Frisbee's contributions would not be overlooked he asked David Di Sambatino, whom he describes as "perhaps the leading authority on the Jesus People," to write an essay about Frisbee's life. Jackson includes this essay as an appendix in his book *The Quest for the Radical Middle*.[94] According to Sambatino, Kenn Gulliksen, whom he describes as "an early member of the Calvary Chapel pastoral staff and founder of the Vineyard churches," was influenced by Frisbee. Sambatino says that Frisbee mentored Gulliksen in the "deeper things of the Holy Spirit." [95] Gulliksen was the person who arranged for Dylan's Bible course.

Evangelical Christians would understand that by "deeper things of the Holy Spirit" Gulliksen means supernatural phenomena associated with Pentecostalism and the Charismatic movement—speaking in tongues, prophetic utterances, faith healing, and treating believers possessed by the devil. In evangelical circles these phenomena are referred to as "Signs and Wonders,"[96] a phrase made famous by John Wimber, a theologian

---

90. Bill Jackson, *The Quest for the Radical Middle*, 28.
91. Ibid., 33.
92. Frisbee was gay, and after his death Hank Hanegraaff, an American author, radio talk-show host and advocate of evangelical Christianity, who was known as "the Bible Answer Man," attacked Vineyard's senior pastor, John Wimber, "for turning his pulpit over to a . . . hypnotist struggling with homosexuality." David Di Sabatino quotes Hanegraaff in "Lonnie Frisbee: A Modern Day Samson," in Bill Jackson, *The Quest for the Radical Middle*, 389. According to De Sabatino, Frisbee "never believed that homosexuality was a natural inclination. Rather, in line with most conservative evangelicals, he always believed that homosexual behavior was the conscious choice of the participant" (388). Sabatino says that Frisbee testified that "God saved him from homosexuality" (383).
93. Bill Jackson, *The Quest for the Radical Middle*, 377.
94. David Di Sabatino, "Lonnie Frisbee: A Modern Day Samson," in Bill Jackson, *The Quest for the Radical Middle*, 377-391.
95. David Di Sabatino, "Lonnie Frisbee: A Modern Day Samson," 379.
96. "Signs and wonders" are mentioned in Deuteronomy 26:8: "And the Lord brought us forth out of Egypt with a mighty hand, and with an outstretched arm, and with great

and preacher who urged first the Calvary Church and then the Vineyard Fellowship to accept these "Pentecostal emphases" in their worship. Chuck Smith, the founder of the Calvary Church, did not totally reject them but he was opposed to aggressive Pentecostalism—to things like "shaking and being 'slain in the Spirit." He preferred "a more biblical low-key approach to spiritual gifts."[97] Kenn Gulliksen and the Vineyard, however, embraced them and in 1982 John Wimber, realizing his "signs and wonders" were no longer welcome at Calvary, joined the Vineyard. Gulliksen turned over the leadership of the Vineyard churches to him.

According to the Vineyard's webpage, "John Wimber's influence profoundly shaped the theology and practice of Vineyard churches from their earliest days until his death in November 1997."[98] Wimber studied at the Fuller Theological Institute of Evangelism and Church Growth, an institution in Pasadena, California founded by a radio evangelist named Charles E. Fuller to provide an alternative to the elite, mainstream seminaries. In *Empowered Evangelicals*, a book dedicated to John Wimber, Rich Nathan and Ken Wilson explain that professors at Fuller's School of World Missions had observed that Christianity could be spread in the third world "through addressing disease and demonic oppression in the power of the Spirit."[99] They observed the gospel spreading more effectively when it was accompanied by biblical signs and wonders.[100] Wimber concluded that this approach was needed in the US. Later, in January 1982, he taught a course at the Fuller Theological Institute called "Signs, Wonders and Church Growth."

John Wimber and, to a lesser extent, Kenn Gulliksen, provided the theological underpinning for the Vineyard's approach, but it was Lonnie Frisbee, the Jesus Freak, who showed them how it could work in practice. David Di Sabatino explains that Frisbee provided John Wimber "with a model of Pentecostal experimentalism that would influence the Vineyard's 'signs and wonders' theology."[101] At the end of the 1960s Frisbee was, by his own admission, a heavy drug user and drug pusher. "When I first turned on to drugs I thought that was the truth," he explains, "so I turned

---

terribleness, and with signs, and with wonders." See also Acts 2:4 and Mark 16:20.
97. Bill Jackson, *The Quest for the Radical Middle*, 87.
98. "Vineyard History," Vineyard USA, http://www.vineyardusa.org/site/about/vine-yard-history (accessed March 20, 2012).
99. Rich Nathan and Ken Wilson, *Empowered Evangelicals*, 34.
100. Ibid. 34-35.
101. David Di Sabatino, "Lonnie Frisbee: A Modern Day Samson," 378.

everyone on to drugs."[102] But then one day when he was "high on acid" walking through the California hills near Tahquitz Falls, the Lord appeared to him. "I was a nudist-vegetarian-hippie when the Lord called me," he explains.[103] Chuck Smith of Calvary Chapel recruited Frisbee in 1968 to help him attract hippies to his church. Frisbee was a skillful evangelist and quickly boosted Calvary's membership by conducting services like this one described in a sociological study conducted in 1971:

> A 22-year-old lay minister—a former drug user, with flowing robe, long hair and beard—leads the service . . . Informal songs are sung by the congregation, mostly centering on the person of Jesus and his imminent return to earth. Prayers for the sick are offered and testimonies are heard . . . Lonnie affirms that God desires to heal anything from 'warts to cancer.' The 'flashes' from previous LSD trips can also be cured. One woman (older than most present) testifies that she has been cured of dandruff. 'Praise the Lord!' says Lonnie. An examination of her head reveals no trace of dandruff.[104]

It is not clear whether the Vineyard's emphasis on "signs and wonders" appealed to Dylan. He may not have known about the Vineyard's openness to "gifts of the Spirit" before enrolling in the Vineyard's Bible's course. Dylan, however, has always been fascinated by the surreal and the irrational. In an interview with Mikal Gilmore in 2012 Dylan talks about how he was "transfigured" after the death of a Hells Angel who had the same name—Robert Zimmerman. Despite persistent questioning by Gilmore, Dylan never makes clear what he means by "transfigured," but clearly it refers to some kind of miraculous event.[105] Dylan may not have embraced the Vineyard's Pentecostalism, but he was fascinated by similar miraculous events, especially those associated with the end of the world—events like the rapture of believers that Hal Lindsey describes as "The Ultimate Trip."[106] "Talk about mind expansion drugs!" Lindsey says. "We are told that we [those who are raptured] shall expand in under-

---

102. David Di Sabatino in "Lonnie Frisbee: A Modern Day Samson" quotes what Lonnie Frisbee said in a 1971 film *The Sun Worshipers* produced by Pyramid Films.
103. Qtd. by David De Sabatino in "Lonnie Frisbee: A Modern Day Samson," 380. He cites the following source: "Lonnie Frisbee Testimony, Anaheim: Vineyard Ministry International. Tape 003."
104. Qtd. by David De Sabatino in "Lonnie Frisbee: A Modern Day Samson," 382. He cites Robert Lynn Adams and Robert Jon Fox, "Mainlining Jesus: The New Trip," *Society* (February 1972), 50.
105. Bob Dylan, interview by Mikal Gilmore. See "Bob Dylan: The Rolling Stone Interview" in *Rolling Stone* (September 27, 2012), 46.
106. Hal Lindsey, *The Late Great Planet Earth* (Grand Rapids, MI: Zondervan, 1970), 135, 173.

standing and comprehension beyond that of any earthbound genius."[107] Comparisons of trips on drugs to trips with Jesus were common in the Jesus movement and in the evangelical groups that proselytized among the hippies. In a between-song sermon on his Gospel Tour Dylan said that "walking with Jesus is no easy trip, but it's the only trip. I'm afraid to say I've seen a lot of other kinds of trips."[108] There was a bit of the Jesus freak in Dylan. Like Lonnie Frisbee and many of the hippies that flocked to Calvary Chapel and the Vineyard, Dylan had problems with drugs at various times in his life. Certainly the Vineyard helped Dylan, as it helped the hippies in the Jesus Movement, to "get high on Jesus."

Other aspects of the Vineyard program, however, may have appealed to Dylan more than its openness to "gifts of the Holy Spirit." Scott Marshall explains that although the Vineyard was not flexible about doctrine, it was very flexible about worship style. "The free and easy style that character-ized the services attracted musicians like a magnet," Marshall says.[109] The Vineyard's pastors had learned that music was useful in recruiting young people dissatisfied with the more traditional churches, and so they made it an important part of their services. Leading pastors at both Calvary Chapel and the Vineyard were music promoters and/or singers and musicians. Chuck Smith, the founder of Calvary Chapel, of which the Vineyard was an offshoot, started Maranatha Music in 1971. According to the Maranatha Music webpage, Smith wished "to promote the 'Jesus Music' that his young hippie followers were writing and singing up and down the California coast."[110] In the early 1960s John Wimber, who became the senior pastor at the Vineyard, was, according to David Neff, a "beer-guzzling, drug-abusing pop musician" who played saxophone for "The Righteous Brothers."[111] Their song, "You've Lost that Lovin' Feeling," was a big hit in 1964.[112] Kenn Gullikson was a singing pastor who released his own album of Christian songs.[113]

The Vineyard attracted other musicians besides Dylan, including Keith Green and Debby Boone, two singers who were recording Christian

---

107. Ibid., 144.
108. Excerpt from remarks Dylan made at a concert in Hartford, CT, on May 7, 1980. See Clinton Heylin, ed., *Saved! The Gospel Speeches of Bob Dylan*, 72-73.
109. Scott M. Marshall with Marcia Ford, *Restless Pilgrim*, 27.
110. "About Us," Maranatha! Music, https://www.maranathamusic.com/about (accessed December 3, 2018).
111. David Neff, "Wimber's Wonders," *Christianity Today* 42, no. 2 (February 9, 1998), 15.
112. Bill Jackson, *The Quest for the Radical Middle*, 44.
113. Howard Sounes, *Down the Highway*, 324.

songs when Dylan was releasing his own Christian albums. Green was a friend of Dylan's and like Dylan was a Jew who became an evangelical Christian. Before Kenn Gullikson welcomed Dylan to the Vineyard, he had helped both Keith Green and his wife Melody, who was also Jewish, find Jesus.[114] In a book about her husband Melody describes how first Keith and then she herself "received Jesus" after a Bible study session led by Gullikson. She describes Gullikson's approach, which is probably similar to the one he later used with Dylan. The study sessions the Greens attended were held in a big yellow house in the Coldwater Canyon section of Beverly Hills, an area, she says, that was "definitely on the 'Map to the Movie Stars' Homes.'"[115] She describes Gullikson as "a young man with yellow-blond hair, a round friendly face, and warm and smiling eyes."[116] The session at which Keith accepted Jesus began with people singing songs while sitting cross-legged on the floor—songs like "Father I Adore You" composed by Chuck Smith, the pastor of Calvary Chapel. Then after a simple prayer Gulliksen began talking about God in a homespun way that both Keith and Melody found very appealing. He started by saying that earlier in the day he had become impatient with his wife and felt like he had "blown it" with her but then he remembered John 1:9 where "it says that if we come to Jesus and confess our sins, he's faithful to forgive our sins." So he begged first God to forgive him and then his wife to forgive him. "It was beautiful," he concluded.[117] Both Melody and Keith were impressed by Gullikson's approach. "He made Jesus sound like his best friend or something," Melody Green says. "It didn't seem abstract or mystical at all."[118]

Scott Marshall reports that Keith Green "had no problem seeing himself as a Jewish Christian," another similarity to Dylan, though Green's case is a little different.[119] Dylan was raised in a Jewish household, had a bar mitzvah, etc., but Green's parents hid their Jewishness. According to a

---

114. The Jesus Movement of the 1960s and 1970s attracted many Jews. The parachurch organization Jews for Jesus was created in the early 70s to support them. The entry for "Late 1960s" on its "Jews for Jesus Timeline" reads as follows: "The Jesus Movement in full swing and many Jewish young people are coming to believe in Jesus." See "Jews for Jesus Timeline," https://web.archive.org/web/20130124124243/http://www.jewsforjesus.org/about/timeline (accessed January 9, 2013).

115. Melody Green with David Hazard, *No Compromise: The Life Story of Keith Green* (Nashville, TN: Thomas Nelson, 2008), 132.

116. Ibid., 133.

117. Ibid., 134.

118. Ibid.

119. Scott M. Marshall with Marcia Ford, *Restless Pilgrim*, 64.

biographical sketch on a website devoted to his life and work, when Green learned the truth he readily accepted his Jewishness and "proudly told the world, 'I'm a Jewish Christian.'"[120]

In her biography of her husband, Melody Green says that she and Keith first met Dylan as a result of their both being associated with the Vineyard. They spent time with Dylan in his apartment and office near Santa Monica. Dylan was working on songs that would appear on his first Christian album, *Slow Train Coming*, and, according to Melody, he showed them some lyrics and asked their opinion of them.[121] In 1980 Green released his album *So You Wanna Go Back to Egypt*. Bob Dylan plays harmonica on one of the songs, "Pledge My Head to Heaven." Two years later on July 28, 1982, Green and two of his small children died in a plane crash.[122]

In *Tangled Up in the Bible* Michael J. Gilmour considers whether Dylan was influenced by Green's songs. One might think it more likely that the more famous Dylan influenced Green, but it is an interesting question. Melody Green says that when Keith was recording *So You Wanna Go Back to Egypt* Dylan told Keith's producer, Bill Maxwell, that Keith's earlier album, *For Him Who Has Ears to Hear* (1977), "was one of his favorite albums of all time."[123] Gilmour arranges lyrics from this album of Green's next to lyrics from Dylan's gospel albums. His chart reveals similarities. Comparing Green and Dylan's songs, Gilmour says, "helps us appreciate that at least some of Dylan's Christian and biblical vocabulary was absorbed from those he associated with in 1978 and later."[124] Not only vocabulary but "sentiments and moods" as well. In "Saved" Dylan sings "I'm so glad / So Glad / I want to thank You, Lord" and in "Heart of Mine" he says "Heart of mine, so malicious and so full of guile." Such outbursts of joy and self-deprecation, Gilmour points out, were common in "the form of evangelical Christianity Dylan connected with."[125] He suggests that although there may have been no direct influence in either direction in the Green-Dylan relationship, there was "a shared milieu." They also

---

120. "About Keith Green," Last Days Ministries, https://www.lastdaysministries.org/Groups/1000008700/Last_Days_Ministries/Keith_Green/Bio/Bio.aspx (accessed December 4, 2018).
121. Melody Green and David Hazard, *No Compromise*.
122. Ibid., 431-436. See also Scott M. Marshall with Marcia Ford, *Restless Pilgrim*, 64.
123. Melody Green and David Hazard, *No Compromise*, 340-341.
124. Michael J. Gilmour, *Tangled up in the Bible*, 81.
125. Ibid.

seemed to share a passion for Jesus and a conviction that one could be both a Jew and a Christian.

In the 1960s and 1970s both the Jesus Movement and the Vineyard emphasized a simple gospel: "Jesus Saves!" It is a gospel that Dylan preaches in his Christian songs, including "Saved":

> *By His grace I have been touched*
> *By His word I have been healed*
> *By His hand I've been delivered*
> *By His spirit I've been sealed*
> *I've been saved*
> *By the blood of the lamb*

And in "What Can I Do For You?"

> *Pulled me out of bondage and You made me renewed inside*
> *Filled up a hunger that had always been denied*
> *Opened up a door no man can shut and You opened it up so wide*
> *And You've chosen me to be among the few*
> *What can I do for you?*

The simple gospel preached by the Vineyard and other evangelical churches is also primarily a personal or individualistic gospel, not a social gospel. The focus is on personal redemption—on saving oneself, not on reforming the social order. And once you are saved—one of the "chosen few"—what then? "What can I do for you?" as Dylan asks in his song. Based on what I have read, including books and articles written by Vineyard insiders, the Vineyard's answer is: Win new converts and then teach them to win more. All Vineyard leaders are passionate about "planting" new churches. They are less passionate about attacking poverty and social injustice. According to the Vineyard's Core Values & Beliefs booklet, "the mission of Vineyard USA is to join God's mission in the world by building a community of churches that are proclaiming and practicing the full message and reality of the kingdom of God."[126] The Vineyard's focus is not just on the US. In fact only a third of its churches are in the US; the majority are overseas. Vineyard founders believe they have been "called to bring the gospel of the kingdom to every nook and cranny of creation, faithfully translating the message of Jesus into language and forms that are relevant

---

126. Core Values & Beliefs booklet, Vineyard USA, https://web.archive.org/web/20131207055604if_/http://www.vineyardresources.com/CoreValuesAndBeliefs.pdf.

to diverse people and cultures."[127] These "forms" include Wimber's "signs and wonders," which helped Lonnie Frisbee convert hippies in California and have proven useful to the Vineyard in converting people around the world.

Dylan's own answer to his question—What, after being saved, can I do for you?—is similar to the Vineyard's: Convert others. Early in his career, in his protest songs, Bob Dylan attacked the sinfulness of the social order, but after his conversion his focus was on saving himself and others before it was too late. We see this emphasis on personal redemption and evangelism in songs like "Gonna Change My Way of Thinking" which includes these lines:

> Jesus said, "Be Ready
> For you know not the hour in which I come"
> He said, "He who is not for Me is against Me"
> Just so you know where He's coming from

And also in "Are You Ready?":

> When destruction cometh swiftly
> And there's no time to say a fare-thee-well
> Have you decided whether you want to be
> In heaven or in hell?
>
> Are you ready for the judgment?
> Are you ready for that terrible swift sword?
> Are you ready for Armageddon?
> Are you ready for the day of the Lord?
> Are you ready, I hope you're ready

If the world is going to end soon—so soon there's no time for a "fare-thee-well"—then there is no time for a social gospel. I will explore Dylan's apocalyptic view of the world in my next chapter.

---

127. "Core Values and Beliefs," Vineyard USA, http://www.vineyardusa.org/site/about/vineyard-values (accessed November 15, 2012).

27

PROPHET OF THE APOCALYPSE

There is a sense of urgency in songs like "Are you Ready?" because after he was born-again Dylan, along with those in the Jesus Movement and in most evangelical churches, believed that the end of the world was coming soon. Along with the simple gospel (Jesus saves!), a belief in an imminent apocalypse, followed by the second coming of Christ, is a defining trait of both the Jesus Movement and evangelical Christianity. In the 1960s members of the Christian Foundation, a part of the Jesus Movement, would pass out handbills on Hollywood Boulevard saying "Repent of your sins. Jesus is coming soon!"[1] Chuck Smith, founder of Calvary Chapel, the church from which the Vineyard emerged, believed that "the last days are upon us, and the Spirit of God is being poured out upon us. And it's just God's plan. It's just coming to completion."[2] According to Bill Jackson, Chuck Smith predicted that the rapture would occur in 1981.[3]

In 1974, the same year that Kenn Gulliksen founded the Vineyard as an offshoot of Calvary Chapel, he conducted a Bible study class in the home of the Christian musician Larry Norman.[4] In 1969 Larry Norman

---

1. Ronald M. Enroth, Edward E. Ericson, Jr., and C. Breckinridge Peters, *The Jesus People: Old-Time Religion in the Age of Aquarius* (Grand Rapids, MI: William B. Eerdmans Publishing, 1972), 54.
2. Ibid., 179.
3. Bill Jackson, The Quest for the Radical Middle (Cape Town, South Africa: Vineyard International Publishing, 1999), 86.
4. Ibid.,78.

had written "I Wish We'd All Been Ready," a song about the end of the world. Norman conveys urgency by describing the sad separation of a couple. Both husband and wife are asleep in their bed when the husband is raptured up to heaven but the wife is not:

> *A man and wife sleep in bed she hears a noise*
> *And turns her head he's gone*
> *I wish we'd all been ready*

I mention Larry Norman and his song to emphasize that the coming apocalypse was a common theme of Christian music in the late 1960s and 1970s. Like John Wimber's "Signs and Wonders" it was no doubt useful in recruiting converts. Who wants to see their spouse or friend raptured to heaven and be left behind to face the possibility of eternal damnation? Dylan, however, was interested in the apocalypse before his dramatic conversion to evangelical Christianity. Because apocalyptic themes pervade both his pre- and post-conversion songs we need to look more closely at Dylan's fascination with End Times.

In a 1984 interview Robert Hilburn asked Dylan: "Do you actually believe the end is at hand?" Dylan's reply: "I don't think it's *at hand*. I think we'll have *at least* two hundred years."[5] In another 1984 interview, when Dylan was on a European tour, Mick Brown of the *Sunday Times* asked Dylan if he believed in evil. "Sure, I believe in it," Dylan responded. "I believe that ever since Adam and Eve got thrown out of the garden that the whole nature of the planet has been heading in one direction—toward apocalypse. It's all there in the Book of Revelations [sic], but it's difficult talking about these things to most people because most people don't know what you're talking about, or don't want to listen."[6] "Apocalypse" comes from a Greek word meaning "revelation" and Dylan was, as the passage just quoted suggests, fascinated by "Revelation," the book of the Bible which prophecies that the world will end in a cataclysmic battle between good and evil at Armageddon. Thirty years later Dylan was still talking about the Book of Revelation. When Mikal Gilmore interviewed Dylan in 2012 soon after the release of *Tempest*, his thirty-fifth studio album, he mentioned to Dylan that the Bible was still providing imagery for his

---

5. Bob Dylan, Interview with Robert Hilburn, The Los Angeles Times, November 23, 1980. Reprinted in Jonathan Cott, ed., Bob Dylan: The Essential Interviews (New York: Wenner Books, 2006), 288.
6. Bob Dylan, Interview with Mick Brown, Sunday Times, July 1, 1984.

songs, "Of course," Dylan replied. "What else could there be? I believe in the Book of Revelation."[7]

Many people believe that the end is near. A TIME/CNN poll conducted after the September 11, 2001, attack on the World Trade Center, found that 59% of Americans believed that the events of Revelation were going to come true, and one-quarter thought the Bible predicted the September 11 attack. Interest in the apocalypse rises in times of crisis and subsides in calmer periods. The attacks on the World Trade Center created a crisis atmosphere and this may explain the high results of this poll. In 2010, however, a somewhat calmer period, a Pew Research Center report indicated that 41% of Americans believed that Christ definitely (23%) or probably (18%) will have returned to earth by 2050. That percentage jumped to 58% for white evangelical Christians.[8] Scholars suggest that apocalyptic thinking has deep roots in American culture—deeper, it seems, than many liberal secularists are aware. In *Apocalypse Jukebox: The End of the World in American Popular Music* David Janssen and Edward Whitelock argue that "apocalypse is a permanent and central part of the American character."[9]

There are positive and negative views of end times. Paul Boyer point outs that when Christopher Columbus arrived in the new world he "quoted passages from Revelation and Isaiah which prophesize 'a new heaven and a new earth.'"[10] Later in his life Columbus wrote: "God made me the messenger of the new heaven and the new earth of which he spoke in the Apocalypse of St. John after having spoken of it through the mouth of Isaiah; and he showed me the spot where to find it."[11] The Puritans believed that in America they were building this new heaven and new earth described in Revelation—"a shining city on a hill," a "beacon to the world." They saw their "errand into the wilderness" as part of God's plan. Like the Puritans, evangelicals today are more likely to have a positive attitude toward end times because they see apocalyptic events—even the

---

7. Bob Dylan, Interview with Mikal Gilmore. See "Bob Dylan: The Rolling Stone Interview" in *Rolling Stone* 1166, September 27, 2012, 51.

8. Pew Research Center, "Jesus Christ's Return to Earth," http://pewresearch.org/databank/dailynumber/?NumberID=1043 (accessed October 23, 2012).

9. David Janssen and Edward Whitelock, *Apocalypse Jukebox: The End of the World in American Popular Music* (Brooklyn, NY: Soft Skull Press, 2009), 3.

10. Paul Boyer, *When Time Shall Be No More: Prophecy Belief in Modern American Culture* (Cambridge: Belknap Press, 1992), 223. Qtd. by David Janssen and Edward Whitelock in *Apocalypse Jukebox*, 16.

11. Paul Boyer quotes Columbus in *When Time Shall Be No More*, 225.

most tragic ones—as part of God's plan. Believers in a "sacred apocalypse," Janssen and Whitelock point out, "know there is a better world on the other side"; believers in a secular apocalypse lack that comforting notion: They fear that "apocalyptic catastrophe will simply bring an end to humanity."[12]

DYLAN'S SECOND BIBLE: *THE LATE GREAT PLANET EARTH*

For proof that many Americans were fascinated with end times in the 1970s one need look no further than the phenomenal success of Hal Lindsey's *The Late Great Planet Earth*, which we now know he wrote with Carole C. Carlson.[13] Released in 1970, it was the best-selling non-fiction book of its decade and it played a major role in increasing interest in end times and evangelical Christianity.

This book clearly influenced Dylan profoundly. His view of Revelation is based on Lindsey and Carlson's account. When he talked about end times in his between-song sermons on his Gospel Tour, which he did often, he presented Lindsey and Carlson's view, arguing, for example, as they do, that the biblical Gog and Magog mentioned in Ezekiel and Revelation are the modern countries of Russia and China.[14] In Appendix B I summarize in more detail their account of events leading to Armageddon, but basically in *The Late Great Planet Earth* they tie biblical prophecies to contemporary events—to Russia's alliance with Arab countries, which threatens Israel, and to China's support of Vietnam and wars of liberation in Africa and the Middle East. When Dylan's Gospel Tour was in Tempe, Arizona on November 26, 1979, Dylan concluded a five-minute rap with a retelling of Lindsey and Carlson's Armageddon scenario. Here's a sampling from it:

> Russia will come down and attack in the Middle East. China's got an army of two million people—they're gonna come down in the Middle East. There's gonna be a war called the Battle of Armageddon which is like something you never even dreamed about. And Christ will set up His kingdom and He'll rule it from Jerusalem. I know, far out as that may seem, this is what the Bible says.[15]

---

12. David Janssen and Edward Whitelock, *Apocalypse Jukebox*, 4.
13. Hal Lindsey with Carole C. Carlson, *The Late Great Planet Earth* (Grand Rapids, MI: Zondervan, 1970).
14. Gog and Magog were two legendary powers who served Satan (Ezekiel 38:2; Revelation 20:8). Clinton Heylin, *Bob Dylan: Behind the Shades* (New York: Summit Books, 1991), 339. See also Clinton Heylin, ed., *Saved! The Gospel Speeches of Bob Dylan* (Madras and New York: Hanuman Books, 1990), 36, 47.
15. My quotation is taken from Clinton Heylin, *Bob Dylan: Behind the Shades*, 338. In this book Clinton Heylin says it was this second show in Tempe on Dylan's Gospel Tour at

Dylan's biographers emphasize the influence of Lindsey and Carlson's book on the songwriter. Clinton Heylin reports that it was Dylan's "second Bible" and says "it added an apocalyptic edge to his worldview."[16] Dylan's song "Ye Shall Be Changed," Heylin says, is based on Chapter 11 of Lindsey and Carlson's book. In this chapter, titled "The Ultimate Trip," they talk about the rapture during which dead Christians will be resurrected to meet Christ in the air. They cite First Corinthians 15:52 where it is stated that "in the twinkling of an eye," when "the trumpet shall sound," the "dead shall be raised incorruptible, and we shall be changed."[17] Dylan echoes this passage in his refrain:

> Ye shall be changed, ye shall be changed
> In a twinkling of an eye, when the last trumpet blows
> The dead will arise and burst out of your clothes
> And ye shall be changed

In his biography Howard Sounes reports that Dylan had read Lindsey and Carlson's book and told his friend, the singer Maria Muldaur, that "dramatic events would soon unfold"—presumably dramatic events like the rapture Dylan describes in "Ye Shall Be Changed."[18]

There are other treatments of end times, like Tim F. LaHaye's and Jerry B. Jenkins' "Left Behind" series. At the start of *Left Behind* (1995), the first book in this series, the pilot and some of the passengers in a jet headed for Heathrow are "left behind" when the good Christians are raptured up to heaven. If you count graphic novels and children's versions, this series has sold fifty million copies. Book 9 in the series was the best-selling novel of 2001.[19] It was Lindsey and Carlson's book, however, that influenced Dylan. Lindsey was associated with the Vineyard and emerged from a milieu very similar to its founders. He held leadership positions in two Southern California church groups—first the Campus Crusade for Christ, then J. C. Light and Power House—that were similar to Calvary

---

which the audience reacted most negatively to his between-song sermons. The sermon that he quotes from in his book to illustrate the hostility and Dylan's reaction to it, however, is clearly the sermon that was, according to a collection of Dylan's between-song sermons that Heylin himself edited, delivered in San Francisco on November 26, 1979. See Clinton Heylin, ed., *Saved! The Gospel Speeches of Bob Dylan,* 42-48 and 113-114 speeches.

16. Clinton Heylin, *Bob Dylan: Behind the Shades,* 321.
17. Hal Lindsey with Carole C. Carlson, *The Late Great Planet Earth,* 140.
18. Howard Sounes, *Down the Highway: The Life of Bob Dylan,* (New York: Grove Press, 2001), 332.
19. Nancy Gibbs et al., "Apocalypse Now," *Time* magazine, July 1, 2002.

Chapel and the Vineyard Fellowship. Kenn Gulliksen, the founder of the Vineyard, and Lindsey were close friends.[20] Clinton Heylin says Lindsey "was once a leading member of the Vineyard Church" and Bill Jackson mentions that Lindsey was one of the celebrities who was attracted to the Vineyard.[21]

In *The Late Great Planet Earth* Lindsey and Carlson present a view of the end of the world known in theological circles as "pretribulational premillennialism."[22] It is called "pretribulational" because those who subscribe to this view interpret the Bible to say that Christian believers, living and dead, will be raptured up to heaven *before* an intense seven-year period of suffering known as the "Great Tribulation." Those who convert during or after the tribulation will be able to join the millennial kingdom when Christ returns during the second coming. In other words, according to pretribulationalists, there are, in effect, two "second comings." This view is called "premillennialist" because those who hold it believe that the (final) second coming of Christ, the coming associated with the final judgment, will occur *before* the millennium. When He returns, He—not humankind—will establish this millennium, this glorious Kingdom of God, and He will rule over it from the throne of David in Jerusalem.

Postmillennialists, on the other hand, believe that Christ will return *after* a millennium that will have been already established by a faithful cadre of Christian believers. In *The Meaning of the Millennium: Four Views* Loraine Boettner explains that postmillennialists believe that "the kingdom of God is now being extended in the world through the preaching of the gospel and saving work of the Holy Spirit in the hearts of individuals, that the world eventually is to be Christianized and that the return of Christ is to occur at the close of a long period of righteousness and peace commonly called the millennium."[23] Lindsey has nothing but scorn for postmillennialists. World War I "disheartened" the postmillennialists, he says, and World War II "virtually wiped out this viewpoint." "No self-respecting scholar," Lindsey says, holds this view today.[24]

---

20. Rudy Maxa, "Bob Dylan Knocks on Heaven's Door, Accepts Christ, Says a West Coast Pastor as the Music Biz and the Star's Fans Await an Album to Explain It All," *Washington Post*, May 27, 1979.
21. Clinton Heylin, *Bob Dylan: Behind the Shades*, 321; and Bill Jackson, *The Quest for the Radical Middle*, 80.
22. Pretribulational premillennialism is sometimes called "dispensational premillennialism."
23. Loraine Boettner, "Postmillennialism," in *The Meaning of the Millenium: Four Views*, ed. Robert G. Clouse (Downers Grove, IL: InterVarsity Press, 1977), 117.
24. Hal Lindsey with Carole C. Carlson , *The Late Great Planet Earth*, 176.

Scholars like Loraine Boettner, whom I presume is self-respecting, do hold this view, however; and others, like Anthony A. Hoekema, support a view of end times known as amillennialism (also called "realized" or "inaugurated" millennialism).[25] Amillennialists believe that the millennium was inaugurated at Christ's first coming and that it extends to Christ's second coming. In other words, we are now living in the "millennium," a word which—both postmillennialists and amillennialists agree—should not be understood to mean literally 1000 years. Amillennialists believe that by living a sinless life and by dying for our sins Christ won a decisive victory over Satan. In this view Christ is already reigning on earth and that is why sin, while not annihilated, has been curtailed. For amillennialists the Kingdom of God is not only a future hope but also a present reality.

It is very difficult to distinguish postmillennialism from amillennialism because advocates of both views believe that the second coming of Christ will be preceded by an age in which peace and righteousness will gradually increase. Neither claims that the end of the world is near, emphasizing instead that the present age may well continue for a long time. Neither believes that Satan rules the world and neither are obsessed with sin, believing instead that good is the rule and evil the exception. Both emphasize that church members should not wait for the end but work to improve the present age, not simply by converting others, but also through social and political action. These two approaches are called by different names primarily because the amillennialists believe we are now living in the millennium, that Christ is now reigning on earth, and therefore one cannot call them postmillennialists, who believe Christ returns after the millennium. I do not want to belabor the differences between end time scenarios. What I wish to emphasize is that Dylan embraced premillennialism, the most apocalyptic of the various views of the apocalypse available to him, a view that emphasizes the imminent end of the world, that sees Satan as controlling human affairs, and that suggests believers should focus on personal salvation and evangelism, not political or social action.

---

25. Anthony A. Hoekema, "Amillennialism," in *The Meaning of the Millenium: Four Views*, ed. Robert G. Clouse (Downers Grove, IL: InterVarsity Press, 1977), 155-187.

Lindsey's premillennial view prevailed among the Jesus People and in many evangelical churches, including the Vineyard.[26] The authors of *Jesus People* (1972) observe that "Lindsey's approach [pretribulational premillennialism] probably finds favor with a greater number of Jesus People than any of the other approaches."[27] In his history of the Vineyard, Bill Jackson calls *The Late Great Planet Earth* "a classic restatement of pretribulational premillennialism in a package the youth culture could embrace." The popularity of the book, Jackson says, helped boost membership in both the Calvary and Vineyard churches.[28] Dylan, as we have seen, was influenced by it and expressed premillennial views often in his between-song speeches on his Gospel Tour. In these speeches Dylan emphasizes an imminent apocalypse, repeating often that we're living in end times; he stresses Satan's power, repeating often that Satan is the "God of this world"; and he discourages social and political action—even education, commenting repeatedly that these pursuits are futile because "the Devil's got a plan" and the world will soon be destroyed.[29]

Dylan reveals a fascination with the apocalypse in his pre-conversion songs, a fact which suggests we should not overemphasize the influence of Lindsey and Carlson's book or the Vineyard Bible course Dylan took. In pre-conversion songs like "The Times They Are a-Changin'," "Blowin' in the Wind," "A Hard Rain's A-Gonna Fall," and "It's All Over Now, Baby Blue" his "apocalypticism," Cartwright points out, "was relatively a-historical." In these songs, he says, Dylan used apocalyptic images "primarily to express cataclysmic upheavals in society and in personal lives. His emphasis was upon the poetic and artistic imagery which largely conveyed feeling."[30] It is true that in these pre-conversion apocalyptic songs Dylan does not indicate that he is talking specifically about the second coming of Christ, as he does in conversion-period songs like "Are You Ready?"; or in "When He Returns" in which he sings "Don't you cry and don't you die and don't you burn / For like a thief in the night, He'll replace wrong with right /

---

26. It seems that both Calvary and Vineyard churches support a premillennial view of the end of the world. They differ, however, on when the rapture will occur. Calvary pastors believe in a pre-tribulation rapture, Vineyard pastors in a post-tribulation rapture. See Bill Jackson, *The Quest for the Radical Middle*, 86.
27. Ronald M. Enroth et al., *The Jesus People*, 190.
28. Bill Jackson, *The Quest for the Radical Middle*, 32.
29. Bob Dylan talks about living in end times and mentions Satan's power in many of his between-song sermons on this Gospel Tour. See, for example, speeches 7, 8, 10, 15, 21, and 61 in Clinton Heylin, ed., *Saved! The Gospel Speeches of Bob Dylan*.
30. Bert Cartwright, *The Bible in the Lyrics of Bob Dylan* (Bury, Lancashire, England: Wanted Man, 1992), 110.

When He returns."[31] In this second song Dylan echoes Thessalonians 5:2: "For yourselves know perfectly that the day of the Lord so cometh as a thief in the night."

His earlier, pre-conversion songs, however, do contain biblical allusions and imagery; and Dylan, in a between-song sermon at a concert in Albuquerque on December 5, 1979, suggests that he also had Jesus in mind when he wrote them. "I told you 'The Times They Are A-Changin',' he says, "and they did. I said the answer was 'Blowin' in the Wind,' and it was. I'm telling you now Jesus is coming back, and He is."[32] Maybe Dylan is saying: "My prophecies in these first two songs ("Blowin' in the Wind" and "The Times They are a-Changin'") weren't about the second coming of Christ, but they came true, so you should believe my prophecy about the second coming of Christ in my Christian songs." Or maybe Dylan did have the second coming in mind when he wrote these two earlier songs. Note how "The Times They Are a-Changin'" ends:

> The order is rapidly fadin'
> And the first one now
> Will later be last
> For the times they are a-changin'

These lines clearly evoke Matthew 19:30: "But many *that are* first shall be last; and the last *shall be* first." These words of Christ to his disciples are commonly interpreted to mean that those who are first in this life—the rich and powerful, for example—may be the last to enter the Kingdom of God when Christ returns and the Final Judgment occurs. In other words, one shouldn't expect the Kingdom of God to follow the ways of this world.

If Dylan was prophesying the second coming in these early pre-conversion songs, then we should see his dramatic conversion in 1979 as an intensification and reaffirmation of previous beliefs, not the adoption of a whole new belief system. This is the view of Francis J. Beckwith who argues that Dylan, by alluding to this Bible passage from the Gospel of Matthew, "appeals to an ancient understanding of the last judgment found in the Christian Bible." In "The Times They Are a-Changin'," he points out, "it's the *times*, not the moral principles, that are changing."[33] "Apparently,

---

31. *A Thief in the Night*, a Christian end times film that appeared in 1972, takes its title from the same Bible passage that Dylan references in this song, 1 Thessalonians 5:2.
32. Clinton Heylin, ed., *Saved! The Gospel Speeches of Bob Dylan*, Speech #4, 12-13.
33. Francis J. Beckwith, "Busy Being Born Again: Bob Dylan's Christian Philosophy," in *Bob Dylan and Philosophy*, eds. Peter Vernezze and Carl J. Porter (Chicago: Open Court, 2006), 152.

for Dylan," he adds, "the times were changing [in the 1960s] because there was a hearkening back to first principles that should have been but were not applied to those who were oppressed and for whose cause in the American civil rights movement Dylan offered support." Beckwith argues that Dylan's so-called Christian albums are not unusual anomalies but rather should be seen as "seamlessly connected" to a Christian moral tradition that underlies both his pre- and post-conversion songs.[34] At the end of this chapter I will return to this question of how anomalous songs on Dylan's Christian albums are.

FOUR APOCALYPTIC MOTIFS

In discussing Dylan and the apocalypse some scholars find it useful to distinguish songs with an apocalyptic aesthetic (or "ethos," or "poetics," or "imagination") from songs that present the Bible's view of end times (as interpreted by Lindsey and Carlson and other evangelical theologians). Bert Cartwright suggests this distinction when he talks about an "a-historical apocalypticism" in Dylan's pre-conversion songs which differs from the more biblical variety found in many songs on his Christian albums.[35] "First exploring the bible's apocalyptic imagery from an artistic perspective of potent symbol," Cartwright says, "Dylan eventually adopted a quite literal understanding of the way God would get even with evil and, with his chosen few, prevail."[36] In protest songs written in the 1960s—songs like "The Times They Are a-Changin'" and "It's All Over Now, Baby Blue"—it is difficult to know, Cartwright says, whether Dylan's "apocalyptic allusions" are just a poetic way of suggesting drastic change is coming or whether he has in mind the Bible's account of end times.

David Janssen and Edward Whitelock discuss four "apocalyptic motifs" in Dylan's songs: the secular, the profane, the Romantic, and the sacred. They argue that "Dylan's interest in, one might say obsession with, apocalypse has informed his work from the start." Dylan's gospel period, they say, "could be seen as simply the most obvious manifestation of that interest/obsession."[37] Janssen and Whitelock's "central assertion" is that "apocalypse is everywhere"—not just in Dylan's songs but in all rock and roll. "From its earliest formation," they argue, "rock and roll has been the

---

34. Ibid., 151-152.
35. Bert Cartwright, *The Bible in the Lyrics of Bob Dylan*, 110.
36. Ibid., 121.
37. David Janssen and Edward Whitelock, *Apocalypse Jukebox*, 116.

music of apocalypse, a soundtrack for the end of the world, a simultaneously private and public repository for the anxiety of temporality."[38] They say, however, that of all the rock and rollers, Dylan has produced "the most prolific body of work concerned with the apocalypse."[39] Janssen and Whitelock could be accused of overstating their case for rock and roll generally but regarding Dylan I do not think they exaggerate. They make a convincing case for apocalyptic motifs not just in Dylan's Christian songs but in his pre-conversion songs as well. In fact, they spend very little time discussing songs from Dylan's so-called "Christian albums."

Much depends, of course, on what one means by an "apocalyptic motif." Here are some examples to clarify what Janssen and Whitelock mean by the term. In explaining apocalyptic motifs of the *secular* variety they mention "Talkin' World War III Blues" from *The Freewheelin' Bob Dylan* (1962). The speaker in this song has had a crazy dream about "walkin' into World War III" and goes to see a doctor. "Tell me about [the dream]," the doctor says, and the speaker does, recounting incidents like this one:

> *Well, I spied a girl and before she could leave*
> *"Let's go and play Adam and Eve"*
> *I took her by the hand and my heart it was thumpin'*
> *When she said "Hey man, you crazy or sumpin'*
> *You see what happened last time they started"*

After listening the doctor tells the speaker that he has been having a similar dream, except that he "dreamt that the only person left after the war was me / I didn't see you around." In songs about the apocalypse, Janssen and Whitelock point out, Dylan often combines "ribald humor, utter doom, and world destruction."[40] Songs like "Talkin' World War III Blues" and also "Highway 61 Revisited," which include comedic elements, contrast with the "tragic mien" of "A Hard Rain's a-Gonna Fall."[41] These songs are primarily about a secular apocalypse. They are not, Janssen and Whitelock say, "promoting" Armageddon, at least not the Armageddon of the Book of Revelation. Often, however, Janssen and Whitelock point out, Dylan mixes "the sacred and the secular to the point that one cannot make clear

---

38. Ibid., 6.
39. Ibid., 101.
40. Ibid., 103.
41. Ibid.

distinctions between the two, which just may be the point."[42] The authors make this observation about songs on Dylan's *The Basement Tapes*, but it could apply to songs on many albums.

By *profane* apocalyptic motifs Janssen and Whitelock mean portrayals of the end that are terrible, frightening, and disorienting but also humorous. They argue that unlike "pulpit-pounders" (people like Hal Lindsey, Tim LaHaye and Jerry Jenkins) Dylan doesn't hesitate to explore the "comic absurdities" of being left behind.[43] They agree with Robert Shelton that to understand Dylan's profanely apocalyptic works one should place them in the context of the grotesque,[44] and they cite Mikhail Bakhtin, a leading theorist on the grotesque, who argues that the grotesque can take away our fears by turning what frightens us into "amusing or ludicrous monstrosities."[45] Janssen and Whitelock find profane and grotesque apocalyptic motifs in many songs—"It's Alright, Ma (I'm only Bleeding)," "Ballad of a Thin Man," "Desolation Row," for example—but the epitome of Dylan's grotesque vision is found, they say, in "Stuck Inside of Mobile with the Memphis Blues Again." In this song Shakespeare in pointed shoes is talking to a French girl, railroad men are drinking blood like wine and smoking eyelids, and a preacher is dressed in twenty pounds of headlines. These are ludicrous images, but there's "apocalyptic fear," Janssen and Whitelock argue, in the refrain: "Oh, Mama, can this really be the end / To be stuck inside of Mobile / With the Memphis blues again."[46]

In explaining *Romantic* apocalyptic motifs in Dylan's songs Janssen and Whitelock distinguish Romanticism from romance. Romanticism, or "Romantic idealism," is, they explain, "the constant sense of personal quest, in which the artist is hero, along with an intense interest in creative revision."[47] They suggest that Dylan resembles the English Romantics— Blake, Lord Byron, Shelley, and Coleridge—and argue that there is "a direct line from Dylan to Allen Ginsberg to Walt Whitman, America's great Romantic poet."[48] By "romance" Janssen and Whitelock mean "the pursuit of love in all its human forms, but especially the passions

---

42. Ibid., 104.
43. Ibid., 108.
44. Ibid., 107. See also Robert Shelton, *No Direction Home: The Life and Times of Bob Dylan* (New York: Morrow, 1986), 389.
45. Ibid., 107-108. Janssen and Whitelock quote Mikhail Bakhtin, *Rabelais and His World*, trans. Hélène Iswolksy (Cambridge: MIT Press, 1968), 47.
46. Ibid., 110.
47. Ibid., 111.
48. Ibid.

of the heart."[49] Dylan, they argue, is both a Romantic and a romantic. Merging these two roles, however, is almost always going to fail—or lead to some kind of personal apocalypse—because "Romanticism is a mode of idealistic expression that can never be complete or fulfilled, due to our very real limitations, but for those who are attracted to Romanticism, it is the pursuit that matters, not the endpoint."[50]

Janssen and Whitelock do not mention Ralph Waldo Emerson, but Dylan's Romanticism can also be traced back to this champion of individualism. In "Self-Reliance" Emerson argued that society hampers the Romantic quest. "The voices which we hear in solitude . . . grow faint and inaudible as we enter into the world. Society everywhere is in conspiracy against the manhood of every one of its members. . . . Whoso would be a man must be a nonconformist." Elizabeth Brake relates Dylan's concept of freedom to Emerson's.[51] Like Emerson, she says, Dylan worries about a "deforming conformity," and warns his lovers about it frequently, like in these lines from "To Ramona":

> But it grieves my heart, love,
> To see you tryin' to be a part of
> A world that just don't exist
> It's all just a dream, babe
> A vacuum, a scheme, babe
> That sucks you into feelin' like this

It is this fear of conformity which leads Dylan to oppose conventions of *romance*, which, if he were willing to observe them, might save a loving relationship—thereby preventing a personal apocalypse. "To challenge *romantic* conventions is a *Romantic* impulse inasmuch as it suggests change," Janssen and Whitelock say, and they see this impulse operating in "It Ain't Me, Babe":[52]

> You say you're lookin' for someone
> Who'll pick you up each time you fall
> To gather flowers constantly
> An' to come each time you call
> A lover for your life an' nothing more

---

49. Ibid.
50. Ibid.
51. Elizabeth Brake, "'To Live Outside the Law, You Must Be Honest': Freedom in Dylan's Lyrics," in *Bob Dylan and Philosophy*, eds. Peter Vernezze and Carl J. Porter (Chicago, IL: Open Court), 78-89.
52. David Janssen and Edward Whitelock, *Apocalypse Jukebox*, 113.

> *But it ain't me, babe*
> *No, no, no, it ain't me, babe*
> *It ain't me you're lookin' for, babe*

"All I Really Want to Do," they say, "works in a similar vein." Here's the last stanza:

> *I don't want to fake you out*
> *Take or shake or forsake you out*
> *I ain't lookin' for you to feel like me*
> *See like me or be like me*
> *All I really want to do*
> *Is, baby, be friends with you*

According to Janssen and Whitelock, Romantics love "creative change." Dylan's anti-love songs, they suggest, can be explained as a *Romantic's* refusal to be *romantic*, to play the game of love in the old, boring, and conventional way—by bringing flowers, fawning over one's lover, etc. Attempts to merge the Romantic and the romantic lead to failure. Songs like "New Morning," in which Dylan finds love, are, Janssen and Whitelock say, "not representative of Dylan." There is, they say, "a lot more breaking up than making up in his songs."[53]

In calling Dylan's doomed love affairs romantic apocalypses Janssen and Whitelock may reveal a fondness for hyperbole. Doomed love affairs are not the end of the world, at least not literally the end of the world. As Bert Cartwright explains, at first Dylan's apocalypses appeared to be disasters in the world or in his personal life; people did not understand them to be references to biblical accounts of how the world would end. As Janssen and Whitelock argue Dylan's apocalypses first were *secular*; then, in the songs he sang on his Gospel Tour, they became *sacred*.

Why was Dylan so fascinated with the apocalypse generally and, specifically, with Lindsey and Carlson's account of it? One possible reason is that the nation of Israel, the spiritual home of Dylan's Jewish ancestors, is a key player in Lindsey and Carlson's prophetic scenario. In their interpretation of the Bible, Israel must be restored and the Jews converted before Christ's second coming. "What has happened and what is happening right now to Israel," they insist, "is significant in the entire prophetic picture."[54] They argue that the end of the British mandate and the proclamation of

---

53. David Janssen and Edward Whitelock, *Apocalypse Jukebox*, 112.
54. Hal Lindsey with Carole C. Carlson, *The Late Great Planet Earth*, 44.

the state of Israel on May 14, 1948 are predicted in Matthew 24: 32, 33 and 4, where it is said Christ will return when the fig tree puts forth leaves. The "fig tree," they say, "has been a historic symbol of national Israel."[55] They distinguish Israel's "physical restoration" from its "spiritual restoration."[56] The former will occur "shortly before the Messiah's coming" and the latter "just after His return to this earth."[57] The spiritual rebirth, which would involve the conversion of Jews to Christianity, would be "the beginning of the everlasting kingdom which the Messiah is promised to bring."[58] Lindsey and Carlson are certainly not the first eschatologists to stress the importance of Israel. Lindsey and Carlson themselves cite Increase Mather who emphasized the importance of Israel's restoration in *The Mystery of Israel's Salvation* (1669).[59] "It was generally agreed by all Christian eschatologists through the centuries," says Ernest Lee Tuveson in *Redeemer Nation*, "that the predictions of Christ's second advent could not be fulfilled before the conversion and ingathering of the people of the promise [the Jewish people]."[60] The New England Puritans carried this view to America.

Some theologians and scholars are not as certain as Lindsey and Carlson that the Bible predicts the literal return of Jews to Israel and the physical restoration of the nation. Theologians call Lindsey and Carlson's view of end times "dispensational premillennialism." It is premillennialism because they believe that Christ will return *before* the millennium and play a key role in ushering it in. It is dispensational because they believe that true believers will be raptured up to heaven before Christ's second coming. Dispensationalism was introduced by John Nelson Darby (1800-1882) who argued that human history was divided into dispensations, or stages during which God dealt with his chosen people in different ways. Darby, an Anglo-Irish evangelist who was associated with the Plymouth Brethren, brought dispensational views from Great Britain to the United States. Lindsey and Carlson, like Darby, believe that there will be two "second comings"—that Christ will return before the Great Tribulation to snatch (or rapture) believers, living and dead, up to heaven,

55. Ibid., 53.
56. In discussing the restoration of Israel, Lindsey and Carlson cite passages from Chapters 36 through 39 of Ezekiel.
57. Ibid., 48.
58. Ibid., 62.
59. Hal Lindsey with Carole C. Carlson, *The Late Great Planet Earth*, 50.
60. Ernest Lee Tuveson, *Redeemer Nation: The Idea of America's Millennial Role* (Chicago: University of Chicago Press, 1968), 138.

an experience Lindsey and Carlson refer to as the "ultimate trip."[61] Christ will return again after the Great Tribulation, which will end with the battle of Armageddon, to save the world and judge the wicked.

Based on their reading of Scripture, Lindsey and Carlson conclude that the physical restoration of Israel entails three important events: "First, the Jewish nation would be reborn in the land of Palestine. Secondly, the Jews would repossess old Jerusalem and the sacred sites. Thirdly, they would rebuild their ancient temple of worship upon its historic site."[62] They see the first event as having occurred when David Ben-Gurion announced the formation of the state of Israel on May 14, 1948.[63] They see the second event, the repossession of sacred sites, as having occurred during the Six-Day War in 1967 when Israel defeated the United Arab Republic, Jordan, and Syria. More specifically they say it occurred when Moshe Dyan, the Israeli general, "marched to the wailing wall, the last remnant of the Old Temple, and said, 'We have returned to our holiest of holy places, never to leave her again.'"[64] Referring to the Israeli victory in the Six-Day War, Lindsey and Carlson say that "Again, against incredible odds, the Jews had unwittingly further set up the stage for their final hour of trial and conversion."[65]

The last event, the rebuilding of the Temple in old Jerusalem, is still in the future. It will occur, they say, "shortly before" Jesus Christ's return to establish his ever-lasting Kingdom.[66] For Lindsey and Carlson this sign was crucial. They are encouraged when, after the Six-Day War and the recapture of Jerusalem, Israeli leaders began to talk about rebuilding the Temple.[67] For them the occurrence of the first two events and talk of the third sets the stage for the unfolding of other events that will soon lead to Armageddon and the coming of the millennium. Many evangelical Christians have adopted Lindsey and Carlson's view of end times, or a view very similar to it. They see Israel not only as a democratic ally in America's struggle to keep Iran and other Muslim countries at bay but also as a sacred place where events must unfold in a certain way to ensure the second coming of Christ.

---

61. Hal Lindsey with Carole C. Carlson, *The Late Great Planet Earth*, 135, 137, 144.
62. Ibid., 50-51.
63. Ibid., 53.
64. Ibid., 55.
65. Ibid.
66. Ibid., 52.
67. Ibid., 57.

Evangelicals supporting Israel for these reasons is not a new phenomenon. In *When Time Shall Be No More*, Paul Boyer describes how Christian premillennialists have supported Israel over the years and how Israeli politicians have courted and welcomed this support. These Israeli politicians played "the fundamentalist card," Boyer writes, while "privately ridiculing premillennialist readings of prophecy as those of a six-year old child."[68] In 1971 Prime Minister David Ben-Gurion welcomed 1500 delegates from different countries to a prophecy conference in Jerusalem. At this conference, Chaim Herzog, Israel's U.N. ambassador at the time, gave an interview for the film version of Lindsey and Carlson's *The Late Great Planet Earth*.[69] What Boyer calls an "Israeli-premillennial nexus" has existed for a long time and continues to the present day. In 1982 Louis Goldberg of the Moody Bible Institute wrote that Israel and prophecy went together like lox and bagels.[70]

They are still linked. Their belief that events must unfold in Israel in a certain way to ensure the second coming of Christ is one reason why evangelical Christians support conservative politicians who are pro-Israel—politicians like Ronald Reagan and Donald Trump. During Reagan's administration Hal Lindsey was a consultant on Middle East affairs in the Pentagon. Reagan's Secretary of the Interior, James Watt, a pentecostalist, once said: "I don't know how many future generations we can count on until the Lord returns." Reagan's Secretary of Defense, Caspar Weinberger, worried that the end of the world was coming soon. "I have read the Book of Revelation," he said, "and, yes, I believe the world is going to end—by an act of God, I hope—but every day I think time is running out."[71]

Evangelical Christians are strong supporters of the Trump administration whereas American Jews are not. (More than 75% of American Jews voted for the Democrats in the mid-term election in 2018.)[72] When on May 14, 2018, President Trump moved the American Embassy from Tel Aviv to Jerusalem, two evangelical pastors, John Hagee and Robert Jeffress,

---

68. Paul Boyer, *When Time Shall Be No More*, 204.
69. Ibid.
70. Louis Goldberg, *Turbulence over the Middle East* (Neptune, NJ: Loizeaux Brothers, 1982), 16. Cited by Paul Boyer, *When Time Shall Be No More*, 189.
71. Nancy Gibbs et al. quote these announcements of belief in the imminent end of the world by members of President Reagan's administration. See Nancy Gibbs et al, "Apocalypse Now."
72. Jonathan Weisman, "American Jews and Israeli Jews Are Headed for a Messy Breakup," *New York Times*, January 4, 2019.

consecrated the ceremony.[73] Pastor Hagee is the Founder and National Chairman of Christians United for Israel. Robert Jeffress, one of Trump's loyal supporters, is pastor of the First Baptist Church in Dallas, Texas, a church with 13,000 members. He is also host of a daily radio program and a frequent guest speaker for Fox News. In the story of end times promoted by Lindsey and Carlson and the Vineyard and other evangelical churches, Jews and Israel and the holy city of Jerusalem play important roles. This feature may have made the form of Christianity they were promoting attractive to Dylan who was raised in a Jewish family.

I return now to the question of whether the songs on Dylan's Christian albums—*Slow Train Coming* (1979), *Saved* (1980), and *Shot of Love* (1981)—are similar to or very different from songs on his pre- and post-conversion albums. Francis J. Beckwith, as I pointed out at the end of the last section, argues that Dylan's songs, both pre- and post-conversion, are "seamlessly connected to a similar, if not the same, moral tradition."[74] He discusses "Gospel Plow," "The Lonesome Death of Hattie Carroll" and "With God on Our Side," all pre-conversion songs, and "When You Gonna Wake Up?" and "Slow Train" from *Slow Train Coming*, Dylan's first post-conversion album, and finds in all of them a commitment to the same Christian moral principles that all people in all times should abide by.

I find it difficult to accept Francis Beckwith's claim that Dylan's "lifelong project" was to preach Christian virtues.[75] Dylan explains in his autobiography that he never wanted to be a spokesman for a cause. In the mid-1960s he had already grown tired of "finger-pointing songs," especially topical or protest songs. By that time, as Mike Marqusee explains, the vindictiveness toward wrongdoers that Dylan expressed in songs like "Masters of War" and "The Lonesome Death of Hattie Carroll" had become abstracted from politics—a "strictly person to person" problem.[76] In his anti-love songs, I argue in Chapter Six, it became a man to woman problem. The speakers in "It Ain't Me, Babe," "Like a Rolling Stone" and "Just Like a Woman" are angry at women for relatively minor character flaws—for being too possessive, for dressing too fine, for acting immaturely; they don't accuse them of breaking the Christian moral rules that Beckwith seems to have in mind.

---

73. Ibid.
74. Francis J. Beckwith, "Busy Being Born Again," 152.
75. Ibid., 145.
76. Mike Marqusee, *Chimes of Freedom* (New York: The New Press, 2003), 153.

I find Bert Cartwright's view more convincing. "Dylan's conversion in late 1978 to a fundamentalist born-again form of Christian expression," Cartwright argues, "marks a sharp change in his knowledge and use of the Bible."[77] He acknowledges that Dylan was interested in the Bible throughout his career, but says that his conversion made his religion more personal and more joyful. Before, Cartwright argues, Dylan saw the Bible as a book of moral rules but after his conversion it became "a source book for personal piety."[78] He suggests that the Vineyard course taught by Kenn Gulliksen helped bring about Dylan's change in outlook. He quotes Gulliksen who told a reporter that the course Dylan took was "designed primarily so the person would know the Lord as a person, not just the book."[79] Cartwright also emphasizes the joy that Dylan found in his religion after his conversion, a joy that is expressed in "Saved." Here is the second stanza:

> *I've been saved*
> *By the blood of the lamb*
> *Saved*
> *By the blood of the lamb*
> *Saved*
> *Saved*
> *And I'm so glad*
> *Yes, I'm so glad*
> *I'm so glad*
> *So glad*
> *I want to thank You, Lord*
> *I just want to thank You, Lord*
> *Thank You, Lord*

The biggest difference between the pre- and post-conversion Dylan, however, is that after his conversion Dylan wanted to convert others to his brand of fundamentalist Christianity. Kenn Gulliksen and Hal Lindsey were good friends and had a similar (dispensationalist premillennialist) view of end times, a view that Dylan accepted and began preaching about in his between-song sermons on his Gospel Tour. Dylan had, Cartwright says, "long been intrigued by apocalyptic imagery," but before he was converted this imagery was "relatively ahistorical"—used "primarily to

---

77. Bert Cartwright, "The Bible in the Lyrics of Bob Dylan," 105.
78. Ibid., 112-113.
79. Ibid., 113. Cartwright cites this source: Dan Wooding, "Bob Dylan—By His Pastor," *Buzz* (U.K.), November 1980, 4-5.

express cataclysmic upheavals in society and personal lives. Cartwright has in mind songs like "A Hard Rain's Gonna Fall," "The Times They Are a-Changin'" and "It's All Over Now, Baby Blue."[80] In his post-conversion songs, however, his apocalyptic imagery became "historical." It was used to present the Bible's account—as interpreted by Lindsey and Carlson— of end times. When David Janssen and Edward Whitelock in *Apocalypse Jukebox* contrast "secular apocalypse" with "sacred apocalypse," they make a similar distinction.[81]

---

80. Bert Cartwright, "The Bible in the Lyrics of Bob Dylan," 110.
81. David Janssen and Edward Whitelock, *Apocalypse Jukebox*, 102-103 and passim.

28

GOD'S WRATH & DYLAN'S DEVIL

R evelation, Dylan's favorite book in the Bible, is, among other things, an account of how God will pour down his wrath on unbelievers. In Hal Lindsey and Carole C. Carlson's pretribulational, premillennial account believers will be raptured to heaven before tribulation begins; non-believers, however, will experience seven years of terrible suffering. According to Lindsey and Carlson the Great Tribulation will begin when the Great Dictator—the Antichrist, the leader of the revived Roman empire—signs a pact with the Israelis and allows them to rebuild their Temple.[1] Just before and during Christ's return, seven vials or bowls of wrath will be unleashed on the "Christ-rejecting world."[2] These seven vials, also referred to as the seven plagues, include painful sores and other physical afflictions, as well as natural disasters like fires that scorch the earth, and earthquakes.

Postmillennialists and amillennialists have a kinder, gentler view of end times. They both believe that the world is getting better through the efforts of Christian believers. They tend to downplay the terrors of the tribulation period, predicting that Christian believers will usher in the millennium through good works (for postmillennialists) or that a better

---

1. Hal Lindsey with Carole C. Carlson, *The Late Great Planet Earth* (Grand Rapids, MI: Zondervan, 1970), 152. See also my "Events Leading to Armageddon in Dylan's 'Second Bible' " in Appendix B, item #5.
2. Hal Lindsey with Carole C. Carlson, *The Late Great Planet Earth*, 163. See also verses 15 and 16 of the Book of Revelation.

world—the millennium—has already been realized thanks to Christ's sacrifice (for amillennialists). For Lindsey and Carlson, however, and I believe for Dylan, the world is too awash in sin to be saved by the efforts of a few uncorrupted believers. When you got "Adulterers in churches and pornography in the schools / You got gangsters in power and lawbreakers making rules," as Dylan says in "When You Gonna Wake Up?", you need an angry God threatening eternal damnation of the wicked to clean up the mess. Well-meaning Christians are no match for Satan.

The God of both the Hebrew Scriptures or Old Testament and the New Testament is definitely an angry and vengeful God. The Bible contains more references to God's wrath than to his love and kindness.[3] Some sample passages:

Psalms 7:11—God judgeth the righteous, and God is angry with the wicked every day.

Nahum 1:2—God is jealous, and the Lord revengeth; the Lord revengeth, and is furious; the Lord will take vengeance on his adversaries, and he reserveth wrath for his enemies.

Nahum 1:6—Who can stand before his indignation? And who can abide in the fierceness of his anger? His fury is poured out like fire, and the rocks are thrown down by him.

Romans 1:18—For the wrath of God is revealed from heaven against all ungodliness and unrighteousness of men, who hold the truth in unrighteousness.[4]

Revelation 6:17—For the great day of his wrath is come; and who shall be able to stand?

Christians believe, however, that God's wrath is a "*corollary* or *function* of divine care."[5] "His wrath," explains Abraham J. Heschel, "is not regarded as an emotional outburst, as an irrational fit, but rather as a part of His continual care."[6] The word "anger" in the Bible, Herschel says, "denotes what we call righteous indignation, aroused by that which is considered

---

3. Bob Deffinbaugh, "The Wrath of God," Bible.org—World's Largest Bible Study Site, http://bible.org/seriespage/wrath-god (accessed July 29, 2011).
4. In the New International Version of the Bible, the clause that ends this verse ("who hold the truth in unrighteousness") is translated as "who suppress the truth by their wickedness."
5. Robert Oakes, "The Wrath of God," *Philosophy of Religion* 27 (1990), 130.
6. Abraham J. Heschel, *The Prophets* (New York: Harper and Row, 1962), 293.

mean, shameful or sinful; it is impatience with evil." And, he adds, "Indifference to evil is more insidious than evil itself."[7]

The prophets in the Bible—Isaiah, Jeremiah, Ezekiel, Daniel, and John the Divine—whose prophecies Dylan and Lindsey and Carlson see coming true in the present age all predicted that God would pour his wrath down on unbelievers. Dylan clearly admired the Old Testament prophet Jeremiah and quotes him on the sleeve of his album *Saved*.[8] Because Jeremiah talked so much about the wrath that God would inflict on the people of Israel, he has been called the "prophet of wrath."[9] "Behold, a whirlwind of the Lord is gone forth in fury, even a grievous whirlwind," Jeremiah prophecies. "It shall fall grievously upon the head of the wicked."[10] Biblical prophets described the wrath of God because they wanted their people to mend their ways and avoid it. Emphasizing God's wrath was a way to bring sinners and non-believers into the fold. Modern day Evangelical Christians adopt a similar strategy. "May the doctrine of God's wrath be an incentive to evangelism and the proclamation of a pure gospel," writes Bob Deffinbaugh in his article for the Evangelical website Bible.org.[11] Dylan was a careful reader of the Bible and also someone disturbed by present day problems—militant and corrupt leaders and the lack of social justice, for example—and so it is not surprising that he speaks like a prophet angry at his people's sins. As Bert Cartwright notes, "Dylan relishes the vengeance of a biblical god who in righteous indignation wreaks havoc upon ones held in contempt."[12]

But it is not the Bible alone that helps us understand Dylan's angry tone: It is also the American tradition of the jeremiad, a type of political sermon that originated with the biblical prophets but underwent special development in America. "The term *jeremiad*," David Howard- Pitney explains, which means "a lamentation or doleful complaint," derives from the biblical prophet, Jeremiah, who warned of Israel's fall and the destruction of the Jerusalem temple by Babylonia as punishment for the people's failure to keep the mosaic covenant. The "Mosaic covenant" refers

---

7. Ibid., 283 and 284.
8. Dylan quotes Jeremiah 31:31: "Behold, the days come, saith the Lord, that I will make a new covenant with the house of Israel, and with the house of Judah."
9. Abraham J. Heschel, *The Prophets*, 106.
10. Jeremiah 23:19.
11. Bob Deffinbaugh, "The Wrath of God."
12. Bert Cartwright, *The Bible in the Lyrics of Bob Dylan* ([Place of publication not identified]: [publisher not identified], 1992), 44. An earlier edition was published in 1985 in Bury, Lancashire, England, by Wanted Man.

to the agreement that God made with the people of Israel, represented by Moses, that if they obeyed the Ten Commandments then they would be "a peculiar treasure unto me above all people" (Exodus 19:5)."[13]

The jeremiad, Sacvan Bercovitch says, was "a mode of public exhortation that originated in the European pulpit, was transformed in both form and content by the New England Puritans, persisted through the eighteenth century, and helped sustain a national dream through two hundred years of turbulence and change." It was designed, he adds, "to join social criticism to spiritual renewal."[14] Allen Ginsberg's poem "Howl" and Martin Luther King's "I Have a Dream" speech are examples of the genre. Many of Dylan's songs are jeremiads. It is a genre, Alan Jacobs says, that "has been deeply embedded in American culture since its origins. To condole the innocent downtrodden and condemn their wicked oppressors, preferably in a very loud voice, has for much of our country's history been a highly favored and much-relished practice." And, Jacobs adds, "Few have done it with more flair than Dylan."[15]

Dylan's Judeo-Christian heritage and the tradition of the jeremiad encourage a "loud voice," an angry impatience with suffering and injustice.[16] They help us understand the anger that Dylan expresses toward immoral leaders and other obvious sinners in many songs, not just those on his overtly Christian albums. They help us understand his passion for "finger-pointing." But is Dylan's Judeo-Christian heritage and the jeremiad tradition also at work in his anti-love songs, in which he hits back at former lovers and other people who have incurred his disfavor for one reason or another?[17] At a concert in England on May 4, 1966 after Dylan "went electric"—moved from folk to rock—the crowd booed

---

13. David Howard-Pitney, *The African American Jeremiad: Appeals for Justice in America* (Philadelphia: Temple University Press, 2005), 5.
14. Sacvan Bercovitch, *The American Jeremiad* (Madison, WI: University of Wisconsin Press, 1978), xi.
15. Alan Jacobs, "It Ain't Me Babe," *A Visit to Vanity Fair: Moral Essays on the Present Age* (Grand Rapids, MI: Brazos Press, 2001), 102.
16. David Howard-Pitney calls the American jeremiad "a rhetoric of indignation." See *The African American Jeremiad*, 5.
17. Dylan was the first to refer to his early protest songs as "finger-pointing songs" and journalists and Dylan biographers have adopted the term. See Nat Hentoff, "The Crackin', Shakin', Breakin' Sounds," in *Bob Dylan: The Essential Interviews*, ed. Jonathan Cott (New York: Wenner Books, 2006), 23. Robert Shelton talks about Dylan's "finger-pointing" and "anti-love" songs. See *No Direction Home: The Life and Music of Bob Dylan* (Milwaukee, WI: Backbeat Books, 2011), 185, 192. Alan Jacobs mentions "Dylan's contemptuous insult-songs," giving "Idiot Wind" as an example. His "insult-songs" seem roughly equivalent to Shelton's "anti-love songs." See Alan Jacobs, "It Ain't Me Babe," 103.

and shouted "Sing a protest song."[18] "Oh come on, these are all protest songs," Dylan shouted back. "Aw, it's the same stuff as always. Can't you HEAR?" In a sense that's true: Dylan is always protesting something, either some social injustice or some possessive lover who "wasted his precious time."[19] His political "finger-pointing" songs and his anti-love songs both seem motivated by anger.

But does the Bible justify getting angry at possessive lovers and other people that one finds irritating? In a much discussed biblical passage Christ says that "whosoever is angry with his brother without a cause shall be in danger of the judgment" (Matthew 5:22). This passage is understood not as a condemnation of all anger, only unrighteous anger—anger "without a cause." Christ himself gets angry, as many biblical references attest. "The passion Jesus exhibits the most in the Gospels, with thirty such references," observes Paul Gondreau, "is anger."[20] Perhaps the best known passage is the description of Christ's rage when he found people selling oxen and changing money in the temple (John 2:13-16). On this occasion Christ becomes not just verbally but also physically violent: He whips the money changers with a "scourge of small cords," overturns tables, etc.

The author of the Epistle to the Ephesians says "Be ye angry, and sin not" (4:26), a passage usually interpreted to mean there can be anger without sin, but one has to be careful with anger because it can lead to sin.[21] But a few verses later this same author tells the Ephesians to put away "all bitterness, and wrath, and anger, and clamor" and "be kind to one another."[22] William V. Harris, who discusses anger in classical antiquity and the early Christian period, concludes that the "early Christian tradition about the suppression of human anger was somewhat ambiguous." The New Testament's message regarding anger, he says, is ambivalent: It fails to distinguish "sinful from acceptable anger."[23]

---

18. Martin Scorsese includes this concert in his film *No Direction Home: Bob Dylan* (Hollywood, CA: Paramount Pictures, 2005). See also Mike Marqusee, *Chimes of Freedom: The Politics of Bob Dylan's Art* (New York: The New Press, 2003), 199.
19. See Dylan's song "Don't Think Twice, It's All Right."
20. Paul Gondreau, *The Passions of Christ's Soul in the Theology of St. Thomas Aquinas* (Munster: Aschendorff, 2002), 37.
21. Some scholars consider Paul to be the author of "A Letter to the Ephesians" but others argue it was written in Paul's name by a later author strongly influenced by Paul's thought.
22. Ephesians 4:31-32.
23. William V. Harris, *Restraining Rage: The Ideology of Anger Control in Classical Antiquity* (Cambridge, MA: Harvard University Press, 2001), 396, 399.

Some modern interpretations of the Bible message concerning anger are less ambiguous. One Evangelical Christian website cites key passages and concludes that "Anger, while very likely to become sinful, is not really sinful in itself." Anger at sin and the unrighteousness of men (sic) is "righteous indignation" and is "sinless" but "when anger arises because of wounded or aggrieved personality or feelings, it is sinful and punishable."[24] Dylan frequently sounds "aggrieved," particularly in his anti-love songs in which he criticizes women for various personality flaws. He may only be using women to attack a culture of materialism, but he still sounds mean-spirited and vindictive in these songs. In his early protest songs and in his songs on his Christian albums, Dylan, like the prophet Jeremiah, seems to be in sympathy with divine anger at sin and corruption. It seems likely that some of this same anger spilled over into Dylan's anti-love songs, and this is why there is a bitterness in them that seems out of proportion to the alleged "sins" of the women he addresses.

We see Dylan aligning himself with divine anger in a between-song talk he gave on May 8, 1980, in Hartford, CT, when he was about six months into his Gospel Tour.[25] In this talk he connects God's slaughter of the Amorites with the punishment that Dylan suggests God will rain down on homosexuals in San Francisco for their immoral behavior. God's instrument for the slaughter of the Amorites was Joshua, an assistant of Moses, to whom God says: "And I brought you into the land of the Amorites, which dwelt on the other side Jordan; and they fought with you: and I gave them into your hand, that ye might possess their land; and I destroyed them from before you" (Joshua 24:8). Dylan talks about Joshua in his between-song sermon and also evokes Genesis 15:16: "But in the fourth generation they shall come hither again: for the inequity of the Amorites is not yet full." Its fullness (and the slaughter of the Amorites) would indicate the time when the ancestors of Abraham would return from Egypt and repossess the land of Canaan. "We started out [began the Gospel Tour] in San Francisco," Dylan tells his Hartford, CT audience. "It's

---

24. Entry for "Wrath, (Anger)," in *International Standard Bible Encyclopedia*, ed. James Orr, http://www.searchgodsword.org/enc/isb/view.cgi?number=T9245 (accessed Nov. 30, 2011). Biblical passages cited include Psalms 97:10; Ephesians 4:26; and Mark 3:5.
25. This speech of Dylan's is not included in *Saved!: The Gospel Speeches of Bob Dylan*, ed. Clinton Heylin, but Scott M. Marshall discusses it in *Restless Pilgrim The Spiritual Journey of Bob Dylan* (Orlando, FL: Relevant Books, 2004),47. Marshall quotes from a transcription of Dylan's onstage rap that appeared in an article by Patrick Webster in Freewheelin' Vol. 18, No. 180 (August 2000). P. 31.

kind of a unique town these days. I think it's either one third or two thirds of the population that are homosexuals in San Francisco. I've heard it said. Now, I guess they're working up to a hundred percent. . . . Anyway, I would just think, well, I guess the iniquity's not yet full. And I don't wanna be around when it is!"[26]

In this between-song speech Dylan behaves like the speakers in many of his songs: He is uncompromisingly moralistic, aggrieved by other people's behavior, and certain—when that inequity gets full—of an apocalyptic ending. It seems that Dylan regarded homosexuality as a sign that the end was near. It's not here yet, the iniquity is not yet full, but homosexuality for Dylan is a sure sign that inequity and the apocalypse are "picking up speed," as Dylan would say when he introduced his song "Slow Train" on his Gospel Tour.[27] Dylan's near-fullness of inequity resembles Lindsey and Carlson's ripeness in *The Late Great Planet Earth*. "The time is ripe and getting riper for the Great Dictator, the one we call the 'Future Fuehrer,'" Lindsey and Carlson write. "This is the one," they say, "who is predicted in the Scriptures very clearly and called the 'Antichrist.'"[28] Lindsey and Carlson don't mention homosexuality but they list other signs of ripeness: sun-god worship by fraternity members in California, for example, and drug addiction,[29] and an increase in interest in witchcraft and astrology.[30] Most evangelical churches, including the Vineyard, condemn homosexuality as a sin, and so Dylan may have been revealing his Vineyard training in his remarks at Hartford.[31]

---

26. Ibid.
27. See, for example, Dylan's between-song sermons numbered 10 and 25 in *Saved! The Gospel Speeches of Bob Dylan*, 23, 52.
28. Hal Lindsey with Carole C. Carlson, *The Late Great Planet Earth*, 103.
29. Satan, Lindsey and Carlson say, uses hallucinatory drugs to "take man to a deeper level of approach with him." In *The Late Great Planet Earth* they tell the story of a fraternity member at a university who told him he wanted to know about Christ. The student, however, started "taking trips" and began worshiping the "King of Darkness." See Hal Lindsey with Carole C. Carlson, *The Late Great Planet Earth*, 126.
30. Ibid., 124-126.
31. "We believe that homosexuality is a deviation from the Creator's plan for human sexuality," reads a policy report titled "Homosexuality 2004," issued by the National Association of Evangelicals. See National Association of Evangelicals, https://web.archive.org/web/20110615021140/http://www.nae.net/government-relations/policy-resolutions/181-homosexuality-2004- (accessed March 26, 2013). The Vineyard's opposition to homosexuality is revealed in David Di Sabatino's account of Lonnie Frisbee, the apparently gay Jesus Freak who attracted many young people to the Vineyard. See David Di Sabatino, "Lonnie Frisbee: A Modern Day Samson," Appendix III of Bill Jackson's *The Quest for the Radical Middle* (Cape Town, South Africa: Vineyard International Publishing, 1999), 377-391.

WAS DYLAN'S CHRISTIAN PERIOD AN ANOMALY?

Is the Dylan who links the iniquity of the Amorites to the alleged transgressions of homosexuals really the "typical" Dylan? This question brings us back to a question raised earlier: Was Dylan's Christian period an anomaly, or only a time when Dylan expressed his lifelong Christian views in a more explicit and more "in your face" manner? I believe the latter is closer to the truth. Bert Cartwright analyzes Dylan's use of biblical language and describes five phases, but in all five Dylan expresses Christian ideas, which forces Cartwright to struggle mightily, it seems to me, to distinguish some of his phases from the others.[32] Dylan has been singing so long that it is easy to forget that he sang songs about Jesus on his very first album, *Bob Dylan*, released in 1962. It included two original songs and the rest were covers of old blues and gospel songs like "In My Time of Dyin'," "Fixin' to Die," "Gospel Plow," and "See That My Grave is Kept Clean." If you listen to "In My Time of Dyin'" you will discover that Dylan was singing about the rapture long before Lindsey and Carlson published *The Late Great Planet Earth*. Here is the second stanza of "In My Time of Dyin'" (also called "Jesus Make Up My Dying Bed"), a gospel song written by Blind Willie Johnson in the 1920s. The song alludes to I Thessalonians 4:17[33] and Psalms 41:3.[34] Here is Dylan's second stanza:

> *Well, meet me Jesus, meet me, meet me*
> *in the middle of the air*
> *If these wings should fail to me*
> *Lord, won't you meet me with another pair*
>
> *Well, well, well, so I can die easy*
> *Well, well, well*
> *Well, well, well, so I can die easy*
> *Jesus gonna make up, Jesus gonna make up*
> *Jesus gonna make up my dying bed*

Francis Beckwith begins an article about Dylan's Christian philosophy by quoting these lines from "Gospel Plow":

> *Mary wore three links of chain*
> *Every link was Jesus name*

---

32. Bert Cartwright, *The Bible in the Lyrics of Bob Dylan*.
33. "Then we which are alive and remain shall be caught up together with them in the clouds, to meet the Lord in the air: and so shall we ever be with the Lord."
34. "The Lord will strengthen him upon the bed of languishing: thou wilt make all his bed in his sickness."

Keep your hand on that plow, hold on
Oh Lord, Oh Lord, keep your hand on that plow, hold on

This song "would be, by most accounts of Dylan's life and work," Beckwith says, "better suited for his so-called Christian albums" but by his own account both "Gospel Plow" and these albums are "part of a lifelong project to come to grips with the deeper moral and metaphysical questions that have always found a place in Dylan's art, both before and after his Christian conversion."[35] Beckwith suggests that a deep sense of morality had always "lurked behind" (or "percolated beneath") the surface of Dylan's art, and therefore his conversion to Christianity should not be seen as surprising or inconsistent.[36] Most of the songs he discusses were written before or during his Christian period, but he suggests his post-conversion works also express Christian moral principles.[37]

Beckwith identifies four "aspects" of Dylan's pre-conversion work. He implies that they are all Christian, but only the first—and maybe the second—strike me as specifically Christian or Judeo-Christian; I do not believe the other two are unique to Christianity. The first aspect is Dylan's "assimilation of the Christian narrative," which is, he says, "a story of betrayal, separation, and redemption that has a beginning, a middle, and an end. It is a linear history that began at some finite point in the past and is destined to end at some point in the future, the eschaton [final event in the divine plan]."[38] Dylan read all kinds of books, including some by authors unsympathetic to Christianity, but all were, Beckwith says, "immersed in, shaped by, reacting to, or influenced the formation of the Christian narrative."[39] Dylan's fascination with the apocalypse, as I've already discussed, certainly indicates he was interested in how this narrative ends.

The second Christian aspect of Dylan's pre-Christian work, according to Beckwith, is the assumption that we live in a "moral universe"—that "human beings have an intrinsic moral purpose" and therefore we are fully within our rights to pass judgment on those who don't know right from wrong, on people like the judge (who doubly should know better, being a

---

35. Francis J. Beckwith, "Busy Being Born Again: Bob Dylan's Christian Philosophy," in *Bob Dylan and Philosophy*, ed. Peter Vernezze and Carl J. Porter (Chicago: Open Court, 2006), 145.
36. Ibid., 146, 155.
37. Ibid., 151-152.
38. Ibid., 146.
39. Ibid.

judge himself) in Dylan's "The Lonesome Death of Hattie Carroll" who lets a rich man who killed a hotel maid get off with only a six-month jail term. In this song, Beckwith says, Dylan's understanding is like that expressed by St. Paul who, in his letter to the Romans, says that the wrath of God will fall on wicked men who "suppress the truth by their wickedness."[40] I, too, have argued that Dylan in many songs approves of God's judgment of the sinful and corrupt and sometimes assumes a god-like persona and judges people harshly himself.

Beckwith's third Christian aspect that he sees underlying all of Dylan's work is related to the second. It is a belief in "an objective moral law, one that is universal, unchanging, and applies to all persons in all times and in all places."[41] Beckwith discusses "With God on Our Side," one of Dylan's early songs that Joan Baez praised and sang with Dylan when they toured together. This is the song in which Dylan mentions by name America's wars—the Indian wars, Spanish-American War, the World Wars, Cold War confrontations, etc.—and says the makers of these wars justified them, and their accompanying atrocities, by claiming they had God on their side. This song is not an attack on Christianity, Beckwith says, but rather "an indictment against religious people, especially Christians, who have drifted from the absolute moral principles that they claim to accept."[42]

The final Christian aspect of Dylan's work, according to Beckwith, is his emphasis on the importance of practicing virtue, a theme she finds in Dylan's song "Forever Young," the song that Dylan apparently wrote with his own children in mind:

> *May you always do for others*
> *And let others do for you*
>
> *May you grow up to be righteous*
> *May you grow up to be true*
> *May you always know the truth*
> *And see the lights surrounding you*

He finds this "practicing virtue" theme also in "The Lonesome Death of Hattie Carroll." The light sentence for the aristocrat who killed the maid did not match the crime and therefore, he suggests, it would not encourage people to practice virtue.

---

40. Romans 1:18-19.
41. Francis Beckwith, "Busy Being Born Again: Bob Dylan's Christian Philosophy," 153.
42. Ibid., 151.

DYLAN AND THE DEVIL

Beckwith's last two aspects seem too general to be labeled "Christian." A much more specifically Christian aspect of Dylan's art, one which Beckwith does not discuss, is his focus on sin and the Devil. Sin, the Devil, and redemption are, of course, included within the Christian narrative that Beckwith says Dylan has assimilated, but they are too important to Dylan's worldview and his art to be brushed over quickly. Here is Dylan speaking to Bill Flanagan in a 1986 interview:

> We're all sinners. People seem to think that because their sins are different from other people's sins, they're not sinners. People don't like to think of themselves as sinners. It makes them feel uncomfortable. "What do you mean sinners?" It puts them at a disadvantage in their mind. Most people walking around have this strange conception that they're born good, that they're really good people— but the *world* has just made a mess out of their lives. I have another point of view. But it's not hard for me to identify with anybody who's on the wrong side. We're all on the wrong side, really.[43]

Sin, of course, was surely emphasized in his Vineyard Bible course. That all people are sinners is a key Vineyard belief, one stated in this way on its webpage: "We believe that the whole world is under the domination of Satan and that all people are sinners by nature and choice."[44] In this belief the Vineyard resembles other evangelical churches and fellowships. The *Chambers Dictionary* defines "evangelical" in this way: "Of the school that insists especially on the total depravity of unregenerate human nature, the justification of the sinner by faith alone, the free offer of the Gospel to all, and the plenary inspiration and exclusive authority of the Bible."[45] We have seen that Satan, or the Antichrist, plays a key role in the version of end times emphasized by Vineyard pastors and in Lindsey and Carlson's *The Late Great Planet Earth*. The Antichrist, or the Great Dictator or Future Fuhrer, is the leader of the revived Roman Empire that, Lindsey and Carlson say, will lead the forces of Western civilization in a climatic battle at Armageddon against "the vast hordes of the Orient probably united under the Red Chinese war machine."[46]

---

43. Bill Flanagan, *Written in My Soul* (Chicago: Contemporary Books, 1986), 104.
44. See "Core Values & Statement of Faith," pamphlet by Vineyard USA, available for download at https://vineyardusa.org/about/core-values-beliefs/ (accessed November 2, 2022).
45. Quoted in Clinton Heylin, *Bob Dylan: Behind the Shades* (New York: Summit Books, 1991), 320.
46. Hal Lindsey with Carole C. Carlson, *The Late Great Planet Earth*, 162.

That Dylan was concerned—perhaps even obsessed—about sin and the Devil during his Christian period is beyond all doubt. He referred to both often in the songs he sang and the speeches he gave on his Gospel tour. One song he sang on that tour, "Man Gave Names to All the Animals," from *Slow Train Coming*, ends as follows:

> *Man gave names to all the animals*
> *In the beginning, in the beginning*
> *Man gave names to all the animals*
> *In the beginning, long time ago*

> *He saw an animal as smooth as glass*
> *Slithering his way through the grass*
> *Saw him disappear by a tree near a lake . . .*

After singing this song at a concert in Pittsburgh, May 15, 1980, Dylan explained exactly what animal he was talking about:

> The animal there, in case you haven't guessed, was a snake—the same snake that was in the Garden of Eden. The same snake that was Satan, Lucifer, god of this world. Prince of the power of the air. That's the same snake. Just like he was out deceiving Eve, he's out there deceiving us right now.[47]

In other words, Dylan fully accepts the idea of original sin. "Temptation's not an easy thing, Adam given the devil reign," he sings in "Pressing On." "Because he sinned I got no choice, it run in my vein." And in "Saved" he sings,

> *I was blinded by the devil*
> *Born already ruined*
> *Stone-clad dead*
> *As I stepped out of the womb*

Because we are all sinners, the only thing one can do is to keep "pressing on / To the higher calling of the Lord." In his between-song speeches Dylan explained to his audiences that Adam gave the keys to the world to Lucifer but they were returned to humankind by Christ on the cross. "If you're a descendant of Adam—anybody here a descendant of Adam?" Dylan asked an audience in Buffalo on May 1, 1980. "Well, Adam got those keys (to Paradise) offa you, and Jesus Christ went to the cross to get those keys back."[48]

---

47. *Saved! The Gospel Speeches of Bob Dylan*, 97-98.
48. Ibid., 79.

Evangelicals emphasize that the Devil is a master of deceit. When he returns as the Antichrist he will talk about peace and safety while he leads the world toward destruction. This Antichrist, this "Future Fuehrer," "will have a magnetic personality, be personally attractive, and a powerful speaker," Hal Lindsey and Carol Carlson say. "He will be able to mesmerize an audience with his oratory."[49] Dylan captures this deceitful quality of Satan in his song "Man of Peace" released in 1983:

> Look out your window, baby, there's a scene you'd like to catch
> The band is playing "Dixie," a man got his hand outstretched
> Could be the Führer
> Could be the local priest
> You know sometimes Satan comes as a man of peace

Satan could be someone with the "sweet gift of gab," Dylan explains in this song. He could appear as a great "humanitarian" or as a "philanthropist." In a 2008 article Hal Lindsey suggests he could be someone like former US President Barack Obama. Actually, he implies that Barack Obama *is* the Antichrist. "Obama is correct in saying that the world is ready for someone like him—a messiah-like figure, charismatic and glib," Lindsey wrote in an essay in *WorldNetDaily* in 2008. "The Bible calls that leader the Antichrist. And it seems apparent that the world is now ready to make his acquaintance."[50]

The Dylan songs and sermons discussed above were, however, a product of his born-again Christian period—1978-1981. Was Dylan's focus on sin and the Devil during this period an anomaly, or only a surfacing of beliefs that Dylan has expressed, albeit in more muted form, throughout his career? Christopher Ricks in *Dylan's Visions of Sin* leans toward the latter view. "The claim in this book," Ricks says, "isn't that most of Dylan's songs, or even most of the best ones, are bent on sin. Simply that (for the present venture in criticism) handling sin may be the right way to take hold of the bundle."[51] Bert Cartwright, a minister of a mainline (Disciples of Christ) Protestant church, goes further, arguing that "the

---

49. Lindsey, *The Late Great Planet Earth*, 108.
50. *Time* correspondent Amy Sullivan quotes Lindsey in an article about an online ad by Senator John McCain's campaign when he was running for President against Senator Obama in 2008. The ad included images suggesting Obama was the Antichrist. See Amy Sullivan, "An Antichrist Obama in McCain Ad?", *Time*, August 8, 2008. I read Sullivan's article at https://web.archive.org/web/20120318075456/http://www.time.com/time/politics/article/0,8599,1830590,00.html (accessed March 21, 2012).
51. Christopher Ricks, *Dylan's Visions of Sin* (New York: Harper Collins, 2003), 6.

power of the Devil is never far from Dylan's mind. It is a haunting pre-supposition of all he sings." For Dylan, he says, "the Devil is a much more lively character than Christ" and is "much more alive and interesting than God."[52] To make his case Cartwright discusses pre-conversion as well as post-conversion songs. He mentions two songs about the devil that Dylan wrote very early in his career—in 1963.[53] The first is "Talkin' Devil" which ends as follows:

> *Well, he wants you to hate and he wants you to fear,*
> *Wants you to fear something that's not even there,*
> *He'll give you your hate, and he'll give you his lies,*
> *He'll give you the weapons to run out and die.*
> *And you give him your soul.*

The other is "Whatcha Gonna Do?" in which Dylan asks

> *What you're gonna do*
> *When the devil calls your cards*
> *O Lord, O Lord*
> *What shall you do?*

Cartwright then discusses songs from Dylan's album *John Wesley Harding* (1967), an album Dylan has described as "a fearful album—just dealing with fear [laughing], but dealing with the devil in a fearful way, almost."[54] Cartwright sees Dylan struggling with the devil in most of the songs on this album. Dylan does not refer explicitly to the Devil (or Satan, or Lucifer) in these songs: Cartwright *interprets* them as being about the Devil. Some of his interpretations seem forced, but others, if not completely convincing, are plausible.[55] Take, for example, his comments on "As I Went Out One Morning." In this song the speaker goes for a walk in the morning near "Tom Paine's," presumably a reference to a bar

---

52. Bert Cartwright, "Talkin' Devil with Bob Dylan," *The Telegraph* 49 (Summer, 1994). I found this article on the website "Expecting Rain: Bob Dylan," http://www.expectin-grain.com/dok/who/d/devil.html (accessed March 29, 2013).
53. Dylan recorded "Talkin' Devil", which is not listed on his official website, for a magazine called *Broadside* but never performed it. The second song, "Whatcha Gonna Do?", first recorded in 1963, does appear on Dylan's website and on his album *The Bootleg Series, Vol. 9: The Witmark Demos: 1962-1964.*
54. See Bob Dylan, an interview with Jonathan Cott in Rolling Stone (November 16, 1978) which is reprinted in Bob Dylan: The Essential Interviews, ed. Jonathan Cott (New York: Wenner Books, 2006), 251–270. Dylan talks about the devil on page 260.
55. Bert Cartwright is tentative about some of his interpretations. For example, he says that "it is *conceivable* that 'Dear Landlord' is a pact between Dylan and the Devil"; and he says that "The subject of 'I Am a Lonesome Hobo' may also be the Devil. See Bert Cartwright, "Talkin' Devil with Bob Dylan."

in Greenwich Village where Thomas Paine wrote "The Crisis Papers." He spies "the fairest damsel / That ever did walk in chains." He offers this damsel his hand, but when she takes it he realizes immediately that she intends to harm him.

> *"Depart from me this moment"*
> *I told her with my voice*
> *Said she, "But I don't wish to"*
> *Said I, "But you have no choice"*

She pleads with him, promising to "secretly accept him" and says they can fly south together. At that moment Paine himself runs up and tells the girl to let him go. As she is releasing her grip, Tom Paine apologizes to the speaker for what the girl has done.

On December 13, 1963, only a short time after President Kennedy had been assassinated, Dylan received the Tom Paine Award from the Emergency Civil Liberties Committee in the Grand Ballroom of the Americana Hotel in New York. Lord Bertrand Russell had won the award the year before. The ECLC gave Dylan the award because—its Chairman, Corliss Lamont, later explained—Dylan had become "the idol of the progressive youngsters of today" and the organization wanted to help older progressives better understand the youthful protest movement.[56] The evening was a disaster. Dylan had begun drinking early that night and gave a rambling acceptance speech in which he said, among other bizarre things, that he empathized with Lee Harvey Oswald. This didn't sit well with the older progressives who, only three weeks after Kennedy's death, were still mourning their fallen hero. In interpreting "As I Went Out One Morning" Cartwright refers to Dylan's embarrassing talk and also to a 1984 interview with Nat Hentoff in which Dylan explains that he was turned off by the aging, well-dressed liberals attending the dinner. The women were in "minks and jewels" and "it was like they were giving the money out of guilt," he told Hentoff.[57]

In interpreting "As I Went Out One Morning," Cartwright says that the damsel "appears to represent those who claimed the name of Tom Paine," in other words, the older progressives who were giving Dylan the award. In his song, Cartwright says, Dylan innocently reaches out his hand, but then, "instantly recognizing the Devil at work, Dylan, in

---

56. See Letter from Corliss Lamont to attendees of the dinner. It can be found at "Bob Dylan and the NECLC," http://www.corliss-lamont.org/dylan.htm (accessed April 5, 2013).
57. Nat Hentoff, "The Crackin', Shakin', Breakin' Sounds," 26.

good biblical fashion, resists [so] that the Devil may be forced to flee, saying 'Depart from me this moment.'" This remark is in "biblical fashion" because it echoes James 3:7: "Submit yourselves therefore to God. Resist the devil, and he will flee from you." Dylan cites this Bible passage in a between-song talk on his Gospel Tour: "It's hard not to go to Hell you know . . . As soon as you get rid of the enemy outside, the enemy comes inside. He got all kinds of ways. The Bible says 'Resist the Devil and the Devil will flee.' You got to stand to resist him."[58]

The Devil for Dylan is not only the "God of the World" but also, as Dylan says, an inside enemy, or as, Cartwright puts it, "a perverse force lurking within one's own spirit." Cartwright analyzes several songs in which Dylan, in his interpretation, is acknowledging that he is "complicit" in the Devil's work. He finds this complicity theme in both pre- and post-conversion songs—in, for example, "The Ballad of Frankie Lee and Judas Priest," "I Dreamed I Saw St. Augustine," "I Pity the Poor Immigrant," and "The Wicked Messenger" from *John Wesley Harding* (1967); and in "Jokerman" from *Infidels* (1984). Cartwright argues that in this last song Dylan perceives that this Satanic spirit, represented by the Jokerman, has wormed itself into his own being and become "a persecutor within":

> *Shedding off one more layer of skin*
> *Keeping one step ahead of the persecutor within*
> *Jokerman dance to the nightingale tune*
> *Bird fly high by the light of the moon*
> *Oh, oh, oh, Jokerman*

Commenting—unclearly, in my view—on these lines, Cartwright says, "Recognizing the Devil as 'the persecutor within,' the best he [the persona, Dylan?] can do is keep running as fast as he can before he is grabbed from behind."[59]

Although a critic like Cartwright, who is also a pastor and theologian, may see the Devil in more songs than the rest of us, it seems clear that notions of the Devil and sin were integral to Dylan's view of the world and

---

58. *Saved! The Gospel Speeches of Bob Dylan*, ed. Clinton Heylin, 89.
59. This song has challenged critics. Michael Gray—in a long, detailed analysis—identifies the "persecutor within" with Jung's notion of a dark side that mythic heroes must repress. In this song, Gray says, Dylan seems at times to be talking about Jesus and at other times talking about himself. He argues that in it Dylan mocks superheroes, including rockstars like himself, and that he betrays some negative feelings about another superhero, Christ. See Michael Gray, *Song and Dance Man III* (London: Continuum, 2000), 481-516.

to his view of himself. He accepted the notion of original sin and what it implied, namely that there "Ain't no man righteous, no not one," which is the title of a song Dylan wrote in 1979.[60] It also seems true that he viewed women as temptresses who were in league with the Devil and led men to sin. "I gaze into the doorway of temptation's angry flame," Dylan sings in "Every Grain of Sand," "And every time I pass that way I always hear my name." In "Trouble in Mind" Dylan sings: "Satan whispers to ya, 'Well, I don't want to bore ya / But when ya get tired of Miss So-and-So I got another woman for ya." Dylan has toured all his adult life as a famous figure, and so temptresses are everywhere. Vineyard pastor Kenn Gulliksen has said that after his hedonistic Alimony Tour Dylan was "apparently ready to ask for God's forgiveness for sin."[61]

Dylan was probably speaking from personal experience when, in introducing his song "Solid Rock" at a concert on his Gospel Tour, he said: "But you watch when you do need some help—when you've exhausted everything else, when you've had all the women you can possibly use, when you've drunk all you can drink. You can try Jesus. He'll still be there."[62] The Devil and sin are defeated on the cross, as Dylan makes clear in "Ain't No Man Righteous, No Not One":

> *Done so many evil things in the name of love, it's a crying shame*
> *I never did see no fire that could put out a flame*
>
> *When I'm gone don't wonder where I be*
> *Just say that I trusted in God and that Christ was in me*
> *Say He defeated the devil, He was God's chosen Son*
> *And that there ain't no man righteous, no not one*

My conclusion is that Dylan's Christian period was not an anomaly. The songs he wrote from 1978 to 1981 differed in some ways from earlier and later songs but Dylan's deep immersion in the Christian narrative is evident in all his work, in songs written both before and after his conversion. His preconversion songs are more poetic, subtle, and—in my opinion—more pleasing, perhaps because these songs reflect not recent and direct Bible teaching but rather a longer acculturation in a culture that

---

60. This title, repeated often in the song, echoes Paul's epistle to the Romans 3:10: "There is none righteous, no not one."
61. Howard Sounes quotes Gulliksen in *Down the Highway: The Life of Bob Dylan* (New York: Grove Press, 2001), 325.
62. Clinton Heylin, ed., *Saved: The Gospel Speeches of Bob Dylan* (Albany, NY: April 27, 1980). Dylan talked about the devil in many of his gospel speeches. See, for example, pages 23, 24, 29.

is predominately Judeo-Christian. This acculturation included learning Jewish prayers and rituals, reading the Bible as literature, and listening to folk, country, blues, and gospel songs. "In Dylan the prophet meets the bluesman," says Alan Jacobs. "The ancient laments of Israel rejoin songs born in slavery and the cottonfields."[63]

If Dylan's Christian period was not an anomaly then why was there such a hullabaloo when Dylan began singing Christian songs on his Gospel Tour? As we have seen, Dylan had been covering gospel songs throughout his career, sometimes tweaking them a little, sometimes singing them more or less as they were sung by traditional singers. So, when he began to write and sing songs like those on *Slow Train Coming*, why didn't fans and the media accept them? Why didn't they think, "That's cool. Now Dylan's writing his own gospel songs." At least in part it was all the factors already discussed—the "Jesus gonna getcha," evangelistic quality of the songs (and his between-song speeches); Dylan's refusal to sing any of his old "protest" songs; the initial negative publicity; etc. But I suggest there are other causes. Dylan's gospel songs were understood to be personal songs about his own born-again experience. When he performed "Saved," singing "I was blinded by the devil" but "I've been saved / By the blood of the lamb," people understood Dylan to be speaking from personal experience, "testifying," as an evangelical Christian would say. Many Americans, however, associate the gospel or spiritual song with the suffering of slaves and poor people, many of them African American, people like Blind Willie Johnson (1890-1947), a street preacher-singer from Texas who was blinded as a child when his stepmother poured acid in his eyes. Johnson died of pneumonia when the hospital refused to treat him, either because of his disability or his race.[64] Many fans no doubt concluded that Bob Dylan's background did not qualify him to write songs like "Saved." It was fine to cover and tweak songs sung by other gospel singers—that was paying tribute to past artists and to African American culture—but Dylan was now writing and performing his own gospel songs, and that was different.

There is also the quality of Dylan's singing. In 2003 Sony Music Entertainment released *Gotta Serve Somebody: The Gospel Songs of Bob Dylan*, an album of eleven songs from *Slow Train Coming* and *Saved*.

---

63. Alan Jacobs, "It Ain't Me Babe," 101.
64. Gérard Herzhaft, *Encyclopedia of the Blues*, 2nd ed., trans. Brigitte Debord (Fayetteville, AR: University of Arkansas Press, 1997), 103-104.

Dylan sings the last song, "Gonna Change My Way of Thinking," with an old friend, Mavis Staples, a member of The Staple Singers, the family group of singers that Dylan used to listen to when he was in high school in Hibbing, Minnesota.[65] All the other songs are sung by some of the best gospel singers and gospel choirs in America. In 2005 a DVD of the singers working in the studio on the songs on this album was released. Also included on this DVD are interviews with the singers who perform the songs.[66] I believe that many people, including non-Christians, would find watching and listening to this DVD to be a joyful, uplifting experience. It is impossible to hear Dottie Peoples sing "I Believe in You," or Regina McCrary and the Chicago Mass Choir sing "Pressing On," or Joe Ligon and Mighty Clouds of Joy sing "Saved," and not be moved by the music and by the obvious pleasure the singers and musicians are experiencing by performing it.

Dylan did have four African American backup singers on his Gospel Tour—Carolyn Dennis,[67] Regina McCrary (then Regina Havis), Helena Springs, and Monalisa Young—and they opened the show with five or six songs. Dylan, however, was the lead vocalist on the rest of the songs and the act people came to see. It is instructive to listen to Dylan singing songs like "Pressing On" and "I Believe in You" on his album *Saved* and compare his performances to those on *Gotta Serve Somebody*—either the CD or the DVD. There is a world of difference. Interviewed on the DVD, Shirley Caesar, who sings the opening song, "Gotta Serve Somebody," says that "you got to be careful how you present the gospel because if you don't present it right, then they're going to react as though it's another kind of music and it isn't." In another interview Regina McCrary makes a similar point. What makes the songs different on Dylan's album, she says, "is that Bob Dylan sung them. Because you take the same Bob Dylan song and let the Fairfield Four or Shirley Caesar sing it and it's gonna go right back into the church to that thing that we grew up with." McCrary then sings some lines from "In the Garden" in what she feels is the wrong way to sing a gospel song: "When they came for him in the Garden. . ." she sings, tapping out the beat. "Did they know . . . ."

---

65. It has been rumored that Dylan once asked Mavis' father, Roebuck "Pops" Staples, if he could marry his daughter. Mavis jokes about the rumor in an interview in *Time*. See Mavis Staples, "10 Questions," *Time*, July 1, 2013.
66. The DVD is called *Gotta Serve Somebody: The Gospel Songs of Bob Dylan*. It is distributed by Image Entertainment.
67. Dennis and Dylan were later secretly married in 1986, the same year their daughter, Desiree, was born.

"Well," she continues, "if I'm in church singing, I'm not gonna sing it like that. I'm gonna probably say [singing] 'When they came for him in the garden / Did they know . . . .' Different. The only difference is who's singing the song." Perhaps it was not the only difference, but it was a big difference, one that probably affected how audiences reacted to Dylan on his Gospel Tour.[68]

---

68. "In the Garden," a song from Dylan's album *Saved*, is sung in the video *Gotta Serve Somebody*, but, for some reason, it was left off the DVD.

29

DYLAN, MESSIANIC JUDAISM, & THE JUDEO-CHRISTIAN TRADITION

I have explained that some Jewish Dylanophiles have argued that Dylan's commitment to Christianity was transitory—a reaction to stress—and that he later abandoned Christianity and returned to Judaism. There is scant evidence to support this view. He did visit Israel, he did arrange bar mitzvahs for his children, and he did continue to do benefit concerts for the Lubavitchers, a Hasidic movement. Jewish Dylanophiles apparently seized on these facts and convinced themselves that he had returned to Judaism. A poorly sourced, misleading article titled "Dylan Ditching Gospel" that appeared in *New York Magazine* in 1982 also gave hope to Jewish fans.[1] The article quoted an unidentified source who maintained that Dylan's Christian period was over. Following his born-again experience in 1979, however, Dylan has continued to affirm his Christian faith in various ways for over three decades. Scott M. Marshall and Marcia Ford document these reaffirmations in *Restless Pilgrim*, mentioning, among other things, the following:

1. Dylan's release in 1989 of his album *Oh Mercy,* which Scott M. Marshall and Marcia Ford call "practically a companion piece" to *Slow Train Coming,* Dylan's first "Christian" album, which was

---

1. "Dylan Ditching Gospel," *New York Magazine*, no author listed (March 15, 1982): 15.

561

released a decade earlier.[2] A song like "Shooting Star" from this album reveals that Dylan was, at least in 1989, still a prophet of the apocalypse, still warning people that the time was growing short, and still telling them that they should listen to Jesus:

> *Listen to the engine, listen to the bell*
> *As the last fire truck from hell*
> *Goes rolling by*
> *All good people are praying*
> *It's the last temptation, the last account*
> *The last time you might hear the sermon on the mount*

2. The fact that Dylan has continued to sing explicitly Christian songs—his own and covers of traditional Christian songs—at concerts. In 1991, Marshall and Ford report, "Dylan sang 'Gotta Serve Somebody' in more than eighty concerts, 'I Believe in You' in twenty-nine, and 'In the Garden' in ten."[3] In 2002 Dylan included "Solid Rock," perhaps the most fervent of his Christian songs, in the set for his European tour, a song in which the speaker talks about Christ having been "chastised" and "rejected" for the speaker's sake, and so, though others are waiting for "a false peace to come," he is "hanging on to that solid rock."[4]

Along with his own Christian songs, Dylan sang covers of traditional religious songs including "Hallelujah, I'm Ready to Go," "Somebody Touched Me," "Pass Me Not, O Gentle Savior," "Rock of Ages," and "I Am the Man, Thomas." At a concert in Atlanta in 1999 he opened with this last song, a practice that, Marshall and Ford say, he continued in many shows that followed.[5] In the song, written by Ralph Stanley and Larry Sparks, Christ speaks to the Apostle Thomas, who is called "doubting Thomas" because he refused to believe in the crucifixion and resurrection until he saw the nail prints on Jesus' hands.[6] Here is the second verse:

---

2. Scott M. Marshall and Marcia Ford, *Restless Pilgrim: The Spiritual Journey of Bob Dylan* (Relevant Media Group Inc., 2002), 98.

3. Ibid., 107.

4. The rock mentioned by Paul in 1 Corinthians 10:4: "And did all drink the same spiritual drink: for they drank of that spiritual Rock that followed them: and that Rock was Christ."

5. Scott Marshall and Marcia Ford, *Restless Pilgrim*, 98. Ibid., 144.

6. St. John 20:4: "The other disciples therefore said unto him, We have seen the Lord. But he [the Apostle Thomas] said unto them, Except I shall see in his hands the print of the nails and put my finger into the print of the nails, and thrust my hand into his side, I will not believe."

I am the man, Thomas
I am the man
Look at these nail scars
Here is my hand

Dylan's covers of songs like "I Am the Man, Thomas," Clinton Heylin says, "testify to both a world-weary yearning for release and an abiding faith in Christ's promise of redemption."[7]

3. Dylan's release of *Bob Dylan Live: 1961-2000*, an album in which Dylan covered the traditional Christian songs "Somebody Touched Me" and "Wade in the Water" and sang some of his own Christian songs—"Knockin' on Heaven's Door" and "Slow Train."

4. His willingness in 2003 to participate in the making of the tribute album, *Gotta Serve Somebody: The Gospel Songs of Bob Dylan*, which I discussed in Chapter Twenty-Seven.

5. The fact that Dylan continued, in the second decade of the twenty-first century, to open his shows with a religious song. For example, on his Asian tour in 2011 he opened his Hồ Chí Minh City and Shanghai concerts with his song "Gonna Change My Way of Thinking." Here is the last stanza:

Jesus said, "Be ready
For you know not the hour in which I come"
Jesus said, "Be ready
For you know not the hour in which I come"
He said, "He who is not for Me is against Me"
Just so you know where He's coming from

It seems clear that in 1979 when he had his born-again experience Dylan, as Scott Marshall and Marcia Ford argue, "bought the entire gospel message" and that he has been a committed Christian ever since.[8] It also seems clear that he never abandoned Judaism and is both interested in and proud of his Jewish heritage. Some might see this as "spiritual schizophrenia," Scott Marshall and Marcia Ford say, but apparently Dylan did

---

7. Quoted by Scott Marshall and Marcia Ford, *Restless Pilgrim*, 148. Marshall and Ford cite Clinton Heylin, *Bob Dylan: Behind the Shades Revisited* (New York: William Morrow, 2001), 719-720.
8. Scott Marshall and Marcia Ford, *Restless Pilgrim*, 177.

not.[9] Paul Emond, the Vineyard pastor who taught Dylan the Bible, has said that Dylan "is one of those fortunate ones who realized that Judaism and Christianity can work very well together."[10] Judaism and Christianity are indeed compatible in many ways. The majority of the "Christian" Bible is, after all, Jewish scripture, and Jews and Christians share a similar sacred history and similar ethical values based on the Ten Commandments. They also both believe in an apocalyptic ending of the world. "Revelation completed Christianity's assimilation of Jewish apoc-alypticism," the *Encyclopedia Britannica* explains. Evangelical Christians like Hal Lindsay draw on both the Old Testament book of Daniel and the New Testament's final book, Revelation, in constructing their vision of how the world will end.

Where Judaism and Christianity differ, however, is in regard to the Messiah. Jews believe the Messiah has not yet come, while Christians believe that he has come, and will come again. The anonymous author of Daniel speaks of a "Son of Man," a heavenly being who will redeem the world.[11] Most people who call themselves Jews, however, do not believe that Christ is that being. "Modernist movements in Judaism have attempted," an entry in the *Encyclopedia Britannica* explains, "to maintain the traditional faith in an ultimately redeemed world and a messianic future without insisting on a personal messiah figure."[12] For many people these different views regarding the presence or absence of a personal messiah are too crucial to be set aside.

Some Jews, however—people who call themselves Messianic Jews—do believe that Jesus is the Messiah. In 1970 when the Jesus Movement was in full swing, Moishe Rosen, a Baptist minister who was born Jewish, moved to California to preach the gospel to Jews in the counterculture movement. His message was that it was possible to be Jewish and also accept Jesus as the Messiah. In 1973 he founded Jews for Jesus in San Francisco, an organization that still exists today. Though he believed in Jesus, Rosen—like Dylan—observed Jewish customs. According to his 2010 obituary in the New York Times, he "held seders at Passover, fasted

---

9. Ibid., 110.
10. Quoted in Clinton Heylin, *Bob Dylan: Behind the Shades*, 353.
11. Daniel 7:13-14.
12. "Messiah," Encyclopedia Britannica Online Academic Edition, http://www.britannica. com.ezproxy.humboldt.edu/EBchecked/topic/377146/messiah (accessed November, 2012).

on Yom Kippur and married couples under a huppah, the Jewish wedding canopy."[13]

Messianic Judaism is controversial in the mainstream Jewish community. For devout Jews, belief in Jesus is apostasy and Messianic Judaism just another name for evangelical Christianity.[14] In his book *Jews for Jesus* (1974) Rosen describes being attacked by a Jewish woman while he and his group were protesting a strip club in the North Beach area of San Francisco. Rosen was wearing a denim jacket with "Jesus Made Me Kosher" on the back. "That's my religion you're ridiculing!" the woman shouted. (Rosen also wore campaign buttons saying "Jews for Jesus" and "Torah is good for the soul.")[15] That was in the early 1970s. Jews for Jesus is still opposed by Jewish leaders. Rabbi James Rudin, the senior inter-religious affairs adviser of the American Jewish Committee, had this to say about the leaders of Jews for Jesus when a *New York Times* reporter interviewed him after Rosen's death: "People should know that they really are Christian missionaries. I would have had much more respect for him [Rosen], and for his organization, if they had just come out and said, 'We are Christian missionaries, trying to convert Jews.'"[16] According to Scott Marshall and Marcia Ford, Christians also—after a "heady-honeymoon phase" in the 1970s—began to distrust Messianic Jews, "labeling them Judaizers and charging them with polluting the gospel by allegedly insisting that their converts became more Jewish than they had ever been before."[17] According to Marshall and Ford, Dylan's "involvement with any single Messianic Jewish ministry was incidental at best," though, they add, "he almost certainly had to be aware of the tension between those ministries and the gentile church. In typical Dylan fashion, he apparently ignored the bickering and went on with his spiritual life."[18]

It is tempting to label Dylan a Messianic Jew because in some ways the label fits. Like people of Jewish descent in the organization Jews for Jesus he does not just believe that Jesus is the Messiah, he accepts the entire Christian Gospel—the Trinity, the resurrection, the idea that we are all

13. Margalit Fox, "Moishe Rosen Dies at 78; Founder of Jews for Jesus," *New York Times*, May 22, 2010.
14. See the *Evangelical Dictionary of Theology*, 2nd edition, ed. Walter A Elwell (Grand Rapids, MI: Baker Academic, 2001), 766.
15. Moishe Rosen with William Proctor, *Jews for Jesus* (Old Tappan, NJ: Fleming H. Revell Company, 1974), 11-13.
16. Margalit Fox, "Moishe Rosen Dies at 78.".
17. Scott Marshall and Marcia Ford, *Restless Pilgrim*, 110-111.
18. Ibid., 111.

sinners "by nature and practice,"[19]—and, at the same time, he also talks proudly of his Jewish roots and observes Jewish holidays and customs. "Roots, man—we're talking about Jewish roots, you want to know more?" he asked an interviewer in 1983. "Check on Elijah the prophet. He could make rain. Isiah the prophet, even Jeremiah, see if their brethren didn't want to bust their brains for telling it right like it is, yeah—these are my roots, I suppose."[20]

A story Scott Marshall tells reveals how Dylan (in his own mind at least) made the Old and New Testament—his Jewishness and his Christianity—fit together harmoniously. Before Dylan's Gospel Tour arrived in Montreal in late April of 1980 for a series of concerts, a cartoon drawn by "Aislin" (Terry Mosher) appeared in the *Montreal Gazette*. It depicted St. Joseph's Oratory, a Roman Catholic basilica and Montreal landmark, with a sign in front of it reading "Welcome Bob Dylan." The joke was that the Catholic church was so desperate to attract followers that it would welcome even Dylan. Apparently Dylan loved the cartoon and asked Mosher for the original. The cartoonist sent it to him in return for a signed copy. On the copy he sent Mosher, Dylan wrote "To Aislin, 'The law was given by Moses but grace & truth thru Jesus Christ' (John 1:17) Love, Bob Dylan."[21] Although at first glance this may seem to be an unremarkable inscription, I think Marshall is right to see deeper meanings in it. When Dylan's album *Saved* was released in June—about two months after the Montreal concerts—Dylan chose the following passage from Jeremiah to be printed on the album sleeve: "Behold, the days come, saith the Lord, that I will make a new covenant with the house of Israel, and with the house of Judah."[22] The old covenant, also called the Mosaic or Sinai Covenant, was the agreement that God made with the people of Israel, represented by Moses, that if they obeyed the Ten Commandments then they "shall be a peculiar treasure unto me above all people."[23]

According to Christian theologians, the new covenant that Jeremiah refers to is the covenant mentioned in Chapter 8 of Paul's Epistle to the

---

19. See the Jews for Jesus "Statement of Faith" on the organization's webpage, https://www.jewsforjesus.org/about/statement-of-faith (accessed March 14, 2013).

20. Quoted in Larry Yudelson, "Dylan: Tangled up in Jews," in *The Bob Dylan Companion*, ed. Carl Benson (New York: Schirmer Books, 1998), 174-175.

21. See Scott Marshall and Marcia Ford, *Restless Pilgrim*, 49-50.

22. Jeremiah Chapter 31, verse 31.

23. Exodus Chapter 19, verse 5: "Now therefore, if ye will obey my voice indeed, and keep my covenant, then ye shall be a peculiar treasure unto me above all people: for all the earth *is* mine."

Hebrews. A new covenant was needed because the people of Israel broke the old one. This new covenant would be written not on stone tablets but in people's hearts.[24] Less harsh than the old one, it includes God's promise to be merciful and to forget people's sins and iniquities.[25] This new covenant does not need to be earned but rather is freely given—a gift of "grace," as Dylan, by quoting St. John 1:17, indicates in his inscription that he sent to the cartoonist. Marshall and Ford say that Dylan chose to print Jeremiah's promise of this new covenant on his album *Saved* because "to him, and to many other Jewish believers in Jesus, the verse signified the fulfillment of their Jewishness in the new covenant—salvation through Jesus—that God made with the house of Israel. Today, many Messianic Jews prefer to be called 'completed' Jews for the same reason."[26] Should we then call Bob Dylan a "messianic Jew"? I do not use the term because it is controversial and also misleading: It correctly indicates the ethnicity of a believer like Dylan, but perhaps overstates the Jewishness of his beliefs. Perhaps we should dispense with labels and simply conclude, as Scott Marshall and Marcia Ford do, that despite his Jewish roots and his Christian beliefs, Dylan is a man comfortable in his own skin.

Another term, one with an interesting history, is "Judeo-Christian." It is rarely used to describe an individual—we don't commonly say, "He's a Judeo-Christian"—but Americans use it often to describe their country, or culture, or tradition. It is a controversial term and very hard to define. It has been used to advance both inclusive liberal and exclusive conservative agendas. Though it existed previously, it did not become widely used, Mark Silk has explained, until the 1930s when liberal Jewish and Christian leaders and American communists used it to oppose "fascist fellow-travelers and anti-Semites" who had "appropriated 'Christian' as an identifying mark."[27] After World War II, Mahmood Mamdani explains, "The notion of a Judeo-Christian civilization crystallized as a post-Holocaust antidote to anti-Semitism."[28] In other words, when the term first became popular it was used to advance an inclusive/liberal agenda, at least as far

---

24. Hebrews Chapter 8, verse 10: "For this is the covenant that I will make with the house of Israel after those days, saith the Lord; I will put my laws into their mind and write them in their hearts: and I will be to them a God, and they shall be to me a people."
25. Hebrews 8, verse 12: "For I will be merciful to their unrighteousness, and their sins and their iniquities will I remember no more."
26. Scott Marshall and Marcia Ford, *Restless Pilgrim*, 50.
27. Mark Silk, "Notes on the Judeo-Christian Tradition in America," *American Quarterly* 36, no. 1 (Spring, 1984), 66.
28. Mahmood Mamdani, *Good Muslim, Bad Muslim: America, the Cold War, and the Roots of Terrorism* (Westminster, MD: Knopf Publishing Group, 2004), 36.

as attitudes toward Jews were concerned. Henry Wallace, Vice President of the US from 1940-1945, wrote in 1940 that the "Jewish tradition, the Christian tradition, the democratic tradition and the American tradition are all one."[29]

Since the 1980s, however, and continuing into the twenty-first century, the term "Judeo-Christian" has been used more to exclude than include and has been used more by conservatives than by progressives. Conservatives have used it to identify and preserve what they consider to be the cultural core of the nation. Note how conservative commentator and Republican presidential candidate Pat Buchanan employed the term in a 1991 editorial that appeared in the *St. Louis Post-Dispatch*: "Our Judeo-Christian values are going to be preserved and our Western heritage is going to be handed down to future generations and not dumped on some landfill called multiculturalism."[30] After the terror attacks on 9/11 generated fear and debate about the role of Muslims in the US, some American Muslim leaders suggested "Judeo-Christian" be replaced with "Judeo-Christian-Islamic." Some Christians, however, including Ted Haggard, the president of the National Association of Evangelicals, rejected the proposal, arguing that before they can be included Muslims first have to contribute to American society.[31]

What does the term "Judeo-Christian" imply? Sam Sobel says "it is a term popularized by persons who use it in lieu of the more restrictive term, Christian," and then goes on to say that those who use it "imply with some degree of condescension the possibility of Hebrew involvement in Christian morality."[32] The term suggests, he says, a marvelous and harmonious synthesis of Jewish and Christian "theology, morality, and general outlook." Sobel argues that in this sense Judeo-Christianity is a myth because, he says, "The two religions could scarcely be further apart

---

29. Deborah Dash Moore quotes Henry Wallace in "Jewish GI's and the Creation of the Judeo-Christian Tradition," in *Religion and American Culture: A Journal of Interpretation* 8, no. 1 (Winter, 1998), 34-35. Moore cites the following source: Henry A. Wallace, "Judaism and Americanism," *Menorah Journal* 28, no. 2 (July-September 1940), 137.
30. Pat Buchanan, "Editorial," *St. Louis Post-Dispatch*, December 13, 1991. This editorial is cited in Douglas Hartmann, Xuefeng Zhang, and William Wischstadt, "One (Multicultural) Nation Under God? Changing Uses and Meanings of the Term 'Judeo-Christian' in the American Media," *Journal of Media and Religion* 4, no. 4 (2005), 208.
31. Douglas Hartmann, et al., "One (Multicultural) Nation Under God?" 230. The authors refer to an article about the Muslim leaders' proposal that appeared in the *Washington Post* (May 17, 2003).
32. Sam Sobol, "The Myth of Judeo-Christianity," *Humanist* 41 (1981), 24.

in almost all detail."[33] Sobel argues that Judaism is more humanistic than Christianity for a variety of reasons, including the following: because its focus is on improving this world, not on a world after death; because it is less obsessed with sin; and because it encourages better treatment of women.

In an article called "The Violence of the Hyphen in Judeo-Christian," Marshall Grossman considers the terms "post-colonial"[34] and "Judeo-Christian." He argues that in the second term the Jew—the "Judeo-"—is the "subjugated other" described in post-colonial scholarship.[35] In other words, the Jew in a "Judeo-Christian" country becomes comparable to a colonial subject, say a Nigerian, or a Vietnamese, who may live in a country liberated from colonial oppression, but for whom, within their "post-colonial self," "the subjugated other" still persists. Grossman says that "the rhetorical form of the two hyphens provides for a seductive chiasmus"—an antithesis with the parts reversed: "Judeo" is superimposed on "colonial" and "Christian" on "post."[36]

Is there any evidence that Bob Dylan felt "subjugated" because he was a Jew in a predominantly Christian country? None that I could find. When he was registered and circumcised he was assigned two names: a Hebrew name, Shabtai Zisel ben Avraham, and an English name, Robert Allen Zimmerman.[37] Growing up in Hibbing he was called Robert or Bobby. Later he changed his name to Bob Dylan because, he suggests in his autobiography, he was looking for a catchy name, something "exotic and inscrutable."[38] If he wanted something that would appear *really* exotic and inscrutable to Christian America, he could have chosen Shabtai

---

33. Ibid.
34. After World War II, "post-colonial" had a chronological meaning. It referred to the post-independence period of countries that become liberated from colonial rule. Beginning in the late 1970s the term began to be used by literary critics (for example, Edward Said, H. K. Bhabha, and Gayatri Chakravorty Spivak) to refer to "the political, linguistic and cultural experience of societies that were former European countries." See Bill Ashcroft, Gareth Griffiths, and Helen Tiffin, *Post-Colonial Studies: The Key Concepts* (London: Routledge, 2000), 186.
35. Marshall Grossman, "The Violence of the Hyphen in Judeo-Christian," *Social Text* 22 (1989), 115.
36. Ibid.
37. Howard Sounes, *Down the Highway: The Life of Bob Dylan* (New York: Grove Press, 2001), 14.
38. Many people think Dylan named himself after the poet Dylan Thomas. He did—sort of. Dylan says he had "seen some poems by Dylan Thomas," but before that he had read about a saxophone player named David Allyn. He liked "Allyn" but "the letter D came on stronger" than the "A" so he went with "Dylan," finally settling on "Bob Dylan." See Bob Dylan, *Chronicles: Volume One* (New York: Simon and Schuster, 2004), 78.

Zisel ben Avraham! There is no evidence that Dylan ever considered that option, but there is also no evidence that he was greatly troubled by antisemitism. When he arrived in Greenwich Village, he did create a fictitious past—claiming that he had been a carnival performer and blues singer in New Mexico, for example—but he did so, it seems, not primarily to hide his Jewishness but because he admired the wandering ways of singers like Woody Guthrie and those singers he listened to on Harry Smith's *Anthology of American Folk Music,* the anthology I have discussed in Chapter Twenty-One: "Dylan's Musical Roots: The Basement Tapes".

In his literary analysis of the term "Judeo-Christian" Marshall Grossman emphasizes that the hyphen in the phrase both "conjoins" and "disjoins." He concludes his article by talking about the old and new covenants—the same two covenants that Dylan sees as working harmoniously together. Grossman argues that one's attitude toward the two covenants depends on from which side of the hyphen in "Judeo-Christian" you read them. Read from the Christian side, the hyphen marks the "synchronizing moment" when the people of the first covenant are "sublated" into the body of Christ. Read from the Jewish side, however, the hyphen conceals "the subsumption of the first term by the second."[39] Grossman quotes from Saint Paul's first epistle to the Corinthians: "The Letter Killeth but the Spirit giveth Life." In other words, Grossman says, the Jews, the people of the first covenant, the people of the Law, must be "transformed into the people of the Spirit." The phrase "Judeo-Christian," he says, "preserves the Jew as textual presence [but] only by sending the Jews as historical actor below the bar of 'Judeo-Christian' consciousness."[40] Dylan chooses to read the phrase from the Christian side, but occasionally, perhaps worried that others (or maybe he himself) will forget his Jewish background, he stands up and talks about his "Jewish roots," or visits Israel, or does another benefit concert for a Jewish cause.

Debates about the limits of cultural pluralism and how to define America's cultural core will continue within the US, but most informed citizens of the world, I suggest, perceive America to be—and refer to it as—a "Christian" or "Judeo-Christian" nation. They understand, however, that the increasing number of Muslims from the Middle East and Buddhists from Asian countries, including Vietnam, are testing the tolerance of some Americans who insist that America remain a Judeo-Christian

---

39. Marshall Grossman, "The Violence of the Hyphen in Judeo-Christian," 120-121.
40. Ibid., 121.

country. People in foreign countries also recognize that many Americans consider themselves to be secular humanists or agnostics or atheists. In a 1969 article titled "Myth of the Judeo-Christian Tradition," the Jewish theologian and novelist Arthur A. Cohen argued that Jews and Christians in the US had set aside their theological differences—the messiah issue, for example—to reinforce themselves against a common enemy: "the religion of American secularism."[41] One senses that Dylan saw himself as a warrior in this Jewish-Christian anti-secularism battle when he opened his Gospel tour in San Francisco, where secular humanism thrives.

Though America is changing, I would argue that those who look at America from afar are correct: The United States *is,* not exclusively but predominantly, a Judeo-Christian country. Dylan's songs have resonated deeply with Americans because they express—very powerfully and artistically—the Judeo-Christian values, assumptions, and beliefs that I have discussed: the conviction that we are all by nature sinners, the assumption that anger is justified if it is righteous, a focus on end times, and the belief that one day a redeemer will come to save us and lead us to a better world.

---

41. Arthur A. Cohen, "The Myth of the Judeo-Christian Tradition," *Commentary* (November 1969). Accessed online at https://www.commentary.org/articles/arthur-cohen/the-myth-of-the-judeo-christian-tradition (accessed September 10, 2022).

30

TRỊNH CÔNG SƠN & BOB DYLAN: A BUDDHIST-CHRISTIAN DIALOGUE

As I explained in the Introduction, in late March 2011, when I first learned that there would be a Bob Dylan-Trịnh Công Sơn concert in Hồ Chí Minh City, a fan fantasy began to develop in my mind. When introduced, Bob Dylan, in some hastily learned Vietnamese, would acknowledge Trịnh Công Sơn's accomplishments, especially his anti-war songs, and then he would sing, in his honor, his famous protest song, "Blowin' in the Wind." Then Trịnh Công Sơn's sister, Trịnh Vĩnh Trinh, would sing one of Trịnh Công Sơn's anti-war songs, maybe "Lullaby of Cannons for the Night" [Đại bác ru đêm], and Dylan, his Vietnamese rapidly improving, would join her on the final chorus. For the finale Joan Baez and Khánh Ly, both aging but still beautiful, would emerge from the wings and sing bilingual versions of Dylan's "Forever Young" and Trịnh Công Sơn's "Love Each Other" [Hãy yêu nhau đi] inviting all singers, band members, and the audience to join them for the final choruses.

If some of these elements had been included it might have been a better concert. At least it would have been more respectful of Vietnamese sensibilities. But if it succeeded in suggesting that Trịnh Công Sơn and Bob Dylan truly were "harmonious souls," as the promoters in their pre-concert publicity claimed, it would have been a triumph of showmanship over substance, because Trịnh Công Sơn and Bob Dylan are very different people who in their songs suggest very different ways of living in this world. Their differences, in my view, are largely attributable to their different religious backgrounds. Off-the-cuff comments like "Trịnh Công Sơn is the Bob Dylan of Vietnam," and "They are two harmonious souls" create warm feelings by suggesting commonalities, but they obscure real differences that are bound to come up later when intercultural and interreligious dialogue becomes more thoughtful. Differences should not prevent this dialogue from occurring.

We have seen that Bob Dylan and Trịnh Công Sơn differ profoundly in how they react both to personal misfortune—a failed or troubled love affair, for example—and to political catastrophes like war and social injustice. Whereas Trịnh Công Sơn typically reacts to personal and political disappointments with sadness and loving-kindness, Bob Dylan often responds with a mixture of defiance, anger, and resentment. Their different reactions result in songs with a very different tone and a very different message about how to live in this world. In explaining these differences I have discussed key events in the composers' lives, differences in literary and musical traditions, and differences in personality. Now I shall discuss religious differences: the fact that Dylan grew up within a culture that was predominantly Judeo-Christian whereas Trịnh Công Sơn grew up within a culture that was predominantly Buddhist. I emphasize this difference in religion because I believe it is the most important difference between these two singer-songwriters, and helps us understand other differences that I have discussed. In other words, I am suggesting that religion affects people deeply, even those who profess to be only nominal followers of their faith.

Many Christians in the U.S. are nominal Christians: They will check "protestant" or "catholic" on a form to indicate their religious affiliation but they may never have been baptized, rarely or never attend church services, and would not claim to have a special relationship with Jesus Christ. Even a nominal Christian in the U.S., however, will be influenced by Christian ideas and images because they permeate American culture. It is more difficult to distinguish a nominal Buddhist from a devout Buddhist than to distinguish a nominal Christian from a devout Christian. Many Buddhists *tu Phật tại gia* [practice Buddhism at home] and so failure to visit a pagoda regularly does not mean that one is not devout.[1] For Christians, however, attendance at Sunday services or at fellowship meetings is generally a

---

1. See Chapter Twenty-Four, where I explain terms Vietnamese use for "Buddhist" [*người Phật tử*] and "lay Buddhist" [*người Phật tử cư sĩ*] and consider which term best describes the role Buddhism played in Trịnh Công Sơn's life.

sign that one is more than a nominal Christian. Most devout Vietnamese Buddhists have a Buddhist name, but so do many nominal Buddhists: It does not necessarily indicate intense devotion to one's faith.

Dylan is not simply a nominal Christian. Although his parents were Jewish, he has embraced Christianity and has issued several albums completely devoted to Christian songs. Though he resents people trying to turn him into a spokesperson for anything, Dylan became, at least for part of his career, a spokesperson for his faith. Donald Mackenzie argues that Dylan "was able to reveal much more religious truth prior to his conversion." This was, he says, because Dylan's "pre-conversion songs had subtlety and poetry and so they struck a responsive chord." In his overtly Christian songs, however, he expressed a "simplistic approach to Christianity" that made it more difficult for many people to say, "'he speaks for me.'"[2] Trịnh Công Sơn's spiritual seeking led him deeper into Buddhism. His "soft philosophy" was primarily Buddhist. Dylan's spiritual seeking led him to Evangelical Christianity. Exploring how the two singer-songwriters were influenced by their respective faiths is, I believe, the best way to appreciate the depth of their differences.

Kristin Beise Kiblinger presents a useful framework for comparing religions and so I will refer to it in the following discussion of what is an ongoing dialogue between Buddhist and Christian scholars. First, however, I will explain her framework.

"Each religious community," Kiblinger says, "must face and decide how best to respond to the situation of religious plurality."[3] She mentions three options: inclusivism, exclusivism and pluralism. She prefers inclusivism, which she says, "has to do with willingness to incorporate the other or something of the other's," a doctrine or a practice, for example, within one's own religion.[4] She gives examples of beliefs and practices that would indicate an inclusive approach. One might, she says, "accept as true or good a doctrine or practice from a foreign religious system. Or one might believe that a religious other could attain ultimate fulfillment or salvation as conceived by the home tradition."[5]

Kiblinger's second option, exclusivism, is "problematic and rare," she says, because it "commits the whole group to the claim that no

---

2. Donald Mackenzie, "The Conversion of Bob Dylan," *Theology Today* 37 (1980), 358.
3. Kristin Beise Kiblinger, *Buddhist Inclusivism: Attitudes Towards Religious Others* (New York: Routledge, 2017), 1.
4. Ibid.
5. Ibid.

other religious community teaches or practices anything that the home group does." It also suggests that only members of this group can obtain salvation.[6] Kiblinger describes her third option, pluralism, as a "different strokes for different folks" position. Pluralists, she says, quoting Paul J. Griffiths,[7] "Think that all religions are equally effective in bringing salvation about."[8]

This framework provided by Kiblinger will be useful in comparing the views of other known scholars eager to promote Buddhist-Christian dialogue. I will begin with Rudolf Otto.

RUDOLF OTTO

Rudolf Otto, who was born in the German state of Prussia in 1869, was an influential German Lutheran scholar of comparative religion and the first modern German scholar to engage in a dialogue with Buddhist teachers. In October 1911 he began a journey that included travels in India, where he visited with Muslims, Hindus, Sikhs, and Parsees. He also visited the predominantly Buddhist countries of Burma, Thailand and Japan.[9] He found Japanese Buddhism particularly attractive. Otto believed, however, that all religions begin with a "sense of the holy," and argued that Christianity develops this sense better than all other religions. In a lecture delivered in 1913, he said that Christians value "emotion and feeling" whereas Buddhists value "the monastic ideal of apathy and complete stillness and calmness."[10] For Buddhists, he says, the goal is to become free of emotional agitation and excitement. This central difference, he continues, is found in the "opposing natures" of the two founders: "On the one hand, there is Jesus of Nazareth who, in rage, in a truly human act, drove the profaners from the temple with a whip; and on the other, the calm, silent, stilled, Buddha, the ideal of the extinction of the world of feeling, of passion, of excitement."[11]

---

6. Ibid., 2.
7. Kristin Beise Kiblinger quotes Paul J. Griffiths, *Problems of Religious Diversity*, (Malden, MA: Blackwell publishers, 2001) xv.
8. Kristin Beise Kiblinger, *Buddhist Inclusivism*, 2.
9. Philip C. Almond, "Translators' Introduction," in Rudolf Otto and Philip C. Almond, "Buddhism and Christianity:—Compared and Contrasted," *Buddhist-Christian Studies* Vol. 4 (1984), 87-88.
10. Ibid. 87-101. This lecture has been translated by Philip C. Almond. See Rudolf Otto and Philip C. Almond, "Buddhism and Christianity: Compared and Contrasted," in *Buddhist-Christian Studies* Vol. 4 (1984), 87-101. See page 98 for the passage about the rage of Jesus and the calmness of Buddha.
11. Rudolf Otto and Philip C. Almond, "Buddhism and Christianity: Compared and Contrasted," 98.

Christ in an angry rage and the Buddha calm and quiet. Clearly Christians like Dylan are influenced by the first image and Buddhists like Trịnh Công Sơn by the second. Note that Otto says Christ's rage is "a very human act,"[12] but implies that Buddha's calmness is sub- or super-human. For a Christian like Rudolf Otto, Buddhism is too passionless, too impersonal. Buddhists, he suggests, believe that one extinguishes suffering by extinguishing desire. They envision the impersonal transcendent reality of Nirvana whereas Christians believe in a personal and loving God whom they can reach through prayer.

Otto, however, in his 1913 lecture, also mentions "parallels" or "convergencies" between Buddhism and Christianity. Among the parallels he lists are these:

1. He finds a parallel between two "supra-mundane ideals: on the one hand the Kingdom of God, and on the other Nirvana." Both ideals, he says are "world-transcending salvations envisaged as comforting and delivering."[13]

2. Both religions, Otto says, "have opposed to the same extent the emphasis on cult and ritual; both have opposed the prejudice that religion could be encapsulated in the externals of ritual purity." Both religions, he says, "advocate a middle way between worldliness and asceticism."[14]

3. In both Buddhism and Christianity, Otto observes, "monasticism is both legitimate and responsible." Christianity, he says, was not monastic in the beginning but became so later.[15]

4. Buddhists and Christians, Otto says, have an analogous relation to an earlier version of their religion. He mentions the relationship between Theravada Buddhism, preserved in the Pali Canon, and Mahayana Buddhism, known as "the Great Vehicle" which he describes as "an all embracing religion." "It is only popular claptrap," he says, "that this later form of Buddhism had defiled itself, had degenerated and who knows what else." "Mahayana degenerate? No! Mahayana Buddhism is to early Buddhism what Catholic and later Protestant Christianity is for us to the primitive form of the first phase."[16]

---

12. Ibid. 98.
13. Ibid. 90.
14. Ibid.
15. Ibid., 91.
16. Ibid., 93.

5. Otto's most famous work, which I will discuss later, is *The Idea of the Holy*. In his introduction to his translation of Otto's 1913 lecture, Philip C. Almond defines holy as "that mysterious, transcendent in general that lives in the religious feeling of devotion and humility."[17] Almond says that Otto's idea of the holy was "aroused" by an experience of synagogue worship in Morocco.

Otto says that although this feeling of religious awe is "not completely lacking" in Buddhism, it is not "a determinative element."[18] This parallel between Christianity may not be pronounced—"not completely lacking" is not the same as "contains"—but it *is* a parallel.

In 1917, four years after he gave this lecture in 1913, Otto published his first edition of what became his best known work: *The Idea of the Holy*. This idea of the holy is Otto's *a priori,* his basic assumption about how religions function in people's lives. Otto is thought of as someone who emphasizes—in some people's view over-emphasizes—non-rational aspects of religion. John W. Harvey, who translated Otto's book into English, addresses this issue in a preface to his translation. In Otto's book, he admits, there is "an overplus of meaning which is non-rational, but neither in the sense of being *counter* to reason on the one hand nor *above* reason on the other. The two elements, the rational and the non-rational, must be regarded (in Otto's favorite simile) as the warp and woof of the complete fabric, neither of which can dispense with the other."[19]

In his preface John W. Harvey says that a passage by Blaise Pascal in *Pensées*, an unfinished work that Pascal wrote in 1657-1658, accurately sums up Otto's position. "If one subjects everything to reason our religion will lose its mystery and its supernatural character. If one offends the principals of reason our religion will be absurd and ridiculous. . . . There are two equally dangerous extremes, to shut reason out and to let nothing else in."[20] Otto did not deny the rational aspect of Christianity, but he wanted to emphasize its non-rational elements. His term for these elements is "holy." Otto explains that people understand "holy" to mean "moral" or "ethical" or "completely good." This word does suggest these things, he

---

17. Ibid., 96.
18. Rudolf Otto and Philip C. Almond, "Buddhism and Christianity: Compared and Contrasted," 97.
19. John W. Harvey, "Translator's Preface," in Rudolf Otto, *The Idea of the Holy,* second edition (London: Oxford University Press, 1957), page xvii. Otto mentions this simile on page 46 of *The Idea of the Holy.*
20. Ibid., xviii-xix.

explains, but he insists that what he calls "holy" also has "a clear overplus of meaning" that is non-rational. Otto's term for this non-rational element is "numinous," coined from the Latin *numen*—divine power or divine presence.[21] For Otto the holy is a "purely an *a priori* category."[22] It proceeds from theoretical deduction, not from observation or experience. In his introduction to his translation of Otto's 1913 lecture Philip C. Almond points out that Otto's conviction that religions are, "in the first instance, the result of the operation of a religious *a priori*," is already present.[23]

Kiblinger does not discuss Otto's approach but she would likely classify him as an inclusivist, and Almond would agree. Almond quotes a passage from an article Otto wrote discussing "parallels" between Buddhism and Christianity. All religions, those in the East and those in the west, Otto says in this article, can actualize the religious *a priori*, a sense of the Holy.[24]

THÍCH NHẤT HẠNH

I have discussed Thích Nhất Hạnh in other chapters, most extensively in Chapter Twenty-Four, so I will not repeat here information about his life and his view of Trịnh Công Sơn, but instead focus on his approach to Buddhist-Christian dialogue. Kiblinger classifies Thích Nhất Hạnh's approach as inclusivist. He is the first scholar that she discusses in a chapter titled "Case Studies of Two Prominent Buddhist Inclusivists." (The other scholar is Masao Abe.)[25]

In *Living Buddha, Living Christ,* Thích Nhất Hạnh[26] doesn't suggest complete agreement between Buddhism and Christianity but he does find what are best described as parallels. For example, he says that the Buddhist concept of mindfulness is "very like the Holy Spirit. Both are agents of healing."[27] Mindfulness, he points out, is also present in the Christian Eucharist. "In Christianity," he says, "when we celebrate the Eucharist, sharing the bread and the wine as the body of God, we do it in the same spirit of piety, of mindfulness, aware that we are alive, enjoying dwelling in the present moment."[28] Thích Nhất Hạnh says that "we do not speak of

21. Rudolf Otto, *The Idea of the Holy*, trans. John W. Harvey (London, Oxford University Press, 1957), 5-6.
22. John W. Harvey, "Translator's Preface," 88.
23. Ibid.
24. Ibid.
25. Kristin Beise Kiblinger, *Buddhist Inclusivism*, 91-102.
26. Thích Nhất Hạnh, *Living Buddha, Living Christ* (New York: Riverhead Books, 1995.
27. Ibid., 14.
28. Ibid., 29.

Original Sin in Buddhism, but we do talk about negative seeds that exist in every person—seeds of anger, ignorance, intolerance, and so on—and we say that these seeds can be transformed when we touch the qualities of Buddha, which are also seeds within us.[29] Thích Nhất Hạnh also sees parallels between the Buddhist *sangha* [Vn. *Tăng già*[30]] and the Christian church.[31] He also distinguishes between the historical Buddha, the person who was born near the border between India and Nepal, got married,[32] died at the age of 80, et cetera, and the living Buddha, "the Buddha of the ultimate reality, the one who transcends all the ideas and notions and is available to us at any time." This distinction, Thích Nhất Hạnh says, parallels the distinction that Christians make between the historical Christ who was born in Bethlehem, was the son of a carpenter, was crucified at the age of thirty-three, et cetera, and "the living Christ who is the son of God, who was resurrected and who continues to live."[33]

Thích Nhất Hạnh also talks about similarities between Buddhism and Christianity in *Going Home: Jesus and Buddha as Brothers.*[34] In this book he points out that "there is a real danger of being caught up in words and doctrines." Instead, he says we should concentrate on direct experience. He illustrates this point by discussing the Buddhist concept of Nirvana, the final goal of Buddhism, a state in which there is no more suffering and one is released from the cycle of death and rebirth. Nirvana, he says, cannot be described in words. It must be experienced. With any word you use to point at the noumenal dimensions[35] you have to be careful. You should not get caught in that word.[36] Thích Nhất Hạnh even finds a similarity between the holy spirit in Christianity and "the energy of mindfulness."[37]

---

29. Ibid., 44. Some of these negative seeds that Thích Nhất Hạnh mentions are included in the Three Poisons [Vn.: Tam Độc; Skt.: trivisa] that I have discussed in previous chapters. The Three Poisons are Greed [Vn.: tham], Anger [Vn.: sân], and Delusion [Vn.: [si]
30. Vietnamese sometimes call a Sangha a *tăng thân*.
31. Thích Nhất Hạnh, *Living Buddha, Living Christ*, 66-69.
32. In the sixth century B.C.E, the young man named Siddhatta Gotama, who had a wife and a son, decided to abandon his family and join a group of men and a few women who lived in the forest in the plain of the Ganges river. See Karen Armstrong, *Buddha* (NY: Penguin Books, 2001), 1-2.
33. Thích Nhất Hạnh, *Living Buddha, Living Christ*, 34-35.
34. Thích Nhất Hạnh, *Going Home: Jesus and Buddha as Brothers* (New York: Riverhead Books, 1999).
35. Noumenal dimensions are dimensions that exist independently of human perception and understanding. The term is associated with the philosophy of Immanuel Kant.
36. Thích Nhất Hạnh, *Going Home: Jesus and Buddha as Brothers*, 10-12.
37. Ibid., 194. See also Thích Nhất Hạnh, *The Miracle of Mindfulness: An Introduction to the Practice of Meditation*, trans. Mobi Ho (Boston, MA: Boston Beacon Press, 1975).

Thích Nhất Hạnh's emphasis on similarities between Buddhism and Christianity probably results from his belief in the Buddhist concept of non-duality [Skt. *Advaita*: Vn. *Bất Nhị*], the concept that everything is a part of one nondual consciousness. In his last chapter in *Living Buddha, Living Christ*, Thích Nhất Hạnh writes that Buddhists and Christians will find similarities between their two religions because both contain "the same elements of stability, joy, peace, understanding and love."[38]

I find Thích Nhất Hạnh's conviction that Christianity and Buddhism are very similar difficult to accept. I see more differences than similarities, perhaps because I have not passed through the gate of non-duality.

TWO IMPORTANT BUDDHIST CONCEPTS: NO-SELF AND LOVING-KINDNESS[39]

The concept of no-self is one of the most important concepts in Buddhism. It is one of the three "marks of existence": *anitya* (impermanence), *dukkha* (suffering, unsatisfactoriness), and *anatman* (no-self).[40] These three marks of existence are emphasized by some exclusivists, who are, as I am, impressed by differences between Buddhism and Christianity. Because no scholar has discussed the concept of no-self more thoroughly than Lynn de Silva does in his book *The Problem of the Self in Buddhism and Christianity*, I will summarize his views.

De Silva was born in Sri Lanka in 1919 and died in 1982. He was Director of the Study Centre for Religion and Society in Colombo. In an introduction to his book he acknowledges that the doctrine of *anatman* [no-self] is "the bedrock of Buddhist teaching,"[41] but this fact does not lead him to adopt what Kiblinger calls an exclusivist perspective. Instead he takes an approach that has many aspects of the position Kiblinger calls inclusivism. De Silva sees similarities as well as differences between Buddhism and Christianity and this perspective is evident in his discussion

---

38. Thích Nhất Hạnh, *Living Buddha, Living Christ* (New York: Riverhead Books, 1995), 194-195.
39. Some scholars spell the names of these concepts the way they are spelled in the Pali Canon, the oldest collection of scriptures in the Theravada Buddhist tradition. Other scholars use the later Sanskrit spellings. I will spell them as they are spelled in Sanskrit. However, to avoid confusion that may result when readers encounter Pali spellings in other books and articles, here is the way no-self and loving-kindness are spelled in Pali and Sanskrit: No-self [Pali: *annata*; Sanskrit: *anatman*]; Loving-kindness and Compassion [Pali: *metta*; Sanskrit: *matri*].
40. Scholars writing in English translate the Sanskrit word *anatman* in three different ways: non-self, not-self, and no-self. I will translate it as no-self.
41. Lynn A. de Silva, *The Problem of the Self in Buddhism and Christianity* (New York: Harper & Row Publishers, 1979), 1.

of no-self. "There is no notion of an immortal soul in the Bible," he argues, "rather there is much in the biblical view of man that is in accord with the Buddhist doctrine of *anatman* (non-self)."[42] But he also at times sounds like an exclusivist; "How can you," he asks his readers, perhaps primarily his Buddhist readers, "reconcile the doctrine of *anatman*, which denies the self, with the doctrine of karma and rebirth, which affirms the identity and continuity of the self?" There is also, he points out, the problem of Nirvana. "If in reality there is no self," he asks, "who is it that obtains *Nirvana* and experiences happiness?"[43]

De Silva, who refers only to "man" but presumably has women in mind also, says that "it is in the understanding of man as *anatta-pneuma* (non-egocentric relationality) that one should seek a solution to the problems of the self."[44] In his foreword to de Silva's *The Problem of the Self in Buddhism and Christianity*, John Hick explains that *anatta-pneuma* expresses the idea that "human selves" should not be seen as "atomic entities, permanently excluding one another, but as parts of a living system of inter-personal relationships, within which their separating walls of egoity may ultimately be transcended."[45] The term *pneuma* is derived from the Greek *pneuma*, meaning a blast of wind, breath or spirit. De Silva says that *pneuma* has many meanings but he emphasizes three:
1. the Holy Spirit of Christ
2. "a purely Christian spirit created in the believer which enables him to hold communion with God because spirit with spirit can meet."[46]
3. "the natural possession of every man, which of itself is neither good nor bad, and is not easily distinguished from *psyche*."[47]

In Chapter 14, "The Practical Relevance of the Anatta-pneuma Concept," de Silva says that this concept is one that "Marxists, Maoists and followers of other secular ideologies are as much involved with as theologians and philosophers, mystics and hippies."[48] He quotes a passage from Marx's *Das Kapital* in which Marx says that "Peter (disciple of Jesus) grasps his relation to himself as a human being through becoming aware of his relation to the

---

42. Ibid., 2.
43. Ibid.
44. Ibid., 74.
45. John Hick, "Foreword," in Lynn A. de Silva, *The Problem of the Self in Buddhism and Christianity*, page x.
46. Lynn A. de Silva, *The Problem of the Self in Buddhism and Christianity*, 88.
47. Ibid.
48. Ibid., 146.

man Paul (the apostle) as a human being of like mind with himself."[49] This is one aspect of what we mean by *pneuma*" De Silva says: "the fact that man is by nature communal, that to *be* is to be related."[50]

De Silva argues that "selflessness is a great virtue" and mentions that it is a virtue that Mao Tse-tung "ceaselessly upheld and exemplified in his life."[51] De Silva quotes a tribute that Chairman Mao made to a comrade who died. In this statement Chairman Mao says that "We must learn the spirit of absolute selflessness" from this comrade.[52]

Selflessness is a virtue that is highly valued in Confucian countries like China and Vietnam. As I have explained in Chapter Sixteen, "The New Poetry [*Thơ Mới*] Movement Part One," no-self [Vn. *vô ngã*; Skt. *anatman*] is ingrained in Vietnamese language and culture. When a child addresses his father he refers to himself as "child" [*con*] and his father as *cha* [father] or *bố*.[53] What is important is not his own self but rather his relation to his father. After Vietnamese poets were exposed to French poetry, however, things changed. Hoài Thanh and Hoài Chân explain the change in *Thi Nhân Việt Nam*. Before the Vietnamese New Poets arrived on the scene, they point out, "there was only the collective: a large one, the country, and a small one, the family. The individual aspect was submerged in the family and the country like a drop of water in the sea."[54]

De Silva quotes comments by Mao Tse-tung about the evils of selfishness and the positive aspects of selflessness and suggests that "There is something religious in these 'Thoughts of Mao.' Has not religion something to contribute to create that kind of selfless man?"[55] Clearly, de Silva believes that it does.

In *Understanding Vietnam*, Neil L. Jamieson explains that in countries like China and Vietnam, "the individual can be no more than a member of the family. The ideas or actions of the individual must be subjugated to the family hierarchy... And a nation is just a larger family, also with a hierarchy just like the one in a small family."[56] In other words, selflessness,

---

49. Ibid., 150.
50. Ibid., 151.
51. Ibid., 152.
52. Ibid.
53. Ibid. *Bố* is more common in north Vietnam and *cha* more common in the south.
54. Hoài Thanh and Hoài Chân, *Thi Nhân Việt-Nam* [Vietnamese Poets] (South Vietnam: Hoa Tiên, 1967), 52.
55. Lynn A. de Silva, *The Problem of the Self in Buddhism and Christianity*, 153.
56. Neil L. Jamieson, *Understanding Vietnam* (Berkeley, CA: University of California Press, 1993), 173.

no-self, the necessity of yielding to the needs of others, has been built into the system.

We also see selflessness in the way Vietnamese celebrate *Tết*, Việt Nam's New Year festival, the most important holiday in Vietnam. Vietnamese do not celebrate their individual birthdays on the day they were born, as most people do in America. Instead, when the first day of *Tết* arrives, everyone in the family becomes one year older. Vietnamese young people have come to embrace the idea of an individual birthday celebrated on the day they were born, but this a relatively new custom.

Americans value their individual freedoms and don't think that in pursuing them they are being selfish. De Silva, however, in Chapter 3, "The No Soul Theory," discusses the Buddhist concept of *tanha*[57] which refers to thirst, desire, longing and greed. *Tanha*, De Silva says, is primarily the thirst for self. "Therefore," he says, "it is by self-emptying, realizing the truth of *anatman* (no-self), that the new man can come into being."[58] Simply put, no-self is good because it combats selfishness.

De Silva ends his chapter three, "The No-Soul Theory," by connecting two important Buddhist concepts: *dukkha* (suffering, unsatisfactoriness), and *annatman* (Vn. *vô ngã*). The conflict between these two concepts disappears, de Silva says, when one sees that they are identical. "Hence," he says, "it is of the utmost importance for one to realize the fact of soullessness (*annatman*)" because "It is this realization that leads to freedom from *dukkha*."[59]

It is not surprising that de Silva associates the Buddhist concept of no-self with Mao Tse-tung. A google search for "Comparisons of Communism and Buddhism" will lead one to many articles that point out similarities. The compilers of the website *Encylopedia.com*, for example, mention that "Neither Buddhists nor communists believe in a creator deity, and both Buddhism and Communism are based on a vision of universal egalitarianism."[60] They mention also that the Buddhist concept of the *sangha* resembles a communist society.[61]

---

57. Skt. *trsna*; Vn. *aí anatman.*
58. Lynn de Silva, *The Problem of the Self in Buddhism and Christianity*, 152. See also pages 28-29.
59. Ibid.
60. Encylopedia.com, https://www.encyclopedia.com/religion/encyclopedias-alma-nacs-transcripts-and-maps/communism-and-buddhism (accessed March 3, 2023).
61. Ibid.

De Silva discusses Chairman Mao because he believes they share the view that selflessness is an important, perhaps the most important, quality. *Anatman*, de Silva says, "with its rejection of the notion of the immortal soul within man, serves to dispel the illusion of the egocentric 'I', which is, as the Buddha taught, the root cause of all evil."[62]

LOVING-KINDNESS [SKT.: *MAITRI*; VN.: *TỪ BI*]

I focus on the Buddhist concept of loving-kindness and compassion [Vn. *từ bi*] because, like the concept no-self I have just discussed, it is one of the most important concepts in Buddhism. The Vietnamese author of a dictionary of Buddhist terms refers to *từ bi* as "one of the basic tenets of Buddhism."[63] I also focus on *từ bi* because it refers to qualities, loving-kindness and compassion, that Trịnh Công Sơn revealed in his life and in his songs. "Lullaby for you" [Ru em],* for example, a song he wrote after the love of his life, Ngô Vũ Dao Ánh, broke up with him and married someone else, contains these lines:

> *A lullaby for you for unfortunate lives*
> *Loving you I love betrayal more*
> *Loving you suddenly loving-kindness and compassion [từ bi] fill*
> *my heart*

As explained in previous chapters the dominant form of Buddhism in Vietnam is Mahayana, a form which emphasizes the role of bodhisattvas, enlightened beings who postpone their own liberation to help others achieve enlightenment. Rudolf Otto contrasts earlier versions of Mahayana Buddhism, sometimes called small vehicle Buddhism, with later versions of Buddhism, referred to as large vehicle Buddhism.[64] Small vehicle Buddhism, Otto says, "teaches one to become like that sage who sits in the monastery and egotistically broods about his own salvation."[65] We want something different. Otto says: "We want to become Buddha."[66] Otto wants himself and others to be like bodhisattvas who postpone their own liberation to help others achieve nirvana. He doesn't want to be like those small vehicle egotistical Buddhists who worry only about their own

---

62. Lynn A. de Silva, *The Problem of the Self in Buddhism and Christianity*, xi.
63. Tâm Tuệ Hỷ, ed., *Danh từ Phật học thực dụng* [Useful Buddhist Terms] (Hà Nội: Tôn Giáo, 2004), 549.
64. Philip C. Almond, "Translators' Introduction," in Rudolf Otto and Philip C. Almond, "Buddhism and Christianity: Compared and Contrasted," *Buddhist-Christian Studies*, Vol. 4 (1984), 93.
65. Ibid.
66. Ibid.

salvation. Then Otto relates this discussion of unselfish bodhisattvas to *Từ bi* or *maitri*. In Mahayana Buddhism, he says, "something quite new bursts forth: *maitri* in the sense of the Bodhisattva ideal, love in an abnormally altruistic form."[67]

Scholars of comparative religion frequently compare *maitri* to *agape*, a Greek word that in John 3:16 refers to the love that moved God to send his only son for the world's redemption. (Scholars refer to this Greek word for love because most agree that the New Testament was originally written in Greek.) Vietnamese translate *maitri* as *từ tâm* and refer to everyday love as *tình yêu*. In Trịnh Công Sơn's songs, however, as we have seen, *tình yêu* often dissolves into *từ tâm*, a universal love that arises when one realizes that oneself and others are equally empty. As Thích Thiên-Ân points out, "Loving-kindness in Buddhism is an impartial and universal love, free from every trace of egocentric grasping."[68] This is one reason why in Trịnh music we find no love songs as earthy as works like Dylan's "Lay, Lady, Lay":

> *Lay, lady, lay, lay across my big brass bed*
> *Stay, lady, stay, stay while the night is still ahead*
> *I long to see you in the morning light*
> *I long to reach for you in the night*
> *Stay, lady, stay, stay while the night is still ahead*

Or "I'll Be Your Baby Tonight":

> *Close your eyes, close the door*
> *You don't have to worry anymore*
> *I'll be your baby tonight*
>
> *Kick your shoes off, do not fear*
> *Bring that bottle over here*
> *I'll be your baby tonight*

Or "Make You Feel My Love," a beautiful song that many other singers have covered:

> *When the rain is blowing in your face*
> *And the whole world is on your case*
> *I could offer you a warm embrace*
> *To make you feel my love*

---

67. Ibid.
68. Thich Thien-An, *Buddhism and Zen in Vietnam in Relation to the Development of Buddhism in Asia* (Rutland, VT: Charles E. Tuttle, 1975), 62.

In my introduction I mentioned that when western journalists sought information about Trịnh Công Sơn, the Vietnamese they interviewed told them that he was "the Bob Dylan of Vietnam." I would like to suggest a rough, and admittedly rather far-fetched, parallel between this tag phrase used by Vietnamese to describe Trịnh Công Sơn to westerners, and attempts by Christian theologians and missionaries to make Christianity more palatable to Buddhists in Asia. During the war the Vietnamese diplomat and writer Trần Văn Dĩnh[69] and Western journalists who said Trịnh Công Sơn was "Vietnam's Dylan" were trying to make Trịnh Công Sơn more understandable to the primarily Christian West. Some Christian theologians who were also missionaries were eager to convert Buddhists to Christianity. Lynn de Silva's motivation, the scholar Perry Schmidt-Leukel, explains, "was clearly a missionary one."[70] Schmidt-Leukel describes the *tilakkhana*, the three marks of existence—impermanence [*anitya*], suffering [*dukkha*] and no-self [*anatman*]—and then explains de Silva's argument that all three marks are rendered harmless if one embraces Christianity. This is possible, according to de Silva, because of "the Christian teaching of a trinitarian God." Here is a summary of how, in de Silva's view, this teaching overcomes the three marks of existence:

Mark 1, the impermanence of all life [*anitya*] is overcome by the imperishable eternal father.

Mark 2, the suffering of unredeemed existence [*dukkha*] is overcome by the Son the Redeemer.

Mark 3, *no-self* [*anatman*] is overcome by the divine spirit who transforms us into persons who can live in an eternal relationship with God.[71]

This scheme seems too neat and simple to me—and condescending. Buddhism raises these troubling questions, de Silva seems to saying, and Christianity provides the answers. De Silva's approach seems to be motivated by missionary impulses. Showing how the religion that they wish potential converts to convert to solves problems raised by

---

69. See Tạ Ty, "Trịnh Công Sơn và tiếng ru máu lệ" [Trịnh Công Sơn and Lullabies of Blood and Tears], in *Mười khuôn mặt văn nghệ hôm nay* [Ten Faces of Art Today] (Saigon: Lá Bối, 1971), 23-64.

70. Perry Schmidt-Leukel, "Buddhism and Christianity: Antagonistic or Complementary?," *Studies in World Christianity*, No. 2 (January 1, 2003), 265.

71. Perry Schmidt-Leukel discusses the three marks of existence in his article "Buddhism and Christianity: Antagonistic or Complementary?" He explains in note 25 that "this correlation of tilakkhana and trinity was presented in de Silva; 1967." I presume he is referring to an earlier edition of *The Problem of Self in Buddhism and Christianity*.

the potential convert's home faith is no doubt an effective strategy for missionaries to adopt. This is true for Christian missionaries but also for Buddhist scholars like Thích Nhất Hạnh, who adopts a similar strategy. He emphasizes similarities between Buddhism and Christianity to make Buddhism attractive to people in the West.

In all these attempts people eager to make the strange familiar take one or two superficial similarities and based on this skimpy evidence argue for an overall sameness. The result is that deep underlying differences are ignored. Though Easterners as well as Westerners are involved, something akin to Edward Said's "Orientalism," which I mentioned in my introduction, may be operating both in the tag "Trịnh Công Sơn is the Bob Dylan of Vietnam" and in arguments for Buddhist-Christian complementarity. Both seem to reflect what Said describes as "a certain will or intention to understand, in some cases to control, manipulate, even to incorporate, what is a manifestly different (or alternative and novel) world."[72]

There are some similarities between Trịnh Công Sơn and Bob Dylan and between Buddhism and Christianity but I am more impressed by the profound differences between the two composers and their two religions. As a Buddhist Christian or Christian Buddhist myself, I tend to regard Buddhism and Christianity as Sallie King, a professor of philosophy and religion and both a Quaker and a Buddhist, regards these two traditions: as "two languages, each of which speaks with great profundity truths of the spiritual life, yet neither of which (like any language) is really translatable into the other."[73] But then perhaps neither Professor King nor I have yet passed through the dharma gate of non-dualism. Possibly I am too close to my Christian self—too inclined to see "two" when I should see "one." I am aware of the irony inherent in arguing that Trịnh Công Sơn and Bob Dylan are not harmonious souls while talking of non-dualism.

In fact I do feel there are some important—not just superficial—similarities between the two composers. Both singers began their careers singing about social issues. Trịnh Công Sơn sang about the war, and his songs expressed the views of many Vietnamese who longed for an end to a war that was tearing their country apart. Dylan did write some songs

---

72. Edward W. Said, *Orientalism* (New York: Vintage Books, 1978), 12.
73. Sallie B. King, "The Mommy and the Yogi," in *Beside Still Waters: Jews, Christians, and the Way of the Buddha*, eds. Harold Kasimow, John P. Keenan, and Linda Klepinger Keenan (Boston: Wisdom Publications, 2003), 157-170.

protesting war and economic and racial inequality. Though he hated the label, he *was* a spokesperson for progressive causes. His song "My Back Pages," included on his 1964 album *Another Side of Bob Dylan*, contains these lines:

> *"Equality," I spoke the word*
> *As if a wedding vow*
> *Ah, but I was so much older then*
> *I'm younger than that now*

These lines are difficult to interpret. Is Dylan repudiating or approving the vow he made when he was young to work for equality? Did Dylan ever stop believing in the struggle for equality and social justice? I do not believe that he did. In an interview with Nat Hentoff in 1964, when he was recording *Another Side of Bob Dylan,* he told Hentoff that there were not any "finger-pointing songs" in this album. "Now a lot of people," he said, "are doing finger pointing songs. You know, pointing to all the things that are wrong. Me, I don't want to write for people anymore. You know, be a spokesman."[74]

I agree, however, with those who argue that progressive principles like racial equality and social justice that Dylan pushed in the early 1960s have continued to inform his work.[75] He has never wanted to be considered a spokesperson for these principles, but he didn't abandon them. What he repudiated was the self-righteous indignation of the 1960s radicals and their belief that reason, new laws, and social programs alone could solve the world's problems.

While it may be wrong, as some theologians suggest, to equate Christian love with Buddhist loving-kindness and compassion, both singer-composers expressed concern for the other—for humankind. Dylan never completely abandoned his concern for the downtrodden and his hope for a more just society. In 1989 Dylan wrote a song called "What Good Am I?" in which this concern for the other is very evident. Here are the second and last stanzas:

---

74. Bob Dylan, interview with Nat Hentoff, "The Crackin', Shakin', Breakin', Sounds" in *The New Yorker*, October 24, 1964. This interview is included in *Bob Dylan: The Essential Interviews*, ed. Jonathan Cott (New York: Wenner Books, 2006), 16.

75. See, for example, Alan Jacobs, *"It Ain't Me Babe" A Visit to Vanity Fair: Moral Essays on the Present Age* (Grand Rapids, MI: Brazos Press, 2001), 102; and Jordy Rocheleau, "'Far Between Sundown's Finish An' Midnight's Broken Toll': Enlightenment and Postmodernism in Dylan's Social Criticism," in *Bob Dylan and Philosophy*, ed. Peter Vernezze and Carl J. Porter (Chicago, IL: Open Court 2006), 66-77.

What good am I if I know and don't do
If I see and don't say, if I look right through you
If I turn a deaf ear to the thunderin' sky

What good am I?
What good am I if I say foolish things
And I laugh in the face of what sorrow brings
And I just turn my back while you silently die
What good am I?

I sense that Trịnh Công Sơn would have liked this song but I cannot imagine him writing one like it. It is a gentle, loving song, but a sense of guilt pervades it. Perry Schmidt-Leukel, a professor of theology and religious studies, says Buddhists see the human predicament as suffering caused by impermanence; Christians understand the human predicament as sin.[76] Cynthia Eller makes a similar point: "Where Buddhism begins with suffering and the search for its solution," she says, "Christianity begins with sin and the search for its redemption and forgiveness."[77] Trịnh Công Sơn sees the human predicament in Buddhist terms, and one senses that Buddhism provided him with some solace. Bob Dylan sees the human predicament in Christian terms, and one senses Christianity provides him some solace. The common ground here is finding peace of mind, becoming more content with oneself.

In this respect perhaps Buddhism and Christianity are complementary and the souls of Trịnh Công Sơn and Bob Dylan can be seen as harmonious. For who hasn't, in some part of their life, needed help in dealing with life's impermanence—with the quick passing of youth, with the loss of a loved one? Bob Dylan would seem to be more in need of forgiveness for sins than Trịnh Công Sơn, but who hasn't worried about their own sins, big or small—about mistakes made as a son or daughter, as a brother or sister, as a lover, as a husband or wife, or as a parent? Who doesn't wish to ease the pain?

---

76. Perry Schmidt-Leukel, "Buddhism and Christianity", 273.
77. Cynthia Eller, "The Impact of Christianity on Buddhist Nonviolence in the West," in *Inner Peace, World Peace: Essays on Buddhism and Nonviolence*, ed. Kenneth Kraft (Albany, NY: State University of New York Press, 1992), 97.

APPENDICES

SONGS PERFORMED AT THE
"BOB DYLAN—LIVE IN VIETNAM" CONCERT
HỒ CHÍ MINH CITY, APRIL 10, 2011

SONGS BY TRỊNH CÔNG SƠN[1]

1. Xin mặt trời ngủ yên [Please Sun Sleep Peacefully], sung by Cẩm Vân
2. Sóng về đâu [Where Will the Wave Go?], sung by Cẩm Vân
3. Lời mẹ ru [Words of a Mother's Lullaby], sung by Mỹ Linh
4. Em hãy ngủ đi [Sleep, My Love], sung by Mỹ Linh
5. Hạ trắng [White Summer], performed on saxophone by Trần Mạnh Tuấn
6. Ru tình [Lullaby for Love], sung by Hồng Nhung
7. Thuở bống là người [When the Goby Fish was a Person], sung by Hồng Nhung
8. Tình nhớ [Love Remembered], sung by Quang Dũng and Hồng Nhung
9. Biển nhớ [The Sea Remembers] and Một cõi đi về [A Place for Leaving and Returning], sung by Quang Dũng
10. Bốn Mùa Thay Lá [Four Seasons of Changing Leaves], sung by Quang Dũng

---

1. Apparently there were some last minute changes to this schedule. Linh Phạm complains that only ten Trịnh Công Sơn songs were performed and that Mỹ Linh and Thanh Lam did not sing. According to Linh Phạm, the Vietnamese portion of the concert lasted less than an hour. The ten songs, she says, were performed in a hurried fashion. Linh Phạm, "Nhạc Trịnh 'lạc' trong buổi diễn Bob Dylan" [Trịnh Music Was "Lost" in the Bob Dylan Concert], http://www.baomoi.com/Nhac-Trinh-lac-trong-buoi-dien-Bob-Dylan/71/6044594.epi (accessed July 1, 2012).

11. Vết lăn trầm [Quiet Imprint], sung by Thanh Lam

12. Ru ta ngậm ngùi [To Lull Oneself in Sorrow], sung by Thanh Lam

13. Xin cho tôi [Please Give Me], sung by Đức Tuấn

14. Con mắt còn lại [The Eye That Remains], sung by Đức Tuấn

15. Hãy yêu nhau đi [Love Each Other], sung by a group (Tốp ca)

SONGS BY BOB DYLAN

1. Gonna Change My Way of Thinking (Dylan on keyboard)

2. It Ain't Me, Babe (Dylan on guitar)

3. Beyond Here Lies Nothin' (Dylan on guitar, Donnie Herron trumpet)

4. Tangled Up In Blue (Dylan center stage on harp)

5. Honest With Me (Dylan on keyboard)

6. Simple Twist Of Fate (Dylan on guitar)

7. Tweedle Dee & Tweedle Dum (Dylan on guitar)

8. Love Sick (Dylan on keyboard)

9. The Levee's Gonna Break (Dylan on keyboard)

10. A Hard Rain's A-Gonna Fall (Dylan on keyboard)

11. Highway 61 Revisited (Dylan on keyboard)

12. Spirit On The Water (Dylan on keyboard and harp)

13. My Wife's Home Town (Dylan on keyboard)

14. Jolene (Dylan on keyboard)

15. Ballad Of A Thin Man (Dylan center stage on harp)

First encore

16. Like A Rolling Stone (Dylan on keyboard)

17. All Along The Watchtower (Dylan on keyboard then center stage on harp)

Second encore

18. Forever Young (Dylan on keyboard then center stage on harp)

EVENTS LEADING TO ARMAGEDDON IN DYLAN'S "SECOND BIBLE," *THE LATE GREAT PLANET EARTH*

1. The presence of a reborn and prosperous Israel provokes "a great enemy from the uttermost north of Palestine" to launch an attack on Israel.[1] Ezekiel called the leader of this northern enemy "Gog" of the land of "Magog."[2] Citing scholars who say this northern enemy is Russia, Lindsey and Carlson see Ezekiel's prophecy fulfilled in the growing strength of the Soviet Union.[3]

2. In its coming attack on Israel this northern power will be aided by a "southern confederacy," an "Arab-African" alliance consisting of Egypt, Libya, and Ethiopia. Russia will either conquer these countries or convince them to join its "northern confederacy."[4]

3. The author of Revelation describes vicious angels who dry up the Euphrates River to facilitate an invasion by the "kings of the east." According to Revelation 9:16, "the number of the army of the horseman were two hundred thousand." In a chapter titled "The Yellow Peril," Lindsey and Carlson see these passages as predicting an invasion of the Middle East by the forces of Mao Tse-tung. Lindsey and Carlson mention a television documentary in which Chinese leaders boasted that they could field an army of 200 million men—the same number as mentioned in Revelation 9:16. "Coincidence?" Lindsey asks.[5]

4. A revived Roman Empire headed by the Antichrist will come to power. This empire will not be identical, geographically speaking, to the ancient Roman Empire but it will include countries whose people have inherit-

---

1. Hal Lindsey and Carol C. Carlson, *The Late Great Planet Earth* (Grand Rapids, Michigan: Zondervan, 1970), 52.
2. Ezekiel, 38:1-3.
3. Hal Lindsey and Carol C. Carlson, *The Late Great Planet Earth*, 59-66. For a more thorough discussion of what country Ezekiel refers to in 38:1-3 see Paul Boyer, *When Time Shall Be No More: Prophecy Belief in Modern American Culture* (Cambridge: Belnap Press, 1992), 223.
4. Lindsey and Carlson base these predictions on Daniel 12:40-44. They are coming true, they say: "The territory of Northern Africa is becoming solidly pro-Soviet."
5. Ibid., 86.

ed Roman culture and traditions.[6] Lindsey sees the Common Market and the unification of Europe as signs that this empire is being formed. This new Roman empire will be aided by an "all-powerful religious system" which will "dominate the world in the time before the return of Christ."[7] This will not be the true Christian church, but rather the perverted church predicted in Revelation 17:3-5:"THE MOTHER OF HARLOTS AND OF THE ABOMINATIONS OF THE EARTH."[8] According to Lindsey and Carlson, increased drug use, sun worship on college campuses, the growing interest in astrology, and the rise of "apostate" Christian churches that stray from the teaching of the Bible are all signs that this one-world religious system is gaining in power.[9] And, Lindsey and Carlson say, the existence of "ecumenical mania," which has led to organizations like the National Council of Churches and the World Council of Churches, is a sign that this false religion is beginning to dominate the world.[10]

5. The Great Dictator, the Antichrist who leads the revived Roman empire, will sign a pact with the Israelis and allow them to rebuild their Temple. With the signing of this pact, the Great Tribulation begins.[11] This is a period of intense suffering—disease, war, starvation—which will last for seven years. True believers, however, will not suffer. Before the Tribulation begins, they will be raptured—snatched from earth to meet Jesus Christ in the air, as explained in 1 Corinthians 15:52: "In a moment, in the twinkling of an eye, at the last trump: for the trumpet shall sound, and the dead shall be raised in- corruptible" Dylan evokes this biblical passage in his song, "Ye Shall Be Changed." First believers who have died will be raptured, then those who are alive.[12] By assuming there will be a pretribulation rapture Lindsey and Carlson align themselves with dispensationalists who believe that Jesus will return to earth twice—once to remove (or rapture out) believers before the earth is devastated during the Great Tribulation; and again when he comes to judge the living and the dead and set up his Kingdom.[13]

6. War will break out when Russia invades Israel[14] in an attempt to gain a foothold in the Middle East. In a "classic double-cross," Russia will decide to turn on the countries of the Arab-African alliance. Russia will defeat them and soon conquer the Middle East.

7. The Roman Dictator will mobilize his forces to defeat Russia and, based on Ezekiel 39:6, Lindsey believes the Dictator will use nuclear weapons

---

6. Ibid., 94.
7. Ibid., 94, 185.
8. Ibid., 122.
9. Ibid., 122-130.
10. Ibid., 130-131.
11. Ibid., 152.
12. Lindsey and Carlson cite 1 Thessalonians 4:13-18.
13. Lindsey belongs to a long line of dispensationalists that goes back at least as far as J. N. Darby (1800-1882). See Robert G. Clouse, ed., *The Meaning of the Millennium: Four Views* (Downers Grove, IL: IVP Academic, 1977), 11-13.
14. Lindsey and Carlson cite Ezekiel 38:14-16.

in this battle, though this seems to be a creative interpretation of Ezekiel's prophecy that the Lord will "send a fire on Ma-gog."

8. With the Russians and their allies out of the picture, only two powerful forces remain to fight "the final climatic battle of Armageddon: the combined forces of the Western civilization united under the leadership of the Roman Dictator and the vast hordes of the Orient probably united under the Red Chinese war machine."[15] As the battle between these two forces reaches its climax, when it seems as if all life will be destroyed, Christ will return and "save man (sic) from extinction."[16]

9. Christ will separate the surviving believers[17] from the unbelievers. The believers will enjoy a thousand years of peace in a Kingdom of God ruled by Jesus, the Messiah. The unbelievers will be "cast off the earth."[18]

10. At the end of the millennium, Satan, who has been bound for 1000 years, "is released momentarily so that he could reveal the rebellion in the unbelieving hearts of those who rejected Christ as Savior."[19] Christ will crush this rebellion before fighting breaks out. At this point the history of mortal human beings will end for "all mortals will be changed into immortality" and the Kingdom of God, which existed during the millennium, will be transformed into the "new heaven and new earth," the "holy Jerusalem" described in Revelation 21.

---

15. Ibid., 162.
16. Ibid., 168.
17. Lindsey and Carlson explain that some people will become believers during the seven-year Tribulation. In other words, some people will miss the pre-tribulation rapture, but will receive a second chance at the second coming. Ibid., 143.
18. Lindsey and Carlson cite Revelation 20:11-15 and Matthew 25:31-40.
19. Ibid., 178.

THREE STRANDS OF AMERICAN PROTESTANT CHRISTIANITY: A SHORT SUMMARY*

Note: Not all protestants in the U.S. will fit neatly into one of these strands. Some people combine views from the different strands to form their own belief system.

STRAND ONE: FUNDAMENTALIST PROTESTANTS

A. Fundamentalists believe in the literal truth of the Bible. They believe that the world was created in six days as stated in Genesis, the first book of the Bible. They therefore do not accept Darwin's theory that the earth and humans developed slowly over many thousands of years. They object to the teaching of evolution in the schools if biblical creationism (the Bible's story of creation) is not also taught.

B. Some fundamentalists believe that not only the Bible but also scientific evidence supports the Genesis story of creation, a position that is called "scientific creationism" or "intelligent design."

C. Fundamentalists believe in Pre-millennialism—that Christ's return will usher in the Kingdom of God and a thousand years of peace (Revelations 20:1-5). Until He arrives there is not much that can be done to make the world better. Only personal repentance and self-purification can prepare one for the end of the world. In other words, they differ from post-millennialists who believe that Christ will return only after Christians have established a peaceful kingdom. Their belief in pre-millennialism makes fundamentalists unenthusiastic about organizations like the United Nations.

D. Fundamentalists believe in original sin which makes it impossible for people to save themselves. To be saved one must let the Holy Spirit enter one's soul. One must accept Christ's sacrifice—recognize that Christ died on the cross for our sins. Fundamentalists believe that this conversion experience, referred to as being "born again," is quick, sudden and life changing. It is an experience tied to a datable event; it is not a gradual process.

E. Fundamentalists accept a very apocalyptic vision of the end of the world and the Last Judgement. They believe that Satan (the Anti-Christ) will stage a revolt, that believers will suffer, but ultimately Christ will triumph and rule over a new heaven and a new earth (Revelations 21: 1).

F. Fundamentalists stress the differences between Christians and non-Christians.

G. Fundamentalists generally hold conservative views on political and social issues. Most do not want the government to limit their freedom. They object, for example, to laws controlling the use and sale of guns. Most fundamentalists are opposed to abortion and same-sex marriage.

STRAND TWO: LIBERAL PROTESTANTS

A. Liberal protestants are skeptical about biblical creationism. They find inspiration in stories like that of the world being built in six days, and the story of Noah's flood, and the resurrection of Christ, but they doubt the literal truth of these stories. They portray Christ as a moral teacher, not a supernatural being.

B. Liberal protestants do not have an apocalyptic vision regarding the end of the world and so they do not talk about pre-millennialism and post-millennialism. They know that in Revelation, the last book of the Bible, it is predicted that the world will end in a terrible struggle between the forces of good and evil, but they believe that if everyone works together a just and peaceful world can be achieved. They believe in working for progressive political causes and support international organizations like the United Nations.

C. Most liberal protestants do not believe in original sin. This is another reason why they are more optimistic than fundamentalists about the ability of humans to improve themselves and the world.

D. Partly because they don't believe in original sin, liberal protestants do not talk about "born again" experiences—sudden conversions in which one is visited by the Holy Ghost and one's life is suddenly changed. They tend to emphasize a gradual deepening of faith and conviction.

E. Liberals protestants tend to minimize differences between Christianity and other religions. They believe that Buddhists, Muslims, and Christians can agree on what is right and what is wrong.

F. Liberal protestants often belong to a mainline church affiliated with a long established denomination—to an Episcopalian, Methodist, Congregational, Lutheran, or Presbyterian church, for example. Many fundamentalists, on the other hand, prefer to belong to smaller denominations or Christian "fellowship groups" where there is general agreement about important doctrines.

G. Many liberal protestants accept gay marriage and are "pro-choice," or favor a woman's right to have an abortion.

STRAND THREE: EVANGELICAL PROTESTANTS

First some definitions:

The following three words derive from a Greek word, *evangelion*, which means "good news"; the word "gospel" has the same origin. They differ in the placement of the stress.

Evan*gel*ical: a member of a Protestant group who follows the beliefs and practices listed below (A through G); also used as an adjective as in the phrase "Evangelical Protestant."

*evan*gelism: the zealous preaching and dissemination of the gospel, as through missionary work.

*evan*gelist: One who practices evangelism—who preaches and disseminates the gospel

A. Evangelical protestants share some beliefs with both fundamentalists and liberal protestants. On a continuum ranging from conservative to liberal they are somewhere in between, but closer to the conservative side.

B. They believe in biblical inerrancy—that the Bible is never wrong—but are less determined to force their position on others. For example, many evangelicals may reject Darwinian evolution but they don't insist that it can't be taught in schools and don't withdraw their children from schools where it is taught.

C. Many, though not all, evangelicals reject pre-millennialism, the idea that Christ arrives first and ushers in the Kingdom of God, a view widely held by fundamentalists. Therefore many are more optimistic than fundamentalists about the possibility of moral progress. They believe humans can improve their lives.

D. Evangelicals, like fundamentalists, believe that quick and sudden conversions or "born again" experiences in which the Holy Spirit enters someone's soul are both possible and fairly common. Because of this acceptance of "born again" experiences, many Americans consider "born-again Christian" and "Evangelical Christian" as synonymous terms.

E. Evangelicals are more ecumenical than fundamentalists, more willing to reach out to and cooperate with other Christian churches.

F. Some evangelical protestants embrace an offshoot of Evangelical Protestantism called pentecostalism. Pentecostalists believe that they must experience a second baptism of the Holy Spirit, not just the widely accepted water baptism. This second baptism is similar to the "born again" experience emphasized by fundamentalists except for pentacostalists it may involve going into a trance, "speaking in tongues," the making of prophecies, and the miraculous healing of the sick. Some churches that emphasize these experiences call themselves "charismatic," not pentecostal, but the experiences charismatic churches emphasize are similar to those one might see in a pentecostal church.

G. Evangelicals believe that salvation is available to everyone, not just a select few, but that to be saved one must accept Christ. They favor cooperating with non-believers in human welfare projects.

H. Most Evangelical Christians are opposed to abortion and marriage equality.

WHAT STRAND DID BOB DYLAN BELONG TO?

The Vineyard Fellowship where Bob Dylan took Bible classes in 1979 was an Evangelical church. Clinton Heyland in his biography of Dylan says that the "Vineyard Church brand of Christianity transformed him into a Bible-thumping evangelist." However, Dylan's belief in pre-millennialism, his very apocalyptic vision of the end of the world, and his conviction that there was little people could do to improve the world are all fundamentalist traits.

APPENDIX D

A SELECTION OF SONGS BY TRỊNH CÔNG SƠN

All translations are by Cao Thị Như Quỳnh and John C. Schafer unless another translator is indicated. After the title we have included the date of composition.

Age of Stony Sadness (1961)

It's still raining rain falls everywhere
You with sad fingers on your hands
I go to church on a sad Sunday
Where is that girl with a rose pinned in her hair
Oh, the road is long
A lullaby for a thousand years, a thousand years
Lulling you warmly, lulling you warmly

It's still cloudy clouds drift aimlessly
The strands of your hair drift quickly drift quickly
Like a kind current on a sad Sunday
Where is the girl and why now is the rose forgotten in my hand
Oh, the road is long
Calming words for a thousand years, a thousand years
Lulling your anger, lulling your anger

It's still raining rain falls, rain falls
Icy cold sheets flow down my limp arms
My sad life you take with you into emptiness
Days pass indifferently

It's still raining rain falls, rain falls
Each pink cloud you carry on your shoulders
My sad life is like a leaf carried endlessly by the wind
Spinning all the way to the end of the sky

It's still raining rain falls everywhere
Your exposed heels you forget you forget
Oh, the church on a sad Sunday
Where is the girl, I wonder, as I kiss the wilted rose
You who are slender with long fingers
Calming words for a thousand years, a thousand years
Lulling your sadness, lulling your unfaithfulness

Tuổi đá buồn

Trời còn làm mưa mưa rơi mênh mang
Từng ngón tay buồn em mang em mang
Đi về giáo đường ngày chủ nhật buồn
Còn ai còn ai đóa hoa hồng cài lên tóc mây
Ôi đường phố dài
Lời ru miệt mài ngàn năm, ngàn năm
Ru em nồng nàn, ru em nồng nàn

Trời còn làm mây mây trôi lang thang
Sợi tóc em bồng trôi nhanh trôi nhanh
Như dòng nước hiền ngày chủ nhật buồn
Còn ai còn ai đóa hoa hồng vùi quên trong tay
Ôi đường phố dài
Lời ru miệt mài ngàn năm, ngàn năm
Ru em giận hờn ru em giận hờn

Trời còn làm mưa mưa rơi mưa rơi
Từng phiến băng dài trên hai tay xuôi
Tuổi buồn em mang đi trong hư vô
Ngày qua hững hờ

Trời còn làm mưa mưa rơi mưa rơi
Từng phiến mây hồng em mang trên vai
Tuổi buồn như lá gió mãi cuốn đi
Quay tận cuối trời

Trời còn làm mưa mưa rơi thênh thang
Từng gót chân trần em quên em quên
Ôi miền Giáo Đường , ngày chủ nhật buồn
Còn ai còn ai, đóa hoa hồng tàn hôn lên môi
Em gầy ngón dài
Lời ru miệt mài ngàn năm, ngàn năm
Ru em muộn phiền, ru em bạc lòng

Diễm of the Past (1960)

The rain still falls on the old tower
Your long arms, your pale eyes
Autumn leaves raining down, the tapping of
small feet
I look in the distance, straining to see

The rain still falls on small leaves
In the afternoon rain I sit waiting
In your footsteps leaves quietly fall
Coldness suddenly pervades my soul

This afternoon rain still falls why don't you
come
What if tomorrow there is pain
How can we be with each other, marks of pain
appear
I beg you to return soon

The rain still falls, life's like a stormy sea
How do you remember traces of migrating
birds
Please let the rain pass over a vast region
Let the wanderer forget he's wandering

The rain still falls, life's like a stormy sea
How do you know a gravestone feels no pain
Please let the rain pass over a vast region
In the future even stones will need each other

Diễm xưa

Mưa vẫn mưa bay trên tầng tháp cổ
Dài tay em mấy thuở mắt xanh xao
Nghe lá thu mưa reo mòn gót nhỏ
Đường dài hun hút cho mắt thêm sâu

Mưa vẫn hay mưa trên hàng lá nhỏ
Buổi chiều ngồi ngóng những chuyến mưa
qua
Trên bước chân em âm thầm lá đổ
Chợt hồn xanh buốt cho mình xót xa

Chiều này còn mưa sao em không lại
Nhỡ mai trong cơn đau vùi
Làm sao có nhau hằn lên nỗi đau
Bước chân em xin về mau

Mưa vẫn hay mưa cho đời biển động
Làm sao em nhớ những vết chim di
Xin hãy cho mưa qua miền đất rộng
Để người phiêu lãng quên mình lãng du

Mưa vẫn hay mưa cho đời biển động
Làm sao em biết bia đá không đau
Xin hãy cho mưa qua miền đất rộng
Ngày sau sỏi đá cũng cần có nhau

Don't Despair I Tell Myself (1992)

Don't despair, I tell myself, don't despair
Autumn leaves fall in the midst of winter
Don't despair, my dear, don't despair
You are I and I am you

A kite flies but the soul stays cold
The kite falls making the abyss more sad
Who am I who still hides my tears
Who am I to be still of this world
Who am I, who am I, who am I
To love this life so much

Don't despair I tell myself, don't despair
Golden sunlight fades like a private life
Don't despair, my dear, don't despair
Be yourself and the dawn will come
The road is long and the afternoon sun's rays
are lonely
Within some soul sadness softly rises

Tôi ơi đừng tuyệt vọng

Đừng tuyệt vọng, tôi ơi đừng tuyệt vọng
Lá mùa thu rơi rụng giữa mùa đông
Đừng tuyệt vọng, em ơi đừng tuyệt vọng
Em là tôi và tôi cũng là em.

Con diều bay mà linh hồn lạnh lẽo
Con diều rơi cho vực thẳm buồn thêm
Tôi là ai mà còn khi dấu lệ
Tôi là ai mà còn trần gian thế
Tôi là ai, là ai, là ai?
Mà yêu quá đời này.

Đừng tuyệt vọng, tôi ơi đừng tuyệt vọng
Nắng vàng phai như một nỗi đời riêng
Đừng tuyệt vọng, em ơi đừng tuyệt vọng
Em hồn nhiên rồi em sẽ bình minh
Có đường xa và nắng chiều quạnh quê
Có hồn ai đang nhè nhẹ sầu lên

Do You Remember? (1972)

Christ has abandoned humankind
Buddha has abandoned humankind
So please abandon someone
So please abandon me
Life around here has thousands of invitations
Life around here is full of voices welcoming
you
We are all used to separations

Christ has abandoned humankind
Budda has abandoned humankind
Please save a life
Please come to me
Because the rivers are drying up
Because the wind tonight sings a prison song
Come to me and stand near my sorrow

Christ has abandoned humankind
Buddha has abandoned humankind
Do you remember life
Do you know humankind
Do you remember me at all

Này Em Có Nhớ

Chúa đã bỏ loài người
Phật đã bỏ loài người
Này em xin cứ phu người
Này em hãy đến tìm tôi
Đời sống quanh đây có vạn lời mời
Đời sống quanh đây tiếng người mừng gọi
em vào
Đời đã quen với những kiếp xa nhau.

Chúa đã bỏ loài người
Phật đã bỏ loài người
Này em xin cứu một người.
Này em hãy đến tìm tôi
Vì những con sông đã cạn nguồn rồi
Vì gió đêm nay hát lời tù tội quanh đời
Về cùng tôi đứng bên âu lo này.

Chúa đã bỏ loài người
Phật đã bỏ loài người
Này em có nhớ cuộc đời
Này em có biết loài người
Này em có nhớ gì tôi

Each Day I Choose a Little Happiness (1977)

Each day I choose a little happiness
Choose flowers and smiles
I pick wind from sky and invite you to take it
So your eyes will smile like flying leaves

And in this way I live happily each day
And in this way I enter life
A life I love with all my heart

Each day I choose a road to walk
A road that leads to brothers, sisters, and friends
I wait for you to return, for those familiar foot-
steps
Crossing a golden carpet of tamarind leaves

Each day I choose a little happiness
With brothers and sisters I search for everyone
I choose this place to sing together
So noisy laughter fills the air

Each day I choose one time only
Choose a lullaby for a child softly stepping into life
I choose full sunshine, choose a rainstorm
So rice plants cry joyfully and wave like hands

Each day I choose to sit quietly
Looking closely at my native land, thinking about
myself
I suddenly realize why I live
Because the country needs a good heart

Mỗi ngày tôi chọn một niềm vui

Mỗi ngày tôi chọn một niềm vui
Chọn những bông hoa và những nụ cười
Tôi nhặt gió trời mời em giữ lấy
Để mắt em cười tựa lá bay

Và như thế tôi sống vui từng ngày
Và như thế tôi đến trong cuộc đời
Đã yêu cuộc đời này bằng trái tim của tôi

Mỗi ngày tôi chọn đường mình đi
Đường đến anh em đường đến bạn bè
Tôi đợi em về bàn chân quen quá
Thảm lá me vàng lại bước qua

Mỗi ngày tôi chọn một niềm vui
Cùng với anh em tìm đến mọi người
Tôi chọn nơi này cùng nhau ca hát
Để thấy tiếng cười rộn rã bay

Mỗi ngày tôi chọn một lần thôi
Chọn tiếng ru con nhẹ bước vào đời

Tôi chọn nắng đầy chọn cơn mưa tới
Để lúa reo mừng tựa vẫy tay

Mỗi ngày tôi chọn ngồi thật yên
Nhìn rõ quê hương ngồi nghỉ lại mình
Tôi chợt biết rằng vì sao tôi sống
Vì đất nước cần một trái tim

Evening in My Native Land (1980)

Evening in my native land
Sometimes a rain-filled sky
Sometimes sun-drenched pine trees on a hill
Sometimes a distant river in the mist

Evening in my native land
Sunlight on bright red tile roofs
Wind brings news of a season to come
With long rains or many days of sun

Evening in my native land
With private places for everyone
Streets that couples stroll along
Happy street corners in the towns
Drops of evening on the leaves
Like smiling eyes as evening fades

Evening in my native land
Sun rays fold like wings at end of day
Red and gold traces at the edge of clouds
Homeward footsteps here and there
Evening fades but some light remains
As cooking fires start to glow

Evening in my native land
Wind comes to play from the distant sea
Mountains the purple of myrtle flowers
A city kissed by sunlight in the dusk

Evening in my native land
Wishes for many things that have passed
A lifetime of memories for you alone
Our native land will remain forever

Chiều Trên Quê Hương Tôi

Chiều trên quê hương tôi
Có khi đây một trời mưa bay
Có nơi kia đồi thông nắng đầy
Có trên sông bờ xa sương khói

Chiều trên quê hương tôi
Nắng phơi trên màu ngói non tươi
Gió mang tin một mùa sẽ tới
Sẽ mưa lâu hoặc cơn nắng dài

Chiều trên quê hương tôi
Có những chốn riêng cho mọi người
Những con đường lứa đôi
Những góc hè phố vui
Giọt chiều trên lá
Như mắt người cười giữa chiều phai
Chiều trên quê hương tôi
Nắng khép cánh chia tay một ngày
Vết son vàng cuối mây
Tiếng chân về đó đây
Chiều đi nhưng nắng vẫn cho đời
Lửa bếp hồng khơi

Chiều trên quê hương tôi
Gió đến chơi từ bờ biển xa
Núi đồi khi màu sim tím lạ
Nắng như môi hoàng hôn trên phố

Chiều trên quê hương tôi
Ước bao nhiêu điều đã trôi qua,
Có riêng em cuộc đời sẽ nhớ
Nét quê hương nghìn năm vẫn là

The Eye That Remains (1992)

There's still two eyes and for people one eye cries
There's still two eyes and one eye cries for people
The eye that remains looks at my life
Looks at me climbing high, looks at me going
down low
The eye that remains looks at a love that's faded
Love in two hands that one day vanished
The eye that remains, whose eye is it
The eye that remains looks at me sighing

There's still two eyes and for people one eye cries
There's still two eyes and one eye cries for people
The eye that remains looks at one becoming two
Looks at you as loving, looks at you as fierce
The eye that remains suspects my love
Loves like crazy and misses like crazy
The eye that remains looks at white clouds fly
The eye that remains looks at me sadly

There's still two eyes and for people one eye cries
There's still two eyes and one eye cries for people

Con mắt còn lại

Còn hai con mắt khóc người một con
Còn hai con mắt một con khóc người
Con mắt còn lại nhìn cuộc đời tôi
Nhìn tôi lên cao nhìn tôi xuống thấp
Con mắt còn lại nhìn cuộc tình phai
Tình trong hai tay một hôm biến mất
Con mắt còn lại là con mắt ai
Con mắt còn lại nhìn tôi thở dài

Còn hai con mắt khóc người một con
Còn hai con mắt một con khóc người
Con mắt còn lại nhìn một thành hai
Nhìn em yêu thương nhìn em thú dữ
Con mắt còn lại ngờ vực tình tôi
Cuồng điên yêu thương cuồng điên nỗi nhớ
Con mắt còn lại nhìn mây trắng bay
Con mắt còn lại nhìn tôi bùi ngùi

Còn hai con mắt khóc người một con
Còn hai con mắt một con khóc người

The eye that remains looks at life as nothingness
Looks at you as emptiness, looks at you as sun
and shade
The eye that remains is gentle and loving
Looks at you leaving and your heart faraway
The eye that remains is a dark and gloomy night
The eye that remains is a passionate night

Con mắt còn lại nhìn đời là không
Nhìn em hư vô nhìn em bóng nắng
Con mắt còn lại nhẹ nhàng từ tâm
Nhìn em ra đi lòng em xa vắng
Con mắt còn lại là đêm tối tăm
Con mắt còn lại là đêm nồng nàn

Huế Saigon Hanoi (1969)

Huế, Saigon, Hanoi—native land why still so far
Huế, Saigon, Hanoi—why indifferent for all these
years
Oh Vietnam
How much longer must people sit missing each
other
A million sisters
A million brothers
In all three regions rise up and revolt
The time has come for young people to join
together
Young people
It's time to take pioneering steps
From the Center, the South, and the North

To light torches hailing freedom
On the road where there are prisons
We'll build schools and markets
Our people will return to till the fields and will be
well clothed and fed
As our hands work to rebuild the country the old
hatred fades
There will be roofs on our houses, fruits in our
gardens
So you can go to the mountain top to sing happy
love songs
North, South, Center—come together and make
one region
Break down borders, widen roads, and build a
peaceful land

Huế, Saigon, Hanoi—twenty years weeping tears
of misery
Huế, Saigon, Hanoi—within each of us a Vietnam-
ese heart is hurting
There's bullets and bombs and human greed but
no weapons can kill our people
Oh Vietnam, wake up from dreams so eyes can
drive away hatred
Erase all traces of the old sadness
Tomorrow flowers will bloom along the roads in
the North and the South
Friendly hands, hearts without borders
Oh brothers and sisters, listen to our love for each
other

Huế Sài gòn Hà Nội

Huế Sài Gòn Hà Nội
Quê hương ơi sao vẫn còn xa
Huế Sài Gòn Hà Nội
Bao nhiêu năm sao vẫn thờ ơ
Việt Nam ơi
Còn bao lâu những con người ngồi nhớ
thương nhau
Triệu chân em
Triệu chân anh
Hỡi ba miền vùng lên cách mạng
Đã đến lúc nối tấm lòng chung
Tuổi thanh niên
Hãy đi bằng những bước tiến phong
Từ Trung Nam Bắc
Chờ mong nung đốt
Những bó đuốc reo vui tự do
Đường đi đến những nơi lao tù
Ngày mai sẽ xây trường hay họp chợ
Dân ta về cày bừa đủ áo cơm no
Bàn tay giúp nước bàn tay kiến thiết
Những dấu căm hờn xưa nhạt mờ
Nhà ta xây mái vườn ta thêm trái
Cho em ra đầu núi ca tình vui
Bắc Nam Trung ơi đoàn kết một miền
Phá biên thuỳ mở rộng đường thêm
Dựng nước bình yên

Huế Sài Gòn Hà Nội hai mươi năm tiếng khóc
lầm than
Huế Sài Gòn Hà Nội trong ta đau trái tim Việt
Nam
Đạn bom ơi
Lòng tham ơi khí giới nào diệt nổi dân ta
Việt Nam ơi
Bừng cơn mơ cho mắt nhìn sạch tan căm thù
Hãy xoá hết dấu tích buồn xưa
Ngày mai đây những con đường Nam Bắc nở
hoa
Bàn tay thân ái lòng không biên giới
Anh em ơi lắng nghe tình nhau
Ngày vui lớn sẽ qua trăm cầu
Mẹ dâng miếng cau rồi dâng ngọn trầu
Cho hai miền trùng phùng lòng thấy nao nao
Ngày-nam-đêm-bắc tình chan trong mắt
Sẽ thấy trăm bình minh ngọt ngào

On happy days crossing a hundred bridges
Mothers offering the areca nut and the betel leaf*
uniting the two regions
On southern days and northern nights
Eyes overflowing with love will see a hundred
sweet dawns
Our hearts gallop like a horse flying in the wind
Our people will grow up in freedom
North, South, Center—deep feelings for each other
Step away for once from extermination
Build one common house for all

Ngựa bay trong gió lòng reo muôn vó
Cho dân ta bừng lớn trong tự do
Bắc Nam Trung ơi tình nghĩa mặn nồng
Bước ra ngoài một lần diệt vong
Dựng mái nhà chung.

I Sing You to Sleep (1967)

I sing you to sleep
On a morning in Winter
You go out to the rice field
And greet a branch of new rice
I sing you to sleep
On a morning in Fall
You go in the mist
And call the leaves into the season

The road is truly sad
On a day at the end of Winter
The road is unclear
On a day at the end of Fall
You go into Summer
Sunshine lights up the sky
And on some spring
Stirred by a new love

Go lightly into life
Tapping your feet softly
You call the bud of a rose
Just wilted at the end of the yard
Hearing a love suddenly turning sad
In the bustling leaves
So the following Spring
I acquire a sad love

I sing you to sleep
On a morning in Spring
You kiss the bud of a rose
And greet drops of sunshine
I sing you to sleep
Summer's just passed
You kiss your hand
Feeling sorry for love in the world

Tôi ru em ngủ

Tôi ru em ngủ
Một sớm mùa Đông
Em ra ngoài ruộng đồng
Hỏi thăm cành lúa mới
Tôi rue em ngủ
Một sớm mùa Thu
Em đi trong sương mù
Gọi cây lá vào mùa

Con đường thật buồn
Một ngày cuối Đông
Con đường mịt mù
Một ngày cuối Thu
Em vào mùa Hạ
Nắng thắp trên cao
Và mùa xuân nào
Ngẩn ngơ tình mới

Đi nhẹ vào đời
Thầm thì gót chân
Em gọi nụ hồng
Vừa tàn cuối sân
Nghe tình chợt buồn
Trong lá xôn xao
Để mùa Xuân sau
Mua riêng tình sầu

Tôi ru em ngủ
Một sớm mùa Xuân
Em hôn một nụ hồng
Hỏi thăm về giọt nắng
Tôi ru em ngủ
Hạ cũng vừa sang
Em hôn lên tay mình
Để chua xót tình trần

---

* Chewing a quid of the areca nut and a betel leaf is an ancient custom in Vietnam. Offered at engagements and weddings and other ceremonies, it symbolizes a union destined to last for a long time.

Let the Wind Blow It Away (1971)

To live in this life
One needs a good heart
To do what with do you know
To let the wind blow it away
To let the wind blow it away

The wind blows so clouds pass over rivers
The day's just arisen or night vastly falls
Oh the heart can fly with time
Becoming a shadow and spreading lies

But when evening comes
There needs to be laughter
To think about as the leaves fly
Then the water carries them away
Then the water carries them away

Consider life from a different angle
Look carefully at this love
Just listen quietly don't say a word
To hurt the heart
To hurt the heart

In the heart a sick bird lies still
Sleeping a long time with a wound that's deep
One morning the bird flies away forever
And its singing dissolves in the rising wind

Love the day that's coming
Though tired of life
As long as there's life be happy
Though someone is gone
Though someone is gone

Để gió cuốn đi

Sống trong đời sống
Cần có một tấm lòng
Để làm gì em biết không
Để gió cuốn đi
Để gió cuốn đi

Gió cuốn đi cho mây qua dòng sông
Ngày vừa lên hay đêm xuống mênh mông
Ôi trái tim đang bay theo thời gian
Làm chiếc bóng đi rao lời dối gian

Những khi chiều tới
Cần có một tiếng cười
Để ngậm ngùi theo lá bay
Rồi nước cuốn trôi
Rồi nước cuốn trôi

Hãy nghiêng đời xuống
Nhìn suốt một mối tình
Chỉ lặng nhìn không nói năng
Để buốt trái tim
Để buốt trái tim

Trong trái tim con chim đau nằm yên
Ngủ dài lâu mang theo vết thương sâu
Một sớm mai chim bay đi triền miên
Và tiếng hót tan trong trời gió lên

Hãy yêu ngày tới
Dù quá mệt kiếp người
Còn cuộc đời ta cứ vui
Dù vắng bóng ai
Dù vắng bóng ai.

Like the Wing of a Flying Heron (1964)

Is the sunshine as rosy as your lips
Is the rain as sad as your eyes
Your hair in small strands
Falls on life and makes the waves drift

The wind's happy because your hair flies,
The cloud sulks and sleeps on your shoulder
A shoulder slender and small
Like the wing of a heron returning to a far off place

Is the sunshine still jealous of your lips
Is the rain still sad in your clear eyes
From the time I took you home
I knew we would be far apart.

The stream greets your passing feet,
The leaves sing in your scented hands,
The leaves are dry because they wait

Như cánh vạc bay

Nắng có hồng bằng đôi môi em
Mưa có buồn bằng đôi mắt em
Tóc em từng sợi nhỏ
Rớt xuống đời làm sóng lênh đênh

Gió sẽ mừng vì tóc em bay
Cho mây hờn ngủ quên trên vai
Vai em gầy guộc nhỏ
Như cánh vạc về chốn xa xôi

Nắng có còn hờn ghen môi em
Mưa có còn buồn trong mắt trong
Từ lúc đưa em về
Là biết xa nghìn trùng

Suối đón từng bàn chân em qua
Lá hát từ bàn tay thơm tho
Lá khô vì đợi chờ
Cũng như đời người mãi âm u

Like someone's life that's always somber

Is it happy where you are
Is the sky blue where you are
I hear every single tear drop
Falling to become a sparkling lake

Nơi em về ngày vui không em
Nơi em về trời xanh không em
Ta nghe từng giọt lệ
Rớt xuống thành hồ nước long lanh

Like Words of Good By (1981)

All my rendezvous now closed,
Body light as a cloud;
A little light's just hurried off too
Closing each happy night.

Well trodden streets wait all day long
For feet from old times that pass uncertain
How can you know each private life
To love more and with more passion

A rose from the past remains
Next to my life here,
A little love passes like a hurried breeze,
I suddenly recognize myself

I want one time to thank life
That's given me some passion
At times I lie down and hear laughter
But it's just a dream

Love's like light that at sunset rushes off
Love's not far but not so near
Love's like a rock full of endless longing,
Love's uncertain and leaves us sad and worried

I remember the whispering each night
It seems like drunkenness now
Delicate golden flowers at the edge of the sky
Like words of good by

Như một lời chia tay

Những hẹn hò từ nay khép lại
Thân nhẹ nhàng như mây
Chút nắng vàng giờ đây cũng vội
Khép lại từng đêm vui

Đường quen lối từng sớm chiều mong
Bàn chân xưa qua đây ngại ngần
Làm sao biết từng nỗi đời riêng
Để yêu thêm yêu cho nồng nàn

Có nụ hồng ngày xưa rớt lại
Bên cạnh đời tôi đây
Có chút tình thoảng như gió vội
Tôi chợt nhìn ra tôi

Muốn một lần tạ ơn với đời
Chút mặn nồng cho tôi
Có những lần nằm nghe tiếng cười
Nhưng chỉ là mơ thôi

Tình như nắng vội tắt chiều hôm
Tình không xa nhưng không thật gần
Tình như đá hoài nỗi chờ mong
Tình vu vơ cho ta muộn phiền

Tiếng thì thầm từng đêm nhớ lại
Tưởng chỉ là cơn say
Đóa hoa vàng mỏng manh cuối trời
Như một lời chia tay

Love Song of a Mad Person (1967)

I love someone killed in the Battle of Pleime
I love someone killed in Battlezone D
Killed at Dong Xoai, killed in Hanoi
Killed suddenly near the border

I love someone killed in the battle of Chu Prong
I love someone whose corpse floats on the river
Killed in a rice field, killed in a dense jungle
Killed coldly, the body charred like coal

I want to love you, to love Vietnam
In the storm my lips whisper your name
And the name Vietnam
Bound together by our golden-skin tongue

I want to love you, to love Vietnam
Growing up our ears became used to gunfire

Tình ca của người mất trí

Tôi có người yêu chết trận Pleime,
Tôi có người yêu ở chiến khu "Đ"
Chết trận Đồng xoài, chết ngoài Hà Nội
Chết vội vàng, dọc theo biên giới

Tôi có người yêu chết trận Chu Prong
Tôi có người yêu bỏ xác trôi sông
Chết ngoài ruộng đồng, chết rừng mịt mùng
Chết lạnh lùng, mình cháy như than

Tôi muốn yêu anh yêu Việt Nam
Ngày gió lớn tôi đi môi gọi thầm
Gọi tên anh, tên Việt Nam
Gần nhau trong tiếng nói da vàng

Tôi muốn yêu anh, yêu Việt Nam
Ngày mới lớn tai nghe quen đạn mìn

My hands and lips are useless now
I've forgotten my human voice

I love someone killed in the Battle of Asao
I love someone now a twisted corpse
Killed in a mountain pass, killed under a bridge
Killed and left unclothed, choking in anger

I love someone killed in the Battle of Ba Gia
I love someone just killed yesterday
Killed by chance, killed with no appointment
Killed without hate, dead as a dream

Thừa đôi tay dư làn môi
Từ nay tôi quên hết tiếng người

Tôi có người yêu chết trận Asao
Tôi có người yêu nằm chết cong queo
Chết vào lòng đèo, chết cận gầm cầu
Chết nghẹn ngào, mình không manh áo

Tôi có người yêu chết trận Ba Gia
Tôi có người yêu vừa chết hôm qua
Chết thật tình cờ, chết chẳng hẹn hò
Không hận thù, nằm chết như mơ

Lullaby for You (1965)

A lullaby for you late in the night
A lullaby for you in the dark months
A lullaby for you on the the rough nights
A lullaby for you though we're far apart

A lullaby for you for nights in the past
A lullaby for you for betraying me
A lullaby for you I kneel like a slave
A lullaby for you because of your regal manner

A lullaby for you for sweetness in the past
A lullaby for you for unfortunate lives
Loving you I love betrayal more
Loving you suddenly loving kindness and
compassion fill my heart

A lullaby for you the luxury you crave
A lullaby for you full of passion
A lullaby for you a vague sense of love and duty
A lullaby for you a lullaby for you submerged
in a storm

A lullaby for you exhausted from pain
A lullaby for you returning in a dream
A lullaby for you carrying a child
A lullaby for you a lullaby for you thin and
suffering

At the end of life there's nothing more
The dream I craved is gone
Sometimes the heart makes arrangements

Grieving because a rainy day begins

Ru em

Ru em ngủ những đêm khuya
Ru em ngủ tháng âm u
Ru em cùng những u mê
Ru em, ru em dù đã chia xa

Ru em vì những đêm xưa
Ru em phụ rẫy trong ta
Ru em quì gối vong nô
Ru em, ru em vì dáng kiêu sa

Ru từng ngọt bùi đã qua
Ru người lận đận héo khô
Yêu em, yêu thêm tình phụ
Yêu em lòng chợt từ bi bất ngờ

Ru em thèm khát xa hoa
Ru em đầy những đam mê
Ru em tình nghĩa vu vơ
Ru em, ru em chìm dưới phong ba

Ru em mệt lả cơn đau
Ru em về giữa chiêm bao
Ru em bồng bế con theo
Ru em, ru em gầy yếu hư hao

Thôi rồi còn gì nữa đâu
Đã tàn mộng mị khát khao
Đôi khi con tim hò hẹn
Ngậm ngùi vì một ngày mưa bắt đầu.

A Lullaby of Cannons for the Night (1967)

Every night cannons resound in the town
A street cleaner stops sweeping and listens
The cannons wake up a mother
The cannons disturb a sad young child
At midnight a flare shines in the mountains

Every night cannons resound in the town
A street cleaner stops sweeping and listens
Each flight of the planes frightens the child
Destroying the shelter, tearing golden skin
Each night the native land's eyes stay open wide

Thousands of bombs rain down on the village
Thousands of bombs rain down on the field
And Vietnamese homes burn bright in the hamlet
Thousands of trucks with Claymores and grenades
Thousands of trucks enter the cities
Carrying the remains of mothers, sisters, brothers

Every night cannons resound in the town
A street cleaner stops sweeping and listens
Every night cannons, the future falls like golden leaves
Cannons like a chant without a prayer
Children forget to live and anxiously wait

Every night cannons resound in the town
A street cleaner stops sweeping and listens
Every night cannons sing a lullaby for golden skin
The cannons sound like a prelude to a familiar sad song
And children are gone before they see their native land

Đại bác ru đêm

Đại bác đêm đêm dội về thành phố
Người phu quét đường dừng chổi đứng nghe
Đại bác qua đây đánh thức mẹ dậy
Đại bác qua đây con thơ buồn tủi
Nửa đêm sáng chói hoả châu trên núi

Đại bác đêm đêm dội về thành phố
Người phu quét đường dừng chổi đứng nghe
Từng chuyến bay đêm con thơ giật mình
Hầm trú tan hoang ôi da thịt vàng
Từng đêm chong sáng là mắt quê hương

Hằng vạn tấn bom trút xuống đầu làng
Hằng vạn tấn bom trút xuống ruộng đồng
Cửa nhà Việt Nam cháy đỏ cuối thôn
Hằng vạn chuyến xe Clay-more lựu đạn
Hằng vạn chuyến xe mang vô thị thành
Từng vùng thịt xương có mẹ có em

Đại bác đêm đêm dội về thành phố
Người phu quét đường dừng chổi đứng nghe
Đại bác đêm đêm tương lai rụng vàng
Đại bác như kinh không mang lời nguyện
Trẻ thơ quên sống từng đêm nghe ngóng

Đại bác đêm đêm dội về thành phố
Người phu quét đường dừng chổi đứng nghe
Đại bác đêm đêm ru da thịt vàng
Đại bác nghe quen như câu dạo buồn
Trẻ con chưa lớn để thấy quê hương

Morning in Spring (1969)

On a morning in spring
A child plays in a field
Steps on a buried mine
His legs fly away

On a morning in spring
His chest lies in pieces
Thousands of flowers
Gaze down on his heart

My child, your school has reopened
On the playground no word is spoken
On new paper a lesson of love
Why now is the ink so faded

On a morning in spring
A child lies quiet and still
His hands holding wild flowers
Fragile petals of gold

Một buổi sáng mùa xuân

Một buổi sáng mùa xuân
Một đứa bé ra đồng
Đạp trái mìn nổ chậm
Xác không còn đôi chân

Một buổi sáng mùa xuân
Ngực đứa bé tan tành
Ngàn hoa đồng cỏ nội
Cúi xuống nhìn con tim.

Em thơ ơi chiều nay trường học lại
Trong sân chơi bạn và thầy im lời
Bài học về yêu thương trên giấy mới
Sao hôm nay nét mực đã phai.

Một buổi sáng mùa xuân
Một đứa bé yên nằm
Bàn tay cầm cỏ dại
Có hoa vàng mong manh

On a morning in spring	Một buổi sáng mùa xuân
A child lies quiet and still	Một đứa bé im lìm
His lips form a question	Bờ môi đường thẩm hỏi
Is there a paradise?	Có thiên đường hay không?

A Mother's Legacy (1965)

Gia tài của mẹ

A thousand years slaves of the Chinese*	Một ngàn năm nô lệ giặc Tàu
A hundred years dominated by the French†	Một trăm năm đô hộ giặc Tây
Twenty years of daily civil war‡	Hai mươi năm nội chiến từng ngày
A mother's legacy, to leave for her children	Gia tài của mẹ để lại cho con
A mother's legacy, the sad country of Vietnam	Gia tài của mẹ là nước Việt buồn
A thousand years slaves of the Chinese	Một ngàn năm nô lệ giặc Tàu
A hundred years dominated by the French	Một trăm năm đô hộ giặc Tây
Twenty years of daily civil war	Hai mươi năm nội chiến từng ngày
A mother's legacy, a forest of dry bones	Gia tài của mẹ một rừng xương khô
A mother's legacy, a mountain of graves	Gia tài của mẹ một núi đầy mồ
Teach the children truthful speech	Dạy cho con tiếng nói thật thà
Mother hopes her children won't forget the color of their skin	Mẹ mong con chớ quên màu da
Children don't forget the skin color of the old Vietnam	Con chớ quên màu da nước Việt xưa
Mother waits for her children to come home	Mẹ trông con mau bước về nhà
Mother hopes that her children far away	Mẹ mong con lũ con đường xa
Oh children of the same father, will forget hatred	Ôi lũ con cùng cha quên hận thù
	Một ngàn năm nô lệ giặc Tàu
	Một trăm năm đô hộ giặc Tây
	Hai mươi năm nội chiến từng ngày
A thousand years slaves of the Chinese	Gia tài của mẹ ruộng đồng khô khan
A hundred years dominated by the French	Gia tài của mẹ nhà cháy từng hàng
Twenty years of daily civil war	
A mother's legacy, rice fields all dry	Một ngàn năm nô lệ giặc Tàu
A mother's legacy, rows of burned homes	Một trăm năm đô hộ giặc Tây
	Hai mươi năm nội chiến từng ngày
A thousand years slaves of the Chinese	Gia tài của mẹ một bọn lai căng
A hundred years dominated by the French	Gia tài của mẹ một lũ bội tình
Twenty years of daily civil war	
A mother's legacy, a mixed-blood gang	
A mother's legacy, an unfaithful horde§	

---

* The Han Chinese annexed the country of the Vietnamese, called Au Lac, in 207 B.C. In 939 A.D. the Vietnamese defeated the Chinese and achieved independence. That adds up to about a thousand years—1146 years—of Chinese control.

† French forces captured Saigon in 1861 and established the colony of Cochinchina in south Vietnam. The French ruled Tonkin (north Vietnam) and Annam (central Vietnam) indirectly as "protectorates." The Vietnamese defeated the French in 1954. This adds up to around 100 years of French domination.

‡ The First Indochina War, in which the French (and Vietnamese allied with them) fought Việt Minh forces inspired by Hồ Chí Minh, began in 1946 and ended in 1954. The Second Indochina War, or "American War," in which Americans (and Vietnamese allied with them) fought the North Vietnamese and Vietcong (troops of the National Liberation Front), began in 1964 or 1965. After 1954 there were some years of peace but the country was still divided and tensions between the north and south were high. Thus, Trịnh Công Sơn's reference to twenty years makes sense. He refers, it seems, to the period from 1946 to 1965.

§ In Chapter One I suggest that "mixed-blood gang" and "unfaithful horde" could refer to those who embraced the communist-led revolution (with help from Russia and China); or to those who supported the Republic of Vietnam and its ally, the US. These final two lines could be Trịnh Công Sơn's way of acknowledging the international dimensions of the conflict.

Pink Rain (1964)

The sky nurtures sunshine to make pink clouds
The clouds pass quickly, you bend in sorrow
The rain falls as on another day you visited
Clouds quietly make the wind rise

A person sits there watching a big storm
Oh, love feels like sadness
Out there leaves still seem green
Out there far away the river rises and flows for
miles

You cried on a rainy afternoon on a high hill
There's nothing left, it's been foggy for a long time
You go home on the bridge, the rain wets your
dress
Flying poinciana flowers are clouding the way
Lines of green leafed trees are touching each other

A person sits down, head surrounded in clouds
Waiting many afternoons for you to come
Arms for embracing have weakened
Oh, time has worn out wandering feet

A person sits and asks for plentiful rain
On two hands a long-lasting pain
A person lies down and listens to a lullaby
Life is too brief to be indifferent

Mưa hồng

Trời ươm nắng cho mây hồng
Mây qua mau em nghiêng sầu
Còn mưa xuống như hôm nào em đến thăm
Mây âm thầm mang gió lên

Người ngồi đó trông mưa nguồn
Ôi yêu thương nghe đã buồn
Ngoài kia lá như vẫn xanh
Ngoài sông vắng nước dâng lên hồn muôn
trùng

Nay em đã khóc chiều mưa đỉnh cao
Còn gì nữa đâu sương mù đã lâu
Em đi về cầu mưa ướt áo
Đường phượng bay mù không lối vào
Hàng cây lá xanh gần với nhau

Người ngồi xuống mây ngang đầu
Mong em qua, bao nhiêu chiều
Vòng tay đã xanh xao nhiều
Ôi tháng năm gót chân mòn trên phiếm du

Người ngồi xuống xin mưa đầy
Trên hai tay cơn đau dài
Người nằm xuống nghe tiếng ru
Cuộc đời đó có bao lâu mà hững hờ

A Place for Leaving and Returning (1974)

For years I've wandered here and there
Going in circles, growing weary of life
On my shoulders the sun and the moon
Lighting a lifetime, a place for leaving and
returning

What word from the trees, what word from
the grass
An evening of pleasure, a life so light as time
passes
First spring is gone, then summer too
In early fall one hears horses returning from afar

Clouds overhead, sun on my shoulders
I walk away, the river stays
From love's spirit an unbidden call
While in me human shadows rise

Rain makes me miss rain long ago
Rain falling in me drop by small drop
Years without end and never a meeting
One doesn't know which place is home

The road goes in circles, miserable and sad
One side's new grass, the other dreams of the
past

Một cõi đi về

Bao nhiêu năm rồi còn mãi ra đi
Đi đâu loanh quanh cho đời mỏi mệt
Trên hai vai ta đôi vầng nhật nguyệt
Rọi suốt trăm năm một cõi đi về

Lời nào của cây lời nào cỏ lạ
Một chiều ngồi say, một đời thật nhẹ ngày qua
Vừa tàn mùa xuân rồi tàn mùa hạ
Một ngày đầu thu nghe chân ngựa về chốn xa

Mây che trên đầu và nắng trên vai
Đôi chân ta đi sông còn ở lại
Con tinh yêu thương vô tình chợt gọi
Lại thấy trong ta hiện bóng con người

Nghe mưa nơi nầy lại nhớ mưa xa
Mưa bay trong ta bay từng hạt nhỏ
Trăm năm vô biên chưa từng hội ngộ
Chẳng biết nơi nao là chốn quê nhà

Đường chạy vòng quanh một vòng tiểu tụy
Một bờ cỏ non một bờ mộng mị ngày xưa
Từng lời tà dương là lời mộ địa
Từng lời bể sông nghe ra từ độ suối khe

Trong khi ta về lại nhớ ta đi
Đi lên non cao đi về biển rộng

Each sunset's call is also the grave's At the sea's edge one hears a stream far away	Đôi tay nhân gian chưa từng độ lượng Ngọn gió hoang vu thổi buốt xuân thì
Returning I remember leaving I climb the high mountain, descend to the wide sea But my arms have yet to cover this world In this young life a sad wind blows	Hôm nay ta say ôm đời ngủ muộn Để sớm mai đây lại tiếc xuân thì
Today I'll drink, then wake up late At early morn I'll regret my lost spring	

## Sad Sacred Words (1959)	## Lời buồn thánh
A sad Sunday afternoon Lying in a lonely room Oh, the pale sad singing of an afternoon Rain, rain without end Oh, how lonely I still am	Chiều chúa nhật buồn Nằm trong căn gác đìu hiu Ôi tiếng hát xanh xao của một buổi chiều Trời mưa, trời mưa không dứt Ô hay mình vẫn cô liêu
A sad Sunday afternoon Lying in a lonely room Hearing the pale sad singing of an afternoon, Friends far from sleeping mat and blanket Desolate for how long	Chiều chúa nhật buồn Nằm trong căn gác đìu hiu Nghe tiếng hát xanh xao của một buổi chiều Bạn bè rời xa chăn chiếu Bơ vơ còn đến bao giờ
A sad Sunday afternoon, Lying in a lonely room Please give me the five fingers of your angel hand In the midst of regret, through fits of sulking Please enter loneliness with the five fingers of your hand	Chiều chúa nhật buồn Nằm trong căn gác đìu hiu Tôi xin em năm ngón tay thiên thần Trong vùng ăn năn, qua cơn hờn dỗi Tôi xin năm ngón tay em đi vào cô đơn.
A sad Sunday afternoon, listening to the wind return A sad Sunday afternoon, listening to the wind return A sad Sunday afternoon, listening to the wind return Afternoon ...	Chiều chúa nhật buồn lặng nghe gió đi về Chiều chúa nhật buồn lặng nghe gió đi về Chiều chúa nhật buồn lặng nghe gió đi về Chiều, chiều

## Tears for the Native Land (1965)	## Nước mắt cho quê hương
Tears of love for a child The child sleeps, the mother's pleased Tears of love for a river Hugging the water plants Tears of love for the earth Barren for years Tears of love for the people Our people suffer a hard fate	Giọt nước mắt thương con Con ngủ mẹ mừng Giọt nước mắt thương sông Ấp ủ rêu rong Giọt nước mắt thương đất Đất cằn cõi bao năm Giọt nước mắt thương dân Dân mình phận long đong
Tears of love for the clouds The clouds sleep above the forest Tears of love for the trees Trees fall in the mountains	Giọt nước mắt thương mây Mây ngủ trên ngàn Giọt nước mắt thương cây Cây ngả trên non

Tears of love for you [anh]*	Giọt nước mắt thương anh
Your blood-dry body	Khô giòng máu châu thân
Tears of love for the native land	Giọt nước mắt quê hương
Oh they flow without end	Ôi còn chảy miên man

Oh the endless streams of tears	Ôi giòng nước mắt chảy hoài
Flowing forever	Giòng nước mắt đời đời
Tears of love for someone	Giọt nước mắt thương ai
Oh streams of tears from the heart	Ôi giòng nước mắt trong tim
Drenching the soul	Chảy lai láng vào hồn
They wake us in the dead of night	Nửa đêm gọi đến mình

Tears of love for the birds	Giọt nước mắt thương chim
Birds flee the forest	Chim bỏ xa rừng
Tears of love for the night	Giọt nước mắt thương đêm
The night pushes the hearse	Đêm đẩy xe tang
Tears of love for you [em]†	Giọt nước mắt thương em
During this troubled time	Trên vận nước điêu linh
Tears with no name	Giọt nước mắt không tên
Tears shed for the native land	Xin để lại quê hương

Thank Life a Little (1993) — Cho đời chút ơn

In town one day I glimpsed you across the street	Hôm chợt thấy em đi về bên kia phố
Suddenly my heart filled with a very strange glee	Trong lòng bỗng vui như đời rất lạ
I found myself following your steps	Tôi tìm thấy tôi theo từng gót xa
Rustling leaves along the road sounded like words	Làm lời lá bay trên đường đi
I saw myself as that ray of sunshine	Tôi tìm thấy tôi như giọt nắng kia
That brought a rosy tint to your lips	Làm hồng chút môi cho em nhờ

Lips of paradise that sing like a small bird	Môi thiên đường hót chim khuyên
Hair as fragrant as sandalwood falls on your shoulders	Ôi tóc trầm ướp vai thơm
I heard the vastness of life	Ta nghe đời rất mênh mông
In the slow steps you take	Trong chân người bước chầm chậm

Keep walking so the dawn quickly comes	Hãy còn bước đi cho bình minh lên sớm
I thank life a little for the flap of that dress	Cho đời chút ơn biết tà áo nọ
You're the perfume dust that makes the forest fragrant	Em là phấn thơm cho rừng chút hương
The song words for the world	Là lời hát ca cho trần gian
Down in the town a person thinks of you	Dưới phường phố kia có người nhớ em
Dreaming of paradise the whole night through	Nằm mộng suốt đêm trong thiên đường.

Vietnamese Girl (1965) — Người con gái Việt nam

Vietnamese girl with golden skin	Người con gái Việt Nam da vàng
Loves her native land as she loves fields of ripe rice	Yêu quê hương như yêu đồng lúa chín
Vietnamese girl with golden skin	Người con gái Việt Nam da vàng
Loves her native land	Yêu quê hương nước mắt lưng tròng

---

* "Anh" is a masculine second-person singular pronoun used to refer to an older male, an older brother, a husband, or a lover.

† "Em" is a second-person singular pronoun used to address a young child, a younger sister, a wife, or a lover.

Until her eyes fill with tears

Vietnamese girl with golden skin
Loves her native land so she loves those who
suffer.
The girl sits and dreams of peace
Loves her native land as she loves herself

You've never known your land in peace
You've never seen the old Vietnam
You've never once sung a folk song
You've been left with hate in your heart

One day the girl goes to her village
She goes in the night, gunshots echo noisily
She suddenly clutches her heart
Blood slowly spreads on fragrant skin

Vietnamese girl with golden skin
Dies with her dreams for her native land
Vietnamese girl with golden skin
Loves her native land but is no more

Oh, this sorrowful and cruel death
Oh, a land a thousand years in the dark
You arrived at your native land alone
And I, I'm worrying and searching still

Người con gái Việt Nam da vàng
Yêu quê hương nên yêu người yếu kém
Người con gái ngồi mơ thanh bình
Yêu quê hương như đã yêu mình

Em chưa biết quê hương thanh bình
Em chưa thấy xưa kia Việt Nam
Em chưa hát ca dao một lần
Em chỉ có con tim căm hờn

Người con gái một hôm qua làng
Đi trong đêm, đêm vang ầm tiếng súng
Người con gái chợt ôm tim mình
trên da thơm, vết máu loang dần

Người con gái Việt Nam da vàng
Mang giấc mơ quê hương lìa kiếp sống
Người con gái Việt Nam da vàng
Yêu quê hương nay đã không còn

Ôi cái chết đau thương vô tình
Ôi đất nước u mê ngàn năm
Em đã đến quê hương một mình
Riêng tôi vẫn âu lo đi tìm

Waiting for a Day (1972)

Waiting for love upon the cross
Waiting to wipe out anger in the shade of the
bodhi tree
Waiting for vultures on a branch shedding tears
Waiting for smiles in the midst of worry

Waiting to walk around the world
To see the world's heart petty and mean
Waiting to hear the return of humanity's con-
science
Waiting while mornings become worn and dry

How many years waiting using hatred as a weapon
Words of love from the heart are heard no more
How many murky years and bombs and bullets
still fall
In our native land heroes slowly pass from view

There are tears of hardship, let me weep with them
Waiting to see brothers and sisters in the light of
the sun
Save in the immensity a road real small
Waiting for the day when you step happily on it

Waiting for the native land to grow from sorrow
Waiting for the blood of brothers and sisters to
turn into rose buds
Waiting for trees to turn green in forests of misery
Waiting to see roads free of obstructions

Đợi có một ngày

Đợi chờ yêu thương trên cây thánh giá
Đợi xóa sân si dưới bóng bồ đề
Đợi con kên kên trên cành nhỏ lệ
Đợi có tiếng cười trong nỗi lo

Đợi làm đôi chân đi quanh thế giới
Để thấy con tim thế giới hẹp hòi
Đợi nghe lương tâm con người trở lại
Đợi đã héo mòn những sớm mai

Bao nhiêu năm chờ đợi oán thù là khí giới
Trong con tim lời nói yêu thương mất rồi
Bao nhiêu năm mịt mùng dấu đạn bom chưa
dứt
Trên quê hương dần khuất những anh hùng

Giọt lệ gian nan cho ta khóc với
Đợi thấy anh em dưới ánh mặt trời
Dành trong bao la con đường thật nhỏ
Đợi sẽ có ngày em bước vui

Đợi từ đau thương quê hương sẽ lớn
Đợi máu anh em chớm những nụ hồng
Đợi cây lên xanh trên rừng hoạn nạn
Đợi thấy những đường không cách ngăn

Where Will the Wave Go? (1995)

Sea and wave sea and wave don't push me
Don't push me and knock me down
Sea and wave sea and wave don't push each
other
If we push the sea back where will the wave
go?

White crested waves and sunken mountains
Where to return to
Return to a place with dreams covered in
clouds
Rivers all dried up calamities all around

Where can I find you
Sea and wave sea and wave don't push each
other
If we push the sea back the wave will lie hurt
Sea and wave sea and wave don't push me
Don't push me and make me fall in human
hearts

Sea and wave sea and wave don't push me
Don't let me see all of a human heart
Sea and wave sea and wave don't push each
other
If we push the sea back where will the wave go

Some slumber with no partner
Dim moon in the old [native?] land
A person stands waiting, a breeze whistles
Golden sunlight reminds us of eternity
Remembering a thousand years that have
passed

Sea and wave sea and wave don't drift far
Many years we've waited for the wave to come
near
Sea and wave sea and wave don't be sad
Don't nurture within a hating heart

Sea and wave don't push each other

Sóng về đâu

Biển sóng biển sóng đừng xô tôi
Đừng xô tôi ngã dưới chân người
Biển sóng biển sóng đừng xô nhau
Ta xô biển lại sóng về đâu

Sóng bạc đầu và núi chìm sâu
Ta về đâu đó
Về chốn nào mây phủ chiêm bao
Cạn suối nguồn bốn bể nương dâu
Ta tìm em nơi đâu

Biển sóng biển sóng đừng xô nhau
Ta xô biển lại sóng nằm đau
Biển sóng biển sóng đừng xô tôi
Đừng xô tôi ngã giữa tim người

Biển sóng biển sóng đừng xô tôi
Đừng cho tôi thấy hết tim người
Biển sóng biển sóng đừng xô nhau
Ta xô biển lại sóng về đâu

Giấc ngủ nào giường chiếu quạnh hiu
Trăng mờ quê cũ
Người đứng chờ gió đồng vi vu
Vạt nắng vàng nhắc lời thiên thu
Nhớ ngàn năm trôi qua

Biển sóng biển sóng đừng trôi xa
Bao năm chờ đợi sóng gần ta
Biển sóng biển sóng đừng âm u
Đừng nuôi trong ấy trái tim thù
Biển song đừng xô nhau

"A RECOLLECTION" [*HỒI ỨC*]
BY TRỊNH CÔNG SƠN

In this essay Trịnh Công Sơn talks about Ngô Thị Bích Diễm, the girl who inspired him to compose what is probably his most famous love song, "Diễm xưa"* [Diễm of the Past]. The location of the scene described is in the southern part of the city of Huế. Diễm lived on the southern side of the Bến Ngự [Royal Wharf] River, so named because this was where the king docked the royal barge. Trịnh Công Sơn lived on the north side in an apartment complex on Nguyễn Trường Tộ Street. The bridge Diễm crossed was called the Phú Cam Bridge because it led to the Phú Cam Church.

Once there was a very slender girl who walked through rows of camphor trees with tiny green leaves on her way to the Faculty of Letters at the University of Huế.

For many days, many months, during that period, this girl would walk under the dome of these camphor trees.

For numerous sunny seasons and wet seasons she would pass by. During the sunny seasons the cicadas would noisily sing a summer song in the leaves. When she passed by during the Huế's spring rainy season, she would appear dimly in the rain between the two dark rows of camphor trees.

Her house was across the river and each day to get to school she had to cross a bridge and walk along the street lined with camphor trees.

From the balcony of my home I watched her pass by, going and returning, four times each day. At that time girls in Huế did not ride noisy vehicles that moved at dizzying speeds as they do now. Except for people who lived far away and had to go by bicycle, most slowly walked to school, moving in a leisurely and regal manner. They walked to be admired, to feel quietly in their hearts that they were beautiful. Whether they showed off their beauty to be admired by many people or only one person is not important. Those footsteps from many directions lead to many schools with familiar and sometimes very old names. They walked so others could observe them but also so, at the same time, they had time to observe the earth, the rivers, the flowers and trees of nature. Camphor, almond, red royal Poinciana, sumac, laurel, and also the Perfume River that flows around the city—all these things had been blowing a pure romantic mist into their souls since they were young. That's why Huế never ceases to be a source of inspiration. An ancient citadel, temples and palaces, imperial tombs—all these things make people long for the past and help free them from the troubles of the world. As a result Huế becomes a private space, a private world. It's not as enticing as a large metropolis but it is the source of gentle personal emotions which suddenly turn people into dreamers who wish for worlds that are not completely real.

But what are reality and dreams? Truthfully, when all is said and done, the former is an illusion of the latter. And after having those illusions for a rather long time, people who grow up in that small city weave and embroider their own dreams.

That also was a time when on each pure morning, each afternoon, each evening, the bell at Linh Mụ Pagoda echoed in the air above the river, arriving at each partially shuttered or closed in house.

Time passed very quietly here—so quietly that people did not have a perception of time. It was a time with no shape, no color. Only when old people died in the coldness of winter did one wake up and suddenly become aware of the whisperings of tombs and graves in the surrounding hills and mountains.

In that quiet and dreamy time, and in that vaguely surreal [*liêu trai*] atmosphere, that girl continued to pass by each day between the two rows of camphor trees on her way to school. She was going to school but sometimes it seemed as if she were headed toward an indefinite place, a direction that was not a direction, because those steps seemed to float on a happy cloud of dreams.

In harsh hot and rainy seasons that girl crossed a bridge and walked under camphor trees to arrive finally at her rendezvous location. But a rendezvous doesn't mean something is promised. Because in that surreal time a promise was an unbelievable fantasy. No surreal dream will ever come true: All are bound to disappear.

That girl who walked through those rows of camphor trees now lives in a faraway place and has a different life. Everything that remains is only a memory. All memories are worth remembering but at some point must be forgotten. That girl was Diễm of bygone days.

"PLAYING GAMES" [*TRÒ CHƠI*]

BY TRỊNH CÔNG SƠN

I do not know where this article first appeared. To my knowledge it has not been reprinted in any journal or book, but it can be found online at the following website: https://trinhcongsonblog.wordpress.com/2013/08/17/tro-choi/.

The following translation is by Cao Thị Như Quỳnh.

When you feel that the game of life has something disturbing about it, then look for a quiet place, close the doors and pretend that you have thrown yourself into a fit of dreamlike pain. Choose whatever pain you like but make sure it's painful—so excruciatingly painful that death has the opportunity to gaze at you and test your fate. And when you reach a point that seems the most hopeless, suddenly from distant meadows healthy breezes arrive, bringing with them a fragrance of green rice, mint, and wild flowers. These breezes revive you and bring to life again the spring seasons that lie asleep, forgotten in your veins. That is also a time of rebirth of small living things in the swamps and of the awakening of wise men on high mountains or in deep grottos.

In a month when you must visit five or seven seriously ill patients, attend ten funerals and twenty weddings (including in one case two or three in an hour), then that fiendish month is no longer fun. It is a hellish game. When a game becomes hellish there is no reason to play it anymore. It's better to withdraw and run away quickly.

Perhaps of all the games the game of friends causes the least grief. It can be either a lot of fun or only a little fun, but it doesn't cause heartrending pain. But if you are unlucky and the game of friends suddenly leads to a heartrending situation, you should be polite and open your heart several more times and reflect on what happened. Don't let a misunderstanding lead to more misunderstanding. Don't let the traces of jealousy affect your trust in your friends.

There are houses that collapse because of unstable foundations. There are gardens that are scraggly because they lack fertilizer. Don't make things already very heavy even heavier because the added burden will only weigh down our minds even more. Know how to forget and how to leave behind things that cannot travel forward with us.

There are games that we never grow tired of. On the other hand, there are quite a few games that we lose interest in after playing them only a few times. Once you've begun the game of drinking alcohol or tea it's hard to withdraw. Drinking tea has become a *tao* [path, way, religion; Vn: đạo]. Almost everyone has heard of the tao of tea. It is one of the high class leisure games of old sages. The game of drinking alcohol is closer to real life. It is a friend, a lover. It is happiness and also sadness. It is words of comfort. It is a source of inspiration. It is sharing and returning a favor. To sum up, for people who know how to drink alcohol as an elegant game it is everything. Drink alcohol to love life and people more and to love even the ghost-like, firefly-like flickering of betrayal in love.

If you keep your promise with the fields of grain and grapes, the game of drinking alcohol never causes any calamities. I have passed through those fields and walked through the doors that lead to the home of very high oak barrels filled with an amber liquid, and in each of those fragrant drops a silent and mysterious life is developing each day, even each minute, continuing in the silent darkness a process that has been going on for hundreds of years. During those hundreds of years alcohol does not sleep: It is awake. Awake and transforming itself. Transforming itself into a body that is soft and supple, transparent, and fragrant.

When the game of drinking alcohol does not invite us anymore we sigh for a while and tell ourselves this does not mean we have been abandoned. This is only a brief separation and it won't be too long before drops of fragrant alcohol fill crystal glasses again during quiet and private parties or in animated and cozy gatherings with friends.

There are a thousand and one games but for me the dearest and most splendid games are love, life, and alcohol. Those are the games that have chosen me and I have accepted them—accepted them like the first and last choice of a fate that is neither colorful nor gloomy. I circle around these games as I circle around compassion. These games sometimes liberate me, help me rise up from dark and hellish holes of decline; and sometimes they press me deeply into suffering.[†]

I don't applaud and promote any particular game because I want to preserve my integrity and compassion. Ever since I entered this life I have encountered love and alcohol. Now I am saying good-bye once more. Good-bye to those glasses of warm alcohol in the morning, noontime, afternoon and night. My life is now free of games. A white colorless life. Playing the game of life without color forces me to find myself, to search for a face that does not look like the one in the past.

---

† "Suffering" here is our translation of *trầm luân*, a word which means "suffering" or "misfortune." It evokes the Buddhist concept of *samsara*, the cycle of births and deaths, the cycle of existence.

SOME NEW POEMS [THƠ MỚI]

"The Sound of Autumn II" [Tiếng Thu II]

By Lưu Trọng Lư
Translated by Mary Cowan et al.

The nighttime anguish has lulled,
Shivers of falling leaves do not last long,
The doe has found her trail once more, my love;
Villages and cities echo to the sound of gongs,
Fledgling birds waken in their dreams,
Broken destinies are born again;
In the rebirth of my soul, dearest one,
Can you feel the changed song of yours?
The sudden downpour on the wharf expanded,
The autumn sun strokes your lashes,
Brocade and silk weave steps that lead away,
The faithful moon casts its light into the hearts remaining,
Forests stir beneath the wind,
A hundred gusts of autumn leaves fly past-
Between earth and heaven in turmoil,
The doe of a thousand leagues pricks up its ears,
And quivers on the trail of warhorses.

"O, the Supply Carrier" [O tiếp tế]

By Lưu Trọng Lư
Translated by Neil L. Jamieson

Learning of life's deep intent
Off to carry supplies O went.
At her twenty years of age,
What knew she of life's darker page?
Looking forward, to and fro,
O passed by camps of the foe.
O moved on without delay,
Asking sisters on her way.
Moving with a stealthy step,
down deserted roads she crept.
O sang a tune, she hummed a lay.
The enemy camps were far away.
O laughed, and then she chattered.
All over the road her echo scattered.
Sometime she could rest again.
It didn't matter where or when.
O went on, and on and on.
Light of day would soon be gone.

A ravine forced her to wading
And her pants got soaking wet.
Suddenly she stopped to rest,
Looked at the water and saw her face.
O noticed, all at once,
The bloom of spring was fading.
Her white complexion was turning brown.
O feared her husband's frown,
But she walked on at a steady pace.
She was working for her nation.
If he didn't like it, let him frown.

In Every Heart the American Imperialists Are Our Special Enemies
[Đế quốc Mỹ là kẻ thu riêng của mỗi trái tim ta]

By Chế Lan Viên

They tear up the bodies of children, they burn down houses
They kill our rice fields with chemicals
They chop down trees still young and growing
They stab through the saffron robes of monks

What's horrifying is that they still have human faces
Are molded like us from the finest gold
Woven like us in the silk of life
The face of the killers is like the face of the killed
When they shoot at us, when they shout their commands
Why is it still in a human voice
Scooping from the sparkling stream of life
They yell and laugh we are bleeding

If these killers had the face of a devil
Humankind would recognize them right away as they passed by
The American flag still has forty-eight stars*
A flag that kills people still has the colors of flowers

What if Americans when talking gave off a strong stench of blood
Birds flying by would escape in the air
Animals would look for a place to hide
But the face of the enemy is a smiling face

Between battles they kiss the hand of a pretty girl
They drop napalm bombs in churches where people pray
They know how to mix peace with atomic bombs
Like mixing rose water with the blood of innocent children

Oh South Vietnam!
A booby trap is the most humane of weapons
Those who burn houses must burn in the fire they started
So life returns to its original goodness
And snakes no longer ambush in gardens of flowers

So people's faith in people returns
So they have faith in a bright shining candle and in a pearl as sparkling as dawn
Kill all the demons of darkness
Oh rifles, you are the rifles of humanity

* Chế Lan Viên probably was unaware that Alaska and Hawaii became states in 1959, which
  brought the total number of states to 50.

APPENDIX H

SOME PRE-WAR SONGS

Autumn Raindrops (1942)

By Đặng Thế Phong
Translated by Jason Gibbs

Outside on the veranda, the autumn rain is gently falling
The somber sky is quieting, suspended clouds are scattering
Amidst the muffled wind blowing past in the autumn rain
Who's crying? who's grieving?
A couple of young birds chirp from the branch
As if auguring blue skies
"Stop wind
Why bring sad rain
To a plaintive heart?"

Autumn's spirit arrives announcing the sadness it brings along
Feelings empty on all sides, for there's no screen to block the returning wind
Who's sobbing, lamenting life,
Teardrops rush down,
The world's immeasurably sad.

We hope the clouds will scatter bringing sweet gentle breezes.
The clouds open up to blue sky
Could such happiness be?
The rain continues to fall,
How many more incarnations until this melancholy subsides?

The distant wind still returns,
The unyielding rain spreads its gloom
Oh sky, for how many more years
Will tears pour from the sky because of autumn?

Giọt mưa thu

Ngoài hiên giọt mưa thu thánh thót rơi
Trời lắng u buồn mây hắt hiu ngừng trôi
Nghe gió thoảng mơ hồ trong mưa thu
Ai khóc ai than hờ!

Vài con chim non chiêm chiếp kêu trên cành
Như nhủ trời xanh
Gió ngừng đi
Mưa buồn chi
Cho cõi lòng lâm ly

Hồn thu tới nơi đây gieo buồn lấy
Lòng vắng muôn bề không liếp che gió về
Ai nức nở thương đời
Châu buông mau
Dương thế bao la sầu

Người mong mây tan cho gió hiu hiu lạnh
Mây ngỏ trời xanh
Chắc gì vui
Mưa còn rơi
Bao kiếp sầu ta nguôi

Gió xa xôi vẫn về
Mưa giăng mù lê thê
Đến bao năm nữa trời...
...Vợ chồng Ngâu* thôi khóc vì thu.

---

* "Vợ chồng Ngâu" [wife and husband named Ngâu] refers to a Vietnamese story about a keeper of water buffalos and a weaver who, when they fell in love, neglected their duties and angered the Jade Emperor. To punish them, he turned them into stars and placed them in different parts of the Milky Way, allowing them to meet only once a year. Jason Gibbs does not include this allusion in his translation.

Innermost Feeling (1951?)

By Nguyễn Văn Khánh

When we love someone we love for our whole lives
Love's harsh and fills our lives with heartbreak
Because when we love our love's always on our
mind

Months and years drift coldly by
We're reminded always of our love
We miss someone immensely
That love that we can't ever forget

We know when one falls in love
It comes with pain
So why do we keep loving and missing our love
Even though, even though if a day comes
And we're struck by love
That love will fall apart
And we still love, still miss someone
Our love pains us
[Even] [Then] after days living quietly
The pain still lasts always

When we fall in love who can understand us
We keep our pain a secret in our hearts
Coldly cherishing a love about which our love is
unaware

Nỗi lòng

Yêu ai, yêu cả một đời
Tình những quá khắt khe khiến cho đời ta
Đau tủi cả lòng vì yêu ai mà lòng hằng nhớ

Năm tháng trôi lạnh lùng hoài
Tình đó nhắc nhở luôn đến ta tình ai
Nhớ cả một trời
Tình yêu kia mà lòng nào quên.

Lòng vẫn biết nếu yêu rồi một ngày
Là đến với đớn đau
Nhưng sao trong ta cứ vẫn yêu vẫn nhớ
Dẫu sao, dẫu sao nếu có một ngày
Một ngày ai reo tim ta
Là tình yêu kia ly tan
Và lòng vẫn thương vẫn nhớ
Tình đó khiến sui lòng ta đau
Rồi với bao ngày lặng lẽ sống
Nỗi đau trong lòng người yêu vẫn yêu hoài.

Yêu ai, ai hiểu được lòng
Thầm kín những đớn đau với riêng lòng ta
Ấp ủ lạnh lùng tình yêu kia mà người nào hay

Melancholy [Ngậm ngùi] (1940)

Huy Cận's poem:

The afternoon sun slants across the yard
In an untended garden the sad leaves of the mimo-
sa plant close
A spider quickly spreads a sad thread
Sleep, love, let me fan for you
My heart opens with this fan
A hundred birds bring dreams to the head of your
bed
Sleep, love, and dream an ordinary dream
Sleep, love, and dream an ordinary dream
A lullaby for you, the sound of willows along the
river banks
Sleep, love! Sleep, love! Sleep and dream an ordi-
nary dream
The sound of willows on the banks
The long shadows of the trees at end of day

Your soul has ripened in sadness through the
seasons
Rest your head on my arm
Let me hear the heavy fruit of sadness fall

Phạm Duy's song version:

Nắng chia nửa bãi chiều rồi
Vườn hoang trinh nữ xếp đôi lá rầu.
Sợi buồn con nhện giăng mau;
Em ơi ! Hãy ngủ... anh hầu quạt đây.
Lòng anh mở với quạt này
Trăm con chim mộng về bay đầu giường
Ngủ đi em, mộng bình thường
Ngủ đi em, mộng bình thường
Ru em sẵn tiếng thùy dương đôi bờ...
Ngủ đi em! Ngủ đi em! Ngủ đi mộng vẫn bình
thường
À ơi có tiếng thùy dương mấy bờ
Cây dài bóng xế ngẩn ngơ
Hồn em đã chín mấy mùa buồn đau
Tay anh em hãy tựa đầu,
Cho anh nghe nặng ư ứ trái sầu rụng rơi

Predestined Love (1960)

By Lam Phương

My love, what happens if dreams don't come true?
High mountains wide earth how can we find each other?
On life's dark road full of twists and turns
I wait for fate to lead us across the bridge

My love, remember when we met long ago
On the dike as the evening market was ending
Hesitating each time I came to see you
Your cheeks blushed red from shyness
My love, do you remember those times
When the sun slowly set

You would return on a distant road
We'd meet but not dare smile
We'd gaze at each other with happy hearts?
My love, did at that moment that day
Our two beating hearts speak our dream?
Though the road of life blocked our love
That first moment will never fade

Send the Wind to Make the Clouds Fly (1952)

Blue dresses fluttering in autumn
Withered flowers and cold trees standing in a row
One by one each golden leaf
Falls silently on old ground

Send the wind to make the clouds fly
Send colorful butterflies to the flower
Send also moonlight the pale blue of a love letter
Send them here with the autumn of the world

Send the wind to make the clouds fly
Send strands of silk to look for love
Send also a blue letter of love
And eyes like an autumn lake

I'm full of feelings of regret
The boat has gone to the other bank
From where there's no way home
I'm now in the afternoon of life
But my heart's still full of love
I want to break the old mirror to find the old image
But what use are regrets
Birds fly away, I have left
The earthly way back has been forgotten
Separated forever
The pain of earthly love cannot be healed

Send the wind to make the clouds fly
Send amorous butterflies to the flower
Send also moonlight the pale blue of a love letter
Send them here with the autumn of the world

Duyên kiếp

Em ơi nếu mộng không thành thì sao
Non cao đất rộng biết đâu mà tìm
Đường đời mịt mời vạn nẻo về đâu
Mong chờ duyên kiếp đưa lối bắc cầu

Em ơi nhắc lại phút xưa gặp nhau
Trên đê vắng người lúc tan chợ chiều
Ngại ngùng mỗi lần anh đến tìm em
Má em ửng hồng vì quá thẹn thùng

Em ơi nhớ chăng thuở ấy
Mỗi khi bóng chiều xuống dần
Em về trên quãng đường xa
Gặp nhau dù không dám cười
Nhìn nhau, nhìn nhau mà lòng vẫn vui

Em ơi phải chăng phút giây ngày ấy
Đôi tim ước mộng bấy lâu thành lời
Dù rằng đường đời ngăn cách tình ta
Phút giây ban đầu mãi không phai nhòa.

Gửi Gió Cho Mây Ngàn Bay

Với bao tà áo xanh đây mùa thu
Hoa lá tàn, hàng cây đứng hững hờ
Lá vàng từng cánh rơi từng cánh
Rơi xuống âm thầm trên đất xưa

Gửi gió cho mây ngàn bay
Gửi bướm muôn màu về hoa
Gửi thêm ánh trăng màu xanh lá thư
Về đây với thu trần gian

Gửi gió cho mây ngàn bay
Gửi phím tơ đồng tìm duyên
Gửi thêm lá thư màu xanh ái ân
Về đôi mắt như hồ thu
Thấy hối tiếc nhiều
Thuyền đã sang bờ
Đường về không lối
Giòng đời trôi đã về chiều
Mà lòng mến còn nhiều
Đập gương xưa tìm bóng
Nhưng thôi tiếc mà chi
Chim rồi bay, anh rồi đi
Đường trần quên lối cũ
Người đời xa cách mãi
Tình trần khôn hàn gắn thương lòng

Gửi gió cho mây ngàn bay
Gửi bướm đa tình về hoa
Gửi thêm ánh trăng màu xanh lá thư
Về đây với thu trần gian.

APPENDIX I

SOME PERFORMANCES OF NHAC TRINH

Trịnh Công Sơn's songs have remained extremely popular in Vietnam and in the Vietnamese diaspora. Proof of this popularity is the large number of videos of famous singers singing his songs that are available on YouTube. Most of these songs are sung by Khánh Ly and Hồng Nhung who, as I explain in Chapter Eight: Personae and Personalities, were talented singers who were friends of Trịnh Công Sơn. His fame was enhanced by their fine performances of his songs. Here are links to some videos of their performances (accessed September 2023):

Khanh Ly
Như cánh vạc bay: https://www.youtube.com/watch?v=kIpM-KqrnXYk&ab_channel=CaS%C4%A9Kh%C3%A1nhLy
Như một lời chia tay: https://www.youtube.com/watch?v=kmhidpSD-vgE&ab_channel=FMusic
Khanh Ly's YouTube channel: https://www.youtube.com/channel/UC534KI6NPbnDFVJc6GrMyDg

Hong Nhung
Bống Bồng Ơi: https://www.youtube.com/watch?v=_GiiTDb9afQ&ab_channel=Nh%E1%BA%A1cX%C6%B0a
DVD Liveshow: https://www.youtube.com/watch?v=wrMhI6CB-w3U&ab_channel=NH%E1%BA%ACTMINH
Her YT: https://www.youtube.com/@HongNhungOfficial

Hoang Trang

Some Trịnh Công Sơn songs on YouTube are sung by a young student and singer, Hoàng Trang. In 2020 her songs went viral on social media after clips of her performing songs by Trịnh Công Sơn garnered millions of views on YouTube.

Ta đã thấy gì trong đêm nay: https://www.youtube.com/watch?v=8uOM-mhdJUeA&ab_channel=BAODUCTV

Ru Em Từng Ngón Xuân Nồng: https://www.youtube.com/watch?v=PH-Q9b8uZZF8

Her YouTube channel: https://www.youtube.com/@TrangHoangSinger/featured

WORKS CITED

Abrams, M. H. *A Glossary of Literary Terms*. Fort Worth: Harcourt Brace Jovanovich, 1985.
ACLU of Southern California. *Day of Protest, Night of Violence*. Los Angeles: Sawyer Press, 1967.
Aymonier, Etienne. *La langue française et l'enseignement en Indochine*. 1880. Paris: Armand Colin et Cie.
Baez, Joan. *And a Voice to Sing With: A Memoir*. New York: Summit Books, 1987.
Ballaban, John. *Ca Dao Việt Nam: Vietnamese Folk Poetry*. Greensboro: Unicorn Press, 1980.
Bằng Phong Đặng Văn Âu. "Nhạc sĩ Trịnh Công Sơn—một thien tài đồng lõa với tội ác" [Trịnh Công Sơn—A Genius Who Allied Himself With Cruelty]. *Tiền Vệ*, April 12, 2009. https://www.tienve.org/home/activities/viewThaoLuan.do?action=viewArtwork&artworkId=8532 (accessed Nov. 3, 2016).
Ban Mai. *Trịnh Công Sơn: Vết chân dã tràng* [Trịnh Công Sơn: The Footprint of the Sand Crab]. Hanoi: Lao Động, 2008.
——. "Trịnh Công Sơn, người tình của cuộc sống" [Trịnh Công Sơn, A Lover of Life, Part 1]. Trinh Cong Sơn Cultural Association, 2008. http://www.tcs-home.org/ban-be/articles/trinh-cong-son-nguoi-tinh-cua-cuoc-song-phan-1 (accessed February 19, 2016).
Bảo Định Giang. "Điếu Văn" [Funeral Oration]. *Văn Nghệ* [Literature and Art] 26 (1989).
Barthes, Roland. *S/Z*. Translated by Richard Miller. New York: Hill and Wang, 1974.
——. *Image – Music – Text*. Translated by Stephen Heath. New York: Hill and Wang, 1977.
Batchelor, Stephen. *Buddhism Without Beliefs: A Contemporary Guide to Awakening*. New York: Riverhead Books, 1998.
Beckwith, Francis J. "Busy Being Born Again: Bob Dylan's Christian Philosophy." In *Bob Dylan and Philosophy*, edited by Peter Vernezze and Carl J. Porter. Chicago: Open Court, 2006.
Bowden, Betsy. *Performed Literature: Words and Music by Bob Dylan*. Bloomington: Indiana University Press, 1982.
Bowser, Kenneth. Interview for PBS's *American Masters*, January 22, 2012. http://www.pbs.org/wnet/americanmasters/phil-ochs-but-there-for-fortune-interview-director-kenneth-bowser/1960/ (accessed Aug. 31, 2018).
——. *Phil Ochs: There but for Fortune*. First Run Features: 2011.
Brake, Elizabeth. "'To Live Outside the Law, You Must Be Honest': Freedom in Dylan's Lyrics." In *Bob Dylan and Philosophy*, edited by Peter Vernezze and Carl J. Porter. Chicago: Open Court, 2006.
Brooks, Cleanth. *The Well Wrought Urn*. New York: Harcourt, Brace and World, 1947.
Bùi Bảo Trúc. "Về Trịnh Công Sơn" [About Trịnh Công Sơn]. *Văn* [Literature] 53 & 54 (May and June 2001).
Bùi Vĩnh Phúc. *Trịnh Công Sơn ngôn ngữ và những ám ảnh nghệ thuật* [Trịnh Công Sơn: Language and Artistic Obsessions]. Gardena: Văn Mới, 2005.
Bushman, Brad J., Roy F. Baumeister, and Angela D. Stack. "Catharsis, Aggression, and Persuasive Influence: Self-Fulfilling or Self-Defeating Prophecies?" *Journal of Personality and Social Psychology* 76, no. 3 (1999).
Buttinger, Joseph. *Vietnam: A Dragon Embattled*, vol. 2: *Vietnam at War*. New York: Frederick A. Praeger, 1967.
Bửu Chỉ. "Nhạc phản chiến Trịnh Công Sơn" [Trịnh Công Sơn's Anti-war Music]. *Diễn đàn* [Forum] 110 (2001).
——. "Về những ca khúc phản chiến của Trịnh Công Sơn" [On Trịnh Công Sơn's Anti-war Songs]. *Diễn đàn* [Forum] 110 (Sept. 2001).
Bửu Ý. Interview by Phan Quỳnh Anh, "Bửu Ý: Trầm ngâm ngồi nhớ bạn hiền, vợ yêu" [Thoughtfully Sitting and Remembering a Kind Friend, a Beloved Wife]. https://cand.com.vn/Nhan-vat/Buu-Y-Tram-ngam-ngoi-nho-ban-hien-vo-yeu-i314686/ (accessed Jan. 9, 2014).
——. *Trịnh Công Sơn: Một nhạc sĩ thiên tài* [Trịnh Công Sơn: A Genius of a Musician]. HCMC: Trẻ, 2003.

Cao Huy Hóa. "Cư sĩ giữa dòng đời" [Lay Buddhists in the Flow of Life]. In Cao Huy Hóa, *Thiền một chút* [A Little Zen]. HCMC: Phương Đông, 2014.

Cao Huy Thuần. Introductory remarks at a concert titled "Đêm hoài niệm Trịnh Công Sơn" [An Evening to Remember Trịnh Công Sơn]. May 26, 2001.

——. Introductory remarks at "Đêm Trịnh Công Sơn: Hòa Bình và Tình Yêu" [An Evening of Trịnh Công Sơn: Peace and War]. Paris, May 3, 2001.

——. "Buồn bã với những môi hôn" [Sadness with the Kisses]. In Cao Huy Thuần, *Nắng và hoa* [Sunshine and Flowers]. HCMC: Văn hóa Sài gòn, 2006.

——. "Chiến tranh trong Trịnh Công Sơn" [The War in Trịnh Công Sơn]. In Cao Huy Thuần, *Khi tựa gối khi cúi đầu* [He'd Hug His Knees, Hang Down His Head]. Hanoi: Văn Học, 2011.

——. "Phật giáo Huế trong dòng chảy của lịch sử" [Huế Buddhism in the Flow of History]. *Liễu Quán* 1 (January 2014).

Cartwright, Bert. *The Bible in the Lyrics of Bob Dylan.* Bury: Wanted Man, 1992.

"Ca sĩ Hồng Nhung và câu chuyện về người mẹ kế đặc biệt" [The Singer Hồng Nhung and Stories about Her Special Stepmother]. Báo Mới, http://www.baomoi.com/ (accessed Aug. 22, 2016; site now defunct).

Chân Không (Cao Ngọc Phương). *Learning True Love: How I Learned and Practiced Social Change in Vietnam.* Berkeley: Parallax Press, 1993.

Chappell, David W. "From Dispute to Dual Cultivation: Pure Land Responses to Ch'an Critics." In *Traditions of Meditation in Chinese Buddhism*, edited by Peter N. Gregory. Honolulu: University of Hawai'i Press, 1986.

Chế Lan Viên. *Những bài thơ đánh giặc* [Fighting Poems]. Hà Nội: Thanh Niên, 1972.

Chesneaux, Jean. *The Vietnamese Nation: Contribution to a History.* Translated by Malcolm Salmon. Sydney: Current Book Distributors, 1966.

Child, Francis James. *The English and Scottish Popular Ballads*, 5 vols. Boston: Houghton-Mifflin, 1982-98.

Chu Xuân Diên. "Ca Dao" [Folk Verses]. In *Từ Điển Văn Học* [Cultural Dictionary], edited by Đỗ Đức Hiểu, Nguyễn Huệ Chi, Phùng Văn Tửu, and Trần Hữu Tá. Hà nội: Thế giới, 2003.

Công Huyền Tôn Nữ Nha Trang. "The Role of French Romanticism in the New Poetry Movement in Vietnam." In *Borrowings and Adaptations in Vietnamese Culture*, edited by Trương Bửu Lâm. Manoa: Center for Asian and Pacific Studies, University of Hawaii, 1987.

Cổ Ngư. "Đôi dòng về Trịnh Công Sơn" [Some Lines about Trịnh Công Sơn].*Văn Học* [Literary Studies] special edition (October 10 & 11, 2001).

Conze, Edward et al. *Buddhist Wisdom: The Diamond Sutra and the Heart Sutra.* New York: Vintage, 2001.

Cooke, Nolo. "The Myth of the Restoration: Dang-Trong Influences in the Spiritual Life of the Early Nguyen Dynasty (1802-47)." In *The Last Stand of Asian Autonomies: Responses to Modernity in the Diverse States of Southeast Asia and Korea, 1750-1900*, edited by Anthony Reid. New York: St. Martin's Press, 1997.

Cott, Jonathan. *Bob Dylan: The Essential Interviews.* New York: Wenner Books, 2006.

Cuong Tu Nguyen. *Zen in Medieval Vietnam: A Study and Translation of the Thiền Uyển Tập Anh.* Honolulu: University of Hawai'i Press, 1997.

Đặng Tiến. "Trịnh Công Sơn: Tiếng hát hòa bình" [Trịnh Công Sơn: Voice of Peace]. *Văn Học* [Literary Studies] 186 & 187 (Oct.-Nov., 2001).

——. "Trịnh Công Sơn: đời và nhạc" [Trịnh Công Sơn: Life and Music]. *Văn* [Literature] 53 & 54 (2001).

Đặng Vương Hưng. "Bí ẩn 'Những mối tình trai'của nhà thơ Xuân Diệu" [The Secrets of Xuân Diệu's 'Male Loves']. *Việt Times*, March 15, 2016. https://viettimes.vn/bi-an-nhung-moi-tinh-trai-cua-nha-tho-xuan-dieu-post22219.html (accessed June 8, 2020).

DeFrancis, John. *Colonialism and Language Policy in Viet Nam.* The Hague: Mouton, 1977.

Đinh Cường. "Gửi Sơn, Những đoàn ghi rời của người bạn ở xa" [For Sơn, Scattered Notes from a Friend Far Away]. In *Trịnh Công Sơn: Cuộc đời, âm nhạc, thơ, hội họa, suy tưởng* [Trịnh Công Sơn: Life, Music, Poetry, Painting, Reflections], edited by Trịnh Cung and Nguyễn Quốc Thái. HCMC: Văn Nghệ, 2001.

Đoàn Lê Giang. "Nguyễn Thị Manh Manh—nữ sĩ tiền phong trong Phong trào Thơ mới" [Nguyễn Thị Manh Manh—A Vanguard Member of the New Poetry Movement]. Khoa Việt Nam Học [Faculty of Vietnamese Studies], November 10, 2018. http://www.vns.edu.vn/index.php/vi/nghien-cuu/van-hoa-viet-nam/569-nguyen-thi-manh-manh-a-nu-si-tien-phong-trong-phong-trao-tho-moi (accessed October 26, 2020).

Đỗ Hồng Ngọc. "Con mắt còn lại" [The Eye That Remains]. Tạp *Chí Văn Hóa Phật Giáo* [Journal of Buddhist Culture] no. 57. http://tapchivanhoaphatgiao.com/ (accessed June 23, 2014; site now defunct).

Dowd, Maureen. "Blowin' in the Idiot Wind." The New York *Times*, Apr. 9, 2011.

Durand, Maurice M. and Nguyen Tran Huan. *An Introduction to Vietnamese Literature.* Translated from the French by D.M. Hawke. New York: Columbia University Press, 1985.

Duy Lân. "Bob Dylan ở Việt Nam: Thương nhau như thế quá mười ghét nhau" [Loving Each Other Like That Is Like Hating Each Other Ten Times Over]. http://vn.news.yahoo.com/bob-dylan-%E1%BB%9F-vi%E1BB%87t-nam--th%C6%BO (accessed Apr. 14, 2011; site now defunct).

Dylan, Bob. "How Does It Feel?: Don't Ask," interview by Robert Hilburn. *Los Angeles Times*, Sept. 16, 2001.

———. *Chronicles: Volume One.* New York: Simon and Schuster, 2004.

———. *Saved! The Gospel Speeches of Bob Dylan.* Edited by Clinton Heylin. Madras and New York: Hanuman Books, 1990.

———. "Bob Dylan's Late-Era, Old-Style American Individualism," interview with Douglas Brinkley. *Rolling Stone*, May 14, 2019. https://www.rollingstone.com/music/music-news/bob-dylans-late-era-old-style-american-individualism-90298/ (accessed Feb. 13, 2023).

———. "Banquet Speech." The Nobel Prize, December 10, 2016. https://www.nobelprize.org/prizes/literature/2016/dylan/25424-bob-dylan-banquet-speech-2016 (accessed July 7, 2019).

Eller, Cynthia. "The Impact of Christianity on Buddhist Nonviolence in the West." In *Inner Peace, World Peace: Essays on Buddhism and Nonviolence*, edited by Kenneth Kraft. New York: State University of New York Press, 1992.

Eppsteiner, Fred. "Editor's Preface." In *The Path of Compassion: Writings on Socially Engaged Buddhism.* Berkeley: Parallax Press, 1988.

Fall, Bernard. *Street Without Joy: Indochina at War.* Harrisburg, PA: Telegraph Press, 1961.

Fitzgerald, Frances. *Fire in the Lake: The Vietnamese and the Americans in Vietnam.* Boston: Little, Brown and Company, 1972.

Foster, Nelson. "To Enter the Marketplace." In *The Path of Compassion: Writings on Socially Engaged Buddhism*, edited by Fred Eppsteiner. Berkeley: Parallax Press, 1988.

Gegenhuber, Kurt. "Hollis Brown's South Dakota." The Celestial Monochord, March 15, 2006. https://www.celestialmonochord.org/hollis_browns_s/ (accessed Apr. 14, 2013).

Gelles, David. "Talking Mindfulness on the C.E.O. Beat." The New York *Times*, November 28, 2018. https://www.nytimes.com/2018/11/28/reader-center/ceos-mindfulness-meditation.html (accessed December 5, 2018).

Giao Hương and Dạ Ly. "Công bố hàng trăm bức thư tình của nhạc sĩ Trịnh Công Sơn: Trịnh Công Sơn-Dao Ánh qua hồi ức của Trịnh Vĩnh Trinh" [Making Public Hundreds of Trịnh Công Sơn's Love Letters (Part 7): Trịnh Công Sơn—Dao Ánh as Remembered by Trịnh Vĩnh Trinh]. *Thanh Niên* [Youth Online], March 4, 2011. https://thanhnien.vn/cong-bo-hang-tram-buc-thu-tinh-cua-nhac-si-trinh-cong-son-ky-7-trinh-cong-son-dao-anh-qua-hoi-uc-cua-trinh-vinh-trinh-post297058.html (accessed Apr. 12, 2011).

Giao Vy. "Huế lang thang trong tháng tư" [Wandering in Huế in April]. *Diễn đàn* [Forum] 118 (2002).

Gibbs, Jason. "Nhac Tien Chien: The Origins of Vietnamese Popular Song." ThingsAsian, http://thingsasian.com/story/nhac-tien-chien-origins-vietnamese-popular-song (site now defunct).

———. "Reform and Tradition in Early Vietnamese Popular Song." ThingsAsian, http://thingsasian.com/story/reform-and-tradition-early-vietnamese-popular-song (accessed March 17, 2015; site now defunct).

Gilmour, Michael J. *Tangled Up in the Bible: Bob Dylan and Scripture.* New York: Continuum, 2004.

Ginsberg, Allen. "Wichita Vortex Sutra." In *Planet News.* San Francisco, CA: City Lights Books, 1974.

———. Interview by Peter Barry Chowka, Modern American Poetry, 1995.

Goldberg, J. J. "Bob Dylan at 60: 'We Used to be Young Together'; A Musical Seer Who Disdained Role of Prophet." *Forward*, May 18, 2001.

Goldstein, Richard. "Bob Dylan and the Nostalgia of Patriarchy." *The Nation*, Apr. 27, 2006.

Gray, Michael. *Song and Dance Man III: The Art of Bob Dylan.* London: Continuum, 2000.

Greene, Andy. "The Inside Story of Bob Dylan and Martin Scorsese's New 'Rolling Thunder Revue' Doc." *Rolling Stone*, June 10, 2019. https://www.rollingstone.com/movies/movie-features/the-inside-story-of-bob-dylan-martin-scorseses-rolling-thunder-revue-doc-844268/ (accessed July 11, 2019).

Griffin, Sid. *Million Dollar Bash: Bob Dylan, The Band, and The Basement Tapes*. London: Jawbone Press, 2007.

Hajdu, David. *Positively 4th Street*. New York: Farrar, Straus and Giroux, 2001.

Hà Minh Đức. "Chế Lan Viên." In *Nhà văn Việt Nam* [Vietnamese Writers], edited by Phan Cư Đệ and Hà Minh Đức. Hà Nội: Đại Học và Trung Học Chuyên Nghiệp, 1979.

Harvey, Peter. *An Introduction to Buddhism*. Cambridge: Cambridge University Press, 1990.

Hạ Vĩnh Thi. "Vài nét về tiểu sử Xuân Diệu [Some Comments on the Life of *Xuân Diệu*]. In *Hoàng tử của thi ca Việt Nam hiện đại* [Xuân Diệu: The Crown Prince of Modern Vietnamese Poetry], edited by Hạ Vĩnh Thi. Hanoi: Hanoi Publishing, 2000.

Hentoff, Nat. "The Crackin', Shakin', Breakin' Sounds." In *Bob Dylan: The Essential Interviews*, edited by Jonathan Cott. New York: Wenner Books, 2006.

Heylin, Clinton. *Bob Dylan: Behind the Shades*. New York: Summit Books, 1991.

——. *Bob Dylan: Behind the Shades Revisited*. New York: Harper Entertainment, 2003.

——. *Revolution in the Air*. Chicago: Chicago Review Press, 2009.

Hillis Miller, J. "Narrative." In *Critical Terms for Literary Study*, edited by Frank Lentricchia and Thomas McLaughlin. Chicago, IL: University of Chicago Press, 1990.

Hinds, John. "Reader Versus Writer Responsibility: A New Typology." In *Writing Across Languages: Analysis of L2 Text*, edited by Ulla Connor and Robert B. Kaplan. Reading: Addison-Wesley, 1987.

Hirsch, E. D. *The Aims of Interpretation*. Chicago: University of Chicago Press, 1976.

Hoài Thanh and Hoài Chân. *Thi Nhân Việt Nam* [Vietnamese Poets]. 1967.

Hoàng Cát. "Mối 'tình trai' của nhà thơ Xuân Diệu và nhà thơ Hoàng Cát" [The 'Male Love' between Xuân Diệu and the Poet Hoàng Cát], interview with Thiên Kim. *An Ninh Thế Giới* [World Security], January 30, 2016. http://antg.cand.com.vn/Kinh-te-Van-hoa-The-Thao/Moi-tinh-trai-cua-nha-tho-Xuan-dieu-va-nha-tho-Hoang-Cat-381592/ (accessed June 20, 2020).

Hoàng Diệp Lạc. "Âm hưởng Kinh Thánh trong âm nhạc Trịnh Công Sơn" ["Biblical Echoes in the Music of Trịnh Công Sơn"]. Giáo Phận Qui Nhơn [Diocese of Qui Nhơn]. https://web.archive.org/web/20140414212023/http://gpquinhon.org/qn/news/tap-chi-muon-phuong/Am-huong-Kinh-Thanh-trong-am-nhac-Trinh-Cong-Son-2209/#.U0xRJEfLeUk (accessed September 21, 2014).

Hoàng Phủ Ngọc Tường. "Nói chuyện với Hoàng Phủ Ngọc Tường về biến cố Mậu Thân ở Huế" [Talking to Hoàng Phủ Ngọc Tường about the Events in Huế], interview by Thụy Khuê. Radio France Internationale, July 12, 1997. http://thuykhue.free.fr/tk97/nchpngoctuong.html (accessed Oct. 21, 2016).

——. "Hành tinh yêu thương của Hoàng tử Bé" [The Little Prince's Planet of Love]. In *Trịnh Công Sơn: Một người thơ ca một cõi đi về* [Trịnh Công Sơn: A Singer-poet, a Place for Leaving and Returning], edited by Nguyễn Trọng Tạo, Nguyễn Thụy Kha, and Đoàn Tử Huyến. Hanoi: Âm Nhạc, 2001.

——. *Trịnh Công Sơn và cây đàn lya của hoàng tử bé* [Trịnh Công Sơn and the Lyre of the Little Prince]. HCMC: Trẻ, 2004.

Hoàng Trung Thông. "Tiểu sử nhà thơ Xuân Diệu" [Life History of the Poet Xuân Diệu]. In *Tuyển tập Xuân Diệu Thơ* [Selected Poems of Xuân Diệu], edited by Hoàng Trung Thông and Vũ Quần Phương. Hanoi: Văn Học, 1986.

——. "Tiểu sử nhà thơ Xuân Diệu" [Life History of the Poet Xuân Diệu]. In *Văn Nghệ* [Literature and Arts Magazine], no. 52 (December, 1985).

Hoàng Xuân Sơn. "Hoàng Xuân Sơn: nơi tôi sinh sống thì hát nhạc Trịnh cũng nên dè dặt" [Hoàng Xuân Sơn: Where I Live (Montreal, Canada) You Should Be Careful about Singing Trịnh Music], interview by Bùi Văn Phú. http://damau.org/archives/19866 (accessed Jan. 15, 2012; site now defunct).

Hồng Nhung. "Hồng Nhung & Trịnh Công Sơn những ngày đầu quen nhau" [Hoàng Nhung & Trịnh Công Sơn—First Days Together]. http://wwwcomp.nus.edu.sg/--nguyenvu/artists/TC_Son/TCS _articles/About_TCS/TCSon (accessed Feb. 7, 2005; site now defunct).

——. "Xuất xứ 'Bống bồng ơi'" [How "Bống bồng ơi" Came to Be]. http://www.comp.nus.edu.sg/-nguyenvu/Artists/TC_Son/TCS_articles/About_TCS/TCSon (accessed Feb. 7, 2005; site now defunct).

Hue-Tam Ho Tai. "Religion in Vietnam: A World of Gods and Spirits." *The Vietnam Forum* 10 (Summer-Fall, 1987).

Hương Bùi. "Khánh Ly lặng lẽ viếng mộ Trịnh Công Sơn" [Khánh Ly Quietly visits Trịnh Công Sơn's Grave]. 24h, May 2, 2014. https://web.archive.org/web/20140507031225/http://us.24h.com.vn:80/ca-nhac-mtv/khanh-ly-lang-le-vieng-mo-trinh-cong-son-c73a627448.html (accessed May 26, 2014).

Huỳnh Ngọc Trảng. "The Kitchen God Returns to the Heavens." *Vietnam Heritage* 1, no. 4 (2014).

Huỳnh Sanh Thông. *An Anthology of Vietnamese Poems*. New Haven: Yale University Press, 1996.

Huỳnh Sanh Thông, Nguyễn Du. *The Tale of Kiều: A Bilingual Edition of Truyện Kiều*. New Haven: Yale University Press, 1983.

Jacobs, Alan. "It Ain't Me Babe." In *A Visit to Vanity Fair: Moral Essays on the Present Age*. Grand Rapids, MI: Brazos Press, 2001.

Jamieson, Neil L. *Understanding Vietnam*. Berkeley, CA: University of California Press, 1993.

——. "Shattered Identities and Contested Images: Reflections of Poetry and History in 20th-Century Vietnam." *Crossroads* vol. 7, no. 2 (1992).

Janssen, David, and Edward Whitelock. *Apocalypse Jukebox: The End of the World in American Popular Music*. Brooklyn: Soft Skull Press, 2009.

Jara, Joan. *The Unfinished Song: The Life of Victor Jara*. New York: Ticknor & Fields, 1984.

Karnow, Stanley. *Vietnam: A History*. New York: Viking Press, 1983.

Khánh Ly. *Chuyện kể sau 40 năm* [Stories Told after 40 Years]. 4 Phuong. https://web.archive. org/web/20170924021848/http://4phuong.net/ebook/12182147/chuyen-ke-sau-40-nam. html (accessed Aug. 8, 2017).

——. "Khánh Ly nói về đời mình, về Trịnh Công Sơn" [Khánh Ly Talks about Her Own Life and about Trịnh Công Sơn], interview by Bùi Văn Phú. *Văn* [Literature] 92 (2004).

——. *Đằng Sau Những Nụ Cười* [Behind the Smiles]. HCMC: Văn Học, 2015.

——. "Bên Đời Hiu Quạnh" [Next to a Desolate Life]. In *Trịnh Công Sơn: Một người thơ ca một cõi đi về* [Trịnh Công Sơn: A Singer-poet, a Place for Leaving and Returning].

Khuất Đầu. "Người nữ trong nhạc Trịnh Công Sơn" [Women in the Music of Trịnh Công Sơn]. In *Trịnh Công Sơn: Ánh nến và bạn bè* [Trịnh Công Sơn: The Light of a Candle and Friends], edited by Tạ Duy Anh, et al. Hanoi: Hội Nhà Văn.

Kim Nhật, *Những Nhà Văn Tiền Chiến Hà Nội Hôm Nay* [Pre-War Hanoi Literary Figures Today] (Los Alamitos CA: Xuân Thu, 1991).

King, Sallie B. "Thich Nhat Hanh and the Unified Buddhist Church of Vietnam: Nondualism in Action." In *Engaged Buddhism: Buddhism Liberation Movements in Asia*, edited by Christopher S. Queen. Albany: State University of New York Press, 1996.

Knitter, Paul F. *Without Buddha I Could Not Be a Christian*. UK: One World Publications, 2013.

Krashen, Stephen D. *The Input Hypothesis: Issues and Implications*. New York: Longman, 1985.

Krein, Kevin, and Abigail Levin. "Dylan, Authenticity, and the Second Sex." In *Bob Dylan and Philosophy*, edited by Peter Vernezze and Carl J. Porter. Chicago, IL: Open Court, 2006.

Lại Nguyên Ân and Alec Holcombe. "The Heart and Mind of the Poet Xuân Diệu: 1954-1958." *Journal of Vietnamese Studies* 5, No. 2 (Summer, 2010).

Landau, Jon. *It's Too Late to Stop Now: A Rock and Roll Journal*. San Francisco: Straight Arrow Books, 1972.

Lang Mai. "Thực tập thiền ca" [Practicing Zen Songs]. Làng Mai [Plum Village]. http://langmai. org/dai-may-tim/thien-ca (accessed November 11, 2015).

Lã Xưa. "Giải mã nghi án giới tính của 'ông hoàng thơ tình' Xuân Diệu," [Solving the Case of the Sexuality of Xuân Diệu, the "Prince of Love Poetry"]. Saigon Ocean. https://saigonocean. com/gocchung/html/xuandieu.htm (accessed April 8, 2020).

Lê Bá Hán, Trần Đình Sử, and Nguyễn Khắc Phi. *Từ Điển Thuật Ngữ Văn Học* [Dictionary of Literary Terms]. HCMC: Giáo Dục, 2006.

Lê Hữu. "Từ 'Diễm xưa' đến 'Một cõi đi về'" [From 'Diễm xưa' to 'Một Cõi Đi Về']. *Văn Học* [Literary Studies] 186 & 187 (Oct.-Nov., 2001).

Lê Minh Quốc, ed. *Trịnh Công Sơn: Rơi lệ ru người* [Trịnh Công Sơn: Shedding Tears, Singing Lullabies]. Phụ Nữ, 2004.

Lê Minh Quốc. "Bùi Giáng—thi sĩ tinh quái của nên thi ca Việt Nam hiện đại" [Bùi Giáng— The Mischievous Poet of Modern Vietnamese Poetry and Song]. Lê Minh Quốc, https:// leminhquoc.vn/the-loai-khac/tac-pham-cua-ban-be/1610-toa-dam-%20khoa-hoc-ve-thi-si-bui-giang.html?start=4 (accessed June 6, 2016).

Lemon, Lee T. and Marion J. Reis, trans. and eds. *Formalist Criticism: Four Essays*. Lincoln: University of Nebraska Press, 1965.

Lê Trắc / Lê Tắc. *An Nam Chí Lược* [Brief Records An Nam]. Huế: Huế University Press, 1961.

Lê Văn Đức. *Tự điển Việt Nam* [Vietnamese Dictionary]. Saigon: Khai Trí.

Liên Thành. *Biến Động Miền Trung: Những bí mật lịch sử trong các giai đoạn 1966-1968-1972* [Disorder in the Central Region: Historical Secrets from the Periods 1966-1968-1972], 11th Edition. California: Ủy Ban Truy Tố Tội Ác Đảng Cộng Sản Việt Nam [Committee to Prosecute Crimes of the Vietnamese Communist Party], 2014.

——. *Huế thảm sát mậu thân* [Huế—The Massacre of Tết Mậu Thân]. Southern California: Published by the author, 2011.

——. "Liên Thành trả lại một số thắc mắc trong bài về Trịnh Công Sơn" [Liên Thành Answers Some Questions Regarding His Article about Trịnh Công Sơn]. Biến Động Miền Trung, June 30, 2009. http://biendongmientrung-lienthanh.blogspot.com/2009/06/lien-thanh-viet-bai-2-ve-trinh-cong-son.html (accessed Jan. 9, 2017).

——. "Trịnh Công Sơn và những hoạt động nằm vùng" [Trịnh Công Sơn and Underground Activities]. Khai phóng [Emancipation], May 28, 2009. http://khaiphong.org/showthread.php?1929-Tr%26%237883%3Bnh-C%F4ng-S%26%23417%3Bn-v%E0-nh%26%237919%3Bng-ho%26%237841%3Bt-%26%23273%3B%26%237897%3Bng-n%26%237857%3Bm-v%F9ng (accessed Nov. 1, 2016; site now defunct).

Light, Alan. "'In 'Rolling Thunder Revue,' Scorsese Tries to Capture a Wild Dylan Tour." *New York Times,* June 12, 2019.

Lindsey, Hal and Carole C. Carlson. *The Late Great Planet Earth*. Grand Rapids, MI: Zondervan, 1970.

Linh Phạm. "Nhạc Trịnh 'lạc' trong buổi diễn Bob Dylan" [Trịnh Music Was "Lost" in the Bob Dylan Concert]. Báo Mới, April 11, 2011. https://web.archive.org/web/20110417073031/ http://www.baomoi.com/Nhac-Trinh-lac-trong-buoi-dien-Bob-Dylan/71/6044594.epi (accessed July 1, 2012).

Li Tana. *Nguyễn Cochinchina: Southern Vietnam in the Seventeenth and Eighteenth Centuries*. Ithaca, NY: Southeast Asia Program Publications, Cornell University, 1998.

Lomax Hawes, Bess. "Folksongs and Function: Some Thoughts on the American Lullaby." *Journal of American Folklore* 87, no. 344. April-June 1974.

Lopez, Donald S. *The Heart Sutra Explained: Indian and Tibetan Commentaries*. New York: State University of New York Press, 1987.

Luce, Don and John Sommer. *Vietnam—The Unheard Voices*. Ithaca, NY: Cornell University Press, 1969.

Lưu Kường. "Còn hai con mắt, khóc người" [There's still two eyes, crying for people]. *Công An Nhân Dân*, 2011. http://ww.baomoi.com/ (accessed November 7, 2011; site now defunct).

Lưu Trọng Lư. *Nửa đêm sực tỉnh* [Waking in the Middle of the Night]. Thuận Hóa, 1989.

Lý Hải Châu et al. *Tuyển tập Chế Lan Viên*, Tập một [A Collection of Works by Chế Lan Viên, Vol. 1]. Hà Nội: Văn học, 1985.

Maguire, Jack. *Essential Buddhism: A Complete Guide to Beliefs and Practices*. New York: Pocket Books, 2001.

Malpas, Simon, and Paul Wake. *The Routledge Companion to Critical Theory*. London: Routledge, 2006.

Marcus, Greil. *Like a Rolling Stone: Bob Dylan at the Crossroads*. New York: PublicAffairs, 2005.

——. *The Old Weird America: The World of Bob Dylan's Basement Tapes*. New York: Picador, 2011.

Marqusee, Mike. *Chimes of Freedom: The Politics of Bob Dylan's Art*. New York: The New Press, 2003.

——. "The Song that Got Away." *Guardian*, May 27, 2005.

Marr, David G. "Concepts of 'Individual' and 'Self' in Twentieth-Century Vietnam." *Modern Asian Studies* 34, no. 4 (2000).

McAllister, James. "'Only Religions Count in Vietnam': Thich Tri Quang and the Vietnam War." *Modern Asian Studies* 42, no. 4 (2008).

McCallister, Patrick, and Thi Cam Tu Luckman. "The Kitchen God Returns to Heaven [Ông Táo Về Trời]: Popular Culture, Social Knowledge, and Folk Beliefs in Vietnam." *Journal of Vietnamese Studies* 10 (Winter 2015).

McHale, Shawn Frederick. *Print and Power: Confucianism, Communism, and Buddhism in the Making of Modern Vietnam*. Honolulu: University of Hawai'i Press, 2004.

McKeen, William. *Bob Dylan: A Bio-Bibliography*. Westport, CT: Greenwood Press, 1993.

McLeod, Mark W. and Nguyen Thi Dieu. *Culture and Customs of Vietnam*. Westport, CT: Greenwood Press, 2001.

McT. Kahin, George. *Intervention: How America Became Involved in Vietnam*. New York: Alfred A. Knopf, 1986.

Meade, Marion. "Does Rock Degrade Women?" The New York *Times*, Mar. 14, 1971.

Minh Chi, Ha Van Tan, and Nguyen Tai Thu. *Buddhism in Vietnam*. HCMC: The Gioi, 1993.

Moyar, Mark. *Triumph Forsaken: The Vietnam War, 1954-1965*. Cambridge: Cambridge University Press, 2006.

Muller, René. *Beyond Marginality: Constructing a Self in the Twilight of Western Culture*. Westport, CT: Praeger, 1998.

Mu Soeng. *The Diamond Sutra*. Boston MA: Wisdom Publications 2000.

Negherbon, William. "The Story of Lady Kieu." In *Some Aspects of Vietnamese Culture: Four Lectures by Nguyễn Đình Hòa, Nguyễn Ngọc Bích, William Negherbon, and Võ Đình*. Carbondale, IL: Southern Illinois University Center for Vietnamese Studies, 1972.

Ngọc Văn. "Diễm của ngày xưa" [Diễm of Bygone Days]. *Tiền Phong* [Vanguard], Mar. 14, 2010. http://www.tienphong.vn/Tianyon/Index.aspx?ArticleID=188748&ChannelID=7 (accessed Mar. 20, 2010).

Ngo Tay. "Khánh Ly: 'Xin cho quê hương mãi bình an'" [Please Make the Native Land Forever Peaceful]. *Khampha.vn*, October 5, 2014. https://web.archive.org/web/20141019075107/http://khampha.vn:80/giai-tri/khanh-ly-xin-cho-que-huong-mai-binh-an-c6a189609.html (accessed January 7, 2015).

Người Đưa Tin [Person Who Delivers News]. "Trịnh Công Sơn – Hồng Nhung: Những ngày 'không ngày tháng'" [Trịnh Công Sơn – Hồng Nhung: Days without Days or Months]. http://www.nguoiduatin.vn/trinh-cong-son-hong-nhung-ngung-ngay-khong https://ngoisao.vn/am-nhac/tin-tuc/trinh-cong-son-hong-nhung-nhung-ngay-khong-ngay-thang-66725.htm (accessed Apr. 13, 2012; site now defunct).

Ngô Văn Tao. "Bùi Giáng và Trịnh Công Sơn." https://www.tcs-home.org/ban-be/articles/bui-giang-va-trinh-cong-son (accessed July 21, 2022).

Nguyễn Hoàn. "Con người minh triết trong nhạc Trịnh Công Sơn" [The Wise Person in the Music of Trịnh Công Sơn]. Trinh Cong Son Cultural Association, April 2011. https://www.tcs-home.org/ban-be/articles/con-nguoi-minh-triet-trong-nhac-trinh-cong-son (accessed July 19, 2022).

Nguyễn Huệ Chi. "Nguyễn Thị Manh Manh." In *Từ Điển Văn Học* [Cultural Dictionary], edited by Đỗ Đức Hiểu, Nguyễn Huệ Chi, Phùng Văn Tửu, and Trần Hữu Tá. Hà nội: Thế giới, 2003.

——. "Trần Khâm." In *Từ điển Văn Học* [Dictionary of Literature], edited by Đỗ Đức Hiểu et al. Hanoi: Thế Giới, 2004.

Nguyễn Hưng Quốc (Hoàng Ngọc Tuấn). "Viết, giữa truyền thống và nhu cầu sáng tạo" [Writing, Culture and the Need to Create]. Tien Ve, https://web.archive.org/web/20140716052451/http://www.tienve.org/home/literature/viewLiterature.do?action=viewArtwork&artworkId=852 (accessed March 17, 2015).

Nguyễn Khắc Viện and Hữu Ngọc. *Vietnamese Literature: Historical Background and Texts*. Hanoi: Red River, Foreign Languages Publishing House, n.d.

Nguyễn Khoa Điềm and Ngô Văn Phú. *Nhà văn Việt Nam hiện đại* [Modern Vietnamese Writers]. Hanoi: Hội Nhà Văn, 1997.

Nguyễn Ngọc Bích, translator. *A Thousand Years of Vietnamese Poetry*. New York: Alfred A. Knopf, 1975.

Nguyễn Quốc Vinh. "Love of Men: Xuân Diệu, Translations and Interview with Tô Hoài." *Việt Nam Forum* 16 (1997).

Nguyễn Thành Long. "Hai câu chuyện về Chế Lan Viên" [Two Stories about Chế Lan Viên]. *Văn Nghệ* [Literature and Art] no. 27-28 (1989).

Nguyễn Thanh Ty. *Về một quãng đời Trịnh Công Sơn* [On a Period of Trịnh Công Sơn's Life]. (Place of publication and publisher not listed: 2001).

Nguyễn Thế Anh. "Buddhism and Vietnamese Society throughout History." *South East Asia Research* 1 No. 5 (March 1993).

——. "The Vietnamization of the Cham Deity Pô Nagar." In *Essays into Vietnamese Pasts*, edited by K.W. Taylor and John K. Whitmore. Ithaca, NY: Southeast Asia Program, Cornell University.

Nguyễn Thị Manh Manh. "Có nên bỏ chế độ đa thê không?" [Should We Abandon Polygamy?]. *Phụ nữ tân văn* [Women's News] no. 268 (November 29, 1934).

——. "Dư luận nam giới đối với phụ nữ tân tiến" [The Male View of Progressive Women]. *Phụ nữ tân văn* [Women's News] no. 243 (April 24, 1934).

——. "Có nên tự do kết hôn không?" [Should We Be Free to Choose Whom We Marry?]. *Phụ nữ tân văn* [Women's News] no. 267 (November 21, 1934).

Nguyễn Thị Minh Hà, Nguyễn Thị Thanh Bình, and Lady Borton, editors. *The Defiant Muse: Vietnamese Feminist Poems from Antiquity to the Present: A Bilingual Anthology*. New York: The Feminist Press, 2007.

Nguyên Thuận. "Trịnh Công Sơn và Bob Dylan: Tri ân hay hát lót?" [Trịnh Công Sơn and Bob Dylan: A Sign of Gratitude or Singing to Fill In?]. http://www.vietnamplus.vn/Home/Trinh-Cong-Son-va-Bob-Dylan-Tri-an-hay-hat-lot/20114/84995.vnplus (accessed July 5, 2012).

Nguyễn Trọng Tạo. "Chatting about Lyrics and Music." *Vietnam Cultural Window* 47 (February, 2002).

Nguyễn Trọng Tạo et al., editors. *Trịnh Công Sơn:Một người thơ ca một cõi đi về* [Trịnh Công Sơn: A Singer-Poet, a Place for Leaving and Returning]. Hanoi: Trung Tâm Văn Hóa Ngôn Ngữ Đông Tây.

Nguyen Van Huyen. *The Ancient Civilization of Vietnam.* Hanoi: Thế Giới, 1995.

Nguyễn Văn Long. "Anh Thơ." In *Từ Điển Văn Học* [Cultural Dictionary]. Đỗ Đức Hiểu, Nguyễn Huệ Chi, Phùng Văn Tửu, and Trần Hữu Tá, editors. Hà nội: Thế giới, 2003.

——. "Tiểu sử" [Life History]. In *Tuyển Tập Lưu Trọng Lư* [Lưu Trọng Lư: Selections], edited by Nguyễn Văn Long. Hanoi: Văn Học, 1987.

Nguyễn Vỹ. *Văn thi sĩ tiền chiến* [Pre-war Poets]. Hanoi: Hội Nhà Văn, 1994.

Nguyễn Xuân Nam and Vũ Thị Thường. *Tuyển tập Chế Lan Viên* [Selections: Chế Lan Viên]. Hanoi: Văn Học, 1985.

Nguyễn Đắc Xuân. "Nhà Văn Nguyễn Đắc Xuân một chứng nhân của những năm sáu mươi ở Huế" [The Writer Nguyễn Đắc Xuân, A Witness of the 1960s in Huế], interview by Dương Minh Long. http://dongduongthoibao.net/view.php?storyid=561 (accessed Sept. 12, 2012).

——. *Trịnh Công Sơn: Có một thời như thế* [Trịnh Công Sơn: There Was Such a Time]. HCMC: Văn Học, 2003.

——. "Hậu quả của 'Cái Chết' của tôi" [The Consequences of my "Death"]. http://sachhiem.net/NDX/NDX020.php (accessed Sept. 30, 2012).

——. "Sự thực 'Thư gửi Ngô Kha của Trịnh Công Sơn'" [The Truth about Trịnh Công Sơn's "Letter to Ngô Kha"]. In *Ngô Kha hành trình,* edited by Bửu Nam and Phạm Thị Anh Nha.

——. "Vài điều về Liên Thành, Tắc giả 'Biến động, Miền Trung'" [A Few Things about Liên Thành, the Author of *Disorder in the Central Region*]. https://sachhiem.net/NDX/NDX017.php (accessed Oct. 30, 2016).

Nguyễn Đình Hòa. *Vietnamese Literature: A Brief Survey.* San Diego: San Diego State University, 1994.

Nguyễn Minh Nhựt, Phạm Sỹ Sáu, Nguyễn Duy and Nguyễn Trọng Chức, editors. *Trịnh Công Sơn: Tôi là ai, là ai . . .* [Trịnh Công Sơn: Who Am I, Am I . . .]. Hồ Chí Minh City: Trẻ, 2011.

Nguyễn Trọng Tạo, Nguyễn Thụy Kha, and Đoàn Tử Huyến, editors. *Trịnh Công Sơn: Một người thơ ca một cõi đi về* [Trịnh Công Sơn: A Singer-poet, a Place for Leaving and Returning]. Hanoi: Âm Nhạc, 2001.

Nhã Ca. *Giải khăn sô cho Huế* [Mourning Headband for Huế]. Saigon: Đất Lành, 1971. For an English translation, see Nhã Ca, *Mourning Headband for Huế,* translated by Olga Dror. Bloomington, IN: Indiana University Press, 2014.

Ninh, Kim N. B. *A World Transformed: The Politics of Culture in Revolutionary Vietnam.* Ann Arbor, MI: The University of Michigan Press, 2005.

Oberdorfer, Don. *Tet!* Garden City, NY: Doubleday, 1971.

Ochs, Phil. "An Open Letter from Phil Ochs to Irwin Silber, Paul Wolfe, and Joseph E. Levine." *Broadside* 54 (1965).

——. "The Need for Topical Music." *Broadside* no. 22 (March, 1963).

Phạm Duy. *Hồi ký* [Memoirs], Vol. III. *Thời phân chia quốc-cộng* [The Period of Nationalist-Communist Division]. Midway City, CA: Phạm Duy Cường Musical Productions, 1991.

——. *Tân nhạc Việt Nam thuở ban đầu* [Modern Vietnamese Music in the Early Days]. Hồ Chí Minh City: Trẻ, 2006.

——. *Thời phân chia quốc-cộng* [The Period of Nationalist-Communist Division]. Midway City, CA: Phạm Duy Cường Musical Productions, 1991.

——. *Đặc khảo về dân nhạc ở Việt Nam* [Research on the Folk Music of Vietnam]. Saigon: Hiện Đại, 1972.

——. *Đường về Dân Ca* [The Road Back to Folk Songs]. Los Alamitos CA: Xuân Thu.

——. "Những bước đầu (trong nửa thế kỷ tân nhạc)" [First Steps (in half a century of modern music)]. *Hợp lưu* [Convergence] 17 (June & July, 1992).

——. "Nói về ca khúc và thơ phổ nhạc" [Speaking about Songs and Poems Put to Music]. *Văn: Tạp Chí Văn Học Nghệ Thuật* [Literature: a Journal of Literary Studies and Art] 66 and 67 (June and July, 2002).

Phan Bùi Bảo Thy. "Liên Thành, kẻ sát nhân trong những ngày miền Trung biến động" [Liên Thành, The Assassin During the Days of Disorder in the Central Region]. An Ninh Thế Giới Online, May 27, 2012. http://antg.cand.com.vn/Tu-lieu-antg/Lien-Thanh-ke-sat-nhan-trong-nhung-ngay-mien-Trung-bien-dong-303297/ (accessed May 4, 2017).

Phan Cư Đệ. *Tuyển Tập* [Selected Works], vol. 3. Huế: Giáo Duc, 2006.

Phan Khoi. "Một lối thơ mới trình chánh giữa làng thơ" [A New Way of Writing Poems is Presented to the Village of Poetry]. *Phụ Nữ Tân Văn* [Women's News], March 10, 1932.

——. "Phép làm thơ" [Rules for Writing Poetry]. *Phụ-nữ Tân-vân* [Women's News] 73, October 9, 1930.

Phan Thị Vàng Anh. "Chế Lan Viên: A Daughter's Memories." Translated by Huỳnh Sanh Thông. *Vietnam Review* (Spring-Summer, 1997).

Phan Thị Đào. *Tìm hiểu thi pháp tục ngữ Việt Nam* [Understanding the Prosody of Proverbs]. Huế: Thuận Hóa, 2001.

Plum Village. "Thich Nhat Hanh Returns Home: Official Announcement." https://plumvillage. org/news/thich-nhat-hanh-returns-to-vietnam/ (accessed February 5, 2019).

Prebish, Charles S. *Luminous Passage: The Practice and Study of Buddhism in America.* Berkeley: University of California, 1999.

Ricks, Christopher. *Dylan's Visions of Sin* (New York: Harper Collins, 2003).

Rotolo, Suze. *A Freewheelin' Time: A Memoir of Greenwich Village in the Sixties.* New York: Broadway Books, 2008.

Russell, Tim. "Sub Par Homesick Blues: Bob Dylan Live in Vietnam." *The Quietus*, April 12, 2011. http://thequietus.com/articles/06062-bob-dylan-live-in-vietnam-review (accessed Apr. 13, 2011).

Sagnier, Thierry J. *The Fortunate Few: IVS Volunteers From Asia to the Andes* (Portland, OR: NCNM Press, 2015).

Said, Edward W. *Orientalism* (New York: Vintage Books, 1978).

Sâm Thương. "Những ngày cuối của Sơn ở cõi tạm" [Sơn's Last Days in this Temporary Abode]. Trịnh Công Sơn Cultural Association, www.tcs-home.org/ban-be/vinh-biet-anh-son/ SamThuong (accessed Feb. 28, 2005).

——. "Đi tìm thời gian đã mất" [In Search of Lost Times]. https://www.sachhiem.net/ VANHOC/Samthuong.php (accessed Apr. 27, 2022).

Scaduto, Anthony. *Bob Dylan.* London: Helter Skelter Publishing, 1996.

Schafer, John C. and Thế Uyên. "The Novel Emerges in Cochinchina." *Journal of Asian Studies* 52, no. 4 (Nov. 1993).

Lê Thị Phương Dung. Interview by John C. Schafer. Huế, 2007.

Schafer, John C. *Trịnh Công Sơn-Bob Dylan: Như trăng và nguyệt?* [Trịnh Công Sơn-Bob Dylan: Like Trăng and Nguyệt?], translated by Cao Thị Như-Quỳnh. HCMC: Trẻ, 2012.

——. "Thi ca đối với người Việt và người Mỹ" [Poetry in Regard to Vietnamese and Americans]. *Đặc San Văn Khoa* [Special Issue of the Faculty of Letters] *1972-1973.* Huế: Viên Đại Học Huế.

Schumacher, Michael. *There But for Fortune: The Life of Phil Ochs.* New York: Hyperion, 1996.

Schwartz, Alexandra. "The Rambling Glory of Bob Dylan's Nobel Speech." *The New Yorker,* June 6, 2017. https://www.newyorker.com/culture/culture-desk/the-rambling-glory-of-bob-dylans-nobel-speech (accessed August 8, 2019).

Scorsese, Martin. *No Direction Home: Bob Dylan.* Paramount Pictures, 2005.

Shaar Murray, Charles. *Crosstown Traffic: Jimi Hendrix and the Post-War Rock 'n' Roll Revolution.* New York: St. Martin's Press, 1989.

Shaplen, Robert. *The Lost Revolution.* New York: Harper Colophon Books, 1955.

Shelton, Robert. *No Direction Home: The Life and Music of Bob Dylan.* Milwaukee, WI: Backbeat Books, 2011.

Shklovsky, Victor. "Art as Technique." In *Russian Formalist Criticism: Four Essays,* translated and edited by Lee T. Lemon and Marion J. Reis. Lincoln, NE: University of Nebraska Press, 1965.

Silber, Irwin. "An Open Letter to Bob Dylan." *Sing Out!* November, 1964. http://www.edlis.org/ twice/threads/open_letter_to_bob_dylan.html (accessed Apr. 19, 2018).

Smith, Patti. "How Does It Feel." *The New Yorker,* Dec. 14, 2016. https://www.newyorker.com/ culture/cultural-comment/patti-smith-on-singing-at-bob-dylans-nobel-prize-ceremony (accessed June 9, 2019).

Soucy, Alexander. "Nationalism, Globalism and the Re-establishment of the Trúc Lâm Thiền Buddhist Sect in Northern Vietnam." In *Modernity and Re-enchantment: Religion in Post-revolutionary Vietnam,* edited by Philip Taylor. Singapore: Institute of Southeast Asian Studies, 2007.

Sounes, Howard. *Down the Highway: The Life of Bob Dylan.* New York: Grove Press, 2001.

Springsteen, Bruce. *Born to Run.* New York: Simon & Schuster, 2016.

Stevenson, Seth. "Tangled Up in Boobs: What's Bob Dylan Doing in a Victoria's Secret Ad?" *Slate* (April, 2004). https://slate.com/business/2004/04/bob-dylan-shills-for-victoria-s-secret.html (accessed June 6, 2018).

Tâm Nhiên. "Thế giới thi ca tư tưởng Bùi Giáng" [Bùi Giáng's World: His Poetry, Song and Thought]. *Thư Viện Hoa Sen*, March 18. 2013. http://thuvienhoasen.org/a17034/the-gioi-thi-ca-tu-tuong-bui-giang (accessed June 13, 2016).

Tâm Tuệ Hỷ, editor. *Danh từ Phật học thực dụng* [Useful Buddhist Terms]. Hà Nội: Tôn Giáo, 2004.

Tạ Ty. "Trịnh Công Sơn và tiếng ru máu lệ" [Trịnh Công Sơn and Lullabies of Blood and Tears]. In *Mười khuôn mặt văn nghệ hôm nay* [Ten Faces of Art Today]. Saigon: Lá Bối, 1971.

Taylor, Keith. "Nguyen Hoang and the Beginning of Vietnam's Southward Expansion." In *Southeast Asia in the Early Modern Era: Trade, Power, and Belief*, edited by Anthony Reid. Ithaca, NY: Cornell University Press, 1993.

Taylor, Philip. *Modernity and Re-enchantment: Religion in Post-revolutionary Vietnam*. Singapore: Institute of Southeast Asian Studies, 2007.

Trịnh Cung and Nguyễn Quốc Thái, editors. *Trịnh Công Sơn: Cuộc đời, âm nhạc, thơ, hội họa và suy tưởng* [TCS: Life, Music, Poetry, Painting, Reflections]. HCMC: Văn Nghệ, 2001.

Trịnh Vĩnh Trinh. "Tiểu Sử Trịnh Công Sơn" [Biography of Trịnh Công Sơn].

Thanh Thương Hoàng (Quốc Oai). *Phật Giáo Tranh Đấu* [The Buddhist Struggle]. Saigon: Tân Sanh, 1963.

Thế Lữ. "Một hy vọng trong làng âm nhạc: Ông Nguyễn Văn Tuyên" [Something Hopeful in the Village of Music: Mr. Nguyễn Văn Tuyên]. *Ngày Nay* [Today] 116 (26 June 1938).

——. "Tựa tập 'Thơ Thơ'" [Preface to *Poésies*]. In Mã Giang Lân, *Thơ Xuân Diệu: Những lời bình* [The Poetry of Xuân Diệu: Reviews]. Hanoi: Văn Hóa—Thông Tin, 1999.

Thích Giác Tâm. "Con mắt còn lại" [The Eye That Remains]. Giác Ngộ Online, https://giacngo.vn/con-mat-con-lai-post11286.html (accessed December 12, 2022).

Thích Nhất Hạnh. *Being Peace*. Berkeley: Parallax Press, 1996.

——. *Lotus in a Sea of Fire*. New York: Hill and Wang, 1967.

——. *No Death, No Fear*. New York: Riverhead Books, 2002.

——. *The Heart of Buddha's Teaching*. New York: Broadway Books, 1999.

——. "Thông điệp thương yêu của Trịnh Công Sơn" [Trịnh Công Sơn's Message of Love]. Làng Mai [Plum Village]. https://langmai.org/thien-duong/nghe-phap-thoai/pt-phien-ta/pt-su-ong-lm/binh-tho-nhac/noi-vong-tay-lon-trinh-cong-son/ (accessed Sept. 3, 2015).

Thich Thien An. *Buddhism and Zen in Vietnam*. Rutland, VT: Charles E. Tuttle Company, 1975.

——. *Buddhism and Zen in Vietnam in Relation to the Development of Buddhism in Asia*. Rutland, VT: Charles E. Tuttle, 1975.

——. *Zen Philosophy, Zen Practice*. Berkeley: Dharma Publishing, 1975.

Thiên Đỗ. "The Quest for Enlightenment and Cultural Identity: Buddhism in Contemporary Vietnam." In *Buddhism and Politics in Twentieth-Century Asia*, edited by Ian Harris. London: Pinter, 1999.

Thu Hà. "Cái gì đã thuộc về nguyên tắc thì không có ngoại lệ" [There Are No Exceptions to Matters of Principle]. *Tuổi trẻ* [Youth], Apr. 18, 2003.

Titmuss, Christopher. "Interactivity: Sitting for Peace and Standing for Parliament." In *The Path of Compassion: Writings on Socially Engaged Buddhism*, edited by Fred Eppsteiner. Berkeley, CA: Parallax Press, 1988.

Topmiller, Robert J. *The Lotus Unleashed*. Lexington, KY: University Press of Kentucky, 2002.

Tô Vũ. "Nhạc vàng là gì?" [What Is Yellow Music?]. *Văn hóa nghệ thuật* [Culture and Art] 5 (1976).

Trager, Oliver. *Keys to the Rain: The Definitive Bob Dylan Encyclopedia*. New York: Billboard Books, 2004.

Trần Hoàng Thiêm Kim. "Bà Tôn Lệ Minh—Vợ nhà thơ Lưu Trọng Lư: 'Em chải lại đời anh'" [Mrs. Tôn Lệ Minh—Wife of the poet Lưu Trọng Lư: 'You Groom My Life']. *An ninh thế giới Online*, February 27, 2018. http://antg.cand.com.vn/Kinh-te-Van-hoa-The-Thao/Ba-Ton-Le-Minh-vo-nha-tho-Luu-Trong-Lu-Em-chai-lai-doi-anh-479752 (accessed July 21, 2020).

Trần Hữu Thục. "Một cái nhìn về ca từ Trịnh Công Sơn" (One View of Trịnh Công Sơn's Lyrics). *Văn học* [Literary Studies] 186 & 187 (Oct.-Nov., 2001).

Trần Ngọc Bảo. *Từ Điển ngôn ngữ văn hóa du lịch Huế xưa* [A Tourist Language and Culture Dictionary about Huế in the Past]. Gia Định: Thuận Hóa, 2005.

Trần Nhật Vy. "Nữ phóng viên đầu tiên" [The First Woman Reporter]. *Tuổi Trẻ* [Youth], June 18, 2015. https://tuoitre.vn/nu-phong-vien-dau-tien-763227.htm (accessed January 7, 2021).

Trần Tuyết Hoa. "40 Năm Hành Trình Âm Nhac Trịnh Công Sơn, Thái Hòa và Tôi" [A 40 Year Musical Journey with Trịnh Công Sơn, Thái Hòa and I]. Trinh Cong Son Cultural Association, April 2006. https://www.tcs-home.org/ban-be/articles/40-nam-hanh-trinh-am-nhac-trinh-cong-son-thai-hoa-va-toi (accessed July 18, 2022).

Trần Văn Khê. "Phong Cách Tán Tụng trong Phật Giáo Việt Nam" [The Way of Recitation in Vietnamese Buddhism]. Giác Ngộ Online. http://giacngo.vn/PrintView.aspx?Language=vi&ID=524658 (accessed August 17, 2015; site now defunct).

Trần Việt. "Nguyễn Phúc Liên Thành, Chống Tôi Lên Tiếng" [We Raise Our Voices]. Chung Toi Len Tieng, April 2, 2012. http://chungtoilentieng.blogspot.com/2012/04/phan-vii-nguyen-phuc-lien-thanh-theo.html (accessed Feb. 28, 2017).

Trịnh Công Sơn. "Hồi Ức" [A Recollection].

———. "Tôi Đã Tận Hưởng Những Tình Cảm Nhân Loại" [I Have Benefited from Humane Emotions], interview by Lữ Quỳnh. In *Trịnh Công Sơn: Một người thơ ca một cõi đi về*, eds. Nguyễn Trọng Tạo et al.

———. Interview with Thích Tâm Thiện. In *Nguyệt San Giác Ngộ* [Enlightenment Monthly Review] no. 1, April 1996.

———. Interview with Vĩnh Xương. In the journal *Đất Việt* [Vietnamese Land], June 6, 1986.

———. "Lá thư gửi cho người đang ở trong tù hay đã bị thủ tiêu" [A Letter for a Person Who is Now In Prison or Has Been Exterminated]. In *Ngô Kha hành trình*, edited by Bửi Nam and Nguyễn Thị Anh Nga.

———. "Thông điệp thương yêu của Trịnh Công Sơn" [Trịnh Công Sơn's Message of Love]. Làng Mai [Plum Village]. https://langmai.org/phapduong/binh-tho-nhac/ (accessed September 3, 2015; the site is now defunct).

———. "Trò Chơi" [Playing Games].

———. "Đò đưa" [A Boat that Carries Us]. In *Trịnh Công Sơn: người hát rong qua nhiều thế hệ* [A Troubadour Who Sang for Many Generations], edited by Trần Thanh Phương et al. HCMC: Trẻ, 2004.

———. *Trịnh Công Sơn: Thư tình gửi một người* [Trịnh Công Sơn: Love Letters for Someone]. HCMC: Trẻ, 2011.

Trịnh Cung "Bi kịch Trịnh Công Sơn" [The Tragedy of Trịnh Công Sơn]. *Văn* [Literature] 53 & 54 (2001).

———. "Sơn Trong Trí Nhớ Nhỏ Nhoi Của Tôi" [Sơn in My Limited Memory]. In *Trịnh Công Sơn: Cuộc đời, âm nhạc, thơ, hội họa, suy tưởng* [Trịnh Công Sơn: Life, Music, Poetry, Painting, Reflections], edited by Trịnh Cung and Nguyễn Quốc Thái. HCMC: Văn Nghệ, 2001.

———. "Trịnh Công Sơn không quan tâm đến chính trị?" [Did Trịnh Công Sơn Not Pay Attention to Politics?]. Tạp Chí Da Màu. http://damau.org/archives/5055 (accessed Nov. 3, 2016; site now defunct).

Trịnh Vĩnh Trinh. "Công bố hàng trăm bức thư tình của nhạc sĩ Trịnh Công Sơn (Kỳ 7): Trịnh Công Sơn—Dao Ánh qua hồi ức của Trịnh Vĩnh Trinh" [Making Public Hundreds of Trịnh Công Sơn's Love Letters (Part 7): Trịnh Công Sơn—Dao Ánh as Remembered by Trịnh Vĩnh Trinh], interview with Giao Hương and Dạ Ly. *Thanh Nien*, March 4, 2011. https://thanhnien.vn/cong-bo-hang-tram-buc-thu-tinh-cua-nhac-si-trinh-cong-son-ky-7-trinh-cong-son-dao-anh-qua-hoi-uc-cua-trinh-vinh-trinh-post297058.html (accessed Apr. 12, 2011).

Xuan Dieu. *Truyện Dài: Những Bước Dường Tư Tưởng Của Tôi* [A Long Story: My Ideological Development]. *Văn Học Quê Hương* [Literature of the Native Land]. http://vanhoc.quehuong.org/viewtruyen.php?ID=6741&cat=15 (accessed May 28, 2020).

Tuấn Huy. "Trịnh Công Sơn, có sót xa người" [Trịnh Công Sơn: Painful Memories of Someone]. *Văn học* [Literary Studies] 186 & 187 (Oct.-Nov., 2001).

Tuck, William P. "Toward a Theology of the Proclaimed Word." *Review and Expositor*. Jan. 1, 1984.

Van, T. "Vietnamese Singer Khánh Ly to perform in Hanoi." VietNamNet, Apr. 10, 2014. https://web.archive.org/web/20140902061713/http://english.vietnamnet.vn/fms/art-entertainment/99543/veteran-singer-khanh-ly-to-perform-in-hanoi.html (accessed May 11, 2014).

Văn Ngọc. "Trịnh Công Sơn, Khánh Ly và những khúc tình ca một thời" [Trịnh Công Sơn, Khánh Ly, and the Love Songs of an Era]. *Diễn đàn* [Forum] 110 (September, 2001).

———. "Trịnh Công Sơn, Khánh Ly và những khúc tình ca một thời" [Trịnh Công Sơn, Khánh Ly and the Love Songs of an Era]. *Diễn đàn* [Forum] 110 (Sept. 2001).

Van Ronk, Dave and Elijah Wald. *The Mayor of MacDougal Street*. Philadelphia: Da Capo Press, 2005.

Viet Thanh Nguyen. *Nothing Ever Dies: Vietnam and the Memory of War*. Cambridge: Harvard University Press, 2016.

Vĩnh Nguyên. "Hồi ức về Trịnh Công Sơn" [A Recollection of Trịnh Công Sơn]. In *Trịnh Công Sơn Cát Bụi Lộng Lẫy* [Trịnh Công Sơn: Resplendent Sand and Dust], edited by Trần Thùy Mai et al. Huế: Thuận Hóa, 2001.

Võ Phiến. *Văn học miền nam tổng quan: 1954-1975* [Literature in South Vietnam: 1954-1975]. Westminster, CA: Văn Nghệ, 1986.

Võ Quang Yến. "Nhạc Trịnh Công Sơn từ Paris qua Nhất Bản" [Trịnh Công Sơn Music from Paris to Japan.] *Diễn Đàn* [Forum], March 28, 2014. https://www.diendan.org/sang-tac/nhac-trinh-cong-son-tu-paris-qua-nhat-ban?searchterm=Nh%E1%BA%A1c+Tr%E1%B-B%8Bnh+C%C3%B4ng+S%C6%A1n+t%E1%BB%AB+Paris (accessed February 17, 2020).

Vũ Hạnh. *Đọc lại Truyện Kiều* [Rereading the Tale of Kiều]. Saigon: Cảo Thơm, 1966.

Ward, Geoffrey C. and Ken Burns. *The Vietnam War: An Intimate History*. New York: Alfred A. Knopf, 2017.

Watson, Burton, translator. *The Vimalakirti Sutra*. New York: Columbia University Press, 1997.

Weber, Max. *The Religion of India: The Sociology of Hinduism and Buddhism*. Translated and edited by Hans H. Gerth and Don Martindale. Glencoe, IL: The Free Press, 1958.

Weller Taylor, Keith. *The Birth of Vietnam*. Berkeley, CA: University of California Press, 1983.

Whitmore, John K. "Social Organization and Confucian Thought in Vietnam." *Journal of Southeast Asian Studies* 15, No. 2 (Sept., 1984).

Widdicombe, Lizzie. "The Higher Life." *The New Yorker*, July 6 & 13, 2015.

Williams, Paul. *Bob Dylan, Performing Artist: The Early Years, 1960-1973*. London: Omnibus Press, 2004.

——. *Bob Dylan, Performing Artist: The Middle Years, 1974-1986*. New York: Omnibus Press, 2004.

——. *Dylan—What Happened?* Glen Ellen, CA: Entwistle Books, 1980.

Wills, David S. "Allen Ginsberg and Bob Dylan." *Beatdom.* http://www.beatdom.com/allen-gins-berg-and-bob-dylan/ (accessed Mar. 24, 2019).

Wimsatt, William K. and Monroe C. Beardsley. "The Intentional Fallacy." In *The Verbal Icon*, edited by William K. Wimsatt. Lexington, KY: Farrar, Straus, and Cudahy, 1954.

Wolfe, Paul. "The 'new' Dylan." *Broadside* 53 (December, 1964).

Wolff, Daniel. *Grown-Up Anger*. New York: Harper, 2017.

Woodside, Alexander B. "The Historical Background." In Huỳnh Sanh Thông and Nguyễn Du, *The Tale of Kiều: A Bilingual Edition of Truyện Kiều*.

Xuân Diệu. *Những bước đường tư tưởng của tôi* [Stages on My Journey of Thought]. Hà Nội: Văn hóa, 1958.

——. "Truyện Dài: Những Bước Đường Tư Tưởng Của Tôi" [A Long Story: My Ideological Development]. *Văn Học Quê Hương* [Literature of the Native Land], May 28, 2020. http://vanhoc.quehuong.org/viewtruyen.php?ID=6741&cat=15 (accessed May 28, 2020).

——. "Vai trò lãnh đạo của Đảng" [The Party's Leadership Role]. *Văn Nghệ*, no. 110, March 1, 1956.

Yoshikawa, M. "Some Japanese and American Cultural Characteristics." In *The Cultural Dialogue: An Introduction to Intercultural Communication,* edited by M. H. Prosser. Boston, MA: Houghton Mifflin, 1978.

Zinoman, Peter. "Nhân Văn Giai Phẩm on Trial." *Journal of Vietnamese Studies*, Vol. 11, No. 3/4 (Summer-Fall, 2016).

ABOUT THE AUTHOR

John C. Schafer, Professor Emeritus of English at Cal Poly Humboldt in Arcata, California, has taught English in Vietnam with International Voluntary Services (1968-1970) and the Fulbright Program (1971-73; 2001). His articles about Vietnamese literature have appeared in the *Journal of Southeast Asian Studies*, the *Journal of Vietnamese Studies*, *Crossroads*, the *Journal of Asian Studies*, the *Vietnam Forum*, and other journals. With the Press at Cal Poly Humboldt he has republished *Võ Phiến and the Sadness of Exile* (2016) and *Vietnamese Perspectives on the War in Vietnam* (2019).